D0548673

FASHION MERCHANDISING

An Introduction

Fifth Edition

Elaine Stone

Professor, Merchandising and
Marketing, and Coordinator
of the Small Business Center
Fashion Institute of Technology
New York, New York

Contributor
Jean A. Samples

Formerly Instructor
Houston Community College
Houston, Texas

Training Coordinator
C.U.C. International
Houston, Texas

Gregg Division
McGraw-Hill Publishing Company
New York   Atlanta   Dallas   St. Louis   San Francisco
Auckland   Bogotá   Caracas   Hamburg   Lisbon
London   Madrid   Mexico   Milan   Montreal   New Delhi
Paris   San Juan   São Paulo   Singapore
Sydney   Tokyo   Toronto

Sponsoring Editor: Mary McGarry
Editing Supervisor: Angela Piliouras
Design and Art Supervisor: Caryl Valerie Spinka
Production Supervisor: Mirabel Flores
Photo Supervisor: Ellen Meehan

Text Designer: Delgado Design Inc.
Cover Designer: Scott Silvers
Cover Photographer: Ken Karp
Picture Editor: Natalie Goldstein

Library of Congress Cataloging-in-Publication Data

Stone, Elaine.
    Fashion merchandising: an introduction / Elaine Stone;
  contributor, Jean A. Samples.— 5th ed.
      p. cm.
    Includes index.
    ISBN 0-07-061744-9 : $25.25
    1. Fashion merchandising—United States.   2. Clothing trade-
-United States.   I. Samples, Jean A.   II. Title.
HD9940.U4S78   1990
687'.068'8—dc20   89-34104
                                                  CIP

Copyright © 1990, 1985, 1981, 1976, 1971 by McGraw-Hill, Inc. All
rights reserved. Printed in the United States of America. Except as
permitted under the United States Copyright Act of 1976, no part
of this publication may be reproduced or distributed in any form or
by any means, or stored in a data base or retrieval system, without
the prior written permission of the publisher.

1 2 3 4 5 6 7 8 9 0 DOCDOC 8 9 4 3 2 1 0 9 8 7

ISBN 0=07-061744-9

PREFACE

The fashion business is exciting, stimulating, fascinating! Because it is also ever-changing, we have developed *Fashion Merchandising: An Introduction,* Fifth Edition, to provide a structured learning process to help students discover the innovation and challenges of today's fashion business.

Fashion Merchandising: An Introduction, Fifth Edition, reflects the survey nature of an introductory course by covering all the interdependent levels of the fashion business so that students can be made aware of the many careers in fashion. The concepts and practices developed are equally applicable to the merchandising of all fashion-influenced goods, although the text treats them largely in terms of men's, women's, children's apparel and accessories. To keep our readers current in the most recent happenings in the fashion business, each chapter concludes with a discussion of the latest developments and upcoming trends.

This fifth edition provides hundreds of new up-to-date examples and illustrations. In addition, the text has been substantially rewritten to sharpen its focus on fashion and to allow space for expanded material on: (1) the business of fashion, (2) domestic and foreign markets, (3) the impact of technology on each level of fashion, and (4) the global sourcing that is so important to the internationalization of fashion.

ORGANIZATION OF THE TEXT

The fifth edition of *Fashion Merchandising: An Introduction* uses the successful classroom-tested organization of the previous editions. It is structured in the following sequential learning order: Unit 1, The Dynamics of Fashion; Unit 2, The Producers of Fashion; Unit 3, The Markets for Fashion; Unit 4, The Merchandising of Fashion.

Unit 1: The Dynamics of Fashion

The first five chapters acquaint the student with the fundamentals of fashion and the basic principles that govern all fashion movement and change. This unit also teaches the fundamentals of the business of fashion. Many new examples and illustrations have been provided.

Chapter 1, "The Nature of Fashion," introduces fashion terminology, examines the components of fashion, and explains why fashion is always subject to change. Chapter 2 explores the manner in which economic, sociological, and psychological factors influence fashion demand. Chapter 3 discusses the rhythmic changes in silhouette, the cyclical movement of fashion, and how to predict fashion trends with relative accuracy. Chapter 4 explains how fashions start; the roles and responsibilities of designers, manufacturers, and retailers; the major theories relating to fashion adoption and dissemination; and why most people follow rather than lead fashion change. Chapter 5 explores the scope of the fashion business, explains the different types of business organizations, and allows the student to investigate the different forms of business structure.

Unit 2: The Producers of Fashion

The next seven chapters trace the history and development, organization and operation, merchandising and marketing activities, and trends in industries engaged in producing fashion. Chapter 6 discusses textile fibers and fabrics. Chapter 7 explains the fur industry and the leather apparel and accessories industry. Chapter 8 explores the women's apparel business with emphasis on current changes and future trends. Chapter 9 covers children's apparel, both boys and girls. Chapter 10 details the operations of the menswear market and the innovations occurring in recent years. Chapter 11 explores the excitement and opportunities of the many-faceted fashion accessories market. Chapter 12 explains the different levels of the intimate apparel industry and also spotlights the cosmetic industry.

Unit 3: The Markets for Fashion

This unit has been reorganized to give detailed information on domestic and foreign markets and how fashion inspiration comes from many areas around the world. In Chapter 13 the domestic fashion markets are individually detailed. Chapter 14 explores the major foreign markets and their importance as sources of fashion inspiration. The global nature of fashion is detailed in a new chapter, Chapter 15, which emphasizes world-wide sourcing for both imports and exports.

Unit 4: The Merchandising of Fashion

The distribution and promotion of fashion is covered in the last unit. Chapter 16 examines the major types of retail organizations that operate as distributors of fashion goods to consumers. Chapter 17 explores trends in fashion retailing and explains new, exciting, and innovative methods of distribution. In Chapter 18, the fashion auxiliary services are explained with emphasis on advertising and publicity. Also covered in this chapter are resident buying offices and the major changes that are occurring in them.

Appendices

Four appendices have been added to this edition. They address themselves to the career goals of students in the fashion business. The career information from the last edition has been updated and significantly reorganized for greater ease of use.

TEXT FEATURES

The fifth edition has many exciting special features that make the people, principles, practices, and techniques of the fashion business come alive in the minds of students. We believe that these features will help the students to learn about the fashion business in an enjoyable manner. All these features are appropriate for class discussion and library research projects.

Fashion Focus

A popular feature added in the last edition, the "Fashion Focus," highlights interesting people, places, and/or products that impact on the subject matter. This feature is found in every chapter.

Technology Talk

"Technology Talk" is a new feature that covers the latest technology and highlights how the implementation of "high tech" has caused dynamic changes on every level of the fashion business. These "Tech Talks" can be used as current events projects with students following the changes, successes, or failures of these technological innovations. This feature is found in Units 2 and 4.

Briefly Speaking

Another new feature, "Briefly Speaking," is a short, interesting article about a specific new development in the fashion business. These "briefs" can be used as examples, so that students can research the current literature on fashion and write their own "briefly speaking" articles. This feature is found in Units 2, 3, and 4.

Glossary

The glossary contains over 250 industry terms. A knowledge and understanding of the "language" of fashion gives students a firm footing upon which they can "step-out" into the industry and know they are speaking the right language.

End-of-Chapter Activities

Each of the 18 chapters in the text concludes with three kinds of student-oriented activities designed to enrich and reinforce the instructional material. A "Merchandising Vocabulary" section in each chapter explains fashion and merchandising terms introduced for the first time in that chapter. The student will recognize these terms when they appear in subsequent chapters. These terms are also in the Glossary.

"Merchandising Review" asks questions about the key concepts of each chapter. These questions provoke thought, encourage classroom discussion, and develop recall of the material presented in the text.

The section called "Merchandising Digest" consists primarily of an excerpt from the text. It asks the student to explain the significance of the excerpt and to support the explanation with specific illustrations. This activity affords the student an opportunity to apply theory to actual situations and to draw on his or her own background and experiences.

End-of-Unit Activities

Another popular feature that has been repeated in this edition is the "Fashion Project," drawn from authentic merchandising situations, which ends each unit. These fashion projects emphasize and reinforce the instructional elements brought out in each unit. The projects enrich instruction and suggest to students that fashion merchandising is a dynamic and exciting field.

Instructor's Manual

An instructor's manual is available to adopters at no cost. It includes a number of options for organizing the fashion merchandising curriculum and contains general suggestions for teaching the course. It also contains supplementary assignments for each unit. The key to the text includes answers to all end-of-chapter and end-of-unit exercises.

A useful feature is a test bank of five tests containing test material for the units, and a final examination. The tests are composed of 100 objective questions each and are ready to duplicate.

ACKNOWLEDGMENTS

The author is grateful to the many educators and businesspeople who have given her encouragement, information, and helpful suggestions. Among these, Jean Samples, who also worked on the last edition, stands out. Jean has contributed many insights, ideas, and above all, enthusiasm, to this project. Her use of the previous editions in the classroom has greatly enriched this one.

The following educators reviewed the fourth edition in depth and made many significant suggestions for improvement:

Elaine McCain
Lee College
Baytown, Texas

Audra Shields
Houston Community College
Houston, Texas

The following educators reviewed the manuscript for this edition and provided a wealth of information and inspiration:

Alfred V. Sloan, Jr.
Fashion Institute of Technology
New York, New York

Anyse Winston
New York City Technical College
Brooklyn, New York

The author is also indebted to the following industry experts who read and critiqued the specific chapters mentioned for accuracy, up-to-date information, and completeness:

Anne K. Bernard (Ch. 18)
Associate Professor, Advertising and Communications Department
Fashion Institute of Technology

Patricia Breen (Chs. 7 & 11)
Associate Professor, Fashion Buying and Merchandising Department
Fashion Institute of Technology

Addie Roback Goldstrom (Ch. 15)
Director of Product Development
Fashion Stores Association

Gloria Hartley (Ch. 14)
President, Creative Imports

Jack Hyde (Ch. 10)
Assistant Professor, Advertising and Communications Department,
Fashion Institute of Technology

John Karl (Ch. 10)
Chairman, Menswear Design and Marketing Department
Fashion Institute of Technology

Edward Newman (Ch. 6)
Chairperson, Fabric Styling Department
Fashion Institute of Technology

Nurie E. Relis (Ch. 12)
Assistant Chairperson, Fashion Design Department
Fashion Institute of Technology

Jack Rittenberg (Ch. 12)
Dean of Students and Consulting Chairman, Cosmetics Department
Fashion Institute of Technology

Rose Rosa (Ch. 9)
Professor, Fashion Design Department
Fashion Institute of Technology

Jill Vander Putten (Ch. 7)
Consulting Chairman, Fur Program
Fashion Institute of Technology

I regret that space does not allow me to mention all the fashion industry experts I consulted; they were very generous with their time and expertise.

Elaine Stone

CONTENTS

Photo Credits

J. Donoso, Sygma: 1, 117 (bottom right), 326. Robert Roth, LGI: 5. P. Vauthey, Sygma: 7, 71 (top left, top right, bottom). AP/World Wide: 9 (bottom left), 63 (middle), 323, 368. Daniel Simon, Gamma-Liaison: 9 (bottom right), 21, 63 (right), 117 (bottom right), 332 (right), 336. Reuters, Bettmann Newsphoto: 10, 84, 332 (left). Woodfin Camp: 15. © 1949, renewed 1975 by the Conde Nast Publications, Inc.: 17. The Ganger Collection (top left and right): 19. James Andanson, Sygma: 26. Gamma Liaison: 32. Art Resource (left): 34. The Bettmann Archive: 34 (middle, right), 63 (left), 229. Peter Gould, Image Press: 36. Alcott & Andrews: 40. Patrice Habans, Sygma: 48. Reprinted courtesy of *In Fashion* magazine: 56. Tim Ryan, Gamma-Liaison: 60. Karen Filter: 74. Marmel Studios, The Stock Market (top right): 76. Geri Engberg, The Stock Market (middle): 76. Richard Gross, The Stock Market (bottom right): 76. Jim Rolan, LGI: 82. I. Hartman, LGI: 85. NBC, Inc.: 86. Steven E. Sutton, Duomo: 88. Barbara Rios, Photo Researchers: 95, 189. Fendi: 100. Liderno Salvador (top): 103. Krizia (bottom): 103. Esprit: 105, 198. Sygma: 108, 316. Murjani (top right): 117. Luca Babini (top left): 117. American Textile Manufacturer's Institute, Inc. (top): 119. Wolfgang Kaehler (middle, bottom): 119. Fiber Industries: 125. Wool Industries: 127. Ideacomo: 128. Hoechst Celanese: 131. DuPont Photo: 132. West Point/Pepperell, Inc.: 139. Ulrike Welsch, Photo Researchers: 146. American Leather Tanning Industry: 149. N.Y. Fashion Club/Gingette: 151. The Fur Vault: 152. Helen Frustick for James Hirch Furs: 159. Vittoriano Rastelli, N.Y.T. Pictures: 161. Blackgama/Great Lakes Mink Association: 162. The International Fur Wholesalers: 165. International Ladies Garment Worker's Union: 169, 170. Anne Klein II: 179. Forgotten Woman: 183. Mother Care: 184. Richard Pasley,

Stock Boston: 185. The Addis Company: 187. John Barr, Gamma-Liaison: 196. Theo Westenberger, Sygma: 200. Pepsi, 202. Hartmarx Corp.: 214. Pierre Cardin: 217. Jeffrey Banks, Pres., Jeffrey Banks Ltd.: 218. Fineberg Publicity for the Greif Companies: 223. Bloomingdale's: 224, 341. Ebony Man: 226. C.D.I. Technologies: 231, 343. Images Press: 236. © 1986, Reebok International, Ltd.: 240. Polo Ralph Lauren: 242, 394. R. Marino, Sygma: 245. Walborg: 249. Tiffany & Company: 251. Scott Halleran, Images Press: 253. Macy's: 257. Neiman-Marcus: 259, 263 (top, middle), 379. Olga (bottom): 263. Vanity Fair: 265. Spiegel (left): 269. Brownstone Studio, Inc. (right): 269. The Limited/Victoria's Secret: 270. Adrien Arpel: 273. Tom Tracy, The Stock Market: 276, 278. Crabtree & Evelyn: 280. Estee Lauder: 282. Spencer Grant, Photo Researchers: 285. Mattel: 286. Chicago Apparel Center: 294. The Dallas Apparel Center: 297. Robert F. Carl, Men's Fashion Association: 298. The Dallas Menswear Mart: 299. Miami Merchandising Mart: 300, 305. California Mart: 311. L'Unico Mipel Al Mondo (top left, top right, bottom): 321. Igedo: 325. Canadian Fashion Inc.: 329. Hong Kong Trade Development Council: 334. Spring Apparel Fabrics Division: 347. Bengali, Benetton: 350, 363. John Chaisson, Gamma-Liaison (bottom left): 359. John Perkell, The Stock Market (top): 359. Rich's Department Store: 366. Zayre's: 370, 391. The Gap: 372. Gerd Ludwig, Woodfin Camp: 382. *Stores:* 388. Larry Fleming: 390. Cable Value Network: 397. Jim Knowles: 398. *Elle* magazine: 404. The Leichman Group, Ltd.: 405. F. Meylan, Sygma: 359 (middle right, bottom right), 406. Patrick Group Media: 408. The Fashion Newsletter, International Forecast of Incoming Fashions, © Newsletter Service, Inc.: 411. Federation Francaise Dupret a Porter Feminin: 412. G. Schachmes, Sygma: 414.

UNIT ONE

the dynamics of fashion

Fashion on its most basic level is about the making and selling of clothes. On another equally important level, though, it is about the making and selling of image and style. Fashion is the most dynamic of American businesses. It thrives on change. If the fashion business did not change, it would not survive. After all, the most important thing the fashion business does is to show the world what is new. It does this through the merchandising of apparel and accessories.

As a business, fashion is composed of many, often paradoxical, elements. It is an art and a science, an industry that is at the same time both highly personal and incredibly public.

Fashion can be viewed as an art because so much creativity is required to make its products. Unlike most other businesses where conformity is the norm, fashion nurtures innovation and creativity in those who work in the industry.

Fashion has always been considered a science as well. Modern fashion manufacturing was born during the industrial revolution and has matured in the age of technology. Without machines, clothing could never be mass-produced. Technology has revolutionized the way fashion is made. Almost all stages of clothing production from design to delivery rely to some extent on technology.

Fashion, always a highly personal business, is in the process of becoming even more so. Clothing design has always been about one person's—the designer's—ideas. Today, though, one cannot examine the personal element in fashion without also talking about the customer.

A decade ago, fashion designers and leaders virtually dictated what the consumer of fashion wore. Today's fashion users, however, are more sophisticated, more knowledgeable, and most important, more individualistic. They are not afraid to express their own ideas about how they want to look against the designers' ideas about how people should look. For the first time in the history of fashion, customers are unabashedly taking an active role in choosing what they wear.

The result has been role reversal: Where the makers of fashion once got their ideas entirely from their own world of style, they now borrow freely from the external world. New fashion ideas now come from the world around us: the streets, innovative teenagers, a new play, a celebrity with his or her unique look.

But however personal fashion is on one level, the making of clothes is still very much a public business. Always, the fashion business must cater to a mass market, and these days, even to one with rapidly rising expectations. Thanks to television, new ideas and trends now sweep across the country and are adopted in a matter of days.

When we speak of fashion as a public business, we are also referring to the external forces that affect the business. Shifts in the economy, sociological influences, and demographic changes all contribute to change in fashion and therefore affect the fashion business.

All these contradictory elements work to keep the fashion business dynamic and ever-changing. In this unit, you will examine how and why fashion changes. You'll begin to develop a basic vocabulary and a working knowledge of the principles around which the fashion world revolves (in Chapter 1). You'll examine the various forces that come together to make fashion dynamic and alive:

▶ The environmental forces—the role that economic, sociological, and psychological elements play in the fashion business—in Chapter 2.

▶ The cyclical forces—how fashions change and how an understanding of this constant cycle of change can be used to predict and analyze current and future fashion—in Chapter 3.

▶ The design forces—the role played by designers, manufacturers, and retailers in creating fashion—in Chapter 4.

▶ The business forces—the scope of the industry, its recent growth and expansion, and various new forms of ownership—in Chapter 5.

Not only does fashion thrive on change, but the business of fashion is itself changing. The world of fashion operates in a far different way today than it did 10 years ago. It moves faster and reaches more people. It is more sophisticated. And perhaps most important, it is more businesslike. In order to understand the changes that have occurred and will occur in the future of the fashion industry, you must first understand the dynamics that underlie the fashion business.

THE NATURE OF FASHION

❝Fashion is and has been and will be, through all ages, the outward form through which the mind speaks to the universe. Fashion in all languages designs to make, shape, model, adapt, embellish, and adorn.❞[1]

Fashion, then, involves our outward, visible lives. Fashion involves the clothes we wear, the dances we dance, the cars we drive, and the way we cut our hair. Fashion also influences architecture, forms of worship, and lifestyles. It has an impact on every stage of life from the womb to the tomb.

People started covering their bodies with clothes to keep warm and be modest, but adornment—decoration—was already an important part of dressing. Pressure from peer groups and changes in lifestyle influence the type of adornment considered acceptable in a particular time or for a particular group. Basically, of course, the reasons people have for wearing clothes have not changed. Today people still wear clothes to keep warm or cool and for the sake of modesty, but what we select for those purposes is very much influenced by a desire to adorn ourselves.

Because people are social animals, clothing is very much a social statement. By looking at the way a person dresses, you can often make good guesses about his or her social and business standing, sex-role identification, political orientation, ethnicity, lifestyle, and aesthetic priorities. Clothing is a forceful and highly visible medium of communication that carries with it information about who a person is, who a person is not, and who a person would like to be.

THE IMPORTANCE OF FASHION

During recent years the general interest in fashion has increased enormously. Fashion is one of the greatest economic forces in present-day life. To a great extent, it determines what people will buy. Change in fashion is the motivating factor for replacing clothes, cosmetics, furniture, housewares, and automobiles. Fashion causes changes in consumer goods and at the same time makes people want the new products, since the thought of being unfashionable is a fate worse than death to many people!

As important as fashion is to the individual consumer and to fashion businesses, probably less is commonly known about fashion than about most other human activity. Although reams of material have been written about fashion, relatively little explains why and how a fashion begins, becomes popular, and declines, and what the principles are that govern fashion trends. Students of human nature want to know what fashion means—both in the past and in the 1990s. Is fashion a political statement? A social statement? Is fashion a measure of the national economy or an art form? Sociologists, psychologists, and historians study fashion in order to better understand society, human nature, and the past. Their findings provide us with insight into the meanings of current fashion.

Webster defines fashion as "prevailing custom, usage, or style,"[2] and in this sense it covers a wide range of human activity. The term is used in this book in a narrower sense: **fashion** here means the style or styles of clothing and accessories worn at a particular time by a particular group of people.

THE FASHION BUSINESS

Fashion today is big business; millions of people are employed in fashion-related activities. The **fashion industries** are those engaged in manufacturing the materials and finished products used in the production of apparel and accessories for men, women, and children. Throughout this book any reference to "fashion industries" means the manufacturing businesses unless others are specifically mentioned. The broader term **fashion business** includes all the industries and services connected with fashion: design, manufacturing, distribution, retailing, advertising, publishing, and consulting; in other words, any business concerned with fashion goods or services.

Marketing

Today, marketing has become a major influence in the fashion business. What does marketing mean? Most people think of marketing only as promotion and selling. However, promotion and selling are only two aspects of marketing. The process of **marketing** includes diverse activities that identify consumer needs, develop good products, and price, distribute, and promote them effectively so that they will sell easily. "The aim of marketing is . . . to know and understand the customer so well that the product or service hits him and sells itself."[3]

Fashion Marketing and Merchandising

The fashion business has been rather slow in adopting the marketing techniques that have been so successful in the growth of consumer goods such as automobiles, packaged foods, and health and beauty aids. For many years fashion producers were only concerned with what was economical and easy for them to produce. They would spend considerable time and money trying to convince the consumer that what they had produced was what the consumer wanted. The producer had little or no interest in the wants and needs of the consumer.

Recently, however, the total process of marketing has been adopted by the fashion business and is being applied to the products and services of the fashion industries. The result is called **fashion marketing:** that is, the marketing of apparel and accessories to the ultimate consumer.

The topic of this book is narrower than fashion marketing; we are concerned with **fashion merchandising,** which refers to the *planning* required to have the right fashion-oriented merchandise at the right time, in the right place, in the right quantities, at the right prices, and with the right sales promotion.

MISCONCEPTIONS ABOUT FASHION

As the power of fashion to influence our lives grows, three misconceptions about it continue to be widely held. The first and most common misconception is that designers and retailers dictate what the fashion will be and then force it upon helpless consumers. It has been said that the industry is composed of "obsolescence ogres." In reality, consumers themselves decide what the fashion will be by influencing new designs and by accepting or rejecting the styles that are offered. Consumers are, in truth, "variety vultures."

Spangles, sequins, and see-through are a mark of the distinctive fashion style of Cher, who is seen here in an Egyptian-inspired outfit.

The second misconception is that fashion acts as an influence on women only. Today, men and children are as influenced by and responsive to fashion as women. Fashion is the force that causes women to raise or lower their skirt lengths, straighten or frizz their hair, and change from sportswear to dressy clothes. Fashion is also the force that influences men to grow or shave off their mustaches and beards, choose wide or narrow ties and lapels, and change from casual jeans into three-piece suits. Fashion is also the force that makes children demand specific products and styles.

The third misconception is that fashion is a mysterious and unpredictable force. Actually, its direction can be determined and its changes predicted with remarkable accuracy by those who study and understand the fundamentals of fashion. Fashion was once considered an art form controlled by designers who dictated its content. But fashion has now evolved into a science that can be measured and evaluated.

THE TERMINOLOGY OF FASHION

What is the difference between fashion, style, and design? Just what do high fashion, mass fashion, taste, classic, and fad mean? To avoid confusion when discussing fashion, we must first understand the meanings of these terms. The definitions that follow are based on the work of Dr. Paul H. Nystrom, one of the pioneers in fashion merchandising.[4]

Style

The first step in understanding fashion is to distinguish between "fashion" and "style," words that most people use interchangeably although there is an immense difference in their meanings. In general terms, a style is a characteristic or distinctive artistic expression or presentation. Styles exist in architecture, sculpture, painting, politics, and music, as well as in popular heros, games, hobbies, pets, flirtations, and weddings.

In apparel, **style** is the characteristic or distinctive appearance of a garment—the combination of features that makes it unique and different from other garments. For example, T-shirts are as different from silk blouses as they are from peasant blouses. Riding jackets are as different from safari jackets as they are from blazer jackets.

Although styles come and go in terms of acceptance, a specific style always remains a style, whether it is currently in fashion or not. Some people adopt a style that becomes indelibly associated with them and wear it regardless of whether it is currently fashionable. Joan Crawford's platform shoes, Katherine Hepburn's pleated trousers, the Duchess of Windsor's hairdo, Woody Allen's sneakers, Michael Jackson's glove, and Bruce Springsteen's T-shirts are all examples of personal style.

Some styles are named for the period of history in which they originated—Grecian, Roman, Renaissance, Empire, flapper era (1920s), Gibson Girl era (early 1900s). When such styles return to fashion, their basic elements remain the same. Minor details are altered to reflect the taste or needs of the era in which they reappear. For example, the flapper style of the 1920s was short, pleated, and body skimming. That style can be bought today, but with changes for current fashion acceptance.

Fashion

On the other hand, a **fashion** is a style that is accepted and used by the majority of a group at any one time, no matter how small that group. A fashion is always based on some particular style. But not every style is a fashion. A fashion is a fact of social psychology. A style

Is it a bird? A plane? Superwoman? No—just a "high-fashion" leader viewed by a "mass-fashion" follower.

is usually a creation from an artist or a designer. A fashion is a result of social emulation and acceptance. A style may be old or new, beautiful or ugly, good or bad. A style is still a style even if it never receives the slightest acceptance or even approval. A style does not become a fashion until it gains some popular acceptance, and it remains a fashion only as long as it is accepted. Miniskirts, square-toed shoes, mustaches, and theatrical daytime makeup have all been fashions. And no doubt each will again be accepted by a majority of a group of people with similar interests or characteristics—for example, college students, young career men and women, retired men and women.

Fashions appeal to many different groups and can be categorized according to the group to which they appeal. **High fashion** refers to a new style accepted by a limited number of fashion leaders who want to be the first to adopt changes and innovation in fashion. High-fashion styles are generally introduced and sold in small quantities and at relatively high prices. These styles may be limited because they are too sophisticated or extreme to appeal to the needs of the general public, or they are priced well beyond the reach of most people. However, if the style can appeal to a broader audience, it is generally copied, mass-produced, and sold at lower prices. The fashion leaders or innovators who first accepted it then move on to something new.

To contrast with high fashion, **mass fashion** or **volume fashion,** consists of styles that are widely accepted. These fashions are usually produced and sold in large quantities at moderate to low prices, and appeal to the greatest majority of fashion-conscious consumers. Mass fashion accounts for the majority of sales in the fashion business. Mass fashion is the "bread and butter" of the fashion banquet!

Design

There can be many variations of detail within a specific style. A **design** is a particular or individual interpretation, or version, of a style. A style may be expressed in a great many designs, all different, yet all related because they are in the same style. A sweatshirt, for example, is a distinctive style, but within that style, individual variations may include different types of necklines, pockets, and sleeves. Another example is a satchel handbag which may be interpreted with different closures, locks, or handles. These minor variations are the different interpretations that change the design of a style.

In the fashion industries, manufacturers and retailers assign a number to each individual design produced. This is the **style number.** The style number of a product identifies it for manufacturing, ordering, and selling purposes. In this instance, the term "style number" is used rather than "design number," even though a design is being identified.

Taste

In fashion, **taste** refers to prevailing opinion of what is and what is not attractive and appropriate for a given occasion. Good taste in fashion, therefore, means sensitivity not only to what is artistically pleasing but also to what is appropriate for a specific situation. A style, such as an evening gown, may be beautiful. But if it is worn to a morning wedding, for example, it may not be considered in good taste.

There are many styles that are beautiful, but because they are not in fashion, good taste prevents their use. On the other hand, there may be a present-day fashion that is inartistic or even ugly, but its common acceptance means that it is in good taste.

Nystrom described the relationship between good taste and fashion this way: "Good taste essentially is making the most artistic use of current fashion . . . bridging the gap between good art and common usage."[5]

Even during the height of acceptance of a particular fashion, it is considered in good taste only if it is worn by people on whom it looks appropriate. For example, miniskirts, tight pants, bikinis, and halter tops are considered in good taste only for slim people in good physical shape.

Timing, too, plays a part in what is considered good or bad taste. British costume authority James Laver saw the relationship between taste and fashion in terms of its acceptance level. A style, he said, is thought to be:[6]

"indecent"	10 years before its time
"shameless"	5 years before its time
"outré"	1 year before its time
"smart"	in its time
"dowdy"	1 year after its time
"hideous"	10 years after its time
"ridiculous"	20 years after its time

While the time an individual fashion takes to complete this course may vary, the course is always a cyclical one. (See Chapter 3.) A new style is often considered daring and in dubious taste. It is gradually accepted, then widely accepted, and finally gradually discarded.

For many decades, Laver's cycle has been accepted as the movement of most fashions. However, in the last few decades some fashions have deviated from this pattern. The fashion cycles have become shorter and have repeated themselves within a shorter space of time. For the student of fashion this presents an interesting challenge. What factors determine which fashions will follow the accepted cycles and which fashions will not? To understand the movement of fashion, it is important to understand that fashions are always in harmony with the times in which they appear. During the upheaval and unrest of the late 1960s, short skirts made their appearance everywhere, from campus to office. In the late 1980s another wave of social unrest appeared and short skirts reappeared.

A Classic

Some styles or designs continue to be considered in good taste over a long period. They are exceptions to the usual movement of styles through the fashion life cycle. A **classic** is a style or design that satisfies a basic need and remains in general fashion acceptance for an extended period of time.

Depending upon the fashion statement one wishes to make, a person may have only a few classics or may have a wardrobe of mostly classics. A classic is characterized by simplicity of design which keeps it from being easily dated. The "Chanel" suit is an outstanding example of a classic. The simple lines of the Chanel suit has made it acceptable for many decades, and although it reappears now and then as a fashion, many women always have a Chanel suit in their wardrobes. Other examples of classics are shirtwaist dresses, blazer jackets, cardigan or turtleneck sweaters, button-down oxford shirts, and loafers. Among accessories, the pump-style shoe, the one-button glove, and the clutch handbag are also classics. For young children, overalls and one-piece pajamas have become classics.

Long or short, the Chanel suit has been a fashion classic for decades.

FASHION

VIVIENNE WESTWOOD: THE MOTHER OF PUNK

Fashion would not be fashion if it did not change and constantly challenge established style. And among the hundreds of prominent designers who have made it their business to stretch the boundaries of fashion, one in particular stands out: Vivienne Westwood.

A former schoolteacher who grew up in the north of England, Westwood began sewing clothes for herself at age 12. In the late 1960s, when she was in her twenties, Westwood broadened her design talents to include copying and customizing "whatever cult clothes were in vogue at the moment."[1] With her business and romantic partner, Malcolm McLaren, she opened a shop on King's Road in London, where she began selling her dramatic designs and using fashion to explore contemporary culture.

Striving to "destroy the world conformity"[2] in the early 1970s, Westwood created a new look highlighted by ripped T-shirts and studded black leather jackets and became the founder and "high priestess" of punk,[3] in both its fashion and its ideology. As she herself expressed her goal: "My job is always to confront the establishment to try and find out where freedom lies and what you can do. . . . [Fashion] is only interesting to me if it's subversive."[4]

But again, proving that fashion is synonymous with change, Westwood

A typical daring and innovative look from Vivienne Westwood.

FOCUS

ventured closer to the mainstream in 1980 and took the fashion world by storm with a much more accessible "pirate" look. Originally created by her for the rock group Adam and the Ants, the new look featured romantic and colorful garments such as roomy, ruffled shirts, baggy knicker pants, and brocade vests.

The pirate craze was followed by the popular "Buffalo Gals" collection full of wool frock coats and sheepskin vests, and in October 1985, Westwood wowed the fashion world with the launch of her mini-crini—a short, bell-shaped crinoline skirt that was widely copied and became the fashion focus of 1986.

With such a diverse series of style statements behind her, one might think that Westwood had nowhere else to go with designs that would surprise fashion observers. But true to form, in the spring of 1987, Westwood introduced yet another innovative collection, this time borrowing on the staid styles of British royalty.

"It is a pleasure to feast on the surprises of tradition,"[5] Westwood said of the collection, which was composed of classic British tailored woolens, fitted coats, and suits whose lapels curved into a heart shape when buttoned. Predictably, there were unpredictable touches, too, such as plaid schoolgirl dresses topped with fake ermine capes, and "criniscule" minicrinoline skirts. As true proof of Westwood's new-found acceptance, the collection was featured in Manhattan's trendy Charivari stores, as well as in Bloomingdale's, which even created a series of display windows for the line.

In short, Vivienne Westwood stands as the perfect example that everything in fashion—including a designer's philosophy—is based on change and the ability to look forward. As one writer noted: "Westwood has always stood stridently and stylishly in the fashion front."[6] And that is doubtless where she will stay.

[1] "Vivienne Westwood: Shock Treatments," *Gentleman's Quarterly*, January 1983, p. 132.
[2] Jon Savage, "Rich Pickings at the World's End . . .," *The Face*, January 1981, p. 25.
[3] Cathleen McGuigan, with Rita Dallas, "Breaking All the Rules," *Newsweek*, January 23, 1984, p. 53.
[4] Savage, p. 25.
[5] "The Mother of Punk Fashion," *Women's Wear Daily*, March 19, 1987, p. 26.
[6] Robert Elms, "Coming West to the New World's End," *Soho News Style Supplement*, October 6, 1981, p. 56.

This Fashion Focus is based on information from the articles cited above and from these sources:

"High Priestess of the Crinoline Craze That Swept Fashion in 1986," *Women's Wear Daily*, January 12, 1987, p. 1.
Bonnie Johnson, "For Britain's Vivienne Westwood, the Mother of Punk, It's the Prophet Motive That Counts," *People*, October 1987, pp. 66–68.

A Fad

A fashion that suddenly sweeps into popularity, affecting a limited part of the total population, and then quickly disappears is called a **fad.** It comes into existence by the introduction of some feature or detail, usually exaggerated, that excites the interest of the customer. The fad starts by being quickly accepted and then quickly imitated by others. Fads often begin in lower-price ranges, are relatively easy to copy, and therefore flood the market in a very short time. Because of this kind of market saturation, the public tires of fads quickly and they end abruptly.

Fads follow the same cycle as fashions do, but their rise in popularity is much faster, their acceptance much shorter, and their decline much more rapid than that of a true fashion. Because most fads come and go in a single season, they have been called "miniature fashions." In recent decades we have had the "punk" hairdo fad, the "King Tut" design fad, the "Nehru" collar fad, the "Urban Cowboy" fad, and the "Vanna White" fad. Fads, like fashions, invade every field, sports, literature, religion, politics, and education.

However, many things that come in as fads become fashions and can carry over for several seasons. In fact, it is very difficult to draw the line between fads and fashions. The chemise, or sack dress, is probably the outstanding example of this phenomenon. After an instant rise to popularity in the late 1950s, it quickly passed from the fashion scene. A few years later, the chemise reappeared as the shift. In 1974, the chemise again appeared in the Paris collections, modified to eliminate its former disadvantages. American manufacturers quickly reproduced it in several versions and in a wide price range. That the chemise, in its various manifestations, again appeared in the late 1980s is strong evidence that it, too, will become a fashion classic.

For decades, ballet dancers used leg warmers to protect their valuable legs during and after strenuous exercise and dancing. And there the knowledge and use of leg warmers ended. But in early 1982, leg warmers were suddenly adopted by high school and college students, doubtless made aware of them by the movie and TV show *Fame.* Worn over panty hose or pants, they provided the wearer with warmth as well as a very "in" look. Finally leg warmers were being worn with short shorts on the streets of Southern California where the temperatures are far from chilly, and on men and women runners all over the country. Another fad became a fashion.

COMPONENTS OF FASHION

Fashion design does not just happen, nor does the designer wave a magic wand to create a new design. Fashion design involves the combination of four basic elements or components: silhouette, detail, texture, and color. Only through a change in one or more of these basic components does a new fashion evolve. This is true of any fashion-influenced product, from kitchen appliances to automobiles, from apartment houses to office buildings, and from accessories to apparel.

Silhouette

The **silhouette** of a costume is its overall outline or contour. It is also frequently referred to as "shape" or "form."

It may appear to the casual observer that women have worn countless silhouettes throughout the centuries. Research shows, however, that there are actually only three basic forms—straight, or tubular; bell-shaped, or bouffant; and the bustle, or back fullness—with many variations.[7]

Since the mid-eighteenth century, these three basic silhouettes have consistently come into fashion in the same sequence, each recurring approximately once every 100 years and lasting for about 35 years. For example, the triangle shape (a variation of the straight, or tubular, silhouette) of the 1930s and 1940s reoccurred as the wide-shoulder, narrow-hip silhouette of the late 1970s. The widespread sociological change and rapid technological developments of recent decades, however, may have altered both the traditional life span and the sequence of these silhouettes.

Details

The individual elements that give a silhouette its form or shape are called **details.** These include trimmings; skirt and pant length and width; and shoulder, waist, and sleeve treatment.

Silhouettes evolve gradually from one to another through changes in detail. When the trend in a detail reaches an extreme, a reversal of the trend takes place. For example, dresses and suits featured wide shoulders with much padding in the 1940s and 1950s. This was reversed in the late 1960s and 1970s, when the look became casual and unstructured. This casualness reached such extremes that by the start of the 1980s, structured clothing was back in fashion and dress and suit shoulders began once again to grow wider as padding was inserted.

The spiked-heel, pointed-toe shoe of the 1950s gave way to the "clunky" flat shoe with broad toe of the late 1960s. Again, extremes were eventually reached and the heel went higher, first becoming a wedge and then, by 1980, a regular heel. Toes narrowed somewhat, and soon the American woman was reunited with her favorite shoe fashion—the classic pump.

Variations in detail allow both designer and consumer to freely express their individuality within the framework of the currently accepted silhouette. To emphasize a natural-waistline silhouette, for example, a slender woman might choose a simple wide belt, a heavily decorated belt, or a belt in a contrasting color to suit her personality and the occasion. To express his individuality, a man might emphasize the wide-shoulder look with epaulets or heavy shoulder pads.

Texture

One of the most significant components of fashion is texture. **Texture** is the look and feel of material, woven or nonwoven.

Texture can affect the appearance of a silhouette, giving it a bulky or slender look depending on the roughness or smoothness of the materials. A woman dressed in a rough tweed dress and a bulky knit sweater is likely to look larger and squarer than she does in the same dress executed in a smooth jersey and topped with a cashmere sweater.

Texture influences the drape of a garment. Chiffon clings and flows, making it a good choice for soft, feminine styles, while corduroy has the firmness and bulk suitable for more casual garments.

Texture affects the color of a fabric by causing the surface to either reflect or absorb light. Rough textures absorb light, causing the colors to appear flat.

Smooth textures reflect light, causing colors to appear brighter. Anyone who has tried to match colors soon discovers that a color which appears extremely bright in a shiny vinyl, satin, or high-gloss enamel paint seems subdued in a rough wool, a suede, or a stucco wall finish. Pile surfaces such as velvet both reflect and absorb light; thus the colors of pile surfaces look richer and deeper than those of flat, smooth surfaces.

Color

Color has always been a major consideration in women's clothing. Since World War II, color in men's clothing has been regaining the importance it had in previous centuries. Today color is a key factor in apparel selection for both sexes. Color is important in advertising, packaging, and store decor as well.

Historically, colors have been used to denote rank and profession. Purple, for instance, was associated with royalty and in some periods could be worn only by those of noble birth. Black became customary for the apparel of the clergy and for members of the judiciary.

Color symbolism often varies with geographical location. While white is the Western world's symbol of purity, worn by brides and used in communion dresses, it is the color of mourning in India.

Color has been importantly affected by developments in technology. Better ways of tanning leather and dyeing and finishing fabrics have produced a wider variety of colors and color combinations than ever before for fashion designers to work with. Colors today are also more permanent, more resistant to fading or changing, and thus more acceptable to consumers. Colors change appearance depending on adjacent colors. Thus blues are brightened by nearby oranges or dulled by adjacent grays or blacks.

Today a fashion designer's color palette changes with consumers' preferences. In some seasons, all is brightness and sharp contrast, and no color is too powerful to be worn. In other seasons, only subdued colors appeal. Fashion merchants must develop an eye for color—not only for the specific hues and values popular in a given season, but also for indications of possible trends in consumer preference.

THE INTANGIBLES OF FASHION

Fashion itself is intangible. A style is tangible, made up of a definite silhouette and details of design. But fashion is shaped by such powerful intangibles as group acceptance, change, the social forces important during a certain era, and people's desire to relate to specific lifestyles.

Acceptance

The fig leaf, the first fashion creation, was widely accepted and since then we have come a long way. Basically, fashion is acceptance: group acceptance or approval is implied in any definition of fashion. Most people have a deep-seated wish to express themselves as individuals but also to be part of a group. To dress in the latest fashion means that they are trying to be individual yet also belong.

Acceptance need not be universal, however. A style may be adopted by one group while other segments of the population ignore it. For example, the fashions shaped by big-city lifestyles are rarely popular with the suburban crowd. The carefree, nonconformist fashions on

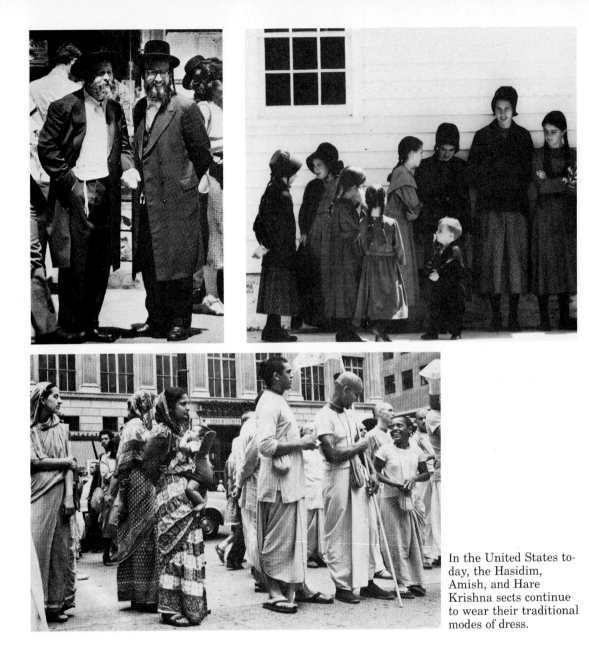

In the United States today, the Hasidim, Amish, and Hare Krishna sects continue to wear their traditional modes of dress.

college campuses bear little or no relationship to those accepted by businesspeople.

A style may also be accepted and become a fashion in one part of the world while it is ignored or rejected elsewhere. Each of the following is considered fashionable by its own inhabitants: the igloo of the Inuit, the thatched hut of some African tribespeople, and the ranch-style house of many American suburbanites. Similarly, many ethnic and religious groups have distinctive styles of dress.

The way we dress is a personal signature. The dress or suit we wear is not just a confirmation of the old adage that "Clothes makes the man . . . or woman," but rather an example of the fact that our need for acceptance is expressed largely in the way we dress. Acceptance also means that a fashion is considered appropriate to the occasion for which it is worn. Clothes considered appropriate for big-business boardrooms would not be considered acceptable for casual weekends.

If any of you should doubt the power of acceptance in fashion, try a simple experiment. Put on clothes worn 10 or 20 years ago, or totally different in style from what is considered the fashion. Then go out casually among your friends, acquaintances, or even strangers, and note their reactions toward you and then your feelings toward yourself. There will be quizzical looks, doubtful stares, and in some cases smirks and laughter. No one can really "belong" to their chosen group and at the same time choose to be completely "out" of present-day fashion. Such is the power of fashion acceptance.

Change

Fashion changes because ideas about politics, religion, leisure, democracy, success, and age change. Fashion is also a complex means for facilitating orderly change within a mass society. This is particularly true when the society is no longer able to provide identity and maintain social order via custom or tradition.[8] In the United States, where different immigrant and ethnic groups must adjust to one another, fashion is one means of providing a social bond.

Fashion is subject to change—both rapid and gradual. Modern communi-cations play a major role in today's accelerated rate of fashion change. The mass media spreads fashion news across the face of the globe in hours, sometimes seconds. Live TV coverage of events around the world enables us to see not only what people are doing but also what they are wearing. Our morning newspapers show us what fashion leaders wore to a party the night before. Even slight fashion changes are given faster and wider publicity than ever before. Consumers who like these changes demand them from merchants, who in turn demand them from manufacturers.

New technology is constantly producing new fibers and blends of fibers. Each seems to offer more than the one before and encourages the discarding of the old. Also, the consumer finds the moderately priced, "off-the-rack" dress easier to discard than the more expensive hand-sewn or hand-knitted creation.

The Futility of Forcing Change

Fashion expresses the spirit of the times, and in turn influences it. Fashion designers are successful or not depending on their ability to sense and anticipate changes if not to initiate them. Changes can be initiated, but there are as many examples of failures as there are of successful changes. Efforts have been made from time to time to force changes in the course of fashion but they usually fail. Fashion is a potent force which by definition requires support by the majority.

As an example, in the late 1960s, designers and retailers decided that skirts had reached their limit in shortness and that women would soon be seeking change. So the designers designed and the retailers stocked and promoted the "midi," a skirt mid-calf in length. The designers and retailers were right in

After World War II, Christian Dior met the demand for change from the tailored short-skirted look of the early 1940s by providing women with the full-skirted feminine "New Look."

theory but wrong in timing and choice of skirt length. Consumers found the midi too sudden and radical a change and did not accept or buy the style in sufficient numbers to make it a fashion. In the late 1980s, designers and retailers did it again—this time they tried to force a change to very short skirts. Again, the public disliked the radical change and refused to buy miniskirts, causing a financial crisis in the women's apparel business.

Occasionally, necessity and government regulation can interrupt the course of fashion. During World War II, the U.S. government controlled the type and quantity of fabric used in consumer goods. One regulation prohibited anything but slit pockets on women's garments to avoid using the extra material that patch pockets require. Skirts were short and silhouettes were narrow, reflecting the scarcity of material.

Meeting the Demand for Change

After World War II, a reaction to these designs was to be expected. A new French designer, Christian Dior, caught and expressed the desire for a freer line and a more feminine garment in his first collection, which achieved instant fashion success. Using fabric with a lavishness that had been impossible in Europe or America during the war years, he created his "new look," with long, full skirts, fitted waistlines, and feminine curves.

Dior did not change the course of fashion; he accelerated it—from an evolutionary course to a revolutionary one. He recognized and interpreted the need of women at that time to get out of stiff, short, narrow, unfeminine clothes and into soft, free, longer, feminine ones. Consumers wanted the change, and the lifting of the very strict wartime restrictions made it possible to meet their demand.

Another example of a consumer demand for change occurred in menswear just before World War II. Year after year, manufacturers had been turning out versions of a style that had long been popular in England—the padded-shoulder, draped suit. A number of young men from very influential families, who were attending well-known northeastern colleges, became tired of that look. They wanted a change. They took their objections to New Haven clothing manufacturers, and the result was the natural-shoulder Ivy League suit that achieved widespread popularity for the next 15 to 20 years.

A Mirror of the Times

Fashion is a nonverbal symbol. It communicates that the wearer is in step with the times. Because fashions are shaped by the forces of an era, they in turn reflect the way we think and live. Each new fashion seems completely appropriate to its time and reflects that time as no other symbol does. A study of the past and careful observation of the present makes it apparent that fashions are social expressions that document the tastes and values of an era just as the paintings, sculpture, and architecture of the times do. The extreme modesty of the Victorian era was reflected in bulky and concealing fashions. The sexual emancipation of the flappers in the 1920s was expressed in their flattened figures, short skirts, "sheer" hosiery (the first time the bare leg was exposed), and

short hair. The individualistic fashions of the late 1980s were a true reflection of the current freedom of expression and lifestyle.

Social Class

Fashions mirror the times by reflecting the degree of rigidity in the class structure of an era. Although such ideas are difficult to imagine today, throughout much of history certain fashions were restricted to the members of certain rigidly defined social classes. In some early eras, royal edicts regulated both the type of apparel that could be worn by each group of citizens and how ornate it could be. Class distinctions were thus emphasized. Certain fashions have also been used as indications of high social standing and material success. During the nineteenth century, the constricted waists of Western women and the bound feet of high-caste Chinese women were silent but obvious evidence that the male head of the household was wealthy and esteemed.

Now, on the verge of a new century, social classes are far more fluid and mobile than ever before. Because there is no universal way of life today, people are free to choose their own values and lifestyles—and their dress reflects that choice. Many fashions exist simultaneously, and we are all free to adopt the fashions of any social group. If we do not wish to join others in their fashion choices, we can create our own modes and standards of dress. The beatniks of the 1950s and the hippies of the 1960s had their typical fashions, as did the bohemians of the 1920s and the liberated groups of the 1970s. In the 1980s we had the phenomenon of the punk rockers existing side by side with the yuppies.

Fashions are social expressions of their time. These medieval fashions emphasize class distinctions; the aristocrats wore elegant, impractical garments, while the peasants wore sturdy, practical clothes.

Lifestyle

Fashions also mirror the times by reflecting the activities in which people of an era participate. The importance of court-centered social activities in seventeenth and eighteenth century Europe was in evidence in men's and women's ornately styled apparel. Fashions became less colorful and more functional when a new working class was created by the industrial revolution.

Currently, our clothes also vary according to lifestyle. More casual and active sportwear in wardrobes reflect our interest in active sports and leisure pastimes. The difference in the lifestyle of an urban, career-oriented woman and that of a suburban housewife is totally reflected in their choice of wardrobes.

PRINCIPLES OF FASHION

Diversification of fashion has added new dimensions to the interpretation of the principles of fashion. While the intangibles of fashion can be vague and sometimes difficult to predict and chart, certain fundamental principles of fashion are tangible and precise. For many decades these principles served as the solid foundation for fashion identification and forecasting—they still do—but the astute student of fashion recognizes that in today's vibrant and changing atmosphere the application of these principles becomes a more intricate and challenging task.

The five principles we will discuss are the foundations upon which the study of fashion is based whether this study concerns the history of fashion, the spread of fashion, or the techniques related to fashion merchandising and marketing.

1. Consumers establish fashions by accepting or rejecting the styles offered. The popular belief that designers create artistic designs with little regard for the acceptance of these designs by the public is quite false. No designer can be successful without the support and acceptance of the customer.

It is true that new fashions can be introduced by famous designers, but it is relatively rare. A few examples are the loose, boxy jacket of the Chanel suit, the famous bias cut clothes designed by Vionnet, and the "new look" by Christian Dior. However, the designers who are considered to be the "creators" of fashion are those who have consistently given expression to the silhouette, color, fabric, and design that are wanted and accepted by a majority of the consumers.

A **customer** is a patron or potential purchaser of goods or services. Thus, a retail store's dress buyer is a customer of a dress manufacturer, and the dress manufacturer is a customer of a fabric producer. The **consumer** is the ultimate user; the person who uses the finished fashion garment.

Designers create hundreds of new styles each season, based on what they think may attract customers. From among those many styles, manufacturers choose what they think will be successful. They reject many more than they select. Retailers choose from the manufacturers' offerings those styles they believe their customers will want. Consumers then make the vital choice. By accepting some styles and rejecting others, they—and only they—dictate what styles will become fashions.

2. Fashions are not based on price. Just because something is expensive it does not follow that it will be successful. Although new styles that may eventually become fashions are often introduced at high prices, this is happening less and less today. What you pay for an item of apparel is not an indication of whether the item is considered to be fashionable.

In the fashion diversity offered to consumers today, successful fashions are to be found at every price level. Upper income consumers will accept fashions at very low prices, and consumers at the opposite end of the income scale will often splurge and buy a very expensive item—if it is in fashion. In many cases, consumers coordinate fashions that are both inexpensive and expensive with little regard to the price. For example, an expensive piece of jewelry can be pinned to a inexpensive T-shirt, or conversely, a fashionable piece of costume jewelry can be pinned to an expensive designer gown.

Another example is the total fashion acceptance of sneakers and running shoes. At every price level the consumer accepted the style, and the fashionability of sneakers was assured.

3. Fashions are evolutionary in nature; they are rarely revolutionary. In these days of rapid cultural and national revolutions, it is hard to believe that a worldwide phenomenon such as fashion is evolutionary in nature—not revolutionary. To the casual observer it appears as though fashion changes suddenly. Actually, fashion change comes about as a result of gradual movements from one season to the next.

Throughout history there have probably been only two real revolutions in fashion styles. One of these occurred during the twentieth century: the Dior "new look" of 1947. The other was the abrupt change of styles brought about by the French Revolution when the fashion changed overnight from elaborate full skirts, low-cut daring bodices, and ornate and glamorous fabrics to simple, drab costumes in keeping with the political and moral upheaval.

Fashions usually evolve gradually from one style to another. Skirt lengths go up or down an inch at a time, season after season. Shoulder widths narrow or widen gradually, not suddenly. It is only in retrospect that fashion changes seem marked or sudden.

Fashion designers understand and accept this principle. When developing new design ideas, they always keep the current fashion in mind. They know that few people could or would buy a whole new wardrobe every season, and that the success of their designs ultimately depends on sales. Consumers today buy apparel and accessories to supplement and update the wardrobe they already own, some of which was purchased last year, some the year before, some the year before that, and so on. In most cases, consumers will buy only if the purchase complements their existing wardrobe and does not depart too radically from last year's purchases.

4. No amount of sales promotion can change the direction in which fashions are moving. Promotional efforts on the part of producers or retailers cannot dictate what consumers will buy, nor can it force people to buy what they do not want. The few times that fashion merchants have tried to promote a radical change in fashion, they have not been successful.

This micro-mini dress of the late 1980s illustrates the fifth principle of fashion.

As the women's liberation movement grew in the late 1960s, women rebelled against the constriction of girdles and bras. The overwhelming majority stopped wearing girdles and began wearing panty hose instead. Various "counterculture" looks were adopted by some and a more relaxed look was adopted by nearly everyone. Reflecting this change was the reemergence of the soft, no-seam natural bra. Regardless of promotion by the intimate-apparel industry, nothing could persuade the majority of American women to submit again to the rigid control of corsets and girdles.

Also, promotional effort cannot renew the life of a fading fashion unless the extent of change gives the fashion an altogether new appeal. This is why stores have markdown or clearance sales. When the sales of a particular style start slumping, stores know they must clear out as much of that stock as possible, even at much lower prices, to make room for newer styles in which consumers have indicated interest.

5. All fashions end in excess. This saying is sometimes attributed to Paul Poiret, a top Paris designer of the 1920s. Many examples attest to its truth. Eighteenth century hoopskirts ballooned out to over 8 feet in width, which made moving from room to room a complicated maneuver. The French tried to accommodate these skirts and designed doors that could be opened to a width far beyond that of regular doors. They became known as "French doors" and can still be found in architecture today. Similarly, miniskirts of the 1960s finally became so short that the slightest movement caused a major problem in modesty. See also the mini-skirted gown on page 21. This same trend toward excess can be found in examples of menswear. Just think of the growth of the width of a tie. It will start as a thin string tie, and become wider and wider until that original string tie is as wide as a bib!

Once the extreme in styling has been reached, a fashion is nearing its end. The attraction of the fashion wanes and people begin to seek a different look—a new fashion.

REFERENCES

[1] George P. Fox, *Fashion: The Power That Influences the World. The Philosophy of Ancient and Modern Dress and Fashion.* Lange and Hellman, Printers & Sterotypers 1850–1860–1872, Introduction, p. 20.

[2] *Webster's Ninth New Collegiate Dictionary,* G & C Merriam Company, Springfield, Mass., 1988, p. 450.

[3] Peter F. Drucker, *Management Tasks, Responsibilities, Practices,* Harper & Row, New York, 1973, pp. 64–65.

[4] Paul H. Nystrom, *Economics of Fashion,* The Ronald Press, New York, 1928, pp. 3–7; and *Fashion Merchandising,* The Ronald Press, New York, 1932, pp. 33–34.

[5] Nystrom, *Economics of Fashion,* p. 7.

[6] James Laver, *Taste and Fashion,* rev. ed., George C. Harrop & Co., Ltd., London, 1946, p. 202.

[7] Agnes Brooke Young, *Recurring Cycles of Fashion: 1760–1937,* Harper & Brothers, New York, 1937, reprinted by Cooper Square Publishers, Inc., New York, 1966, p. 30.

[8] Cathy Teevon, "The Psychology of Fashion", *Apparel Industry Magazine,* September 1984, p. 62.

MERCHANDISING VOCABULARY

Define or briefly explain the following terms:

Classic
Consumer
Customer
Design
Details
Fad
Fashion

Fashion business
Fashion industries
Fashion marketing
Fashion merchandis-
ing
High fashion
Marketing

Mass or volume
fashion
Silhouette
Style
Style number
Taste
Texture

MERCHANDISING REVIEW

1. What group ultimately decides whether a style will be "fashionable" or not? Explain your answer.
2. Apparel styles are often named for the period in history in which they were introduced. Name three such styles and the historic period in which they originated.
3. Give two examples of "classics" that are in style today for each of the following groups: (*a*) men, (*b*) women, and (*c*) children.
4. Distinguish between (*a*) style, fashion, and design, and (*b*) classic and fad.
5. List and briefly explain the interrelationships between the four components of fashion.
6. Fashion apparel change has accelerated during the past 100 years. Which factors, in your opinion, have had the greatest influence on change? Why?
7. Give examples of how fashion mirrors the times today.
8. Can designers, manufacturers, or retailers force unwanted fashion on consumers? Explain your answer.
9. What are the five basic principles relating to fashion? Discuss the implications for fashion merchants.
10. Name at least three types of consumer products, other than apparel and accessories, in which fashion plays a major role today. What fashion elements or components are featured in each?

MERCHANDISING DIGEST

The following statements are from the text. Discuss the significance of each, giving examples of how each applies to merchandising fashion goods.

1. "Men today are as influenced by and responsive to fashion as women."
2. "Acceptance . . . means that a fashion is considered appropriate to the occasion for which it is worn."
3. "Many fashions exist simultaneously" today.

THE ENVIRONMENT OF FASHION

A cardinal rule in any business is "know your customer"—a rule that is especially true in the fashion business. How many potential customers for your products and services are there in a given community? How old are these customers? How much are they willing to spend on your product? What level of service do they expect? Are they married or single, homeowners or renters? How many children do they have? What kind of work do they do? What is their annual income? What is more important to them, value or style? Prestige or price? How much do they have to spend on "extras"? Do they like to shop early or late in the day? Weekdays or weekends? What motivates them to shop in a particular store? How do they spend their leisure time? *Who are your customers?*

Accurate facts about customers, properly interpreted, help the designers, manufacturers, and retailers of fashion merchandise make major decisions about what to offer them. Guesswork and misinterpreted facts can lead to major business failures. One major source of information about the consumer market is the U.S. Bureau of the Census.

The U.S. census produces over 3 billion separate statistics about how many Americans there are, what they work at, where they live, and how they are doing as measured by income and creature comforts.[1] These seemingly dull statistics are a treasure of vital information, not only for government, but also for every business interested in translating the data and projections drawn from them into new product and profit opportunities.

Used properly, census data provide us with all-important information about conditions that affect our lives and influence our actions. Collectively, the conditions under which we live are called our **environment.**

Just as the environment of one nation or society differs from that of another nation or society, so the environment of one neighborhood differs from that of another. In fashion merchandising, it is important to be aware of the conditions that affect a particular target customer's environment and to know how the environment differs from one target group to another.

Four major environmental factors affect fashion interest and demand:

1. Demographics and psychographics.
2. The degree of economic development and well-being of a country or society.
3. The sociological characteristics of the class structure.
4. The psychological attitudes of consumers.

Each will be discussed in turn in this chapter.

DEMOGRAPHICS AND PSYCHOGRAPHICS

Both manufacturers and retailers try to identify and select target markets for their goods. (**Target markets** are specific groups of potential customers that a business is attempting to turn into regular customers.) Businesses attempt to determine who their customers are, what those customers want, how much the customers are willing to pay for goods, where potential customers are located, and how many targeted customers there are. Today, demographic and psychographic studies are a vital part of determining these important factors.

Demographics are population studies that divide broad groups of consumers into smaller, more homogeneous target segments. The variables covered in a demographic study include population distribution by regional, urban, subur-

ban, and rural areas; age; sex; family life cycle; race; religion; ethnicity; education; occupation; and income.

Psychographics are studies that develop fuller, more personal portraits of potential customers and their lifestyles. Psychographic studies more fully predict consumer purchase patterns and distinguish users of a product. The variables covered in a psychographic study include personality; attitude, interests, and personal opinions; and actual product benefits desired. These studies help greatly in matching the image of a company and its product with the type of consumer using the product. Psychographics help companies understand and predict the behavior of present and potential customers.

THE ECONOMIC ENVIRONMENT

The growth of fashion demand depends on a high level of economic development, which is reflected in consumer income, population characteristics, and technological advances. In his book *On Human Finery*,[2] Quentin Bell underscores the relationship between economics and fashion. He explains that most economically sophisticated countries discard their national costumes long before other nations begin to abandon theirs. England, for example, which led the Western world into the industrial revolution, was the first country to stop wearing traditional national dress. Bell points out that Greece, Poland, and Spain, countries with little in common except for being in similar stages of economic development, retained their national costumes when countries with more industrialized economies—Germany, Belgium, Denmark, and Japan—were abandoning theirs.

A striking example of how countries with swift economic development also move ahead in fashion is The People's Republic of China. Long restricted to the traditional blue Mao jacket and pants for both sexes, the Chinese have increased their interest in contemporary fashions with their increased economic growth, complete with a limited number of fashion shows and boutiques!

Consumer Income

Consumer income can be measured in terms of personal income, disposable income, and discretionary income. Many groups of people use the amount of personal income as an indicator of "arriving" in their particular social set. The more personal income they have, the more socially acceptable they consider themselves to be.

At present, many U.S. families may be earning more personal income, but enjoying it less. Measurements have shown sharp increases in personal income in the past decades, but decreases in amounts of disposable and discretionary income.

Personal Income

The total or gross income received by the population as a whole is called **personal income.** It consists of wages, salaries, interest, dividends, and all other income for everyone in the country. Divide personal income by the number of people in the population and the result is **per capita personal income.**

Disposable Personal Income

The amount a person has left to spend or save after paying taxes is called **disposable personal income.** It is

An increased interest in fashion in China is obvious as the bicyclist is intrigued by the latest fashion look—dare she get one for herself?

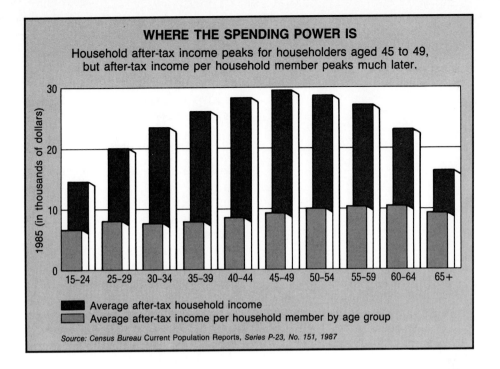

WHERE THE SPENDING POWER IS

Household after-tax income peaks for householders aged 45 to 49, but after-tax income per household member peaks much later.

Average after-tax household income
Average after-tax income per household member by age group

Source: Census Bureau Current Population Reports, *Series P-23, No. 151, 1987*

roughly equivalent to take-home pay and provides an approximation of the purchasing power of each consumer during any given year.

The chart above shows disposable income per household and per capita by various age groups. While household after-tax income starts to drop after age 49, individual after-tax income does not peak until ages 60 to 64, showing that consumers in the 50- to 64-year-old age bracket have the highest disposable income of any group.

Consumers spend about 6 percent of their disposable income on clothing and shoes—about $165 billion per year.

Discretionary Income

The money that an individual or family can spend or save after buying necessities—food, clothing, shelter, and basic transportation—is called **discretionary**

income. Of course, the distinction between "necessities" and "luxuries" or between "needs" and "wants" is a subjective one.

Purchasing Power of a Dollar

Average income has been increasing each year, but this has not meant that people have an equivalent increase in purchasing power. The reason for this is that the value of the dollar—its **purchasing power** or what it will buy—has steadily declined since 1940.

A decline in the purchasing power of money is caused by inflation. **Inflation** is defined as an increase in available money and credit, with relative scarcity of goods, resulting in a significant rise in prices.[3] Inflation, therefore, is an economic situation in which demand exceeds supply. Scarcity of goods and services, in relation to demand, results in

TABLE 2-1 • PURCHASING POWER OF THE DOLLAR: 1940–1985

Year	Average as Measured by Consumer Prices
1940	$ 2.381
1945	1.855
1950	1.387
1955	1.247
1960	1.127
1965	1.058
1967	1.000
1970	.860
1975	.620
1980	.405
1985	.310

Source: U.S. Bureau of Labor Statistics; monthly data in U.S. Bureau of Economic Analysis, "Survey of Current Business."

ever-increasing prices. Table 2-1 shows the changes in the purchasing power of the consumer dollar from 1940 to 1985.

When income taxes increase, the purchasing power of the family income drops; a decrease in income taxes has the reverse effect. With an inflationary economy, the working time required to acquire the necessities of life—basic food, clothing, transportation, and shelter—increases. The increase is not, however, uniform among all items.

In a **recession,** which represents a low point in a business cycle, money and credit become scarce, or "tight." Interest rates are high, production is down, and the rate of unemployment is up. People in the lower-income groups are the hardest hit; those with high incomes are the least affected. Yet these groups are small when compared with the middle-income group. It is the reaction of these middle-income people to any economic squeeze that is the greatest concern of the fashion merchant. For not only is the middle-income group the largest, it is also the most important market for fashion merchandise.

Effect on Fashion Marketing

Both inflation and recession affect consumers' buying patterns. Fashion merchants in particular must thoroughly understand the effects of inflation and recession when planning their inventory assortments and promotional activities. Manufacturers must also understand how consumers are affected by economic factors.

Most manufacturers are concerned with national trends. Retailers, however, must consider the impact of statistics in their local areas as well as the statistics from national studies. **Market segmentation** is the separating of the total consumer market into smaller groups. These are known as **market segments.** Through identifying and studying each market segment, producers and retailers can target their goods and services to their special markets.

Population

The majority of the population of the United States has some discretionary income and thus can influence the course of fashion. Two factors relating to population, however, have an important bearing on the extent of fashion demand:

1. The size of the total population and the rate of its growth.
2. The age mix of the population and its projection into the future.

Size of Population

The size of the population relates to the extent of current fashion demand. The rate of population growth suggests what tomorrow's market may become. In 1920 the United States had a population of about 106 million. By 1950 that figure had reached 151 million, and by 1980, 227.6 million. The U.S. Census Bureau has projected that by 1995 our population will reach the staggering figure of 259,559,000 people—a tremendous increase of well over 150 million people, or almost 145 percent, in 75 years.

Age Mix

The age mix and its projection into the future affect the characteristics of current fashion demand and suggest what they may be in the future. While the overall population continues to grow, the growth rate is not the same for all age groups or for both sexes. Since each group has its own special fashion interests, needs, and reactions, changes in the age mix serve as vital clues to future fashion demand.

For example, as the baby-boom generation reaches middle age, one of the largest and fastest growing age groups in the United States is the 35- to 54-year-old group. This is a new factor. The under-age 14 group, however, declined in the 1980s, a result of the lower birthrate in the 1970s. The results of that lower birth rate will continue to be apparent in the 1990s, when the group falls into the next age category, the 15- to 24-year-olds. The 15- to 24-year-old group, although not as large as other age groups, will probably continue to be the group most responsive to change and eager for the new. But, because of the decrease in the size of the group, its impact on the fashion scene will actually be reduced. The chart on page 30 shows the relative growth of the different age groups through the year 2000.

Because both men and women are living longer, the over-age 65 group is steadily growing. Statistician Stanley Kranczer, estimating that the number of Americans 100 years old or older—about 25,000 in 1987—will rise rapidly, projects that this group will reach 1 million by the year 2050. Those 50 years old and older account for over one-half of all discretionary spending power. This mature group becomes increasingly important in the fashion world as their earlier retirement, and in many cases increased retirement incomes, allows them to spend many active years wherever and however they choose. They are healthier, better educated, more active, and will live longer. Their interests and discretionary purchases vary radically from those of their younger counterparts, offering a real challenge to businesses to meet the demands of the "new old." The demand of older consumers for items such as package travel tours, cosmetic aids, and apparel that suits their ages and retirement lifestyles will offer growth opportunities for marketers, especially in fashion.

Technological Advances

In few if any countries has business competition been as keen and fast-growing as in the United States. The competition has fostered countless technological advances, many of which have had impact on the fashion field. As the variety and availability of new products have been increased by technological advances, the demand for new fashions has also increased.

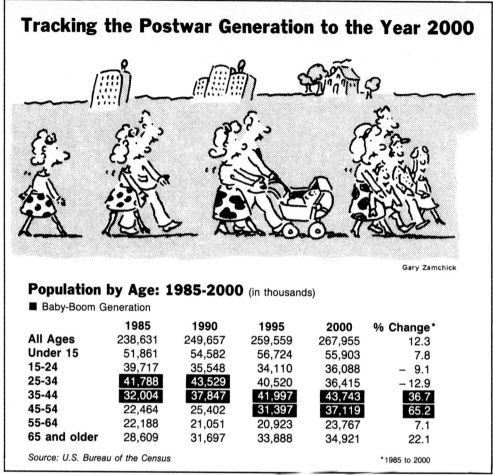

Tracking the Postwar Generation to the Year 2000

Gary Zamchick

Population by Age: 1985-2000 (in thousands)

■ Baby-Boom Generation

	1985	1990	1995	2000	% Change*
All Ages	238,631	249,657	259,559	267,955	12.3
Under 15	51,861	54,582	56,724	55,903	7.8
15-24	39,717	35,548	34,110	36,088	− 9.1
25-34	41,788	43,529	40,520	36,415	−12.9
35-44	32,004	37,847	41,997	43,743	36.7
45-54	22,464	25,402	31,397	37,119	65.2
55-64	22,188	21,051	20,923	23,767	7.1
65 and older	28,609	31,697	33,888	34,921	22.1

Source: U.S. Bureau of the Census   * 1985 to 2000

© 1988 by The New York Times Company. Reprinted by permission.

Manufacturing Equipment and Processes

Improved spinning and weaving machines, which helped start the industrial revolution, were the first major advances in the fashion industry. The mechanical sewing machine was the next advance, in the mid-1800s. Today, almost every phase of fabric and apparel manufacture is automated.

Modern sewing machines are powered to operate at high speeds; some specialized machines can produce 5,000 to 6,000 stitches a minute. High-speed knitting machines are equally efficient. Embroidery machines can not only stitch different patterns at the turn of a dial but can also produce a design on many pieces of cloth at one time. Hems can be power-stitched at high speed or even "welded" by ultrasonic waves. Bonding machines for welding two thicknesses of cloth are available. Some machines can also weld fibers into new types of nonwoven fabrics more supple and delicate than felt, which is the original non-woven fabric.

New processes have burgeoned, too. These include ways to make and use a wide variety of man-made fibers, separately or in blends. The industry also is producing blends of man-made and natural fibers for improved quality, appearance, and performance. For example, a new finishing process, called Sanfor-Set, when used on a 100 percent cotton fabric "irons itself in the dryer." The advantages of the natural cotton fiber combined with the Sanfor-Set process make ironing unnecessary.

The development of new methods of treating fabrics has made possible many fashions that could not have been introduced in the past. Bright colors were more readily accepted when they became resistant to fading from sun, rain, and laundry soaps. Pleats became more popular when they were treated to retain their creases through many washings or dry cleanings. Bulky fashions met less resistance when the bulk was achieved without weight.

Computer technology has affected every area of fashion production and marketing. Computer-assisted pattern drafting, research and planning, inventory control, product distribution, and countless other areas in the fashion business have benefited from the computer age.

Agriculture

Agricultural developments have affected the fashion field most strongly in the areas of cotton, wool, fur, and leather. In general, improved agricultural techniques have resulted in more and better-quality products.

Improved seed strains and better control of insect pests and plant diseases have helped increase the quality and quantity of cotton grown on an acre. Mechanized equipment helps farmers plant the crop, tend it, and harvest it more efficiently and with less labor. Scientific breeding has produced sheep that yield increasingly better grades of wool and has increased the amount of wool that can be clipped from each animal. Improved methods of fur farming and ranching have contributed to better pelts and hides for the fur and leather industries.

Communications

Not many years ago, news of every sort traveled more slowly. This meant that life moved more slowly and fashions changed more slowly. It took weeks or months for people in one section of the country to learn what was being worn in another part of the country. Fashion trends moved as leisurely as the news.

Our electronic age has changed all that. Today we enjoy rapid communication in ever-increasing quantities and infinite varieties. By means of satellites and round-the-clock broadcasting, television brings the world to our homes. Thus it has become a most important medium for transmitting fashion information. Famous designers create special costumes for stars, and we all take note. Changes in the dress and hairstyles of our favorite newscasters, talk-show personalities, series characters, and even sports stars have a great impact on us. For instance, in the mid-1980s, the "Miami Vice" look swept the country, as men in all walks of life tried to emulate the style of stars, Don Johnson and Philip Michael Thomas.

Popular movies also influence fashion. Back in 1983, *Flashdance* caught the fancy of millions of young people. Soon the one-bare-shoulder look was seen everywhere. A few years later, *Top Gun* and its star Tom Cruise helped to popularize aviator-style sunglasses; and on

The "Miami Vice" look spread throughout the world in the late 1980s as young men copied Don Johnson's sunglasses, t-shirts, casual jackets, and 5 o'clock shadow!

a broader scale, the blockbuster *Crocodile Dundee* and its sequel launched a craze for all things Australian.

At the same time, a continuing enthusiasm for exercise has kept interest in fashions for fitness high. The support of major celebrities in this area influences the public as well. For instance, Jane Fonda has devoted ongoing promotion to her enormously popular workout through exercise studios, a book, and an ever-growing number of videocassettes. Other celebrities, such as Cher, have contributed to the appeal of exercise and exercise apparel by acting as spokespeo-

ple for exercise centers and health clubs.

While television informs us about fashion on a national and international scale, radio also has a valuable place. Radio is an excellent medium through which local merchants can inform their audiences of special fashion events.

Transportation

Improved trucks and superhighways and the growth of the air-freight business bring the producer of fashion goods and the stores that sell them much closer together. Instead of weeks, the transportation of goods from vendor to store now takes days—sometimes only hours if the speed is worth the cost. Consolidated shipping, in which two or more shippers put together a truckload or carload, helps get merchandise to the stores more quickly and at reduced transportation costs.

Developments in transportation have also influenced fashions themselves. The earliest automobiles created a need for dusters, veils, and gauntlets. Today, sports cars and motorcycles require practical dress such as jeans, pants, scarfs, and short or divided skirts. Air travel has made any part of the world and any climate accessible in a matter of hours. This, plus the new affluence of such a large segment of the population, has created a demand for travel and vacation clothes that grows every year.

The old "resort season," which took place only among the extremely wealthy in late December and January, has become a "fifth season," which begins in October and lasts until late March. Increasingly, retailers need to have appropriate fashions for warm or cold climates almost year-round. The demand for wrinkle-free, packable clothing also continues to grow.

THE SOCIOLOGICAL ENVIRONMENT

To understand fashion, one needs to understand the sociological environment in which fashion trends begin, grow, and fade away. The famous stage and screen designer Cecil Beaton saw fashion as a social phenomenon that reflects "the same continuum of change that rides through any given age." Changes in fashion, Beaton emphasized, "correspond with the subtle and often hidden network of forces that operate on society . . . In this sense, fashion is a symbol."[4]

Simply stated, changes in fashion are caused by changes in the attitudes of consumers, which are in turn influenced by changes in the social patterns of the times. The key sociological factors influencing fashion today are leisure time, ethnic influences, status of women, social and physical mobility, and wars, disasters, and crises.

Leisure Time

One of the most precious possessions of the average U.S. citizen today is leisure time, because it is also one of the most scarce. The demands of the workplace compete with the demands of family and home for much of people's waking hours, leaving less and less time for the pursuit of other activities, whether those activities include a fitness regimen, community work, entertainment, relaxation— or even shopping.

The ways in which people use their leisure time are as varied as people themselves. Some turn to active or spectator sports; others prefer to travel. Many seek outlets for self-improvement, while growing numbers fill their time and enhance their standard of living with a second job. The increased importance of leisure time has brought changes to people's lives in many ways—in values, standards of living, and scope of activities. As a result, whole new markets have sprung up. Demand for larger and more versatile wardrobes for the many activities consumers can now explore and enjoy has mushroomed.

Casual Living

A look into the closets of the American population of the 1980s would probably reveal one aspect that is much the same from coast to coast, in large cities and in small towns: Most would contain an unusually large selection of casual clothes and sportswear. The market for casual apparel developed with the growth of the suburbs in the 1950s, and has had a continuous series of boosts in the years since. The "do your own thing" revolution of the 1960s made a casual look for men and women acceptable in what had been more formal places and occasions. The 1970s saw a tremendous surge in the number of women wearing slacks and pantsuits and in the number of men and women wearing jeans just about everywhere.

Even with the return to more formal styles for many occasions in the 1980s, comfortable styling and casual influence continue to strongly influence dress in all segments of society, at work and at play. The choice as to what is suitable for an activity is still largely left to the individual.

Active Sportswear

There is no doubt about it, the superstar of the fashion market in the 1970s and the 1980s has been sportswear. The

What a difference some decades make! Swimming, biking, and tennis in days gone by had sports clothes much different than today's.

sportswear growth has been phenomenal! While sports clothes have been around since the turn of the century, when they first appeared they were not particularly distinctive. Women's sport dresses for playing tennis or golf were not much different from their regular streetwear, and men's outfits similarly varied little from business suits. By the 1920s, consumers began demanding apparel that was appropriate for active sports or simply for relaxing in the sunshine. But it is the emphasis on health and self in the last two decades that has caused the fantastic growth of the active sportswear market. Sports-minded people play tennis in specially designed tennis fashions. Golfers want special golf-

wear. Joggers want only jogging outfits. And bikers seem able to bike only in appropriate fashions. The same goes for skaters, skiers, runners, hang gliders, sky divers, and climbers. Health clubs, exercise classes, and workout gyms exploded in popularity in the 1980s and a whole new and vast world of leotards, exercise suits, warm-up suits, and other self-improvement fashions and accompanying accessories were born. Whatever the activity, the specialized fashions—from jogging suits to bicycle shorts—quickly followed and became a vital need. Today, even those who do not participate in a particular sport beyond watching the pros on television feel the need to look the part!

Ethnic Influences

In recent years, minority groups in the United States, representing over 20 percent of the nation's total population, have experienced vast population increases and sociological changes.

Blacks

Blacks are better educated and hold higher-level jobs than they did in the past. With better education comes a stronger sense of oneself and one's heritage. Today many black people show the pride they feel in their African heritage by wearing African styles, fabrics, and patterns. Nonblacks have adopted these styles as well. Fashion companies have acknowledged the changes that have occurred among the black population and have reflected these changes in the products they market and the models they use. Today, cosmetics are available that emphasize rather than hide the beauty of dark skin. Black men and women have become world-famous modeling clothing and advertising various items in magazines and on television.

Hispanics

The Spanish-speaking market within the United States is growing so fast that market researchers can't keep up with it. In 1987 there were an estimated 18,312,000 Hispanics. In addition, 6 to 10 million undocumented Hispanics are estimated to be here. Together, these groups form the fastest-growing minority in the United States and the world's fifth largest Spanish-speaking population, following only Mexico, Spain, Colombia, and Argentina. By the year 2000, the Hispanic population is expected to reach over 25 million.

Until 1930, immigration to the United States was almost exclusively from Europe. Then for the following three decades, Latin Americans, mostly from Mexico and Puerto Rico, comprised 15 percent of the immigrants. By 1970, that portion had grown to 40 percent, with an influx of Central and South Americans. Since 1980, an estimated 153,000 Haitians and Cubans have also sought refuge in the United States.[5] The Hispanic population has made its impact on the fashion scene with the introduction of fiery colors, prints reminiscent of lush South American rainforests, and dance and music styles that have been accepted by the entire American public.

Asians

The end of the Vietnamese war and the influx of thousands of refugees from Cambodia and Vietnam brought additional traditions and costumes to be shared. These refugees joined the other segments of Asians already part of our country: the Koreans, the Chinese, and the Japanese. This stimulated interest in some of the more exotic fashions of the East and in the everyday comfort of the Chinese sandal and quilted jacket. The early 1980s brought Japanese designers to the attention of the American fashion scene with the highly exaggerated Japanese look. These oversized, multilayered clothes were styled in materials of somber tones and with an old, worn look. The latter was achieved by artfully designed "holes" actually cut in the garments and with edges left ragged. This "ragged" look was accepted by the most avant-garde of young women who had a large supply of self-confidence. To the majority of women, the influence of the Japanese designers was accepted only as it was translated by other designers into more subdued, mainstream fashions.

FASHION

DONNA KARAN: A FASHION STAR IS BORN

There is no sure road to becoming an "overnight" sensation in the fashion world. Even those who have made a name for themselves designing for a company have been known to strike out when they've designed under their own names. But then there is Donna Karan.

For about 10 years, Donna Karan was chief designer for Anne Klein & Co., a job she stepped into after Anne Klein's death in 1974. An unquestionable success in that position, Karan received two coveted Coty Awards; but with time, she felt she wanted something different and took the giant step of leaving Anne Klein to launch her own company.

Karan unveiled her premiere collection under her own name in May 1985—and was immediately hailed as the hit of the season. In less than a year, the Karan line had caught on so completely with consumers that the prestigious department stores carrying it were selling out of the clothing faster than with any other designer line. Plus, at Bergdorf Goodman, the collection was producing the highest sales per square foot of any American designer space in the store.[1]

What was the key to Karan's spontaneous success? As many saw it, her designs struck a responsive note; they fit the times.[2] Or put another way, as an executive woman herself, Karan knew what executive women wanted—in fact, she said, "I will design only clothes and accessories that I myself would wear."[3]

In essence, what Karan designs is a "no-fuss" collection[4] of separates, consisting of easy, flowing skirts, form-fitting bodysuits, dusters, and pants, all in styles and fabrications that can be wrapped, draped, tied, and mixed and matched, using just a few basic essentials. The look created by the apparel is then topped off by a full line of Donna Karan accessories, including jewelry, stockings, handbags, belts, and gloves.

While Karan states that she is designing for a working woman, her clothes are very different from the more traditional "office" looks of a Liz Claiborne or Calvin Klein. Rather, she says she de-

FOCUS

signs her clothing for the top professional woman, the woman who is so sure of herself and her career that she can enjoy wearing sophisticated, curvy, almost sexy clothing even at work.[5]

Of course, not all Donna Karan customers are top executives and some probably do not work at all, but what they all have in common, besides their taste for this designer's line, is money to spend on their wardrobe—since the clothing is among the most expensive produced by an American designer. Most of her outfits can be assembled for around $1,000, although another $1,000 would have to be spent to accessorize them as Karan intends.

The result of that spending for consumers, though, is a look that more than a few fashionable women have found comfortable and flattering to wear; the result for Donna Karan's company is projections of between $200 and $250 million of retail business a year.[6] And that does not include new directions Karan has been pursuing for her name, such as a fragrance, eyewear, watches, and underwear.

One of the newest directions is her DKNY line, which debuted in 1988 just three years after her start on her own. The DKNY label cost approximately one-half the price of the Karan collec-

tion and is a "bridge line" devoted to a total lifestyle.[7]

Street-smart Karan literally went to the street for her DKNY inspiration. "I always loved the sound of NYPD [New York Police Department]. DKNY has the same energy."[8] She describes her DKNY line of apparel and accessories as "the other side of me—the fun and spirited side."[9]

In addition, she plans to open her own retail shops offering their entire collection of apparel and accessories. That's a major accomplishment in a relatively short time—but what else could one expect from an overnight sensation?

[1] Carrie Donovan, "How a Fashion Star Is Born," *The New York Times Magazine,* May 4, 1986, p. 27.

[2] Ibid., p. 30.

[3] Bobbi Queen, "Split Personalities," *Women's Wear Daily,* October 31, 1984, p. 40.

[4] Susan Snell, "Donna Karan Bares Body Suit and Soul," *Dallas Apparel News,* August 1985, p. 32.

[5] Donovan, p. 30.

[6] Ibid., p. 28

[7] Pat Sloan, "Karan Sets Second Clothes Line," *Ad Age,* September 26, 1988, p. 76.

[8] Kathleen Bayes, "Donna Hits the Streets," *Women's Wear Daily,* September 19, 1988, pp. 6–7.

[9] Jill Newman, "DKNY: The Fun Side of Donna Karan," *Women's Wear Daily,* November 18, 1988, p. 96.

This Fashion Focus is based on information from the articles cited above and from these sources:

Newman, Jill, "Doing Them Her Way," *Women's Wear Daily,* May 15, 1987, pp. 10–11.

Cathy Cook, "Dresses for Successes," *Review,* September, 1988, pp. 37–38, 87–88, 90–96.

Status of Women

In the early 1900s, the American woman was, in many ways, a nonperson. She could not vote, serve on a jury, earn a living at any but a few occupations, own property, or enter public places unescorted. She passed directly from her father's control to her husband's control, without rights or monies. In both households, she dressed to please the man and reflect his status.

Profound changes began to occur during World War I, and have accelerated ever since. The most dramatic advances have happened since the mid-1960s and the advent of the women's movement. Women's demands for equal opportunity, equal pay, and equal rights in every facet of life continue to bring about even more change. These changes have affected not only fashion but the entire field of marketing.

Jobs and Money

In early 1981, predictions were that by 1985, half of all American women over the age of 16 would be in the workplace. At the end of 1981, that figure had already been reached and surpassed. The U.S. Department of Labor reported that the figure of all such working women was 52.3 percent, and today it has climbed even higher. This represents a staggering increase of over 5 million women who have entered the workforce since 1977, when the figure was 48.4 percent. The Department of Labor also predicted that before 1990, 75 percent of all two-parent families would have both parents employed.

The following graph illustrates the steady increase in the number of women in the workforce between 1965 and 1985, a figure that has almost doubled, despite the relatively small increase in women's salaries during the same period when compared to men's salaries. Both financial pressures and career satisfaction should keep the number of working women growing.

The dramatic increase in working women has led to a surge in fashion interest, because a woman who works is continuously exposed to fashion. It is everywhere around her as she meets people, shops during her lunch hour, or is on her way home. As a member of the workforce, she now has the incentive, the opportunity, and the means to respond to fashion's appeal. Periodicals, such as *Ms.* and *Working Woman,* make this market reachable.

Finally, women in general today have more money of their own to spend as they see fit. Approximately four women in every six have incomes, earned and unearned, of their own. These women

	Numbers of Women Working	Salaries as a Percentage of Men's Salaries
1985	51.1 million	65%
1980	45.5 million	60.5%
1975	37.5 million	59.7%
1970	31.5 million	59.2%
1965	26.2 million	59.9%

and their acceptance or rejection of offered styles have new importance in the fashion marketplace.

Education

Often the better educated a woman becomes, the more willing she is to learn new things. She is also more willing to try new fashions, which of course serves to accelerate fashion change. And with more women today receiving more education than ever before, the repercussions on fashion are unmistakable. Today's educated women have had wider exposure than their mothers or grandmothers to other cultures and to people of different backgrounds. Consequently, they are more worldly, more discerning, more demanding, and more confident in their taste and feel for fashion. Fashion marketers must recognize these new customers.

No wonder Edward Sapir, a leading social scientist, considered education a major factor in fashion change. "Fashion is custom in the guise of departure from custom," said Sapir.[6] To him, fashion is a resolution of the conflict between people's revolt against adherence to custom and their reluctance to appear lacking in good taste.

Social Freedom

Perhaps the most marked change in the status of women since the early 1900s is the degree of social freedom they now enjoy. Young women today are free to apply for a job, and to earn, spend, and save their own money. They are free to go unescorted to a restaurant, theater, or other public place. Women travel more frequently than they did in the past. They travel to more distant locations at a younger age and often alone. Many own their own cars. If they can

afford it, they may maintain an apartment or share one with others.

Short skirts, popular in the 1920s, the early 1940s, the 1960s, and the 1980s, are commonly interpreted as a reflection of women's freedom. So, too, is the simplicity of the styles that prevailed in those periods: chemises, sacks, tents, shifts, other variations of loose-hanging dresses, and pants.

Different theories exist about why these changes came about. Some people believe that stiff, unyielding corsets went out with a stiff, unyielding moral code. Others believe that the changes had no particular social significance. They believe that women rejected inflexible corsets not because of a change in the moral code but because the new materials were simply more comfortable. Similarly, pants may be viewed as an expression of women's freedom or merely as suitable garments for hopping in and out of the indispensable car.

Whatever the reasons, the lifestyles of American women, and their opinions and attitudes about fashion, have changed radically in the past three decades. American women have gained hard-won freedoms in their social and business lives. They are just as definite about their freedom of choice in fashion. The thought of today's independent women accepting uncomfortable and constricting clothing or shoes just to follow the dictates of some fashion arbiter, as they did years ago, is ludicrous. Today's busy, active women, whether at home or at the office, have very carefully defined preferences for fashions that suit their own individual needs and comfort. Today's successful designers recognize these preferences and make sure that their drawing boards reflect them.

ALCOTT&ANDREWS

THE NEW STORE FOR WOMEN OPENS TOMORROW.

THE OUTSTANDING WOMAN IN THE CORPORATE WORLD DOESN'T WEAR A UNIFORM.

The executive woman needs an elegant, versatile, beautifully-made wardrobe that projects her authority and personal style.

But the woman who runs from meeting to meeting has no time to run from store to store. She needs one store that offers an abundance of well-tailored clothing, not man-tailored clothing, in depth she just won't find anywhere else. Floors of wonderful clothing made exclusively of natural fibers because the finest clothing can be made from nothing less.

A store where professional personnel will help her build a wardrobe almost as easily as she can buy a blouse. Where individual attention and personal service, from pre-selection to shopping-by-appointment to alterations, are a matter of course.

And a store whose prices don't insult her intelligence.

In short, a store that affords the executive woman the quality of clothing and service that has always been available to the executive man.

Alcott & Andrews. We open tomorrow.

Today's career woman shows her independence by having her own fashion look—not constrained by a "uniform" look either at home or in the office.

Social Mobility

Almost all societies have classes, and individuals choose either to stand out from or to conform to their actual or aspired-to class. Bell viewed fashion as the process "whereby members of one class imitate those of another, who, in turn, are driven to ever new expedients of fashionable change."[7]

Bell considered the history of fashion inexplicable without relating it to social classes. He is not alone in his thinking. Other sociologists have related fashion change to changes in social mobility and to the effort to associate with a higher class by imitation.

The United States is sometimes called a classless society, but this is valid only in that there are no hereditary ranks, royalty, or untouchables. Classes do exist, but they are based largely upon occupation, income, residential location, education, or avocation, and their boundaries have become increasingly fluid. They range from the immensely wealthy (self-made millionaires or their descendants—the Vanderbilts, Whitneys, and Rockefellers, for example) at the top through the very wealthy (mostly nouveau riche) through the many middle-income levels and finally to the low-income and poverty levels. At the very bottom are the so-called hardcore unemployed and those people who have no homes and whose possessions can be carried from place to place.

Middle-Class Growth

Most fashion authorities agree that there is a direct relationship between the growth and strength of the middle class and the growth and strength of fashion demand. The middle class has the highest physical, social, and financial mobility. Because it is the largest class, it has the majority vote in the adoption of fashions. Members of the middle class tend to be followers, not leaders, of fashion, but the strength of their following pumps money into the fashion industry. And the persistence of their following often spurs fashion leaders to seek newer and different fashions of their own.

The United States has a very large middle class with both fashion interest and the money to indulge it. It is growing in proportion to the total population. Despite fluctuations in the economy, this growth generally means a widespread increase in consumer buying power, which in turn generates increased fashion demand.

Physical Mobility

Physical mobility, like social mobility, encourages the demand for and response to fashion. One effect of travel is "cross-pollination" of cultures. After seeing how other people live, travelers bring home a desire to adopt or adapt some of what they observed and make it part of their environment.

Thus Marco Polo brought gunpowder, silks, and spices from the Orient, introducing new products to medieval Europe. In the nineteenth century, travelers brought touches of Asian and African fashions to Western dress and home furnishings. In the twentieth century, Latin American and pre-Columbian influences were introduced into North America, dramatically changing the direction and emphasis of fashion in this country.

In the United States, people enjoy several kinds of physical mobility. For example, the daily routine for many people involves driving to work or to a shopping center, often in a different city.

Among the broad range of influences they are exposed to during their daily trips are the fashions of others and the fashion offerings of retail distributors.

A second form of physical mobility popular among Americans is vacation travel. Whether the travelers are going to a nearby lake or around the world, each trip exposes them to many different fashion influences and each trip itself demands special fashions. Living out of a suitcase for a few days or a few months requires clothes that are easy to pack, wrinkle-resistant, suitable for a variety of occasions, and easy to keep in order.

A third form of physical mobility is change of residence, which, like travel, exposes an individual to new contacts, new environments, and new fashion influences. Record unemployment figures have caused shifts in population in the 1980s in many parts of the country.

War, Disaster, and Crisis

War, widespread disaster, and crisis shake people's lives and focus attention on ideas, events, and places that may be completely new. People develop a need for fashions that are compatible with changes in their attitudes and also changes in their environment.

Such changes took place in women's activities and in fashions as a result of the two world wars. World War I brought women into the business world in significant numbers and encouraged their desire for independence and suffrage. It gave them reason to demand styles that allowed freer physical movement. World War II drew women into such traditionally masculine jobs as riveting, for which they previously had not been considered strong enough. It put them in war plants on night shifts. It even brought women other than nurses into the military services for the first time in the country's history. All these changes gave rise to women's fashions previously considered appropriate only for men, such as slacks, sport shirts, and jeans.

The Depression of the 1930s was a widespread disaster with a different effect on fashions. Because jobs were scarce, considerably fewer were offered to women than had been before. They returned to the home and adopted more feminine clothes. And because money also was scarce, wardrobes became skimpier. A single style often served a large number of occasions. Women who did hold jobs felt pressure to look younger so they could compete with younger applicants. This encouraged an increased use of lipstick and cosmetics.

In the late 1970s and early 1980s, a combination of the energy crisis and exceptionally cold weather brought a mass of warm clothing to the marketplace. Thermal underwear, formerly seen only in sporting goods catalogs, was featured in department and specialty shops. Retailers stocked up on sweaters, tights, boots, mittens, leg warmers, scarfs, coats, jackets, and vests with down fill. Not only the Northeast and West but the normally temperate Sun Belt was struck by bitter-cold weather. The record-breaking cold and unfamiliar snow and sleet created demand for warm clothing in areas formerly not interested in such apparel.

THE PSYCHOLOGICAL ENVIRONMENT

"Fashion promises many things to many people," according to economist Dr. Rachel Dardis. "It can be and is used to attract others, to indicate success, both social and economic, to indicate leadership, and to identify with a particular social group."[8] Fashion interest and demand at any given time relies heavily on prevailing psychological attitudes.

The five basic psychological factors that influence fashion demand are boredom, curiosity, reaction to convention, need for self-assurance, and desire for companionship.[9] These factors motivate a large share of people's actions and reactions in general.

- **Boredom.** People tend to become bored with fashions too long in use. Boredom leads to restlessness and a desire for change. In fashion, the desire for change expresses itself in a demand for something new and satisfyingly different from what one already has.

- **Curiosity.** Curiosity causes interest in change for its own sake. Highly curious people like to experiment; they want to know what is around the next corner and how color combinations, changes in silhouette, and details affect the look of fashion. There is curiosity in everyone, though some may respond less dramatically than others to it. Curiosity and the need to experiment keep fashion demand alive.

- **Reaction to Convention.** One of the most important psychological factors influencing fashion demand is the reaction to convention. People's reactions take one of two forms: rebellion against convention or adherence to it. Rebellion against convention is characteristic of young people. This involves more than boredom or curiosity: it is a positive rejection of what exists and a search for something new. However, acceptance by the majority is an important part of the definition of fashion. The majority tends to adhere to convention, either within its own group or class or in general.

- **Need for Self-Assurance.** The need for self-assurance or confidence is a human characteristic that gives impetus to fashion demand. Often the need to overcome feelings of inferiority or of disappointment can be satisfied through apparel. People who consider themselves to be fashionably dressed have an armor that gives them self-assurance. Those who know that their clothes are dated are at a psychological disadvantage.

- **Desire for Companionship.** The desire for companionship is fundamental in human beings. The instinct for survival of the species drives individuals to seek a mate. Humans' innate gregariousness also encourages them to seek companions. Fashion plays its part in the search for all kinds of companionship. In its broader sense, companionship implies the formation of groups, which require conformity in dress as well as in other respects. Flamboyant or subdued, a person's mode of dress can be a bid for companionship as well as the symbol of acceptance within a particular group.

IMPLICATIONS OF ENVIRONMENTAL INFLUENCES

At the 1987 Convention of the National Retail Merchants Association, Peter Francese, president of *American Demographics,* stressed that changes in demographics and psychographics make it essential for retailers to know their potential customers and understand them. Who is the customer? What do customers really want? Are they sophisticated, unsophisticated? What is their purchasing behavior? Francese stressed that merchandising must be done on a store-by-store basis. "Retailers need customer information systems. The customer market is fragmented. We have to see how this manifests itself in merchandise. Stereotypes don't work."[10]

Projections based on demographic and psychographic research can be used by manufacturers and retailers alike to determine their target customers. When demographic and psychographic data are ignored, business is likely to fall off. In 1987 and 1988, for example, there was a sharp drop in women's apparel sales. Women were not buying the latest fashions, among them the miniskirt. Retailers appeared to have ignored the fact that the baby-boomers, who buy the most clothing, were over 30 years old. In addition, the 14- to 24-year-old group had decreased by almost 13 percent in the previous 8 years. Not only do the older baby-boomers have different body shapes than the 14- to 24-year-olds for whom many of the fashions were designed, but the more mature customers have a lifestyle in which fashion extremes such as short miniskirts have little or no place.[11]

Broadly speaking, the consumer of the future will be better educated, more affluent or upscale, more mature, and more concerned with receiving greater value. Working women will be a prime target market segment—but all working women don't wear Gucci shoes and make $100,000! The manufacturer and retailer who take time to truly know their customers and the changes in their lives will be leaders in the fashion industry of the future.

REFERENCES

[1] Robert Levy, "Cashing In on the Census," *Dun's Business Month,* April 1983, p. 52.

[2] Quentin Bell, *On Human Finery,* The Hogarth Press, Ltd., London, 1947, p. 72.

[3] *Webster's Ninth New Collegiate Dictionary,* Merriam-Webster, Inc., Springfield, Mass., 1988, p. 620.

[4] Cecil Beaton, *The Glass of Fashion,* Doubleday & Company, Inc., New York, 1954, pp. 335, 379–381.

[5] Udajan Gupta, "From Other Shores," *Black Enterprise,* March 1983, p. 51.

[6] Edward Sapir, "Fashion," *Encyclopedia of the Social Sciences,* Vol. VI, London 1931, p. 140.

[7] Bell, p. 72.

[8] Rachel Dardis, "The Power of Fashion," *Proceedings of the Twentieth Annual Conference, College Teachers of Textiles and Clothing, Eastern Region,* New York, 1966, pp. 16–17.

[9] Paul H. Nystrom, *Economics of Fashion,* The Ronald Press, New York, 1928, pp. 66–81.

[10] "New Trends in Consumer Demographics", from 1987 NRMA's 76th Annual Convention Coverage, as reported in *Stores,* February 1987, p. 73.

[11] Robert Metz, "Women's Fashion Retailing Hurt by Misreading of Demographics," *The Providence Journal,* June 26, 1988, p. F4.

MERCHANDISING VOCABULARY

Define or briefly explain the following terms.

Demographics
Discretionary income
Disposable personal
 income
Environment

Inflation
Market segmentation
Market segments
Per capita personal
 income

Personal income
Psychographics
Purchasing power
Recession
Target market

MERCHANDISING REVIEW

1. Name the four major environmental influences on fashion interest and demand in any era.
2. Market segmentation is vitally important to producers and retailers of fashion merchandise. Explain why, giving at least two examples of how such information could be used by the fashion industry.
3. How does the size and age mix of a population affect current fashion demand? What does information about size and age mix today tell us about the future of fashion demand?
4. In what ways has increased availability of leisure time affected the fashion market?
5. How has the changing status of ethnic groups affected fashion interest and demand? Cite at least two examples.
6. How does a higher level of education affect fashion interest and demand?
7. What is social mobility? How does the degree of social mobility affect fashion interest and demand? Illustrate your answer with examples.
8. Upon what factors are classes in the United States usually based? Why is it more difficult to identify an individual's social class in this country than it is in other countries?
9. Describe three kinds of physical mobility that people in the United States enjoy today, explaining how each influences fashion demand.
10. Five basic psychological factors motivate much of human behavior. List them, explaining how each affects fashion interest and demand.

MERCHANDISING DIGEST

1. Is discretionary income or disposable personal income the more significant figure to fashion producers and marketers? Why?
2. Discuss how technological advances in the following areas affect rate of change and interest in fashion: (a) manufacturing equipment and processes, (b) transportation, (c) communications.
3. How has the status of women changed during the twentieth century? How have these changes affected fashion interest and demand?

THE MOVEMENT OF FASHION

Fashion is, in many ways, like a river.

A river is always in motion, continuously flowing—sometimes slowly and gently, other times rushing and turbulent. It is exciting, never the same. It affects those who ride its currents and those who rest on its shores. Its movements depend on the environment.

All of this is true of fashion, too. The constant movements of fashion depend on an environment made up of social, political, and economic factors. These movements, no matter how obvious or how slight, have both meaning and definite direction. There is a special excitement to interpreting these movements and estimating their speed and direction. Everyone involved in fashion, from the designer to the consumer, is caught up in the movement of fashion.

The excitement starts with the textile producers. Fully 12 to 18 months before they offer their lines to manufacturers, the textile people must choose their designs, textures, and colors. From 3 to 9 months before showing a line to buyers, the apparel manufacturers begin deciding which styles they will produce and in which fabrics. Then, 2 to 6 months before the fashions will appear on the selling floor, the retail buyers make their selections from the manufacturers' lines. Finally, the excitement passes on to the consumers, as they select the garments that will be versatile, appropriate, and suitably priced for their individual needs and wants.

How can all these people be sure their choices are based on reliable predictions? Successful designers, manufacturers, buyers, and consumers have a good understanding of basic cycles, principles, and patterns that operate in the world of fashion. Their predictions are based on this understanding.

THE FASHION CYCLE

All fashions move in cycles. The term **fashion cycle** refers to the rise, wide popularity, and then decline in acceptance of a style. The word "cycle" suggests a circle. However, the fashion cycle is represented by a bell-shaped curve. (See page 53.)

Some authorities compare the fashion cycle to a wave, which shows first a slow swell, then a crest, and finally a swift fall. Like the movement of a wave, the movement of a fashion is always forward, never backward. Like waves, fashion cycles do not follow each other in regular, measured order. Some take a short time to crest; others, a long time. The length of the cycle from swell to fall may be long or short. And, again like waves, fashion cycles overlap.

Stages of the Fashion Cycle

Fashion cycles are not haphazard; they don't "just happen." There are definite stages in a style's development that are easily recognized. These stages can be charted and traced, and in the short run, accurately predicted. Being able to recognize and predict the different stages is vital to success in both the buying and the selling of fashion.

Every fashion cycle passes through five stages: (1) introduction, (2) rise, (3) culmination, (4) decline, (5) obsolescence. A comparison of these stages to the timetable suggested by Laver in Chapter 1 would look like this:

Introduction	"indecent/shameless"
Rise	"outré"
Culmination	"smart"
Decline	"dowdy/hideous"
Obsolescence	"ridiculous"

The fashion cycle serves as an important guide in fashion merchandising. The fashion merchant uses the fashion cycle concept to introduce new fashion goods, to chart their rise and culmination, and to recognize their decline and obsolescence.

Introduction

The next new fashion may be introduced by a producer in the form of a new style, color, or texture. The new style may be a flared pant leg when slim legs are popular, vibrant colors when earth tones are popular, or slim body-hugging fabrics such as knit jersey when heavy-textured bulky looks are being worn.

New styles are almost always introduced in higher-priced merchandise. They are produced in small quantities since retail fashion buyers purchase a limited number of pieces to test the new styles' appeal to targeted customers. This testing period comes at the beginning of the buying cycle of fashion merchandise, which coincides with the introduction stage of the fashion cycle. The test period ends when the new style either begins its rise or has been rejected by the target customer. Because there can be many risks, new styles must be priced high enough so that those that succeed can cover the losses on those that don't succeed. Promotional activities such as designer appearances, institutional advertising, and charity fashion shows, which will appeal to the fashion leaders of the community and also enhance the store's fashion image, take place at this point.

Rise

When the new original design (or its adaptations) is accepted by an increasing number of customers, it is considered to be in its **rise stage.** At this stage, the fashion buyer reorders in quantity for maximum stock coverage.

During the rise stage of a new original design, many retailers will offer **line-for-line copies** or "**knock-offs,**" as they are referred to in the fashion industry. These are versions of the original designer style duplicated by manufacturers. These copies look exactly like the original except that they have been mass-produced in less expensive fabrics. Because production of the merchandise is now on a larger scale, prices of the knock-offs are generally lower.

As a new style continues to be accepted by more and more of the customers, **adaptations** appear. Adaptations are designs that have all the dominant features of the style that inspired them, but do not claim to be exact copies. Modifications have been made, but distinguishing features of the original, such as a special shoulder treatment or the use of textured fabric, may be retained in the adaptation. At this stage, the promotion effort focuses on regular price lines, full assortments, and product-type ads to persuade the customer of the store's superiority in filling his or her fashion needs.

Culmination

The **culmination stage** of the fashion cycle is the period when a fashion is at the height of its popularity and use. At this stage, also referred to as the **plateau,** the fashion is in such demand that it can be mass-produced, mass-distributed, and sold at prices within the range

New styles are almost always introduced in higher-priced merchandise amid much excitement and hoopla. Here Yves Saint Laurent shows his newest styles to appreciative press and buyers.

of most customers. This stage may be long or brief, depending on how extended the peak of popularity is. The quilted coat, which began as an expensive down-filled style in the late 1970s, reached its culmination stage when mass production in acrylic fill had made a quilted coat available to practically every income level. At the culmination stage, the high-price line fashion buyer stops reordering the fashion and begins reducing stock.

The culmination stage of a fashion may be extended in two ways:

1. If a fashion becomes accepted as a classic, it settles into a fairly steady sales pattern. An example of this is the cardigan sweater, an annual steady seller.
2. If new details of design, color, or texture are continually introduced, interest in the fashion may be kept alive longer. Shoulder-strap handbags are a perfect example. Another example is the continued fashion interest in running shoes, fostered by new colors, designs, and comfort innovations.

Decline

When boredom with a fashion sets in, the result is a decrease in consumer demand for that fashion. This is known as the **decline stage.** It is a principle of fashion that all fashions in excess end.

As a fashion starts to decline, consumers may still be wearing it, but they are no longer willing to buy it at its regular price. The outstanding fashion merchandiser is able to recognize the end of the culmination stage and start markdowns early. At this point, production stops immediately or comes slowly to a halt. The leading fashion stores abandon the style; traditional stores take a

moderate markdown and advertise the price reduction. This will probably be followed in a short while by a major price-slash clearance or closeout. At this stage the style may be found in bargain stores at prices far below what the style commanded in earlier stages.

Obsolescence

When strong distaste for a style has set in and it can no longer be sold at any price, the fashion is in its **obsolescence stage.**

Lengths of Cycles

Predicting the time span of a fashion cycle is impossible since each fashion moves at its own speed. However, one guideline can be counted on. Declines are fast, and a drop to obsolescence is almost always steeper than a rise to culmination. At this point, as they say in merchandising, "You can't give it away."

As the world moves closer and closer to the twenty-first century, the speed with which products move through their cycles is accelerating. Rapid technological developments and "instant" communications have much to do with this speedup, as do fast-changing environmental factors. The result is an intense competition among manufacturers and retailers to provide consumers with what they want and expect—constantly changing assortments from which to choose.

The cycle of innovation, demand, wide acceptance, and rejection occurs in most products, from home computers to automobiles to sports equipment, from women's apparel to menswear. The cycle starts with a new idea from a designer. This is introduced to the public as a product. It commands interest and begins to be accepted by the innovators in the buying public. The product gains in popularity and "everybody has to have it." And then, its popularity declines—sometimes because it has become too common, more often because people have been impressed by a newer idea. This is the pattern that all fashions follow. All that varies is the speed of passing from one stage to the next, which dictates the lifetime of the cycle.

American society at the end of the twentieth century accepts as routine live TV pictures of astronauts working in outer space, of battles being fought in various parts of the world, and of personalities participating in social occasions at every point of the globe. Our appetite for constant newness and change seems to be insatiable. The vast choice of new styles that consumers are offered continuously by the fashion world provides them with an important role in the movement of fashion cycles. Consumers either give a new style enough acceptance to get it started, or they immediately reject it. Since more new fashions are always ready to push existing ones out of the way, it is no wonder that with each passing year the time required for a fashion to complete its cycle becomes shorter and shorter.

Breaks in the Cycle

In fashion, as in everything else, there are always ups and downs, stops and starts. The normal flow of a fashion cycle can be broken or abruptly interrupted by outside influences. The influence can be simply unpredictable weather or a change in group acceptance. Or it can be much more dramatic and far-reaching—war, worldwide economic depression, or a natural disaster, for example.

Although no formal studies have been made of the phenomenon of the broken cycle, manufacturers and merchants have a theory about it. They believe that a broken cycle usually picks up where it has stopped once conditions return to normal or once the season that was cut short reopens. Consider the effect that a shortage of petroleum can have on the movement of man-made fibers. Although the success of man-made fibers—with all their easy-care attributes—is tremendous, their availability was interrupted by petroleum shortages both in 1973 and again in 1979. However, when the petroleum supply increased, the popularity of these fibers returned to what it had been.

Widespread economic depressions also temporarily interrupt the normal progress of a fashion cycle. When there is widespread unemployment, fashion moves much more slowly, only resuming its pace with economic recovery and growth.

Wars also affect fashion. They cause shortages which force designers, manufacturers, retailers, and consumers to change fashions less freely or to restrict styles. People redirect their interests, and fashion must take a back seat. When fashion apparel is in a cycle break, interest in cosmetics usually picks up. Women switch cosmetics or use them differently to satisfy their desire for something new. After wars have ended, interest in fashion picks up and it flourishes once again.

Long-Run and Short-Run Fashions

The length of time individual fashions take to complete their cycles varies widely. **Long-run fashions** take more seasons to complete their cycles than what might be considered average; **short-run fashions** take fewer seasons.

Some fashions tend to rise in popular acceptance more slowly than others, thereby prolonging their life. Some stay in popular demand much longer than others do. The decline in popular demand for some fashions may be slower than for others.

Silhouettes, colors, textures, accessories, classics, and fads may be classified as long-run or short-run fashions. The length of time each takes to complete a full demand cycle varies widely. As discussed in Chapter 2, the level of technological development, existing lifestyles, psychological factors, and prevailing social and economic conditions also influence these timetables.

Silhouettes and Details

Three basic fashion silhouettes form the basis for all clothing, as noted in Chapter 1. These are straight, or tubular; bell-shaped, or bouffant; and the bustle, or back fullness.[1] Therefore, it is obvious that silhouettes are long-run fashions. They do not change drastically from one season to another. Instead, it is through a series of changes in detail that a silhouette changes. The changes may be so imperceptible that a year-old garment may not look out of fashion. However, as these subtle changes add up over a period of four or five years, older apparel may take on a look that seems badly proportioned and definitely dated. And when the same silhouette goes through more and more years of detail changes— it is then replaced by another silhouette. In her book, *Recurring Cycles of Fashion,* Young pointed out that approximately every 35 years the silhouettes changed completely.[2] See the drawing on page 59.

Since the more detailed an item of apparel is, the sooner it becomes dated, obviously the simple, understated styles will generally have a longer fashion life. Is it any wonder that many high-fashion designers here and abroad aim for styles that will remain fashionable for 10 to 15 years . . . or longer?

Colors and Textures

Colors and textures were once thought of as secondary and short-run fashions. However, with new scientific studies about its potentially beneficial emotional and psychological effects, color has gained importance as an element of fashion. Thus color in today's fashions has taken on a new meaning, and designers and retailers herald new seasons, silhouettes, and details with exciting new colors. The traditional white and pastels for summer and black for winter are limitations of the past, as year-round air conditioning has blurred the once-sharp distinctions between the seasons in many parts of the world.

Textures, too, are less seasonally oriented. Whether a fabric is smooth or nubby, crisp or soft, sheer or opaque, light or heavyweight has more to do with the fashion needs of the customer than of the season. This has become possible with the technological advances in man-made fibers and the new texture finishes for natural fibers.

Accessories

For many years shoes, handbags, jewelry, millinery, gloves, belts, scarfs, and cosmetics were thought of merely as finishing touches for apparel, with only seasonal or short-run fashion cycles. Today many accessories are regarded as apparel items and have full-run fashion cycles of their own. Handbag and shoe "wardrobes" are owned by many consumers and are used to prolong or change the fashion cycles of their basic apparel. Scarfs are also considered important fashion accents. Today's scarfs come in many sizes, lengths, fabrics, and colors. They are used as belts or sashes, head coverings, and blouse fill-ins, and in any other exciting or innovative way the customer wishes.

Jewelry moves in both long-run and short-run cycles. Pearls had a long cycle of popularity during the fifties and sixties but declined because of the unstructured and casual look of the seventies. In the eighties, with the return of the fifties' look and the classic and extravagant look and feel of fashion in general, pearls once again began a fashion cycle.

Classics

The longest-running fashions are classics—those fashions that seem permanently arrested in the culmination stage of their cycles. Classics are usually practical and universally appealing. The shirtwaist dress, cardigan sweater, plain pump, neutral hosiery shades for women, and oxford-type shoe and sports jacket for men are examples.

Classics change, but only superficially. Material, texture, detail, and even silhouette may vary, but the style itself continues in fashion. A woman's pump may be made of any leather, fabric, or plastic. It may have a blunt or a pointed toe and a high or low heel. It may be made in a single color or a combination of colors. Although it changes superficially to relate to current fashions, it remains a pump—not an oxford, a loafer, or a T-strap. Similarly, a shirtwaist dress, whatever its fabric, color, sleeve length, and skirt fullness, remains a shirtwaist.

Fads

The here-today-and-gone-tomorrow nature of fads qualify them as the shortest-lived of short-run fashions. Fads rise with meteoric speed and decline even more quickly. Just think of platform shoes, baggy jeans, and punk hairstyles to recognize a typical short-run fad.

However, sometimes a fad does not behave in the expected way and then the fashion experts are fooled. The fad starts normally, with a limited and highly subjective group accepting it. But then, instead of following the usual pattern of rapid saturation and sudden death, the fad is accepted by the general public and leaves the "fad" category to become a legitimate fashion. In some cases the fad even becomes a classic.

When jogging became the rage with health-conscious men and women in the early 1980s, specially designed jogging shoes and warm-up suits began to appear. Gradually, business women used the comfortable shoes to go back and forth to work instead of wearing regular shoes on the hard city sidewalks. Warm-up suits began to be used as standard leisure-time wear for men, women, and children, with no regard to serious exercise. Today, jogging shoes and warm-ups are a standard part of almost everyone's wardrobe.

Consumer Buying and the Fashion Cycle

Every fashion has both a consumer buying cycle and a consumer use cycle. (See the next page.) The curve of the consumer buying cycle rises in direct relation to that of the consumer use cycle. But when the fashion reaches its peak, consumer buying tends to decline more rapidly than consumer use. Different

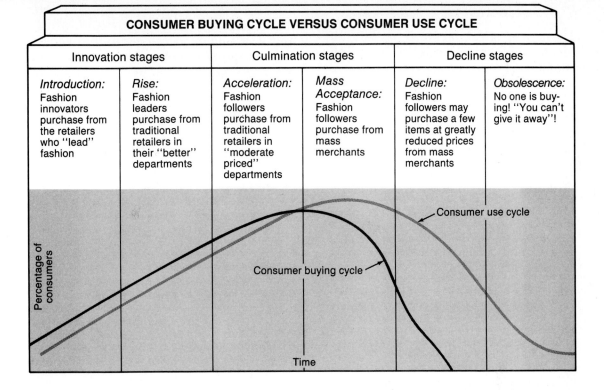

CONSUMER BUYING CYCLE VERSUS CONSUMER USE CYCLE					
Innovation stages		Culmination stages		Decline stages	
Introduction: Fashion innovators purchase from the retailers who "lead" fashion	*Rise:* Fashion leaders purchase from traditional retailers in their "better" departments	*Acceleration:* Fashion followers purchase from traditional retailers in "moderate priced" departments	*Mass Acceptance:* Fashion followers purchase from mass merchants	*Decline:* Fashion followers may purchase a few items at greatly reduced prices from mass merchants	*Obsolescence:* No one is buying! "You can't give it away"!

segments of society respond to and tire of a fashion at different times. So different groups of consumers continue to wear fashions for varying lengths of time after they have ceased buying them. While each group is using and enjoying a fashion, the producers and merchants serving that group are already abandoning the style and marketing something newer. Their efforts in this direction are most profitable when they anticipate, rather than follow, the trend of consumer demand.

Consumer buying is often halted prematurely. This happens because producers and sellers no longer wish to risk making and stocking an item they believe will soon decline in popularity. Instead, they concentrate their resources on new items with better prospects for

longevity. This procedure is familiar to anyone who has tried to buy summer clothes in late August or skiwear in March.

FACTORS INFLUENCING FASHION MOVEMENT

At the beginning of this chapter, the movement of fashion was likened to the movement of a river. As Laver said, in comparing the fashion cycle to a force of nature, "Nothing seems to be able to turn it back until it has spent itself, until it has provoked a reaction by its very excess."[3] However, just as a river can swell to turbulent flood stage or be slowed or diverted by a dam, so the movement of fashion can be accelerated or retarded by a variety of factors.

Accelerating Factors

There are seven general factors that speed up fashion cycles. These influences are, themselves, ever growing and accelerating as the pace of life in the last years of the twentieth century becomes more and more rapid and geographically all-encompassing. The accelerating factors are:

1. Increasingly widespread buying power.
2. Increased leisure.
3. More education.
4. Improved status of women.
5. Technological advances.
6. Sales promotion.
7. The changes of the seasons.

Increasingly Widespread Buying Power

More widely diffused discretionary income means there are more people with the financial means to respond to a fashion change. The more consumers flock to a new fashion, the sooner it will reach its culmination. The more widespread the financial ability of consumers to turn to yet a newer fashion, the sooner the current fashion will plunge into obsolescence.

Increased Leisure

In the past, long hours of work and little leisure permitted scant attention to fashion for the great majority of the population. More leisure time usually means more time to buy and enjoy fashion of many kinds. In the last 20 years, sharp decreases in working hours and increases in paid vacations have encouraged more use of at-home wear, casual clothes, sports apparel, travel clothes, and different types of ordinary business dress. Increased purchases of these types of apparel give impetus to their fashion cycles.

One result of today's increased leisure time has been the return to catalog buying. Catalog buying originally evolved because people in farming societies lived far from stores and had little leisure time for shopping. Today's leisure time has allowed people to add new physical and mental activities to their lives, such as sports and hobbies, leaving little time for shopping once again. Realizing that their customers are using leisure time in other pursuits, retailers are producing catalogs that come into the consumers' homes and can be read at night or during other spare time. Many department stores employ this technique for special events such as anniversary sales, white sales, Mother's Day, Father's Day, Easter, and Christmas.

More Education

The increasingly higher level of education in the United States helps to speed up fashion cycles in two ways. First, more people's horizons have been broadened to include new interests and new wants. And second, more people are equipped by education to earn the money to satisfy those wants. These two factors provide significant impetus to the adoption of new fashions.

Improved Status of Women

In a society with few artificial social barriers, women with discretionary income can spend it as they choose. No law or custom prevents any woman from buying the newest and most prestigious styles in dresses, hats, or shoes if she can afford to—thus giving impetus to a fashion cycle in its earliest phases. Sex discrimination in the job market has steadily decreased, and social acceptance of women who manage both homes and jobs has steadily increased. As a result, today's women have more discretionary income and are influencing the speed of fashion cycles in the way they use that income.

Technological Advances

Today we live in an "instant" world. The stunning advances in technology in almost every area have put us in immediate possession of facts, fantasies, and fashions. We see news as it happens around the world. Goods are sped to retail stores by land, air, and sea more rapidly than would have been dreamed of just a few decades ago.

New fibers, finishes, and materials with improved qualities are constantly being developed. Computer technology has improved production techniques and statistical control and analysis for more efficient product marketing. The result has been control of price increases, and in many cases, reduced prices on many fashion goods. All of these technological advances combine to make goods available almost at the instant that the consumer is psychologically and financially ready to buy. Thus the cycle of fashion becomes more and more accelerated.

Sales Promotion

The impact of sales promotion is felt everywhere in the fashion world today. Magazines, television, newspapers, billboards, and direct mail all expose the public to new fashions in a never-ending procession. While there is no way to force consumers to accept new fashions, nor any way to save a fashion if consumers reject it, sales promotion can greatly influence a fashion's success by telling people it exists. Sales promotion can help to speed up acceptance of a new fashion or sometimes extend its peak or duration. The jeans of the 1970s and the miniskirts of the late 1980s are looks that were made available to women through sales promotion. Promotion, therefore, can frequently help a fashion reach its culmination more speedily.

Seasonal Change

Nothing is so consistent in bringing about change in fashions as the calendar. As the seasons change, so do consumer demands. After months of winter, people want to shed their heavy clothing for lightweight spring and summer fashions. In climates where there are radical seasonal changes, this is only natural, even though our homes, schools, cars, and places of business are kept at desired temperatures through central heating and air conditioning. However, even in areas such as Florida and Hawaii, where the weather is moderate year-round, people change their wardrobes with the seasons. Even if the twenty-first century brings complete climate control, people will never accept the boredom of a year-round wardrobe.

Because people today are so geared to travel at all times of the year to all types of climates, the seasonal changes are accelerated and a kind of preseason testing can go on. Resort wear appears in retail stores in time for selection by the public for winter vacations in tropical areas. The late-June appearance of the first fall fashions in leading stores makes it possible for the style-conscious to make their selections well in advance of the first cold wind. Consumer responses to these early offerings allow manufacturers and retailers alike to know what does and does not appeal.

Retarding Factors

Factors that retard the development of fashion cycles either discourage people from adopting incoming styles or encourage them to continue using styles

A HOP, SKIP AND JUMPSUIT

The looks before you leap-
bright, light and
slightly mad

Down-to-earth patterns complement the bounce of baggy jumpsuits: Aztec print jumpsuit in off-white and black, $155, and bathing suit, $174, both from Guy Paulin. Hat, David, Inc.; earrings, Jim Calderon; shoes, Calvin Klein.

Accelerating factors include sales promotion, such as this magazine photo of a jumpsuit and its "slightly mad" accessories. Note that the copy tells who produced these items and what they cost.

that might be considered on the decline. Retarding factors include the opposites of the accelerating factors; for example, decreased buying power during recessionary periods. Major retarding factors are habit and custom, religion and sumptuary laws, the nature of the merchandise, and reductions in consumers' buying power.

Habit and Custom

By slowing acceptance of new styles and prolonging the life-spans of those already accepted, habit and custom exert a braking effect on fashion movement. Habit slows the adoption of new skirt lengths, silhouettes, necklines, or colors whenever shoppers unconsciously select styles that do not differ perceptibly from those they already own. It is easy for an individual to let habit take over, and some consumers are more susceptible to this tendency than others. Their loyalty to an established style is less a matter of fashion judgment than a natural attraction to the more familiar.

Custom slows progress in the fashion cycle by permitting vestiges of past fashions, status symbols, taboos, or special needs to continue to appear in modern dress. Custom is responsible for such details as buttons on the sleeves of men's suits, vents in men's jackets, and the sharp creases down the front of men's trousers. Custom usually requires a degree of formality in dress for religious services. The trend toward similarity of dress for men and women in this country has permitted women to wear trousers, but custom still discourages men from wearing skirts.

A classic example of the influence of custom is the placement of buttons. They are on the right side for men, originating with the need to have the weapon arm available while dressing and undressing. And they are on the left for women, who tend to hold babies on that side and can more conveniently use the right hand for buttons. The stitching on the backs of gloves is another example; it dates back to a time when sizes were adjusted by lacing at these points.

Religion

Historically, religious leaders have championed custom, and their ceremonial apparel has demonstrated their respect for the old ways. In the past, religious leaders tended to associate fashion with temptation and urged their followers to turn their backs on both. Religion today, however, exerts much less of a restraining influence on fashion. Ex-amples of the new relaxation may be found in the modernization of women's dress in most religious orders and in the fact that most women no longer consider a hat obligatory when in church.

In the 1970s and 1980s a countertrend arose to religion's diminishing impact on fashion. It is particularly evident in the dress adopted by the young followers of Hare Krishna and in the adoption of ancient dress by the followers of the revolution in Iran. In both cases, the religious leaders of these movements have decreed that modern fashions lead to temptation and corruption.

Sumptuary Laws

Sumptuary laws regulate what we can and cannot purchase. Today, there are sumptuary laws which, for example, require that children's sleepwear be flame-retardant. In the past, sumptuary laws have regulated extravagance and luxury in dress on religious or moral grounds. Height of headdress, length of train, width of sleeve, value and weight of material, and color of dress have all at times been restricted to specific classes by law. Such laws were aimed at keeping each class in its place in a rigidly stratified society.[4]

Other laws, such as those of the Puritans, attempted to enforce a general high-mindedness by condemning frippery. An order passed in 1638 by the General Court of Massachusetts stated:

No garment shall be made with short sleeves, and such as have garments already made with short sleeves shall not wear same unless they cover the arm to the wrist; and hereafter no person whatever shall make any garment for women with sleeves more than half an ell wide.[5]

And in the eighteenth century, a bill was proposed (but rejected) that stated:

All women of whatever age, rank, profession, or degree, whether virgin, maid, or widow, that shall impose upon, seduce, and betray into matrimony any of His Majesty's subjects by scents, paints, cosmetic washes, artificial teeth, false hair, Spanish wool, iron stays, hoops, high-heeled shoes, or bolstered hips, shall incur the penalty of the law now in force against witchcraft and the like demeanours, and that marriage, upon conviction, shall stand null and void.[6]

People have a way of ignoring local ordinances, however, if they conflict with a fashion cycle that is gathering strength. In New York in the 1930s, fines could be imposed on individuals who appeared on the streets wearing shorts, or whose bathing-suit shoulder straps were not in place on public beaches. What was considered indecent exposure then—shorts and strapless bathing suits—is commonplace today. More recently, the late 1960s and 1970s saw a dramatic change in high school dress codes, although many private schools still have strict requirements in regard to acceptable dress.

Nature of the Merchandise

Not all merchandise moves at the same pace through a fashion cycle. Often the very nature of the merchandise is responsible for the rate of movement. Over the years it has been accepted as normal that men's fashion cycles move more slowly than women's. In recent years, however, the changing lifestyles of the male population have resulted in accelerating menswear cycles. Women's apparel generally moves in slower cycles than accessories, though as was pointed out earlier in this chapter, some accessories now have full-run cycles comparable to those of apparel.

Reductions in Consumers' Buying Power

Consumers' buying power has a powerful effect on the movement of fashion cycles. When buying power increases, fashion cycles often speed up. Decreased buying power, conversely, can retard the movement of fashion cycles. During economic recessions and resultant high unemployment, consumers' buying power is sharply reduced. Many people make do with clothes they have, buying only necessities. A similar caution is shown by consumers affected by strikes, inflation, high taxes, or interest rates. All these factors have a slowing influence on fashion cycles. The poorer people are, the less impact they have on fashion's movements. They become bystanders in matters of fashion, and as a result do not keep cycles moving. Laver emphasized the importance of buying power when he said that nothing except poverty can make a style permanent.[7]

RECURRING FASHIONS

In the study of fashion history, we see that styles reoccur, with adaptations that suit the times in which they reappear. Occasionally an entire look is reborn. The elegant, simple look of the late 1940s and early 1950s, for example, was born again for the generation of the 1980s. Nostalgia influenced choices not only in apparel, but also in hairstyles and makeup.

Sometimes a single costume component or a minor detail that had exhausted its welcome stages a comeback, like the "chandelier" earring in the mid-

1980s. At other times, a single article of clothing, like the sandals of the ancient Greeks, returns to popularity.

An outstanding example of a recurring men's fashion is the T-shirt. T-shirts originated in France as cotton underwear. They were discovered during World War I by American soldiers who preferred them to their own itchy wool union suits. In the 1940s they re-emerged as "tee" shirts for golfing and other active sports. In the sixties they became part of the women's fashion scene as well.

Today the T-shirt has put ego into fashion. T-shirts are bought for both fashion and antifashion reasons, and in both cases they announce to all what the wearer stands for. A T-shirt can project nationality (*Je suis Américaine*), affiliation (Boys Town), aspiration (Superman), or rock-star preference (the Rolling Stones). T-shirt wearers can identify themselves outright by names, initials, telephone numbers, or even blown-up photographs of themselves transferred onto the T-shirt.[8]

Research indicates that in the past, similar silhouettes and details of design in women's apparel have recurred with remarkable regularity.

In *Recurring Cycles of Fashion,*[9] Young studied skirt silhouettes and their variations in connection with her interest in theatrical costumes. From data she collected on the period from 1760 to 1937, she concluded that despite widely held opinions to the contrary, there were actually only three basic silhouettes. These three basic silhouettes always followed each other in the same sequence, each recurring about once every 100 years. Each silhouette with all its variations dominated the fashion scene for a period of approximately 35

According to Agnes Brooks Young, there are only three basic silhouettes: (a) bell-shaped, (b) back-fullness, and (c) straight. They tend to follow each other in regular sequence. "Back interest" has recurred for the first time since the bustle!

years. Having reached an excess in styling, it then declined in popularity and yielded to the next silhouette in regular sequence.

The anthropologist A. L. Kroeber studied changes in women's apparel from the early 1600s to the early 1900s. His conclusions confirm Young's findings that similar silhouettes recur in fashion acceptance approximately once every 100 years. In addition, Kroeber found that similar neck widths recurred every 100 years, and similar skirt lengths every 35 years.[10] In more recent times, this rate of change has altered. There was the short skirt in the 1940s, the long skirt in the 1950s, the super-short skirt in the 1960s, and the mid-length skirt in the 1970s. Interestingly, in the last years of the twentieth century, it seems that all lengths are acceptable—from the super-short skirt to ankle length, and every length in between!

FASHION

When adventurous spirits yearn to hear the call of the wild, they need not pack up and head for darkest Africa or the Amazon jungle. Instead, they can simply saunter down to their nearest Banana Republic store and "explore" to their hearts' content.

A true adventure in retailing, the Banana Republic Travel & Safari Clothing Co. was begun in 1978 by Mel and Patricia Ziegler—and its innovative concept immediately struck a chord in the fashion merchandising business. That impact was felt perhaps even more strongly because the couple who launched Banana Republic had absolutely no prior experience in either fashion or retailing.

Both avid travelers, Mel Ziegler was an author and reporter for the *San Francisco Chronicle,* while Patricia had been a *Chronicle* staff artist. When they both felt the urge to get out of the newspaper business, their personal love of

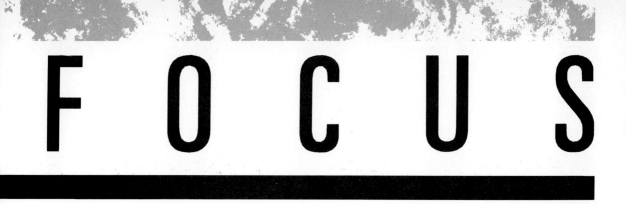

F O C U S

comfortable, practical clothing gave them the idea of selling it—and the concept of Banana Republic was born.

The Zieglers opened their first store in their hometown of Mill Valley, California, and decorated it, 1950s Hollywood style, to look like a jungle trading post. One store led to another, and another, and in less than 10 years, there were more than 65 Banana Republic stores scattered in urban markets across the country—some looking like a jungle trading post, some like an African hunting lodge, and some like a decaying British officers' club. All are embellished with (plastic) elephant trunks, (plaster) big-game heads, and sometimes military surplus jeeps. A Beverly Hills branch even features an elephant crashing through a wall and a bush plane hanging from the ceiling!

As for the merchandise, Banana Republic offers a wide range of safari dresses, bush shirts and shorts, Gurkha pants, and leather aviator jackets, all made from natural fabrics and only in "sunproof" colors: khaki, gray, white, olive drab, faded indigo, and dusty plum. Much of the apparel is bought from military surplus outlets the world over; and what can't be found ready-made, Patricia Ziegler designed herself.

While the store's safari-style gear is deliberately outside the mainstream of fashion, that is part of its appeal to many fashionable consumers. The clothing expresses a casually chic lifestyle image—and its style caused the retailer's popularity to soar so quickly that in 1983, The Gap persuaded the Zieglers to sell them the chain.

With The Gap providing capital for expansion, Banana Republic reached an estimated $115 million in gross sales in 1986. However with the change in ownership, differences in operating and merchandising styles caused the Zieglers to retire from the business. This change adversely affected the growth pattern and the Banana Republic became a "problem child" to Gap management. But in 1989, the Banana Republic refurbished its image, and customers once again responded to the mystery and excitement of its merchandise mix.

It all adds up to fashion retailing that's a little bit off the beaten track—but then, that's what makes the business *fashion*.

This Fashion Focus is based on information from these sources:

Macintosh, Jeane, "Wall Street Eyes Banana Republic," *Women's Wear Daily,* March 8, 1989, p. 10.

Salholz, Eloise, with Pamela Abramson, "Hail the Khaki Republic," *Newsweek,* May 13, 1985, p. 89.

Walsleben, Elizabeth C., "Banana Republic: Adventures in Retailing," *California Apparel News/National Edition,* February 27–March 5, 1987, p. 82.

Weil, Henry, "Keeping Up With the (Indiana) Joneses," *Savvy,* February 1986, pp. 41–46.

PLAYING THE APPAREL FASHION GAME

According to Madge Garland, a well-known English fashion authority: "Every woman is born with a built-in hobby: the adornment of her person. The tricks she can play with it, the shapes she can make of it, the different portions she displays at various times, the coverings she uses or discards . . ." all add up to fashion.[11]

Many clothing authorities read a clear message into the alternate exposure and covering of various parts of the body—sex. J. C. Flügel cited sexual attraction as the dominant motive for wearing clothes.[12]

Laver explained fashion emphasis in terms of the sexuality of the body. "Fashion really began," he said, "with the discovery in the fifteenth century that clothes could be used as a compromise between exhibitionism and modesty."[13] Laver also suggested that those portions of the body no longer fashionable to expose are "sterilized" and are no longer regarded as sexually attractive. Those that are newly exposed are **erogenous,** or sexually stimulating. He viewed fashion as pursuing the emphasis of ever-shifting erogenous zones, but never quite catching up with them. "If you really catch up," he warned, "you are immediately arrested for indecent exposure. If you almost catch up, you are celebrated as a leader of fashion."[14]

Men's apparel has long played the fashion game, too, but, since the industrial revolution, in a less dramatic manner than women's. Women's fashions have tended to concentrate mainly on different ways to convey sexual appeal. Men's fashions have been designed to emphasize such attributes as strength, power, bravery, and high social rank.

When a male style does emphasize sex, it is intended to project an overall impression of virility.

Pieces of the Game

The pieces with which the women's fashion game is played are the various parts of the female body: waist, shoulders, bosom, neckline, hips, derriere, legs, and feet, as well as the figure as a whole. Historically, as attention to a part of the anatomy reaches a saturation point, the fashion spotlight shifts to some other portion.

In the Middle Ages, asceticism was fashionable. Women's clothes were designed to play down, rather than emphasize, women's sexuality. The Renaissance was a period of greater sexual freedom. Women's apparel during this period highlighted the breasts and the abdomen, particularly the latter.

By the eighteenth century, however, the abdomen had lost its appeal. Although the bosom continued to be emphasized, a flatter abdomen was fashionable, and heels were raised to facilitate upright carriage. The Empire period, with its high waistline, also stressed the bosom. But the entire body was emphasized with sheer and scanty dresses— some so sheer they could be pulled through a ring. Some advocates of this fashion even wet their apparel so that it would cling to the figure when worn.

During the nineteenth century, fashion interest shifted to the hips, and skirts billowed. Later, the posterior was accented with bustles and trains.

Early in the twentieth century, emphasis switched from the trunk to the limbs, through short skirts and sleeveless or tight-sleeved dresses. Flügel interpreted accent on the limbs, together with the suggestion of an underdeveloped torso, as an idealization of youth. He foresaw continued emphasis on youth and boyishness as a result of women's participation in varied activities, the steady march of democracy, and increasing sexual freedom.[15]

In the 1960s, fashion interest was focused on short skirts and the legs. As the sixties drew to a close, interest shifted from legs to bosom. By the early 1970s, the natural look of bosoms was in. The unconstructed, natural look was followed by the "no-bra" look. This fashion reached its culmination and began its decline when bosoms were only slightly concealed beneath see-through fabrics or plunging necklines. As this excess led to obsolescence, the 1980s ushered in a reemergence of the 1950s bosom. Manufacturers of bras and inner wear are featuring soft-side bras, strapless bras, T-back bras, and sports bras to once again give a firmly supported look to the bosom.

The Figure as a Whole

According to Garland, the fashions of the 1950s and early 1960s showed off the entire figure:

The modern girl manages at the same time to bare her shoulders, accentuate her bust, pull in her waist, and show her legs to above the knees. It is a triumph of personal publicity over the taboos of the past and the previous limitations of fashion.[16]

The emphasis on the legs has occurred many times during the 20th Century. The "flappers" of the 1920s, the "mods" of the 1960s, and the "chics" of the 1980s all were delighted to show and "shake a leg!"

Until the late 1960s brought the "youth cult" and its attendant revolt against conventional sexual and political attitudes, previous fashion eras had centered attention only on parts of the body. The "triumph of personal publicity" achieved in the late 1960s and early 1970s broke all records for calling attention to just about every area of the human body. It was, indeed, an allover feast for the eye of the observer.

Rules of the Game

In the game of emphasizing different parts of the female body at different times, as in any game, there are rules.

The first and strongest rule is that fashion emphasis does not flit from one area to another! Rather, a particular area of the body is emphasized until every bit of excitement has been exhausted. At this point, fashion attention turns to another area. For example, as has been noted, when miniskirts of the 1960s could go no higher and still be legal, the fashion emphasis moved on.

The second rule of the fashion game may well be, as Garland suggested, that only certain parts of the body can be exposed at any given time.[17] There are dozens of examples throughout fashion history that back up this theory: floor-length evening gowns with plunging necklines, high necklines with miniskirts, turtlenecks on sleeveless fashions.

A third rule of the fashion game is that, like fashion itself, fashion attention must always go forward. "A fashion can never retreat gradually and in good order," Dwight E. Robinson said, ". . . like a dictator it must always expand its aggressions or collapse. Old fashions never fade away; they die suddenly and arbitrarily."[18]

PREDICTING THE MOVEMENT OF FASHION

Producing and selling fashion merchandise to consumers at a profit are what fashion merchandising is all about. To bring excitement and flair to their segment of merchandising, producers and retailers must have a well-defined plan and must follow the movement of general fashion preferences.

The success of fashion merchandising depends upon the correct prediction of which new styles will be accepted by the majority of consumers. The successful forecaster of fashion must:

1. Distinguish what the current fashion trends are.
2. Estimate how widespread they are.
3. Determine when these fashions will appeal to the firm's target customer groups.

With information on these three points, projections—a prime requisite in successful fashion merchandising—become possible.

Identifying Trends

A **fashion trend** is a direction in which fashion is moving. Manufacturers and merchants try to recognize each fashion trend to determine how widespread it is and whether it is moving toward or away from maximum fashion acceptance. They can then decide whether to actively promote the fashion to their target customers, to wait, or to abandon it.

For example, assume that short jackets have developed as a fashion trend. At the introduction and rise stages, retailers will stock and promote more and more short jackets. When customer response begins to level off, retailers will realize that a saturation point is being reached with this style and will begin introducing longer jackets into their stocks in larger and larger numbers. If the retailers have correctly predicted the downturn in customer demand for short jackets, they will have fewer on hand when the downturn occurs. And while some customers may continue to wear the short-jacket style, they will not be buying new short jackets, and certainly not at regular prices.

Sources of Data

Modern fashion forecasters bear little resemblance to the mystical prognosticators of old. Their ability to predict the strength and direction of fashion trends among their customers has almost nothing to do with what is often called a "fashion sense." Nor does it depend upon glances into the future via a cloudy crystal ball. Today's successful fashion forecasters depend upon that most valuable commodity—information. Good, solid facts about the willingness of customers to accept certain goods are the basis of successful merchandising decisions.

In today's computerized business world, merchants can keep "instant" records on sales, inventories, new fashion testing, and myriads of other contributing factors that aid the fashion merchandising process. In addition, wise merchants keep their eyes open to see what is being worn by their own customers as well as by the public as a whole. They are so familiar with their customers' lifestyles, economic status, educational level, and social milieu that they can determine at just what point in a fashion's life cycle their customers will be ready to accept or reject it. Merchants turn to every available source for information that will help ensure success.

They use their hard-gained sales experience but don't just rely on their own judgment; they rely on the judgment of others too. From the producers of fashion, from resident buying offices, and from special fashion groups such as the predictive services I.M. International, Nigel French, and Here & There, they learn about the buying habits of customers other than their own. Successful merchants look at the large fashion picture to predict more ably just where their local scene fits in.

Interpreting Influential Factors

An old theater saying goes, "It's all in the interpretation." In other words, written or spoken words gain their importance by the way they are presented to the audience. That is where the special talents of the performer come in. The same is true of fashion forecasting. All the data in the world can be collected by merchants, producers, or designers, but this is of little importance without interpretation. That is where the forecasters' knowledge of fashion and fashion principles comes into the picture. From the data they have collected, they are able to identify certain patterns. Then they consider certain factors that can accelerate or retard a fashion cycle among their target group of customers. Among these factors are current events, the appearance of prophetic styles, sales promotion efforts, and the canons of taste currently in vogue.

Current Events

The news of what is going on in the country or the world can have a long-term or short-term influence on consumers and affect their response to a fashion. By 1984, for example, the media was reporting at length on the nomination of a woman Vice President for the country. Numerous papers and magazines discussed current events in the corporate business world with articles about the business opportunities for women at mid- and upper-management levels. Success in responsible positions in the business world demanded "dressing for success," and career-minded women responded by adopting the business-oriented suit look. By their very appearance these women indicated their determination to succeed in the still male-dominated world of business.

Prophetic Styles

Good fashion forecasters keep a sharp watch for what they call **prophetic styles.** These are particularly interesting new styles that are still in the introduction phase of their fashion cycle. Taken up enthusiastically by the socially prominent or by the flamboyant young, these styles may gather momentum very rapidly or they may prove to be nonstarters. Whatever their future course, the degree of acceptance of these very new styles gives forecasters a sense of which directions fashion might go in.

Sales Promotion Efforts

In addition to analyzing the records of past sales, fashion forecasters give thought to the kind and amount of promotion that helps stimulate interest in prophetic styles. They also consider the kind and amount of additional sales promotion they can look forward to. For example, a fiber producer's powerful advertising and publicity efforts may have helped turn slight interest in a product into a much stronger interest during a corresponding period last year. The forecaster's problem is to estimate how far

the trend might have developed without those promotional activities. The forecaster must also assess how much momentum remains from last year's push to carry the trend forward this year, and how much promotional support can be looked for in the future. The promotional effort that a forecaster's own organization plans to expend is only one part of the story; outside efforts, sometimes industrywide, also must be considered in forecasting fashions.

Canons of Taste

According to Nystrom, fashions that are in accord with currently accepted canons (standards) of art, custom, modesty, and utility are most easily accepted.[19] Today's forecasters are careful to take current canons of taste into consideration as they judge the impact of new styles. In the 1960s, when it was "anything goes" in behavior and values for a large segment of the population, the subdued traditional styles had very little place in fashion. At the end of the twentieth century, while both ends of the spectrum can be found in the fashion world, the more conservative styles continue to dominate the fashion scene as a more moderate way of life continues to please more of the people more of the time. The development of good taste by the fashion merchant is a must. It comes from acquired merchandise knowledge as well as careful observation of people who possess good taste.

Importance of Timing

Successful merchants must determine what their particular target group of customers is wearing now and what this group is most likely to be wearing 1 month or 3 months from now. The data these merchants collect enable them to identify each current fashion, who is wearing it, and what point it has reached in its fashion cycle.

Since merchants know at what point in a fashion's cycle their customers are most likely to be attracted, they can determine whether to stock a current fashion now, 1 month from now, or 3 months from now.

A good example were "Shaker knit" sweaters in the late 1980s, when they moved from being "classics" to become the hottest item in the sweater business. The look began in expensive sweaters carried in better stores and quickly moved into the medium-price range in specialty stores. From there they moved to low-end stores and you couldn't give them away. However, because of their "classic" look, they soon returned to the sweater stocks of most stores and have been carried each year as a basic.

REFERENCES

[1] Agnes Brooke Young, *Recurring Cycles of Fashion: 1760–1937,* Harper & Brothers, New York, 1937, reprinted by Cooper Square Publishers, Inc., New York, 1966, p. 30.

[2] Ibid.

[3] James Laver, *Taste and Fashion,* rev. ed., George G. Harrap & Co., Ltd., London, 1946, p. 52.

[4] Pearl Binder, *Muffs and Morals,* George G. Harrap & Co., Ltd., London, 1953, pp. 162–164.

[5] Elisabeth McClellan, *History of American Costume,* Tudor Publishing Company, New York, 1969, p. 82.

[6] John Taylor, *It's a Small, Medium, and Outsize World,* Hugh Evelyn, London, 1966, p. 39.

[7] Laver, p. 201.

[8] Clara Pierre, *Looking Good: The Liberation of Fashion,* Reader's Digest Press, New York, 1976, p. 149.

[9] Young, p. 30.

[10] A. L. Kroeber, "On the Principles of Order in Civilizations as Exemplified by Change in Fashion," *American Anthropologist,* Vol. 21, July–September 1919, pp. 235–263.

[11] Madge Garland, *The Changing Form of Fashion,* Praeger Publishers, New York, 1971, p. 11.

[12] J. C. Flügel, *The Psychology of Clothes,* International Universities Press, New York, 1966, p. 163.

[13] Laver, p. 200.

[14] Ibid., p. 201.

[15] Flügel, p. 163.

[16] Garland, p. 20.

[17] Ibid., p. 11.

[18] Dwight E. Robinson, "Fashion Theory and Product Design," *Harvard Business Review,* Vol. 36, November–December 1958, p. 128.

[19] Paul H. Nystrom, *Fashion Merchandising,* The Ronald Press, New York, 1932, p. 94.

MERCHANDISING VOCABULARY

Define or briefly explain the following terms:

Adaptations	Fashion trend	Plateau
Culmination stage	Line-for-line copies	Prophetic styles
Decline stage	or knock–offs	Rise stage
Erogenous	Long-run fashions	Short-run fashions
Fashion cycle	Obsolescence stage	Sumptuary laws

MERCHANDISING REVIEW

1. Fashions go through a five-phase life cycle. Name and explain each cycle.
2. How do line-for-line copies of fashions differ from adaptations of fashions?
3. In what ways can the culmination stage of a fashion be extended?
4. What disruptions can occur in the normal progress of a fashion cycle? Can the cycle be resumed once it is disrupted? Give examples.
5. Explain the differences in short-run and long-run fashions. Give two examples of each.
6. What conclusions did Agnes Brooke Young reach in her study of skirt silhouettes from 1760 to 1937? Give recent examples of how the back fullness silhouette has been revived.
7. In what respects does the consumer buying cycle differ from the consumer use cycle? How is such information useful to fashion merchants?
8. List the "pieces" of the women's fashion game, according to Madge Garland. What happened to these "pieces" in the 1960s and 1970s?
9. According to leading fashion authorities, what are the three basic rules that govern the fashion game?
10. What basic resources are available to the fashion merchant to predict fashion trends?

MERCHANDISING DIGEST

1. Give at least one current example of each of several factors that are accelerating the forward movement of fashions today.
2. Certain factors tend to retard the development of fashion cycles by discouraging the adoption of newly introduced styles. List these factors and give at least one example of how each factor exerts a braking influence on fashion development.
3. From your study and appraisal of currently popular styles, define what the "pieces of the game" are today, that is, where the current fashion spotlight is focused. Do you see any signs of change? Explain your views.

THE LEADERS OF FASHION

In mid-December 1987, American politicians and media were poised for the arrival in Washington, D.C., of Soviet leader Mikhail Gorbachev for meetings with President Reagan and the signing of the history-making nuclear arms control treaty.

At the same time, the American fashion world was poised for the arrival of that other influential Russian, Raisa Gorbachev. At her first public appearances, the wife of the Soviet leader had surprised the world with her chic look and fashion sense. After decades of projecting a decidedly gray and dumpy image, the U.S.S.R. had a style-setting first lady.

And so, as their husbands met to hammer out international policy, Nancy Reagan and Raisa Gorbachev met to share their interests, humanistic programs, and remarkable fashion sense. Through live television coverage, the whole world watched. And within moments, fashion designers were making notes, fashion writers were preparing releases, and fashion-conscious women around the globe were mentally seeing themselves in the clothes of the two first ladies.

Once again, fashion had proven to be a potent force influencing people around the world. Fashion news was sharing the spotlight with momentous political and cultural events. This meeting between the superpowers was a dramatic example of how fashion is associated with almost every occurrence in world affairs. It also demonstrated the role that prominent people play in influencing fashion.

But how do fashions generally begin? Who starts them, who sponsors them, and what influences consumers to accept them? Answers to these questions are complex and involve designers, manufacturers, retailers, and most of all, consumers.

The myth that every change in fashion is caused by a designer seeking a new way to make money is, of course, not true. It is consumers who bring about changes in fashion. The needs and wants of consumers change. Their ideas about what is appropriate and acceptable change. And their interests in life change. These are all reasons that influence fashion designers and manufacturers to produce new and different styles for consumers' consideration. The charting, forecasting, and satisfaction of consumer demand are the fashion industry's main concerns.

BIRTH OF A FASHION

Current trends in consumers' purchasing, lifestyles, and attitudes are noted and analyzed. Subsequently the trends are interpreted and presented to consumers in the form of new styles. Designers and manufacturers influence fashion by providing an unending series of new designs from which consumers choose to best express their individual lifestyles.

Many precautions are taken to ensure that designers are presenting what customers want. Even so, at least two-thirds of the new designs introduced each season by the fashion industry fail to become fashions. Some designs are introduced too early, before the public is ready to accept them. Other designs fail because they are too extreme for consumer acceptance. Still other designs fail to become fashions because although they are commonly accepted in many places, they meet pockets of resistance in certain areas of the country. What is worn in New York today is not necessarily what consumers in less urban areas of the United States are ready to accept. Witness the hot pants, the harem pants, the peasant looks of the 1970s, and the punk-rock extremes of the 1980s! Only a trend that reflects a nationwide mood will successfully cross the United States from ocean-to-ocean and affect the lives and wardrobes of all those in-between.

THE DESIGNER'S ROLE

The days when the design world was populated by a few visionaries whose ideas produced all the designs for the public are long gone. Today there are unlimited opportunities in the field of design for those who have the special talents, both artistic and practical, that are needed to shape the consumer's world. Designers are everywhere and they design everything—fashions, furnishings, housewares, office equipment. Their tools range from pencil and sketchpad to computer programs that can produce many variations of a design with a few keystrokes.

Designers must continually study the lifestyles of those consumers for whom their designs are intended. Because designers work far in advance of their designs' final production, they must be able to predict future fashion trends. Designers must be aware of the effects of current events, socioeconomic conditions, and psychological attitudes on fashion interest and demand.

In creating designs that will not only reflect consumer attitudes and needs but also give expression to artistic ideas, fashion designers are continually influenced and limited by many factors. Of particular importance are practical business considerations. All designs must be produced at a profit and within the firm's predetermined wholesale price range. Consequently, designers must consider the availability and cost of materials, the particular image that the firm wants to maintain, available production techniques, and labor costs. Great designers use their creativity to overcome all these limitations and to produce salable, exciting designs.

Types of Designers

Most American designers who are using their artistic and innovative talents to design fashion-oriented merchandise fall into one of three categories:

1. High-fashion, or "name," designer
2. Stylist-designer
3. Freelance artist-designer

High-Fashion Designer

A high-fashion designer is usually referred to in this country as a "name" designer. Because of the success and originality of their designs, name designers are well-known to fashion-conscious customers. High-fashion designers are responsible not only for creating the designs but also for the choice of fabric, texture, and color in which each is to be executed. They may often be involved in development of the production model, as well as plans for the promotion of the firm's line. Some name

From concept to creation, from photos to fittings, the fashion designer eats, sleeps, and drinks the excitement of bringing new designs to life. But designers like Karl Lagerfeld are also involved in checking details to insure the success of that season's fashion.

designers work for fashion houses, as do Karl Lagerfeld for Chanel and Gianni Ferre for Dior. Others like Bill Blass and Yves Saint Laurent own their own firms or are financed by a "silent partner" outside the firm.

Until recently, designer names were associated only with original, expensive designs in apparel. Today, many designers whose names have come to be associated with what is new and original license their names to manufacturers of accessories, home furnishings, cosmetics, and fragrances.

Stylist-Designer

A second type of designer—the stylist-designer—uses his or her creative talents to adapt or change the successful designs of others. A stylist-designer must understand fabric and style construction as well as the manufacturing process because designs are usually adapted at lower prices. Stylist-designers usually create designs at the late rise or early culmination stage of the fashion cycle. They are usually not involved in details relating to the production of the firm's line or the planning of its promotional activities, but must design within the limits of the firm's production capacity and capability. Stylist-designers whose company sells to major chains often accompany the salesperson to define the look or to better understand what the buyer wants.

Freelance Artist-Designer

The third type of designer—the freelance artist-designer—sells sketches to manufacturers. These sketches may be original designs by the freelancer or adaptations, and may reflect the freelancer's own ideas or the manufacturer's specifications. The freelancer usually works out of a design studio and sells sketches and designs to the general apparel market. With the delivery of a sketch to the manufacturer, a freelancer's job ends.

Insight and Intuition

A designer takes a fashion idea and embodies it in new styles. Even the most creative designers, however, disclaim any power to force acceptance of their styles. Few have said so more effectively than Paul Poiret, one of the twentieth century's great Parisian couturiers. He once told an American audience:

I know you think me a king of fashion . . . It is a reception which cannot but flatter me and of which I cannot complain. All the same, I must undeceive you with regard to the powers of a king of fashion. We are not capricious despots such as wake up one fine day, decide upon a change in habits, abolish a neckline, or puff out a sleeve. We are neither arbiters nor dictators. Rather we are to be thought of as the blindly obedient servants of woman, who for her part is always enamoured of change and a thirst for novelty. It is our role, and our duty, to be on the watch for the moment at which she becomes bored with what she is wearing, that we may suggest at the right instant something else which will meet her taste and needs. It is therefore with a pair of antennae and not a rod of iron that I come before you, and not as a master that I speak, but as a slave . . . who must divine your innermost thoughts.[1]

Insight and intuition always play a large part in a designer's success. Constant experimentation with new ideas is a must. As one fashion reaches the excess that marks its approaching demise, a designer must have new styles ready and waiting for the public.

Sources of Design Inspiration

Where does the designer get ideas and inspiration for new fashion? The answer, of course, is: everywhere! Through television the designer experiences all the wonders of the entertainment world. In films the designer is exposed to the influences of all the arts and lifestyles throughout the world. Museum exhibits, art shows, world happenings, expositions, the theater, music, dance, and world travel are all sources of design inspiration to fashion designers. The fashions of the past are also a rich source of design inspiration.

While always alert to the new and exciting, fashion designers never lose sight of the recent past. They know that consumers need to anticipate something new each season. But they also recognize that whatever new style is introduced will have to take its place with what consumers already have in their wardrobes. No one starts with all new clothes each season. Rarely does a revolutionary new style succeed. Instead, it is the evolutionary new style that so often becomes the best-selling fashion.

The 1980s Looked to the 1960s

In the last years of the 1980s a modern-day Rip Van Winkle, awakening after a 20-year sleep, might have thought he was still in the late 1960s. Folk singers Peter, Paul, and Mary were entertaining coast-to-coast, as were Judy Collins and the Smothers Brothers. The Rolling Stones, David Bowie, and The Beach Boys were front-page entertainment news. Fervent people marched for peace and joined hands across America to fight against hunger. "Cabaret" with Joel Grey was playing to capacity houses on Broadway. And "Flora, the Red Menace," the show that introduced Liza Minnelli to theater audiences in the 1960s, was delighting new audiences of the 1980s with its music and wit. Women in the audience were wearing fashions that reflected the 1960s—with short skirts, fashions of denim and leather, fashions that had garter belts and nylon stockings worn underneath. And, of course, boots . . . boots . . . boots!

The 1980s Looked to the 1950s

For some years, television had been showing young people and reminding their parents what life had been like in the 1950s. While *Happy Days* and *Laverne and Shirley* presented the 1970s version of the fifties, reruns of actual TV shows like *Father Knows Best, Leave It to Beaver,* and *Ozzie and Harriet* were brought back. A whole new group of people, born in the 1960s and 1970s, were introduced to sock hops and hula hoops.

Fashion designers were ready! The looks of the 1950s were brought out and updated for the times and were seized upon by the young people and the not so young. The "little black dress" immortalized by Marilyn Monroe, the legend of the fifties, came back from coast to coast. Shortie gloves, button earrings, blouses and skirts, shorter hair, and fashions with form all added to the impact. The looks cut across all income levels, with adapted 1950s silhouettes from famous designers at one end of the scale and poodle skirts and toppers at the other. The only steady ingredient was nostalgia. In the troubled 1980s a highly romanticized picture of the more settled 1950s was a very comforting thing to think about, and, as far as possible through fashions and customs, to attempt to recreate.

Happily shopping for 1950s furniture and knick-knacks, these 1980s fashion rights look at what was new and "hot" back then.

The 1980s Looked to the 1930s and 1940s

Meanwhile at the same time, another trend was underway in America, one that belonged to a more mature customer. Again, movies, television, music, and personalities had combined to give it impetus.

Television programs such as *Brideshead Revisited* and *The Winds of War* evoked the 1930s and 1940s. Motion pictures added their impact with *An Officer and a Gentleman* and *Frances*, each reflecting the fashions, dreams, and customs of the period. Music of the 1930s and 1940s came back upon the American scene after two decades of rock, first led in by disco; then, as disco faded, by the rebirth of the Big Band sound. The emphasis was very definitely on the romantic.

Fashion responded with 1980s adaptations of the looks of the earlier years.

Clothes once again had form. Soft fabrics and sweeping silhouettes evoked the mood. People began to dress up again for various functions. Some of the niceties of life, such as debuts and proms, which had been subjected to ridicule in the turbulent 1960s and 1970s, were once again embraced by ever-larger groups. Designers reached for ways to provide elegance that was viable in the 1980s. Glittering productions on Broadway replaced the angry underside of life that had commanded the theater for the previous two decades. Hollywood once again dared to film stories of hope and humor, and *E.T.* and *Alf* became the country's best friends from outer space. Romance novels, long derided as reading matter worthy only of the lowest intellects, were revealed as the nation's secret passion and the source of a huge multimillion-dollar industry. In the music world, the words and meaning of a song once again became important ... even as the beat went on. The fashion world responded by translating the needs and wants of these romantically inclined customers into fashions and accessories that reflected the mood—and seemed to do it with almost uncanny speed and ease, proving, as ever, that fashion is the most fluid of all the industries.

THE MANUFACTURER'S ROLE

Manufacturers would agree with Dwight E. Robinson that "every market into which the consumer's fashion sense has insinuated itself is, by that very token, subject to [the] common, compelling need for unceasing change in the styling of its goods."[2]

Even in such mundane items as writing paper, the need for change has produced rainbows of pastels, brilliant deep shades, and the traditional white with dainty or bold prints. Similarly, in basics such as bedsheets or men's dress shirts, the once traditional white has yielded to a variety of colors, stripes, and prints. There is scarcely an industry serving consumers today in which the manufacturer's success does not depend, in part, upon an ability to attune styling to fashion interest and demand. A current trend is to hire merchandisers who do market research for the manufacturer, specializing in identifying the correct customer and his or her needs and wants.

Types of Manufacturers

In general, manufacturers of fashion goods can be divided into three groups. One group is made up of firms that produce innovative, high-fashion apparel. This group is usually identified as the "better market." A second group of firms sometimes produces originals. But it usually turns out adaptations of styles that have survived the introduction stage and are in the rise stage of their fashion life cycle. This group of firms is usually identified as the "moderate-priced market." A third group of manufacturers makes no attempt to offer new or unusual styling. Rather, these firms mass-produce close copies or adaptations of styles that have proved their acceptance in higher-priced markets. This group is usually identified as the "budget market."

Fashion Influence

In the field of women's apparel, manufacturers are committed to producing several new lines a year. A **line** is an assortment of new designs with a designated period for delivery to the retailer. Some of these may be new in every sense of the word and others merely adaptations of currently popular styles. Producers hope that a few of the designs in a given line will prove to be "hot"—so precisely in step with demand that their sales will be profitably large. When such designs are reordered frequently, they are known as **Fords** in the industry.

For the most part, the fashion industries are made up of manufacturers whose ability to anticipate the public's response to styles is excellent. Those who do badly in this respect, even for a single season, usually reap small sales and large losses. Unless they are unusually well financed, they quickly find themselves out of business. In the fashion industry, the survival of the fittest means the survival of those who give the most able assistance in the birth and growth of fashions that consumers will buy.

THE RETAILER'S ROLE

Although retailers do not create fashion, they can encourage or retard its progress by the degree of accuracy with which they anticipate the demands of their customers. They seek out from the manufacturer styles that they believe are most likely to win acceptance from these target groups.

Types of Retailers

There are many ways to classify retail firms. However, when firms are evaluated on the basis of their leadership positions, they tend to fall into three main categories.

First there are firms that are considered "fashion leaders." They feature newly introduced styles that have only limited production and distribution. These styles are usually expensive. A second group, called "traditional retailers"—by far the largest in number—features fashions that have captured consumer interest in their introduction stage and are in the late rise or early culmination stage of their life cycles. Since these styles are usually widely produced by this time, they are most often offered at moderate prices. A third group of retailers, often called "mass merchants," features widely accepted fashions that are well into the culmination phase of their life cycles. Since fashions at this stage of development are usually mass-produced, mass merchants can and do offer fashions at moderate to low prices.

Fashion Influence

Sometimes, because of their constant and intimate contact with their customers, retailers are so intuitive or creative that they lead their suppliers in anticipating the styles their customers will

"Fashion leader" stores like Bonwit Teller, Bergdorf Goodman, and I. Magnin feature newly introduced styles in their stores across the country.

accept. Such retailers accelerate the introduction and progress of new fashions by persuading manufacturers to produce styles that answer an upcoming need or demand. Because of this ability, retailers are doing more and more product development for their own customers.

However, most retailers simply select from what is offered to them by producers that they have been successful with in the past. There is a constant flow, back and forth, of information about the styles that the customer is buying. The systems that producers and retailers have today for this purpose are very rapid and accurate, mainly because of the development of the computer.

Because of these instantly available and accurate records, retailers can monitor sudden or gradual changes in the preferences of their own customers. The variations in what consumers are buying at a particular store are reflected in what the store buys from the manufacturers of fashion merchandise. From these manufacturers come information about customer preferences that flows in several different directions. One flow is back to the retail stores to alert them to trends they may not have noticed themselves.

Retailers can influence fashion by failing to stock styles that consumers are ready to buy if given the opportunity. Conversely, retailers can make the mistake of exposing new styles prematurely. No amount of retail effort can make customers buy styles in which they have lost interest or in which they have not yet developed interest. The more accurately a retailer understands his or her customers' fashion preferences, the more successful the operation will be. And the more successful the operation, the more important the retailer's fashion influence will be.

THEORIES OF FASHION ADOPTION

Fashions are accepted by a few before they are accepted by the majority. An important step in fashion forecasting is isolating and identifying those fashion leaders and keeping track of their preferences. Once these are known, the fashion forecaster is better able to forecast which styles are most likely to succeed as fashions, and how widely and by whom each will be accepted.

Three theories have been advanced to explain the "social contagion" or spread of fashion adoption: the downward-flow theory, the horizontal-flow theory or "mass-market" theory, and the upward-flow theory. Each attempts to explain the course a fashion travels or is likely to travel, and each has its own claim to validity in reference to particular fashions or social environments.

Downward-Flow Theory

The oldest theory of fashion adoption is the **downward-flow theory** (or the "trickle-down theory"). It maintains that in order to be identified as a true fashion, a style must first be adopted by people at the top of the social pyramid. The style then gradually wins acceptance at progressively lower social levels.

This theory assumes the existence of a social hierarchy in which lower-income people seek identification with more affluent people. At the same time, those at the top seek disassociation from those they consider socially inferior. The theory suggests that (1) fashions are accepted by lower classes only if, and after, they are accepted by upper classes, and (2) upper classes will reject a fashion once it has flowed to a lower social level.

Early economists, such as Roe in 1834 and Foley and Veblen at the turn of the twentieth century, were among the first to observe this type of social behavior and its effect upon fashion. In 1903, French sociologist Gabriel Tarde described the spread of fashion in terms of a social water tower from which a continuous fall of imitation could descend.[3] The German sociologist Georg Simmel, one of the first of his discipline to undertake a serious study of fashion, wrote in 1904:

Social forms, apparel, aesthetic judgment, the whole style of human expression, are constantly being transformed by fashion in [a way that] . . . affects only the upper classes. Just as soon as the lower classes begin to copy their styles, thereby crossing the line of demarcation the upper classes have drawn and destroying their coherence, the upper classes turn away from this style and adopt a new one. . . . The same process is at work as between the different sets within the upper classes, although it is not always visible here.[4]

The downward-flow theory has had among its twentieth-century proponents such authorities as Robinson, Laver, Sapir, and Flügel. Flügel, in fact, suggested that sumptuary laws originated with the reluctance of upper classes to abandon the sartorial distinctiveness that to them represented superiority.[5]

Implications for Merchandising

To some extent, the downward-flow theory has validity. Some fashions may appear first among the socially prominent. Eager manufacturers then quickly mass-produce lower-priced copies that many consumers can afford, and the wealthier consumers seek newer styles.

Because our social structure has radically changed, this theory has few adherents today. The downward-flow theory of fashion dissemination can apply only when a society resembles a pyramid, with people of wealth and position at the apex and followers at successively lower levels. Our social structure today, however, is more like a group of rolling hills than a pyramid. There are many social groups and many directions in which fashion can and does travel.

This altered pattern of fashion acceptance is also a result of the speed with which fashion news now travels. All social groups know about fashion innovation at practically the same time. Moreover, accelerated mass production and mass distribution of fashion goods have broadened acceptance of styles. They are available at lower prices and more quickly than ever before.

Industry Practice

For the reasons given above, those who mass-produce fashion goods today are less likely to wait cautiously for approval of newly introduced styles by affluent consumers. As soon as significant signs of an interesting new style appear, the producers are ready to offer adaptations or even copies to the public.

Horizontal-Flow Theory

A newer theory is the **horizontal-flow theory** (or mass-market theory) of fashion adoption. This theory claims that fashions move horizontally between groups on similar social levels rather than vertically from one level to another.

One of the chief exponents of this theory was Dr. Charles W. King. He proposed that the social environment, including rapid mass communications and the promotional efforts of manufacturers and retailers, exposes new styles to

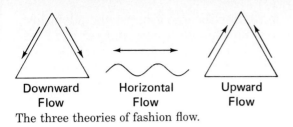

| Downward Flow | Horizontal Flow | Upward Flow |

The three theories of fashion flow.

the fashion leaders of all social groups at approximately the same time. King noted that there is almost no lag between the adoption of a fashion by one social group and another.[6] Paris fashions, for example, are now bought and copied for mass distribution sometimes even before the originals are available to the more affluent markets. Trade buyers at couturier openings purchase models, ship them home by air, and get copies into retail stores often before the custom client—whose garments are made to order by the same couturiers—has had to wear the new clothes.

This horizontal flow also has been observed by some modern supporters of the older downward-flow theory. Robinson, for example, said that any given group or cluster of groups takes its cues from contiguous groups within the same social stratum. He claimed fashions therefore radiate from a center of each stratum or class.[7]

Implications for Merchandising

The theory of horizontal fashion movement has great significance for merchandising. It points out the fallacy of assuming that there is a single, homogeneous fashion public in this country. In reality, a number of distinctly different groups make up the fashion public. Each group has its own characteristics and its own fashion ideas and needs. The horizontal-flow theory recognizes that

what wealthy society people are wearing today is not necessarily what suburbanites, college students, or office workers will either wear tomorrow or wait until tomorrow to accept. This theory acknowledges that there are separate markets in fashion goods as in any other type of merchandise.

Retailers who apply the horizontal-flow theory will watch their own customers closely rather than be guided solely by what more exclusive stores are selling. They will seek to identify the groups into which customers can be divided in terms of income, age, education, and lifestyle. Among their customers, they will look for the innovators and their style choices as well as the influentials and their selections. King defined a **fashion innovator** as a person who is quicker than his or her associates to try out a new style. A **fashion influential** is a person whose advice is sought by associates. A fashion influential's adoption of a new style gives it prestige among a group. The two roles may or may not be played by the same individual within a specific group.

The news that socially prominent women are wearing plunging necklines in exclusive New York restaurants will have less significance for the retailers in a small Midwestern city than the observation that the leader of the country-club set in their community is abandoning bright colors for black on formal occasions. If the latter is a fashion influential in the community, she is a more important bellwether for them than the New York socialites.

Industry Practice

King drew a distinction between the spread of fashion within the industry itself and its adoption by consumers. A vertical flow definitely operates within the industry, he conceded: "Exclusive and famous designers are watched closely and emulated by lesser designers. Major manufacturers are studied and copied by smaller and less expert competitors."[8] And, as any reader of *Women's Wear Daily* knows, the hottest news in the industry concerns what the top designers and the top producers are showing.

King pointed out, moreover, that the innovation process in the industry represents a "great filtering system." From an almost infinite number of possibilities, manufacturers select a finite number of styles. From these, trade buyers select a smaller sampling. Finally, consumers choose from among retailers' selections, thereby endorsing certain ones as accepted fashions.

This process, King maintained, is quite different from the consumer reaction outlined by Simmel and other proponents of the downward-flow theory. The difference lies in the fact that today the mass market does not await the approval of the "class" market before it adopts a fashion.

Upward-Flow Theory

The third theory that attempts to explain the process of fashion adoption is relatively new. It reflects the enormous social changes that have occurred in the past three decades. Because the process of fashion dissemination that evolved in the 1960s, 1970s, and 1980s was the exact opposite of that which prevailed throughout much of recorded history, this theory has important implications for producers and retailers alike.

This theory of fashion adoption is called the **upward-flow theory.** It holds that the young—particularly those of low-income families and those in higher-income groups who adopt low-income lifestyles—are quicker than any social group to create or adopt new and different fashions. As its name implies, this theory is exactly the opposite of the downward-flow theory. The upward-flow theory holds that fashion adoption begins among the young members of lower-income groups and then moves upward into higher-income groups.

The decades of the fifties, sixties, seventies, and eighties had outstanding examples of the upward-flow theory. In the fifties young people discovered Army-Navy surplus stores and were soon wearing khaki pants, caps, battle jackets, fatigues and even ammunition belts. In the sixties, led by the Hell's Angels, the motorcycle clubs introduced the fashion world to black leather . . . in jackets, vests and studded armbands. Soon the jet set was dressed in black leather long coats, skirts, and pants. Meanwhile, other young people were discovering bib overalls, railroad worker's caps, and all-purpose laborer's coveralls that were soon translated into jumpsuits. Peasant apparel, prairie looks, and styles and designs from various minority groups followed the same pattern. They began as part of a young and lower-income lifestyle and were then quickly adopted among older people with different lifestyles and incomes.

One of the more dramatic illustrations of this has been the T-shirt. In its short-sleeved version, it has long been worn by truckers, laborers, and farm workers. In its long-sleeved version, it was the uniform of local bowling and softball teams. In the seventies, the T-shirt became a messageboard and sprouted a brand-new fashion cottage industry. The ultimate T-shirt was the Chanel No. 5, first the perfume . . . then the T-shirt. Actually, the Chanel T-shirt was a logical application of a tenet long held by the late Coco Chanel, who believed that fashion came from the streets and was then adapted by the couture.

In the eighties sources of inspiration for fashion styles representing the upward-flow theory were everywhere, especially in the world of rock and roll. By following the fashion statements of rock and roll idols, America's youth were arrayed in worn denim, metal, leather, lace, bangles, spandex, and glitter. Colors ranged from Cyndi Lauper's peacock looks to Roy Orbison's basic black. Madonna became a style-setter and introduced the country to her underwear worn on the outside. And Boy George and Annie Lennox flaunted an androgynous wardrobe of no sex at all.

Implications for Merchandising

For producers and retailers, this new direction of fashion flow implies radical changes in traditional methods of charting and forecasting fashion trends. No longer can producers and retailers look solely to name designers and socially prominent fashion leaders for ideas that will become tomorrow's best-selling fashions. They also must pay considerable attention to what young people favor, for the young have now become a large, independent group that can exert considerable influence on fashion styling.

As a result, today fewer retailers and manufacturers attend European couture showings, once considered fashion's most important source of design inspiration. Now producers and retailers alike are more interested in ready-to-wear (prêt-à-porter) showings. Here they look for styles and design details that reflect trends with more fashion relevance for American youth.

Industry Practice

Apparently, fashion will never again flow in only one direction. Of course, customers will always exist for high fashion and for conservative fashion. But producers and retailers must now accept that they will be doing a considerable proportion of their business in fashions created or adopted first by the lower-income young and by those who choose to be allied with them.

FASHION LEADERS

As different as they may be, the three theories of fashion flow share one common perspective: they recognize that there are both fashion leaders and fashion followers. People of social, political, and economic importance here and abroad are seen as leaders in the downward-flow theory. The horizontal-flow theory recognizes individuals whose personal prestige makes them leaders within their own circles, whether or not they are known elsewhere. Finally, the important fashion role played by young, lower-income groups in the last half of the twentieth century is recognized in the upward-flow theory.

The theories of fashion adoption stress that the fashion leader is not the creator of the fashion; nor does merely wearing the fashion make a person a fashion leader. As Bell explained: "The leader of fashion does not come into existence until the fashion is itself created . . . a king or person of great eminence may indeed lead the fashion, but he leads only in the general direction which it has already adopted."[9] If a fashion parade is forming, fashion leaders may head it and even quicken its pace. They cannot, however, bring about a procession; nor can they reverse a procession.

FASHION

Anyone even marginally interested in fashion is familiar with the names of most fashion trend setters, or those who influence what the "stylish people" will be wearing each season. After all, many are almost household names, like Chris-tian Dior, Calvin Klein, Oscar de la Renta, Donna Karan, Madonna—Ma-donna, you say?

Actually, some of the most powerful influences on fashion do not necessarily come from the established fashion

F O C U S

houses or designers, but from popular figures in the entertainment world—like Madonna. Many of these highly visible entertainers have a distinct look and style that is all their own—until, that is, thousands of their fans start to imitate it and a new fashion craze is born. And while the looks popularized by these celebrities may not have a long-lasting effect on the direction of fashion, their effect is frequently more immediately visible than that of a designer.

Taking a fashion cue from a favorite pop star or movie actor is hardly a new trend for the consuming public. How many little girls in the thirties wore ringlet curls and patent-leather shoes to look like Shirley Temple? And when the Beatles burst on the scene in the early sixties, millions of young men started wearing "Beatle boots" and growing their crewcuts into longer "Beatle cuts."

Today, perhaps because of the heightened exposure for rock stars through media outlets like MTV, their style influence is more powerful than ever. Many young women, for instance, picked up in recent years on the eclectic, kinky, thrift-shop looks favored by Cyndi Lauper; others turned to the sexier, short-skirted, body-stockinged outfits popularized by Madonna. In the meantime, Michael Jackson may have

shed his distinctive one-gloved image—but until he did, it was a widely recognizable fashion statement.

Musical performers are not the only ones to influence fashion. One of the strongest fashion trends of the 1980s can be traced directly to the popular *Miami Vice* television show, and particularly its star, Don Johnson. Within one season of the program's being on the air, stylish men all over the country were wearing the "Miami Vice" look—from the loafers with no socks, to the collarless T-shirts under open jackets, right down to the Ray-Ban "shades," and haven't-shaved-in-two-days stubble.

Of course, not every popular musician or actor starts a fashion trend in his or her image. The masklike makeup of rock group KISS, for instance, never caught on with the general public; and despite the spectacular success of the *Rambo* movies, Sylvester Stallone did not popularize ammunition belts as part of an everyday wardrobe. Those may be considered silly examples; but even when a "hot" personality does not set a style, there is no denying that fashion followers are always watching for a lead to follow. After all, how many millions of people have tuned in to *Wheel of Fortune* simply to see what Vanna was going to wear that night?

Innovators and Influentials

Famous people are not necessarily fashion leaders, even if they do influence an individual style. Their influence usually is limited to only one striking style, one physical attribute, or one time. The true fashion leader is a person constantly seeking distinction and therefore likely to launch a succession of fashions rather than just one. People like Beau Brummel, who made a career of dressing fashionably, or the duchess of Windsor, whose wardrobe was front-page fashion news for decades, influence fashion on a much broader scale.

What makes a person a fashion leader? Flügel explained: "Inasmuch as we are aristocratically minded and dare to assert our own individuality by being different, we are leaders of fashion."[10] King, however, made it clear that more than just daring to be different is required. In his analysis, a person eager for the new is merely an innovator or early buyer. To be a leader, one must be influential and sought after for advice within one's coterie. An influential person, said King, sets the appropriate dress for a specific occasion in a particular circle. Within that circle, an innovator presents current offerings and is the earliest visual communicator of a new style.[11]

Royalty

In the past, fashion leadership was exclusively the province of royalty. New fashions were introduced in royal courts by such leaders as Empress Eugenie and Marie Antoinette. In the twentieth century, the duchess of Windsor, although an American and a commoner by birth, was a fashion innovator and influential from the 1930s through the 1960s. When the King of England gave up his

Princess Diana in another "working girl" outfit for modern royalty. What would be a glamorous formal gown for us is just another working outfit for royalty who attend formal affairs as part of their daily duties.

throne to marry "the woman he loved," style and fashion professionals throughout the world copied her elegance. The Sotheby auction in the late 1980s of the duchess of Windsor's jewelry sparked new interest in her style, and designers are showing copies of her jewelry.

Until Princess Diana and Sara Ferguson married into the British royal family, few royal personages in recent years have qualified as fashion leaders. Despite the belief held by some that kings and queens wear crowns and ermine, the truth is that modern royalty has become a hard-working group whose daily life is packed with so many activities that sensible and conservative dress is necessary for most occasions.

The Trumps, Ivana and Donald, are the darlings of the media. Their every business move, charity ball, or mansion purchase is avidly reported, and the fashion statements they make are copied by the fashion public.

The Rich

As monarchies were replaced with democracies, members of the wealthy and international sets came into the fashion spotlight. Whether the members of "society" derive their position from vast fortunes and old family names or from recent wealth, they bring to the scene a glamor and excitement that draws attention to everything they do. Today, through the constant eye of television, magazines, and newspapers, the average person is able to find fashion leadership in a whole new stratum of society—the jet set.

What these socialites are doing and what they are wearing are instantly served up to the general public by the media. As far as fashion is concerned, these people are not just *in* the news; they *are* the news. Any move they make is important enough to be immediately publicized. What they wear is of vital interest to the general public. The media tell us what the social leaders wear to dine in a chic restaurant, to attend a charity ball, or to go shopping. Because they are trendsetters, their choices are of prime interest to designers and to the world at large.

This inundation of news about what social leaders wear of course influences the public. The average person is affected because so many manufacturers and retailers of fashion take their cue from these social leaders. Right or wrong, fashion merchants count on the fashion sense of these leaders. They know that the overwhelming exposure of these leaders in the media encourages people of ordinary means to imitate them—consciously or unconsciously.

The Famous

Fashion today takes its impetus and influence from people in every possible walk of life. These people have one thing in common, however: they are famous. Because of some special talent, charisma, notoriety, or popularity, they are constantly mentioned and shown on television, in fashion magazines, and in newspapers. They may or may not appear in the society pages.

In this group can be found presidents and princesses, movie stars and religious leaders, sports figures and recording stars, politicians and television personalities. Because they are seen so frequently, the public has a good sense of their fashions and lifestyles and can imitate them to the extent of the public's means and desires.

Prominent individuals have been responsible for certain fashions that continue to be associated with them. Many times, however, these individuals are not what would be considered fashion leaders. Although the cornrow braiding of hair had been practiced among blacks in Africa and America for decades, it was adopted by many young black women only after Cicely Tyson appeared with the hairstyle in the movie *Sounder* in 1972. In 1979, Bo Derek wore it in the film *10* and gave the style new impetus. In the 1930s, a tremendous impact was felt by an entire menswear industry when Clark Gable appeared without an undershirt in *It Happened One Night.* Practically overnight, men from all walks of life shed their undershirts in imitation of Gable. In the late 1930s, women dared to wear slacks after seeing Greta Garbo and Marlene Dietrich wearing them in the movies. In the early 1960s, when Mrs. John F. Kennedy appeared in little pillbox hats, both the style and the hat market blossomed under the publicity. Some styles are so closely associated with the famous people who wore them that they bear their names (see the table on page 87).

Athletes

Today there is strong emphasis on sports. And what prominent sports figures wear is of great importance to the people who seek to imitate them. Television has increased the public acceptance of several sports. For example, people have enjoyed going to baseball, football, or basketball games for years. But sports of a more individual nature, such as tennis and golf, were of minor interest. Now these sports are brought into the living rooms of an increasing number of viewers. As a result, fashions for participating in these sports have grown remarkably in importance. Tennis is now a very popular participation sport and has given rise to an entire specialized fashion industry. Today, every aspiring tennis player has endless fashion styles, colors, and fabrics to choose from. A wide selection of fashions

Dr. and Mrs. Huxtable, better known as Bill Cosby and Phylicia Rashad, are welcome guests into our home every week. The Bill Cosby "sweater look" has become a major fashion, and in the 1980s his "sweater man" replaced the 1940s "sweater girl" Lana Turner.

FASHION STYLES NAMED FOR THE FAMOUS

Amelia Bloomer	Bloomers
Earl of Chesterfield	Chesterfield jacket
Dwight D. Eisenhower	Eisenhower jacket
Geraldine Ferraro	"Gerry cut" (hairstyle)
Mao Tse Tung	Mao jacket
Jawaharlal Nehru	Nehru jacket
Madame de Pompadour	Pompadour (hairstyle)
Nancy Reagan	"Reagan plastics" (costume jewelry)
Duke of Wellington	Wellington boots
Earl of Cardigan	Cardigan sweater
Duke of Windsor	Windsor knot (tie)
Duke of Norfolk	Norfolk jacket

is also available for golf, jogging, running, swimming, skating, biking, snorkeling, and other sports.

FASHION FOLLOWERS

Filling out forms for his daughter's college entrance application, a father wrote of his daughter's leadership qualities: "To tell the truth, my daughter is really not a leader, but rather a loyal and devoted follower." The dean of the college admissions responded: "We are welcoming a freshman class of 100 students this year and are delighted to accept your daughter. You can't imagine how happy we are to have one follower among the 99 leaders!"

Most people want to be thought of as leaders, not followers. But there are many people who are followers, and good ones. In fact, followers are in the majority within any group. Without followers the fashion industry would certainly collapse. Mass production and mass distribution can be possible and profitable only when large numbers of consumers accept the merchandise.

Though they may say otherwise, luckily, more people prefer to follow than to lead. The styles fashion leaders adopt may help manufacturers and retailers in determining what will be demanded by the majority of consumers in the near future. Only accurate predictions can ensure the continued success of the giant ready-to-wear business in this country, which depends for its success on mass production and distribution. While fashion leaders may stimulate and excite the fashion industry, fashion followers are the industry's lifeblood.

Reasons for Following Fashion

Theories about why people follow rather than lead in fashion are plentiful. Among the explanations are feelings of inferiority, admiration of others, lack of interest, and ambivalence about the new.

Feelings of Insecurity

Flügel wrote, "Inasmuch as we feel our own inferiority and the need for conformity to the standards set by others,

When "Flo Jo" (Florence Griffith-Joyner) set Olympic records, she became a fashion leader. Women everywhere copied her hairstyle and rushed to get their fingernails lengthened.

we are followers of fashion."[12] For example, high school boys and girls are at a notably insecure stage of life. They are therefore more susceptible than any other age group to the appeal of fads. A person about to face a difficult interview or attend the first meeting with a new group carefully selects new clothes. Often a feeling of inadequacy can be hidden by wearing a style that others have already approved as appropriate.

Admiration

Flügel also maintained that it is a fundamental human impulse to imitate those who are admired or envied. A natural and symbolic means of doing this is to copy their clothes, makeup, and hairstyles. Outstanding illustrations of this theory have been provided by movie stars and models—Mary Pickford, "America's Sweetheart" of the 1910s; Clara Bow, the "It" girl of the 1920s; Veronica Lake and Ann Sheridan, the "Oomph Girls" of the 1940s; Doris Day and Marilyn Monroe in the 1950s; Twiggy in the 1960s; Farrah Fawcett in the 1970s; and Christie Brinkley in the 1980s. Their clothes and hairstyles were copied instantly among many different groups throughout this country and in many other parts of the world. On a different level, the young girl who copies the hairstyle of her best friend, older sister, or favorite aunt demonstrates the same principle, as do college students who model their appearance after that of a campus leader.

Lack of Interest

Sapir suggested that many people are insensitive to fashion and follow it only because "they realize that not to fall in with it would be to declare themselves members of a past generation, or dull people who cannot keep up with their neighbors."[13] Their response to fashion, he said, is a sullen surrender, by no means an eager following of the Pied Piper.

Ambivalence

Another theory holds that many people are ambivalent in their attitudes toward the new; they both want it and fear it. For most, it is easier to choose what is already familiar. Such individuals need time and exposure to new styles before they can accept them.

Varying Rates of Response

Individuals vary in the speed with which they respond to a new idea, especially when fashion change is radical and dramatic. Some fashion followers apparently need time to adjust to new ideas. Merchants exploit this point when they buy a few "window pieces" of styles too advanced for their own clientele and expose them in windows and fashion shows to allow customers time to get used to them. Only after a period of exposure to the new styles do the fashion followers accept them.

FASHION AS AN EXPRESSION OF INDIVIDUALITY

As the twentieth century entered its ninth decade, a strange but understandable trend became apparent across the nation. People were striving, through their mode of dress, to declare individuality in the face of computer-age conformity.

People had watched strings of impersonal numbers become more and more a part of their lives—ZIP Codes, bank and credit card account numbers, employee identification numbers, department store accounts, automobile registrations, social security numbers, and so on. An aversion to joining the masses—to becoming "just another number"—began to be felt. So while most people continued to go along with general fashion trends, some asserted their individuality. This was accomplished by distinctive touches each wearer added to an outfit. A new freedom in dress, color and texture combinations, use of accessories, and hairstyles allowed people to assert their individuality without being out of step with the times. Most social scientists see in this a paradox—an endless conflict between the desire to conform and the desire to remain apart.

We have all known people who at some point in their lives found a fashion that particularly pleased them. It might have been a certain style dress, a certain shoe, or a hairstyle. Even in the face of continuing changes in fashion, the person continued to wear that style in which she or he felt right and attractive. This is an assertion of individuality in the face of conformity. Although superbly fashion-conscious, the late famous actress Joan Crawford never stopped wearing the open-toed, slingback, wedge shoe of the 1940s. When the pointed toe and stiletto heel of the fifties gave way to the low, chunky heel of the sixties, she continued to wear the same style. She was perfectly in step with fashion when the wedge shoe finally returned to popularity in the early 1970s. Woody Allen achieved special recognition for wearing—anywhere and everywhere—sneakers! At formal occasions he conforms by wearing appropriate formal attire. But his feet remain sneakered, and Woody retains his individuality. Recently, Cybill Shepard, the star of the former TV series *Moonlighting,* also wore sneakers . . . both on and off TV.

Most people prefer to assert their individuality in a less obvious way, and today's ready-to-wear fashions lend themselves to subtle changes that mark each person's uniqueness. No two people put the same costume together in exactly the same way.

Fashion editor Jessica Daves summed up the miracle of modern ready-to-wear fashion. It offers, she said, "the possibility for some women to create a design for themselves . . . to choose the color and shape in clothes that will present them as they would like to see themselves."[14]

The Paradox of Conformity and Individuality

For decades, experts have tried to explain why people seek both conformity and individuality in fashion. Simmel suggested that two opposing social tendencies are at war: the need for union and the need for isolation. The individual, he reasoned, derives satisfaction from knowing that the way in which he or she expresses a fashion represents something special. At the same time, people gain support from seeing others favor the same style.[15]

Flügel interpreted the paradox in terms of a person's feelings of superiority and inferiority. The individual wants to be like others "insofar as he regards them as superior, but unlike them, in the sense of being more 'fashionable,' insofar as he thinks they are below him."[16]

Sapir tied the conflict to a revolt against custom and a desire to break away from slavish acceptance of fashion. Slight changes from the established form of dress and behavior "seem for the moment to give victory to the individual, while the fact that one's fellows revolt in the same direction gives one a feeling of adventurous safety."[17] He also tied the assertion of individuality to the need to affirm one's self in a powerful society in which the individual has ceased to be the measure.

One example of this conflict may be found in the off-duty dress of people required to wear uniforms of one kind or another during working hours, such as nurses, police officers, and mail carriers. A second example is seen in the clothing worn by many present-day business executives. Far from the days when to be "The Man in the Gray Flannel Suit" meant that a man had arrived in the business world, today executives favor a much more diversified wardrobe. While suits of gray flannel are still worn, so are a wide variety of other fabrics and patterns. And some top executives favor a more relaxed look altogether, preferring to wear appropriately fashioned separate jackets or blazers with their business slacks.

Retailers know that although some people like to lead and some like to follow in fashion, most people buy fashion to express their personality or to identify with a particular group. To belong, they follow fashion; to express their personality, they find ways to individualize fashion.

Fashion and Self-Expression

Increasing importance is being placed on fashion individuality—on expressing your personality, or refusing to be cast in a mold. Instead of slavishly adopting any one look, today's young person seeks to create an individual effect through the way he or she combines various fashion components. For instance, if a young woman thinks a denim skirt, an ankle-length woolen coat, and a heavy turtlenecked sweater represent her personality, they will be considered acceptable by others in her group.

Forward-looking designers recognize this desire for self-expression. Designers say that basic wardrobe components should be made available, but that consumers should be encouraged to combine them as they see fit. For instance, they advise women to wear pants or skirts, long or short, according to how they feel, not according to what past tradition has considered proper for an occasion. They suggest that men make the same choice among tailored suits, leisurewear, and slacks, to find the styles that express their personalities.

Having experienced such fashion freedom, young people may never conform again. Yet despite individual differences in dress, young experimenters have in common a deep-rooted desire to dress differently from older generations.

REFERENCES

[1] Quentin Bell, *On Human Finery,* The Hogarth Press, Ltd., London, 1947, pp. 48–49.
[2] Dwight E. Robinson, "Fashion Theory and Product Design," *Harvard Business Review,* Vol. 36, November–December 1958, p. 129.
[3] Gabriel Tarde, *The Laws of Imitation,* Henry Holt and Company, New York, 1903, p. 221.
[4] Georg Simmel, "Fashion," *American Journal of Sociology,* Vol. 62, May 1957, p. 545.
[5] J. C. Flügel, *The Psychology of Clothes,* International Universities Press, New York, 1966, p. 139.
[6] Charles W. King, "Fashion Adoption: A Rebuttal to the Trickle-Down Theory," *Proceedings of the Winter Conference,* American Marketing Association, New York, December 1963, pp. 114–115.
[7] Dwight E. Robinson, "The Economics of Fashion Demand," *The Quarterly Journal of Economics,* Vol. 75, August 1961, p. 383.
[8] King, pp. 114–115.
[9] Bell, p. 46.
[10] Flügel, p. 140.
[11] King, p. 124.
[12] Flügel, p. 140.
[13] Edward Sapir, "Fashion," *Encyclopedia of the Social Sciences,* Vol. VI, 1931, p. 140.
[14] Jessica Daves, *Ready-Made Miracle,* G. P. Putnam's Sons, New York, 1967, pp. 231–232.
[15] Simmel, pp. 543–544.
[16] Flügel, p. 140.
[17] Sapir, p. 140.

MERCHANDISING VOCABULARY

Define or briefly explain the following terms:

Downward-flow theory	Fashion innovator	Line
Fashion influential	Fords	Upward-flow theory
	Horizontal-flow theory	

MERCHANDISING REVIEW

1. What are the practical obstacles that limit fashion designers? What additional factors must be considered in developing each fashion design?
2. List the three types of designers commonly serving the American fashion industry today, giving the responsibilities of each.
3. What are the key sources of inspiration for the majority of today's fashion designers? Choose a current fashion designer and illustrate your answer by explaining how his or her designs were influenced by one such source over the past year.
4. Name the three groups into which fashion manufacturers may be classified, indicating the identifying characteristics of each.
5. Name the three groups into which fashion retail firms may be classified, indicating the identifying characteristics of each.
6. Is the downward-flow theory of fashion adoption as valid today as it was in years past? Explain your answer.
7. How does the horizontal-flow theory of fashion adoption affect fashion merchants today? How are merchants today affected by the upward-flow theory?
8. Why are (a) rich people, (b) famous people, and (c) athletes, prime candidates for positions of fashion leadership?
9. Give four reasons why most people follow, rather than lead, in regard to fashion. Explain each.
10. How can fashion be used as a means of expressing individuality?

MERCHANDISING DIGEST

1. Discuss the significance of the following quotation from the text: "Rarely does a revolutionary style succeed. Instead, it is evolutionary new styles that so often become the best-selling fashions."
2. The text states, "Famous people are not necessarily fashion leaders, even if they do influence an individual style." Discuss this statement and how it affects the fashion industry. Name a recent specific style made famous by a famous person who was not necessarily a fashion leader or influential. Name a recent specific style made famous by a famous person who was a fashion leader or influential.
3. Why do people today seek both conformity and individuality in fashion? How does this affect the fashion designer or manufacturer? The fashion retailer?
4. What does the statement, "You're only as good as your last collection," mean in regard to fashion designers?

THE BUSINESS OF FASHION

Fashion is fabulous, fascinating, and fun, and the study of fashion involves history, psychology, sociology, and art. While all this is true, it is important never to lose sight of the fundamental nature of fashion—it is a business. Fashion is affected by technological breakthroughs, changes in investment patterns, shifts in consumer attitudes, world events, and other economic forces. The fashion industry, no less than the auto or steel industries, is shaped by the basic principles of business and economics.

What is business? Business is the activity of creating, producing, and marketing products or services. The primary objective of business is to make a profit. **Profit,** or net income, is the amount of money a business earns in excess of its expenses. Consequently, in this country, **business** can be defined as the activity of creating, producing, and marketing products or services for a profit.

ECONOMIC IMPORTANCE OF THE FASHION BUSINESS

The business of fashion contributes significantly to the economy of the United States, through the materials and services it purchases, the wages and taxes it pays, and the goods and services it produces. The fashion business is one of the largest employers in the country. Of the millions of people employed in manufacturing in the United States, better than one in ten is employed either in factories that produce apparel for men, women, and children or in textile plants that produce the materials from which garments are made.[1]

More people are employed in apparel production than in the entire printing and publishing business or the automobile manufacturing industry. Many more are employed in producing such items as fur and leather garments and accessories and in staffing the retail organizations that distribute these goods.[2] When we add to this a share of the total number of jobs in finance, transportation, advertising, computers, electronics, and other services that devote part of their efforts to the fashion industry, it becomes obvious that the fashion industry has a tremendous impact on our economy.

The growth and development of mass markets, mass-production methods, and mass distribution have contributed to the creation of new job opportunities in the fashion industry—not only in the production area, but in design and marketing as well. Young people are entering the fashion business in greater numbers each year and are having a marked effect on the business. Innovation and change have become increasingly important factors in the economic growth of the fashion business.

SCOPE OF THE FASHION BUSINESS

The fashion business is composed of numerous industries all working to keep consumers of fashion satisfied. A special relationship exists among these industries that makes the fashion business different from other businesses. The four different levels of the fashion business—known as the primary level, the secondary level, the retail level, and the auxiliary level—are composed of separate entities, but they also work interdependently to provide the market with the fashion merchandise that will satisfy consumers. Because of this unique relationship among the different industries, the fashion business is unusually exciting.

The Primary Level

The **primary level** is composed of the growers and producers of the raw materials of fashion—the fiber, fabric, leather, and fur producers who function in the raw materials market. The earliest part of the planning function in color and texture takes place on the primary level. It is also the level of the fashion business that works the farthest in advance of the ultimate selling period of the goods. Up to two years' lead time is needed by primary-level companies before the goods will be available to the consumer. Primary-level goods may often be imports from third world emerging nations, where textiles are usually the earliest form of industrialization.

The Secondary Level

The **secondary level** is composed of industries—manufacturers and contractors—that produce the semifinished or finished fashion goods from the materials produced on the primary level. On the secondary level are the manufacturers of women's, men's, and children's apparel and accessories. Manufacturers who function on the secondary level may be based in America or overseas. Fashion goods are now produced in the Far East, the Caribbean countries, South America, and Europe. Secondary-level companies work from 1½ years to 6 months ahead of the time that goods are available for the consumer.

The Retail Level

The **retail level** is the ultimate distribution level. On this level are the different types of retailers who buy their goods from the secondary level and then supply them directly to the consumer. In many cases the retail level works with both the primary and secondary levels to ensure a coordinated approach to consumer wants. A vertical interrelationship exists between the primary, secondary, and retail levels. Retailers make initial purchases for resale to customers from 3 to 6 months before the customer buying season.

The Auxiliary Level

The **auxiliary level** is the only level that functions with all the other levels simultaneously. This level is composed of all the support services that are working constantly with primary producers, secondary manufacturers, and retailers in order to keep consumers aware of the fashion merchandise produced for ultimate consumption. On this level are all the advertising media—print, audio, and visual—and fashion consultants and researchers.

DIVERSITY AND COMPETITION

The enormous variety and diversity that exists in the kinds and sizes of firms that operate on each level of the fashion industry make it a fascinating and competitive business. There are giant firms, both national and international, and small companies with regional or local distribution, doing business side by side as privately or publicly owned corporations, partnerships, or sole proprietorships. Fashion-producing companies may also be part of conglomerates, which also own, for example, entertainment companies, oil wells, professional sports teams, or consumer foods and products divisions.

Whether large or small, the different types of producers have one need in common—the need to understand what their ultimate customer will buy. Only through complete understanding and co-

Although it is "the world's largest store," even Macy's cannot sell to every customer in the world. Because of the different needs and wants of customers, small stores can also target their own customers and become Davids to Macy's Goliath.

operation can the four levels of the fashion business be aware of new developments in fashion and apply them to satisfy the wants of their customers. This cooperation allows them to have the right merchandise at the right price, in the right place, at the right time, in the right quantities, and with the right sales promotion for their customers.

However, when you begin to try to sell a product or service in our economic system, chances are that someone else will be trying to sell something similar. No matter what the size of the firm involved, potential customers are free to buy where they please and what they please. Each company must compete with the others for those customers' business. A company can choose to compete in one of three ways: price, quality, or innovation.

Competition and Price

Selling blue jeans for less than your competition may bring you more business. However, you are taking in less money than your rival does on each pair sold, and you still have to cover the same cost and expenses. The hope is that your lower price will attract more customers, sell more jeans than your competition, and so come out with a good overall profit. Head-to-head competition like this tends to keep prices down, which is good for the buying public. At the same time, it allows a company to look forward to a promise of profits if it can sell more of its product or service than competitors do.

Competition and Quality

Rather than sell your jeans for less than your competition, you may choose to compete for customers by offering higher-quality goods. Although you may charge more for your jeans, you offer a better fit, more durable fabric, or better styling. This possibility provides a practical incentive for businesses to maintain high standards and increases the choices available to consumers.

Competition and Innovation

Our economic system not only encourages variations in quality and price, it also encourages immense variety in the types of merchandise and services offered to the public. Changes in taste and new technology brought about innovation, so that your jeans could be trimmed or untrimmed, designer-made, or french cut. The economy and the competitive environment are constantly creating new business opportunities. The result is an astonishing diversity of businesses.

GOVERNMENT REGULATION OF BUSINESS

The right of government to regulate business is granted by the U.S. Constitution and by state constitutions. American business originally operated in a **laissez-faire** economy—a government policy of noninterference with business. However, the development of large trusts and monopolies that dominated their markets in the late nineteenth century created the need for regulation.

Because competition benefits our economy, laws have been passed to ensure that no single enterprise becomes too powerful. The ideal is pure competition, in which no single firm or group of firms in an industry is large enough to influence prices and thereby distort the workings of the free-market system. However, this ideal exists in very few industries. Many industries, often called **oligopolies,** are dominated by just a few producers, like the automobile industry. Although oligopolies themselves are not illegal, federal law generally prohibits oligopolies from artificially setting prices among themselves.

Restrictions are also imposed to prevent the development of a monopoly in any particular industry or market. A **monopoly** exists when a company has total control over products and prices and keeps other companies from competing.

A number of factors apart from government intervention help prevent the development of oligopolies and monopolies. In many instances, consumers can find substitute goods or services from other industries if the prices in one industry are higher than they wish to pay. Also, an industry that has only a few producers within a country (such as the auto industry in the United States) often faces competition from abroad.

TABLE 5-1 • KEY FEDERAL LAWS AFFECTING THE FASHION INDUSTRY

Laws Affecting Competition	Purpose and Provisions
Sherman Antitrust Act—1890	Outlawed monopolies. Outlawed restraint of competition.
Clayton Act—1914	Same purpose as Sherman Act but reinforced Sherman Act by defining some specific restraints—e.g., price fixing.
Federal Trade Commission (FTC) Act—1914 (Wheeler-Lee Act of 1938 amended the FTC Act.)	Established the FTC as a "policing" agency. Developed the mechanics for policing unfair methods of competition, e.g., false claims, price discrimination, price fixing.
Robinson-Patman Act—1936	Designed to equalize competition between large and small retailers (i.e., to reduce the advantages that big retailers have over small retailers—outgrowth of 1930 depression and growth of big chain retailers in 1920s).
	Examples of provision of law: 1. Outlawed price discrimination if both small and large retailers buy the same amount of goods. 2. Outlawed inequitable and unjustified quantity discounts (e.g., discounts allowable if (a) available to all types of retailers and (b) related to actual savings that vendor could make from quantity cuttings or shipments). 3. Outlawed "phony" advertising allowance monies—i.e., advertising money must be used for advertising. 4. Outlawed discrimination in promotional allowances (monies for advertising, promotional displays, etc.)—equal allowances must be given under same conditions to small and large retailers alike.
Cellar-Kefauver—1950	This law made it illegal to eliminate competition by creating a monopoly through the merger of two or more companies.

Product and Labeling Laws Designed to Protect Consumers	Purpose and Provisions
Wool Products Labeling Act—1939	Protects consumers from unrevealed presence of substitutes or mixtures. FTC responsible for enforcing law.
Fur Products Labeling Act—1951	Protects consumers and retailers against misbranding, false advertising, and false invoicing.
Flammable Fabrics Act—1953	Prohibits manufacture or sale of flammable fabrics or apparel.
Textile Fiber Identification Act—1960	Protects producers and consumers against false identification of fiber content.
Fair Packaging and Labeling Act—1966	Regulates interstate and foreign commerce by prohibiting deceptive methods of packaging or labeling.
Care Labeling of Textile Wearing Apparel Ruling—1972, 1983	Requires that all apparel have labels attached that clearly inform consumers about care and maintenance of the article.

There are two basic categories of federal legislation that affect the fashion industry: (1) laws that regulate competition, and (2) labeling laws designed to protect consumers. Table 5-1 lists the key federal laws that affect and/or regulate the fashion industry.

FORMS OF BUSINESS OWNERSHIP

Ownership of a fashion business—or of any business—may take many different legal forms, each carrying certain privileges and responsibilities. The three most common forms of business ownership are the sole proprietorship, the partnership, and the corporation. Corporations tend to be large-scale operations that account for the greatest share of the profits earned by American business. However, sole proprietorships are more numerous, accounting for almost 70 percent of all business enterprises.

Each form of ownership has a characteristic structure, legal status, size, and field to which it is best suited. Each has its own advantages and disadvantages and offers a distinctive working environment with its own risks and rewards. (See Table 5-2.)

The Sole Proprietorship

The sole proprietorship is the most common form of business in the United States, as well as in many foreign countries where the economy of the nation depends upon the small businessperson.

In the **sole proprietorship,** the individual who owns the business operates it for his or her own personal interest and assumes all risks. There are many examples of sole proprietorships in all areas of the fashion business—in designing, contracting, retailing, advisory service, and manufacturing. For example, Selma Weiser, owner of the New York specialty store Charivari, was a

TABLE 5-2 • ADVANTAGES AND DISADVANTAGES OF EACH FORM OF OWNERSHIP

FORM OF OWNERSHIP	⬆ Advantages	⬇ Disadvantages
Sole Proprietorship	1 Retention of all profits 2 Ease of formation and dissolution 3 Ownership flexibility	1 Unlimited financial liability 2 Financing limitations 3 Management deficiencies 4 Lack of continuity
Partnership	1 Ease of formation 2 Complementary management skills 3 Expanded financial capacity	1 Unlimited financial liability 2 Interpersonal conflicts 3 Lack of continuity 4 Complex dissolution
Corporation	1 Limited financial liability 2 Specialized management skills 3 Expanded financial capacity 4 Economies of larger-scale operation	1 Difficult and costly ownership form to establish and dissolve 2 Tax disadvantage 3 Legal restrictions 4 Alienation of some employees

From *Contemporary Business,* Fourth Edition, by Louis E. Boone and David L. Kurtz, copyright © 1985 by The Dryden Press, a division of Holt, Rinehart and Winston, Inc. Reprinted by permission of the publisher.

buyer for a department store for many years. She took her savings and opened her first store as a sole proprietorship. Today, Charivari has an international reputation.

Advantages

The sole proprietorship has a number of advantages. One is the ease and low cost of organization and dissolution of the business. Another is the freedom and flexibility of owning and managing your own business. Because of this the proprietor can make decisions promptly and take action at the opportune moment. For many people, personal satisfaction and being one's own boss may be the most significant incentives for establishing a sole proprietorship. Special tax savings and ownership of all profits are the other major advantages of the sole proprietorship.

Disadvantages

There are an equal number of disadvantages in operating a sole proprietorship. The business usually starts with limited financial resources which will most likely curtail the opportunity for profit and growth. Banks and other lending institutions may hesitate to lend large sums of money to sole proprietorships. Since the success of the business depends largely on the talents and managerial skills of one person, difficulties of management can become an obstacle to coordinating and controlling the business, particularly during periods when the owner is absent. Another major difficulty is the unlimited liability of the sole proprietorship. In this instance, the individual owner is liable for all the debts of the business. If the business cannot satisfy these debts, the proprietor's personal and real property may be attached and taken by the creditors. The unlimited liability of the sole proprietor can mean financial ruin to the owner if the business fails. A final disadvantage is lack of continuity. Extended illness, death, or bankruptcy of the owner of a sole proprietorship will terminate the business. Many firms have dissolved because the business is profitable only as long as the owner is able to run it.

The Partnership

A **partnership,** as defined by the Uniform Partnership Act, "is an association of two or more persons to carry on as co-owners of a business for a profit." A contract between or among partners is needed to ensure understanding of the obligations and rewards that each partner agrees to and shares.

Some famous retail establishments such as Abraham & Straus and Lord & Taylor were originally partnerships. Today, many manufacturing firms are partnerships with two or more partners with different expertise working together. The most usual combination is a person with factory and manufacturing know-how partnered with a creative design person or a person with outstanding sales ability.

Types of Partners

Partners' duties and obligations may differ with respect to such factors as management practice, sharing of profits, and extent of liability. Although there are many variations, the following are the most important types:

- A *general partner* is an individual who has unlimited liability and who may be called upon to furnish additional money from his or her own personal assets to pay the debts of the partnership.
- A *limited partner* is an individual whose liability extends up to the amount of his

or her investment and who is not permitted to take an active part in the management of the business.

- A *silent partner* is an individual who does not take an active role in the business, but who is known to the public as a member of the partnership.
- A *secret partner* is an individual who does take an active role in partnership affairs, but who is not known to the public as a member of the firm.
- *Senior and junior partners* are distinguished on the basis of their investment and business experience, and share in the firm's profits.

Advantages

Like sole proprietorships, partnerships are easy to organize. Unlike sole proprietorships, partnerships offer incentives to work hard since a talented or loyal employee can be made a partner. Partnerships generally have more sources of capital (money, property, and other assets) available to them than do sole proprietorships and thus can expand more easily. In addition, multiple owners can supervise and oversee larger facilities. Each partner may handle different functions of the business, thus providing management benefits. This pooling of talent is of tremendous value to the business, as it enables the partnership to operate with a variety of specialists. Tax savings are also accrued to the partnership in much the same manner as to the sole proprietorship.

Disadvantages

As in the sole proprietorship, a major disadvantage is the unlimited liability of the partnership arrangement. If the assets of the partnership are not sufficient to meet its obligations, the creditors may choose to sue any or all of the partners to satisfy the debt. Because the partnership involves two or more indi-

One of the most successful private corporations in fashion—the famous Fendi family—each sister, a specialist in different products from perfume, to purses, to leathers, to furs.

viduals, complicated decision-making and interpersonal problems may occur. Decision making takes longer, and if a stalemate should occur on a vital decision, the only solution to the problem might be to dissolve the partnership. Since the partnership is a temporary form of business and can be terminated by the partners themselves, there is the disadvantage of lack of continuity. The death of any partner leaves his or her heirs no authority to interfere in the affairs of the partnership or to try to carry on the business.

The Corporation

The third form of business ownership is the corporation. A **corporation** is defined by law as "an artificial being, invisible, intangible, and existing only in contemplation of law." The corporate form of organization comprises a relatively small percentage of the total number of business organizations. However, large corporations represent the most powerful segment of the national economy. In the 1980s, many fashion businesses incorporated or became part of large diversified national corporations. Today it is sometimes difficult for small fashion businesses to compete against the large corporations.

Types of Corporations

There are two major forms of corporation ownership. The most common form of ownership is public ownership. A **public corporation** sells shares of its stock on the open market. Anyone can buy a share of stock in the business and become a part owner.

Other corporations are privately owned. In a **private corporation,** no shares of stock are sold on the open market and ownership is usually held by a few people. The public cannot buy shares in this type of corporation.

Not all corporations are independent firms. Subsidiary corporations are partially or wholly owned by another corporation known as a parent company, which supervises the operations of the subsidiary. A holding company is a special type of parent company that exercises very little operating control over the subsidiary, merely "holding" its stock as an investment. See Table 5-3 for examples from the fashion industry of different types of corporations.

Structure of the Corporation

Because corporations have so many owners, they have a special organizational structure that allows efficient operation but still maintains accountabil-

TABLE 5-3 • TYPES OF CORPORATIONS IN THE FASHION INDUSTRY

Type	Description	Example
Public corporation	Business that aims to make a profit for persons or institutions with enough money to purchase shares on the open market.	May Company
Private corporation	Profit-making business with few owners and no open market for its shares.	Esprit
Subsidiary corporation	Corporation that is entirely, or almost entirely, owned by another corporation, known as a parent company or holding company.	Saks Fifth Avenue, parent is Bat Co.

Source: Adapted from D. Rachman and M. Mescon, *Business Today,* 5th ed., 1987, Random House/McGraw-Hill, New York.

ity. In a newly formed corporation, the stockholders elect a board of directors. The directors then select the top officers of the company.

Stockholders The **stockholders** are the owners of the corporation. They are individuals who bought shares of stock that give proof of ownership. The stockholder becomes a part owner of the business whether he or she owns one share or the majority of shares in the firm. This is true in both public and private corporations.

Board of Directors The **board of directors** is the chief governing body of the corporation. Because the individuals who comprise the board hold a position of great trust, directors may be held personally liable to the stockholders for gross negligence, fraud, or the use of corporate assets for their personal gain to the detriment of the company. They cannot be held liable for normal mistakes in business judgment.

Officers The **officers** of the corporation are elected by the board of directors and are directly responsible to the board for carrying out the business objectives of the firm. The board usually appoints a president, executive vice president, secretary, and a number of additional vice presidents who are responsible for various divisions of the firm.

Advantages

The main advantage of the corporation is its *limited liability*. The stockholder can lose no more than the value of his or her original investment. The creditors cannot look beyond the assets of the corporation to settle their debts because the corporation is a separate entity and it, rather than the owners, owes any debt. Unlike the other two forms, the corporation permits ease in transfer of ownership. Stockholders are able to buy and sell shares of stock in the public corporation through brokers in organized markets known as "stock markets or exchanges." The value of these shares changes daily. Therefore, owners may gain or lose money on the sale of their stock. A corporation's continuity of life span is another important advantage. Since corporations are rarely dissolved, they may possess an extremely long life. Because the corporation can divide its ownership into shares of small denominations, the ease of capital formation can help it to expand as long as investors are willing to purchase additional shares of stock. And since the corporation is usually larger than the sole proprietorship or partnership, it can be staffed with management specialists to a greater degree. Stock incentive plans and stock bonuses offer greater incentives for employees than the other forms of ownership usually do.

Disadvantages

The cost of organizing a corporation is burdensome and time-consuming. The legal restrictions can limit the corporation to engage in only those activities that are stated or implied in the original charter. A corporation is taxed at relatively high rates when compared with other types of businesses. Double taxation of corporate income is a result of taxes on the net profit as well as that portion of the profit distributed to the stockholders as individual income. The impersonality and lack of owners' personal interest in the day-to-day operation of the corporation often lead to an inordinate interest in just the amount of dividends each shareholder will receive. This leaves little time for genuine interest in the actual running of the business.

BUSINESS GROWTH AND EXPANSION

For the past few years, business activity has focused on the change in forms of business growth and expansion. The news media is filled with reports of businesses buying and selling other businesses and seeking new methods to make themselves more efficient and competitive.

One of the most distinct changes in the fashion business has been the rise of corporate giants which grew through mergers, acquisitions, and internal expansion. The growth of these giants has changed the methods of doing business,

Internal Growth

A company's ability to grow internally determines its ability to offer more service and broader assortments of merchandise, and to increase profits. This is true because internal growth is real growth, in terms of creating new products and new jobs. Internal growth can be accomplished through horizontal and/or vertical means. When a company has horizontal growth it expands its capabilities on the level on which it has been performing successfully. An apparel company could add new lines to diversify its product offerings; a retail store could open new branches. When a company has vertical growth it expands its capabilities on levels other than its primary function. An apparel company could begin to produce its own fabric, or could retail its manufactured goods in stores that the apparel company owns.

Mergers and Acquisitions

In a **merger** (or acquisition) a sale of one company to another company occurs, with the purchasing company usually remaining dominant. Companies merge to form a larger corporate organization for many reasons. They may wish to take advantage of a large corporation's greater purchasing power, or they may want to sell stock to obtain the financial resources needed for expansion. The desire to constantly increase sales is often able to be fulfilled only by a merger.

Operating economies can often be achieved by combining companies. Many times duplicate facilities can be eliminated, and marketing, purchasing, and other operations can be consolidated. **Diversification,** the addition of various lines, products, or services to serve different markets, can also be a

A fashionable example of vertical growth, Krizia, a famous designer's apparel firm, has branched into its own retail stores.

and has led to the demise of old-time famous-name sole proprietorships, partnerships, and small companies that could no longer compete.

Growth and expansion are fundamental to today's business world. Corporate growth has become a major economic, political, and social issue in recent years. Growth and expansion can occur in a variety of ways—internal growth, mergers, and acquisitions.

motive for a merger. For example, the merger of Levi Strauss, noted for the manufacture of jeans, with Koret of California, a sportswear manufacturer of women's garments, broadened the markets for both types of clothing.

Horizontal Mergers or Acquisitions

In a **horizontal merger** or acquisition, two or more companies with the same type of business are combined. An outstanding example of this type of merger was the absorption by Limited of Lane Bryant, Lerner's, Bendels, and Victoria's Secret.

Vertical Mergers or Acquisitions

In a **vertical merger** or acquisition, a company expands by either absorbing or merging with companies at other levels of the same business in order to be guaranteed a supplier or customers. For example, a fiber company could expand into the production of yarn and also into the production of fabric. Textile companies, such as Burlington and J. P. Stevens, have expanded through combinations of mergers or acquisitions to bring all levels of yarn and fabric production into one corporation. In another example, Hartmarx, a mens clothing manufacturer, acquired the Wallach chain of mens' stores to add to their customer base of distribution.

Conglomerate Mergers or Acquisitions

A **conglomerate** is a company consisting of a number of subsidiary companies in unrelated industries. In a conglomerate merger, two companies in unrelated lines of production or industry are combined. A conglomerate in the fashion world might have one company in the apparel business and other businesses with unrelated product lines. Batus, a British firm, owns the Brown and Williamson Tobacco Company, the Wilkinson Blade Company, maker of razor blades, and Saks Fifth Avenue. Another example is Consolidated Foods, which owns Hanes Hoisery, Sirena Swimwear, as well as food products.

One reason for conglomerate mergers is to diversify a company's sources of income so that economic pressures on one line of business do not seriously jeopardize the entire business. Another reason is that the government has severely restricted vertical and horizontal mergers in the interest of free competition. However, a major disadvantage of the conglomerate has been the difficulties in managing so many unrelated types of business.

Business Terms Used in Expansion and Growth

During the past few years new and different ways that businesses may combine and recombine have become popular. So that you will recognize and understand the terms used in these changes, the following list briefly defines some of these business terms.

Bankruptcy. Legal procedure by which a person or a business unable to meet financial obligations is relieved of debt by having the court divide the assets among the creditors. Example: Murjani.

Divestiture. Sale of part of a company for economic reasons. Example: Campeau selling parts of the original Allied Stores and Federated units.

Factor. Financial institution that specializes in buying accounts receivable at a discount.

Hostile Takeover. Situation in which an outside party buys enough stock in a corporation to take control against the wishes of the board of directors and corporate officers. Example: Campeau takeover of Allied Stores.

Going Public. Act of raising capital by selling shares in a company to the public for the first time. Example: Chaus Co.

Leverage. Use of borrowed funds to finance a portion of an investment.

Leveraged Buyout. Situation in which an individual or group of investors purchases a company with debt secured by the company's assets. Example: Macy's.

Syndicate. Temporary association of two or more firms or individuals, usually for mutual investment.

Trust. Business arrangement established where one company is set up to own a controlling share of the stock of other companies.

Venture Capitalist. Investment specialist who provides money to finance new businesses in exchange for a portion of the ownership with the objective of making a considerable profit on the investment.

The Franchise

A rapidly growing business arrangement is the **franchise.** This arrangement is a contract that gives an individual (or group of people) the right to own a business while benefiting from the expertise and reputation of an established firm. In return, the individual, known as the franchisee, pays the parent company, known as the franchisor, a set sum to purchase the franchise and royalties on goods or services sold. Franchises may be organized as sole proprietorships, partnerships, or corporations, although the form of business organization that the franchisee must use may be designated in the franchise contract.

Franchises generate one-third of all retail sales in the United States today steadily growing in volume according to industry reports. In fact, by 1995 the

Esprit, an apparel manufacturer, has become a major franchiser of Esprit shops around the world.

country-wide franchising network is expected to double.[3] Although the franchise arrangement is most widespread among fast-food restaurants, convenience stores, and automobile dealers, franchises can be found at many levels of the fashion business, especially in retailing.

The growth in the number of designer and manufacturer-franchised shops is phenomenal. One of the outstanding examples of this is found in the operation of Benetton, an Italian manufacturing company. From one franchised store in Italy, opened in 1968, Benetton has grown to over 3,500 franchised stores in 58 countries around the world. Although its first franchised store in the United States opened in 1980, in 1989 the Benetton franchise operation exceeded 1,000 stores coast-to-coast. Another well-known entry in the franchised-shop field is Esprit, the West Coast–based sportswear manufacturer who is franchising Esprit Sport, Esprit Kids, and Esprit de Corp/Shoes shops. Other well-known franchises in the fashion retailing field are Lady Madonna and Maternally Yours maternity shops, the Tennis Lady shops, and the very popular Athlete's Foot stores.

Although we will learn much more about designer-name franchising when we cover the apparel industries, it is important to note that Ralph Lauren, Donna Karan, and Liz Claiborne are all very involved in designer-franchised boutiques and shops in major cities throughout the United States and in some cases in Europe and the Orient.

Advantages

Franchising offers advantages to both the franchisee and the franchisor. The franchisee can get into business quickly, use proven operating methods, and benefit from training programs and mass purchasing offered by the franchisor. The franchisee is provided with a ready market that identifies with the store or brand name, thus assuring customer traffic. The franchisor has a great deal of control over its distribution network, limited liability, and less need for capital for expansion. Expansion is therefore more rapid than would be possible without the franchising arrangement. Royalty and franchise fees add to the profits of the parent company, and the personal interest and efforts of the franchisees as owner-managers help to assure the success of each venture.

Disadvantages

Franchising also has drawbacks for both parties. The franchisee may find profits small in relation to the time and work involved, and often has limited flexibility at the local level. In addition, there is the risk of franchise arrangements organized merely to sell franchises, rather than for their long-range profitability to all parties involved. The franchisor may find profits so slim that it may want to own stores outright rather than franchise them. Attempts to buy back franchises often lead to troubled relations with the remaining franchises.

Licensing

Licensing is an increasingly popular method of expanding an already existing business. **Licensing** is a legal arrangement whereby firms are given permission to produce and market merchandise in the name of the licensor for a specific period of time. The licensor is then paid a percentage of the sales (usually at the wholesale price) called a **royalty fee.** This practice grew tremendously in the late 1970s and 1980s, with sales of all licensed merchandise reaching an estimated $55 billion in 1986. Of that total, apparel and accessories account for about 40 percent of sales, and represent the largest single category of licensed goods sold.[4]

The first designer to license his name to a manufacturer was Christian Dior, who lent his name to a line of ties in 1950. Today, many of the best-known women's and men's apparel designers are licensing either the use of their original designs or just their names without a design for a wide variety of goods, from apparel to luggage and from housewares to chocolates. Among the many American designers involved in licensing are Bill Blass, Calvin Klein, Ralph Lauren, John Weitz, and Oscar de la Renta.

The licensing phenomenon is not limited to name designers. Popular movies and TV shows have spawned apparel and other products based on their themes or characters. Comic or greeting-card characters like Strawberry Shortcake, Garfield, and Snoopy are also frequently licensed, as are most professional sports teams and many players or

Reprinted by permission of NEA, Inc.

athletes. Even the huge Coca-Cola company climbed on the licensing bandwagon and licensed the Coca-Cola name for apparel manufacturing and retail stores.[5]

The advantage of a licensing arrangement to a manufacturer is that the merchandise is identified with a highly recognizable name, which also generally connotes high quality. This recognition factor can be valuable to retailers in presenting their own fashion image. And to consumers, the designer name not only indicates a certain quality of merchandise, but symbolizes status or achievement as well. Because of that built-in appeal, stores have stocked up on designer goods from socks to fragrances and even jewelry.

Retail Programs

A famous designer name is a strong selling point at retail value. For example, Ralph Lauren, who has licensees in women's and men's apparel, fragrances, footwear, scarves, and furs, generated almost $425 million in wholesale volume from foreign and domestic licensed products in 1986.[6] Lauren's company is in the perfect position of having its own Polo/Ralph Lauren shops that can display all the products together.

Established retailers such as Federated Department Stores, Inc., the parent company of Bloomingdale's in New York, Burdine's in Miami, and Filene's in Boston, entered into an exclusive licensing agreement with Cacherel. Similarly, JC Penney, traditionally known as a budget retailer or mass merchandiser, created a licensing program with Halston for an exclusive "Halston" collection. Under the agreement, Halston created a line of moderately priced apparel which could be used by JC Penney to upgrade its budget image and reposition itself as a fashion retailer (see Fashion Focus, p. 108–109).

FASHION

In the late 1960s and early 1970s, Halston, the legendary designer, ruled the world of fashion. He was the first American designer to become a celebrity in his own right and his fashions were worn by many of the richest and most famous women of the day: Jacqueline Kennedy, Lauren Bacall, Liza Minnelli, Bianca Jagger, and Elizabeth Taylor, to name a few.

But by the mid-1980s, all that had changed. Although the Halston name was still appearing on apparel, fragrances, and other products, none were designed by Halston himself. In fact, for all practical purposes, Halston could not use his own name to sell his creations in the field of fashion.

How could such a thing happen? Well, it all stemmed from a business agreement Halston signed in 1973. The deal had its roots in the common practice of designers to license their names, but it took that concept further: rather than simply licensing, Halston actually sold his ready-to-wear line, couture operation, *and* the Halston trademark to Norton Simon, a conglomerate that owned Max Factor cosmetics.

In essence, the agreement allowed Norton Simon to use the Halston name for products the designer did not cre-

FOCUS

ate—and it prohibited Halston from using his name on any design product without Norton Simon's consent. The association gave Halston the working capital he had desired, and it operated smoothly for some time; but in 1983, Norton Simon was itself acquired by Esmark Inc., and Halston Enterprises was put under the control of Esmark's International Playtex division. Then, less than a year later, Esmark was acquired in a hostile takeover by Beatrice Companies, which proceeded to disassemble the Halston company, keeping only the highly successful Halston fragrance and the line of Halston III clothing developed for JC Penney.

Legally, Halston could do nothing to salvage his business. In late 1984, he attempted to buy it back from Beatrice, but the agreement fell through. For over 2 years, Halston simply sat back and watched his name appear on the JC Penney clothing line that he did not design, while virtually his only creations to see light were costumes created (without fee) for the Martha Graham Dance Company, of which he had long been a major backer. Of course, Halston always received royalties for any use of his name, which surely meant a healthy income during this time, but the glamorous life he had once led and the prestigious reputation he had enjoyed were a thing of the past.

The story does not end there, however. In December 1986, one of Playtex's top executives bought the division from Beatrice, and in order to finance his purchase, he sold the Halston business yet again—this time to cosmetics giant Revlon. Once again, Halston was faced with the task of negotiating with his new owners, in an effort to regain some control over his name and his designs.

While Halston's goals to design again may never be as lofty as they were in his heyday, no one could blame him for wanting "to do *something*," or for hoping "it's better than anything I've done before," as he said, acknowledging that "nothing is ever the same as before."[1] Indeed, although the fashion world might someday wait with great anticipation for a glimpse of a new Halston original, it is unlikely that he will ever again rule that world—not since his personal fashion "empire" fell victim to the big business that drives fashion today.

[1] Lisa Belkin, "The Prisoner of Seventh Avenue," *The New York Times Magazine,* March 15, 1987, p. 52.

This Fashion Focus is based on information from the article cited above and from the following:

"Penney Fills Halston Void," *Stores,* June, 1989, p. 22.
    "Roy Frowick Fights for Freedom from the Company That Bought His Middle Name: Halston," *People,* January 6, 1986, p. 83.
    Irene Daria, "Minus Halston, Revlon Puts on a Halston Show," *Women's Wear Daily,* June 19, 1987.

Licensing is also crossing international borders, as an increasing number of designers, foreign and domestic, are making licensing agreements in other countries. In 1986, Christian Dior (the designer who started it all in 1950) generated over $330 billion in wholesale volume in the United States.[7] Major European designers such as Pierre Cardin and Hubert de Givenchy are constantly adding to their licensed products in the United States.

Calvin Klein has licensing arrangements in Canada, Mexico, Brazil, Argentina, Paraguay, and Japan. Klein plans to open stores in London and other European cities. Bill Blass, whose licensing empire does about $250 million of wholesale business each year, has signed several licensing deals for shoes and leather goods, home furnishings, men's apparel, and women's sportswear to be marketed in Japan.

MARKETING

No matter what form of business ownership is chosen for a particular business, success and profits cannot be assured without the appropriate marketing of the product or service.

The American Marketing Association recently devoted a year of study to the definition of marketing and evaluated 25 different definitions before reaching a consensus on the meaning of marketing. Accordingly, **marketing** is defined as the planning and execution of the conception, pricing, promotion, and distribution of ideas, goods, and services to create exchanges that satisfy individual and organizational objectives.[8] One of the reasons the American Marketing Association had so much trouble defining marketing is that marketing is a complex aspect of business as it has to be practised today.

Production-Driven Marketing

Marketing has changed drastically since the early 1920s when many businesses viewed marketing simply as a by-product of production. They concentrated on manufacturing and limited their marketing efforts to taking orders and shipping their production. Early mass-production women's apparel firms were great supporters of this type of marketing.

Sales-Driven Marketing

As the production capacity of the United States increased in the late 1920s the market for manufactured goods became more competitive. This was particularly true in the manufacture of mens, women's and children's apparel and accessories. Because their production output grew, manufacturers learned that they had to persuade more people to buy in order to sell this additional output. To stimulate demand for their goods, they had to spend more time and money on advertising. They began to develop sales forces and trained them to sell to as many potential customers as possible. With the advent of radio, magazine, and television, it became easier to reach more and more people with a sales message. However, most companies were still not consumer-oriented. Instead of asking what the consumer wanted, they were producing what the company could produce and getting their sales efforts to create demand. This thinking was essentially company-oriented rather than consumer-oriented.

The Marketing Concept

Since the late 1940s the focus has shifted to consumer-driven marketing, an approach known as the **marketing concept.** Under this concept companies attempt to identify the consumer's needs and wants, then create goods or services that satisfy them. All the company's efforts are devoted to producing what the consumer wants. Besides giving more attention to consumers, companies now give more thought to the competition so that they can produce a product or service that sets them apart from their competition and makes their product more appealing to customers.

The Marketing Strategy

Because successful marketing can be rather complicated, a business should develop an overall marketing plan for its product. A major concern in a marketing plan is the market—the group of people who want or need a product and who have the money and authority to buy it. Within this market there are market segments or subgroups with distinctive needs and interests and certain common characteristics. When a company approaches their marketing in this manner it is known as market segmentation. According to the American Marketing Association, **market segmentation** means dividing the heterogeneous market into smaller customer divisions with certain relatively homogeneous characteristics that the firm can satisfy.[9] To avoid spreading its resources too thin, they focus on specific **target markets** which are specific groups of customers within the segment to whom a company wants to sell a particular product or service.

A business cannot make a profit unless it has customers. To find out what they need or want takes market research. Once targeted it is important for the business to find the marketing mix that produces the greatest profit. The **marketing mix** is a combination of four major elements—product (ideas, goods, or services), pricing, promotion, and place (distribution)—known as the four P's, that respond to the needs of the intended customer.

REFERENCES

[1] *U.S. Industrial Outlook,* 1987.

[2] Ibid.

[3] Constance Mitchell, "Franchising Fever Spreads," *USA Today,* September 13, 1985, p. 4B.

[4] *The Licensing Letter,* Arnold Bolker, Publisher, February, 1987.

[5] Judy Bloomfield, "New Entries—Superman to Super Sports," *Women's Wear Daily,* June 1, 1987, p. 8.

[6] Lisa Lockwood, "Designer Licensing—The Survivors," *Women's Wear Daily,* June 1, 1987, p. 10.

[7] Ibid., p. 11.

[8] American Marketing Association definition of terms.

[9] Ibid.

MERCHANDISING VOCABULARY

Define or briefly explain the following terms:

Auxiliary level	Laissez-faire	Primary level
Bankruptcy	Leverage	Private corporation
Board of directors	Leveraged buyout	Profit
Business	Licensing	Public corporation
Conglomerate	Marketing	Retail level
Corporation	Marketing concept	Royalty fee
Diversification	Marketing mix	Secondary level
Divestiture	Market segmentation	Sole proprietorship
Factor	Merger	Stockholders
Franchise	Monopoly	Syndicate
Going public	Officers	Target markets
Horizontal merger	Oligopoly	Trust
Hostile takeover	Partnership	Venture capitalist
		Vertical merger

MERCHANDISING REVIEW

1. What is the primary objective of all businesses? Explain your answer.
2. Describe the four levels of the fashion business; give examples.
3. How does the auxiliary level differ from the other levels?
4. What are the five key reasons why an individual would go into business as a sole proprietor? Why take a partner later?
5. In what respect is the sole proprietor "liable" in his business?
6. List and briefly describe the types of partners that may own a business.
7. There are certain disadvantages to the corporate form of business ownership. Name five of them. How is this form of ownership an advantage if the firm decides to expand?
8. If you were the president of a national chain of shoe stores, what are five laws and regulations that would affect how you do business? Which of these laws would *not* affect a small, privately owned bridal shop?
9. Differentiate between vertical mergers and horizontal mergers.
10. How is a licensed designer name an advantage to the manufacturer? To the consumer? To the retailer?

MERCHANDISING DIGEST

1. What initial decisions need to be made by an individual or group of individuals who plan to form a company with regard to the form of ownership which will be most beneficial to all?
2. If you were an officer in a private corporation, how would your situation differ from that of an officer in a publicly held corporation?

Exploring
the Dynamics
of Fashion

D efinite correlations exist between fashions and the times in which they are worn. Fashions change as times change, and when there is a fashion change, the total look changes: accessories, hairstyles, and makeup. As styles are revived, however, they are always variations of the old form, adapted for the new times with its new lifestyles and occasions. Study the table on the next page, and respond to the questions below:

1. Find examples to illustrate one fashion item per decade from the right-hand column of the table (sketch, photo, or cut-out illustrations).

2. Study the decades: what similarities in fashions and their causes can you find?

3. What changes in the environment over the last two decades do you feel will have a lasting effect over the next 10 to 20 years?

4. During what decade was fashion closest to being revolutionary? Describe the causes.

5. During which decades can you find support for the theory that fashion is evolutionary?

6. Develop your own listing of events, public reactions, and interpretation in apparel and dress over the past 2 years.

7. After studying the information on the past decades, what conclusions may be drawn about the evolution of fashions and the relationship of fashion to current events and public personalities?

TABLE 5-4 • SOCIAL AND ECONOMIC INFLUENCES IN FASHION IN THE UNITED STATES (1920–1989)

ERA	Events Taking Place	Public Reactions	Interpretation in Apparel and Dress
1920s	Post World War I, Paris influence Voting rights for women Increasing prosperity Modern art, music, literature Birth of sportswear	Daring looks and behavior Freedom for the body Short hairstyles Women begin to smoke Dancing (Charleston) The roadster	Chemise dresses, short skirts T-strap shoes, cloche hats Luxurious fabrics: silks, satins, crepes Costume looks, long strands of beads
1930s	Depression era Unemployment, no money Hollywood influence: stars & designers Rayon and acetate fabrics Big bands, swing music	Frugality, conservatism "The little woman" "Making do" Take the bus	Soft looks: loose, light fabrics Long hemlines, bias cuts Big hats, big brims The housedress Fox, fur-collared coats
1940s	World War II: Government restrictions Exit France as fashion source Shortage of materials Emergence of American designers Radio, records Crooners: Crosby, Sinatra Dior—1947 "New Look"	Women take men's jobs Glamour, pinup girls Strong nationalism Common cause philosophy Tanks	Tailored, mannish suits, peplum jackets Padded shoulders Knee-length straight skirts Soft, shoulder-length hair (pageboy) Rolled hair Small hats, perched in front Pants for women
1950s	Baby boom Korean war Firms expand, go public, diversify Move to suburbs Incomes rising More imports Improved transportation; communications: TV Development of more synthetics, finishes Birth of rock 'n roll	Buy new homes, appliances, furnishings Conformity Improve quality of family life Use of increased leisure time for sports and recreation The station wagon	Classics: shirtwaist dress At-home clothes Mink stoles Sack dress (too quickly copied) Sportswear Ivy League look, gray flannel suit, skinny ties, buttondown shirts Car coats Wash 'n' wear fabrics
1960s	Rise of shopping centers; boutiques New technology: stretch fabrics, knitting methods Big business expansion; prosperity Designer names	New sexual freedom Experimentation in fashion Antiestablishment attitudes Generation gap Identity seeking, new values	Street fashions: jeans Vinyls, synthetics Miniskirts Wild use of color, patterns Knits, polyester Ethnic clothing and crafts Unisex clothes

ERA	Events Taking Place	Public Reactions	Interpretation in Apparel and Dress
1960s (cont.)	Civil rights movement Vietnam war: youth rebellion, antiwar movement London influence: the Beatles, Twiggy, Mod, Mary Quant, Carnaby Peacock revolution Rock music, youth cult	Divorce, singles Drug experimentation The Volkswagon "Bug"	Fun furs Long hair, wigs Men: turtlenecks, wide ties, Nehru jackets, gold coordinates, nylon printed shirts
1970s	Equal rights, women's liberation movement Women working outside the home Watergate, disenchantment with politics Recessions Ecology, energy crisis Stabilizing economy End of Vietnam war Disco dancing, clubs Consumerism Hostage crisis in Iran	Individualism Return to sanity, reaction to 1960s chaos Back to nature, health foods, natural fibers New conservatism Urban renewal, interest in cities & their problems Equal Rights Amendment Minority organizations Compact cars and subcompact cars	Pantsuits (women) leisure suits (men) Maxi and longuette (1970s disaster) Jeans: bell bottoms, straight leg, tapered leg, peg leg. Jeans for dress and casual wear T-shirts, tank tops, boots Eclecticism Classic look: blazers, investment clothing Separates, not coordinates Romantic look: feminine
1980s	Computer explosion Music videocassettes Nuclear weapons buildup Yuppy (Young Urban Professional) Recession/unemployment Wars in Central America, Middle East Movies: *Fame, E.T., Flashdance, Out of Africa* First black presidential and first woman vice-presidential candidates Japanese fashion explosion Executive-level women; two-income families New baby boom New interest in fitness AIDs crisis Stock market crash, Oct. 1987	Buy home computers Michael Jackson, youth hero Nuclear freeze movement Entrepreneurship Immigration legislation Day-care centers Graffiti art London influence: Punk—Boy George and Culture Club Patriotism flourishes Health education Convertibles return; luxury foreign cars	Return of the chemise Punk hairdos Androgynous dressing Tailored suits and classic dressing for men and women Torn clothes fad Return to pants in mid-decade Furs Oversized silhouettes Return of the miniskirt Warm-ups, aerobic exercise clothing

UNIT TWO

the producers of fashion

Fashion is products. Behind every product there is a story that begins with the raw materials of fiber or fabric, leather or fur, and those who are responsible for their production. Unit 2 starts with a discussion of these, the primary suppliers.

The steps needed to convert these raw materials into the fashions that draw the customers into stores make up the next episodes in the life of a product. This is the business of the secondary suppliers, and there are all kinds—from those that produce men's, women's, and children's apparel to those that specialize in accessories. There are businesses that focus on producing intimate apparel and those that focus on cosmetics. Each of these businesses is a self-contained industry, with its own history, organization, methods of operation, and merchandising and marketing activities. Each is discussed in Unit 2.

In the past few decades, the fashion manufacturing business has grown from an industry composed of many small companies into a far larger one, dominated by a few giants. This has changed the way that apparel is made. Large companies, for example, can afford to invest in the newest technology. Technology, in turn, has helped to make high style and quality accessible to everyone, not just an elite few.

Despite the changes that have resulted from the turmoil of the past decade and the rapidly changing technology, the industry has continued to follow a basic cycle of production that repeats itself season after season. Anyone interested in a career in the fashion field needs to understand this basic cycle and the interrelated roles played by the different fashion producers on both the primary and secondary levels.

TEXTILES: FIBERS AND FABRICS

Have you ever bought a garment simply because you loved the feel of it? Perhaps it was nubby. Or silky smooth. Or maybe it was incredibly soft to touch. If so, then you—like almost everyone else—have responded to a fabric rather than to the style or color of a garment.

So important is the material a garment is made of that Christian Dior, the world-famous haute-couture designer, once said of it: "Fabric not only expresses a designer's dream, but also stimulates his own ideas. It can be the beginning of an inspiration. Many a dress of mine is born of the fabric alone."[1]

The enormous appeal of fabric—and the fibers of which it is composed—lies in its many varied textures, finishes, uses, and colors. These are created, as we shall see, by the textile fiber and fabric industries, two separate industries that work closely together to produce an end product called fashion textiles.

The production of fiber and fabrics is the first step in the manufacture of clothing. As a result, textile fiber and textile fabric manufacturers are considered **primary suppliers.** (Other primary suppliers, who create fur and leather, will be explored in the next chapter.)

THE FIBER INDUSTRY

A **fiber**—an extremely fine, hairlike strand almost invisible to the eye—is the smallest element of a fabric. It is also the starting point of a fabric. Although tiny, fibers have enormous influence on fashion. They are what gives a fabric its color, weight, texture, and durability.

Fibers are either natural or man-made. **Natural fibers** are found in nature, that is, they come from plant or animal sources. The natural fibers are cotton, wool, silk, flax, and ramie. In contrast, the

man-made fibers are made in a chemist's laboratory. They may be made from substances that occur in nature, such as wood pulp, air, petroleum, or natural gas, but these natural substances must be converted into fibers before they can be made into fabric. Because man-made fibers are invented in the laboratory, they are more plentiful than natural fibers. Some of the man-made fibers whose names you may recognize are rayon, triacetate, acetate, acrylic, spandex, and polyester, to name only a few.

History and Development

The use of natural fibers is ancient, while most of the man-made fibers have been invented in the past 50 years. Despite their relatively short life span, however, very rapid advances have been made in the use of man-made fibers. In contrast, the natural fiber industry has developed much more slowly. In fact, many of the recent developments in natural fibers are actually advances made in the man-made fiber industry that were transferred to the natural fiber industry.

The Development of Natural Fibers

The use of natural fibers predates written history. Prehistoric humans are known to have gathered flax, the fiber in linen, to make yarns for fabrics.

Cotton, the most widely used of all the natural fabrics, is the substance attached to the seed of a cotton plant. Cotton fibers are composed primarily of cellulose, a carbohydrate that especially lends itself to the manufacture of fibrous and paper products. Cotton fibers absorb moisture quickly, dry quickly, and have a cooling effect that makes cotton a good fiber for hot or warm weather.

It is easy to see why fibers and fabrics look, feel, and wear differently. See (a) cotton from the cotton plant, (b) silk from silkworms, and (c) wool from sheep.

Wool is the fiber that forms the coat of sheep. An animal fiber, it is composed mostly of protein. Wool fiber is a natural insulator and is used to make warm clothes. Wool fiber, in fact, has a natural crimp that is ideal for the production of bulky yarns which trap air to form insulating barriers against the cold. In contrast to cotton, wool absorbs moisture slowly and dries slowly.

Silk comes from a cocoon formed by a silkworm. The silkworm forms silk by forcing two fine streams of a thick liquid out of tiny openings in its head. These streams harden into filaments, or fibers, upon contact with the air. Silk, best known for its luxurious feel, is a breathable fabric that can be worn year-round. For many years silk required dry cleaning, but today's silk is washable.

Silk all but disappeared from the U. S. fashion market during and after World War II. It has made a dramatic comeback, but it is still not mass-produced.

Flax, used to make linen, comes from the stem of a flax plant. Only after the flax fiber is spun into yarn and woven or knit into fabric is the product called **linen.** Flax is the strongest of the vegetable fibers (it is twice as strong as cotton), and like cotton, it absorbs moisture and dries quickly. This makes linen an excellent fabric for warm-weather apparel. However, even with new technology that makes linen less apt to wrinkle, it still has a tendency to wrinkle and is harder to iron than cotton.

Ramie comes from a woody-leafed Asian plant grown mostly in China. It has only been available in the United States since 1979, when the United States and China reopened trade with one another. Despite its popularity, the importation of ramie was severely reduced in the late 1980s. Ramie, a warm-weather fabric that is linen-like, is also inexpensive.

The Development of Man-Made Fibers

Man-made fibers have been improving the quality of our lives since rayon, the first synthetic fiber, went into production in 1910. Since then, many other man-made fibers have been introduced in literally thousands of new apparel, upholstery, and industrial applications. Today, man-made fibers account for about 75 percent of all fibers used by American textile mills.

Man-made fibers offer a variety of characteristics that are mostly unavailable in natural fibers. Each year, man-made fibers find new uses in our wardrobes, homes, hospitals, and workplaces.

All man-made fibers start life as thick liquids. Fibers of continuous, indefinite lengths are produced by forcing the liquid through the tiny holes of a mechanical device called a **spinnerette.** The process is similar to the way a silkworm produces silk fiber or the way pasta dough is pushed through a pasta machine to make spaghetti.

Fibers are then cut into short lengths and spun into yarn, as is the case with natural fibers, or they are chemically processed into yarn, as are many man-made fibers. In the latter instance, the production of fiber and yarn occurs simultaneously.

There are two basic types of man-made fibers: cellulosic and noncellulosic.

Cellulosic Fibers Cellulose, the same fibrous substance found in plants and used to make natural fibers, is also used to produce **cellulosic fibers.** The three cellulosic fibers are rayon, triacetate, and acetate. Triacetate, for example, is highly drapable and moisture-absorbent, and it makes a fabric that is soft and comfortable. Because these fibers are cellulose-based, they can be produced with a minimum of chemical treatment. The cellulose used to make these fibers comes mostly from soft woods such as spruce.

Noncellulosic Fibers Petroleum, natural gas, air, and water are used to make **noncellulosic fibers.** They are produced from various combinations of carbon, hydrogen, nitrogen, and oxygen. Fiber chemists working in laboratories link the molecules into long chains called **polymers.**

The Federal Trade Commission has assigned **generic names** or nontrademarked names, to eighteen noncellulosic fibers. These are:[2]

acrylic	metallic	polyester
anidex	modacrylic	rubber
aramid	novoloid	saran
azlon	nylon	spandex
glass	nytril	vinal
lastrile	olefin	vinyon

Of these, anidex, azlon, lastrile, and vinal are not currently produced in the United States.

The properties of these fibers greatly influences the behavior of the finished fabric made from them. Polyester, for example, is strong and wrinkle-resistant, which contributes to its durability and washability.

Organization and Operation

Because of the differences in the origin and characteristics of fibers, each industry—the natural fiber industry and the man-made fiber industry—is organized along different lines.

The Natural Fiber Industry

Cotton is produced in four major areas of the United States: the Southeast; the Mississippi Delta; the Texas–Oklahoma

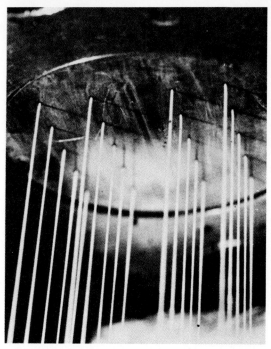

Man-made fibers of varying lengths are produced by forcing thick liquids through the tiny holes of a device known as a spinnerette.

Panhandle; and New Mexico, Arizona, and California.

Nearly all cotton growers sell their product in local markets, either to mill representatives or, more typically, to wholesalers. The cotton wholesalers bargain at central markets in Memphis, New Orleans, Dallas, Houston, New York, and Chicago.

The wool produced in the United States comes from relatively small sheep ranches in the Western states. Boston is the central marketplace for wool, both domestic and imported.

Linen, silk, and ramie are not produced in any great quantities in the United States, and are imported from foreign sources.

The natural fiber industry in the United States has been greatly affected by the advent of man-made fibers. Man-made fibers can literally be constructed to meet current customer demand. If a new lightweight, moisture-resistant fabric is needed, it can be made to order in the laboratory. This ability to tailor the man-made fibers to the demands of the ever-changing marketplace has forced the natural fiber industries to become more attuned to the needs of their customers. In order to compete, the natural fiber industries have become more aggressive about developing new uses for their products and have aggressively promoted themselves. Cotton, usually a warm-weather fiber, is now promoted as a year-round fiber, largely through the introduction of heavier cotton fibers used to make cotton sweaters. And wool, usually designed for cold-weather wear, is now being treated to make new, lightweight fibers that are suitable for year-round wear.

So that they can better promote their new products (and themselves), the natural fiber industries also have organized trade associations that carry their message to the textile industry as well as to the customer.

Originally, the natural fibers were not given the variety of special finishes that we find in them today. Advanced technology, innovative chemical processing, and a need to compete with man-made fibers has changed all that, and natural fibers now have care-and-wear properties that make them equal to the man-made fibers.

The Man-Made Fiber Industry

Obviously, climate and terrain have nothing to do with the production of a man-made fiber. Indeed, chemical plants are extremely adaptable, requiring only supplies of raw chemicals, power, and labor. Chemical companies have thus erected their plants in every part of the United States—up and down the East Coast, in the South, the Midwest, and increasingly on the West Coast. Operations are located wherever companies have found raw materials or railroads and waterways for convenient shipment of those materials. Most of these plants are huge.

With man-made fibers, it is also possible for the producing plant to serve as its own market. It purchases fibers from chemical companies, spins them into yarn and then knits or weaves the yarn into fabric. Burlington Industries, J. P. Stevens, Dan River, and Milliken are just a few of the giants that consolidate all operations, from spun yarn manufacture to finished fabric.

Fiber Development Limited quantities of a new or modified man-made fiber are usually first produced in a pilot plant on an experimental basis. If research indicates that both industry and consumers will accept the new product, mass production begins. New applications of the fiber are then explored and new industries are consulted and encouraged to use it.

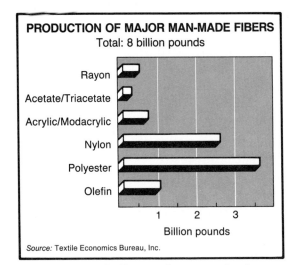

PRODUCTION OF MAJOR MAN-MADE FIBERS
Total: 8 billion pounds

Source: Textile Economics Bureau, Inc.

Of the man-made fibers, polyester and nylon account for about 75 percent of the market.

TABLE 6-1 • MAN-MADE FIBERS AND MAJOR TRADE NAMES

Acetate	Nylon	Olefin	Polyester (cont.)
Acetate by Avtex	A.C.E.	Herculon	Strialine
Ariloft	Anso	Herculon Nouvelle	Trevira
Avron	Antron	Marvess	Ultra Glow
Celanese	Blue "C"	Patlon	Ultra Touch
Chromspun	Cadon		
Estron	Cantrece	**Polyester**	**Rayon**
Loftura	Caprolan	A.C.E.	Absorbit
	Captiva	Avlin	Avril
Acrylic	Celanese	Caprolan	Avsorb
Acrilan	Cordura	Crepesoft	Beau-Grip
Bi-Loft	Courtaulds Nylon	Dacron	Coloray
Creslan	Cumuloft	Encron	Courcel
Fi-lana	Eloquent Luster	Fortrel	Courtaulds HT Rayon
Orlon	Eloquent Touch	Golden Glow	Courtaulds Rayon
Pa-Qel	Enkacrepe	Golden Touch	Durvil
Remember	Enkalon	Hollofil	Enkaire
So-Lara	Enkalure	Kodaire	Enkrome
Zefkrome	Enkasheer	Kodel	Fibro
Zefran	Lurelon	KodOfill	Rayon by Avtex
	Multisheer	KodOlite	Zantrel
Aramid	Natural Luster	KodOsoff	
Kevlar	Natural Touch	Lethasuede	**Spandex**
Nomex	Shareen	Matte Touch	Lycra
	Shimmereen	Natural Touch	
Modacrylic	Softalon	Plyloc	**Triacetate**
SEF	T.E.N.	Polyextra	Arnel
	Ultron	Shanton	
	Zefran	Silky Touch	**Vinyon**
	Zeftron		Vinyon by Avtex

Source: Man-Made Fibers—A New Guide, Man-Made Fiber Producers Association, Inc., 1984, p. 6.

While this procedure is going on in one chemical company, there is always the possibility that another company may be working along similar lines to develop a competitive fiber. The company that is first to develop a new fiber has no assurance that it will have the field to itself for long. There are many brands of such man-made fibers as nylon, rayon, and acetate on the market and a roster of companies producing various acrylics and polyesters. For example, acrylic fibers are produced by Du Pont as Orlon, by Monsanto as Acrilan, by American Cyanamid as Creslan, and by Badische as Zefran. These various companies all have unique specialty variants of the basic acrylic. Another example is polyester, produced by Fiber Industries as Fortrel, by Du Pont as Dacron, by Eastman as Kodel, and by Hoechst as Trevira. Table 6-1 shows trade names of major man-made fibers.

The fierce competition among various producers of man-made fibers is tied to the fact that each product can be made specifically to the customer's demands. In one season, a need may arise for a fiber that is stretchable, offers warmth without weight, and is also wrinkle-resistant. Armed with a list of customer preferences, competing laboratories go to work to develop new products. It is no wonder that several of them come up with the same answer at the same time.

Under the Textile Fibers Products Identification Act of 1960, consumer products that use textile fibers are required to label their products by generic name and to specify the percentage of each fiber that is used. Brand names or trademarks may also be used on the label, but they are not required by law.

Fiber Distribution Producers of man-made fibers sell their fibers to fabric manufacturers in one of three ways:

1. As unbranded products, with no restrictions placed on their end use and no implied or required standards of performance claimed.
2. As branded or trademarked fibers, with assurance to consumers that the quality of the fiber has been controlled by its producer, but not necessarily with assurance as to either implied or required standards of performance in the end product.
3. Under a licensing agreement, whereby the use of the fiber trademark concerned is permitted only to those manufacturers whose fabrics or other end products pass tests set up by the fiber producer for their specific end uses or applications.

Licensing programs set up by different fiber producers and by processors of yarn vary considerably in scope. The more comprehensive programs entail extensive wear testing to back up the licensing agreement. The fiber and yarn producers exercise considerable control over fabric products, sometimes specifying blend levels, that have been li-censed and offer technical services to help correct a fabric that fails to pass a qualifying test. Trademarks used under such licensing agreements are referred to as **licensed trademarks.** Fiber Industries' Fortrel is an example of a licensed trademark.

Merchandising and Marketing

No matter how familiar fashion fabric and apparel producers and consumers may be with the qualities of each fiber, there is always the need to disseminate information about the newest modifications and their application to fashion merchandise. To do this, producers of both natural and man-made fibers make extensive use of advertising, publicity, and market research. They also extend various customer services to manufacturers, retailers, and consumers.

Usually a producer of man-made fibers, such as Du Pont or Monsanto, undertakes these activities on behalf of its own individual brands and companies. The American Fiber Manufacturers Association, a domestic trade association that represents more than 90 percent of the U.S. producers of man-made fibers, filaments, and yarns, also carries on a very active program of consumer education about man-made fibers in general. Originally called the Man-Made Fiber Producers Association, it changed its name to better reflect its products.

Producers of natural fibers, on the other hand, carry on related activities through trade associations, each presenting a particular natural fiber. Examples are the National Cotton Council (the central organization of the cotton industry), Cotton Incorporated (the group specializing in promoting the use of cotton by designers and manufacturers), the American Wool Council, the

Where's Fortrel?

At Buster Brown

And that's just where we want it to be. Because they believe market leadership deserves a few bouquets. Which is why they turn to 50/50 Fortrel*/ cotton blends for Kaboom! by Buster Brown® dresses and trend-setting Buster Brown boyswear. After all, who wouldn't be attracted to a fiber with 27 years of trade and consumer recognition? A fiber that stays true to specification every time. A fiber committed to a beautiful relationship with mills and manufacturers alike. It's a daisy chain that starts with quality and ends with quality. Fortrel and Buster Brown. When you _are_ a leader, you go with a leader.

FORTREL®
The Fiber of Choice

Fiber Industries™

This Fiber Industries ad promotes both Fortrel, a polyester/cotton blend fiber, and Buster Brown, a manufacturer of girls and boys clothing.

Wool Bureau, and the Mohair Council of America.

Advertising and Publicity

As you might suspect, given their greater potential for competition, the man-made fiber industries spend considerably more money on advertising than do the natural fiber industries. They maintain a steady flow of advertising and publicity directed at both the trade and consumer markets. Sometimes an advertising campaign will promote an entire range of textile fibers, while at other times it will concentrate only on a single fiber. Fiber companies give most of their advertising dollars to support the manufacturers who use their fibers.

Among the trade publications used by the man-made fiber industries to promulgate their messages are *Women's Wear Daily, M,* and the *Daily News Record.* Mass-circulation magazines and newspapers as well as radio and television are used to advertise their fashion message—as well as their brand names.

When polyester took a nosedive in popularity in the early 1980s, the Polyester Fashion Council, an offshoot of the then-named Man-Made Fiber Producers Association, began fighting its new negative image. A clever campaign involved the use of "touch test" cards designed to demonstrate that polyester and natural fabrics of identical weight, color, and texture are virtually indistinguishable from one another. The council's efforts were successful and polyester made a quick comeback, both with designers and with the buying public. Today, polyester occupies one-third of the market share of all fibers sold with over 3½ billion pounds produced to make apparel.[3]

Thanks to such advertising and promotion campaigns, consumer recogni-

Monsanto's "Wear-Dated" tag is found only on apparel that passes stringent quality tests.

tion of man-made fibers is high, and producers now concentrate on promoting the qualities of their products rather than the names of individual fibers. For example, Monsanto uses almost every medium including national television to publicize its "Wear-Dated" licensed trademark program. The basis of this program is a guarantee that not only the fabric, but also the buttons, belts, buckles, zippers, lining, padding, thread, and all other appurtenances used in the construction of a garment labeled "Wear-Dated" will give satisfactory normal wear for one full year, or Monsanto will provide the customer with either a refund or a replacement.

Some natural fiber groups are putting more effort and money into campaigns to combat the growing domination of man-made fibers. Because these campaigns are mainly handled by trade associations, they promote the fiber itself, not the products of an individual natural fiber producer. One of the most eye-catching campaigns is that of Cotton Incorporated. The ads and posters not only emphasize cotton's advantages as a fiber but also point to the cotton industry's importance in the economy and to cotton's ecological appeal.

Fiber sources also provide garment producers and retailers with various aids that facilitate mention of their fibers in consumer advertising. This adds a big impact to the recognition already achieved by the fiber producer's name, trademark, slogan, or logotype. For example, the Wool Bureau encourages the use of its ball-of-yarn logotype in producer and retailer advertising of all-wool merchandise, as well as in displays.

Fiber industry producers and trade associations continually provide the press with new information, background material, and photographs for editorial features. Some of this publicity effort is accomplished by direct contact with the press; some of it is done by supplying garment producers and retailers with materials they can use for promotion. A familiar example of fashion publicity on behalf of a natural fiber is the National Cotton Council's annual Maid of Cotton program. A beauty queen is selected to make appearances throughout the United States in a fashionable cotton wardrobe designed by famous designers.

Another form of fiber advertising and publicity is the development of seasonal fashion presentations for use by retail stores. Publicity kits and programs specially prepared for local markets are developed. The objective is to support promotions during peak retail selling periods.

Advertising is also undertaken by fiber producers in cooperation with fabric

Fiber trade associations promote the use of fiber logos in finished garments. These logos are for wool and mohair.

and garment manufacturers and retailers. Such **cooperative advertising,** for which the costs are shared by a store and one or more producers on terms mutually agreed to, benefits the fiber industry in two ways. First, consumers begin to associate the fiber name with other names already familiar, such as the name of the fiber source or the name of the retail store selling the garment. This is particularly important when a fiber is man-made and still new. Second, fabric and garment producers as well as retailers are encouraged to use and promote the fiber because of the fringe benefit they get in the form of subsidized local or national advertising.

Research and Development

Both natural fiber products and man-made fiber producers are constantly seeking ways to improve their products. The large man-made fiber producers handle research and development mainly on an individual company basis. The natural fiber producers, because of the small size of the average company, often work through group efforts.

Man-Made Fibers The research facilities of the giant chemical companies engineer both existing and new fibers to meet the fashion and performance demands of their expanding and varied markets. The producers of man-made fibers are particularly active in instructing the fabric industry in the manipulation of new yarns, in developing optimum blends and constructions, in improving dyeing and finishing techniques, and in evaluating consumer reaction to the fabrics made from their fibers. Technical bulletins on the proper methods of processing their fibers are issued to the trade. These are supplemented by available expert advice on specific problems relating to yarn, fabric, or garment production.

Natural Fibers Producers of natural fibers have increased their research activities in recent years in attempts to impart to their fibers, yarns, and textiles such qualities as dimensional stability, crease retention, wrinkle resistance, luster or matte finish, washability, and any other characteristics that improve their acceptance. For example, some man-made fibers offer dimensional stability, or shrink and stretch resistance. Wool and cotton fabrics can also offer this characteristic when they are preshrunk. Similarly, wash-and-wear and crease-resistant properties, formerly found only in fabrics made from certain man-made fibers, can now be offered in fabrics made of cotton, wool, and flax, primarily as the result of topical chemical finishes.

Customer Services

All major producers of man-made fibers and many smaller firms offer a number of services to direct and secondary users of their products. Producers of natural fibers, working through their associa-

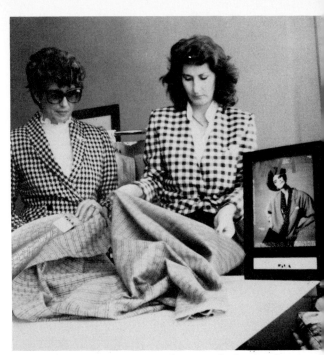

Fibers make up the fabrics that are the basis of the fashion business.

tions, also offer many such services. These include:

- Technical advice as well as technical know-how on weaving and knitting techniques.
- Assistance to textile and garment producers and retailers in locating supplies.
- Fabric libraries that include information about sources, prices, and delivery schedules. Research in a fabric library saves precious time spent shopping the market for trend information.
- Fashion presentations and exhibits for the textile industry, retailers, garment manufacturers, the fashion press, and occasionally, the public.
- Extensive literature for manufacturers, retailers, educators, and consumers about fiber properties, use, and care.
- Fashion experts who address groups of manufacturers, retailers, or consumers,

staging fashion shows and demonstrations.

- Educational films and audiovisual aids for use by the trade, schools, and consumer groups.

Trends in the Fiber Industry

For several years now, regardless of whether they are buying a Ford car or a Du Pont fiber, consumers have been concerned with the quality of the products they buy. While the fiber industries have always been attentive to quality, they have, through advertising and publicity campaigns, striven to be sure that their customers are aware of their interest in quality.

Computers are also playing an important role in the fiber industries' abilities to service their customers more quickly and efficiently. In addition to facilitating communications, they offer important linkage between the various industries and enable them to do such things as coordinate delivery schedules and provide bar coding.

The fiber industry is also fighting hard to overcome another major problem: the encroachment of its domestic markets by imports. Since man-made fibers account for over 75 percent of fiber usage annually in the United States, it is obvious that this will be a continuing and ongoing problem. The American fiber industry will have to fight harder than ever for its share of the international and even the domestic market.

To many observers the man-made fiber story is just beginning, and the next half-century promises to be even more exciting than the previous one. Industry experts predict that the years ahead will see new types of generic fibers with properties not even dreamed of today. In the future, fibers may well be produced with built-in thermostats. Unusual colors will be developed, and light and thermal properties will help to insulate against weather and even protect against disease.[4]

THE TEXTILE FABRIC INDUSTRY

Midway between the fiber and the finished garment is the fabric. **Textile fabric** is any material that is made by weaving, knitting, braiding, knotting, laminating, felting, or chemical bonding. It is the basic material out of which most articles of apparel and accessories are made.

Americans use a lot of textile fabric. Each person consumes nearly 60 pounds of textile fabric annually, about twice what Western Europeans use and nearly ten times as much as most other countries. We use fabric for clothing, home furnishings, transportation, in industry, defense, recreation, health care, and for space exploration.

The production of most fabrics begins with the creation of yarn from fibers. With the exception of felted fabric and a few other nonwoven fabrics, fibers cannot be made into fabrics without first making them into yarn. **Yarn** is a continuous thread formed by spinning, or twisting, fibers together. Yarns are then woven or knit into **greige goods,** or unfinished fabrics. Greige goods (pronounced "gray goods") are converted into finished fabrics for consumer or industrial use.

History and Development

The earliest step toward the mechanization of the textile fabric industry was the introduction of the spinning wheel, brought to Europe from India in the sixth century. Even with the spinning wheel, yarn-making remained tedious work that was mostly done in the home. Not until the eighteenth century did the British develop mechanical methods of spinning cotton fibers into yarn.

The result of mechanized spinning—large quantities of yarn—increased the need for better looms to weave the yarn into fabric. The first power loom was invented by an English clergyman, Dr. Edward Cartwright, and patented in 1785. It used water as a source of energy.

The new mechanization soon spread to America. In 1790, Samuel Slater established a yarn mill in Pawtucket, Rhode Island. The present-day giant in the textile fabric field, J. P. Stevens and Company, is descended from Slater's mill. For decades, though, fabric production remained both a hand operation and a home industry, totally inadequate to meet the demand. Then Francis Cabot Lowell, a New Englander, visited a textile factory in England and memorized the detailed specifications of its power-operated machinery. In 1814 Lowell built the first successful power loom and the first textile fabric mill in the United States.

The demands of a rapidly growing country provided an eager market for the output of American textile mills, and the young industry flourished. Even more automation and mechanization followed. Today it is possible for a single operator to oversee as many as 100 weaving machines if the fabric is not too detailed.

Organization and Operation

For decades, there was no pattern of organization in the textile fabric industry. Some textile fabric companies were large corporations employing thousands of people, but many remained small operations with only a few dozen employ-

TABLE 6-2 • THE FIVE LARGEST PUBLICLY HELD U.S. TEXTILE COMPANIES

Name	Annual Sales (Millions of Dollars)
Burlington	$3,279,300
West Point Pepperell*	2,067,400
Springs Industries	1,661,100
J. P. Stevens*	1,614,700
Fieldcrest/Cannon	1,399,800

*Merged in 1988. J. P. Stevens bought West Point Pepperell.

Source: "Fortune 500 Industrial Corporations," *Fortune,* April 25, 1988, pp. D1–D37.

ees. In 1985, a wave of mergers occurred, involving half of the nation's 15 biggest textile mills. Industry experts predict that the merger mania will result in fewer but stronger companies. Table 6-2 shows the five largest textile companies in the United States.

Textile industry mergers generally assume one of two forms. The first is for a company to buy all or part of a competitor in order to dominate a segment of the market. The second and less popular strategy is for a company to diversify by buying an apparel company that manufactures clothes out of imported apparel fabric.[5]

Mergers have contributed to reduced industry size. The American Textile Manufacturers Institute (ATMI), a trade group, estimates that the industry's productive capacity has shrunk by 10 percent since 1981. Textile companies have closed more than 230 plants, most of which made apparel fabric. The Federal Reserve Bank of Atlanta states that North and South Carolina, the two biggest manufacturing states, have lost more than 60,000 jobs in the past five years.[6]

We're designing a brand new company with one person in mind. Our customer.

When Hoechst and Celanese Corporation joined forces, we never forgot what gave each of us our strength in the first place. Our customer.

And now our unity opens the way to even greater opportunities for you.

We have the diversity of products so vital in today's complex business climate. Products like Trevira‚ Linenesque‚ Comfort Fiber‚ ESP‚ Universe‚ Ceylon‚ Pentaloft‚ Serene‚ Trevira‚ for FR, Celebrate! And the list goes on.

Fibers for nearly every need—from apparel, carpeting and home furnishings to nonwovens and high-loft materials. With the added benefit of knowledge and expertise that extends around the globe.

Enhanced R&D activities assuring you the newest product characteristics, the newest variants and the newest fibers to meet your customer's demands.

Add to this our responsive technical support, our diverse marketing services and a commitment to quality in all that we do.

This is the beginning of a brand new company designed with one person in mind.

You, our customer.

Our unity is your opportunity.

Hoechst Celanese

Hoechst ▣

Shortly after the merger of Hoechst and Celanese, two large fiber and yarn producers, this ad appeared in trade journals to promote the advantages of the newly merged firm.

Textile mills are widely dispersed throughout the country. The industry has tended to seek areas where labor and land costs are low. There has also been little advantage in concentrating production in any one area through the construction of giant mills or complexes. A small mill can operate mainly as efficiently as a large one, because textile machinery has a long useful life and output can be increased by adding extra work shifts. Textile mills used to be concentrated in the northeastern states, but in recent years the southeastern part of the country has offered cheaper labor and land.

TECHNOLOGY TALK

NYLON BLOWS OUT 50 CANDLES

In 1938 Du Pont unveiled a new fiber and named it nylon. This was not the first choice of names for their new baby, originally named "Duparooh"—an acronym for "Du Pont pulls a rabbit out of a hat." The final name nylon came from nylon stocking's widely ballyhooed "no-run" feature.

However, the new baby was not an immediate success. But in 1939 at the New York World's Fair, the 1-year-old put on quite a show! They had a huge machine pull coal, water, and air into one end . . . and out rolled a pair of sheer nylon stockings at the other end. Sheer magic! Every woman visiting the Du Pont exhibit at the World's Fair couldn't wait for these magical nylon stockings to appear in stores so that they could be the first ones to wear them.

Famous for being the first synthetic fiber, nylon is now a $14 billion business worldwide. Since nylon's electrifying entry into the stocking business, it has been made into toothbrushes, apparel, tires.

Its greatest accolade, however, has been as stockings, where it has adorned celebrated legs from Betty Grable's to Cher's. Nylon stockings exploded onto the scene in 1939 and out went saggy cotton hose and expensive silk stockings. Most women could afford nylons, which were sleeker and sexier than anything on the market, and they created "nylon riots" in stores across the country.

By the late 1940s nylon made its way into women's clothing, and the fiber's ability to bounce back to its original shape after being washed made it an instant success. Through the 1950s, nylon appeared in menswear and the 1960s ushered in the nylon family cousins: Orlon, Dacron, and Lycra.

Nylon has also played a major role in the military and has helped us in World War II

After waiting for hours to buy nylons when they first went on sale after World War II, this woman couldn't wait to get home to try them!

where it made mass paratroop drops possible by nylon parachutes replacing the costly silk ones—and lightweight nylon airplane tires meant that planes could carry heavier bomb loads. The same uses apply today, but now nylon parts go into the most sophisticated jet fighters and are a part of the new escape system for space shuttle astronauts.

Looking forward to its 100th birthday in 2038, nylon and its family of famous cousins will continue to create and innovate. In 1986, a combination of nylon and Teflon was made into a carpet fabric called Stainmaster, and helped that segment of the carpet business grow 10 percent in 1 year. Nylon technology will find its way into the leading edges of biotechnology, superconductivity, and computers to create new uses for nylon and its cousins. But it will be in fashion, its first love, where nylon will try to surpass itself.

This Technology Talk is based on information from the following sources:

American Textiles International, "The Nylon Revolution," April 1988, pp. 28–38.
Kevin Maney, "Nylon: 'The Fabric of Everyday Life,'" *USA Today,* January 12, 1988, pp. 1B and 2B.
Marita Thomas and Richard G. Mansfield, "Happy Birthday, Nylon!," *Textile World,* March 1988, pp. 61–66.

Because commitments to specific weaves, colors, and finishes must be made far in advance, the textile fabric industry is extremely well-informed about fashion and alert to new trends. Information about these trends comes from fashion designers, predictive services, fashion directors for fiber or yarn companies, and advance textile shows throughout the world. But because they are geared to mass-production methods, most mills are reluctant to produce short experimental runs for individual designers.

The market centers for textile fabrics are not at the mills but in the fashion capital of the country, New York City. There, on the doorstep of the garment industry, every mill of importance has a salesroom. A fabric buyer or designer for a garment maker, or a retail store apparel buyer or fashion coordinator, only has to walk a block or two to obtain firsthand information on what the fabric market offers.

Types of Mills

Some mills sort and select the fibers to be used, spin them into yarn, then weave or knit them and finish the fabric. Finishing may include dyeing, napping, adding fire retardants, glazing, waterproofing, and pressing. It may also include treating the fabric to ensure such attributes as nonshrinkage and permanent press. Fashion influences decisions every step of the way.

Some mills produce only the yarn. Others weave or knit fabric from purchased yarn but do not carry the process beyond the greige state. There are also plants that bleach, dye, preshrink, print, or in other ways impart desired characteristics to fabrics produced by other mills. The plants that handle the various stages may or may not be under common ownership, and may or may not be geographically close to one another.

For richer and deeper color, yarns may be dyed before being woven or knitted. This process is known as **yarn-dyed.** However, most fabrics are knitted or woven first and then dyed. This process is known as **piece-dyed.** The piece-dyed process gives manufacturers maximum flexibility.

Many mills no longer limit themselves to working with yarns made of a single fiber. Fibers may be used alone or with other fibers, as demand dictates. Any of the types of mills described above may combine a natural fiber with another natural fiber, or, more commonly, a natural fiber with a man-made fiber, to achieve a desired effect. Examination of the fiber content labels on garments shows how widespread the man-made fibers are.

The Converter

It is probably correct to say that the textile converter is the real middleman of the textile industry. **Textile converters** buy greige goods from the mills, have the goods processed to order by the finishing plants, and then sell the finished goods to garment makers. Therefore, textile converters must be on top of trends in colors, patterns, and finishes. They must fully understand fashion and must be able to anticipate demand. Converters work very quickly since they come on the production scene toward the end of the operation, and are primarily interested in the finish and texture applied to the greige goods.

In recent years, converters' know-how has helped American textile producers meet the competition from foreign textile producers who offer more fashion-oriented goods in small yardages. Converters can supply apparel producers with fewer yards of selected fabrics than can larger fabric mills. The latter must produce tremendous yardages of a designated pattern or design in order to maintain a profitable operation. While many converters are small operators, others, such as Springs Industries and Concord, are large.

Merchandising and Marketing

Like Dior, many designers let the fabric act as the creative impetus for their designs. Good designers respond to new fabrics and search for that special fabric that will drape in the way they want or has just the color or texture they need. It is the job of the fabric industry to introduce designers to the particular fabric needed.

The textile industry works several seasons ahead. Fiber producers usually work 2 years ahead of a season. They must present their products this early to textile mills and converters so they will have enough lead time to plan their color and fabric lines. The fabric market presents its products a year ahead of a season. Their first presentation is to the manufacturers of apparel and accessories, after which they present their finished products to retail stores and the press—all ahead of season—so they can publicize upcoming trends.

Since the textile industry must work several seasons ahead of consumer demand, it must also take the lead in recognizing new fashion directions.

The Industry's Fashion Experts

To guide them in future planning, textile firms employ staffs of fashion experts. These experts work with textile designers to create fabrics in the weights, textures, colors, and patterns that they anticipate consumers will want. Since most of the early decisions in both the fiber and the fabric market are based on color, the industry's fashion experts also work closely with specialized associations within the fashion industry that provide advance research and trend information.

Most prominent among these groups are the ones that work exclusively with color, such as the Color Association of the United States, the International Color Authority (ICA), the Color Box, and Huepoint.

Color forecasting services provide their clients with reports and newsletters, color swatches, palette predictions, and color-matching services—all geared to each of the apparel markets (men's, women's, children's).

In addition to making decisions about color, the fabric industry must also consider fabrication and texture. If the trend is toward structured clothing, firm fabrication will be necessary, but when a soft, layered look is in, fabrication can be lightweight and soft.

Since trends must be spotted so far in the future, the fashion experts play an important role as they work with fiber and fabric mills as well as designers and buyers.

Textile Trade Shows and Fairs

New trends are also introduced at trade shows and fairs held throughout the world. Usually semiannual events, these shows are attended by designers, manufacturers, and retailers. The most important of these shows are the Interstoff Textile Fair in Frankfurt, Germany, the Ideocomo in Como, Italy, the Premiere Vision in Paris, France, Textalia in Milan, Italy, and the Canton Trade Fair in Canton, China. Two other well-known shows are the Knitting Yarn Fair and the New York Fabric Show, both in New York City.

The importance of identifying dominant trends becomes more important each year as the competition becomes keener and the market becomes increasingly global. The failure to identify and act on a trend seen at a major textile show, for example, would mean that retailers and apparel manufacturers would be unable to supply the fashions that consumers want.

Advertising and Publicity

Like fiber producers, fabric manufacturers advertise lavishly. Unlike the fiber producers, their advertising usually features the brand names of their products and frequently the names of specific apparel manufacturers that use their goods. Either with the cooperation of fiber sources or on their own, these fabric houses sponsor radio and television programs, run full-color advertisements in a wide variety of mass-circulation magazines and newspapers, and share the cost of brand advertising run by retail stores. Their advertising generally makes consumers aware of new apparel styles, the fabrics of which they are made, and often the names of retail stores where they may be purchased.

Fabric producers compete among themselves for the business of apparel producers. They also compete for recognition among retail store buyers and for consumer acceptance of products made of their goods. They publicize brand names and fabric developments, and stage seasonal fashion shows in market areas for retailers and the fashion press. They provide hang-tags for the use of garment manufacturers. These tags may bear not only the fabric's brand name but also instructions relating to its care. In accordance with federal regulation, fabric producers also supply manufacturers with the required care labels that must be permanently sewn into all garments. Many fabric firms supply information to consumers and the trade press and make educational materials available to schools, consumer groups, and retail sales personnel.

Research and Development

Fabric producers, like fiber producers, now devote attention to exploring the market potential of their products and anticipating the needs of their customers. Success in the fashion industry depends on supplying customers with what they want. Swift changes are the rule in fashion. Anticipation of such changes requires close attention to the market and a scientific study of trends. Market research is used to identify changing lifestyles as well as geographic demands.

Many of the large fabric producers maintain product- and market-research divisions. Their experts work closely with both the trade and consumer markets in studying fabric performance characteristics. Many fabric producers provide garment manufacturers with sample runs of new fabrics for experimental purposes. The market researchers conduct consumer studies relating to the demand for or acceptance of finishes, blends, and other desired characteristics. Such studies also help fabric and garment producers to determine what consumers will want in the future, where and when they will want it, and in what quantities.

Customer Services

Today's well-integrated and diversified fabric companies speak with great fashion authority. They also employ merchandising and marketing staffs whose expertise in fashion trends is available to apparel manufacturers, retailers, the fashion press, and frequently to consumers. Fashion staffs attend fashion forecasts. They conduct in-store sales training programs, address consumer groups, and stage fashion shows for the trade and press. They help retail stores arrange fashion shows and storewide promotions featuring their products, and they assist buyers in locating merchandise made from their fabrics.

TRENDS IN THE TEXTILE FABRIC INDUSTRY

A dramatic change in the mindset of the textile producers and marketing managers has broadened the product mix, quickened the response time required to meet customer demand, and made possible shorter runs of more innovative and fashionable fabrics. Currently, retailers, apparel manufacturers, and the fiber and fabric industries are working together to explore new and innovative ways to move textile products through the pipeline to the ultimate consumer more quickly and efficiently.

Fortunately, the consumption rate of textiles increases every year. Economists forecast that this trend will continue and even accelerate in the 1990s. The role of the textile fiber and fabric industries in the U.S. economy is an important one. These industries employ one out of every ten Americans in manufacturing. All these factors combine to make the textile business one of the nation's most essential industries.

Some of the major trends that affect both the fiber and fabric industries are the growing global market, increased exports, greater diversification of products, increased government regulations, and expanded mechanization and automation.

Briefly Speaking

High-Tech Fabrics

High-tech fabrics—the new breed of textiles specially engineered for athletes and active wear—are finding their way into everyday fashions for streetwear, weekend wear, and spectator sportswear.

These fabrics, engineered to resist extreme temperature changes and athletic stresses from the frigid Alaskan ice fields to the windy heights of the Himalayas, or more ordinary applications for running, cycling, boating, and golfing, are making their way into many new fashion markets.

A sparkling future is forecast for these specialized fabrics—whether made of nylon, polyester, acrylic, or more esoteric fibers. An outstanding example is a knit fabric blending Hydrofil, polyester, and Lycra spandex that moves moisture away from the body. It is currently being used in cross-country ski tights, sports tops, cycling jerseys, jackets, face masks, and gloves. High-tech fabrics can create a situation where the athlete's mind and body is more comfortable . . . allowing the wearer to play that extra set . . . take off those extra seconds . . . or make that added distance.

Consumer reaction to high-tech fabrics is mixed. The experts say it is because high-tech products are generally more expensive and require an educated customer. But as more athletes use these high-tech products, consumers will learn more about them, and jump on the high-tech bandwagon.

This Briefly Speaking is based on information from the following source:

Tina Cantelmi, "High-Tech Fabrics Charge into Fashion," *WWD/DNR* insert, *Retailing Technology and Operations*, May 1988, p. 18.

The Growing Global Market

The major industry concern is the growth of a global market that shows every promise of being permanent. Although the domestic fiber and fabric industries produce a huge amount of goods, the United States still imports large quantities of fiber, yarn, and fabric from around the world. Since 1980 imports have grown an average of 16 percent annually while domestic growth in the textile industry has slowed to less than 1 percent. Over 330,000 jobs have been lost in the U.S. textile industry. Imports now account for more than 52 percent of U.S. clothing sales. The textile and apparel trade deficit hit an astounding $18 billion in 1987.[7]

Like other American industries, the fiber and fabric mills have been adversely affected by overseas competition. Wages are cheaper in those markets, and U.S. apparel makers have turned to such countries as Korea and China for fabrics. As a result, many domestic textile companies have restricted their production of apparel fabrics and gone into the more lucrative production of industrial and household goods.

Not surprisingly, another trend, limited to fabric producers, is toward the acquisition or establishment of mills abroad. Such foreign-based mills may be wholly owned by a U.S. firm or jointly owned by a U.S. firm and a host-country firm. Most mills are located close to the fiber sources. The engineers may be American or American-trained, but the rest of the staff are local workers who are paid according to local wage scales. Advantages to the host-country firm are the availability of the facilities, the fashion knowledge, the technical skill of the U.S. owners or part owners, and increased employment opportunities for its citizens. By producing some goods abroad, domestic manufacturers are able to defend themselves against the competition of foreign-made fabrics. They can also put themselves in a more favorable position to sell in countries where tariff walls limit or keep out goods made in the United States.

Another trend involves foreign business firms buying into fabric or finishing plants here. Some of these firms are becoming partners in, or sole owners of, new facilities being built here. An example is Hoechst, a West German company which bought Celanese, a major American producer.

Despite these trends, domestic producers, particularly given their closeness to their customer, still have a number of important advantages over importers. They can react faster, provide shorter lead time, structure shorter production runs, and in general, remove much of the guesswork that used to hinder the industry.

Increasing Exports

The industry is also directing more of its efforts toward capturing a share of the global market. A number of corporate strategies for the years ahead include:

- Increasing focus on foreign markets and operations for apparel fabrics, since most studies indicate that the major growth in apparel markets will be outside the United States.
- Developing overseas manufacturing operations, or exploring licensing in conjunction with foreign mills, in order to attain a stronger foothold on the international scene.
- Devoting increased resources to market research.

For example, the United States is currently a world leader in home-furnishing textiles, offering more diversified products than any other country. In an attempt to expand this trade, the U.S. textile industry is focusing more of its manufacturing and marketing activities abroad on fabrics for home furnishing and industrial end uses, which are projected to gain larger market shares in the future. The recently enacted Trading Companies Act should significantly assist in increasing export opportunities for the U.S. textile industry. This act was designed to protect American exporters from world currency fluctuations when competing internationally.[8]

Greater Diversification of Products

Today, the textile industry produces a more diversified range of fibers and fabrics than ever before. The specialization that once divided the industry into separate segments, each producing fabrics from a single type of fiber, has all but faded. To meet the needs of consumers, it is often necessary to blend two or more fibers into a yarn or to combine a warp yarn of one fiber with a weft yarn of another. Mills are learning to adjust their operations to any new fiber or combination of fibers.

One of the largest firms in the field illustrate how the industry is moving toward greater product diversification. Burlington, originally a rayon mill specializing in bedspreads, now produces and sells spun and textured yarns of both natural and man-made fibers. Its new products include a variety of finished woven and knitted fabrics, some unfinished fabrics, and hosiery for men, women, and children. It also produces domestic and home furnishings ranging from bed linens to rugs and furniture.

Increased Government Regulation

One of the biggest impacts on the textile industry in the last decade has been the intervention of the federal government in every aspect of the industry: health and safety, noise levels and chemical pollution, consumer product liability, environment, and hiring practices.

Until recently, federal regulation of the textile industry was mainly concerned with the fiber content labeling of fabrics and products made of those fabrics, In 1954, the Flammable Fabrics Act was passed, but it served to ban from the market only a few very ignitable fabrics and apparel made from them. The increasing strength and direction of the consumerism movement, however, resulted in more government regulation of the textile industry on both the federal and state levels.

In July 1972, two important changes in federal textile regulations took effect: the Federal Trade Commission's rule on Care Labeling of Textile Wearing Apparel and the revision of the Flammable Fabrics Act. The FTC's care-labeling rule requires that all fabrics—piece goods as well as apparel and accessories made of fabric—be labeled to show the type of care they require. The label must indicate whether the fabric can be hand washed or machine washed or should be dry-cleaned. If the fabric can be washed, the label must give the temperature at which it should be washed and whether bleach can be used. The label must also indicate whether ironing is required, and if so, at what temperature. The manufacturer must sew a permanent label with these care instructions into each garment.

Other trends in the textile industry that are a result of government environmental and consumer regulations include:

- Fibers and textile products will be made by larger producers with a resulting decrease in the number of small concerns and marginal operations. This will result primarily from the higher production costs related to complying with the new government regulations and the greater capital investment required to stay competitive in a period of continually rising costs.
- Manufacturing operations will function at higher efficiencies, recycling as much material as possible and converting waste to energy.
- Fibers with built-in environmental disadvantages will slowly give way to more suitable replacements, or new processing techniques will be devised to allow their continued use.
- Transfer printing may be an important way to reduce some of the dye-house stream-pollution problems.
- Consumers will be increasingly protected, with particular emphasis on children's apparel and home furnishings.
- Consumers will be better advised on the characteristics of their purchases.

Fabric being quilted by computer. The computer operator types in the program and the machinery automatically forms the desired pattern in quilting.

FASHION

When shopping for clothing most consumers look for features that include style, quality, fashion, fit, price, and ease of care. And increasingly, they are also looking for a label that says Made in U.S.A.—thanks to the efforts of the Crafted With Pride in U.S.A. Council.

Formed in 1984, the Council is dedicated to strengthening the economic and competitive positions of the U.S. textile, apparel, and home-furnishings industries. Its members include cotton growers and shippers, fabric distributors, labor organizations, and manufacturers of man-made fibers, fabrics, apparel, and home fashions, who all together employ about 10 percent of America's manufacturing workforce.[1]

The mission of the Crafted With Pride in U.S.A. Council is simple: "to convince consumers, retailers, and apparel manufacturers of the value of purchasing and promoting United States–made products"—in other words, to demonstrate clearly to the American buying public "why 'buying American' is the right choice for them and for the U.S. economy."[2]

To fulfill that mission, the Council has been working with retailers and manufacturers to improve and increase domestic sourcing. It has also conducted a massive communications campaign, which includes national television advertising packed with celebrities, from Bob Hope to Loretta Swit, telling the country "it matters to me." In-store events have been part of the program, as well, such as a week-long Made in U.S.A. promotion staged by Tampa, Florida–based Maas Brothers in 1987, which drew more than 1,400 consumers to fashion events and a personal appearance by actor Robert Stack.[3]

Also, since 1987, the Council has linked itself with the Miss America pageant, using the reigning "queen" as well as 1979's Miss America, Kylene Barker Brandon, as spokeswomen to spread the "Made in U.S.A." message across the land.

There are certainly plenty of statistics to back up the Council's whole reason for being. For example, in 1985, the United States imported 10 billion

FOCUS

square yards of textiles and apparel, which translated to a loss of one million job opportunities and $40 billion of Gross National Product.[4] What's more, imports of apparel have been growing steadily over the past decade. In 1974, only 15 percent of all apparel sold in the United States was imported; by 1986, imports had climbed to an all-time high of 54 percent.[5]

Despite that dramatic increase, it appears that American consumers like to buy United States–made goods. In a test run by K mart for its Comfort Action slacks, the retailer ran two advertisements that were identical—except that one used the "Made in U.S.A." logo, and the other didn't. The result? The ad with the logo generated 21 percent higher sales.[6] A similar test with Hanover House Industries showed that catalog sales were 10 percent higher when advertised items carried a "Made in U.S.A." logo as compared to those without the logo.[7]

Of course, the Crafted With Pride campaign is not based purely on patriotism. Retailers realize that, especially on more fashionable items, domestic manufacturers are able to respond more quickly to a fashion trend, and deliver orders—and reorders—faster than suppliers overseas. And as long as the quality and price are right, that's a powerful reason to buy American.

Even the Associated Merchandising Corporation, which traditionally imported about two-thirds of its apparel for member stores, recently made the commitment to increase its supply of domestic goods. Said Lee Abraham, AMC's chairman and chief executive officer: "I think most retailers would agree the days of taking extraordinary profits from imports are over. That's one of the reasons AMC's goal now is to strengthen our sourcing in the American market right here on our doorstep."[8] And that's a goal to make Crafted with Pride proud.

[1] From a Crafted With Pride in U.S.A. Council, Inc., brochure.

[2] Ibid.

[3] Robert E. Swift, " 'Made in U.S.A.' Gains Momentum at Retail," *California Apparel News,* June 26–July 2, 1987, p. 32.

[4] From a Crafted With Pride in U.S.A. Council, Inc., brochure.

[5] "Price of Imported Apparel Exceeds Price of Domestic Apparel," Marketing Research Corporation of America, February 1987.

[6] " 'Made in U.S.A.' Logo Increases K mart Sales," press release from Crafted With Pride in U.S.A. Council, Inc.

[7] "Use of Made in U.S.A. Logo Increased Sales by 10%," press release from Crafted With Pride in U.S.A. Council, Inc.

[8] Marvin Klapper, "Patriotism and Profits at AMC," *Women's Wear Daily,* June 23, 1987, p. 14.

This Fashion Focus is based on information from the articles cited above and from this source:

Lena Gilliam, "Former Miss America Focuses on American Fashion," *California Apparel News,* June 26–July 2, 1987, p. 29.

Expanded Mechanization and Automation

The trend toward increased mechanization and automation is clearly apparent throughout the industry as it has changed from one that is labor-intensive to one that is equipment-intensive.

In the mills, new machines combine higher production speeds with lower energy consumption. Automated weaving and knitting machines produce more with fewer operators.

The industry is also experimenting with new printing techniques. Rotary-screen printing is truly the technology of the twenty-first century that will replace flat-screen and roller printing techniques.[9] Powerful computers will enable the industry to set the cost and price of fabrics before they are knitted or woven. These elements are needed to be competitive in the global textile market.

The industry experimented widely with robots in the 1980s, and will probably employ them with increasing frequency in the 1990s. Although the new technology has created job losses, it will ultimately help the industry by attracting bright, ambitious young workers and leaders who want to work in a progressive environment.

One thing is certain: The fully automated textile plant is not just a dream. All the pieces of the puzzle have been laid out on the table. They only need someone to assemble them.[10]

Any student of group dynamics knows that one of the ways to make a group cohesive is to declare a common enemy. With rising imports clearly marked as the common enemy of the American textile industry, the industry finds itself working cooperatively for the first time. One example is the industry-wide campaign "Crafted With Pride in U.S.A.," which is discussed on pages 140–141. By strengthening their numbers, domestic fiber and fabric producers are growing more and more fit. But then, they have no choice.

REFERENCES

[1] Jane Dorner, *Fashion in the Forties and Fifties,* Arlington House, New Rochelle, N.Y., 1975, p. 38.

[2] Man-Made Fiber Producers Association, Inc. *Focus # 9.*

[3] Dianne M. Pagoda, "Polyester Council Striving to Change the Fabric's Image," *Women's Wear Daily,* July 17, 1987, p. 8.

[4] Marvin Klapper, "Man-Mades: In Search of the Right Stuff," *Women's Wear Daily, 75 Years of Fashion, 1910–1985,* Special Section Supplement, Fairchild Publications, November 19, 1987, p. 76.

[5] "Textile Companies Rapidly Stake Out Niches," *Wall Street Journal,* February 5, 1986, p. 6.

[6] Ibid.

[7] Heidi Novotny, "TALA Topics," *California Apparel News,* June 26–July 2, 1987, p. 33.

[8] Stu Campbell, "Study Tells Textile Industry to Pursue International Business," *Daily News Record,* November 22, 1982, p. 12.

[9] Dianne M. Pagoda, "Textile Printing in the 21st Century," *Technology & Operations Supplement, Women's Wear Daily,* March 1987, p. 4.

[10] Cornelius Cahill, "The Textile Automation Puzzle: Fitting the Pieces Together," *American Textiles International,* April 1987, pp. 28–31.

MERCHANDISING VOCABULARY

Define or briefly explain the following terms:

Cellulosic fiber	Licensed trademark	Ramie
Cooperative	Linen	Silk
advertising	Man-made fiber	Spinnerette
Cotton	Natural fiber	Textile converter
Fiber	Noncellulosic fiber	Textile fabric
Flax	Piece-dyed	Wool
Generic name	Polymers	Yarn
Greige goods	Primary supplier	Yarn-dyed

MERCHANDISING REVIEW

1. What is the difference between a natural and a man-made fiber? Give five examples of each, and indicate the source of each natural fiber you name.
2. What has the natural fiber industry done to counteract the effects of man-made fibers in the marketplace?
3. Trace the steps through which a new or newly modified man-made fiber goes from its conception to its general availability.
4. Name and explain the three ways in which producers of man-made fibers usually sell their products to fabric manufacturers.
5. Describe the three major merchandising and marketing activities of natural and man-made fiber producers.
6. Describe the major steps in the production of most fabrics.
7. What is the function of the textile converter? What are the advantages of dealing with a converter for (*a*) a fabric mill, and (*b*) an apparel producer?
8. How do textile fabric producers keep informed about new fashion trends?
9. How have increased fiber, yarn, and fabric imports affected the American textile industry?
10. What are the provisions of the Flammable Fabrics Act of 1954 and the FTC's rule on Care Labeling of Textile Wearing Apparel of 1972?

MERCHANDISING DIGEST

1. What is the role of trade associations in the marketing of fibers and textile fabrics?
2. When a major designer designed his collection for a mass merchandiser, he went directly to the textile mills with specifications for his fabrics in regard to width, pattern repeats, etc. Can most designers do this? Why or why not?
3. Discuss the relationship of the designer and the manufacturer of fashion merchandise to the textile industry.

LEATHER AND FUR

The most glamorous and sought-after textiles—leather and fur—are also the two oldest. Prehistoric people discovered that the animals they killed for food could serve another purpose, that of providing them with warmth and protection from the elements. One side of an animal skin could be worked into leather; the other furnished fur. Today leather and fur are vital to the fashion industry, contributing the raw materials for coats and jackets, handbags, shoes, gloves, and an ever-widening range of garments.

The leather industry is currently in the process of expanding its markets in ways that no one even dreamed of 10 years ago. New processing methods have created leathers so thin and supple that designers can use them for everything from bikinis to shirts to evening wear—all available in an incredible array of colors.

After several years of decline because of environmental concerns over the use of scarce or rare animal skins, furs are making a comeback, especially with the young, first-time customer. The demand for furs has never been greater, at the very time when the fur industry is experimenting with new colors and styles for coats, jackets, capes, and even some new items of apparel, such as vests and scarves.

THE LEATHER INDUSTRY

Leather-making is a highly specialized and time-consuming operation. Because of the time involved, the leather industry must anticipate and predict trends far in advance of other textile suppliers. Leather producers typically decide what production method, textures, finishes, and colors they will use 8 to 16 months before a leather will reach apparel and accessory manufacturers. As a result, those in other fashion industries often look to the leather industry for leadership, particularly in terms of color and texture.

Since leather is a by-product of the meat-packing industry, it is not the target of environmentalists as is the fur industry. No animal is raised specifically for its hide. Animals are raised to feed people, and their skins and hides, which have no food value, are then sold to the leather trade.

History and Development

In the many years that Indian tribes roamed the North American continent, long before the arrival of the first European colonists, the tanning of leather was an important part of tribal life. Indians used deerskins to make clothing, soft yet sturdy moccasins, and tepee homes. By today's tanning standards, their methods would be considered limited and primitive, yet the techniques they used to transform raw animal hides into a variety of products certainly served them well.

In 1623, not long after the arrival of the Pilgrims to Massachusetts, the first commercial tannery in the American colonies was established in Plymouth by an Englishman with the fitting name of Experience Miller. Later Peter Minuit, Governor of New Amsterdam, invented the first machinery used for tanning in the colonies. His invention was a horse-driven stone mill that ground the oak bark then used to convert animal skins into leather.

Many years passed before more important mechanization of the leather industry occurred. But in 1809, a giant step was taken. Samuel Parker invented a machine that could split heavy steer hides 25 times faster than men could do it by hand. The machine also produced a lighter and more supple leather, just what the people wanted for their shoes, boots, and other clothing.

Today new machines do much of the manual work formerly required to stir hides and skins as they soaked. Other machines dehair and deflesh them. Still others split the skins and emboss patterns on them. Machinery has taken much of the human labor out of the processing of leather. In addition, chemistry has provided new tanning agents that reduce the time required to transform hides and skins into leather. These new tanning agents also help achieve a greater variety of finishes.

Mechanization has had little effect, however, in reducing the total amount of time needed for the tanning process. Prolonged exposure to a series of treatments remains necessary to transform hides and skins into leather. What mechanization has brought is an extraordinary new variety of leather colors, textures, and finishes to leather. This variety is possible in spite of restrictions on the commercial use of some animal skins that have been placed on endangered-species lists.

Organization and Operation

Although tanning was once a cottage industry, it has become, relatively speaking, big business. Nearly 16,000 workers are employed in the American tanning industry, and they turn out $1.7 billion worth of tanned leathers annually.[1]

Like the textile industry, the leather business has been subjected to its share of mergers. In 1870, over 4,500 tanneries operated in the United States; today there are fewer than 300. More mergers are predicted for the future, which will lead to fewer and larger plants.

Organization

The American leather industry is divided into three major types of companies: regular tanneries, contract tanneries, and converters. **Regular tanneries** purchase and process skins and hides and sell the leather as their finished product. **Contract tanneries** process the hides and skins to the specifications of other firms (mainly converters), but are not involved in the final sale of the leather. **Converters** buy the hides and skins from the meat packers, commission the tanning to the contract tanneries, and then sell the finished leather. In recent years, converters have been buying finished leather from both regular and contract tanneries.

The leather industry has remained specialized. Calfskin tanners do not normally tan kidskin, and gloveskin tanners do not work with sole leather.

Most U.S. tanneries are located in the northeast and north central states. The industry's major customers—the shoe, apparel, and accessory manufacturers—are clustered in these regions as well. Like textile producers, most leather firms maintain sales offices or representatives in New York City for the convenience of their customers.

Sources of Leather Supply

Almost all leather comes from cattle. But the hides and skins of many other animals from all parts of the world are also used in fashion. Kid and goatskins come from Europe, Asia, Africa, and South America; capeskin comes from a special breed of sheep raised in South Africa and South America; pigskin comes from the peccary, a wild hog native to Mexico and South America; and buffalo comes from Asia.

Kips being tanned in a factory. Many hand processes are still used, and leather craft has remained relatively unchanged.

The variety of glove leathers alone illustrates how worldwide are the sources of leather:

- *Cabretta* from South American sheep.
- *Calfskin* from young calves of the United States and elsewhere.
- *Goatskin* from South America, South Africa, India, and Spain.
- *Kidskin* from Europe.
- *Pigskin* from Yugoslavia, Mexico, and Central and South America.
- *Buckskin* from deer and elk in Mexico, South and Central America, and the People's Republic of China.
- *Mocha* from Asian and African sheep.

Over the next few years, the U.S. tanning and leather finishing industries will show a decline in the value of shipments, due mainly to lower raw materials prices. The U.S. Department of Commerce has predicted that the total employment in leather-related fields will gradually decline.

Leather Processing

Animal pelts are divided into three classes, each based on weight. Those that weigh 15 pounds or less when shipped to the tannery are called **skins.** This class consists mostly of calves, goats, pigs, sheep, and deer. Those weighing from 15 to 25 pounds, mostly from young horses and cattle, are referred to as **kips.** Those weighing more than 25 pounds, primarily cattle, oxen, buffalo, and horse skins, are called **hides.**

The process of transforming animal pelts into leather is known as **tanning.** The word is derived from a Latin word for oak bark, which was used in early treatments of animal skins. Tanning is the oldest known craft.

Three to six months are needed to tan hides for sole leather and saddlery. Less time is required for tanning kips and skins, but the processes are more numerous and require more expensive equipment and highly trained labor. The cowhide that is used for shoe uppers, garments, and accessories can be tanned and finished in 3 to 6 weeks.

The tanning process involves minerals, vegetable materials, oils, and chemicals, used alone or in combination. The choice of a tanning agent depends upon the end use for which the leather is being prepared.

Minerals Two important tanning methods use minerals. One uses alum; the other uses chrome salts. Alum, used by the ancient Egyptians to make writing paper, is rarely utilized today. Chrome tanning, introduced in 1893, is now used to process nearly two-thirds of all leather produced in this country. This is a fast method that produces leather for shoe uppers, gloves, handbags, and other products. Chrome-tanned leather can be identified by the pale, blue-gray color in the center of the cut edge. It is slippery when wet. It is usually washable and can be cleaned by gentle sponging.

Vegetable Materials Vegetable tanning, which is also an old method, uses the tannic acids that naturally occur in the bark, wood, or nuts of various trees and shrubs and in tea leaves. Vegetable tanning is used on cow, steer, horse, and buffalo hides. The product is a heavy, often relatively stiff leather used for the soles of shoes, some shoe uppers, some handbags and belts, and saddlery. Vegetable-tanned leather can be identified by a dark center streak in the cut edge. It is resistant to moisture and can be cleaned by sponging. Vegetable tanning is the slowest tanning method and takes months to complete. Because it is so labor-intensive, relatively little vegetable tanning is done in the United States.

TABLE 7-1 • SPECIAL FINISHES FOR LEATHER

Finishes	Characteristics
Aniline	Polished surface achieved with aniline dyes
Matte (mat)	Flat, eggshell-surface look
Luster or pearl	Soft, opaque finish with a transparent glow
Antiqued	Subtle, two-toned effect like polished antique wood
Burnished	Similar to antiqued, but with less shadowing
Metallic	Surface look of various metals—copper, gold, silver, bronze
Waxy	Dulled, rustic look, as in waxy glove leathers
Patent	Glossy, high-shine finish
Napped	Buffed surface such as in suede or brushed leathers
Suede	Leather finish that can be applied to a wide variety of leathers

Source: William A. Rossi, "What You Should Know About Leathers," *Footwear News Magazine,* June 1982, p. 16.

Oil Processing with oil is one of the oldest methods of turning raw animal skins into leather. A fish oil—usually codfish—is used. Today, oil tanning is used to produce chamois, doeskin, and buckskin—relatively soft and pliable leathers used in making gloves and jackets.

Chemical The most widely used and quickest method of tanning relies primarily on formaldehyde. Because the processing turns the leather white, it can easily be dyed. Formaldehyde-tanned leather is washable. It is often used for gloves and children's shoe uppers.

Combinations It is possible to combine tanning agents. A vegetable and mineral combination is used to "retan" work shoes and boots. Combinations of alum and formaldehyde or oil and chrome are common.

Finishing The finishing process gives leather the desired thickness, moisture, color, and aesthetic appeal. Dyed leather is also sometimes finished with oils and fats to ensure softness, strength, or to waterproof it. Special color effects include sponging, stenciling, spraying, or tie dyeing. Other finishes include matte, luster or pearl, suede, patent, or metallic. Table 7-1 describes the characteristics of different leather finishes.

Merchandising and Marketing

Because of the lead time needed to produce leather, the leather industry not only must stay abreast of fashion, it must be several steps ahead of it. Months before other fashion industries commit themselves to colors and textures, leather producers have already made their decisions. They have started the search for the right dyes and treatments to meet expected future demand. As a result, the leather industry's forecasters are considered the best and most experienced in the fashion industry.

Fashion Information Services

Because they make their assessments of fashion trends so far in advance, others in the industry look to the leather industry for information. Like other fashion industries, the leather industry retains experts to disseminate information about trends and new products in the leather industry.

They often produce booklets that forecast trends, describe new colors and textures, and generally promote the leather industry. Samples of important textures and looks are included.

Fashion experts also work directly with retailers, manufacturers, and the press to help crystallize their thinking about leather products. One-on-one meetings, seminars, and fashion presentations are used to educate the fashion industry and consumers about leather.

Despite all this activity, individual tanners are not known by name to the public. Nor is an editor, in describing a leather garment, likely to mention its manufacturer. Leather producers are not named in retail stores or in leather manufacturers' advertising. Consumers who can name several fabric and fiber producers would have a difficult time naming any leather tanners.

Trade Associations and Trade Shows

Much of the information collected and disseminated by the leather industry comes through its strong trade association, Leather Industries of America (LIA). LIA has worked hard to broaden the market for all types of leathers, often in the face of serious competition. For example, shoe manufacturers, who were important leather users a few years ago, have now turned to other products as well. This has compelled the leather industry to promote and defend its products, and LIA has taken the lead in this activity.

LIA sponsors semiannual color seminars and sells a packet of each season's color swatches to industry members. It supports a Hide Training School and sponsors a student design award. LIA's

LIA publishes many informational papers and booklets, some of which are shown here. Also, LIA is constantly working to promote the benefits and uses of leather.

weekly newspaper, *Council News,* covers the leather industry.

Trade shows are another important source of information within the leather industry. Two years before the ultimate consumer sees finished leather products in retail stores, the leathers are introduced in several industry trade shows. The oldest and most established show, the Semaine du Cuir, is held in Paris in the fall, usually September. The Hong Kong International Leather Fair is held in June, and the Tanners' Apparel and Garment Show (TAG) is held in New York City in October.

Research and Development

The leather industry retains and expands its markets by adapting its products to fashion's changing requirements. Before World War II, relatively few colors and types of leather were available in any one season, and each usually had a fashion life of several years. Today, a major tannery may turn out hundreds of leather colors and types each season, meanwhile preparing to produce more new colors and textures for the next season.

To protect and expand their markets, leather producers constantly broaden their range of colors, weights, and textures. They also introduce improvements that make leather in acceptable material where it formerly had either limited use or no use at all.

Leather has the weight of tradition behind it; people have regarded fine leather as a symbol of luxury for centuries. But today leather shares its hold on the fashion field with other and newer materials. Through product research and development, producers are attempting to meet the competition not only of other leathers but also of other materials.

Industry Trends

Until just a few decades ago, the leather industry concerned itself primarily with meeting consumer needs in relatively few fashion areas—mainly shoes, gloves, belts, handbags, luggage, and small leather goods. The use of leather for apparel was restricted largely to a few items of outerwear, such as jackets and coats. These were stiff, bulky, and primarily functional in appeal.

Today, the leather industry is changing. These changes are the result of three trends: enlarging market opportunities, increased competition from synthetics, and increased foreign trade.

Enlarging Markets

Improved methods of tanning are turning out better, more versatile leathers with improved fashion characteristics. In general, these improvements fall into two categories:

1. The new leathers are softer and more pliable. Tanner's ability to split full-grain leather thinner and thinner creates this new suppleness.
2. The new leathers can be dyed more successfully in a greater number of fashion colors.

Because of these new characteristics, the markets for personal leather goods and leather furniture continue to have the most growth potential.

In cowhide leathers, the demand is high for the lighter-weight, mellow, natural-looking, full-grain leathers. Especially desirable are the glazed, rich-colored, aniline-dyed types that accentuate the natural beauty of the grain that are used predominantly in luggage, portfolios, and furniture. The sheep and lamb tanners are very encouraged by the sustained demand for glazed and suede leathers in the leather apparel market.

Would you believe—leather? Supple and slim, today's leather can be used in styles that show detail and soft styling.

Increased Competition from Synthetics

In the past few decades, the leather market has been eroded by synthetics. Leather heel lifts, which used to be commonplace, are now more often than not replaced with plastic. Synthetics that look and feel like leather but are less susceptible to scratches and easier to maintain are used to make handbags and other small leather goods.

Since most synthetic leather products were not as attractive as leather, synthetics did not offer leather any real competition for a long time. Over a decade ago, however, imitation leathers and suedes that were true substitutes began to be marketed. The most important one, Ultrasuede, quickly became a fashion classic. Although a synthetic, Ultrasuede does not have an image of being fake or cheap, and it is used by such high-fashion designers as Bill Blass, Yves Saint Laurent, and Adolfo.

Increased Foreign Trade

An increased worldwide demand for leather has enabled American hide dealers to obtain higher prices for their products in countries where demand outstrips supply. This, in turn, has led to sharp increases in the export of hides since foreign tanners are able to produce leather more cheaply than their U.S. counterparts.

While the United States has been inundated with cheap leather products in the past few years, its own tanners have turned to exporting their own products. American tanners, known for the high quality of their tanning process and their excellent finishing techniques, have had no trouble expanding into foreign markets.

Industry Growth Factors

Although the leather industry is experiencing a decline in dollar volume, several factors point to overall industry growth. Foremost among these is the trend toward a classic and elegant fashion look with an emphasis on quality. When quality is desired, consumers want real leather with all its mystique and will not settle for substitutes. Another hopeful sign is the fact that the supply of raw hides is large enough to allow for growth in production. Actively supported by a federal export program, the industry's aggressive efforts to develop foreign markets ensures future growth for the industry as does the industry's expanded research programs.

THE FUR INDUSTRY

Long before prehistoric people learned how to plant crops, weave cloth, or build shelters, they figured out how to use fur. They spread it on the floor and used it as rugs. They used it to cover and create walls, thus creating some warmth in an otherwise cold and drafty cave.

By the Middle Ages, the wearing of fur announced one's wealth and status. Sable, marten, ermine, and fox were the favored furs of nobility. Italian cardinals wore ermine as a symbol of purity; English nobles wore it as a sign of power. Fur was also a valued commodity, something that was used in trading. For centuries in Northern Europe, furs were valued more than gold and silver. Fur was still as good as gold in 1900 when Chile banked chinchilla skins as security for a loan.

History and Development

The search for a northwest passage that would shorten the route between Europe and the Orient led to the establishment of the fur trade in North America. When French explorer Jacques Cartier arrived at the mouth of the St. Lawrence River in 1534, he traded furs with the Indians. The next year, when he sailed even farther up the river, he realized what a vast wealth of fur-bearing animals existed on the continent. English and Dutch explorers soon joined the French in setting up trading posts. The first posts were situated along the St. Lawrence and Hudson rivers, but they soon dotted the continent. Early fur-trading posts played a role in establishing such cities as St. Louis, Chicago, Detroit, St. Paul, and Spokane.

The plentiful supply of furs helped the colonists in other ways. They were able to export furs and use the money to bring European necessities—and even some luxuries—to their New World. Furs were an important source of clothing and furnishings. For a while in the mid-eighteenth century, furs were virtually the currency of North America.

It is the beaver, however, that truly deserves a special place in North American history. The discovery of this fur led to a "fur rush" that rivaled the Gold Rush. Beaver was used mostly to make men's hats, but in Canada in 1733, one beaver pelt could also buy a pound of sugar or two combs or six thimbles or eight knives. Settlers pushed west in search of beaver, leaving behind communities with names like Beaver Creek, Beaver Falls, and Beaver Lakes. Fortunes were made. John Jacob Astor was among the first to become a millionaire in the beaver trade. He dreamed of a beaver-fur empire stretching from New York to the Northwest Territory.

Ironically, just as beavers were becoming scarce, the fashion changed. Abraham Lincoln wore a silk top hat to his inauguration, and men stopped wearing beaver hats and began to buy hats made of silk and felt. The demand for beaver ceased overnight.

The interest in women's furs remained strong, however, and during the Civil War, the first mink ranch was established by T. D. Phillips and W. Woodstock. In 1880, silver fox fur farming began on Prince Edward Island, off the eastern coast of Canada. Fur farming and ranching have undergone renewed expansion in the past half century.

Fashions in furs do change, although they change less quickly than do other apparel styles because furs are expensive. While mink coats account for half of all furs sold today, fifty years ago a

Briefly Speaking

Smaller Furriers Market with Celebrities

Smaller fur salons and retailers can now market their furs with a celebrity plug, thanks to a new advertising company catering exclusively to them. Most small furriers and stores search for new ways to get their names known, yet keep the costs down. Advertising takes one of the biggest bites out of a marketing budget.

Star Attractions, Inc., St. Louis, launched its first program in 1988 featuring entertainer Carol Channing in a generic print ad campaign. The Star Attractions package, which costs from $2,000 to $10,000, depending on the population of the retailer's market, includes the use of six photographs showing Channing in furs for print ads in newspapers and magazines, postcards, posters, and counter cards. The retailer just adds the firm's name and address. Retailers can contract to use the package for one year at a time and are guaranteed exclusivity within their market.

The fur retailers are typically small to medium in size and, until this marketing concept came upon the scene, were not able to buy this kind of image advertising. During the first year of the promotion over 30 stores in San Francisco, Charlotte, N.C., and other smaller towns across the U.S.A. used the ad package.

This Briefly Speaking is based on information from the following source:
Constance C. R. White, "Small Retailers Get Market Boost From Celebrity Package," *Women's Wear Daily*, July 19, 1988, p. 9.

woman who wanted to look glamorous chose an ermine cape. Today, an ermine cape would be valuable only as a theatrical prop—and it could be picked up fairly cheaply in a secondhand store.

More than any other time in the history of fur fashion, the current list of furs is long and varied. A new category, called "sport" or "contemporary," includes such furs as raccoon, fox, beaver, coyote, muskrat, Tanuki (Asian raccoon), and nutria (a South American beaverlike animal). Table 7-2 lists furs and their characteristics.

In addition to the use of furs such as Tanuki and nutria, fur manufacturers often reintroduce old ones. Persian lamb, shunned by fur buyers for over two generations, is now making a comeback. Remembered as a fur that was used for grandmother's conservative coat, Persian lamb, which is flat enough to be cut almost like cloth, is now being put to new uses. It is a prime choice in new fur garments such as scarves, sweaters, and jackets.[2]

Sometimes an interest in a fur comes about because fur manufacturers invent a finishing technique that makes a fur seem new. A renewed interest in raccoon can be traced to a technique that eliminated much of its bulkiness. In the 1940s, beaver was invariably sheared to look like a short fur; today it is left unplucked, giving it a totally new look.

Organization and Operation

The fur industry in the United States is divided into three groups, which also represent the three stages of fur production: (1) the trappers, farmers, and ranchers who produce the pelts; (2) the fur-processing companies; and (3) the manufacturers of fur products.

TABLE 7-2 • SELECTED POPULAR FURS AND THEIR CHARACTERISTICS

Fur	Characteristics	You Should Look For
Beaver		
Sheared	Soft, plushy texture.	Silky texture. Well-matched pelts, evenly sheared.
Natural	Long guard hairs over thick underfur.	Lustrous sheen of guard hairs and thickness of underfur.
Calf	Short, sleek, flat hairs. It comes in many natural colors and patterns and may be dyed.	Lustrous, supple pelt with bright luster. Markings should be attractive.
Chinchilla	A short, dense, very silky fur. Originally from South America, but now wholly ranch-raised.	Lustrous slate-blue top hair and dark underfur, although mutation colors are now available.
Coyote	A long-haired fur, often pale gray or tan in color. Durable and warm.	Long guard hair and thick, soft underfur.
Fox	The widest range of natural mutation colors of any fur except mink: silver, blue, white, red, cross, beige, gray, and brown. May also be dyed.	Long, glossy guard hairs and thick soft underfur. Also clarity of color.
Lamb		
American processed	Pelts of fine wool sheep sheared to show the pattern near the skin. Naturally white but may be dyed.	Silky, lustrous moire pattern, not too curly.
Broadtail	A natural (unsheared) flat moire pattern. Color may be natural browns, gray, black, or dyed.	Silky texture and uniformity of pattern.
Mongolian	Long, wavy, silky hair. May be natural off-white, bleached, or dyed.	Silky texture, with wavy—not frizzy—hair.
Mouton	Pelts are sheared, hairs are straightened for soft, water-repellent fur, generally dyed brown.	Uniformity of shearing.
Shearling	Natural sheepskin, with the leather side sueded and worn outside. The fur side is often sheared.	Softness of leather side and even shearing.
Persian lamb	From karakul sheep raised in Southwest Africa, Afghanistan, U.S.S.R. Traditionally black, brown, and gray, new mutation colors available; also dyed.	Silky curls or ripples of fur and soft, light, pliable leather.
Lynx	Russian lynx is the softest and whitest of these long-haired furs, with the most subtle beige markings. Canadian lynx is next, while Montana lynx has stronger markings. Lynx cat or bobcat is reddish black fading to spotted white on longer belly hairs.	Creamy white tones and subtle markings.

TABLE 7-2 • (*continued*)

Fur	Characteristics	You Should Look For
Mink	Soft and lightweight, with lustrous guard hairs and dense underfur.	Natural luster and clarity of color. Fur should be full and dense.
Mutation	Most colors of any natural ranched fur, from white to grays, blues, and beiges.	
Ranch	Color ranges from a true, rich brown to a deep brownish black.	
Wild	Generally brown in color.	
Pieced*	Color and pattern depends on pieces used. This is the least expensive mink.	Pattern and well-made seams.
Rabbit	Generally long hair in a variety of natural colors, including 14 natural mutation colors in ranch rabbit. May be sheared and grooved.	Silky texture and uniformity of color. Ranch rabbit sheds less.
Raccoon	Long silver, black-tipped guard hairs over woolly underfur. May also be plucked and sheared and dyed.	Silvery cast. Plenty of guard hair with heavy underfur.
Sable	Member of marten family. Crown sable is brown with a blue cast. Golden sable, an amber tone, is less expensive.	Soft, deep fur in dark lustrous brown, with silky guard hairs.
Skunk	Underfur is thick and long, keeping guard hairs exact. Stripe may vary in length and width.	Blue-black color, fineness of white marking, thick texture.
Zorina	South American skunk, similar to North American skunk.	Flatter fur with silkier texture.
Tanuki	Also called Japanese raccoon. Color is closer to red fox with distinctive cross markings.	Clarity of color and dense, full texture.

* The same piecing technique can be used for almost any fur. The most common pieced furs are mink, sable, marten, fox, Persian lamb, raccoon, and beaver.

Source: Furs Naturally by Edythe Cudlipp for The American Fur Industry, Inc., New York, pp. 20–22. Reprinted with permission.

Pelt Production

The first step in the production of fur is to obtain the necessary pelts. A **pelt** is the skin of a fur-bearing animal.

Trappers are the primary source of wild-animal pelts, which must be taken only during the coldest season of the year in order to be of prime quality. Trappers sell pelts to nearby country stores or directly to itinerant buyers. In some areas, collectors or receiving houses accept pelts for sale on consignment from trappers or local merchants. When enough pelts have been gathered, a fur merchant exports them or sends them to an auction house, or they are sold at a private sale through a broker.

The majority of furs come from farms or ranches, where fur-bearing animals are bred and raised strictly for their fur.

FASHION

Anyone who thinks that fur coats are only for rich, glamorous ladies of leisure must have been out in the cold too long and therefore hasn't heard the call of Fred Schwartz, otherwise known as "Fred the Furrier."

As chairman emeritus of the Fur Vault, Inc., Schwartz has been credited with leading the business toward greater sales of affordable furs—in part, by targeting the working woman as his prime purchasing customer. And to reach that customer, Schwartz himself beckoned from the company's radio, television, and newspaper advertisements for years, inviting "Barbara," "Evelyn," "Susan," and others to come try on his (relatively) bargain-priced "Creme de Mink" coats or "Freddy" fur jackets.

A fifth-generation furrier, Schwartz first entered the business as a wholesaler with his brother Harold.[1] In 1975, he made the switch to the retail side by

FOCUS

leasing a department he named The Fur Vault in New York's moderate-priced department store, Alexander's.

In 1984, the Fur Vault went public and opened its first two freestanding stores, located in the New York metropolitan area and billed as "fur department stores."[2] And less than a year later, Schwartz upgraded his business by leaving Alexander's and entering a leased department arrangement (called Northern Lights) with upscale Bloomingdale's. Since that time, he opened additional freestanding stores, including several in greater Washington, D.C., and also began operating a leased fur department at Rich's department store in Atlanta.

But what started with so much flair became a commercial and marketing failure. Fred Schwartz resigned in October 1988 and was replaced by Bob Miller, former president of Charles of the Ritz.

What happened? When Fred Schwartz started, he was the only retailer in town promoting mink coats at $2,400 or less. But within five years, many retailers, including Antonovich and Korean-owned Jindo, began to compete at the same price points. Although Fred was the first to build a major fur business selling to the masses, he was lured by the far-fatter profits of mink coats of $3,500 and over and began flirting with richer customers. He began to change the advertising, he appeared in fewer ads, and in 1987 out went the old, good-hearted approach.

"His original outrageous commercials were fun and made you feel good about him," says Miller. "Then they decided to upgrade the company, but there was never really a formal plan. As a result they sent very confusing messages."[3]

What's ahead for Fred the Furrier? He still owns a great deal of Fur Vault stock and is looking to start a new venture. The Fur Vault is changing its image, adding a collection of scarves, and concentrating on the company's leather business under the Andrew Marc label.

[1] Stanley H. Brown, "Coming In Out of the Cold," *Manhattan Inc.*, January 1985, p. 96.
[2] "Fred Vaults Into Fur Department Store Concept," *Fur World*, October 29, 1984, p. 6.
[3] Jeffrey A. Trochtenberg, "R.I.P. Fred the Furrier," *Forbes*, February 20, 1989, pp. 122–123.

This Fashion Focus is based on information from the articles cited above and from these sources:
Helen Burggraf, "Strategies for Selling Furs," *Stores*, March 1987, pp. 23–35.
"Fur Vault to Open Fifth Store in D.C. Area in October," *Fur Age Weekly*, June 16, 1986, p. 5.
Constance C. R. White, "Miller Eyes Fur Vault Turnaround," *Women's Wear Daily*, October 18, 1988, p. 6.
"The Evolution of Fred the Furrier—Or How to Reach $500M by 1993," *The Business of Fur*, April 4, 1988, pp. 1–6–7.
Constance C. R. White, "Fred Schwartz Resigns as Fur Vault Chairman," *Women's Wear Daily*, October 17, 1988.

Almost all mink, rabbit, fox, and more recently, fitch, chinchilla, Persian lamb, and broadtail are ranched. **Fur farming** offers two important advantages. First, animals can be raised under controlled conditions. Second, they can be bred selectively. When wild mink roamed North America, they came in one color, a dark brown with reddish highlights. Today, many beautiful colors, some of which are trademarked and denote a manufacturers private label, are available. Among the better-known names are Jasmin, Scanbrown, Tourmaline, Black Willow, and the most recognizable name of all, Blackgama.[3]

Fur Auctions

Fur pelts are sold at auctions today much as they were in the thirteenth century. Fur buyers and manufacturers bid on the pelts, which are sold in bundles. Buyers look for bundles that are matched in quality and color. This enables a manufacturer to make up a garment of uniform beauty.

Recently, competition has increased among buyers to purchase a "top bundle"—that is, an unusually beautiful bundle that goes for an unusually high price. This, in turn, results in a much touted coat—often costing $100,000 or more—that is made from the top bundle.

The auction trail is an international one, although except for England and more recently, Tokyo, each market sells indigenous furs. U.S. fur buyers travel to England, Scandinavia, China, and the U.S.S.R. To buy North American furs, fur buyers travel to auction houses in New York, Seattle, and Toronto.

Fur Processing

After manufacturers of fur goods buy the pelts, they contract with fur-dressing and fur-dyeing firms to process them.

The job of fur dressers is to make the pelts suitable for use in consumer products. The pelts are first softened by soaking and mechanical means. Then a flesher removes any unwanted substances from the inner surface of the skin. For less expensive furs, this is done by roller-type machines. At this point, the pelts are treated with solutions that tan the skin side into pliable leather. The fur side may be processed at the same time. This involves either plucking unwanted guard hairs or shearing the underfur to make the fur more lightweight. Although fur dressing has traditionally been a handcraft industry, modern technology is turning it into a more mechanical process.

After dressing, the pelts may go to a dyer. Fur dyes were once made from vegetable matter, but are now mostly derived from chemical compounds. New dyes are constantly being developed, making it possible to dye fur more successfully and in more shades than ever before.

Fur Manufacturing

Most fur manufacturers are small, independently owned and operated shops, although a few large companies have emerged largely as a result of the explosion of fur products.

The production of fur garments lends itself neither to mass production nor to large-scale operations. Skill and judgment is required at every stage of manufacture. Doing each step by hand lets a worker deal with each pelt's color, quality, and peculiarities.

The following steps transform pelts into finished garments:

1. A design of the garment is sketched.
2. A paper pattern is made of the garment.
3. A canvas pattern is made.

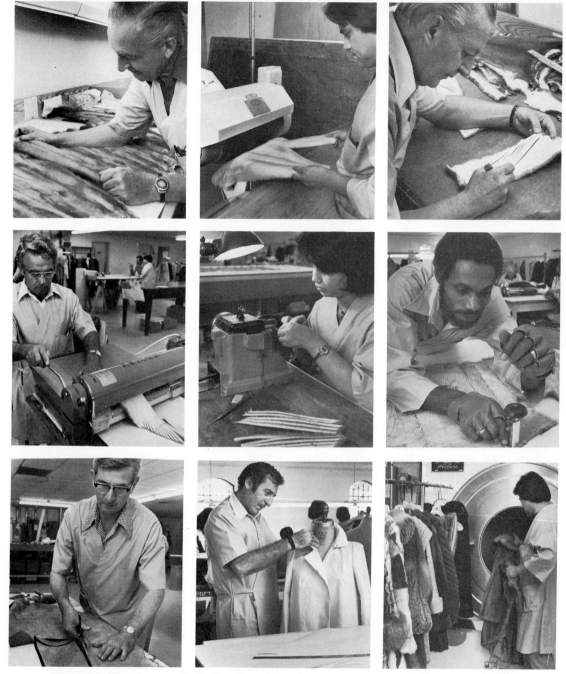

Top—the skins are matched, glazed, and sliced into strips by hand. Center—a machine slices the skins, the slices are sewn together, and wet skins are stapled to the pattern to dry. Below—the pattern is cut, a canvas model is fitted, and finally—the cleaning machine.

4. The skins are cut in such a way as to conform to the designer's sketch, exhibit the fur to its best advantage, and minimize waste.
5. The cut skins are sewn together.
6. The skins are wetted and then stapled to a board to dry, a process that sets them permanently.
7. The garment sections are sewn together.
8. The garment is lined and finished.
9. The garment is inspected.

For some luxurious furs, the cutting operation becomes extremely complex. Short skins must be **let out** to a suitable length for garments. Letting out mink, for example, involves cutting each skin down the center of a dark vertical line of fur (the grotzen stripe). Each half skin must then be cut at an angle into diagonal strips one-eighth to three-sixteenth-inch wide. Then each tiny strip is resewn at an angle to the strips above and below it to make a long, narrow skin. The other half-skin is sewn in a similar manner.

The two halves are then joined, resulting in a longer, slimmer pelt that is more beautiful than the original. Considerable hand labor is required to do all of these operations. Ten miles of thread and over 1,200 staples may be used in a single coat.

Retail Distribution of Furs

The line between manufacturing and retailing is less clear in the fur industry than in most other industries. Retail fur merchants, for example, typically make up an assortment of garments to sell off the rack to customers, but they also maintain a supply of skins in their workroom for custom work.

In retail stores, furs are either leased or sold on consignment. Both operations permit a retail store to offer its customers a large selection without tying up a lot of capital in inventory.

A **leased department** is situated in the store but run by an independent merchant, who pays a percentage of sales to the store as rent. The operator either owns or leases the stock. Lessees often run several similar departments in many stores and can, if necessary, move garments and skins from one location to another. Lessees, who are a unique kind of retailer, are usually well capitalized and have expert knowledge in both furs and retailing.

In **consignment selling** a fur manufacturer supplies merchandise to a retail store, which has the option of returning unsold items. In effect, the manufacturer lends stock to a store. Consignment selling is influenced by the state of the economy. When interest rates are high, stores tend to buy less stock.

Since the early 1980s, fur manufacturers have stepped up their retail activities. The largest manufacturer, Evans, Inc. (operating under the name Arctic Legends) has opened its own retail outlets. Evans, Inc., sold $134.4 million worth of furs in 1987. Eventually, the company hopes to open 100 to 150 Arctic Legends stores across the country, each of which is expected to generate $800,000 to $1.2 million annually.[4]

Fred the Furrier also deserves credit for bringing affordable furs to a new market, namely, women themselves. For many years, women received fur coats only as gifts. They never bought this luxury item for themselves. But when women started working, and also began to get paid more for their work, they started buying furs for themselves, thus creating, in effect, a new market—one that the fur industry has been quick to recognize and expand upon. See the Fashion Focus on pages 156–157.

TECHNOLOGY TALK

FENDI'S FUTURISTIC FURS

In an industry that for generations has produced furs in much the same way as in ancient times, a revolutionary process was developed through technology in 1989.

The famous Fendi sisters showed an entire collection of furs based on a new process that makes them all, from sables to squirrels, reversible. Interfacing, lining, and construction are all eliminated, and the result is fur coats of incredible lightness and minimal bulk. These coats are so light in fact, that a full-length fur coat can be folded up and put into a knapsack. Changing from the fur side to the leather side can be done in a minute and there is no bulky look—no matter which side is outside.

The Fendis had been working on the new technique for over five years. The fact that all inner construction was eliminated changed the look of the coats themselves. Eliminating the shoulder pads makes everything fit naturally, and the lightness of the fur make them swing and swirl as if made of chiffon.

Innovation and technology are a hallmark of Fendi furs. In 1965 after deciding that furs of the time were boring, they decided to do something new. They dyed furs purple, green, and apricot. They braided fur pelts mixing sable with opossum, mink with mole. Fendi is probably the only company in the world to sell dozens of fur coats made of mole and squirrel necks with no linings and hundreds of razor slits, or opossum jackets with polka dots of Mongolian lamb fur on the sleeves. The Fendis have crocheted mink strips, put thousands of holes and slits in fox pelts, and combined bits of beaver with sheer tulle.

The Fendis have one work room that is devoted only to experimentation of fur techniques and technology with new dyes, new sewing techniques, and new designs.

Alda Fendi is the queen of the Fendi fur work rooms. In these surroundings, she and technicians work out what eventually appears on the runways and stores. Most of these innovations have never been tried before. The Fendi's constant interest in new techniques and technology will bring us new and better—but never "boring"—furs.

This Fashion Focus is based upon the following articles.

Marion McEvoy, "Quality In the Works," *W*, October 26–November 2, 1979, pp. 6–8.

Judy Bachroch, "The Roman Empire," *Savvy*, December, 1987, pp. 37–41, 93.

Bernadine Morris, "Revolution: Feather-Light Reversible Furs," *The New York Times*, March 8, 1989, p. C12.

What becomes a Legend most?

Blackglama

BLACKGLAMA® IS THE WORLD'S FINEST NATURAL DARK RANCH MINK. BRED ONLY IN AMERICA, AND IS TRADEMARKED BY THE GREAT LAKES MINK ASSOCIATION, KENOSHA, WI. 53140.

Ann-Margret and mink—glamour and style! Will you one day wear mink and become a legend?

Merchandising and Marketing

Fur traders, dressers, producers, and their labor unions all work through their various trade associations to encourage the demand for fur.

Trade Associations

Trade associations mount their own campaigns to promote furs, and they also work with retailers. The leading associations are the American Fur Industry, Inc., and the Master Furriers, a New York-based organization that represents about 800 U.S. fur retailers. Individual organizations often promote specific furs. There is the Eastern Mink Breeders Association (EMBA is now nationwide); the Great Lakes Mink Association (GLMA), a much smaller group specializing in ranch mink; and the Empress Chinchilla Breeders Cooperative (ECBC).

In 1987, the ranch mink marketing associations, Amerimink and American Legend, merged under the name American Legend, thus putting the Blackgama and EMBA trademarks in one association. With over 1,200 individual ranch memberships, the Legend-owned Seattle Fur Exchange sold a record 2 million mink pelts in 1987.[5]

American Legend has introduced a new program to protect its trademarks from infringement. The association supplies Blackgama and EMBA labels and other point-of-purchase materials only to retailers and manufacturers who can prove they purchased the group's pelts at an American Legend auction.[6]

Trade associations not only monitor the industry, but they help to educate consumers. Fur is a product that is most successfully purchased when the consumer has some specialized knowledge about what he or she is buying. Consumers need to know, for example, that the rarer the breed, the more expensive the fur. A high-quality mink coat costs $10,000 to $15,000, but a Black Willow mink, made up of pelts bred exclusively on one Utah ranch, costs $20,000.

The country of origin also affects price. A top-quality Canadian sable coat costs upward of $60,000, while a Russian sable, considered a superior fur, runs $160,000 or more.[7]

Another important factor in the quality of fur is whether the pelts are female or male. Most female skins are softer and lighter, although there are exceptions, such as fitch, where the male skins are preferred. A coat of female mink or fisher costs, on average, $2,000 more than one of male skins.

Labeling

The Fur Products Labeling Act of 1952 requires that all furs be labeled according to:

1. The English name of the animal.
2. Its country of origin.
3. The type of processing, including dyeing, to which the pelts have been subjected.
4. Whether or not parts have been cut from a used garment or from the less desirable paw or tail sections.

Years ago, such labeling would have been helpful, for example, to prevent a customer from buying a less expensive, dyed muskrat that was touted as the much rarer and more expensive Hudson seal. Today, such labeling is helpful in distinguishing one fur from another in an industry that, without intending to defraud, has learned to capitalize on fashion trends by treating less expensive furs to look like more expensive ones.

Industry Trends

As a general rule, the demand for furs is related to the economy. During the Depression, fur sales dropped off dramatically. After World War II, when the economy was expanding, fur sales boomed. In the early 1970s, conservationists' concerns about the diminishing wildlife species put a temporary damper on fur sales, but the industry rebounded in the 1980s and has remained strong ever since.

Even a 1981–1982 recession failed to slow fur sales, and the stock market crash of 1987 did not affect them. Fur sales topped $1 billion in 1981, up from $944 million in 1980.[8] Mid-1987 saw another milestone, the $2 billion mark. Industry experts say the outlook for the fur industry continues to be good.[9]

Growth will be spurred by renewed fashion interest in furs, increased foreign trade, new channels of retail distribution, and ironically, legislation that is restrictive but nonetheless helpful to the industry.

Renewed Fashion Interest

Once worn only by the rich or for formal occasions, furs are now bought and worn by many kinds of consumers for all occasions. The average customer no longer buys one conservatively cut coat, either. Furs are now sporty and casual, elegant and classic, or faddish and trendy—and with such choices, customers have been persuaded to buy more than one.

Not only have older women—the traditional market—continued to buy furs, but the market has expanded to young and working women as well. Working women now account for over 50 percent of the fur market.[10]

Fur manufacturers are exploring other new markets as well. For most of history, men as well as women wore furs, but in the past 100 years, the fur coat became almost exclusively a woman's garment. In the early 1980s, men once again began wearing fur coats.

In 1987, Parisien Furs, Inc., launched a collection of furs for large-sized women. Considered a sleeper in its first year, this segment of the market is now expected to expand.[11]

Finally, the fur industry is expanding into new products, using fur to make garments, such as vests, sweaters, and dresses, that have not traditionally been made of fur. Big-name designer firms—among them Christian Dior, Yves Saint Laurent, Givenchy, Halston, Oscar de la Renta, Pauline Trigere, and Calvin Klein—also designing furs. Italian designers such as Fendi and Soldano are known for their innovative techniques. In 1989, Fendi introduced a reversible fur/leather coat.

Increased Foreign Trade

The export market is strong for the American fur industry, not only because of the variety of furs that are available but also because of the reputation for quality in U.S. pelt dressing. The United States produces innovative, high-style furs that are in great demand around the world.

In 1979, buyers from Europe, South America, and the Far East traveled to New York to attend the first American International Fur Fair. Today the fair is an important catalyst in bringing foreign fur buyers to the doorstep of domestic fur manufacturers.

New Legislation

The Federal Trade Commission and the fur industry are constantly engaged in talks about fur labeling. Ironically, the most important recent legislation, which was intended to restrict the fur industry, has actually been a boon to sales. The Endangered Species Act of 1973 forbade the sale of furs made from endangered species such as leopard, tiger, ocelot, cheetah, jaguar, vicuna, and a few types of wolf. Since women no longer have to worry about wearing an endangered species, many have returned to the fur market.

New Channels of Retail Distribution

In addition to the retail outlets that have been opened by fur manufacturers like Evans, Inc., and Jindo Furs, fur manufacturers have sought other distribution channels.

Retailers also now sell furs through mail-order catalogs. Spiegel publishes a fur catalog called "Ambiance" that shows over 40 fur products. JC Penney shows and sells furs from a catalog as do other retailers.

Hotel, armory, and arena fur sales are held almost every weekend in New York City and other large cities. Fur manufacturers can conduct these sales for a fraction of the cost in wages and rent if they were to maintain comparable facilities year-round. Even better, the average hotel ballroom, armory, or arena showroom is suitable for displaying thousands of coats, far more than the average fur salon can attractively exhibit. The sales appeal to customers, who like the hands-on approach and lower prices.

The same customers who frequent weekend sales also can shop in manufacturer-leased discount and off-price stores such as Filene's, Syms, Loehmanns, and the Oceanside Factory.

Some manufacturers are opening storefront discount operations. Mademoiselle, the wholesale division of the Fur Vault, Inc., has opened an outlet store called the New York Fur & Coat Co. Its location in the heart of the fur district in New York City is another trend. Today, you cannot walk through the area without passing two or three retail fur stores, a dramatic change from the days when all furs were sold in manufacturers' showrooms, several stories above the street.

Low-Cost Imports

The importation of fur garments produced primarily in the Far East poses a serious problem for the domestic fur industry. Industry estimates suggest that one out of every two fur coats bought in the United States is manufactured offshore.[12] Whereas 10 years ago, no more than 5 percent of the fur business in-

Madison Square Garden/Nassau Veterans Memorial Coliseum

THE GREATEST FUR SALE EVER! FOUR DAYS ONLY!

Thousands of furs at the lowest prices-*guaranteed!**

The largest selection of furs ever assembled. From the collections of over 50 fur wholesalers. Open to the public— free admission.

*If you can show us an ad for a fur of the same style and comparable quality, presently available, priced lower than our show price, we'll beat it!

Mink	$1,699
Raccoon	$1,599
Coyote	$1,599
Fox	$999

You can win a Mink coat.

No purchase necessary. Complete details at show.

madison square garden center exposition rotunda 7th Ave 31st to 33rd Sts.

Sun., December 20, 10 AM–8 PM
Mon., Tues., & Wed.,
December 21, 22 & 23, 12 PM–8 PM

NASSAU VETERANS MEMORIAL COLISEUM

Sun., December 20, 10 AM–8 PM
Mon., December 21, 12 PM–8 PM

INTERNATIONAL *Fur* WHOLESALERS

MINK $1699

Huge arenas are sometimes used to sell furs. Here a customer can choose from thousands of styles from over 50 different manufacturers. Obviously, this could not be done in a store.

volved imports, today 50 percent of the market does.[13] One of the largest manufacturers from the Far East is Jindo, Inc. of Korea. Not only does Jindo manufacture and sell coats to retail stores around the world, but they have their own retail stores in Hong Kong, Hawaii, and the continental United States.

Rising Overhead

In the past decade, rents have more than tripled in Manhattan business districts. Fur manufacturers, traditionally located in the "fur market" along Seventh Avenue between 23d and 30th Streets, have not been exempt from the sensational rent increases. To add to the problem, space has become increasingly difficult to find as businesses with no ties to the fur industry have moved into the fur district in an attempt to escape the higher rents uptown.

As a result, the fur industry has begun to view College Point, Queens, as a new and potentially less expensive home. Plans are underway to build a World Fur Center there. The industry hopes that, like the flower industry and others that have departed from Manhattan in the past decade, it will be able to survive off the beaten path.[14]

Labor Shortage

The fur industry is troubled with a high retirement rate among an older generation of highly skilled fur workers, coupled with a shortage of skilled, young workers ready to enter the field. Many workers now in their late 50s or early 60s who might have worked a few more years are opting for early retirement in the face of rising costs. The problem is offset somewhat by an influx of immigrants, primarily from Greece, who are entering the industry. Unfortunately, not all these workers are highly skilled.

The industry also suffers from a lack of trained middle-management workers on both the wholesale and retail sides. One attempt to remedy this problem has begun at the Fashion Institute of Technology in New York City. The fur industry has pledged to support a program designed to prepare young persons to enter the fur business. Students are trained in fur design, pattern making, merchandising and sales, retailing, production, breeding and wildlife management, and other related industry skills.

REFERENCES

[1] U.S. Industrial Outlook 1986.

[2] Debra Michaels, "Industry to Push Updated Fashion for Persian Lamb," *Women's Wear Daily,* April 23, 1987, p. 6.

[3] Elizabeth Collier, "Mink Color War: Don't Call It Brown," *Avenue,* October 1986, pp 115 117.

[4] Helen Burggraf, "Strategies for Selling Furs," *STORES*, March 1987, p. 8.

[5] "Amerimink Members Agree to Merger with American Legend," *Women's Wear Daily,* April 28, 1987, p. 8.

[6] Kevin Haynes, "American Legend Launches Label," *Women's Wear Daily,* January 1, 1986, p. 15.

[7] Troy Segal, "Now's the Time for Thinking Mink," *Business Week,* April 13, 1987, p. 112.

[8] *Women's Wear Daily,* January 1, 1983, pp. 16–17.

[9] Burggraf, p. 24.

[10] Ruth Feibers, "Fur Industry Adjusts to the 80s," *Chicago Apparel News,* Fall I Edition, March 1987, pp. 61–62.

[11] Debra Michaels, "Fur Expo Scores on Sales, Traffic," *Women's Wear Daily,* June 4, 1987, p. 12.

[12] Feibers, pp. 61–62.

[13] Neil Barsky, "Is Queens too Fur to Travel?" Business section, *New York Daily News,* April 7, 1987, pp. 1–5.

[14] Ibid.

MERCHANDISING VOCABULARY

Define or briefly explain the following terms:

Consignment selling	Hide	Pelt
Contract tannery	Kip	Regular tannery
Converter	Leased department	Skin
Fur farming	Let out	Tanning

MERCHANDISING REVIEW

1. In what ways have technological advances in machinery and chemistry benefited the leather industry?
2. Name and describe the three major types of companies in the leather industry.
3. What are the characteristics of leather tanned by each of the following methods and what consumer goods is each type of tanned leather suited for? (*a*) mineral, (*b*) vegetable materials, (*c*) oil, and (*d*) chemical.
4. What has Leather Industries of America done to broaden the leather market and soften the impact of competition from synthetics?
5. What factors point to continued growth for the leather industry?
6. Describe the history and development of the fur industry in the United States.
7. Into what three groups is the fur industry divided? Briefly describe the function of each.
8. What are the advantages of fur farming over trapping?
9. Outline the steps in transforming processed fur pelts into finished garments.
10. Differentiate between leased departments and consignment selling as these terms apply to retail distribution of fur garments. What major advantages does each have for retail merchants?

MERCHANDISING DIGEST

1. Discuss the following statement from the text and its implications for leather merchandising: "The leather industry not only must stay abreast of fashion; it must be several steps ahead of it."
2. Discuss current trends in the leather industry that relate to (*a*) enlarging markets, (*b*) competition from synthetics, (*c*) increased foreign trade.
3. Discuss (*a*) provisions of the Fur Products Labeling Act of 1952 and how it protects the consumer, and (*b*) recent legislation relating to furs.
4. Discuss current trends in the fur industry as they relate to (*a*) fashion interest, (*b*) increased foreign trade, (*c*) new channels of retail distribution, (*d*) low-cost imports, (*e*) rising overhead, (*f*) lack of skilled workers and managers.

WOMEN'S APPAREL

The street signs read Fashion Avenue. The people who work there call it the "garment center." It is home of the business known as the "rag trade." This 17-block district in midtown Manhattan is where the people who design, make, and sell women's clothing work. The heart of the fashion business, the women's garment industry projects an image of glamour and excitement, and it certainly is that. But it is also a frantically fast-paced, risky, and competitive industry, one that is not for the faint of heart.

The manufacturing and merchandising of women's apparel is a giant multibillion dollar industry employing hundreds of thousands of people. Its influence on the economy is so strong that retail sales figures are one indicator of the health of the nation's economy.

Of necessity, the industry exists in a constant state of change, reacting on an ongoing basis to women's tastes and styles, to an increasingly global economy, and to new technology. It is an industry that truly thrives on change and novelty.

HISTORY OF THE WOMEN'S APPAREL INDUSTRY

For thousands of years, people made their own clothes, often producing their own raw materials and converting them into textiles with which they could sew. A farmer might grow cotton, for example, and his wife would spin and weave it into cotton fabric, which she then used to make the family's clothes. Until the mass manufacturing of clothing began, sewing was considered women's work.

The first step in moving the manufacture of clothes out of the home came around 1800, when professional tailors began to make men's clothing. These clothes were **custom-made**, that is, fitted to the individual who would wear them and then sewn by hand. A few professional dressmakers began to make women's clothes, but only rich women could afford these custom-made designs. Most women still sewed their own clothes at home.

Growth of Ready-to-Wear

The mass production of clothing did not begin until the mid-nineteenth century. After the Civil War, some manufacturers began to mass-produce cloaks and mantles for women. These garments were not fitted, so they could be made in standard sizes and turned out in large numbers.

By the turn of the century, limited quantities of women's suits, skirts, and blouses were being made in factories. Around 1910, someone had the idea of sewing a blouse and skirt together, and the women's ready-to-wear dress business was born. In contrast to custom-made clothes produced by professional dressmakers or made by home sewers,

the term **ready-to-wear** (RTW) refers to clothing made in factories to standardized measurements. In the first decades of the twentieth century, growing numbers of women began to substitute store-bought clothes for home-sewn ones.

Growth of the Garment District

The garment district was created by a committee of clothing manufacturers working with investors and a major real-estate developer. The manufacturers had outgrown their small shops and factories on the Lower East Side and needed to expand. They wanted to move into a new, mostly undeveloped area of the burgeoning city. Between 1918 and 1921, 50 to 60 manufacturers moved uptown to Seventh Avenue along the west side of Manhattan. With more room for expansion in the new area, these entrepreneurs were able to parlay a baby business into a mature industry.

Early apparel factories, called sweatshops, used hand sewers. Very few of these factories even had sewing machines.

New York City, already a major industrial center, was well-positioned to capitalize on the ready-to-wear boom. A large pool of cheap, immigrant labor was available. In addition, New York was ideally located near the textile producers in New England and the South. It was also a port city, so imported textiles could be brought in when needed. By 1923, the city was producing 80 percent of all women's apparel, with 20 percent still being done by home sewers and custom tailors. The 1920s and 1930s saw the emergence of several large clothing manufacturers.[1]

Unionization

The history of the women's apparel business cannot be told without also describing the growth and influence of the clothing unions. The success of the industry in the early twentieth century came about largely because the manufacturers were able to draw upon a substantial supply of immigrant labor. The industry was dominated by Jewish and Italian workers. In 1910, 55 percent of garment workers were Jewish and 35 percent were Italian. Many of the immigrants had no skills, but a sizable number had trained as dressmakers or tailors in their homelands. Skilled and unskilled labor was needed in the garment industry, which seemed to have gotten big overnight. The opportunity to turn a large and quick profit was enormous, at least for the owners.

At the other end of the scale, unfortunately, were the workers, who worked long hours for very little pay under conditions that were totally unregulated. A typical garment factory was dark, overcrowded, unsanitary, and unsafe.

In 1900, the workers began to unionize, a move they saw as their only chance to improve their working condi-

The ILGWU label.

tions. The International Ladies Garment Workers Union (ILGWU) was formed, and it remains today the major garment industry union. Unionization did not happen overnight, and employers resisted the new union's demands as much as they could.

Strikes in 1909 and 1910 paved the way for collective bargaining, but public sympathy for the ladies garment workers was not aroused until the devastating Triangle Shirtwaist Factory fire in 1911. One hundred forty-six workers, most of them young women, were killed. A tragedy of massive proportions, it nonetheless lent strength to the union movement.

At last people began to realize that the union stood for more than collective bargaining, that indeed many of its demands revolved around matters of life and death. The union's new strength opened the door to many concessions that helped the workers, such as strict building codes and protective labor laws. Child labor was outlawed.

The ILGWU managed to survive the Depression years. Under the guidance of David Dubinsky, who took the helm in 1932 and held it for 34 years, the ILGWU enjoyed a period of expansion, and the garment industry underwent a period of innovative growth. ILGWU negotiated a 35-hour, 5-day work week and paid vacations. It instituted health, welfare, and pension programs and financed housing projects and recreation centers.

Since 1975, the ILGWU has been primarily concerned with fighting imports, the first real threat to the American women's apparel industry in several decades. They originated the campaign called "Look for the Union Label" and actively support the current "Crafted With Pride in U.S.A." campaign.

CREATION OF WOMEN'S APPAREL

As the garment industry has grown, the sophistication with which it is able to respond to the demands of customers who seek both style and quality has also grown. The industry has developed from a relatively straightforward one, composed of many small factories, into a complicated one dominated by several industrial giants.

Technology has played a major role in the growth of the garment business. It has helped to make high style and quality accessible to everyone, not just the rich elite. The women's apparel industry must now concern itself with style and fashion more than it ever has in the past.

Despite the new technology, the new emphasis on rapidly changing styles, and the overwhelming growth, the industry has managed to settle into a basic cycle of production that repeats itself more or less unchanged from season to season. Before an article of clothing reaches the retail store racks, much work and planning must be done.

Developing a Line

The first step in the production of a garment is the development of a design con-

cept, which not only encompasses the individual item of apparel or accessories but the entire season's collection from that manufacturer as well. The term **collection** is sometimes used to describe an expensive line.

Seasonal Lines

Lines are created and styled for wholesale presentation several times, or seasons, per year. Designers and merchandisers typically work on two seasons at a time. They put the finishing touches on one line or collection while they begin to develop a new one.

Clothing manufacturers produce between four and six lines every year. These are Spring, Summer, Transitional (also known as Fall I), Fall (or Fall II, as it is called), and Resort/Holiday. Many firms, however, add new styles to lines throughout the year in order to keep buyers "shopping" their lines to see what is new. Conversely, as new styles are added, old ones are dropped. Spring clothes are typically presented to retail buyers in October and November; Summer lines are presented in early January; Fall I is presented in February; Fall II in early April, and Resort/Holiday in August.

Designers, merchandisers and manufacturers start work on their new lines anywhere between three to twelve months before presentation to retail buyers. This means clothes are planned and designed as much as a year before customers will see them in the stores.

Design Concept

The first step involves the work of a designer, or a design staff working under the direction of a "merchandiser." It is these people who are charged with creating a line. They review information on trends and materials, keeping in mind previous fashion successes or failures and the consumer to whom they are trying to appeal. This helps to formulate some idea of what the new line will contain.

Next come designs for individual garments. Each one is sketched or developed in muslin. At this stage, the designer considers his or her work, and weighs it on two points: first, on its own individual merits and, second, for its suitability in the line as a whole. Many designs are discarded at this point. Those that seem most likely to succeed are made up as finished sample garments. A pattern is then made, and the fabric is chosen and cut. Finally, the garment is sewn by a designer's assistant who is also a seamstress. This person is called a **sample hand.**

Now the design is presented to various executives and managers of the

TECHNOLOGY TALK

QUICK RESPONSE— WHAT'S IT ALL ABOUT, ALFIE?

Quick Response—the new industry buzzword is bandied about at trade conferences, seminars, board rooms, and back rooms. Many say this is where the textile, apparel, and retail industries are headed and point to pilot Quick Response (QR) programs already underway . . . with varying degrees of success.

Simply put, **Quick Response** aims at delivering the right product at the right time! It's a strategy designed to give American manufacturers a potent weapon against imports and competitors halfway around the world. Spearheaded by Du Pont in fibers and Milliken in fabrics, the necessary partnerships and electronic high-tech mechanisms are being hammered into place to link all parts of the supply pipeline directly to the nation's retailers.

What QR really means is a far closer association between manufacturer and customer— whether it is apparel and textile or retail and apparel. QR requires the development of trust and communication, and that goes all the way from the cash register to the apparel people and the textile suppliers.

As Kurt Salmon Associates, who were in on the birth of Quick Response, put it: From a manufacturer's point of view, QR can be defined as having in place an operating strategy which has been designed to enable the company to profitably supply its chosen markets with the right product at a competitive price, in the right quantities, at the right time, and with minimum commitment to inventory. Certainly there is nothing new about such a formula. What is new is the change of emphasis and timing, plus the fact that for many companies survival is at stake! It is anticipated that as more QR benefits are demonstrated in practice, doubts about commitment will diminish. As this occurs, implementation will accelerate.

In less than 4 years QR has evolved from a theoretical concept into a comprehensive integrated system that will shorten total cycle time and improve service. There is more to QR than moving goods more quickly to a retailer's shelf, and ultimately more quickly into the consumer's hand. There is a new merchandising strategy evolving that encompasses linkages, partnerships, commitment, and a timetable for fashion that throbs with a new rhythm.

company—people in sales, purchasing, production, and even cost accounting. Many designs are discarded at this point, while others are sent back to the design department for modification. A few are accepted.

Computer-aided Design (CAD). Although the day has not arrived when designers throw away their sketch pads and pencils, the advent of **computer-aided design** (CAD) is giving designers new freedom to explore and manipulate their designs in relatively easy and inexpensive ways. A designer no longer has to take a chance that he or she is having a sample made up in the best color. Now CAD is used to test various colors and color combinations, fabrics, and styles. CAD allows three-dimensional contouring of objects on screen. Folds, creases, and textures are simu-

---

Once belittled as the pipe dream of a few idealistic textile and apparel executives, QR is now more than just a theory. The initiative is gathering steam and test projects are popping up among retailers, domestic apparel manufacturers, and textile mills. While QR is still not the norm throughout the fashion pipeline, the fast replenishment strategy is clearly gaining strength . . . and some ardent influential supporters.

Bar coding and computer-to-computer communications have become integral parts of the QR scenario. Bar coding makes tracking merchandise—from fabric rolls to designer dresses—easier, faster, and more accurate, and electronic data information cuts out human intervention and is faster than mail or messenger service.

So far the success stories center on "staple" goods—jeans, men's and women's tailored pants, hosiery, and innerwear—that manufacturers and retailers stock year-round. But controversy continues to swirl around the application of QR practices to high fashion and seasonal goods. However, the growing segment of companies that has tried Quick Response is gleeful about the payoffs. As for fashion, many respond that the point of QR is not to restock but to let both the retailer and manufacturer see what the customers like and what sizes they wear—tools for planning and implementing the next season's line.

This Technology Talk is based on information from the following sources:

W. A. B. Davidson, "Quick Response: Boon or Boondoggle," *American Textile International*, May 1988, pp. 52–56.
Robert M. Frazier, "Quick Response Strategy for Retailers," *WWD/DNR Retailing Technology & Operations,* December 1988, p. 20.
Holly Haber, "Quick Response: The Sticking Points," *WWD/DNR Retailing Technology & Operations,* April 1988, p. 6.
Holly Haber, "Quick Response Moves Onto the Fast Track," *WWD/DNR Retailing Technology & Operations,* September 1988, pp. 22–24, 52.
Holly Haber, "Dillard's Wants 500 Key Vendors On-line With QR," *Women's Wear Daily,* May 1, 1989, p. 9.
Peter W. Harding, "New Role for Quick Response," *WWD/DNR Retailing Technology & Operations,* September 1988, pp. 30, 52.
Leonard Sloane, "Shortening Links in the Retail Chain," *The New York Times,* October 1, 1988, p. D1.

lated so that CAD-generated garments drape and hang accurately. Once the design is set on the computer, the computer image is used to create a pattern that is complete with darts, seams, and tailor's markings.[2]

Role of the Merchandiser

The merchandiser is the person who channels the creativity of the designer and design staff so that the six "rights" of merchandising can be successfully accomplished. These rights are: the right merchandise, at the right price, at the right time, in the right place, in the right quantity with the right promotion. To these rights must be added another one . . . for the right customer! Because this customer is so important, the merchandiser is given the responsibility to research who the "right" customer is.

Using all their merchandising and marketing skills, the merchandiser helps to form and maintain a positive image in the marketplace for the manufacturer. It is this image that influences a specific consumer group to buy a particular line at the retail level.

In most cases, design has to be disciplined and directed so that the particular image of the manufacturer and the merchandise that is produced will continue to fit the needs and wants of a specific consumer group. Some people in the industry have described the merchandiser as the "glue" that holds the whole design concept together. In fact, the merchandiser is the liaison between the design staff, the production facilities, and the sales staff. The merchandiser has to view the line from the design point of view and also has to be knowledgeable about production and sales efforts.

Producing a Line

Production begins when a pattern maker creates a production pattern in the garment size the company uses to produce its samples. From this pattern, one or more samples are cut and sewn. The samples are used to determine the cost of producing the garment. The design is assigned a style number. At this point, it is officially part of a manufacturer's line.

The samples are then presented to retail buyers at the manufacturers' seasonal shows. Most buyers either accept or reject a line. If they accept it, they will place orders for a number of the individual designs.

Because the manufacturer usually has not yet begun production when a line is shown to the buyers, it may be possible to fine-tune production to the buyers' orders. When a particular style receives a lot of attention from buyers, it is then scheduled for production. Items that generate little or no enthusiasm are dropped from the line.

Cutting

One of the most important steps in the mass production of apparel is the cutting of the garment pieces. Once a garment is slated for production, it is **graded,** or sloped, to each of the various sizes in which it will be made. After a pattern has been graded into the various sizes, the pieces are laid out on a long piece of paper called a **marker.** The success of cutting depends upon the accuracy with which each of the many layers of material are placed on top of one another. A **spreader,** or laying-up machine, carries the material along a guide on either side of the cutting table, spreading the material evenly from end to end. The marker is laid on top of these layers.

For many years, material was cut by hand, but today, the cutting process is either computer-assisted or totally computerized. Computers are given instructions, which are then fed to laser, blade, or high-speed water jet machines that do the actual cutting.

Once the cutting is completed, the pieces of each pattern—the sleeves, collars, fronts, and backs—are tied into bundles according to their sizes. This process is called **bundling.** The bundles are then moved to the manufacturers' sewing operators, who may be on the premises or in a contractors' shops.

Sewing

Technology has dramatically changed the sewing stage of production. Button machines sew on buttons. Computerized sewing machines, those that do embroidery, for example, are set up to stitch whole patterns without a machine operator. A completely automated sewing assembly line is under development in Japan. The only thing humans will do in this new system is supervise.[3]

Once the sewing process is completed, garments are finished, pressed, labeled, and inspected. They are then ready for shipping to retailers.

As the season progresses, manufacturers remain sensitive to retail sales. For example, when reorders come in, they recut only the garments that are most in demand—and therefore, the most profitable.

American manufacturers are increasingly turning to **off-shore production,** that is, the manufacture of American goods in cheap-labor foreign countries. Off-shore production is seen as a way to generally lower costs and therefore compete more effectively with low-cost imports. Some industry insiders view this practice as a threat to the health of American labor; others regard it as a necessity in order for American manufacturers to remain competitive.

Off-shore production is appealing under certain conditions because the federal government gives domestic producers a special tariff advantage, provided only part of the production is done off-shore. Under Section 807 of the Tariff Classification Act, for example, manufacturers can cut and design their own garments and finish them domestically, sending only the sewing to a labor-cheap off-shore country. Duty is paid only on the value added to the garment by the work done abroad.

ORGANIZATION AND OPERATION OF THE WOMEN'S APPAREL INDUSTRY

For many decades, the typical women's apparel company was a small, independently owned, and often family-run, business. Unlike the automobile industry, no Ford or General Motors dominated the women's apparel industry. In the early 1970s, about 5,000 firms made women's dresses, compared to only 300 firms that made radios and televisions. The industry's power came from its collective size. Its 5,000 firms did $3 billion in business every year.

All this changed in the 1960s. An expanding economy led to increased demand for everything, including clothing. Many of the textile companies had grown into huge businesses, as had several major retailers. Pushed from both directions, the clothing manufacturers responded by merging to create large publicly owned corporations.

Within a few years, it became obvious that the large corporations and conglomerates were not as successful as the smaller companies had been. The major problem was that the giants lacked the ability to respond quickly, a necessity in the fashion industry. By the mid-1980s, the merger trend began to reverse, and many women's apparel companies went private again. There are now 15,000 to 18,000 apparel makers, and no one company represents even 1 percent of total apparel sales.[4]

Regardless of whether a company is part of a conglomerate or a family-owned shop, the way in which clothes are produced does not vary. The operation of the apparel industry remains remarkably similar from business to business. The apparel industry is currently undergoing changes, however, that will change its organization if not its operation. Although the merger trend has slowed down and even reversed itself, the emergence of giant apparel producers is changing the face of the women's fashion business. After years of specialization, the women's apparel industry is becoming more diversified.

Briefly Speaking

On Meeting Bill, Carolyn, Oscar, Donna, and Calvin!

Yes, you too can meet these famous American designers and chat about fashion. The magic carpet that takes you to meet them is called a "trunk show." Although trunk shows may mean headaches for designers, this still packs a punch when it comes to selling high-priced clothes.

Designers say that trunk shows account for anywhere from 20 to 43 percent of a line's business. They also give the designer an opportunity to make a personal statement directly to the consumer. Oscar de la Renta says that trunk shows are very important because of the promotional impact, especially if the designer is working with licensees. Adolfo says that he learns a lot from people who buy his clothes. Bill Blass, once known as the "king of the trunk show circuit" has cut back

on personal appearances, but says that trunk shows still account for over 40 percent of his business.

Both Donna Karan and Carolyn Roehm joined the trunk show circuit when they began designing under their own names. Besides being good for profits, trunk shows seem to have a great effect on the designer's designs. Being able to see their clothes on the women who wear them, in the part of the country where they live, helps the designer find out what works and what doesn't.

Most of these clothes retail for over $500, which makes them investing dressing. Many designers say that shore buyers have a limit on how much they may purchase from any one designer. At a trunk show, the consumer can see almost everything that the designer has created and is given a much larger choice and selection.

This Briefly Speaking is based on information from the following source:

Irene Doria, "Trunk Shows: Still 'A Trip to Bountiful,'" *Women's Wear Daily*, April 28, 1986, p. 4.

Pete Born, "Martha's Takes In $410,000 With Bill Blass Trunk Show," *Women's Wear Daily*, May 8, 1989, p. 2.

Size of Producers

The 1970s was an era of organizational change within the industry. It saw the emergence of several women's apparel giants, companies that typically sold over $100 million annually. The largest is Levi Strauss, which does $3 billion in annual sales.

Today the 10 largest apparel companies represent over 20 percent of the total domestic volume, and they continue to grow at a faster rate than the industry overall.[5] The trend toward giantism shows no signs of letting up, at least not in the next decade. It will continue, if for no other reason than the economy demands it. This means that as some firms strive to become giants, many small and medium-sized firms will be swallowed up or will go out of business because they cannot compete.

Types of Producers

The fashion apparel industry consists of three types of producers: manufacturers, jobbers, and contractors. A **manufacturer** is one who performs all the operations required to produce apparel, from buying the fabric to selling and shipping the finished garments. An **apparel jobber** handles the designing, the planning, the purchasing, usually the cutting, the selling, and the shipping, but not the actual sewing operation. A **contractor** is a producer whose sole function is to supply sewing services to the industry, where it is sometimes called an **outside shop.**

Manufacturers

A manufacturer, by definition, is a producer who handles all phases of a garment's production. The staff produces the original design or buys an accepta-ble design from a freelance designer. Each line is planned by the company executives. The company purchases the fabric and trimmings needed. The cutting and sewing are usually done in the company's factories. On certain occasions, however, a manufacturer may use the services of a contractor if sales of an item exceed the capacity of the firm's sewing facilities and if shipping deadlines cannot otherwise be met. The company's sales force and traffic department handle the selling and shipping of the finished goods. One great advantage of this type of operation is that close quality control can be maintained. When producers contract out some part of their work, they cannot as effectively monitor its quality.

Apparel Jobbers

Apparel jobbers handle all phases of the production of a garment except for the actual sewing and sometimes the cutting. A jobber firm may employ a design staff to create various seasonal lines or may buy sketches from freelance designers. The jobber's staff buys the fabric and trimmings necessary to produce the styles in each line, makes up samples, and grades the patterns. In most cases, the staff also cuts the fabric for the various parts of each garment. Jobbers, however, do not actually sew and finish garments. Instead, they arrange with outside factories run by contractors to perform these manufacturing operations. The sales staff takes orders for garments in each line, and the shipping department fills store orders from the finished garments returned by the contractor. (Note that apparel jobbers are involved in manufacturing, whereas most other "jobbers" buy finished goods and sell them to small users who are not able to place large orders.)

FASHION

BRIDGE APPAREL: WHEN A DESIGNER ISN'T A "DESIGNER"

A fashion writer for *The New York Times* once pointed out that "Only in fashion could better be worse."[1] He was referring, of course, to the fact that "better" apparel is "worse" (that is, of lower quality and price) than designer apparel—and now, in recent years, apparel known as **bridge.**

A rapidly growing portion of the women's sportswear business, bridge apparel could basically be defined as designer fashions without the designer price tag. In other words, the clothing is more fashion-forward than most better styles, but less expensive than most designer collections—thereby bridging the gap between the two categories. As a vice president/divisional merchandise manager for Marshall Field put it: "Bridge is for the customer who wants to look like she's wearing designer apparel but who doesn't want to pay for designer apparel."[2]

On the other hand, many customers might not even realize that they are *not* getting designer goods when they buy bridge clothing—thanks to the fact that a number of top designers have developed special bridge collections separate from their regular designer lines. Among them are Perry Ellis with Perry Ellis Portfolio, Calvin Klein with Calvin Klein Classics, and Anne Klein II. In fact, Anne Klein may have actually spawned the entire category when the company launched its "II" line back in 1983.

At that time, the name "bridge" had not yet been dubbed for the clothing, but the concept was clear. Marilyn Kawakami, president of Anne Klein II, described it this way: "The customer we're after is coming from the better market. We're giving her the option to trade up. She's the Evan-Picone customer, the basic customer who is now ready for something new. There is a tremendous market out there that doesn't have the funds to buy designer clothes."[3]

What Anne Klein II has targeted—with other bridge resources following suit—is primarily the female career executive. With the clothing offering many of the same design elements and styling details of a regular designer collection, bridge offers women quality and fashion-forward looks—at about one-third to one-half the price of designer clothes.

How can the design houses chop the price of their clothes down to that extent? The most effective way is through using less expensive fabrics than in their regular collections. However, that is not to say that bridge collections are cheap or poorly made. On the contrary, the companies still "maintain the integrity of the product, using good fabrics and quality styling," said a Calvin Klein spokesman;[4] and, while prices are less

F O C U S

ANNE KLEIN II

than designer, they can still fall in the $150 range for a skirt and $250 range for a jacket.[5]

In addition to the top designer resources that offer bridge collections, there are a number of other names that have established a strong presence in the bridge category, earning themselves an almost designer reputation and following. The best-known of these are Ellen Tracy and Adrienne Vittadini. And as the category grows, it could be a proving ground for other designers to win a following before launching a full-fledged design collection.

But most important, the growth of the bridge apparel category reflects a real need and desire by customers in building their wardrobe. Explained one department store fashion director: "Bridge has a lot to do with what's happening in American style, and with the fact that the bulk of the population is interested in better clothing as opposed to moderate—but not in spending thousands of dollars on clothes."[6]

[1] Michael Gross, "Confusing Clothing Categories," *The New York Times,* July 15, 1987, p. 12.

[2] Penny Gill, "Bridge-(Wo)manship," *Stores,* October 1987, p. 20.

[3] Susan Alai, "Anne Klein II: Seeking Wider Market," *Women's Wear Daily,* February 16, 1983, p. 33.

[4] Gill, p. 25.

[5] Ibid.

[6] Ibid.

This Fashion Focus is based on information from the articles cited above.

Contractors

Contractors usually specialize in just one phase of the production of a garment: sewing. In some cases contractors also perform the cutting operation from patterns submitted by a jobber or a manufacturer. Contractors developed early in the history of the fashion industry, with the beginning of mass-production techniques. Contractors serve those producers who have little or no sewing capability of their own as well as those whose current business exceeds their own capacity.

If a contractor is used, cut pieces of the garment are provided by the manufacturer. For an agreed price per garment, the article is sewn, finished, inspected, pressed, hung or packaged, and returned to the manufacturer for shipment to retail stores.

In the mass production of ready-to-wear, a single sewing-machine operator rarely makes a complete garment. Each operator sews only a certain section of the garment, such as a sleeve or a hem. This division of labor, called **section work** or **piece work,** makes it unnecessary for an operator to switch from one highly specialized machine to another or to make adjustments on the machine. Any change or adjustment in equipment takes time and increases labor costs. In the fashion trade, time lost in making such changes also causes delays in getting a style to consumers. Delays in production could mean the loss of timeliness and sales appeal before an article reaches market.

A contractor may arrange to work exclusively with one or more jobbers or manufacturers, reserving the right to work for others whenever the contractor's facilities are not fully employed. Such agreements are necessarily reciprocal. If a contractor agrees to give preference to a particular jobber's or manufacturer's work, the jobber or manufacturer gives preference to that contractor when placing sewing orders.

Advantages The advantages of the contractor system for the manufacturer are as follows:

- Large amounts of capital are not required for investment in sewing equipment that may soon become obsolete.
- Difficulties in the hiring and training of suitable workers are minimized.
- The amount of capital necessary to meet regular payrolls is greatly reduced.
- By providing additional manufacturing facilities in periods of peak demand, contractors help speed up delivery of orders.
- It is unnecessary to keep one factory busy year-round.

Disadvantages The disadvantages of the contractor system for the manufacturer are as follows:

- No individual has full responsibility for the finished product.
- The quality of workmanship and inspection tends to be uneven.
- Other "manufacturers" (jobbers) may use some facilities and get preferential treatment.

Specialization by Product

Women's apparel producers have typically been specialists, producing apparel of a particular type, a particular size range, and a specific price range. A blouse manufacturer, for example, seldom makes dresses, and a dress manufacturer does not turn out dresses in both women's and junior sizes. A coat and suit manufacturer does not produce both expensive and popular-priced lines.

Despite a move toward greater diversification, producers and retailers still have to think and work like specialists.

For instance, a producer must of necessity choose an inexpensive fabric for a popular-priced line and a more expensive fabric for a better-priced line. Retail buyers still shop one group of producers for sportswear, another for coats, and still another for bridalwear—and this is not likely to change in the future.

Categories

The following are the traditional basic categories in women's apparel and the types of garments generally included in each.

1. *Outerwear*—Includes coats, rainwear, jackets.
2. *Dresses*—Includes one- or two-piece designs and ensembles (a dress with a jacket or coat).
3. *Sportswear and separates*—Includes contemporary activewear; town-and-country and spectator sportswear, such as pants, shorts, tops, swimwear, and cover-ups; bathing caps; beach bags; sweaters; skirts; shirts; jackets; tennis dresses; casual dresses; jumpsuits.
4. *After-five and evening clothes*—Includes dressy apparel.
5. *Suits*—Includes jackets/skirts, jackets/pants combinations.
6. *Bride and bridesmaid attire.*
7. *Blouses*—Includes both dressy and tailored.
8. *Uniforms and aprons*—Includes aprons, housedresses and sometimes career apparel.
9. *Maternity*—Includes dresses, sportswear.

Size Ranges

Women's apparel is divided into several size ranges. Unfortunately, the industry has not yet developed standard industrywide size measurements for each of these ranges, although exploratory work has been undertaken in this direction. In many cases, the manufacturer has the pattern made to fit its targeted customer's approximate size measurement. This is why one manufacturer's misses' size 12 is likely to fit quite differently than another manufacturer's misses' size 12. The traditional size ranges are:

1. *Women's*—Includes even-numbered half-sizes 12½ to 26½ and straight sizes 36 to 52.
2. *Misses'*—Includes regular even-numbered sizes 4 to 20, tall sizes 12 to 20, and sometimes sizes as small as 2.
3. *Juniors'*—Includes regular sizes 5 to 17 and petite sizes 1 to 15.
4. *Petites'*—Includes regular even-numbered sizes 2 to 16 and junior sizes 1 to 15.

Special Sizes

One of the biggest areas of diversification and growth has been in special sizes, specifically petites, large sizes, and maternity. Together petite and large-size apparel sales account for approximately $20 billion in sales. Two-thirds of all women are estimated to fall into one of these two categories, and over three million women will outgrow their clothes every year for at least nine months of pregnancy. Special sizes have become significant enough for some merchandisers to have carved out niches, specializing, for example, in petite or large-size stores that sell primarily private label or only better-priced clothes.[6]

The introduction of special size trade shows was viewed by industry experts as a sign of maturity within the market. The First International Special Size Fashion Fair was held in New York City in 1982. Paris began sponsoring a European special-size show, the Mini Maxi

Tailles, in 1988. Special-size shows exhibit clothes and accessories in large, tall, petite, and maternity sizes.

Petites Forty-seven million women are estimated to be under 5'4" and thus in need of small sizes, a statistic that has caused petites to grow more rapidly than any other segment of the special-sizes market.

Proportioned for short, small-boned women who wear sizes 0–8, petite sizes are worn by both junior and misses customers. In 1980, Evan-Picone, Inc., created a separate division of petite-sized apparel. Within two years, it reached an annual sales volume of over $27 million.[7] Other manufacturers, including Jones New York, Liz Claiborne, and Levi Strauss, added petite lines. Many major department stores, such as Marshall Field, Macy's, and Lord & Taylor, have installed successful petite departments.

The biggest development in petites is entrepreneurial. Special-size stores, not only for petites but also for large sizes, have opened across the country. Karen Austin Petites, a New Jersey–based chain that sells better-priced casual and career wear, was launched in 1986. The company expects to operate 75 stores by 1990. Another chain, Petite Sophisticate, which sells moderate-priced apparel, has opened 178 units since it first opened in 1975.[8]

Large Sizes Approximately 25 percent of all women in the United States wear large sizes—16 through 20, 12½ to 26½, and 36 to 52. Until recently, however, apparel in these sizes made up only a small percentage of apparel production, and large sizes were notable for their lack of style. With the new interest in specialty sizes, this is changing.

Forgotten Woman, a 20-unit chain, has been a pioneer in marketing stylish, better-priced goods to large women. After its success with petites, Petite Sophisticate opened a large-size venture called Sophisticated Woman in 1986. Spiegel entered the market with a large-size catalog in 1984. When their mail-order sales hit $50 million, Spiegel's opened two large-size specialty stores called For You. They spun off a petite catalog in 1985.

In the past, the large-size category suffered from a lack of styling. Major apparel manufacturers used to wait a year before copying their successful styles into large sizes, but many vendors, including many who only made petite sizes, are now making large sizes in fashionable silhouettes and fabrics. Spiegel uses private-label designs for over half the clothes it sells in its stores and is trying to promote greater standardization of large sizes. Resistance to standardization is a problem in large sizes, because unlike petites, there is still a stigma attached to wearing larger sizes.[9]

Maternity Maternity clothes are receiving new emphasis. Now that two out of three pregnant women now stay on the job almost the entire nine months of their pregnancies, pregnant career women have become an important and growing submarket. This trend, combined with a large number of women of child-bearing age, has led to renewed interest in maternity fashion.

When Mothers Work began selling cotton knit dresses by mail order in 1981, the response was so great that the company expanded its line to include business suits, dresses, and jumpers with matching jackets. Another well-known name in maternity wear, Lady Madonna, began with one New York store in 1969 and grew to more than 90 franchises and annual retail sales of $20

Flowing and fabulous! Today manufacturers are producing wanted styles in sizes for larger women. Specialized retailers like The Forgotten Woman sell only larger sizes.

Style, sophistication, and comfort are the major points in today's maternity wear. There are styles to fit many lifestyles!

million.[10] Two of the largest chains are Motherhood, with 315 stores, and Mothercare, which sells maternity clothes and infants' and toddlers' merchandise. Experts believe that each of the chains averages $50 million in annual sales.[11]

Discounters are aggressively going after the maternity wear business. Most notable among them is Marilyn Steinberg Enterprises Inc., which owns 124 stores called Maternity Warehouse.

Wholesale Price Zones

Women's apparel is produced and marketed at a wide range of wholesale prices. Major factors contributing to the wholesale price of a garment are (1) the quality of materials used, (2) the quality of workmanship employed, (3) the amount and type of labor required in the production process, (4) the executive and sales position structure of the organization, and (5) showroom rent and business overhead.

Within this wide range of prices, however, there are certain **price zones,** or series of somewhat contiguous price lines that appeal to specific target groups of customers. The women's apparel market has five price zones:

1. *Designer* (usually the higher prices) —Includes lines of name designers, such as Bill Blass, Ralph Lauren, Oscar de la Renta, Anne Klein, Calvin Klein, and Donna Karan. Only 300 stores in the U.S. carry "designer" clothing, with sales of about $150 million. This is a tiny fraction of the more than $30 billion of women's apparel sold in the other four price zones.[12]

2. *Bridge* (between designer and better prices—usually one-third to one-half of designer prices)—These would include Ellen Tracey, Anne Klein II.

3. *Better* (usually medium to high prices)—Includes lines such as Liz Claiborne, Evan-Picone, J. H. Collectibles, and Jones New York. Also includes some of the better-known national brand names and department store private-label lines, as well as "boutique" lines produced by the prestige designers.

4. *Moderate* (usually the medium prices) —Includes lines of nationally advertised makers, such as Jantzen, Guess, Koret of California, Esprit, and Russ Tog. Sold mostly in chain stores or in main-floor departments in department stores.

5. *Budget* (usually the lower prices; sometimes referred to as the "promotional" or "mass" market)—Includes some national brand names such as Wrangler, but is primarily a

mass market retailer private label such as JC Penney and K mart.

A development of the early 1980s that is expected to reach even greater proportions through the remainder of the century is the appearance of a growing number of **off-price apparel stores,** selling name-brand and designer merchandise at prices well below traditional department store levels. These off-price outlets, such as Marshall's, T. J. Maxx, and Loehmanns, are putting increasing pressure on all the traditional price zones, and are especially affecting moderate to better goods.

MERCHANDISING AND MARKETING

Most fashion producers sell directly to retail stores rather than through intermediaries. The pace of fashion in all but a few staple items is much too fast to allow for the selling, reselling, or warehousing activities of wholesale distributors or jobbers.

As a result, women's apparel producers aim their sales promotion efforts at both retailers and consumers. Such efforts take the form of advertising, publicity, and sales promotion.

Advertising

Today most retail advertising of women's fashion apparel carries the name of the manufacturer. But this was not always the case. As recently as the 1930s, retailers refused to let manufacturers put any tags or labels on the clothes they made. Merchandise shortages during World War II, coupled with government regulations, helped to reverse this situation. Most merchants are now happy to capitalize on the producers' labels that are attached to clothes. They feature manufacturers' names in their own advertising and displays and set up special sections within stores that are exclusively devoted to individual producers' lines.

The apparel manufacturing industry spends less than 1 percent of its annual sales on advertising, but the exposure given to its products is impressive. After all, that 1 percent is usually based on very healthy sales figures.

Filene's Basement Stores, an off-price apparel retailer, keeps the merchandise coming and going—coming from apparel manufacturers, going as purchases by customers.

Print Advertising

Fashion and general-interest magazines and newspapers are prime outlets for apparel advertising, as are trade publications such as *W* and *Women's Wear Daily,* which are primarily for retailers. Fashion magazines provide another forum for exposure, largely directed to the customer, with editorial reports about clothes and fashion trends of the season and with both American and international coverage.

Considering the amount of money that goes into advertising, and the use that retailers are now willing to make of manufacturer's names, it is not surprising that cooperative advertising appears both in magazines and newspapers and now also in store catalogs.

National Brands and Designer Labels

The 1980s saw a tremendous growth in sales for national brands and nationally known designer labels. In part, this resulted from national advertising campaigns directed at consumers. National brands and designer labels are expected to continue to predominate in the industry.

Publicity

In addition to the enormous amount of money spent on advertising, apparel producers also use publicity to promote their names. Many manufacturers, especially in the designer area, retain the services of a public relations firm, whose primary job is to ensure coverage in the editorial pages of magazines and newspapers.

They also supply sports personalities and other celebrities with clothes in an attempt to attract public attention. One rarely watches a sports event these days without hearing mention of the brand names, not only the equipment being used but also of the apparel that is worn, along with endorsements from leading athletes.

Fashion Shows and Press Weeks

The major public relations effort goes into the presentations and fashion shows at which New York designers show their new collections for retailers and the fashion press. These showings are held for two weeks in April, August, and November.

They provide the country's newspaper, magazine, radio, and television fashion editors an opportunity to examine the newest American designer collections as well as those of leading European manufacturers. Editors are deluged with press releases and photo and interview opportunities that will help them tell the fashion stories to their readers. Initially, there were "press weeks" that followed the formal line openings where designers exhibited merchandise lines in all price categories specially to the press rather than to buyers. Gradually, however, the lower-priced merchandise was eliminated. Press weeks as exclusive showcases for high-priced fashion continued; then, as a result of cost and timing factors, they were eliminated. Now the press sees the collections at the same time as the retailers.

Trunk Shows

Trunk shows are another excellent form of publicity for the women's apparel industry. **Trunk shows** present a manufacturer's line to a retail store's sales staff and its customers. A representative of the company, sometimes a designer, typically mounts a fashion show of sample garments. After the show, he or she meets with customers to discuss the styles and their fashion relevance. The retail store's customers may review items they have seen and order them.

CALL OF THE WILD...

A **TRUNK SHOW** OF THE NEW COLLECTION BY **LAUREL BURCH**...
...for those who dare!

Once you catch the fever of the jungle, you'll only be satisfied with designs by Laurel Burch! A popular, contemporary artist and designer, Laurel Burch now brings you original ideas in jewelry, sweatshirts, mugs, tote bags, and stationery. Burch's fabulous oil paintings have been reproduced in new, collectible designs. Sweatshirts in a myriad of tropical colors with mythical creatures and tropical plants set the mood for this collection. M,L, and XL . . **28.00.** Mugs . . . **10.00.** Note cards . . . **1.50.** Assorted earrings, some with matching pins . . . **15.00-30.00.** Canvas tote bags, to carry all your loot home, . . . **28.00-32.00.**

SPECIAL . . . Gift with purchase Beautiful cloissone pin **FREE** with regularly priced Laurel Burch purchase of 15.00 or more.

Come meet James Brown, the Northeast representative for Laurel Burch, at one of our Trunk Shows! Be the first to see new, exciting designs in a wide array of innovative merchandise.
Thursday Oct. 22nd at **Penn Can** . . . **11-4.**
Friday Oct. 23rd at **Downtown** . . . **11-2.**
Saturday Oct. 24th at **Shoppingtown** . . . **11-4.**
You'll also have the opportunity at these shows to see an original Laurel Burch oil painting!

The Addis Co.
When Only The Best Will Do

DOWNTOWN   SHOPPINGTOWN   FAIRMOUNT FAIR   PENN CAN MALL

This unusual "trunk show" by an accessory designer features her entire line.

Everyone benefits from trunk shows. Customers see clothes as the designer planned them and coordinated them, and they experience some of the glamor of the fashion industry. The retailer enjoys the dramatic influx of customers who come to such personal appearances and shows and any profits that result as clothes are ordered. The manufacturer tests the line on real customers and in order to understand real consumers' needs *first hand!* If customer response is enthusiastic, the designer achieves new status—and bigger orders—from the retailer than otherwise expected.

Videotapes

Videotapes that show off a manufacturer's line are another promotional tool. The manufacturers' and designers' seasonal premiers are videotaped with live models; a running commentary is then added by the manufacturer or designer. Videotapes are primarily shown to retailers' sales staffs to explain the fashion importance of items and to give tips on selling, but they are also sometimes shown on the selling floor.

Unfortunately, in-store showings of videotapes have not been the potential goldmine that manufacturers had hoped, perhaps because women who are already in the store to shop do not want to stand around and look at a videotape. Videotape producers have begun to zero in on their market, though, and fashion videotapes are now showing up in restaurants, hospitals, airports, doctors' and dentists' offices, and discos—all places that seem to be more conducive than the store to this form of entertainment. There is no charge to the apparel producer (the video user on location pays a use fee), so this amounts to another form of publicity for the fashion industry. But apparel manufacturers have not given up entirely on the idea of fashion videotapes. They are now experimenting with their use in conjunction with catalogs.

Promotion Aids

Manufacturers also provide retailers with an assortment of other promotional aids designed to assist them and speed the sale of merchandise. A firm may offer any or all of the following:

- Display ideas
- Display and stock fixtures
- Advertising aids
- Suggestions for the design of the department in which their goods are displayed
- Reorder forms and assistance in checking stock for reordering purposes
- Educational and sales training assistance for salespersons and customers
- Promotional talks by producers' representatives
- Assistance in mounting fashion shows
- Statement enclosures or other ads designed to reach customers by mail
- Special retail promotions to tie in with national advertising campaigns
- Advertising mats for smaller stores

In one elaborate but not unusual promotion, a sportswear manufacturer offered assistance to any store that would stage a travel promotion using its merchandise. A major airline was enticed into joining the effort for the publicity it would receive. Its flight attendants made store appearances in which they demonstrated how to pack a suitcase and advised customers on the best clothes to wear for specific trips. The clothes they recommended came from the manufacturers' line, of course, and the destinations they recommended were served by the airline. In this case, a store, an apparel manufacturer, and an airline, to say nothing of the customer, all benefited from the promotion.

INDUSTRY TRENDS

Throughout the rest of the century, the domestic women's apparel industry and the U.S. apparel industry overall will face dramatic changes. American designers have finally succeeded in rivaling Paris designers as definers of high fashion. However, the American design industry faces what may be its toughest competitive challenge ever: the growth of an international clothing market out of which manufacturers must carve their market share, since a rise in imports has threatened the domestic market they have enjoyed.

After decades of domination at home, the American wholesale market has been inundated with imports from countries with cheap labor. The imports, which improve in quality every year, captured 6 percent of the market by 1967 and 22 percent by 1980. Current projections indicate that imports will seize a market share of 40 percent by 1993.[13]

The apparel industry is taking steps, however, to enable it to compete more effectively in an increasingly global marketplace. Some of its tactics include:

- Emergence of manufacturers as retailers
- Greater emphasis on licensing
- Increased emphasis on quick response (see Technology Talk on page 172–173).

Manufacturers as Retailers

In 1987 when Murjani International, then a leading apparel manufacturer, decided to design clothes with Coca-Cola and Jeep labels, it knew it had to show everyone that the red-and-white label could sell something other than a soft drink. To do so, it did something extraordinary: It leased a retail space on Manhattan's fashion-conscious Columbus Avenue. What made this move unusual was not that another clothing

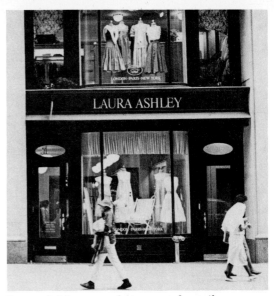

Laura Ashley manufactures and retails.

store had opened on a street filled with them, but that the store was opened by a manufacturer and not a retailer.

Murjani was among an increasing number of clothing manufacturers opening their own stores. Disappointed by the sales, service, and space allotted to them in retail stores and wanting to create the "right" atmosphere for this clothing, they chose to enter the retail business themselves.

Designer Ralph Lauren was the first to do so. Frustrated by the way department and specialty stores were selling his clothes, he opened the first Polo/Ralph Lauren shop on Rodeo Drive in Beverly Hills in 1971. Since then, he has built an empire of over 100 Polo/Ralph Lauren shops that stretches coast-to-coast in the United States and across the oceans in Europe and Asia.[14]

Esprit de Corp, the San Francisco-based apparel manufacturer, opened its first full-priced retail outlet in Los Angeles, having previously opened a discount store in San Francisco in 1981. Since then, Esprit has developed an entire retail division, with 34 stores in the United States, 10 overseas, and plans to expand.

Anne Klein, Calvin Klein, Adrienne Vittadini, Perry Ellis, and Betsy Johnson have also opened their own retail outlets.[15]

But whether manufacturers will be good retailers remains to be seen. A producer first has to compete for good retail talent, which can be expensive, as well as retail space in a prime location. The risks escalate if the manufacturer franchises, which many must do because they cannot personally oversee their retail empire.

Like most franchisers, Yves Saint Laurent discovered that franchises are sometimes sold to persons who lack the experience or financial backing to run a business. Saint Laurent's Rive Gauche boutiques dropped from 28 to 9. Polo/Ralph Lauren reported a smaller failure rate even though all its stores, except the New York and London shops, are franchised. Some designers solve the problem by owning and operating their own shops, but this imposes its own obvious limitations.[16]

Another problem is the reaction of the department and specialty stores that carry the manufacturers' lines. They feel such competition is unfair, and many have decided to stop carrying retail lines that are sold in manufacturers' own outlets.

Liz Claiborne attempted to solve this problem when she opened her retail operation in the mid-1980s by taking pains to separate her retail store from the lines she sold to other stores. Her stores, called First Issue, bore only First Issue stock. It was priced, marketed, and designed differently from lines bearing the Liz Claiborne name.[17]

Despite such efforts, many industry experts feel that the industry cannot sustain everyone, and that ultimately only the strongest will succeed.

Licensing

Licensing, which was described in Chapter 5, experienced a boom in the 1980s. This was largely due to the emergence of an important new market segment—5 million working women who spend $18 billion on apparel yearly. As a group, they are not quite in the income bracket to buy designer clothes, but designers have learned that they can capitalize on the market they represent through licensing ventures.

The first landmark deal in licensing occurred in the 1930s when Mickey Mouse products flooded the market. Shirley Temple was the first human to find a windfall in selling her name for use on dresses, dolls, and an assortment of other products. Not until the 1980s did American designers discover the goldmine that lay in licensing.

The advantage of licensing is that merchandise is identified with a highly recognizable name. Licensed products are estimated at $40 billion annually, with apparel and accessory licensing, the single largest category, accounting for about one-third of the sales.

The disadvantages in licensing are few. When a designer turns over control to a manufacturer as he does when he licenses a product, he may lose some quality control. A bigger problem is that he will move too far afield for his more exclusive customers, but considering the potential profits in licensing, this is unlikely to worry many designers.

Christian Dior was an early pioneer in licensing, having granted his first license in 1949. Even though Dior died in 1957, his name appears on products made by 30 separate manufacturers and total sales of $320 million annually in the United States alone. Pierre Cardin used licenses to create a fashion empire—the largest of its kind—that generates worldwide sales of $500 million. Among the more recent entries into the licensing business are Calvin Klein, with 10 licenses, and Bill Blass, with over 35 licenses. One of the more successful designers at capturing the career-woman market was Anne Klein, with her Anne Klein II line. In its first full year of business in 1981, Anne Klein II sold $50 million. Not all designers are so successful, but for those who are, licensing pays off.

DEVELOPMENT FORECASTS

The women's fashion apparel industry is not immune to the effects of the economy. Coping with a poor economy is just one more challenge that American apparel firms must face creatively. The industry has solved problems with the economy by targeting new retail markets, price points, customers, and even sizes. With such techniques, expansion will undoubtedly continue in coming years, not only in the domestic market but in the new and all-important global fashion market. In the latter, solutions will include increasingly sophisticated licensing and export programs.

The current changes in the American apparel industry make this an exciting and challenging time to be in women's fashion. Those producers who are able to take advantage of the opportunities that exist and to solve their problems creatively will find that the potential for success has never been greater.

REFERENCES

[1] Eileen B. Brill, "From Immigrants to Imports," *WWD/75 Years in Fashion, 1910–1985,* November 1985, p. 10.

[2] Joyce Worley, "3-D Designing," *Women's Wear Daily,* Technology & Operations Section, March 1987, pp. 14–15.

[3] J. D. Kidd, "Japan's Miti-Machine," *Women's Wear Daily,* Technology & Operations Section, June 1986, p. 18.

[4] Leonard Sloane, "Shoppers Stray, Merchants Scramble," *The New York Times,* May 6, 1989, p. 52.

[5] "Outlook for the Apparel Industry," *The KSA Perspective for Apparel Management,* No. 29, Kurt Salmon Associates, New York, January 1983, unpaged.

[6] "Growing Into Special Sizes," *Apparel Merchandising,* April 1988, p. 26.

[7] "Small Clothes Are Selling Big," *Business Week,* November 16, 1981, p. 52.

[8] "Growing into Special Sizes," p. 27.

[9] Ibid., pp. 26–28.

[10] Elaine Louie, "A Ballooning Industry," *Working Woman,* October 1983, p. 174.

[11] Helen Burggraf, "Maternity Shops Grow," *Stores,* March 1987, pp. 63–68.

[12] Woody Hochswender, "Patterns," *The New York Times,* April 18, 1989, p. 36.

[13] "Outlook for the Apparel Industry," unpaged.

[14] Joan Chrissos, "Stores With a Label," *The Miami Herald,* August 16, 1987, Section F, pp. 1–2.

[15] Anne Rosenblum, "SA's Move into Its Own Stores Gains Momentum," *Women's Wear Daily,* March 29, 1988, pp. 1 and 19.

[16] Ibid.

[17] Lisa Lockwood, "Liz Claiborne Unveils First Issue Store," *Women's Wear Daily,* February 2, 1988, p. 12.

MERCHANDISING VOCABULARY

Define or briefly explain the following terms:

Apparel jobber
Bridge apparel
  collection
Bundling
Computer-aided design
  (CAD)
Contractor
Custom-made

Graded
Manufacturer
Marker
Off-price apparel store
Off-shore production
Outside shop
Piece work
Price zones

Quick Response (QR)
Ready-to-wear
Sample hand
Section work
Spreader
Trunk show

MERCHANDISING REVIEW

1. Why did New York City become the center of the garment industry in the United States?
2. Discuss the growth and contributions of the ILGWU to the apparel industry.
3. What are the major advantages of the contractor system? What is the key disadvantage?
4. List the traditional basic categories of women's apparel, giving types of garments in each category.
5. Into what size ranges is women's apparel traditionally divided?
6. List and describe the five major price zones into which women's apparel is divided. What are the major factors contributing to the wholesale price of garments?
7. Why do most fashion producers sell directly to retail stores rather than through wholesalers?
8. Discuss the merchandising activities of women's fashion producers today.
9. How does a manufacturer or designer benefit from attending a trunk show in a retail store?
10. Discuss the major problems facing a manufacturer who is also a retailer.

MERCHANDISING DIGEST

1. Discuss the advantages and disadvantages of standardization of women's apparel sizes.
2. What are the repercussions of a name-brand or designer manufacturer selling current-season apparel to off-price outlets as well as to department and specialty shops?

CHILDREN'S APPAREL

One merchandiser of children's apparel recently summed up the current state of the industry by saying that while the business is not as easy as it used to be, it is considerably more fun.[1] He was referring to the fact that children have at last become style-conscious. After years of paying little attention to and exercising even less control over what they wore, they have become very aware of changing styles. Children are now quick to state what they will and will not wear. This drastic change has come about largely because of television. Children not only see other children on television but they also are deluged with advertisements for children's products, including clothes.

And while being dictated to by little customers may not be everyone's idea of fun, the children's apparel industry has been irrevocably changed.

Everyone from the designers to the customers is looking for a fashion image in children's wear. What once was simply called children's wear can now rightly be called children's fashion.

DEMOGRAPHICS AND THE CHILDREN'S APPAREL INDUSTRY

Children's apparel is unusual in that demographics play an important role in shaping the industry. Patterns of childbearing tend to be cyclical. Although the birth rate had been steadily declining since the end of the nineteenth century, the aftermath of World War II brought about a baby boom. Women who had been working to support the war effort turned over their jobs to the returning soldiers and went home to become full-time housewives—and mothers. The birth rate soared. Three to four children per family was not unusual. Between 1953 and 1964, a whopping 4 million births occurred every year.

In the 1970s, people became concerned that the world population was growing too rapidly and people were urged to have fewer children. Women also began to work outside the home again. The birth rate declined and the average number of children per family sank to fewer than two. The children's wear market tightened its belt accordingly.

The 1980s did not bring about another baby boom, with three to four children per family, but the baby boom babies had themselves reached child-bearing age, and there were a lot of them. While women continued to have a statistical average of 1.5 children, and more women worked every year, the number of babies born increased for the first time since the 1960s. Over 3½ million babies were born in 1987, and almost 3.9 million were born in 1988. After 1990, demographers expect the numbers to drop again.[2]

The good news in the 1980s was that even though women were not having large families again, people were, in an era known for its opulence and wealth, spending more than they ever had before on their children. The number of mothers who worked soared, which meant that two-income families generally had more discretionary income. People not only bought more for each child, but they purchased more expensive goods than in the past, a trend that is expected to continue as long as the economy remains strong.

PSYCHOLOGICAL IMPORTANCE OF CHILDREN'S CLOTHES

The interest in dressing children well is even less likely to abate since psychologists now believe that clothes play an important role in shaping and guiding a child's self-image. As parents under-stand the role that clothes play at various stages of a child's growth, they can help to ensure that a child's appearance will enhance his or her striving to become a mature, self-confident adult.[3]

HISTORY OF THE CHILDREN'S APPAREL INDUSTRY

Although boy's wear is considered part of the men's apparel industry, for our purposes it will be considered as part of children's wear and described in this chapter.

As a commercial activity, the children's wear industry is a phenomenon of the twentieth century. For most of history, children were dressed like miniature adults. Study a portrait from the Renaissance or the American colonial era, and you will see children wearing the same low necklines, bustles, and pantaloons that were currently stylish with adults.

When children's clothes finally began to look different from those that adults wore toward the end of the 1800s, they took on the look of uniforms. All little girls, for example, dressed in a similar drab outfit dark shoes, a mid-calf length skirt, and dark stockings.

Clothes were made extra large so children could grow into them. Their construction was sturdy so they could be handed down to younger children. Many children's clothes were hand-sewn or made by a few apparel manufacturers who never offered any variations on the clothes, nor, for that matter, experienced any growth in their businesses. It did not matter that children's clothes were dull and unattractive because no child would dare to protest what parents wanted him or her to wear.

Although a few designers specialized in high-priced children's wear in the

This 1874 engraving shows children wearing miniature versions of adult apparel.

early 1900s, it was not until after World War I that the commercial production and distribution of stylish children's wear began. Not surprisingly, the growth of the children's wear industry followed in the wake of the developing women's wear industry. When women stopped making their own clothes, they also stopped making their children's clothes.

The children's wear industry also grew because manufacturers found ways to make factory-produced clothing sturdier than homemade clothes. The development of snaps, zippers, and more durable sewing methods were important contributions.

Another important step in the manufacture of children's clothes occurred after World War I when manufacturers began to standardize children's wear sizes. What began as a very primitive method of sizing children's clothing has since turned into a highly sophisticated sizing operation, with many categories and subdivisions.

The next major change in the children's wear industry—really a revolution—was brought about, as noted ear- lier, by the introduction of television into Americans' lives. It did not take advertisers long to discover that children, among the largest group of consumers of television, could be targeted directly. From there it was a short step to gear the advertising in other media— radio as well as magazines and newspapers—toward children.

In addition to establishing children as customers, television helped to create a more sophisticated look in their clothes. Children who modeled children's clothes used to be childlike and cute so they would appeal to parents. But once children themselves became the customers, the models became older-looking and even elegant—all in order to appeal to children.[4]

Beginning as early as age 2, children expect to make their own decisions about what they wear. Even though parents still do the actual purchasing, their choices are heavily influenced by their children's desires.[5]

ORGANIZATION AND OPERATION OF THE CHILDREN'S APPAREL INDUSTRY

Despite the emergence of such giant companies as Carter's and Health-Tex, most children's clothes are still made by small, family-owned businesses. Many adult apparel producers, most notably Danskin, Russ-Togs, Levi Strauss, White Stag, and Blue Bell, also operate children's apparel divisions.

Like adult clothing, children's wear is divided into categories based on price, size, and type of merchandise. Children's clothes are produced in budget, moderate, and better-priced cost ranges. Most children's clothes are bought in the budget and moderate price ranges, although industry figures indicate that parents are spending more on each child and are beginning to buy more of the better-priced goods.

Categories

Children's wear is divided into seven basic size ranges.

1. **Infants**—For babies up to the age of 1 year. Two sizing systems are used, one for sizes 3 to 24 months and another for newborn, medium, large, and extra large.
2. **Toddlers**—For children 2 to 3 years old. Sizes range from 1T to 4T.
3. **Children's**—For girls and boys between the ages of 3 and 6. Sizes include 3 to 6X for girls and 3 to 7 for boys.
4. **Girls'**—For girls between the ages of 7 and 14. Sizes include 7 through 14.
5. **Preteen**—Parallels the girls' size group but offers more sophisticated styling. Sizes range from 6 to 14.
6. **Boys'**—For boys from ages 6 or 7 through adolescence. Includes sizes 8 to 20.
7. **Young men, student, or teen**—Like preteen clothes, this new category was developed to meet the demand for greater sophistication in boys' wear. Includes sizes 8 through 20.

Children's wear is also specialized by product. A producer will make only girls' knits, while another makes only girls' dresses, and another makes only preteen sportswear. But unlike the producers of adult wear, children's wear producers often make a single type of clothing in several size ranges. For example, a producer may make boys' sportswear in sizes 8 through 20, while

0-12 months is the size and department designation. All styles are displayed by size categories.

a producer of girls' dresses may make a product in toddlers through girls sizes.

The same design and production methods that are used in the manufacture of adult apparel are used in children's wear, although they are often simplified.

THE ROLE OF FASHION IN CHILDRENS' WEAR

Even the most basic lines of children's clothing reflect attempts to make the clothes fashionable, and the demand for style, once primarily an urban phenomenon, is now felt in rural areas.

The demand for stylish children's clothes, which has escalated every year, has most recently culminated in designer clothing for children. Children's wear, however, must still be viewed as a business that is a *fashionable* rather than a *fashion* business. The difference is that while the children's wear industry produces fashionable clothing, the styles mirror men's and women's styles. They are not in and of themselves innovative, nor does new fashion ever start in children's wear lines.

The children's wear industry also does not operate with the intensity of the adult clothing industry. Children's clothes, for example, do not follow a ready-to-wear production and design schedule.

Producers of children's clothing have typically operated on a one line per season production schedule, and four lines—spring, summer, winter, and fall—are typical. Lines are not updated during a season. Once a line has been shown and accepted, that is all the manufacturer produces. An exciting and very hot new look might appear at mid-season, but this is still rare. Most manufacturers could not produce a new look until the following season, at which

point demand may even have begun to decline.

The children's wear business has begun to make the kinds of operational changes that are necessary to permit it to stay more on top of changing fashion. Styles in children's wear used to trickle down from the adult fashion world, and typically lagged a year or more behind adult fashions. Today, however, the lag is likely to be only one season, and some manufacturers have geared up to produce hot styles almost immediately.[6] The industry has also begun to use fashion forecasting specialists to enable manufacturers to incorporate new styles into their lines as soon as a trend is spotted. At this point, the smaller (and trendier) manufacturers are still quicker to incorporate new styles and fashion than are the larger companies.

MARKET CENTERS

Most of the children's wear firms are located in the North Atlantic states, particularly in New York City. As is the trend in the women's and men's apparel industries, some factories have moved farther south in order to obtain lower production costs. In many cases goods are produced in foreign countries—the Far East primarily for outerwear, jeans, woven shirts, and sweaters; Greece, Spain, and Israel for infants' knits and apparel items. These countries offer lower production costs than do France, Italy, and Switzerland, which produce prestige merchandise. But the design, sales, and distribution centers of such firms remain in New York City. While New York continues to be the most important market center for children's wear, many producers maintain permanent showrooms in the large regional apparel marts, especially in Miami, and schedule showings there.

FASHION

The word *esprit* means "spirit" in French; and it is therefore a very appropriate name for the $800 million sportswear company that has bounced its way into the fashion consciousness of Americans—and especially, of American kids.

Esprit itself was founded in 1969, and the Esprit Kids division began in 1982. But within four years, the pint-size apparel lines accounted for 20 percent of the company's sales.[1]

The rather lively success of Esprit Kids is based in large part on the company's marketing of its fresh, lifestyle looks for older consumers to the younger generation. As Bonnie Pyle, the division's president, put it: "Our kids' clothes are just scaled down versions of adult clothing. Design is totally sepa-

F O C U S

rate, but the image is the same. We want the customer from the time she's 2 years old all the way up to . . . to my age!"[2]

The Esprit Kids apparel line revolves around a core of basics, including brightly colored Esprit logo T-shirts, tank tops, and sweatshirts, plus classics such as denim jeans, white cotton shirts, and khaki shorts. While the look and styling of the garments borrow from the feel of the regular Esprit line, the kids' line features its own color stories and prints to appeal directly to its own target consumers.

There are, in fact, *three* target consumer groups for Esprit Kids. Originally, there was just one line of apparel for both the toddler and children's age groups. But when Pyle took over the division in 1984, she expanded the product mix and split it into three segments: a "mini" line for ages 3 to 6, a children's line for ages 7 to 11, and a teen line for ages 12 to 15.

Also in 1984, Esprit Kids opened its first freestanding store, located in Corte Madera, California. In less than 3 years, that number grew to more than 12 Esprit Kids stores spread across the country to the East Coast; plus, the company continued to expand its Esprit Kids "shops within shops" in major department stores, including Macy's, Marshall Field, and Bloomingdale's. By 1990, Pyle hopes to have close to 40 freestanding units and up to 50 department store Esprit Kids shops in place.[3]

As far as other directions for the division, the possibility of creating a boys' line is in the back of Pyle's mind, although she plans to take that step cautiously. (A tentative boys' collection for fall '86 was actually cancelled because it "wasn't good enough."[4]) And even as the children's wear line was growing, the division went ahead and cut back on some of the smaller stores that were stocking the apparel "because we found we had too many small stores and we weren't important to a lot of them. We want to be more important to fewer people," Pyle explained.[5]

That's certainly an admirable goal today, and one that typifies the strategic thinking that has helped launch Esprit as a whole into the fashion stratosphere. And with that kind of planning at work—plus apparel that keeps hitting the fashion nail on the head—it's a safe bet that many more kids will be catching the Esprit Kids spirit in the future.

[1] Glynis Costin, "Esprit Slows Racing Pace—Down to Gallop," *Women's Wear Daily,* September 30, 1986, p. 1.

[2] Deborah Brown, "Esprit de Pyle," *Children's Business,* August 1987, p. 59.

[3] Brown, p. 60.

[4] Ibid.

[5] Ibid.

This Fashion Focus is based on information from the articles cited above.

MERCHANDISING AND MARKETING

Many of the features and activities of the children's wear industry are similar, if not identical, to those of the women's and men's apparel industries. Sales promotion and advertising activities for children's wear, however, are considerably more limited.

The few giants in the industry—Carter's, Health-Tex, and Danskin—advertise aggressively to consumers. Smaller firms—the majority of firms producing budget and moderately priced children's wear—leave most consumer advertising to retailers. Firms producing higher-priced, name-designer merchandise do a limited amount of consumer advertising. The high cost of this advertising is often shared with textile firms.

In general the industry limits its advertising to the trade press. Specialized publications that are concerned with children's wear include: *Earnshaw's Infants, Girls-Boys-Wear Review, Young Fashions, Teens & Boys, Children's Business,* and *Kids Fashion.* Trade publications that report on adult fashions, such as *Women's Wear Daily* and *Daily News Record,* also carry children's wear advertising and news reports of interest to retailers on a regular basis.

Trade Shows

In October 1979, the sponsors of the National Fashion and Boutique Show inaugurated a national show for the children's wear industry. Called the National Kids' Fashion Show, it is held every 3 years and features over 350 children's wear lines in every size, price, and product category. The Florida Children's Wear Manufacturers' Guild holds an annual market show every September to promote children's spring and summer apparel lines. Since 1987, the show has been open to non-Florida–based manufacturers, a gesture that may make the show a national market.

Designer Labels

Children's designer-label clothing and accessories are highly visible in stores across the country. The appeal of these items seems to rise above income levels. Designer labels are available in stores geared to middle-income as well as high-income customers.

Contemporary designers often choose vibrant colors and bold patterns for children's wear. Just compare these styles with those shown on page 195.

Although designer wear for children has been around for a while—Izod introduced a boys' line in the late 1960s—the explosion in designer-label children's wear really took off in 1978–1979 with the designer jean craze.[7]

Because they have designer-name status, some children's wear designers, such as Ruth Scharf and Florence Eiseman, have acquired celebrity status. Adult designers have also entered the children's wear arena. Several companies have launched separate divisions of children's wear. Not all have been successful. Although Liz Claiborne reportedly did $15 million (out of a total company volume of $813 million) in 1986 with LizKids, the line never took off as hoped, and the company dropped it in 1988.[8]

Status names are also changing the shape of the boys' wear industry. It is difficult to tell which came first, though—the boys' demand for designer clothes or the designers' efforts to enter the boys' wear market. Whatever the case, well-known fashion designers are now competing for space alongside traditional branded merchandise in boys' wear departments. Boys' wear, in fact, has become a prime area for European and American designers such as Pierre Cardin, Yves Saint Laurent, John Weitz, Ralph Lauren, and Calvin Klein.

When a designer label succeeds in children's wear, its success can often be attributed to what the industry calls the "I can dream, can't I?" syndrome. This refers to a parent who cannot afford a $1,500 Yves Saint Laurent outfit for herself or himself but who sees an opportunity to deck out his or her child in a delectable YSL outfit, thus indulging in the fantasy that at least someone in the family wears designer clothes.

Briefly Speaking

Heel and Toe and Away We Go!

When you talk about "head-to-toe" selling, it helps to have all the merchandise to cover the wearer from head to toe. E. J. Gitano and Mrs. Taki's Kids are two children's wear manufacturers who believe in this concept and have designed collections that show a total look.

In addition to girls' sportswear, E. J. Gitano has added other categories to provide fashion-conscious little girls with a total "coordinated" look. The apparel firm has launched a store with a head-to-toe image that reflects all E. J. Gitano products.

Taking a different and more expensive road, Mrs. Taki's Kids—conceived by Beverly Taki, wife of Anne Klein chairman Tamio Taki—has chosen to present designer children's wear in "sophisticated fun" concept shops in department stores. In order to pull the collection together as a concept within stores, Mrs. Taki's Kids has created a special in-store shop fixture which displays the various aspects of the complete collection.

While the total-concept shops continue selling within the walls of prestigious retailers, Mrs. Taki's Kids plan stores of their own to carry the complete collection, including shoes, accessories, and new products such as toiletries and even cookies. Who knows where "total-concept" selling will go?

This Briefly Speaking is based on information from the following sources:

"E. J. Gitano's Concept Stores: Showcase for Top-To-Toe Style," *Stores*, August 1988, p. 14.
"Mrs. Taki's Kids: Fun Concept at a (High) Price," *Stores*, August 1988, p. 18.

PEPSI and PEPSI-COLA AMERICA are registered trademarks used under license from PepsiCo, Inc.

HERE COMES THE LOOK OF A NEW GENERATION

More Exciting Graphics!
More Sizes!
More Pepsi Power!

Get into it! It's the Pepsi feeling, the Pepsi point-of-view. Now in every kind of fun fashion: T's and sweats, tops and jeans, shirts and shorts for men, women, teens to toddlers. And just wait till you see the scores of super new graphic designs.

The greatest choice... the choice of a new generation.

PEPSI APPAREL AMERICA

Mayfair Industries, Inc.
Empire State Building, Suite 5301, New York, NY 10118
(212) 564-8420

FORTREL
Fortrel® is a trademark of Fiber Industries, Inc. for polyester.

"The choice of a new generation" is the advertising slogan for Pepsi—here we see it being used for both adults and children's wear.

Licensing

Like designer labels, licensed names provide a sense of fashion rightness, in addition to giving a garment or line instant identification in consumers' minds. As a result, as the children's wear industry became more fashion-conscious, manufacturers were quick to produce licensed goods. Today, the ever popular cartoon and toy character licenses, however, share the spotlight with a growing number of corporate and sports licenses.

Licensed cartoon and toy characters, long a staple with children, proliferated during the early 1980s, but the characters were often short-lived. Strawberry Shortcake, Smurfs, Cabbage Patch, and E.T. products each had a moment in the limelight, but were soon replaced by new, more up-to-date characters such as Pound Puppies, GI Joe, Alf, Max Headroom, and Roger Rabbit. About 70 percent of all the licensed apparel and accessories sold in 1985 featured character licenses.[9]

Character licenses dominate in children's T-shirts, sweatshirts, and sleepwear, and are also strong in accessories and sportswear. Their impact is minimal, though, in dresses, suits, and outerwear. Even with the recent boom, children's character licenses proved to be short-lived, and only a few reached the ranks of true stardom (and big profit). As a result, many retailers, particularly department store buyers, have become cautious about overinvesting in them. Department stores, whose promotion is necessary if a licensed character is to be truly successful, tend to stick with the classics that have been around a while—Snoopy, Mickey Mouse, and Beatrix Potter's characters.

Corporate licensing is the latest boom area in children's wear. Children and young adults like wearing clothes that advertise products they use. Among recent successful entrants into this area of children's wear are Coca-Cola; Pepsi-Cola; Burger King; McKids, a joint effort by McDonald's and Sears; and Fisher-Price, a toy manufacturer that has developed a line of children's clothes promoting itself.

Sportswear licensing is the other prospering area of licensing. Sports figures and teams both have high media visibility and thus enjoy instant recognition among children and young adults. Sports figures, who have successfully put their names on sports equipment for years, are now adding them to jogging and running suits, tennis clothes and accessories, as well as less active casual and sportswear lines, with great success. Professional hockey, football, and baseball teams, as well as college and university athletic teams, now routinely license their names for use on clothes, mostly T-shirts and sweatshirts.

INDUSTRY TRENDS

Like women's apparel manufacturers, children's wear producers are constantly on the lookout for ways to increase productivity and reduce—or at least minimize—costs while still maintaining quality. Many manufacturers have found that modernizing and computerizing their operations is a necessity. Even portions of the design process are now computerized in children's wear, mostly because this helps producers respond more quickly to fashion trends in the industry.

Production costs have risen in recent years, and this has forced producers of budget goods to move into moderate lines. Most of the budget-priced children's clothing is produced offshore in labor-cheap foreign countries.

Price Lines

The clear distinctions that once existed between budget, moderate, and better-priced children's wear were eroded in an era of heavy inflation in the 1970s, and the disintegration has continued. Several major moderate-priced sportswear producers such as Pandora and Girlstown were driven out of business by inflation and rising operating costs.

Had they stayed in business, they would have been forced to raise their prices beyond the upper limits of the moderate price range. This would have placed them in competition with established producers of higher-priced apparel and put them in a much smaller segment of the children's wear market—thus making it likely that they would ultimately fail anyway.

Although there was no room for expansion in the upper-priced categories during the upheaval of the 1970s, this was not the case in moderate-priced children's wear. In order to fill the vacuum created in this price range, many budget manufacturers opted to trade up. At the same time, many moderate-priced manufacturers such as Health-Tex and OshKosh, known as suppliers

TECHNOLOGY TALK

"WE TREAT OUR CUSTOMERS LIKE CHILDREN"

Sears Merchandise Group has gotten some very high marks for its new McKids freestanding stores, which were set up through an exclusive licensing agreement with McDonalds Corporation. None of the merchandise in the freestanding McKids stores is duplicated in the 800 Sears stores that carry McKids clothing. McKids stores groupings are mostly boys' and girls' apparel with regular prices that compete directly with department stores rather than discounters. The freestanding McKids stores target their merchandise to dual-income parents who earn more than $40,000 and who have two children.

Presently the McKids stores are located in high-traffic centers and shopping malls, but neighborhood locations are being planned for the future. A 2-year pilot program plans to open 20 to 40 freestanding McKids stores per year. The stores are concentrated in separate selling markets so they will not splinter the impact of the stores around the country.

Everything in a McKids store is designed around a child's perspective, including a 48-inch door which provides a separate entrance for children and dressing-room doors that open to reveal McDonald's characters holding mirrors at low levels appropriate for pint-sized shoppers.

One of the store's technology highlights is a play station located in the rear of the store, equipped with toys, a computer, video screen, and walk-through tower. A video camera records the activity in the play station so that parents can check on their children by glancing at television monitors while they shop. The goal of the design firm that created the McKids interiors was to create a store that was fun. Before the first store was opened, a prototype play station was created and factory, contractor, and office personnel were encouraged to bring their children to test it. Technology aside—the real test was given by the children to the store created by adults—not the standard situation.

To sell children's wear in the past you had to sell to the parents. Today with the rise of technology, the sell is to the kids—with videos, audios, and computers taking over.

This Technology Talk is based on information from the following source:
Tammi Howard, "Sears Hoping McKids Stores Make a Splash," *Womens Wear Daily*, August 29, 1988.

of children's basics, began to supplement their lines with more up-to-date, fashion-oriented garments, a gesture that moved them closer to the better-priced category. And to come full circle, the vacuum created in the budget market by the upgrading of companies such as Health-Tex and OshKosh is now being filled to a large extent by low-cost imports.

Offshore Production

With their promise of delivering low cost and decent quality, imports have made substantial inroads into children's wear. Producers' associations such as the Crafted with Pride in U.S.A. Council and labor unions such as the International Ladies' Garment Workers Union have been diligently applying the same anti-import pressure on behalf of the children's wear industry that they have on behalf of the adult fashion industry. Imports—particularly those involving textiles and apparel—are seen as a major threat to the survival of the American clothing industry.

The government takes a more benign view toward imports and is not inclined to impose any long-term curbs as long as off-shore production works to keep clothing prices (and inflation) low.

But buying foreign-made children's wear has as many pitfalls as pluses. Very early commitment—as much as 8 to 9 months' lead time, for example—is required and there is usually no opportunity for reordering. Despite this, children's retail buyers still favor imports, largely because they feel that foreign-made goods satisfy consumer demand on several levels. In fact, retail buyers not only have been buying imports, but they have often been ordering them to their specifications. In response, manufacturers have also sought out imports.

Influence of Young Adult Fashion

Another important trend is the growing influence of young adult fashions on children's wear. Increasingly, children look to their own peers and to the group just ahead of them, young adults, for pace-setting styles and trends. Successful children's wear producers have learned that they too must look to the young adult fashion world for inspiration. This means watching fads as well as trends. Popular young adult fads and styles are increasingly being translated into children's wear lines.

Specialty Retail Outlets

Children's lines are also receiving special attention due to the opening of many retail outlets specializing exclusively in children's wear. Even among stores that have not opened separate outlets, a trend exists toward opening distinctive stores-within-stores that cater exclusively to children's wear.

Typical of this trend is Esprit. Having built a solid business in sport active wear for juniors and women, they developed an equally successful line for children called Esprit Kids, which they sold in their own children's stores and stores-within-stores. Manufacturer-retailer Benetton developed a successful chain of stores called Benetton 0-12 packed with miniversions of the same stylish merchandise they sold to adults. The Gap has produced a solid venture with its GapKids chain. In the late 1980s Laura Ashley began translating her classic English clothing for adults into children's sizes and opened stores called Mother and Child, which effectively cater to two major markets. Even the toy discount chain Toys 'R' Us got into the act by increasing and upgrading its once-limited selection of children's clothes, and selling them in their Kids 'R' Us stores.

Items Versus Lines

Inevitably, the children's wear industry, with increased pressure to be up-to-date, is going to move away from producing only two distinct and rather limited lines a year. Rather than patterning itself after the adult fashion industry by producing more seasonal lines, however, children's wear producers are dispensing with the idea of lines in favor of producing items—specifically, when they can manage it, "hot" or faddish items. For example, manufacturers who once produced polo shirts or sweatshirts have turned to T-shirts and now rush to get items with the latest logo, character, or saying into the stores. Whether this trend, which revolves around fads, will last is impossible to say.

Unbranded and Discount Goods

Balancing the trend toward instantly produced high fashion is a countertrend toward unbranded and discount children's wear goods. Many children's wear producers are improving their volume of business by increasing their unbranded lines or items, many of which are made to the specifications of chain organizations. Often the chains merchandise these goods under their own brand names, thus developing a product that is theirs exclusively.

In conclusion, most experts are optimistic that the two prevalent trends—a move toward greater fashion in children's wear and another toward buying better children's wear—are unlikely to reverse themselves in the coming years. This should serve to make the children's wear one of the more stable divisions in the overall fashion industry.

REFERENCES

[1] Janet Wallach, "Trendy Little Girls," *Stores,* August 1986, p. 44.

[2] Helen Burggraf, "Maternity Mystique," *Stores,* February 1987, p. 34.

[3] Joyce Brothers, "How Clothes Form a Child's Self-Image," *Earnshaw's Infants,* November 1979, p. 48.

[4] Wallach, p. 44.

[5] "Fashion-Conscious Kids," *Good Housekeeping,* August 1987, p. 68.

[6] Penny Gill, "Kids' Sweaters: Grown-Up Style," *Stores,* August 1987, p. 19.

[7] Susan Ferraro, "Hotsy Totsy," *American Way,* April 1981, p. 61.

[8] Ellen Forman, "LizKids Line Put on Hold," *Children's Business,* August 1987, p. 24.

[9] Penny Gill, "Merchandising Licenses Lines," *Stores,* February 1987, p. 19.

MERCHANDISING VOCABULARY

Define or briefly explain the following terms:

Boys' sizes	Infants' sizes	Young men, student,
Children's sizes	Preteen sizes	or teen sizes
Girls' sizes	Toddlers' sizes	

MERCHANDISING REVIEW

1. Why did demographic trends favor the children's wear industry in the 1980s?
2. What three developments occurred after World War I to cause the growth of the children's wear industry?
3. Name and briefly describe the seven size categories of children's wear.
4. Explain the statement, "Children's wear, however, must still be viewed as a business that is *fashionable* rather than a *fashion* business."
5. How is consumer advertising handled by different types of firms in the children's wear business?
6. What is the appeal of designer-label children's clothing?
7. Why do many retailers limit their purchases of character-licensed children's clothing?
8. Describe what happened to children's wear price categories in the 1970s.
9. What has been the U.S. government's attitude toward the growth of imports in the children's wear industry?
10. Describe the current trend toward specialty retail outlets for children's wear.

MERCHANDISING DIGEST

1. Discuss the importance of licensing in today's children's wear market. How does the licensing system work? Why is it particularly popular with children?
2. Discuss the growing importance of foreign-made children's wear. What are some of the advantages and disadvantages?
3. What trends do you see in the young adult market today that have filtered into the design of children's clothing?

MEN'S APPAREL

While American men have been dressing conservatively for the past 150 years, this has not always been the case. At his inauguration, George Washington wore gold-embroidered stockings and 1½-inch heels.[1] His dress was toned down, as befitted the head of the world's first democracy. For centuries, male courtiers (and other men who could afford it) vied with one another to be seen in the most splendid outfits. At various times, men wore elaborate foot-high, powdered wigs, striped tights, pantaloons, and colorful, extravagantly embroidered silk and velvet coats accessorized with matching silk stockings. Menswear styles often changed as dramatically as women's.

But while fashions in women's clothing continued to be cyclical, menswear had settled into a basically conservative style composed of dark colors and very specifically detailed suits in the late 1700s. Small style changes occurred over the years. Lapels widened and narrowed, collar shapes mutated into various shapes, ties were invented and reinvented. But for a century and a half, men's clothing changed very little. There was no need for a man to be overly concerned about his appearance, because what he wore was virtually dictated by his class and occupation, with very little tolerance for deviation. Fortunately, menswear now seems to have come full circle, and men are once again interested in how they dress.

HISTORY OF THE MENSWEAR INDUSTRY

The oldest of the domestic apparel industries, the menswear industry gave birth to the women's and children's wear industries. It got its start in the late 1700s. Prior to that the rich patronized tailor's shops, where their clothing was custom-made or fitted to them. Everyone else wore homemade clothing.

Dressing for success in the nineteenth century, complete with furled umbrella and top hat.

Birth of Ready-to-Wear

The first ready-to-wear men's clothing was made by tailors in port cities along the Atlantic Coast. Seamen arrived in these cities in need of clothes to wear on land but without the time to have them tailor-made. To meet their needs, a few astute tailors began anticipating the ships' arrivals by making up batches of suits in rough size groupings. Sailors, who could put on the new clothes and walk away in them, liked the idea. Soon plantation owners were ordering the ready-to-wear clothing for their slaves.

The early ready-to-wear stores were called **slop shops,** a name that was appropriate to what they sold. Ready-to-wear clothing offered none of the careful fit or detail of custom-tailored clothes. But the price was right and the convenience was important, so ready-to-wear clothing gradually gained acceptance in ever-widening circles.

Although never considered slop shops, some distinguished menswear retail operations got their start on waterfronts. Brooks Brothers' first store opened in 1818 in downtown New York, and Jacob Reed's Sons first store opened in 1824 near the Philadelphia waterfront.

Role of the Industrial Revolution

The market for ready-to-wear clothing was further increased by the industrial revolution. Ironically, though, the industrial revolution also helped to create the new conservative look that prevailed for so long. The industrial revolution led to the introduction of machinery in all areas of production and replaced the absolute dependence on human hands in the making of goods. Clothing, like much else, could be mass-produced. This, in part, led to standardization in people's tastes. Mass-produced clothes were made for the lowest common denominator, which in menswear led to a conservatively cut, dark-colored suit.

The look, however, was not entirely the result of mass production. The idea of conservative men's suits also had its origins in a new role model that emerged during the industrial revolution—the industrialist. On the one hand, these newly rich tycoons had working-class roots and were not about to dress like the rich peacocks. On the other hand, they had finally gained access to something long denied them—power and money—and they wanted this to show in their dress. Sober and conservative themselves, they chose to wear clothes that were sober and conservative.

The industrial revolution also helped to create a managerial class made entirely of men who were happy to emulate the look of the rich industrialists. Soon all men who worked in offices wore the look, and the tailored, dark-colored worksuit that men would wear for the next 150 years was born.

The industrial revolution helped to move the production of clothing out of the home. The demand for people to operate the new machines was so great that entire families often went to work. This left no one at home to sew, and further boosted the demand for ready-to-wear clothing.

Mid- to Late 1800s

As late as the mid-1800s, rich people still did not consider buying their clothes off the rack in shops that had been slop shops, but had become respectable. The middle class, usually the most important element in making a style acceptable, patronized the stores.

The introduction of the sewing machine in 1846 was another important advance in men's apparel; it sped up production. The California gold rush in 1848 created a market for ready-to-wear clothing. Levi Strauss, a fabric manufacturer, traveled west to the gold fields. But instead of selling his material for tents and covered wagons, it was used to make pants and overalls—sturdy work clothes. The final boost to menswear came during the Civil War, when manufacturers scrambled to make uniforms. The specifications for uniforms led to the development of standardized sizes, thus assuring a better fit in ready-to-wear clothing—the last thing that was necessary to make them popular with all classes.

Store-bought clothes finally broke the class barrier during the last half of the nineteenth century. Financial crises such as the panics of 1869, 1873, and 1907 sent men who had formerly worn only custom-tailored clothes into the ready-to-wear clothing stores. Even though custom-tailoring remained a vital part of the menswear industry far longer than it lasted in women's wear, it was dealt a final blow during the Great Depression. Today, it represents only a small segment of the industry.

World War II

The Great Depression of 1929 brought about a decline in demand for all consumer products, and the economy did not get on its feet again until World War II.

During the war, of course, the entire apparel industry was given over to the war effort. The menswear industry ground to a halt and turned its attention to making uniforms. Restrictions were placed on the design and use of fabric. Once the war ended, however, the restrictions were lifted, and even more important, a long era of post-war prosperity began.

The returning servicemen were eager to get out of their uniforms. The demand for "civvies," or civilian clothes, was so great that for a few years clothing manufacturers worked—with little thought for changing styles—simply to keep up with the demand. By the mid-forties, manufacturers were meeting demand and could even stand back and consider style.

1940s to the Present

The major change in the menswear industry in the post-war period was the emergence of a new class of clothes called sportswear. It originated in

Southern California in the late 1940s, where suburban living and a climate conducive to leisure created a demand for clothes to be worn outside work.

For a while, the demand for sportswear was filled by a group of former New York manufacturers who had gravitated to the West Coast. Not only did

TECHNOLOGY TALK

THE JEANS WAR GOES STAR WARS

Through its pioneering efforts in vendor barcoding, its streetwise advertising campaign for 501 jeans, and its new computer plan to woo retailers, Levi Strauss & Co. makes no secret of its attempt to court the volatile youth market by using new selling techniques and new technologies.

Levi's has introduced a multifaceted electronic data interchange (EDI) program called LeviLink, which ties Levi's sales and shipping departments directly to retailers via computer and telephone modem.

Levi introduced LeviLink at the menswear MAGIC Show in San Francisco, the National Retail Merchants Association's Retail Information Systems Conference in Anaheim, and the Bobbin Show in Atlanta, in September 1986. LeviLink took the industry by storm, making it clear that such quick telecommunications of inventory, order, and shipping data could revolutionize the relationship between retailers and apparel manufacturers.

LeviLink is also having an impact on the "jeans war" between Levi, Lee, and Wrangler. Because of the success of LeviLink, both Lee and Wrangler top management have investigated and begun to implement EDI systems of their own.

What LeviLink offers retailers is a state-of-the-art package of computerized business services developed by Levi for retailers of any size, shape, or description. Included are vendor bar coding and an EDI package that encompasses electronic purchase orders, electronic packing slips, electronic invoicing, and direct electronic transmission of point-of-sale information to trigger automatic stock replenishment.

In addition, smaller retailers, who can't yet afford their own extensive data processing systems for sales analysis and merchandise management, can tie into Levi's own sophisticated computer system and have such services performed for them.

Levi also realized that EDI can work effectively both Levi's suppliers as well as its customers. The real objective is to optimize this pipeline and make it a link that is as efficient as possible among fiber and fabric producers, apparel manufacturers, retailers, and ultimately, consumers.

Some apparel manufacturers are wary of using EDI with retailers because of the implication that it might someday make sales representatives extinct. However, Levi's management do not believe this. They do not see that sales representatives will become extinct, rather they believe that EDI is a tool that helps sales reps do their jobs more effectively.

LeviLink is the EDI pioneer in the jeans business, but other players in the jeans industry have an electronic card or two up their sleeves as well, indicating that the denim world's star wars phase has only just begun.

This Technology Talk is based on information from the following source:

Rob Baker, "The Jeans War Goes Electronic," *Technology & Operations/Womens Wear Daily,* November 1986, pp. 16–21.

they give sportswear to California, but to the entire nation. The California market, as sportswear came to be known in the business, gained further momentum when buyers from major department stores such as Marshall Field, Hudson's, Macy's, and Lord & Taylor traveled to the West Coast to attend the spring sportswear show held every October in Palm Springs. New York clothing manufacturers wasted no time cashing in on the trend. By the mid-1960s, men's sportswear was as much a part of the Eastern market as tailored clothing.

What later become known as designer clothes also got their start in California in the 1940s. Hollywood motion-picture costume designers such as Don Loper, Orry-Kelly, Howard Greer, and Milo Anderson created lines for California sportswear manufacturers. Oleg Cassini and Adrian began licensing agreements with New York neckwear producers.

Designer clothes, à la California, proved to be an idea born before its time, a rare occurrence in the trendy fashion world. The designer sportswear could not compete with the new Ivy League or continental look that emerged on the East Coast. Designer clothes faded away and did not reemerge until the 1960s when designers like Pierre Cardin and John Weitz would try again, with much greater success.

Little happened in men's fashion until the 1960s, when suddenly menswear blossomed. The Mod look brought color to menswear after a 150-year-old absence. It was followed by the Edwardian look, which changed the shape of menswear for the first time in decades. Other styles, such as the Nehru look, were little more than fads.

For the first time since the development of the sewing machine, technology influenced menswear fashions. Knits, made from synthetic fibers, enjoyed a boom in the 1970s. Suddenly a man could outfit himself entirely in knit clothes—a double-knit suit, circular knit shirt, interlock knit underwear, a knit tie, and jersey knit socks. The overexposure of knits, often in poorly designed and contructed clothing, gave polyester a bad image. Its use fell off in the women's apparel industry, but menswear manufacturers continued to use it in a low-key way. Today, 95 percent of men's tailored clothing is made with polyester, most typically blends combining polyester with wool or cotton. Sixty-five percent of men's finer quality suits are made of 55/45 polyester/wool blend; it is the most popular suiting fabric in the United States.

In the 1980s men's fashion took on new life once again, as it had in the 1960s. For the first time, magazines devoted exclusively to men's fashion appeared. Men's fashion types emerged, and a variety of styles became acceptable. A man could be the continental type or the Ivy League type; he could be Edwardian, if he chose. The look that really took off was one of casual elegance, personified by the stars of the popular television show "Miami Vice." The clothes were designed by big designer names, which ensured their elegance, and they were casual, which basically added up to T-shirts worn under Italian sports jackets, classic loafers with no socks, and ever-present designer sunglasses. For the first time, the American menswear market was segmented as the women's market always had been by age, education, and income.

Throughout the 1990s, style is expected to remain an important factor in menswear. It should be noted, however, that in the midst of the interest in new styles, the classic look, fueled by designers such as Ralph Lauren and Giorgio Armani, is particularly strong. The conservative men's suit is not dead yet, nor is it expected to be any time soon.

IMPORTANT ELEMENTS OF THE MENSWEAR INDUSTRY

Throughout the history and growth of the domestic menswear industry, many factors have influenced its development, but few have been as significant as the policy of dual distribution, the use of contractors, and the rise of the labor unions.

Dual Distribution

It is far more common in the menswear industry than in women's apparel for clothes to be distributed on a two-tier system called **dual distribution.** In dual distribution, apparel is made available through both wholesale and retail channels. The practice, which has proven to be cyclical, peaked in the 1960s and 1970s, and has since become less popular.

Dual distribution of menswear got its start in the first half of the nineteenth century when the ready-to-wear business, along with the country's population, was expanding. Interest in dual distribution waned in the last half of the 1900s and did not rise again until the boom business years following each of the two world wars.

The renewed interest in dual distribution in the 1960s and 1970s died out when the industry was threatened with antitrust suits. Federal law forbids the domination by any one company of a segment of any industry.

One of the most successful dual distributors of men's tailored suits has been the Hartmarx Corporation. The company, which also produces outerwear and sportswear, generates $1 billion in annual sales.[2] In addition to its own brand, they produce Hickey Freeman and Austin Reed suits and also produce suits for licensees Christian Dior, Pierre Cardin, Henry Grethel, and Nino Cerutti.

Although the firm functions under the dual distribution system, its lines are also sold to independent specialty and department stores. In 1988, the Hickey Freeman division launched a Savile Row-styled line under a licensing agreement with Gieves & Hawkes, a prestigious London custom tailor.

Use of Contractors

As the men's ready-to-wear business grew, so did its attractiveness as a profitable investment. But going into business as a menswear manufacturer required considerable capital in terms of factory construction, equipment, and labor costs. This situation led to the birth of the contractor business, described in Chapter 8. By hiring a contractor to do the sewing and sometimes the cutting as well, manufacturers eliminated the need for their own factories, sewing machines, or labor force. They could function with just a showroom or space for shipping.

Early contractors of menswear operated in one of two ways. Usually, they set up their own factories where the manufacturing was done. But sometimes they distributed work to operators who would work at home, either on their own machines or on machines rented from the contractors. These workers were paid on a piecework basis.

Right after the Civil War and for the next two decades or so, menswear was manufactured in three different ways: (1) in **inside shops,** or garment factories, owned and operated by manufacturers; (2) in contract shops, or contractors' factories, where garments were

THEN... AND NOW.   THE RIGHT SUIT.

For over a hundred years,
businessmen have known that
Hart Schaffner & Marx
means superior fabrics, superb
tailoring, and styling that fits
the man as well as his times.
Today, the Right Suit is
tailored in Heritage Plus,™ a
fine blend of 55% Dacron®
polyester and 45% wool worsted
woven by Burlington Menswear.
Hart Schaffner & Marx,
the Right Suit® since 1887.
For the Hart Schaffner & Marx
retailer in your area, call toll-free:
1-800-FASHION.

Hart
Schaffner
& Marx.

The Hart Schaffner &
Marx brand is produced
by Hartmarx Corpora-
tion, a dual distributor.

produced for manufacturers; and (3) in homes, where garments were made usually for contractors but sometimes for manufacturers.

A contractor's most important value for apparel manufacturers is the ability to turn out short runs of a style quickly and inexpensively. A **short run** is the production of a limited number of units of a particular item, fewer than would normally be considered an average number to produce. Because short runs are a contractor's specialty, contracting has remained an important factor in women's apparel manufacturing. It was gradually abandoned by menswear manufacturers until recently, when it again became important in the production of men's sportswear because of the impact of faster-moving fashion cycles.

Traditional menswear manufacturers turned away from contractors and stayed away until recently for several reasons.

1. The menswear industry had a pattern of very slow style change, and contracting was not as economical as inside-shop production.
2. Improved equipment and cheaper electric power helped make production in inside shops more practical and efficient.
3. As quality became increasingly important, menswear manufacturers found it easier to control work within their own factories than in the contractors' factories.

Because of escalating labor costs in this country, in the 1970s many menswear manufacturers, including those producing designer collections, returned to the use of contractors, particularly those in Hong Kong and Korea. Hong Kong is favored by better makers, more for quality standards than for cost.

Rise of Unions

As the menswear market and industry grew, so did competition among manufacturers. Factory employees became the victims. To produce ready-to-wear clothing at competitive prices, manufacturers and contractors demanded long hours from workers and yet paid low wages. In addition, factory working conditions, which had never been good, deteriorated further. Contractors were particularly guilty, and their factories deserved the names *sweat* shops or "sweaters" that were given to them. According to an official New York State inspection report of 1887:

The workshops occupied by these contracting manufacturers of clothing, or "sweaters" as they are commonly called, are foul in the extreme. Noxious gases emanate from all corners. The buildings are ill smelling from cellar to garret. The water-closets are used by males and females, and usually stand in the room where the work is done. The people are huddled together too closely for comfort, even if all other conditions were excellent.[3]

What happened next was inevitable. Workers finally rebelled against working conditions, hours, and pay.

Local employee unions had existed in the industry since the early 1800s, but none had lasted long or wielded much power. The Journeymen Tailors' National Union, formed in 1883, functioned (and still functions today) mainly as a craft union. A union representing all apparel industry workers, the United Garment Workers of America, was organized in 1891, but it had little power and soon collapsed. Finally, in 1914, the Amalgamated Clothing Workers of America was formed. It remained the major union of the menswear industry until the 1970s, when it merged with the Textile Workers of America and the United Shoe Workers of America to form the Amalgamated Clothing and Textile Workers Union.

Workers in tailored-clothing plants make up the backbone of the Amalgamated, and the union is a strong force in menswear manufacturing in the North. However, its influence in factories producing mens work clothes, furnishings, and sportswear in the South and other parts of the country was almost nonexistent until the mid-1970s. It was then that a drive to organize support in the South gave the union its first toehold in these areas.

The famous strike during the early 1970s at the El Paso, Texas, factory of the Farah Company, one of the largest manufacturers of mens pants and work clothes, was part of a long and bitter fight. The company had resisted the attempt of the union to organize the Farah workers for many years, and only after a long court battle were the plant and its workers unionized.

ORGANIZATION AND OPERATION OF THE INDUSTRY

The menswear industry traditionally has been divided into firms making different kinds of clothing:

1. *Tailored clothing*—Suits, overcoats, topcoats, sports coats, formal wear, and separate trousers.
2. *Furnishings*—Dress shirts, neckwear, sweaters, headwear, underwear, socks, robes, and pajamas.
3. *Outerwear*—Jackets and active sportswear.
4. *Work clothing*—Work shirts, work pants, overalls, and related items.
5. *Other*—Uniforms and miscellaneous items.

The federal government uses these five classifications. Although it is not an official classification, sportswear (including active sportswear) has become a vital portion of the business, and should be considered a menswear category.

Size and Location of Manufacturers

Menswear, led by the booming sportswear segment, represents a $27 billion market.[4] Unlike women's apparel, the business has been dominated by large firms at the manufacturing level.

In recent years Levi Strauss, Blue Bell, Cluett, Peabody, and Interco have been the four largest manufacturers of menswear and boys' wear. Their combined volume has been estimated to count for approximately one-third of the total volume of the top 30 firms. Because of diversification, mergers, and acquisitions by top menswear producers in the past few years, it has become more difficult to ascertain company size and production figures.

Although there are menswear manufacturers in almost every section of the country, the largest number of plants are in the mid-Atlantic states. New York, New Jersey, and Pennsylvania form the center of the tailored-clothing industry. Over 40 percent of all menswear manufacturers are located in this area.

However, the industry's center is gradually moving south. A number of northeastern manufacturers have set up plant facilities in the South, where both land and labor are less expensive. These include not only apparel manufacturers from the mid-Atlantic states but also some men's shoe manufacturers, who were once found almost exclusively in New England.

Some menswear manufacturers have always been located in the South. For instance, firms manufacturing separate trousers—a segment of the tailored-clothing industry—have always been centered in the South, as have many manufacturers of men's shirts, underwear, and work clothes.

The number of firms located in the West, particularly the Pacific Northwest, and the Southwest is also steadily growing. Most of these plants produce sportswear or casual attire. The Northwest and Upper Midwest are important for sports outerwear and active wear (such as parkas, ski wear, and hunting and fishing gear).

Designing a Line

For generations, tailored-clothing manufacturers in the United States were known as slow but painstakingly careful followers, rather than leaders, in menswear styling. The typical tailored-clothing manufacturer had a staff of tailors to execute existing designs or bought freelance designs. Designers' names were known only within the trade and were seldom considered important by consumers.

Traditionally, the leading fashion influence was English styling. Designers in this country would study the styles currently popular in England (specifically Savile Row), decide which might be acceptable here, and gradually develop a line based on those styles. Production was a slow process because of the amount of handwork involved in making tailored clothing. Usually, a full year passed from the time a style was developed until a finished product was delivered to a retail store.

The first signs of male rebellion against traditional styling came during the late 1940s and early 1950s. As described earlier, year after year manufacturers had been turning out versions of a style that had long been popular on Savile Row—a draped suit with padded shoulders, based originally on the broad-chested uniform of the Brigade of Guards. A number of young men attending well-known northeastern colleges became tired of the traditional look. They took their objections to New Haven clothing manufacturers, and the result was the natural-shoulder, Ivy League suit.

A radical shift in attitudes in the 1960s finally made men willing to wear suits as fashion. The antiwar protests, student activism, black power, and other

The "designer look" of Pierre Cardin in men's formal wear. Since 1961, Cardin has been an important influence in men's fashion.

political movements encouraged American men to express themselves in a nonmainstream manner. They led to the era of the "peacock revolution," when men once again took great pride in their appearance, as in days long ago. Some favored long hair, bold plaid suits, brightly colored shirts, wide multicolored ties, and shiny boots. Others dressed, even for work, in Nehru and Mao jackets, leisure suits, white loafers, polyester double knits, and the "Las Vegas look"—shirts unbuttoned to the waist and gold necklaces in abundance around their necks.

FASHION

At age 15, he was reading the fashion trades and dressing only in Polo apparel. At 17, he became an assistant to Ralph Lauren. At 19, he began working in Calvin Klein's design studio. And at 23, he received a special Coty award for his own first collection of furs for men.

"He" is Jeffrey Banks, a young designer who since that time has continued to earn accolades for his menswear designs—designs that are traditional yet young-spirited. To describe them, he once stated: "I design my clothes for the man who wears suits one day and jeans the next. My clothing also has to be fun. It needn't be serious the way couture is."[1]

Banks may not consider his apparel line serious, but it is certainly not far-out, either. Drawing upon the elegant style of the twenties and thirties and specifically citing the dashing Cary Grant as an inspiration, Banks creates clothes with subtle styling, which he says "can easily be worn from day into evening. They have a subtle mixture of color and they appeal to the classic sophisticated customer."[2]

Banks also describes his customer as the "new traditionalist,"[3] a man with a modern sense of color and style, yet one rooted in traditional classicism. To meet the needs of that customer, the designer

FOCUS

focuses on crisp tailoring and clean lines, emphasizing cut, fit, and understated quality fabrics.

"The man I design for is young at any age, interested in clothes but not a 'clothes horse.' He likes to look good, but he also likes to forget what he's wearing once he has it on," explained Banks. "The man I design for wants a lasting quality in his style; I don't expect him to buy my clothes if he has to replace them every year."[4]

That attitude is something of a departure from the norm for fashion designers, whose new collections often reflect a vastly different style direction from their last. And that is not the only way in which Banks differs from many designers. Rather than seeking the limelight, he chooses to maintain a low profile both in business and socially. "You'll never see me in one of my ads," he has said. "I've always felt if what I did was good, I'd be recognized for it. That lasts longer than any Madison Avenue hype or getting your name in the the paper because you're at the right party."[5]

Certainly recognition for his work has been bestowed liberally on Jeffrey Banks. After his first Coty Award in 1977, he won another in 1982 for his menswear collection. While his Jeffrey Banks Ltd., a division of Oxford Indus-

tries, produces his line of dress sport shirts, accessories, sweaters, neckwear, and knits, he has also formed an affiliation with Hartz & Co. to manufacture his tailored clothing. Also, in 1981, he was named designer for Merona Sport; and in 1984, launched his first women's wear line with Merona—winning Banks a spot on the cover of *Women's Wear Daily* and praise from the fashion editors of *The New York Times*.

That's all pretty heady stuff for a man who had not yet come close to his 40th birthday. Yet success seems to be something Banks takes in his stride as he continues to do what he loves. "I can't imagine doing anything else," he said[6]— and the result of his dedication is a fashion line that any man can bank on.

[1] "Heading for the Top," *The New York Times Magazine,* August 28, 1977, p. 44.

[2] Lela Sabin, "Jeffrey Banks Markets for Perfection," *New York Apparel News,* June 1985, p. 24.

[3] Jeffrey Tay, "Jeffrey Banks: Master Designer in American Menswear," *Ebony Man,* September 1986, p. 23.

[4] "Jeffrey Banks Wears His Own Name on His Jeans and That's Stylish," *Pratt Reports,* Spring 1980, p. 2.

[5] Roberta Burrows, "Jeffrey Banks: New York's New Hot Designer," *Center, The Magazine of Rockefeller Center,* Summer 1985, p. 6.

[6] Ibid.

This Fashion Focus is based on information from the articles cited above and the following:

Stan Gellers, "All the Way to the Banks," *DNR, The Magazine,* November 1984, pp. 47–48.

Importance of Name Designers

By the late sixties, designer names in the menswear industry mushroomed. Most of them were women's wear designers, often from Europe, who decided to exploit their renown by trying out their creativity in the men's field. So popular was the European designer image that even an American designer like Bill Kaiserman gave his firm an Italian name, Raphael.

Among the first American designers who made no bones about being American were Oleg Cassini, John Weitz, Bill Blass, and Ralph Lauren. In fact, Bill Blass, won the first Coty Award ever given for menswear design, in 1968.

Since most of these designers were famous as designers of women's apparel, there was a question about whether men would buy their designs. The movement of men into fashion during the sixties and seventies dispelled that doubt. As reported in *The New York Times*, "The idea that men would wear clothes designed by a women's apparel designer was never considered seriously, and one thing that men have arrived at today is that being interested in clothes does not carry a stigma."[5] The fact that much menswear, particularly furnishings and sportswear, is bought by women for men also aided in the acceptance of name designer styles. Women were familiar with the names and had confidence in the designer's taste.

Although the first foreign country that influenced the design of menswear was England, French and Italian designers became as important in menswear as the traditional English. Pierre Cardin signed his first contract for men's shirts and ties in 1959 and did his first ready-to-wear men's designs in 1961. Christian Dior, Yves Saint Laurent, and other famous women's design-ers followed his example. One important menswear designer who did not come from the ranks of women's wear is Ralph Lauren. He began his career in menswear, designing for women only after he became successful and famous designing for men.

Designer Names Today

Today, an entirely new world of menswear has emerged in which designer labels are promoted as heavily as well-established brand names used to be. Famous foreign and domestic name designers of women's apparel (such as Liz Claiborne) have now entered into licensing agreements for the production of menswear. A designer who licenses his name in suits may also license men's jeans, shirts, jackets, or ties. The manufacturer pays for the design or name of the designer in royalties based on gross sales. Royalties average from 5 to 7 percent on men's suits and 5 percent on men's sportswear, according to industry sources.

Manufacturing companies that license name designers usually establish separate divisions and in many cases allocate separate manufacturing facilities for them. In licensing agreements, the extent of designer involvement varies; designers are not necessarily responsible for all the designs that bear their name.

Today the "name game" is big business in all segments of the menswear industry. While there are no hard figures on the amount of designer business done at the wholesale level, the best market estimates for retail sales are over $1 billion for all categories combined.

One reason for the continuing popularity of designer names is that they are so easily promoted. Consumers associate them with prestige and fashion and rec-

TABLE 10-1 • SELECTED MENSWEAR DESIGNERS/LICENSES

Designer	Company	Classification
Bill Blass	PBM	Clothing
	After Six	Formal wear
	Malcolm Kenneth	Coats, rainwear
	Gates Shirts	Dress, sport shirts
	J. S. Blank	Neckwear
	Buxton	Small leathers
	Revlon	Toiletries
	Royal Robes	Robes
Pierre Cardin	Intercontinental Apparel	Clothing
	Harry Irwin, Inc.	Coats, dress shirts
	Eagle Shirtmakers	Sportswear
	Smerling	Footwear
	Swank	Belts, leathers
	Jacqueline Cochrane	Toiletries
	Sheridane	Neckwear
	Roytex	Robes
	Breezy Point	Active wear
	Gilbert Hosiery	Hosiery
John Weitz	Palm Beach	Clothing
	Casualcraft	Outerwear
	Excello	Shirts
	Glen Oaks	Slacks
	State O'Maine	Swimwear
	Host Pajamas	Pajamas
	Imperial Handkerchief	Handkerchiefs
	Storm Hero Umbrella	Umbrellas
	John Weitz Toiletries	Toiletries
	Camp Hosiery	Hosiery
	Gemini	Footwear

ognize them when they see them. Designers have helped by becoming highly visible. Their names are household words, and their faces frequently appear in newspapers and magazines. They lend themselves to the fantasy of the customer who longs for wealth and excitement.

Designer names also get more exposure than brand names in stores because they often appear on many different kinds of goods displayed in several different departments. Designers often have their own boutiques within stores.

Market Segments

Most market segments are based on style differences, but some exist because they involve different production methods. The five main market segments in menswear are: (1) tailored clothing, (2) sportswear, (3) active sportswear, (4) contemporary apparel, and (5) bridge apparel.

Tailored Clothing

Tailored-clothing firms produce structured or semistructured suits, overcoats, topcoats, sports coats, formal wear, and separate slacks that involve hand-tailoring operations. This kind of clothing once dominated the market, but in recent years, the demand for tailored clothing has steadily declined. Industry statistics show that the number of tailored men's suits dropped from 17.3 million in 1978 to 9.6 million in 1987.[6] Despite the decline, tailored suits have long been—and still are—considered the backbone of the menswear industry.

A tailored suit is structured, or three-dimensional, which gives it a shape even when it is not worn. Tailored clothing is graded according to the number of hand-tailoring operations required to make it. The grades are 1, 2, 4, 4+, 6, and 6+. A grade 1 suit, which represents the lowest quality, is typically carried by stores that feature suits at popular prices. A **grade 6+** suit, which requires between 150 and 200 hand operations to make, is a top-of-the-line suit and is sold at prestige stores. For example, Oxxford, Hickey Freeman, Polo, Hart, Schaffner & Marx, and Armani are all producers of 6+ suits.

Recently, the stock of grade 1 suits has been supplemented by a new grade, known as an **X suit.** X suits are produced using an automation process called **fusing,** in which various parts of a suit are melded together under heat and pressure rather than stitched. New machinery introduced in the 1960s also helped to speed up the production of these cookie-cutter suits. A grade X suit can be produced in 90 minutes with only 90 stitching and pressing operations. Grade X suits cost about $150, compared to $800 or more for a grade 6+ suit, which may take 15 hours of an experienced tailor's time.

Designer Suits Another difference between an inexpensive, low-grade suit and an expensive designer suit is the way each is cut. Designers suits are typically sized on a "7-inch drop." **Drop** refers to the difference between the chest and waist measurements of a jacket. Some jackets designed for young men and other customers who keep in shape may have an even greater drop. Non-designer suits, in contrast, have a 6-inch drop, which gives a suit jacket an entirely different look and fit.

Differences also exist between traditional suits, which have a natural shoulder, and suits with **European styling,** which feature a more fitted jacket, built-up shoulders, and a higher armhole.

Production The production of tailored clothing, as you have probably guessed, is a long, complicated process, although it does parallel the production process for women's apparel. Styles are selected for a new line, after which a manufacturer orders fabrics for the line. Delivery of the fabric may take up to 9 months, so it must be ordered far in advance of when it will be used. Next the line is presented to buyers. Manufacturers do not start to cut suits until enough orders have accumulated to make production of a style worthwhile.

Men's tailored clothing is produced in seven proportioned sizes: *shorts* (36–44), *regulars* (35–46), *longs* (37–48), *extra longs* (38–50), *portly shorts* (39–48), and *large* (46, 48, 50). Not every style is cut in every size range, but the most popular styles are made up in at least half the size ranges.

Suit Separates The steady decline in structured and semistructured tailored menswear has been offset by an increased demand for **suit separates**—jackets and trousers that are worn much as the tailored suit used to be. Tailored suits are now the business uniform only

Suit separates as interpreted by the young moderns. Suit separates allow the fashion-savvy male to demonstrate his initiative in dressing.

cantly lower-priced than tailored garments. When they are made for better-priced lines, they can also be expensive. Because each item is bought separately, the expensive alterations that manufacturers and retailers must often make on tailored clothes are avoided. One industry expert believes that men who buy separates are more fashion-aware than those who need the reassurance of a preassembled look.

Sportswear

Sportswear, or casual wear, which runs the gamut from unconstructed jackets, knits and woven sports shirts, slacks, leisure shorts, to coordinated tops and bottoms, has been the fastest growing segment of the menswear industry since the 1970s. Changes in lifestyle, plus men's growing interest in having more variety and fashion in their wardrobes, have created a demand for leisure clothes.

A generation ago, tailored clothing was office or formal wear, and sportswear was strictly weekend or vacation wear. Today, the real difference between the two lies in the construction rather than the occasion or the styling, colors, or fabrics of the garments.

Sportswear is unstructured, or at minimum, less structured than tailored clothing. Few if any hand-tailoring operations, for example, are required to make a sports jacket. Sportswear lacks padding, binding, and lining, and takes its shape (if indeed it has any shape these days) from the person who is wearing it.

Production Sportswear production also differs from that of tailored wear. Unlike tailored-wear manufacturers, who want staying power for their styles and a lot of lead time, sportswear manufacturers are interested in short runs and a quick

in large, sophisticated cities. Throughout the rest of the country, suit separates are often worn to work—or for almost any occasion except where formal wear is required.

Although an attempt was made in the 1960s to sell menswear consumers on the idea of coordinated sportswear, that is, jackets, vests, and pants that could be mixed and matched with one another, the idea never took hold. Today, suit separates refers to sports jackets and trousers.

Suit separates are usually machine-made, and as a result, can be signifi-

response to customer demand. The quality of workmanship is much less important than the quick production of the styles, colors, and fabrics that customers want.

In addition, unstructured sportswear, regardless of the kind of firm produces it, is likely to be made up in a much narrower size range than tailored clothing. For instance, a sport shirt is not produced in the wide variety of neck sizes, sleeve lengths, and collar and cuff styles in which a dress shirt is made. Instead, a sport shirt is usually produced in four basic sizes (small, medium, large, and extra large), with a choice between short and long sleeves.

This is the kind of production work that contractors handle most successfully. When contractors are used, the sportswear manufacturer may be the designer, or a designer may be hired, or a design may be bought from a freelancer. The manufacturer buys the needed fabric. Then sometimes the cutting and all of the sewing are done by the contractor, as in the women's apparel field. Finally, the finished goods are returned to the manufacturer, who handles the distribution.

Contractors' plants are located wherever production costs can be kept low. They are in many different locations in this country, and an increasing number of American sportswear manufacturers are using contractors in other countries. The use of the contractor system allows the sportswear manufacturers to provide a steady flow of new styles at moderate prices.

Styling and color are a mark of today's men's fashions

Active Sportswear

Another phenomenon of the 1980s was the rapid growth of the **active sportswear** market, which consists of clothing worn during active sports participation as well as during leisure time. In fact, the larger segment of this market are men who want to look as if they are doing something athletic, even when they are ambling to the store for the Sunday paper or flopping down in front of the television set to watch a ball game. As a result, the active sportswear producers make running suits for men who run and men who do not, but want to look as if they do. Sportswear was also responsible for making color a permanent part of men's wardrobes.

Contemporary Apparel

Contemporary menswear refers to a special type of styling that provides high quality and fashion. Contemporary menswear, which produces clothing in all categories, can often be distinguished by its use of bright colors.

Initially, the typical consumer was a young, educated man with the verve to look fashionable. Today, contemporary menswear no longer belongs exclusively to the young but is worn by elegant, style-conscious men of all age groups.

Contemporary merchandise is produced by both tailored-clothing and sportswear firms. It is usually produced under a name designer's licensing agreement, rather than styled by a manufacturer's in-house or freelance designer. When this type of merchandise is produced by a firm already making other types of apparel and furnishings, new operating divisions are usually created to handle the product, give it identity, and enhance its marketability.

Contemporary suits produced are in the following sizes:

1. *Shorts*—Includes sizes 36–40.
2. *Regulars*—Includes sizes 36–42.
3. *Longs*—Includes sizes 38–44.

Bridge Apparel

In the 1980s, the term **bridge apparel** came into play in the menswear industry to define clothing that spanned the style gap between young men's and men's collections, and the price gap between contemporary and designer apparel. In broad terms, the bridge customer is an aging baby-boomer who has grown out of young men's clothing but can't yet afford designer clothes. Bridge customers are between 25 and 40 and have sophistication and style.

Unlike the bridge concept in women's sportswear, for which certain manufacturers and designers have developed collections specifically created as bridge lines, men's bridge apparel is defined much more by retailers than by manufacturers.[7] Each retailer may interpret bridge differently in order to fit its own customer profile. Therefore, one store might have Williwear and Kikit bridge lines, while another might call them contemporary. Whatever their definition of bridge apparel, retailers that identify a portion of their menswear assortment as bridge apparel are seeking to balance fashion with price.

MARKET CENTERS

New York is the largest market center for all kinds of menswear, including tailored clothing, sportswear, contemporary lines, and furnishings. Regional markets in other parts of the country—Chicago, Los Angeles, and Dallas, for example—are growing in importance, but the biggest shows and the largest number of permanent showrooms are still located in New York.

The Clothing Manufacturers Association, the trade association of the tailored-clothing industry, holds two market weeks a year in New York. Fall lines are shown in late March or early April, and spring lines in October. These showings include lines from manufacturers of all types of menswear, including tailored-clothing as well as sportswear and contemporary lines. It is claimed that these showings bring together the offerings of more menswear producers than any other show in the world.

Another important event is the Men's Apparel Guild in California (MAGIC) market week, held twice yearly in Los Angeles since the 1940s. For many years, numerous small regional shows were held around the country, as well as in various cities in each region, but they are declining in popularity. Run for and by salespersons, these shows are called "MAC markets."

As the market for imports and exports has grown in size and importance, more and more domestic manufacturers now attend the important international shows, most notably Pitti Uomo in Italy and SEHM in France.

MERCHANDISING AND MARKETING

Like the women's wear producers, menswear producers back their lines with advertising and publicity. Menswear fiber and textile producers sometimes promote their products. The largest percentage of promotion is done, however, by the menswear producers, who rely on agencies, freelancers, and less often, on an in-house department for advertising and publicity.

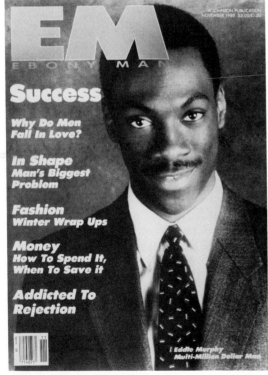

Men's fashion magazines feature many of the same items as do women's fashion magazines, including successful people on the cover.

Advertising

Men's apparel producers began advertising in the late 1800s. Initially, they used trade advertising to establish contact with retailers. Strong, stable relationships were built, and in many large towns and small cities, major manufacturers maintain an exclusive arrangement with one retailer. Not surprisingly, the producers tend to put a lot of their advertising money into cooperative advertising for their long-term retail accounts. Brand-name and designer name producers also sponsor national advertising campaigns.

Sportswear houses, relative newcomers to the marketplace, do not have long-established or exclusive ties with retailers, so they compensate with large national advertising campaigns as well as cooperative advertising with retailers.

Publicity

The new magazines devoted to men's fashions have provided the most interesting and recent forum for publicity for menswear products. They include *Gentlemen's Quarterly (GQ)*, a recognized leader in the field; Fairchild Publication's *M; Men's Guide to Fashion; Esquire,* once the leader in men's fashion and now reasserting itself; and an assortment of ethnically oriented publications such as *Ebony Man* and *Modern Black Man*. Producers make excellent use of the editorial pages of these various publications, and also supply clothes to be modeled.

The major publicity efforts, however, are still undertaken by the trade associations, which sponsor market weeks, trade shows, and other promotions designed to publicize individual producers and the industry as a whole. These include the six trade associations described in Table 10-2.

TABLE 10-2 • MENSWEAR TRADE ORGANIZATIONS

Men's Fashion Association of America (MFA)

Membership:	All segments of the menswear manufacturing industry
Founded:	1955
Major activities:	Three major press preview weeks for fashion editors (Jan.–Feb. in the Southwest or West Coast, June in New York, and Sept.–Oct. in the Southwest or West Coast).
	Semiannual fashion forecast.
	Cosponsor of annual Cutty Sark Awards for outstanding menswear designs.

National Association of Men's Sportswear Buyers (NAMSB)

Membership:	Menswear retailers
Founded:	1953
Major activities:	Three market weeks in New York (Jan., Mar., and Oct.).
	Monthly newsletter on fashion trends to members.
	Seasonal fashion-trend slide kits for member use in merchandising and marketing.
	College scholarship program for children of members and their employees.

Men's Apparel Guild in California (MAGIC)

Membership:	Menswear manufacturers (nationwide)
Founded:	Late 1930s (originally as the Los Angeles Menswear Manufacturers Association)
Major activities:	Semiannual menswear trade shows in Los Angeles, with emphasis on sportswear.

Clothing Manufacturers Association (CMA)

Membership:	Tailored clothing manufacturers
Founded:	1933
Major activities:	Representation of members in negotiations with the union.
	Two market weeks in New York (Jan. and July).
	Publishes trade periodical for international distribution.
	Prepares statistical and technical reports on developments in the tailored clothing industry.

Big and Tall Associates

Membership:	Menswear manufacturers and retailers specializing in apparel for men over 5'11" tall and/or with chest measurements of over 48".
Founded:	1971
Major activities:	Semiannual market weeks.

The Father's Day Council Inc.

Membership:	Nonprofit organization for promoting Father's Day as a gift-giving holiday, supported by manufacturers and major department stores
Founded:	1931
Major activities:	Prepares noncommercial poster and promotional kit around which stores build their own promotion.
	Selects National Fathers of the Year from all walks of life—sports, medicine, politics, theatre, and film.

INDUSTRY TRENDS

The dynamics of population growth as well as developments in the economy today tend to favor certain segments of the menswear market over others. The fastest-growing group at the present time is the age 25–44, upwardly mobile, fashion-oriented executive or managerial man. This group is particularly interested in contemporary styling and tailored separates, which, as a result, are projected to maintain strong sales well into the l990s.

A smaller but related trend is the renewed interest in quality that is apparent in almost all market segments. Other trends include a diversification of products, greater emphasis on style, the automation of production processes, an increase in foreign production and sales, and a proliferation of specialty stores.

Diversification of Product

After years of being highly specialized, often producing only a single type of garment in one grade, menswear producers are now beginning to diversify.

Some of the biggest changes have taken place in an area that was one of the most specialized, that of work clothes. Firms like H. D. Lee and Levi Strauss, which for years never varied their products, began to expand when the casual market took off. In addition to designer jeans, which had saturated the market by the mid-1970s, Lee and Strauss and similar manufacturers moved into slacks, casual pants, and jackets—and even tailored clothing. By the late 1970s, Lee and Strauss were watching style sales reports as keenly as unit sales reports.

Suits provide another example of diversification. In the past, manufacturers of traditional suits turned out a selection of styles in only one or two grades. Today, the trade calls the traditional tailored suit a "suit-suit" because so many other types of suits are now made.

New Interest in Style

The most important trend in men's apparel is the continuing boom in casual and sportswear. A vice-president and director of men's clothing at Neiman-Marcus summed up the men's market, saying: "The clothing business hasn't changed, but the lifestyle has."[8] He correctly noted that because men are now interested in fashion, they are buying different kinds of clothes. Most men's wardrobes today contain three layers: suits for work, active wear for sports, and slacks and sports coats for leisure activities.[9] In addition, a lot of crossover occurs among the three levels. Sports coats and slacks are now acceptable at the office, and active sportswear shows up at Sunday brunch.

When men do wear traditional tailored clothing these days, they favor quality. Spending $700 to $800 for a tailored suit is no longer considered unusual, as indicated by a 1986 review of men's suits in the cost-conscious *Consumer Guide*. Ranked first and second, respectively, were a $710 Oxxford and a $715 Giorgio Armani suit.[10] So style-conscious are some male consumers that they now travel to London several times a year to buy custom-made clothing from Savile Row tailors, much as women have for years traveled to Paris for couture clothing.[11]

Separates

Although the popular-priced blazers, vests, and slacks produced by such companies as Levi Strauss and Haggar have found a permanent place in the mens-

Briefly Speaking

"You're So Vain"

Today's men who shop for skin moisturizers and silk boxer shorts are hardly the innovators of male vanity.

As they sit in salons with "nourishing" skin masques on their faces, they should consider that throughout history, in fact, men have flaunted their finery, fussed with their hair, and painted their faces.

In Elizabethan England, the queen herself led the fashion parade, and men copied her ornate jewelry, wore elaborate ruffs around their necks and kept their stockings up with garters, just as the queen did. But the most conspicuous expression of male vanity, the codpiece, was popular during Elizabeth's reign.

In the late 1980s, "Miami Vice" inspired fashion plates who cultivated a day's growth of stubble and a causal unstructured and unstudied look. In early 17th century France, cavaliers spent hours achieving a look of unstudied chic, and wore their battlefield boots to formal balls, put bright ostrich plumes in their hats, streaked their hair, and smeared on rouge.

During the French Revolution, the *incroyables* exaggerated everything: coattails hung to the ground, bizarre yellow pants rose to the armpits, collars reached the ears. These young men wore gold earrings and applied artificial beauty marks. Across the English Channel, such dandies were known as "macaronies"— which is probably why Yankee Doodle Dandy stuck a feather in his cap and called it what he did!

The most famous dandy of all time was the Englishman George Bryan (Beau) Brummell, who though known as a dandy, did bring an elegant simplicity to male dressing that has remained as the epitome for well-dressed men.

George Brummell.

Although the onset of the Industrial Revolution caused the male image to become a bit drab, the 20s and 30s gave men royalty and movie stars, like the Duke of Windsor, Cary Grant, and Fred Astaire to model themselves after. The 40s brought the "Zoot Suit" with its outrageous padded shoulders and nipped waist, the 60s lapsed into psychedelic colors, bell-bottom pants, and gold medallions and the 70s and 80s brought one of the most visible signs of male vanity. . .the number of publications that have sprung up to serve it.

There is a danger that this male vanity may explode and the fashion scene may become inundated with men who are all wrapped up in their looks. But some women are pleased by this turn of events. They are glad to have men shoulder some of the burden of being attractive, delighted not to have to look at razor burn, relieved that men can go out and buy their own face cream and stop using theirs!

This Briefly Speaking is based on information from the following sources:

Cathleen McGuigan, Sid Atkins, "History's Greatest Fops," *Newsweek*, April 14, 1986, p. 52.
Jerry Adler, Renee Michael, Nikki Finke Greenberg, "You're So Vain," *Newsweek*, April 14, 1986, pgs. 46–55.

wear market, with the renewed emphasis on quality, better-priced tailored clothes are once again selling well. They are unlikely, however, to edge out separates—which at $175 to $195 per item are more attractive than a suit priced at $800 and up.

Sizing

Producers have recently made some changes in sleeve sizes. Men's long-sleeved dress shirt are made in neck sizes 14½ to 17 inches, graduated in half-inches. In each size, the sleeve length has, until recently, also been graduated from 32 to 35 inches. In an effort to reduce inventories and increase stock turnover, though, producers have begun making dress shirts in two sleeve lengths—regular (32–35 inches) and long (34–35 inches). Over 50 percent of all men's dress shirts are now produced only in regular and long sleeve lengths.

Whether this trend will prevail is unclear. Not all shirtmakers have converted to the new sizing, and with the renewed interest in quality, there has also been a reverse trend among some producers toward making exact sleeve sizes again.

Designer and Brand-Name Labels

Although designers such as Ralph Lauren and Calvin Klein have made an impact on men's fashion, no one believes that their impact on men's fashion will equal that of women's fashion. National brands and private labels are more likely to be in competition for retail space than are designer clothes.

National brands, which have already had considerable impact, are expected to remain strong in the foreseeable future. In menswear, brand names are seen as a sign of quality rather than fashion. Private label merchandise is also making inroads. As is the case with women's private labels, they provide menswear with exclusivity and higher profit margins.

Retail operations will strive to provide their customers with a mix of brand names and private labels. Asked about the impact of men's designer wear on brand names, one department store merchandiser commented: "We have no strategic plans for eliminating brands, by any means. It's a matter of balance. [But] our ability to put together private label programs that offer the customer current or wanted fashion, in top quality merchandise, priced fairly, is a significant opportunity for us."[12]

Designer and brand names are part of the push to provide men with up-to-date fashion. And while there will always be a market for classic or traditional men's clothes, industry forecasters predict that menswear will continue to be fashion-oriented. Designers and manufacturers will increasingly take their cues from women's fashion. The menswear industry will become even more seasonal than it is now, and will as a result expand the number of lines offered each year.[13]

AUTOMATION OF PRODUCTION

New equipment and computer systems are helping manufacturers combat one of the more serious problems faced by apparel producers: the rising cost of labor pitted against a dwindling skilled labor force.

The menswear industry has also experienced a turnover rate of between 60 and 70 percent for the past few years. Good tailors and sewers take time to train, and supply has not kept up with demand.

One way that major companies are handling the labor problem is by establishing clusters of plants in the South and other areas where land costs are low and labor is relatively cheap. A large central plant turns out the main segments of a garment, such as the various parts of a shirt. Bundles of those parts are then trucked to small satellite plants in nearby communities for machine-stitching. Since the more intricate work has already been done in the central plant, the work handled at the satellite plants is simple, and the labor cost is relatively low. The satellite plants attract workers because they provide a local source of income, with minimum training required. Workers do not have to travel long distances each day, as they would be required to do in order to earn slightly more at more distant plants.

It is in the central plant of such a cluster, and in other large apparel manufacturing plants, that automation is beginning to be developed. This is being achieved through the installation of equipment that (1) does jobs by machine that formerly had to be done by hand, (2) cuts down on the number of workers needed to do a specific job, and (3) cuts down on the amount of training and skill that workers need.

For example, "pocket-setters" sew a pocket on a shirt automatically. "Sequential buttonhole sewers" stitch all buttonholes on a shirt in a single automated operation. "Collar-makers" reduce the number of workers needed to make a collar on a production-line basis from eight to two. Since the equipment is programmed to follow a set pattern of operations and only a few simple tasks are left to the operators, these workers can be trained to run such collar-making equipment in 2 weeks instead of the 10 to 12 weeks once required to teach

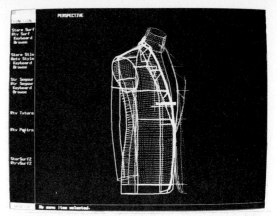

This computer screen displays a computer-aided design for a man's suit jacket.

workers to handle manual collar-making operations.

Automation has also invaded the labor-intensive, better-tailored-clothing industry. In the past, 1 to 1½ hours were required to handpress a man's grade 6 or 6+ suit. Today that time is reduced to a matter of minutes by means of a computer-controlled, automated system that steam-presses each part of the suit. In the last decade, manufacturers of tailored clothing have also turned almost exclusively to computer-assisted machines to mark and cut cloth, and some, such as Brooks Brothers, produce some styles entirely by machine.[14]

In general, the industry is gradually becoming more machine-oriented than operator-oriented. This is a vast change for an industry that, throughout most of its history, prided itself on the individual workmanship that went into many of its products.

Foreign Production and Imports

Price competition is very strong in the menswear market. A very important factor in setting prices at wholesale is the cost of labor. Because of this, an increasing number of menswear producers, particularly sportswear firms, are building plants or contracting to have work done in areas outside the country, where land and labor costs are lower.

The amount and type of work done outside the country, or "offshore," varies greatly. Some firms handle everything except the sewing in their domestic plants and contract to have the sewing done in plants outside the United States. Some have both the cutting and sewing done outside the country. Some ship greige goods to one country for dying and finishing and then ship these goods to another country for cutting and sewing. Some buy fabric outside the country and have the garments cut and sewn outside the country. In some cases, producers never actually see the products in any form until the finished goods are delivered to this country for distribution.

The disadvantages of foreign production include uncertain quality control and a longer wait for delivery of finished garments. Advantages, as discussed in earlier chapters, include lower production costs because of lower building or renting costs and lower costs of labor. This enables manufacturers to charge lower wholesale prices and retailers to pass on savings in lower retail prices. However, since goods produced in foreign countries are subject to import duties, savings are possible only when import duties are relatively low.

Imports have also made inroads in the U.S. menswear market. Their promise of lower production prices and solid quality, plus a demand for exclusivity, have led more retailers to build up their direct-import programs and buy indirect imports (clothing made abroad for U.S. manufacturers).

The menswear industry has become increasingly worried about offshore production and imports. By the late 1980s, approximately 25 percent of all mens' and boys' suits sold in the United States were manufactured overseas. For wool suits, imports and offshore production were as high as 40 percent.[15] The menswear industry attempted to counter this trend by lobbying for increased duties on foreign goods made in several key areas of production, most notably, Taiwan, South Korea, China, the Pacific Basin, and Latin America.

Specialty Trends

Menswear producers may no longer be specializing as much as they once did, but this does not mean that specialization is dying out. In fact, there are several interesting new trends toward specialization, mostly on the retail side of the business.

The number of menswear stores rapidly increased in the 1960s and then decreased in the early 1970s. The 1980s saw a slight increase albeit one that was geared toward specialization. Most notably, stores selling active sportswear sprang up everywhere. Their ability to survive depends, of course, on the continuing popularity of the fitness craze. In addition, retailers that had traditionally catered exclusively to the women's market began to take advantage of the new fashion-oriented men's market by opening specialty stores. In 1987, The Limited, for example, opened a chain of men's sports and leisure wear stores called Express Man.

Also gaining in popularity are men's clothing discounters. Popular discounters were Syms, BFO (Buyer's Factory Outlet), and NBO (National Brands Outlet) on the East Coast, Kuppenheimer Clothing Discount Centers in Texas, The Men's Wearhouse in Los Angeles, National Dry Goods in Detroit, and The Suitery in Chicago.

Catalog sales are another specialty trend. Major retailers, as well as specialty stores, have begun to send out catalogs geared exclusively to men, and stores such as L. L. Bean, which always sold by catalog, report an increase in business. Catalogs are typically slated for a specific market, that is, they specialize in low prices, certain styles or fashions, or exclusivity. Those specialty catalogs that have done thorough market research and have offered their customers exactly what they want have been quite successful.

REFERENCES

[1] Cathleen McGuigan with Sid Atkins, "History's Greatest Fops," *Newsweek,* April 14, 1985, p. 52.

[2] Michael Oneal, "A Retailored Hartmarx Still Needs Some Altering," *Business Week,* March 9, 1987, p. 109.

[3] Harry A. Cobrin, *The Men's Clothing Industry,* Fairchild Publications, Inc., New York, 1970, p. 67.

[4] Carol Hymowitz and Dana Canedy, "Looking Good: Leisure Clothing Revitalizes Dormant Men's Market," *The Wall Street Journal,* June 12, 1987, p. 3.

[5] Barbara Ettore, "Business and Buttonholes," *The New York Times,* October 28, 1979, p. F1.

[6] "Suit Prices Up ... But Purchases Down," *U.S. News & World Report,* April 11, 1988, p. 68.

[7] Jules Abend, "No Bridge for Men's Wear," *Stores,* October 1987, pp. 48–54.

[8] Herbert Blueweiss, "Clothing at Neiman-Marcus," *DNR, The Magazine,* November 30, 1987, p. 10.

[9] Hymowitz and Canedy, p. 31.

[10] William R. Greer, "Suits: Behind Those High Prices," *The New York Times,* March 22, 1987, p. 20.

[11] Ruth La Ferla, "Tailored for Success," *The New York Times Magazine,* April 5, 1987, pp. 68-70.

[12] Jules Abend, "Men's Private Label," *Stores,* October 1986, pp. 66–67.

[13] Ibid., p. 70.

[14] Greer, p. 32.

[15] Ibid., p. 30.

MERCHANDISING VOCABULARY

Define or briefly explain the following terms:

Active sportswear	Dual distribution	Slop shop
Bridge apparel	European styling	Suit separates
Contemporary menswear	Fusing	Tailored-clothing firm
	Inside shops	X suit

MERCHANDISING REVIEW

1. What effect did the industrial revolution have on male apparel? What socioeconomic factors were responsible for the drastic changes that occurred?
2. What three developments in the mid-nineteenth century were largely responsible for the development of the men's ready-to-wear industry in this country? How did each help to accelerate those developments.
3. Discuss the development of sportswear and casual wear in the men's market and the influence they have had on the menswear industry as a whole.
4. Name and describe the three ways in which menswear was manufactured in this country in the latter part of the nineteenth century.
5. For what three reasons did early manufacturers of men's tailored clothing give up the use of contractors?
6. Name the different segments into which the menswear industry is subdivided, on the basis of the type of product lines each produces. What specific products are produced by each segment?
7. Describe the differences between a tailored sports coat and a sports jacket, from a manufacturing standpoint.
8. Contrast the advertising policies of men's tailored-clothing firms with those of firms producing sportswear.
9. Describe two menswear style trends that are likely to continue through the 1990s.
10. How have menswear producers tried to compensate for the rising cost of labor and the shortage of skilled workers in the United States?

MERCHANDISING DIGEST

1. Discuss the following statement from the text: "The conservative men's suit is not dead yet, nor is it expected to be any time soon." Are tailored suits commonly worn in your community? Why or why not?
2. What is the role of designer names in menswear? Which men's designer fashions are currently popular?
3. Discuss why sportswear production can usually be handled successfully by contractors.

ACCESSORIES

Designer Bill Blass once summed up the role of accessories by saying, "You do not need to spend a fortune on apparel, but if you have the best accessories, you will look like you did."[1] Accessories add a finishing touch to a new outfit—and give new life to an old one.

In a business that always moves in the fast lane, it is safe to say that accessory manufacturers must move in a faster lane than anyone else. They have to be able to adapt or change a style in mid-season if that is what is required.

ACCESSORIES AND COORDINATION

The accessory industry differs from other fashion industries in that it exists, in a sense, to serve them. Accessories are designed primarily to coordinate with new fashions, that is, to enhance the latest trends, colors, silhouettes, textures, and designs in apparel. This does not mean, however, that accessory manufacturers are followers. In fact, accessory manufacturers must often be fashion leaders. They require as much, or more, time as others in the garment trade to stay on top of current trends.

Apparel designers occasionally experience resistance to trends and styles, but more often than not, they can introduce a new style with some confidence, knowing that it will be accepted. This is not the case for those who make accessories. They must respond much more to what consumers are asking for. In accessories, consumers often send the first signal of change—usually as they respond to new apparel fashions. Accessory customers, unlike apparel customers, do not necessarily adjust to the new styles. Instead, they either reject or accept them—and they do so early in the season.

If a style is rejected, it is dead. If it is accepted, manufacturers can prepare for a boom. They must produce large quantities of their product in a very short span of time. When an accessory is successful, it is typically stocked and sold in several departments in addition to the accessory department. Stores help out by displaying clothes with a total, or fully accessorized, fashion look. This means scarves are shown with coats when they are the hot accessory of the season. Recent accessory booms have included sunglasses, shawls, headwear, tops, and bodywear.

Unfortunately, accessory manufacturers must also be prepared for the boom to end as suddenly as it began. A raging accessory success can be totally passé in a few months' time.

New accessory lines are shown during fashion market weeks so that merchants can buy a coordinated look. In 1987, a new trade show especially for accessories was launched in New York. Called the Accessorie Circuit, it is designed to be a showcase of better-priced accessories. The show is a reflection of the growing importance of accessories to retailers and consumers.

Specific accessories wax and wane in popularity—here we see hats and earrings sharing the fashion spotlight with boldly striped jumpsuits.

RETAILING ACCESSORIES

Retailers have traditionally viewed accessories as **impulse items**—products that customers typically buy on the spur of the moment. A person who may not want to or is not able to update a wardrobe with the latest apparel styles each season can use accessories to look fashionable. Also, less expensive accessories are still purchased when there is price resistance to larger items of apparel. Accessories are chosen because of their color, style, and newness or simply because one wants to give one's wardrobe—and spirits—a lift.

In recognition of this buying pattern, most department stores position accessories on the main floor, or near the door or cash register in the case of small stores. More recently, they have begun to experiment successfully with "outposts," small accessory departments located next to apparel departments.

Some stores have begun to feature one-stop shopping with boutiques (often stocked exclusively by one designer) that allow customers to buy everything they need—apparel and accessories—in one department. One-stop shopping has proven especially successful with working women who have little time to shop.

It also appeals to the women who are a little unsure of themselves and like the added help that one-stop shopping provides in coordinating their outfits.

Fashion accessories, a category that includes shoes, hosiery, bodywear, handbags, jewelry, gloves, and millinery, are sold in every kind of store, ranging from the largest department stores to smaller boutiques to specialized stores carrying only one kind of accessory. Specific accessories wax and wane in popularity, but some accessories are always popular as most people do not consider themselves fully dressed until they have accessorized an outfit.

In recent years, the business overall has boomed. Many people feel the accessory business, like many other fashion categories, has been given a boost by its association with designer names.

SHOES

Feet have been wrapped, covered, or left uncovered since the beginning of time. Primitive people wrapped their feet in fur, and later people strapped them into sandals.

Customs concerning footwear have differed since the early Greeks and Romans donned sandals and boots. The Greeks generally went barefoot in the house. Romans rarely did so, regarding the wearing of footwear as a mark of superior class.

Making shoes was once a painstaking handicraft. But the commercial production of shoes has developed into an industry providing over 300 variations in shoe lengths and widths and over 10,000 different shapes and styles. Most shoe styles originated in Europe, keeping pace with the growth of European fashion. However, a classic shoe style that originated in America is the moccasin. Favored by both men and women and adored by most children, the moccasin style of shoe still retains its popularity and stands as one of the first examples of unisex fashion.

Organization and Operation

Shoemaking in America was once exclusively a Yankee industry. The major center for footwear production in the United States is still New England, where the industry originated. But another large center of production today is the St. Louis, Missouri, region. The shoe industry moved west when the Midwest became an important source of hide supplies and cheaper labor. Brown Shoe Company, the largest American producer of name-brand footwear, is based in St. Louis.

Shoe production begins with a **last.** Lasts were originally wooden forms in the shape of a foot, over which the shoes were built. Today most modern factories, American and foreign, make lasts of plastic or aluminum. Lasts made from these materials provide more exact measurements, and are easier to handle than the old wooden ones.

The variety of lasts, the quality of materials, and the number and type of manufacturing operations required determine the quality and price of the finished shoe. As many as 200 to 300 operations performed by highly skilled workers are required to make an expensive, high-quality shoe. Shoe manufacturers produce shoes in an enormous range of sizes. The normal range of women's shoe sizes involves 103 width and length combinations. And this does not include sizes shorter than 4, longer than 11, or wider than D.

Inventories, production problems, and capital investments in the shoe business are tremendous compared with those of other fashion-related industries. Thus it is not surprising that giant companies dominate the industry. Among the fashion industries, only cosmetics has a higher percentage of production by giant companies.

The shoe industry is also threatened by imports. From about 50 percent of the market in 1980, imports grew to almost 80 percent by 1986, according to statistics from Footwear Industries of America. The bulk of the imports come from Italy, Taiwan, Brazil, Korea, and Spain. Domestic producers were making 640 million pairs of shoes annually in the late 1960s, but they produced only 255 million pairs in the mid-1980s.[2] In the same period, total shoe sales in the United States rose to 1.3 billion pairs.

Merchandising and Marketing

As with most fashion industries, New York City is the major U.S. market center for shoes. It is there that most producers maintain permanent showrooms, and it is also home to the industry's semi-annual trade show, the National Shoe Fair, which fills a large portion of the enormous Javits Convention Center.

The shoe industry has an active national trade association known as the National Shoe Manufacturer's Association. Together with the National Shoe Retailers Association, it disseminates technical, statistical, and fashion trend information on footwear. In addition, the leather industry and its associations operate as sources of fashion information for shoe buyers and other retail store executives.

Brand names are important in the footwear industry, and manufacturers advertise extensively in national fashion magazines and on national TV.

In contrast with most other fashion industries, many of the large shoe man-ufacturers operate retail chain organizations of their own. This practice is known as "dual distribution." The other industry that practices dual distribution is the menswear industry (see Chapter 10). An outstanding example of dual distribution in the shoe industry is the Brown Group, which manufactures Buster Brown shoes for children, Naturalizer and Air Step shoes for women, and Roblee and Regal shoes for men. The Melville Corporation, which manufactures Thom McAn shoes, and U.S. Shoe Corporation are other examples. All of these shoe brands are sold in retail stores owned by the shoe manufacturers. Frequently these shoe chains also stock related accessories, such as handbags and hosiery.

Some shoe manufacturers also operate in the retail field through leased departments in retail stores. Because of the tremendous amount of capital required to stock a shoe department and the expertise needed to fit and sell shoes, many department and specialty stores lease their shoe departments to shoe manufacturers. Surveys by the National Retail Merchants Association have repeatedly shown that women's shoe departments are among those most commonly leased by its member stores. Examples of manufacturers of shoes who operate leased shoe departments in stores are the U.S. Shoe Corporation and the Brown Shoe Company. Morse Shoe Company and Edison Shoe Company are chain store retailers that import shoes and also operate leased shoe departments in other stores. With the boom in athletic shoes in the 1980s, U.S. Athletics, a chain of specialty footwear stores, began operating leased athletic shoe departments in several major department stores, including Bloomingdale's and Foley's.

TECHNOLOGY TALK

GETTING INTO TECHNOLOGY WITH BOTH FEET

Whether it's men's, women's, or children's—whether it's for dress, casual, or active sports—shoes need to fit and support the foot correctly.

It is primarily in the sports/athletic shoe and the children's shoe classifications that correct fit and the most technologically advanced support and comfort are most important.

Reebok, whose past focus was less on technical performance and more on marketing has changed its focus dramatically and has introduced the Worldtrainer and the World Road (running shoes), as well as an aerobic shoe, Aerobic 600, which incorporates an "Energy Return System" comprised of tubes laid through the midsole of the shoes. The aim, much like Nike's Air System, is to provide not only cushioning, but an extra bounce, or lift, to the wearer. Eventually, Reebok plans to extend the "Energy Return System" into other product categories.

Reebok's advertising is also beginning to focus on the technical performance of its footwear. Reebok has spent millions of dollars on research and development and because of this has originated such innovative footwear features as the "power platform" to help transfer power from the rider of a bicycle to the pedal, a "shockliner" for a more comfortable shoe suitable for walking, and a hytrel film to prevent shoe uppers from stretching.

Because of advanced technology, Reebok was able to structurally give lateral support in their sneakers, not available in regular sports sneakers. Computer technology has also aided in the production and marketing of their shoes. In a year, Reebok markets some 350 different models of sneakers, which extend from simple to complex constructions. To bet-

ter coordinate manufacturing availability with the needs of the marketplace for its wide range of shoes, Reebok developed a computer-based matrix which has reduced production lead times by 25 percent.

The newest kid on the block in the kid's shoe industry is called TU. This stands for Toddler University, which grew in just four years to a business doing over $25 million annually. Unlike traditional rigid high-topped infant shoes, TU's are soft, stitched rather than glued, and built to last with rubber toes and heels. They are also designed so that parents can adjust TU's widths with removable inserts.

One of the fundamental economic problems of the children's shoe business is inventory. There are 11 sizes in children's footwear—and five widths. So for each model, retailers need to stock 55 pairs of shoes. By patenting a single shoe with five inserts for width, TU has retailers going head-over-heels.

Toddler University provides coin-operated "shoe rides"—rocking replicas of TU shoes—which should pay for themselves within a year of placement in a store. With the newest technology at their fingertips, Toddler University looks forward to producing new and innovative shoes for children.

This Technology Talk is based on information from the following sources:

Ellen Benoit, "Lost Youth," *Financial World,* September 20, 1988, pp. 28–31.

Douglas McGill, "Reebok's New Models, Fully Loaded," *The New York Times,* February 14, 1989, p. D1.

James R. Norman, "At Toddler University, The Chairman Is Getting A's," *People,* p. 61.

Beth A Sexer, "Reebok: At the Crossroads," *Sportstyle,* February 22, 1988, pp. 60–63.

FASHION

Twenty years ago, people put on plain old sneakers when they wanted to play tennis, or shoot baskets, or perform calisthenics; and they wouldn't dream of wearing them to the office or to a fancy restaurant.

Today, there are literally dozens of different athletic shoes (never call them "sneakers"!), each specifically designed for a different activity—from walking and jogging to bicycling and volleyball. However, most people don't even wear them for those sporting endeavors: they wear them because they're *fashionable*.

Indeed, thanks to the creative styling and marketing efforts of the leading athletic footwear manufacturers, and most notably Reebok in recent years, their shoes have become status symbols. For many consumers, the name Reebok on their shoes is as impressive as a designer name in their apparel.

Of course, Reebok did not originate the trend to fashion in athletic shoes. In fact, compared to long-established brands like Adidas and Nike, the company is a newcomer to the business, having joined the footwear competition only in the 1980s. But Reebok entered the market when the time was ripe for fashion in athletic footwear; and once the firm's products took off, they took off like a rocket—with sales tripling from 1985 to 1986 alone, ending that year at

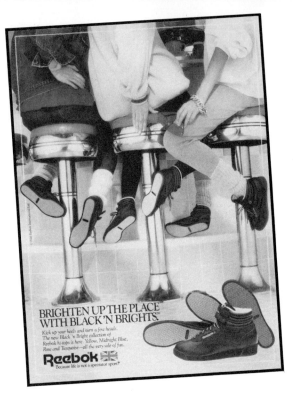

BRIGHTEN UP THE PLACE WITH BLACK 'N BRIGHTS.

Kick up your heels and turn a few heads. The new Black 'n Bright collection of Reebok hi-tops is here. Yellow, Midnight Blue, Rose and Turquoise—all the very sole of fun.

Reebok 🇬🇧
Because life is not a spectator sport.®

over $919 million. That same year, in *Footwear Profile for 1986* published by Kurt Salmon Associates, a New York–based consulting firm, Reebok single-handedly accounted for 39 percent of the total profits of 29 public companies included in the report!

The key to Reebok's phenomenal success lies partly in the consumer lifestyle of the 1980s, which saw an interest in

FOCUS

fitness and exercise combine with a more casual attitude toward street dressing. At the same time, the company set itself on a course of producing a broad line of shoes that would not only meet the functional needs of customers seeking a high-performance sport shoe, but the fashion needs of customers seeking a comfortable, casual, yet good-looking shoe.

And, to further confirm its commitment to fashion, in late 1986, Reebok launched its first line of women's active apparel—following again the footsteps of Adidas and Nike, which introduced apparel lines in 1975 and 1979, respectively. For Reebok, two distinct lines make up the collection: Reebok Sport, a sportswear weekend line with an emphasis on fashion, sold in department and specialty stores; and Reebok, a true performance line, sold exclusively in sporting goods shops such as Herman's World of Sporting Goods.

Reebok further strengthened its commitment to apparel in 1987 by acquiring Ellesse International, a manufacturer of high-end fashion skiwear, sportswear, footwear, and other apparel. And, in the fall of 1988, Reebok launched a line of apparel designed for walking, to complement its walking shoes which debuted a year earlier. The walking clothes involve a "casual lifestyle approach moving into the contemporary vein," according to Douglas Arbetman, Reebok's president of apparel.[1] In 1989, Reebok sent a team of aerobic champions to Russia hoping to sell the firm's shoes and apparel there.[2]

Of course, in its apparel as in its shoes, Reebok continues to seek a balance between function and fashion, even though in many cases customers may not even realize—or care about—the difference between an outfit or shoe designed for marathon running versus one designed to wear to the supermarket. As Arbetman put it, "There is a fine line between true performance and weekend wear,"[3] but in either case, "If fashion isn't there, nothing else is going to matter."[4] It's a far cry from the days of cut-off shorts and sneakers—but that's what fashion's all about!

---

[1] Robert E. Hartlein, "Nike, Adidas, Reebok: Striding Into Fashion," *Women's Wear Daily,* October 7, 1987, p. 13.
[2] "Reebok Exporting Aerobics to Untapped Soviet Market," *Women's Wear Daily,* May 17, 1989, p. 13.
[3] Hartlein, p. 13.
[4] Hartlein, p. 12.

This Fashion Focus is based on information from the article cited above and from this source:

Penny Gill, "Winning Pace for Footwear," *Stores,* July 1987, pp. 36–49.

Women's Shoes

For centuries, little attention was paid to the styling of women's shoes. Their purpose was regarded as purely functional, and it was considered immodest to expose the feminine ankle. Since the 1920s, however, women's feet have been plainly visible, and shoes have developed both in fashion importance and variety. When fashion invaded the shoe industry after World War II, the black or brown all-purpose shoes designed to be worn with any wardrobe disappeared. New and varied leather finishes, textures, plastic and fabric materials, and ranges of colors provided shoe styles that not only kept pace with changes in fashion but in many cases originated fashion trends. Styles have run the fashion gamut from pointed to square toes, from high to flat heels, and from naked sandals to thigh-high boots.

Ralph Lauren creates an elegant ambiance for his designer shoe line. This prototype "shoe shop" can be recreated in department and specialty stores around the world.

Men's Shoes

A shift in thinking and lifestyle on the part of American men has had a dramatic effect on the merchandising of men's shoes. Dress shoes were once the most important sales category in men's shoe departments in retail stores. They are now being replaced by dress/casual and casual shoes. Casual shoes were once considered appropriate only for the 18 to 25 age group, but now are preferred by men of all ages. The return in the 1980s of the classic look, the three-piece suit, and narrower ties has revived interest in loafers, moccasins, and dressier, classic slip-ons.

Although the sales volume for men's shoes is increasing, it is moving at a slower rate than the sales volume for women's shoes.

Children's Shoes

Until they are approximately 10 years old, boys and girls take more interest in their shoes than anything else they wear. Maybe this is due in part to the influence of children's movies—*The Wizard of Oz, Seven League Boots,* and *Cinderella*—in which shoes have magical powers.

Also, boys and girls must be taken along when shoes are bought and are thus involved in the purchase decision. From an early age they are taught that the correct fit and look of their shoes are important. This early training leads children to view shoes as the mainstay of a fashion wardrobe.

Athletic Shoes

Perhaps the most significant development in shoes in the 1980s has been the proliferation of athletic footwear, which is now considered a category in its own right. According to consumer purchase information gathered by MRCA (Marketing Research Corporation of America) Information Services, athletic shoes accounted for 25 percent of all footwear sold in 1986.

The athletic shoe phenomenon is especially striking when one considers that an estimated 80 percent of the footwear is not worn for athletics at all, but simply for comfort and style. One need only look at the legions of women and men walking to work in business suits and sneakers to understand the strength of this phenomenon. Certain brands of athletic shoes have become fashionable, and the shoes are viewed as status items. Leading the pack in both status and sales in recent years has been Reebok, followed closely by Nike and Adidas.

Because of the tremendous consumer demand for athletic shoes, many retailers have begun paying extra attention to the category, often creating a separate department for athletic shoes.

Athletic shoes have even become specialized. Manufacturers now make special shoes for virtually any sports activity—walking, running, aerobics, racquetball, biking. Most of the "super-specialty" shoes are carried in specialty athletic stores, while department stores and other general retailers stock a less specialized and more fashion-oriented range of athletic shoes.

Industry Trends

By the late 1980s, consumers were spending $19 billion on shoes, and the figure was going up every year. Women's shoes represented over half of total sales at $9.6 billion, with men's at $5.2 billion, slightly ahead of children's $4.2 billion total.[3] While footwear imports rose by almost 12 percent in 1986, there are signs that this market has peaked.[4]

In the meantime, to combat foreign sales, domestic manufacturers have been seeking ways to make their own production more profitable and their product more competitive. Many are experimenting with new and upgraded computer technology to aid in the design and manufacture of shoes. The U.S. Department of Commerce's Footwear Revitalization program, in operation since July 1977, has provided grants to manufacturers to update their operations to accommodate the new technology in their U.S. factories. The domestic shoe industry is also trying to increase exports of American-made shoes to the rest of the world.

Whether in athletic or other footwear, there is a strong relationship between shoes and the clothes with which they are worn. Increased emphasis on fashion continues to be the major trend in the footwear industry. Shoe designers and manufacturers regularly attend the Shoe Fair in Bologna, Italy. They also attend European apparel openings, as do shoe buyers from retail stores, gathering information on international trends in styling. More and more, apparel fashions influence both the styling and color of footwear. Skirt lengths, silhouettes, pants, and sporty or dressy clothes are the fashion keys to shoe designs. It is therefore essential for retailers to coordinate shoes and apparel wherever and whenever they can.

HOSIERY

The ancient Greeks were among the first to wear cloth legwear. By the late 1500s, European men and women wore stockings made from a single piece knitted flat, with the two edges sewn together to form a back seam. This technology remained essentially unchanged for centuries.

Until World War I, women's legs were concealed under floor-length skirts and dresses. When skirt lengths moved up and women's legs became visible, interest in adorning them increased, and the hosiery industry began to grow. But it was not until the introduction of nylon that hosiery as we know it today became a fashion accessory. Before the introduction of nylon in 1938, women wore seamed silk, cotton, or rayon stockings. Because of its easier care and greater durability, the new nylon hosiery was eagerly accepted despite its high price.

With the entry of the United States into World War II, nylon production was restricted to war purposes and silk was unavailable. Because the hosiery that was available was heavy and unattractive, women began to go bare-legged and used leg makeup to give the effect of sheer stockings. The bare-legged look became very popular, and when nylon became available again, the industry developed sheerer weights (deniers) and seamless hosiery that would provide this look.

Fashion first entered the hosiery picture in the 1950s with the introduction of colors other than black or flesh tones. But it was not until the 1960s that hosiery became a major fashion accessory. To accessorize the shorter skirt—eventually evolving into the miniskirt and micromini—colors, textures, and weights of stockings were created in great variety. Panty hose were introduced and became a fantastic success. In turn, their popularity led to the introduction of seamless panty hose and figure-control panty hose.

In the 1970s, when women were wearing pants, knee-high and ankle-high hosiery were introduced. Together with panty hose, they captured the major share of the hosiery business. In the 1980s changes in lifestyle produced a

Micro-minied Madonna effectively used patterned panty hose to complete her 1980s "look."

erates. The largest concentration of hosiery plants is found in the Southern states, with more than half of them in North Carolina.

Most hosiery mills perform all of the steps necessary for the production of finished hosiery. Some smaller units may perform the knitting operation only, contracting out the finishing processes.

Full-fashioned seamed hosiery is flat-knit to size and length specifications on high-speed machines. These machines shape the hosiery as it is knitted. The outer edges are then stitched together on special sewing machines, after which the hosiery is dyed. Each stocking acquires its permanent shape through a heat-setting process called **boarding.** Then these stockings are carefully matched into pairs. Their welts are stamped with a brand name or other appropriate information, and the pairs are packaged.

Seamless hosiery and panty hose are circular-knit to size and length specifications on high-speed machines. Again, these machines shape the item during the knitting process. Subsequent steps are dyeing, boarding, pairing, stamping, and packaging.

Since hosiery is knitted in the greige (unfinished) state, most manufacturers can produce branded and unbranded hosiery in the same mill. The greige goods are then dyed, finished, stamped, and packaged to specification for national brand, private brand, or unbranded hosiery.

new set of customer needs and wants which were met with textures in panty hose and tights. Socks in ribs and knits and leg warmers, along with many kinds of athletic socks, revitalized the industry.

Organization and Operation

The hosiery industry consists primarily of large firms, many of which are divisions of huge textile or apparel conglom-

Merchandising and Marketing

Traditionally, the women's hosiery industry concentrated its merchandising activities almost exclusively on the promotion and sale of nationally advertised brands. Recently, however, the industry has been merchandising its products for private labeling or for sale in vending machines and from self-service displays in supermarkets and drugstores. Designer labeling has also become increasingly important.

National Brands

Major hosiery producers sell their brand lines to retail stores across the country. Producers aggressively advertise their lines in national magazines and newspapers and on television. They also usually supply cooperative advertising, display aids, and fashion assistance to help promote these national brands at the store level. Major national brands include Hanes, Burlington, Round-the-Clock, and Kayser-Roth.

Designer-Label Brands

Because designer labeling adds an aura of couture and prestige to any item, designer labels have appeared on a variety of hosiery items, including panty hose, socks, and leg warmers. Many hosiery manufacturers upgrade their designer-label collections with superior yarns and production techniques. Almost all of the designer-label hosiery is the result of licensing agreements between the designer and manufacturers of national brands. In hosiery and panty hose, Hanes uses Oleg Cassini, Kayser Roth uses Calvin Klein, and Round-the-Clock uses Givenchy; in socks, Bonnie Doon uses Geoffrey Beene, Camp Company uses Christian Dior and John Weitz, and Hot Sox uses Ralph Lauren.

Private Brands

Chain organizations, retail stores, and some individual stores have developed their own **private** or **store brands** that compete with nationally advertised brands. A private label offers many advantages for the retailer. The cost of the hosiery is usually less because there is no built-in charge for advertising as there is for national brands. The private brand can be made up in colors and construction that will match customer profile specifications. Because the private brand is not available elsewhere, price promotions are easier. Customer loyalty can also be built upon the exclusivity of the private brand. Some private-label brands are Sears' Best, Macy's Supremacy and Marchioness, and I. Magnin's Magnifique.

Mass-Merchandised Brands

More and more self-service stores such as supermarkets, discount stores, and drug chains are beginning to carry packaged hosiery. With this change in the channels of retail distribution, hosiery manufacturers are developing low-priced, packaged hosiery that can be profitably sold in these stores. Each of these brands offers a good choice of styles and colors. Each manufacturer supplies attractive, self-service stock fixtures and promotes its brand through national advertising. Examples of mass-merchandised brands are L'eggs panty hose, made by Hanes Hosiery, and No Nonsense panty hose, made by Kayser-Roth.

Bodywear

The physical fitness boom of the last decade, which lured millions of Americans into aerobic classes and bodybuilding activities, also was responsible for producing a new fashion category, **bodywear.** It encompasses coordinated leotards, tights, wrap skirts, sweatsuits, exercise outfits, leg warmers, and the shorts, T-shirts, and crop tops that are used for exercise. Sales in this category skyrocketed in the 1980s.

Originally, bodywear was sold in hosiery departments, but many stores are now selling it in separate shops and boutiques. Some stores have focused even more attention on bodywear by staging fashion shows, scheduling personal appearances by designers, and even sponsoring in-store exercise and dance classes.

Today's fashion-conscious women insist on being stylish while they stretch, strain, and sweat to get in shape. Long-time bodywear manufacturers, such as Danskin and Flexatard, capitalized on this new market by creating new exciting leotards with coordinating tights, cover-ups, and other workout apparel necessities. Manufacturers noted for producing other accessories, such as Aris and Evan-Picone, entered the bodywear field with Isotoner Fitnesswear and Highstepper Leotards. Workout celebrity Jane Fonda even tried getting into the bodywear business, although her workout apparel proved far less successful than her workout videos. Designer Ralph Lauren, however, created a bodywear line that has sold very well. Another entry, Marika Bodywear, produces the Mikail Baryshnikov line.

Industry Trends

Fashion trends have a tremendous influence on sales in the hosiery industry. For example, when skirts are shorter or have leg-revealing silhouettes, texture and color in hosiery become important. "All-in-ones"—panty hose with built-in panties—are the answer when tight-fitting pants and skirts are fashionable. Apparel manufacturers have recently worked with hosiery manufacturers to design panty hose that are both texture- and color-coordinated to their sportswear. The hosiery is displayed with the apparel to promote a total fashion look.

The inventory of most hosiery departments includes conventional stockings, panty hose, casual legwear, leg warm-ers, bodywear, and casual footwear. Bodywear and casual footwear are relatively high-priced retail items, while packaged hosiery is low-priced. As a result, some stores have made separate departments out of these two different categories.

The needs and wants of customers prompt hosiery manufacturers to design entirely new items. Control-top panty hose, support hose, queen-sized panty hose, and "all-in-ones" are examples. Most recently, women have shown an interest in the "lingerie look" in hosiery. This has prompted a return to traditional-style stockings and the introduction of such "new" styles as thigh-high hose with delicate lace tops, panty hose with knit-in lace bikini tops, and French-cut briefs. Designed more for special occasions than for everyday wear, the elegant lingerie-look hosiery added a new dimension—and increased sales—to the upper price points of the business.

Another trend that took off was the use of Lycra spandex in sheer panty hose. Lycra spandex fiber, with its excellent stretch and recovery properties, had been used for more than 25 years in swimsuits, girdles, and support hose only. Only in 1979 was its producer, the Du Pont Company, able to make the fiber in fine enough denier for sheer hosiery. First used by L'eggs in its Sheer Elegance brand, the fabrication gradually trickled up to department store brands and today accounts for an estimated 26 percent of all retail class sheer hosiery volume. Some industry experts predict that sheer Lycra hosiery will eventually replace all nylon panty hose.[5]

Men's, women's, and children's hosiery sales are predicted to increase steadily. Athletic, sport, and work socks are exploding in the men's area; knee-highs, tights, leg warmers, and new textures and colors in panty hose are fueling the women's area; and children are emulating their parents in their requests for sport socks, tights, and leg warmers.

In the past decade, innovations in yarn, marketing, and manufacturing have transformed a labor-intensive business into a semiautomated, very competitive industry producing over $5 billion in retail sales. It is estimated that by the year 2000, the domestic hosiery industry will be about 40 percent larger in terms of number of units produced. However, the output will be manufactured by an industry with only one-half as many firms, employing just two-thirds as many people as 20 years earlier.[6]

HANDBAGS

Today the way that people choose to carry their belongings often makes a statement about them, but this was not always the case. Throughout most of history, small, nondescript sacks vied with pockets as places to store one's personal belongings. Even when handbags were invented, they said little about their owners for quite a long time. But the modern handbag, once a mere receptacle for money and makeup, now sends a distinct fashion message as well as statement about its owner's personality and individual style.

As fashion statements, handbags are used to dramatize, harmonize, or contrast with whatever else one is wearing. Styles vary from the most casual, used for sportswear, to the more formal, used for dress-up evening occasions. A handbag may be small or large; its shape, a pouch or a tote, draped or boxy. So important are handbags as fashion accessories that most women own a wardrobe of them.

As personal statements, they also send a message. A woman who chooses to carry a leather briefcase, for example, sends one kind of message, while a woman who uses a backpack sends another. Whether a woman opts for a small, delicate beaded handbag at night or something far more exotic, perhaps a gold box set with unusual jewels, says something about her. The woman who carries a tailored, expensive leather purse creates a different image from the woman who settles on a vinyl or canvas tote.

Organization and Operation

Compared with other fashion industries, the handbag industry is small. The number of domestic firms producing handbags diminishes each year, as imports made in Europe, South America, and the Far East increase. In 1963, over 600 firms made handbags in the United States. In eight years, between 1971 and 1979, the number of domestic firms making handbags dropped from 400 to about 380, and by the late 1980s it had slipped to under 300.[7]

Most American handbag manufacturing has been concentrated in New York and New England, although many plants have recently sprung up in Florida. As small firms close, the remaining firms become larger and more diversified as they seek to capture a broader share of the market.

Merchandising and Marketing

Although manufacturers' brand names are relatively unimportant in the handbag industry (except for certain classics such as Coach Bags and Dooney & Bourke), designer handbags have become popular. Famous names like Pierre Cardin, Bill Blass, Anne Klein, Ralph Lauren, Donna Karan, and Paloma Pi-

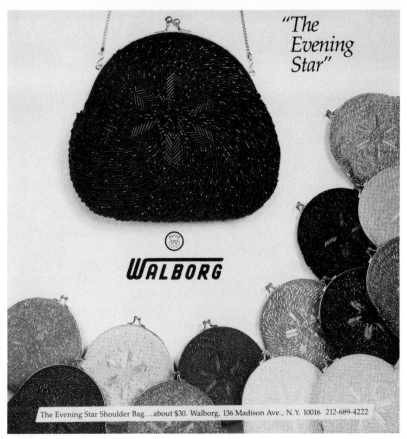

"The Evening Star"

WALBORG

The Evening Star Shoulder Bag...about $30. Walborg, 136 Madison Ave., N.Y. 10016 212-689-4222

Beaded bags are used as a fashion statement for dress-up evenings.

casso have entered licensing agreements with handbag manufacturers. Judith Leiber is famous for her handmade beaded bags in animal shapes and her metal *minaudieres*. Several foreign manufacturers such as Louis Vuitton, Hermes, and Gucci have always enjoyed enormous status at the high end of the market.

Few handbag manufacturers, however, are large enough to advertise on a national basis in newspapers and television. The customer's impression of what is new and fashionable in handbags is mostly gleaned through store displays and advertising in newspapers and magazines. "Total look" advertising, in which models wear fully accessorized outfits, has also helped to create interest in handbags.

Industry Trends

Faced with severe competition from foreign imports, many domestic handbag manufacturers have themselves become importers of foreign-made handbags. These importers employ American designers to create styles and then have the purses made in countries with low-wage scales. In the late 1980s, over 85 percent of all handbags sold in the United States were imports. The industry's trade organization—the National Fashion Accessories Association—has worked closely with government agencies to promote the domestic handbag industry both here and abroad.

To combat imports, some of the larger manufacturers have recently diversified their lines. Many are reaching out to men, who have been flirting with the idea of carrying purses since the 1960s. Still others are adding luggage, small leather goods such as wallets and key cases, and coordinated belts to their product lines.

JEWELRY

Jewelry has always played a significant and varied role in people's lives. In ancient times, some articles of jewelry were worn as amulets to ward off evil. Jewelry was popular among ancient Greeks, Romans, and Africans. The beautiful Roman women who still live in the old frescoes wore long, thin necklaces that encircled their necks two or three times, strands of pearls braided in their hair, and engraved belts decorated with precious stones.

A symbol of wealth and importance, jewelry was at certain times worn only by nobility. Laden with gold chains, their clothing adorned with gems, their fingers covered with rings, they carried on their persons the fortunes of their ruling houses. Medieval noblemen displayed elaborate heraldic emblems symbolizing their knighthood, and military men, another privileged class, used to make a great display of their decorations, which were once jewel-encrusted.

Jewelry styles come and go. In the 1800s, a silver or gold watch was an important accessory. In the late 1980s, people wore throwaway watches. Pearls, a classic accessory for women in the 1940s and 1950s, are once again popular. Sometimes jewelry loses and then regains its symbolic value. The gold chains that are popular now, especially with men, and the popularity of religious symbols in jewelry all seem to hark back to the days when jewelry was worn to protect its owner from evil.

Organization and Operation

Methods of making jewelry have changed little over time. Modern jewelers melt and shape metal, cut and carve stones, and string beads and shells much as jewelers have been doing for centuries. Jewelry designers have always used enamel, glass, ceramic, and natural mineral formations as their raw materials.

Based on the quality of their products, the jewelry industry in the United States can be divided into two primary groups: **fine jewelry** and **costume** or **fashion jewelry.** A third group, **bridge jewelry,** is gaining in importance.

Fine Jewelry

Fine jewelry is the counterpart of haute couture. Only precious metals such as gold and platinum (which includes palladium, rhodium, and iridium) are used to make fine jewelry. Sterling silver is also considered a precious metal, although its intrinsic value is far less than that of gold or platinum. Too soft to be used alone, these precious metals are alloyed, or combined, with one or more other metals to make them hard enough to be fashioned into jewelry.

The stones used in fine jewelry are called **gemstones** to distinguish them from lower-quality stones that are used for industrial purposes. Gemstones, which always come from natural mineral formations, have traditionally been classified as either precious or semiprecious.

Precious stones include diamonds, emeralds, rubies, sapphires, and real, or oriental, pearls. Semiprecious stones in-

THE DIAMONDS OF TIFFANY

The Diamonds of Tiffany. As exceptional as the woman who wears them.

TIFFANY & CO.

NEW YORK LONDON MUNICH HONG KONG BEVERLY HILLS CHICAGO DALLAS HOUSTON BOSTON ATLANTA SAN FRANCISCO 800-526-0649

Still a symbol of wealth and importance . . . diamonds . . . here the specialty of Tiffany's made by Tiffany craftsmen in the Tiffany workshops.

clude amethysts, garnets, opals, jades, and a host of other natural stones that are less rare and costly than precious stones but quite beautiful.

In recent years, chemists have succeeded in creating synthetic precious stones that are chemically identical to real stones. Synthetic stones are now used in combination with 14-carat gold and sterling silver. The most popular of the synthetics is zirconia, which offers the dazzle of diamonds at a fraction of the cost.

Fine-jewelry production is still a handcraft industry. A lapidary, or stone-cutter, transforms dull-looking stones in their natural states into gems by cutting, carving, and polishing them.

In the established fine jewelry houses, as in haute couture houses, design, production, and retail sales typically take place under one roof—and one management. Many fine-jewelry firms sell only the jewelry they create, much of which is custom designed for them. Names such as Cartier and Tiffany have always been used to sell jewelry, but in the past, the designers, who were in the employ of these companies, were not known. In the last decade, though, individual designers have taken on new importance, and customers now look for jewelry designed by Paloma Picasso and Elsa Peretti at Tiffany, as well as independents such as Angela Cummings, Barry Kesselstein-Cord, and Robert Lee Morris.

Costume Jewelry

Costume or fashion jewelry is like mass-produced apparel. A wide range of materials—wood, glass, and base metals such as brass, aluminum, copper, tin, and lead—are used to make it. Base metals are sometimes coated with costlier precious metals such as gold, rhodium, or silver. The stones and simulated pearls used in costume jewelry are made from clay, glass, or plastic. While they are attractive and interesting in their surface appearance, they are less costly and lack the more desirable properties (durability for one) of natural stones.

Prior to the 1920s, costume jewelry as we know it did not exist. Most jewelry was made from gold or, more rarely, silver set with precious or semiprecious stones. Jewelry was worn for its sentimental or economic value and was never used to accessorize one's clothing.

The age of costume jewelry began with designer Coco Chanel. In the 1920s she introduced long, large, and obviously fake strands of pearls to be worn with her clothes. This new accessory was called costume jewelry since it was meant to coordinate with one's costume.

Chanel, it might be noted, not only helped to create an industry, but also continued to wear her trademark pearls for the rest of her life. Today, fake pearls—indeed Chanel-style pearls—are a staple of the costume jewelry industry. First Lady, Barbara Bush, famous for her 3-strand "fake" pearl necklaces, started a resurgence of this style in 1989.

Costume jewelry has always gone through phases. At times, it is intended to look like fine jewelry; at other times, frankly fake-looking jewelry is in style. In the 1960s, Kenneth Jay Lane designed costume jewelry so real-looking that socialites and other fashion leaders favored it over their own authentic jewels. In the 1980s, less well known and highly individualistic designers like Eva Graham, Catherine Stein, Carol Daiplaise, Van Allen, Ellen Joffee, Francine Lambert, Jay Feinberg, Ted Meehling, and Wendy Gell enjoyed success with jewelry that looked real but was fake.

There is always a market in costume jewelry for products that look like the real thing; most mass-produced jewelry, in fact, falls into this category. Large, popular-priced costume-jewelry houses employ stylists who design seasonal lines or adapt styles from higher-priced lines. Most mass-produced costume jewelry is made in Providence, Rhode Island. Facilities are geared toward producing jewelry to the specifications of individual firms, much as apparel manufacturers contract out their work and use jobbers.

Mass-production methods are employed in contrast to the handwork that exemplifies the making of fine jewelry. While a fine jeweler pounds and hand-shapes metal, manufacturers of costume jewelry cast metal by melting it and then pouring it into molds to harden. Designs are applied to the hardened metal surface by painting it with colored enamel or embossing it by machine.

Large firms, such as Monet and Trifari (which have merged), Carolee, Napier, and Accessocraft, dominate the industry, but more than 90% of American jewelry producers are small, family-owned companies with fewer than 25 employees.[8] Individuals with creative talent often open successful small retail and/or wholesale operations that cater to customers who are interested in individualized styling and trend-setting fashions. Such operations are an outgrowth of the handcraft movement of the 1960s and 1970s.

Bridge Jewelry

Dramatic increases in the price of gold and silver in the early 1980s left jewelers seeking new ways to meet the public's demand for reasonably priced, authentic jewelry. The solution was bridge jewelry, that is, jewelry that forms a bridge—in price, materials, and style—between fine and costume jewelry.

The development of bridge jewelry led to increased use of sterling silver and its

Briefly Speaking

Frankly Fake!

In the jewelry business, people are learning that all that glitters is not gold.

The phenomenal popularity of costume jewelry as a fashion accessory is fueling excitement for both manufacturers and retailers. And with its acceptance, the price of *faux* (the French word for fake) has risen to match its improved status.

Nationally, costume jewelry is now a $5 billion industry, with the fastest growth occurring in the "high-end" fashion jewelry ... the "paste with panache." Today, a bauble like those worn by all the society ladies and models in fashion magazines can cost from $500 to $1,000 ... and it is frankly fake!

With its new status, everybody's getting into the act. Yves Saint Laurent signed a deal with Cartier to market YSL fakes in the U.S., while at Chanel, one of the original creators of the fabulous fakes, and still a leader, sales have been growing steadily for the past five years. All over Manhattan's jewelry district, designers are grinding out copies of gems that once belonged to duchesses and queens.

The market in fakes has been booming since gold and silver prices started to soar in the late 70s, pricing even modest fine jewelry out of the grasp of most consumers. Spurred by the expense of precious metals and stones *AND* the anything-goes attitude of fashion, costume jewelry shed its poor step-sister image to become the Cinderella of the industry.

Costume jewelry pieces, containing neither silver or gold, sell for as much as $1,000. Cubic zirconium—the fake diamond—is a favorite material along with high-tech plastics and rhinestones. The pieces are expensive, not because of materials costs, but rather because most of the pieces are hand-made and often heavily detailed. Also, because of the limited size of production runs—sometimes only 1,000 pieces—automation is often not feasible.

The theories of why frankly fake jewelry has become so popular varies. Television shows like "Dynasty" and "Dallas" are credited with creating a desire for a sophisticated look that most women can duplicate only by wearing fakes. Other allege that fakes are popular because of high crime rates!

Even though James Bond believes that "Diamonds Are Forever," rhinestones seem to be just fine with the buying public.

This Briefly Speaking was based on information from the following sources:

Sherl A. Barnett, "Paste With Panache," *Newsday,* November 18, 1987, Part II, p. 7.
Cynthia Rigg, "A Trifle It's Not," *Crains New York Business,* March 31, 1986, p. 3 and p. 44.
Fromma Joselow, "Jewelers Pay a Fancy Price for a More Polished Image," *The New York Times,* April 16, 1989, p. 17.

subsequent elevation to a precious metal. The boom in Native American jewelry in the early 1970s also helped to create interest in bridge jewelry. Many department stores and specialty stores created bridge departments to handle sterling silver and Native American jewelry, and when interest in it faded, they were open to other kinds of bridge jewelry that would help them keep the customer base they had developed.

Bridge jewelry departments at such stores as Marshall Field's, Neiman-Marcus, and the May Company now carry gold-filled, vermeil, sterling silver, and some 14-carat fashion jewelry set with semiprecious stones.

Merchandising and Marketing Activities

Jewelry manufacturers present their new styles and, in the case of costume-jewelry manufacturers, their new lines at semiannual shows sponsored by the industry's trade association, the Jewelry Industry Council. A permanent showroom, the Worldwide Business Exchange (WBE), is also maintained in New York City.

Fine-jewelry manufacturers traditionally have concentrated on providing a wide range of basic pieces, most notably, diamond rings and watches. They support their lines with a variety of services offered to stores. Some advertising assistance is offered, but this has not been common in a business where brand names have been relatively unknown. With the emergence of designer-jewelry names, however, this may change.

Many fine-jewelry departments in stores are leased from manufacturers, mostly because such a large amount of capital is necessary to stock a jewelry department and a specialized sales staff is needed to sell the stock. A percentage of sales is returned to the host store. The Zale Company is an example of a major manufacturer that operates a large leasing operation. In contrast, costume jewelry is sold by the retailer, who may be a department store, a boutique, or a jewelry store carrying a mixture of fine and costume jewelry.

Costume jewelry firms offer seasonal lines designed to coordinate with what is currently fashionable in apparel. Most costume jewelry is produced on a contract basis, which offers the advantage of fast turnaround on individual items. When a particular item is suddenly in demand, costume-jewelry manufacturers can switch gears and produce it quickly in a large quantity. The larger firms also market their goods under their nationally known brand names and advertise widely in national consumer publications. In addition, they offer cooperative advertising to retail outlets. Some manufacturers provide guidance and sales training to retailers.

Industry Trends

Today, all branches of the jewelry industry emphasize the production of designs that complement currently fashionable styles. For example, when turtlenecks are popular, jewelry companies make long chains and pendants that look graceful on high necklines. When sleeveless dresses are in fashion, bracelets become an important piece of jewelry. When prints are popular, jewelry styles become tailored; but when solid or somber colors are popular, jewelry often moves to center stage with more complex designs and bright colors.

In order to compete with costume jewelry, which has gained broad acceptance over the past few decades, fine-jewelry companies have begun to diversify. Some have broadened their lines by moving into bridge jewelry. Others have also diversified into complementary nonjewelry areas. Swank, for example, which for years has manufactured men's small jewelry items, now produces colognes, sunglasses, travel accessories, and a variety of men's gifts.

Swatch made a splash in the market with its casual watches, and has now spread its name and contemporary look into a number of other product categories such as sportswear, sunglasses, and other accessories. The Swatch lines have become so popular that some retailers have created Swatch boutiques.

Designer jewelry is another major market force, especially in costume jewelry. Designers are thought to have been a major contributing factor to the current period of expanding sales. Mary McFadden, Donna Karan, Yves Saint Laurent, Christian Dior, Givenchy, Pierre Cardin, and Anne Klein are some of the apparel designers who have been successful in licensing jewelry lines.

Exports of costume jewelry jumped 26 percent in 1988, but were still only one-sixth of the value of imports! Known more for their skills as producers than as marketers, American costume jewelry makers have long been reluctant to venture into the international market. But growing imports have prodded more of them to explore overseas outlets. In 1988, manufacturers formed a new trade group, the International Jewelry Trade Association, to cultivate foreign business.[8]

GLOVES

Crude animal-skin coverings were the forerunners of mittens, which, in turn, evolved into gloves with individual fingers. Gloves are not new, though; leather gloves were discovered in the tombs of ancient Egyptians.

Gloves have enjoyed a long and varied history, at times even taking on symbolic value. To bring them luck, knights once wore their ladies' gloves on their armor as they went into battle. So long as women wore modest dress, men often cherished the gloves of their beloved as erotic objects. Gloves were once exchanged when property was being sold as a gesture of good faith. And in dueling days, one man would slap another across the face with his glove as an invitation to a duel. Gloves have also been used to denote rank or authority. Prior to the sixteenth century, only men of the clergy or of noble rank were allowed to wear them.

Gloves as fashion accessories have always had their devotees. Queen Elizabeth I of England owned 7,000 pairs of gloves and had a maid whose sole responsibility was to take care of them. Napoleon, who was known to be vain about his hands, once placed a single order for 272 pairs of gloves. And Mary Lincoln at the height of the Civil War was criticized for caring too much about fashion. One much ballyhooed sign of her excessiveness was the fact that she owned 100 pairs of gloves.

Gloves, like most accessories, undergo cyclical popularity. Sometimes, especially when clothes are casual, they are worn only for protection. At other times, they may be used for pure adornment. An example of this is the fingerless, lace glove. Today, glove manufacturers seem to have the best of both worlds: Gloves are being worn both as a fashion accessory and for protection.

To be fashionable, gloves must coordinate in styling, detail, and color with current apparel styles. To be specific, glove styles correlate to the currently popular sleeve length, especially in coats and suits. Some glove styles are considered classics. The untrimmed, white, wrist-length glove is a classic for dress occasions, as is the suit glove, which extends a few inches above the wrist, often made up in leather and used for general wear.

Organization and Operation

In the first half of the twentieth century, the glove business flourished largely because no self-respecting, let alone fashionably dressed, woman went out without wearing gloves. Leather gloves, which were relatively inexpensive, were favored. The 1960s, which saw the onset of a long period of casual dress, also saw the end of gloves as a requirement for a well-dressed woman. They are only now making a comeback, although in new materials. When leather became expensive in the 1980s, manufacturers began to make gloves of knit and woven fabrics, which now dominate the market.

The production of gloves varies, depending upon whether they are made of leather or fabric. Most leather gloves are made, at minimum, with hand-guided operations, and some are still made entirely by hand. At the turn of the century, when gloves were mostly made by hand, the talents of glove cutters were so revered that their employers sent carriages to take them to and from work. Glove cutters earned $60 a week in 1900, an excellent wage for that period.

Leather gloves are typically made in small factories, since few machines and workers are required to run such a factory. Glove producers tend to specialize, performing only one manufacturing operation, such as cutting or stitching. Other operations are farmed out to nearby plants, each of which, in turn, does its own specialty.

In contrast to the methods used to make leather gloves, the fabric-glove in-dustry is much more mechanized. Most fabric gloves are made of some kind of double-woven fiber because this gives them great durability. Knit gloves are made of wool, acrylic, and cotton—even cotton string.

New York City, once the center of the glove-manufacturing industry, has become a virtual ghost town as glove manufacturers have turned to offshore production. Today most gloves are made in the Caribbean and the Philippines.

Merchandising and Marketing

Compared with the dollars spent on consumer advertising for other accessories, the industry outlay for glove advertising is quite modest. Only a few large producers with nationally distributed brand names actively promote their products or offer even limited merchandising support services to retail stores.

Stagnating sales and competition from imports, however, have forced some manufacturers (particularly those who make leather gloves) to reevaluate their merchandising programs. No longer guaranteed a captive audience, producers had to find new ways to entice customers.

Some manufacturers began packaging stretch gloves so they could be sold from self-service counters. They soon moved from that to packing gloves with hats and scarves in a way so they, too, could be sold at a self-service counter. Self-service counters are known to expand the market for gloves, since people will go to one when they sometimes will not take the time to be specially fitted for gloves. Self-service counters are good for manufacturers because they encourage stores to stock a larger inventory.

Manufacturers have also reduced the number of glove sizes, preferring to sell gloves in only small, medium, and large.

Stretch fabric gloves, in which one size fits all, are popular, too.

Manufacturers have learned to make gloves more creatively. Gloves are now lined—and sometimes even made of—a wide array of knitted fabrics, lace, cashmere, fur, and silk.

Finally, while many fashion industries have turned to diversification, the glove industry has moved in the opposite direction, toward specialization. Glove manufacturers, for example, have created a market for gloves for specific sports. Men and women can choose from an array of gloves designed for use at tennis, skiing, bicycling, and golfing—to name just a few.

Industry Trends

Sales of domestically produced leather gloves have suffered considerably in recent years from the competition of less expensive imports. To meet this challenge, the industry is trying to improve manufacturing procedures in order to reduce costs. In addition, improved materials are resulting from product research and development in the leather industry. These are expected to increase the market potential of domestically produced leather gloves. For example, many leather gloves today are handwashable and come in a wide range of fashion colors.

MILLINERY

According to an old saying, whatever is worn on the head is a sign of the mind beneath it. Since the head is one of the more vulnerable parts of the body, hats do have a protective function. But they are also a fashion accessory.

The man's hat of the nineteenth and twentieth centuries in Europe, which was derived from the medieval helmet,

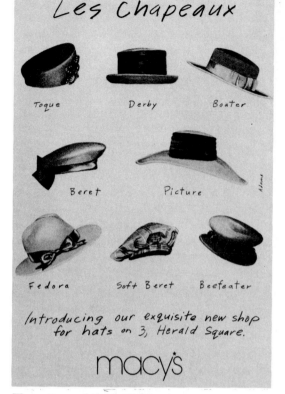

The return of the hat! Macy's announces a new shop for hats—and shows the "new" millinery customer what each style is called.

protected its wearer both physically and psychologically. The heavy crown kept the head safe from blows, and the brim shaded the face from strong sunlight and close scrutiny. In late nineteenth-century America, the hat was a status symbol of a special kind. This was the time of European immigration, and as boatload after boatload of hatless peasants landed, those who wanted to make it plain that they were of a higher class than the immigrants took care to wear hats.[9]

After decades of prosperity and popularity, the millinery industry began to collapse in the years following World War II. Because of the more casual approach to dressing and the popularity of women's beehive and bouffant hairstyles, men's and women's millinery sales hit bottom in 1960. During the freewheeling 1960s and 1970s a hat was worn only on the coldest days, and strictly for warmth, not for fashion. Millinery departments turned to selling wigs to gain sales volume, but wigs also enjoyed only a brief popularity.

During that time, the millinery industry and its active trade association, the National Millinery Institute, researched, publicized, and campaigned in an extensive effort to reverse the trend, with little success. This was not surprising since most experts have noted that no amount of sales promotion can change the direction fashion is moving in.

With the return of glamour and the growing popularity of the classic look in the mid-1980s, the situation in millinery began to change. In fashion shows on both sides of the Atlantic, models paraded the runways with hats adorning their heads. Hats with big brims and little brims; hats decorated with jewels, feathers, veilings; hats made from velvet, felt, and satin—all worn for flattery and fun rather than practicality.

The versatility of the new hats can be attributed to a new breed of designer. The number of established milliners in New York declined sharply over the past three decades, but the millinery field now is attracting fresh young design talent. Young designers are bringing to the industry a vibrant and young appeal to headwear and are successfully interpreting the needs of the new headwear customers. They are the prime reason for the steady growth and success of the renewed millinery industry.

There was a time when a person wasn't considered well-dressed unless he or she was wearing a hat. The industry is hoping for a repeat of that era.

OTHER FASHION ACCESSORIES

Other fashion accessories include neckwear, belts, small leather goods, handkerchiefs, hair goods, sunglasses, umbrellas, and wigs. While some of the industries producing these accessories were quite large at one time, today they are relatively small. The output of industries producing these accessories tends to fluctuate in direct relation to the fashion importance of each to the current popular look. The main showrooms of the producers are in New York City, although the merchandise is manufactured mostly in foreign countries.

One innovative and successful approach to merchandising these various fashion accessories has been to group them all together into one store department. Usually called the "dress accessories department," it features currently fashionable merchandise. When the emphasis is on necks and shoulders, scarves become important. When emphasis is on the waistline, belts are featured. Among the fashion accessories recently in the spotlight is the umbrella. Far from being merely a device for shielding against sun or rain, the umbrella now is a fashion-right item available in vivid colors and prints, and with exciting and exotic handles to please fashion customers. Neckwear and sunglasses are two fashion accessories that are currently enjoying popularity and strong sales.

Neckwear

Neckwear began an upswing in the late 1980s, and many in the business expect

Whether scarves, sunglasses, or another accessory item, stores display the current "hot" seller.

by Collection XIIX), Adrienne Vittadini and Oscar de la Renta (produced by Accessory Street), and Liz Clairborne.

Sunglasses

In recent years, consumers have become increasingly aware of the need to protect their eyes from the sun's harmful rays. At the same time, manufacturers of sunglasses have made a concerted effort to produce sunglasses that are high-fashion. Combine these factors with the high visibility of sunglasses on prominent celebrities like Jacqueline Onassis, Don Johnson, and Tom Cruise, and it is no wonder that sales of this category exploded to the $1.3 billion mark by 1988.[10] Riding the current wave of popularity are many designer names, among them Anne Klein, Christian Dior, Liz Claiborne, Calvin Klein, and Laura Biaghotti. The leading brand name, Ray-Ban (made by Bausch & Lomb), has even managed to achieve designer-name status itself, thanks in large part to its exposure on the *Miami Vice* TV series, popular in the late 1980s.

it to continue. Younger customers have begun wearing scarves, which complement the currently popular ready-to-wear looks. In addition, a number of leading designer names have become associated with neckwear, further enhancing the category's appeal. Among them are Perry Ellis and Anne Klein (produced by Vera), Albert Nipon, Ellen Tracy, and Evan Picone (both produced

REFERENCES

[1] Jill Newman, "Bill Blass: The Shape of Things to Come," *Women's Wear Daily/Accessories,* May, 1987, p. 62.

[2] Pamela G. Hollie, "Shoe Industry's Struggle," *The New York Times,* May 28, 1985, p. D1.

[3] "Footwear 1986," Report from MRCA Information Services, Stamford, Connecticut.

[4] "Footwear Profile for 1986," published by Kurt Salmon Associates, Inc., New York, June 1987.

[5] Alyson Fendel, "Lacy Looks Are Tops," *Stores,* June 1987, p. 20.

[6] Delphi Survey of the United States Hosiery Industry, conducted by Kurt Salmon Associates, Inc., and the National Association of Hosiery Manufacturers, December 1978.

[7] *Women's Wear Daily,* March 4, 1983, p. 21.

[8] Fromma Joselow, "Peddling Trinkets Abroad To Tie the Score in Trade," *The New York Times,* April 16, 1989, p. 17.

[9] Alison Lurie, *The Language of Clothing,* Random House, New York, 1981, p. 177.

[10] "Sales of Sunglasses in U.S. Topped $1.3 Billion for 1988," *Women's Wear Daily,* May 12, 1989.

MERCHANDISING VOCABULARY

Define or briefly explain each of the following terms:

Boarding	Fine jewelry	Private label or brand
Bodywear	Gemstones	Store brand
Bridge jewelry	Impulse items	
Costume or fashion jewelry	Last	

MERCHANDISING REVIEW

1. Why is the accessories department usually on the main floor of a store near the main entrance? What is the value of accessories "outputs"?
2. What are the main locations in the United States for the production of shoes?
3. Discuss the merchandising activities of the domestic shoe industry in terms of (a) advertising, (b) maintenance of retail outlets, and (c) leased departments.
4. How do changes in lifestyle and activities affect the shoe industry? Give examples.
5. Name and briefly describe four methods of merchandising women's hosiery.
6. Give examples of fashion trends that have influenced hosiery.
7. Discuss the fashion importance of handbags. Of what materials are handbags made.
8. Why are shoe and fine-jewelry departments often leased?
9. What are the major materials used in the production of jewelry? Give several examples of how women's apparel fashions influence jewelry fashions.
10. What categories of merchandise are usually to be found in fashion accessories departments today? Discuss the current fashion importance of each category.

MERCHANDISING DIGEST

1. Discuss the following statements and their implications for retail merchants of fashion accessories: "The rise of accessories as a dynamic force in fashion only came about in the past few decades. Although this force diminished for a time, accessories regained a starring role in the mid-1980s and once again play an important part in the look of fashion."
2. Discuss the current importance of bodywear. How important do you feel it will be in the future? Why?
3. List each of the current important fashion accessory items and discuss why they are important to the total fashion look today. At which stage of the fashion cycle is each item, and why do you feel this is so?

INTIMATE APPAREL AND COSMETICS

THE INTIMATE APPAREL INDUSTRY

The wearing of undergarments probably grew out of practical need as people sought something to protect their skins from the chafing of harsh animal skins. And indeed, for many years the purpose of underwear was primarily utilitarian. In the past century, though, as the industry has grown, underwear has also evolved from something functional and merely serviceable into something luxurious, beautiful, and sensual—and these days, fashion-oriented.

Intimate apparel, sometimes called "inner fashions," "innerwear," or "body fashions," is the trade name for women's foundations, lingerie, and loungewear. Originally these three groups of products were separate industries. In recent years, a single industry called intimate apparel has evolved as a result of business mergers, diversification of products, technological advances in fibers and fabrications, and a growing relationship between these industries and the women's ready-to-wear industry. Its three major market segments are foundations, lingerie, and loungewear.

Foundations

Foundations are brassieres, bustiers, garter belts, girdles, corsets, and corselettes (one-piece combinations of a brassiere and a girdle).

History and Development

The foundations industry began after the Civil War with the opening of Warner Brothers corset factory in Bridgeport, Connecticut. The bell-shaped silhouette was then at the height of its popularity. To achieve the tiny waist which was demanded by the bell and its successors, the bustle-back and Gibson Girl silhouettes, women wore corsets made of sturdy, unyielding cotton. Reinforced with vertical stays of whalebone or steel, the corsets laced up the front or back. They were tightly laced to achieve the extreme (in many cases) constriction of the waist—and in some cases of the internal organs, too—that fashion required.

Variations on these stiff corsets were worn by all women until the 1920s, when the rounded and bustled silhouettes that had prevailed for decades gave way to the straight, loose styles of the flappers. Stiff, full-torso corseting was no longer required, but the new silhouette demanded that the bosom and hips be minimized. Bandagelike bras were created to flatten the bust, and new girdlelike corsets controlled any conspicuous bulges below the waist. Women tended to wear these new-style corsets even when they did not need to. While they no longer suffered the internal damage brought on by the old-style corsets, some slender women who insisted on wearing corsets suffered bruised flesh as a result. Still, women considered these corsets essential, if only because they had garters that held up their stockings.

By the 1930s, soft, feminine curves were back in style. Elastic was introduced, and the corset became known as the girdle. Women now coaxed their bodies into two new types of foundations, the two-way stretch girdle and the cup-type brassiere, both of which enjoyed the advantage of being more comfortable than any of their predecessors.

These innovations set a precedent in the foundations industry and in women's lives. Women would henceforth wear inner garments that molded the figure more or less gently, depending upon the whims of fashion. More important, undergarments would now permit freedom of movement.

In the ensuing five decades, further technological advances led to foundations that were softer, more comfortable, and increasingly lightweight. They retained their shapes even after many washings, and were designed for a variety of figure types. A greater variety of styles were available. All this was made possible by the development of spandex and other elasticized fabrics.

In 1986, the Wacoal Company of Japan, a leading manufacturer of foundations, developed an underwire bra made of a nickel and titanium alloy that shaped itself to a woman's body while worn but regained its original shape when washed. Wacoal also pioneered in the computer "mapping" of the female body, which permitted them and other manufacturers to design undergarments that truly supported and enhanced the female figure.

Brassieres offer the best example of the massive style changes that the foundations industry has undergone in the past half century. They have evolved from the original bandage-type bra to a cup form, from plain cotton to fiber-filled to the "no-bra" (or unconstructed) look to the molded (or unseamed) bra. Contemporary foundations coax or mold the body; they do not harness it as garments of the past so often did. Moreover, foundation garments are now comfortable, light, soft, and pretty—all at the same time.

Foundations have become increasingly luxurious over the decades. And fashion has finally invaded this segment of the market, so much so that some beautifully designed undergarments are now worn as outer garments. A lacy silk camisole is too pretty not to show off, and it becomes a dressy top to wear under a suit—or alone. A sexy bustier becomes an evening garment.

Merchandising and Marketing

Since Warner Brothers opened its first factory, brand names have been important in the foundations industry. Most of its merchandising and marketing activities, in fact, are geared toward promoting brand names. The major producers—Lily of France, Playtex, Bali, Maidenform, Formfit-Rogers, and Warner—advertise their own names widely in both trade and consumer publications. Many companies offer cooperative advertising, and ads in consumer publications often mention stores where brand-name products can be purchased.

Foundations manufacturers have also supplied several services to retail stores and their customers. In the early 1980s, intimate apparel producers pioneered with the use of preticketed garments. Timesavers for the retailers, the tickets also gave them immediate access to sales figures, which, in turn, facilitated keeping track of inventory and placing orders. They helped customers by supplying information on style, size, and color.

For decades, the foundations industry encouraged specialized service to the retail customer, and it even helped retailers by providing training to their store employees on sales and fitting techniques. By the late 1970s, though, self-service had become the norm, and foundations were sold from hanging fixtures that provided customers with complete and fast access to a store's stock. The hanging fixtures added excitement to the sales floor and helped customers recognize the increasingly wide range of colors and styles that were becoming available to them.

When women offered some resistance to the displays, the late 1980s found

We've come a long way—not only from the way intimate apparel used to be sold—but also from the stiff standard styling of yesteryear to the frothy feminine styles of the 50s to the sports styling for today's lifestyle.

some stores backtracking and once again offering more personal service to their customers. Wacoal, for example, opened over 100 boutiques in department stores, staffed by clerks who had undergone a week-long training seminar designed to teach them how to fit brassieres. Warner soon followed Wacoal's lead, initially testing the idea of company-trained sales help at Macy's and Bloomingdale's in New York, with the goal of expanding the program nationwide.[1] The future will probably bring a mixture of display racks backed up with expert sales help.

As the market for foundations has become strikingly more fashion-conscious, experts have begun to predict that in coming years it may even take the lead in setting styles rather than taking its cues from the women's apparel industry as it does now.

Lingerie and Loungewear

Lingerie is the market segment made up of slips, petticoats, panties, nightgowns, and pajamas. It has typically been divided into daywear (slips, petticoats, camisoles, chemises, and panties) and nightwear (nightgowns and pajamas). **Loungewear** is the trade term for robes, lounging pajamas, hostess gowns, caftans, floats, and smocks. It is sometimes also known as **leisurewear** or **at-home wear.**

Many lingerie lines have expanded and diversified their product lines to the point where terms like daywear and nightwear no longer apply. It is now so difficult to draw a clear-cut line between lingerie and loungewear that the two market segments have been lumped together for purposes of our discussion.

History and Development

As was the case with foundations, prior to the 1930s mass-produced lingerie and loungewear were purely functional. They offered customers little in the way of style or seasonal variation. Most items were made of cotton, with wool being used in extremely cold climates. Lingerie and loungewear were staple items in a woman's wardrobe, available only in limited styles and colors. Silk, which was expensive and tedious to care for, appeared in custom-made, luxury styles affordable only by the rich.

In the 1930s, a new fiber called rayon changed the face of the intimate apparel industry. Rayon had the luxurious feel of silk, but it was washable and inexpensive. Other similar fibers followed, culminating in the 1950s with the introduction of nylon tricot, a synthetic fiber that was softer and longer wearing than rayon and even more easily maintained. The introduction of these new fibers meant that lingerie and loungewear no longer had to be practical and boring. Available in new fabrics, styles, and colors, these garments became the new luxury item in a woman's wardrobe.

The late 1980s saw still another style revolution in underwear. Although the market was and still is strong for old-fashioned, lacy underwear (a counterbalance, many believe, to the tailored outerwear styles working women wear), another style—imitative of men's underwear and promoted by such designers and manufacturers as Jockey, Calvin Klein, and Swipe—was introduced with great success. Women now buy and wear their own practical—and surprisingly sexy—versions of men's underwear.

Merchandising and Marketing

Brands are as important in lingerie and loungewear as they are in foundations, and like their foundations counterparts, lingerie and loungewear firms advertise their brand names in trade and consumer publications and provide coop ad-

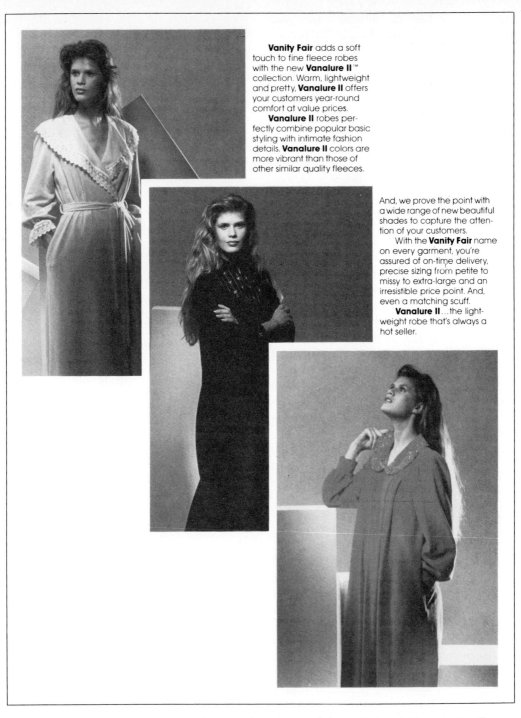

Vanity Fair adds a soft touch to fine fleece robes with the new **Vanalure II**™ collection. Warm, lightweight and pretty, **Vanalure II** offers your customers year-round comfort at value prices.

Vanalure II robes perfectly combine popular basic styling with intimate fashion details. **Vanalure II** colors are more vibrant than those of other similar quality fleeces.

And, we prove the point with a wide range of new beautiful shades to capture the attention of your customers.

With the **Vanity Fair** name on every garment, you're assured of on-time delivery, precise sizing from petite to missy to extra-large and an irresistible price point. And, even a matching scuff.

Vanalure II…the lightweight robe that's always a hot seller.

Robes are known by a variety of names: loungewear, leisurewear, or at-home wear. In this catalog for store buyers, Vanity Fair stresses color, fabric, and styling, but doesn't fail to mention on-time delivery, precise sizing, and a good price!

vertising to retailers. While some old firms such as Vanity Fair, Barbizon, Lady Lynne, Miss Elaine, and Olga continue to promote their names exclusively, the trend is toward less emphasis on brand names and greater promotion of individual styles, colors, fabrics, and designer names.

Like the foundations market, the lingerie and loungewear market is increasingly fashion-oriented. Where previously only the largest companies sent fashion experts to the Paris openings to report on the lines and colors in new apparel styles, now most lingerie and loungewear firms attend the openings and then design fashionable garments to coordinate with the upcoming styles. Today, lingerie and loungewear firms employ top design talent, which they often recruit from the apparel industry.

As a result of covering the fashion markets, manufacturers are able to provide stores with seasonal color and style charts, as well as suggestions for coordinating colors and styles. Companies offer assistance in planning and controlling retail assortments. Some also help to stage retail sales-promotion events, often in cooperation with a textile fiber or fabric producer.

Styling in all three market segments closely follows that of outer apparel. For example, when slim, body-hugging skirts are stylish, the slip and petticoat manufacturers follow suit with slips that are also slim. When vibrant colors and explosive prints were popular in the late 1960s and early 1970s, lingerie and loungewear manufacturers followed suit with their own bright colors and highly creative designs.

The growing visibility of lingerie as a fashion leader has led some well-known designers and celebrities to license their names for intimate apparel lines. While long-established intimate apparel com-

panies such as Playtex with its WOW line have updated their offerings, much of the fashion excitement is coming from the ready-to-wear field and names such as Halston, Ralph Lauren, Christian Dior, and Calvin Klein. They have been joined by other such influential names as Flora Kung and sportswear manufacturer Cherokee. An example of celebrity involvement is the Joan Collins collection introduced in 1987 by Sanmark-Stardust.[2]

Market Centers

New York City is the principal market center for the intimate apparel industry. The major firms maintain permanent showrooms there, as well as in most of the regional clothing marts. Market weeks are held in January and June. Since many store buyers purchase in all three market segments, concurrent market weeks help them to plan and coordinate purchases and promotions. Even when stores employ separate buyers for each segment, the buyers usually work closely with one another to coordinate their purchasing and promotional activities.

New York is also the headquarters of the industry's trade associations, the Associated Corset and Brassiere Manufacturers, the Intimate Apparel Council of the American Apparel Manufacturers Association, and the Lingerie Manufacturers Association. All three associations schedule subsidiary activities for market weeks.

Industry Trends

The use of fashion continues to be the major competitive strategy in the marketing of intimate apparel. A good example of this is the current expansion of the daywear classification. Sexy, sensual silk underdressing is the fashion fillip for the new corporate woman to wear under her more or less severely tailored suit.

This trend is changing the look of lingerie departments. Whereas intimate apparel departments traditionally maintained an 80/20 ratio of basic garments to fashion garments, some retailers now maintain a 50/50 ratio.[3] Daywear trends in lingerie are expected to continue to mirror ready-to-wear styles. Even foundations are now being merchandised to coordinate with outerwear garments. Alphabet bras (T-backs, A-backs, and Z-backs), low-back, and halter-style bras are examples of designs that complement specific outerwear styles.

TECHNOLOGY TALK

DESIGN SYSTEM AN EYE OPENER

Slumbertog, an intimate apparel company that produces Miss Dior loungewear and Jewels daywear, has only praise for their new computer-aided design system that they have nick-named "Star Wars."

The system's extraordinary versatility lets designers build and present an entire line without ever stitching a garment. Even more importantly, they can present lines and create styles while a customer is in the showroom.

And at the Slumbertog plant in Mifflenburg, Pennsylvania, the design system is tied directly into a pattern grading and marking system to help streamline production. "We think it will give us a handle on quick response," affirms Harriet Levenson, company co-chairman.

Slumbertog believes the company is the first intimate apparel maker to computerize its design process. The main reason the company decided to computerize was "to tie everything together and hopefully cut down design costs."

The computer allows operators to look at more fashion styles and more colors to help them come up with better ideas even more rapidly. The initial design can be input by freehand drawing using a tablet and digitizer, or by scanning a photograph into the system. Then the operator defines the image by individual segments and colors them or alters them separately.

Once a design is on the screen, the designer can select from a self-made library of fabrics to see how they will work with the design on screen. The designer can also embellish the image with different trims or findings by pulling them out of the computer's library or sketching them in.

To get the most out of the system, Slumbertogs hired a computer-literate design graduate fresh from the Fashion Institute of Technology; its other four designers received instruction from an FIT professor. It takes about 4 to 6 weeks to learn how to use the system, which is run by selecting color, texture, and other options from on-screen menus.

Harriet Levenson exudes enthusiasm when she talks about the computer-aided design system: "It's exciting because business gets very dull and when you bring in a new dimension it makes it so exciting."

This Technology Talk is based on information from the following source:

Holly Haber, "Slumbertog Design System an Eye Opener," *WWD/DNR Retailing Technology & Operation,* April 1988, p. 18.

Another trend is toward "niche" marketing, that is, the development of products to meet specific customer needs. Among recent successes in this area are sports bras, minimizer bras, maternity lingerie, and large-size lingerie. In loungewear, an entirely new category of garments called leisurewear has been developed to meet women's demands for comfort.

Market Segments

Most intimate apparel manufacturers try to reach specific segments of the market. These may be based on age, lifestyles, or even attitudes.

Loungewear is the most talked-about and rapidly growing segment of the intimate apparel business. It has revived interest in such fabrics as sweatshirting, flannel, and flannelettes, all of which inject a sportswear attitude into these casual clothes. The trend is spearheaded by such companies as Katz Inc., with its popular Kittens line. This new breed of loungewear, which many prefer to call "leisurewear," appeals especially to working women who want to dress comfortably at home, but in clothing that is also acceptable for answering the door or running Saturday errands.

New Markets

Experts predict that intimate apparel producers will seek to expand their markets in aggressive and innovative ways. They may pair their products with ready-to-wear and even move their displays into the ready-to-wear departments. When miniskirts are fashionable, for example, they may be displayed along with minislips. Such products will be advertised and promoted with special manufacturer hangtags designed to educate the consumer.

Intimate apparel manufacturers are also expected to develop multiple sales by designing products to coordinate with sheets and other home decors. Similarly, lingerie sales might be paired with fragrance or cosmetic sales. Stores may even begin offering gift-with-purchase items similar to those offered by the cosmetics industry.

Cross-merchandising is another possible way to expand the market for intimate apparel. Men's silk boxer shorts, for example, might be gift-boxed and offered for sale in women's lingerie departments. And women's lingerie will be gift-boxed and offered for sale in men's departments.

Finally, intimate apparel manufacturers will probably look for totally new markets. Their most likely target will be men's intimate apparel.

Catalogs

In the early 1980s, catalogs provided an important new sales—and image-building strategy for intimate apparel. Today many department stores send out special intimate apparel catalogs, and they regularly include high-fashion intimate apparel in their seasonal catalogs. *Private Lives* by Spiegel, the giant mail-order house, marked that company's entrance into the intimate apparel specialty-catalog field. Other innovators include Hanover House, *Intime* by Brownstone Studio, Victoria's Secret, and many traditional department stores such as Hudson's, The Broadway, Bloomingdale's, and Macy's.

Mergers

Mergers began in the intimate apparel business around 1950. Once customers started to demand color-coordinated foundation garments, many small firms that specialized in one particular garment began to see the advantage in joining forces with other firms to manufacture a complete, color-coordinated line.

Sleek or frilly? It's nice to browse through the styles in intimate apparel catalogs and daydream of how you will look in them.

In time, such collaborative efforts led to more formal mergers. Some intimate apparel companies merged with one another, as was the case with Formfit-Rogers. Others merged with ready-to-wear producers. When elasticized fibers permitted the introduction of figure-control features in bathing suits, another logical merger combination was a foundation manufacturer with a swimsuit manufacturer.

Diversification

Another trend is toward diversification of products. Daywear has expanded to include body shirts, chemises, tap pants, camisole tops, "teddys," and packaged "little nothings." The latter are "nonstructured" bras, pants, and bikinis, which are often prepackaged or sold on self-selection racks in conventional and mass-merchandising stores.

In response to the fact that people have more leisure time, some of which is spent traveling, sleepwear manufacturers have added travel sets of matching robes and gowns. Many items of daywear can be worn as casual tops and dresses outside the home and also for at-home occasions.

FASHION

It's no secret that women enjoy wearing pretty, romantic, or subtly sexy lingerie and daywear. But until recent years, they did not have a store devoted strictly to bringing out the *fashion* in under-fashions—that is, not until the birth of Victoria's Secret.

Founded in 1977 by Roy Raymond and his wife, Gaye, Victoria's Secret started as a single boutique in Palo Alto, California. As legend has it, Roy was "tired of being treated with smirks" when purchasing lingerie for his wife;[1] so the two of them (with no retail background) concocted the name for the venture in front of the fireplace one night,[2] opened the first store—and watched their sales volume double each year for four years!

By 1981, the Raymonds had opened three more stores in the San Francisco Bay area, and had also launched a catalog portion of the business, whose sales quickly matched those of the shops. Just what was the Victoria's "secret?" "Our image is elegant, romantic, and sexy. We believe in subtlety," stated Roy[3]—and customers obviously responded to both the mood and the merchandise.

With $6 million in sales being generated in 1981, Victoria's Secret was no longer a secret—and in 1982, giant retailer The Limited bought from the Raymonds. Said Howard Gross, a former Limited executive who became Victoria's president in 1983: "We looked at intimate apparel and thought 'boring.'

"**Victoria's Secret Catalogue division has experienced a threefold increase in the past three years.** Fourteen catalogues are published each year with an extensive intimate apparel selection as well as ready-to-wear merchandise. Our company provides an unusually high level of service by concentrating on telephone sales and maintaining a knowledgeable staff of associates who respond quickly to customer needs, 24 hours a day. The image of the catalogue reflects the continuing emphasis on Victoria's Secret lingerie and hosiery brands.

Victoria's Secret Catalogue

Cindy Fedus, General Manager

F O C U S

But Roy, on the other hand, had created a fantasy. You couldn't go into his store and walk out empty handed. He made it impossible not to buy."[4]

The fantasy Raymond had created was enhanced by the luxurious and ornate settings for his merchandise, complete with Oriental carpets, antique furniture, and dusty-rose walls. As The Limited took the concept across the country—opening some 250 stores by the end of 1987—the new management refined the presentation to make it less intimidating, and "more like a bedroom setting, very personalized," said Gross.[5] Newer stores, including a 6,000-square-foot flagship opened in late 1986 on New York's 57th Street, are still luxurious, but with an airier look, enhanced by marble floors and mirrored walls.

And what about the merchandise itself? It is broken into major classifications that include: sleepwear; daywear; foundations, meaning bras and panties that match, garter belts and Merry Widows; separate bottoms; and accessories. Three-quarters of the apparel is private-label goods—a number Gross hopes to make 100 percent; and prices average in the $25 to $100 range for sleepwear and daywear, and $30 and up for silk items.[6]

"We try to give the customer superior merchandise for the same prices she would pay in a department store," says Gross. "I believe it is attitude. I believe every woman in America wants to sleep in silk. But every woman in America can't afford a $300 nightgown . . . So it's our job to figure out how to get it to her at a price point she can afford."[7]

If Gross is right, and sleeping in silk is every woman's dream, Victoria's Secret should continue to have customers lining up to fulfill their fantasy. What's more, the retailer is building on its intimate apparel foundation with new collections of fragrances, bath products, jewelry boxes, and other accessories—and projecting to have 400 stores doing $1 billion in sales by 1990.[8] Now that's a fashion "secret" to shout about!

[1] NSM Report Company Profiles, December 28, 1981.

[2] Steve Ginsberg, "Victoria's Secret Is the Subtle, Sexy, Look," *Women's Wear Daily,* November 19, 1981, p. 12.

[3] Ibid.

[4] Lynn Rhodes, "Victoria's Secret Gets Around," *Body Fashions/Intimate Apparel,* November 1986, p. 6.

[5] Joan Bergmann, "It's Victoria's Secret," *Stores,* November 1985, p. 67.

[6] Sandra Palumbo, "Victoria's Secret Is No Longer Hush-Hush as Volume Has Boomed to $100 Million," *Women's Wear Daily,* March 12, 1987, p. 14.

[7] Joan Bergmann, p. 72.

[8] "The Mystery in Victoria's Secret," *Apparel Merchandising,* December 1988, p. 70.

This Fashion Focus is based on information from the articles cited above.

THE COSMETICS AND FRAGRANCE INDUSTRIES

Beauty may only be skin-deep, but tell that to the millions of women—and these days, men—who spend billions of dollars every year trying to improve the look, feel, and smell of their bodies. This quest for beauty is hardly new. For thousands of years people have smeared themselves with lotions and potions of every description in the hope of making themselves as attractive as possible. As far back as 100 B.C., Cleopatra rubbed her face with lemon rinds, took milk baths, accentuated her eyes with kohl, and set her hair with mud.

The cosmetics industry is big business and getting bigger. It turns out hundreds of new products annually, each of which must compete for a share of the market. These days, the fashion-apparel business plays an important role in building the business of the cosmetics industry. Many designers have introduced their own cosmetic and fragrance lines, and they often work with the cosmetic manufacturers to help them design new products that will coordinate with each season's new styles. Thanks to this new link, cosmetics, like fashion, are now cyclical. For example, when sports clothes are popular, and a no-makeup look is in, the cosmetics industry, eager to maintain sales, has learned to respond with appropriately low-key cosmetics. When bright colors and elaborate clothes are in style, the cosmetics industry touts more makeup and brighter palettes.

History and Development

For centuries, the pursuit of beauty was the prerogative of the rich. Special beauty aids concocted in temples, monasteries, alchemists' cells, and kitchens were available only to the privileged few. Only in the past 60 years has the pursuit of beauty found its way into modern laboratories and brought with it an ability to manufacture and distribute cosmetics on a more widespread basis.

Today although an elite segment of the market has survived, cosmetics are available to anyone who wants to use them. What was once a luxury is now viewed by many as a necessity. This in turn has led to more innovation in mass production, advertising, and package design. The market has also become increasingly segmented as different kinds of cosmetics are made available to customers based on their ages, lifestyles, and ability to pay.

Dreams Versus Science

With the move to the laboratory came a new emphasis on the scientific development of cosmetics. Whereas for decades the word "moisturize" alone was enough to sell a skin cream, new, improved creams were now promoted for their abilities to "nourish" and "renew" the skin. Today, one takes a "daily dose" of skin-care products, which are likely to be "pH-balanced." Cosmetics salespersons no longer help their customers select a makeup shade; they are now trained technicians who can "diagnose" the customer's needs and prescribe the right "formula."

The 1970s saw the emergence of "natural" products made from such ingredients as aloe vera, honey, musk, almonds, and henna. The trend toward natural cosmetics in the 1980s turned into a full-blown consumer preoccupation with health and self-image. The new emphasis was on the protective aspects of cosmetics. The buying public began to seek products that maintained and protected their skins rather than merely en-

A beautiful example for the use of her products, Adrien Arpel is one of the innovative, business-oriented personalities in the present cosmetics world.

The cosmetics industry has always been dominated by personalities, a trait that shows little sign of abating. What has changed is the nature and purpose of the personalities.

From the 1950s through the 1970s, a few flamboyant personalities, most notably, Elizabeth Arden, Helena Rubenstein, Charles Revson, Max Factor, and Estee Lauder, dominated the industry and virtually dictated its shape and scope. Lesser known but equally innovative were Dorothy Gray, Hazel Bishop, and Harriet Hubbard Ayer. The drive, intuition, foresight, and promotional abilities of these pioneers is still felt in the industry, and has rarely been duplicated in other industries. By the mid-1980s, only Estee Lauder survived with her beauty empire still intact and run by her personally. The others had become public corporations or part of multinational conglomerates.

The cosmetics industry seems destined, however, to be run by personalities, and a new generation, with names like Adrien Arpel, Madeleine Mono, Christine Valmy, Georgette Klinger, Merle Norman, Flori Roberts, and Don Bochner, soon emerged. Unlike the old stars, though, these new entrepreneurs rely less on personality and more on sound business strategies.

Organization and Operation

The cosmetics industry has undergone significant changes in recent years in terms of its organization and operation. Once made up entirely of many small firms, none of which controlled a significant share of the market, it is now dominated by a few large firms that command large market shares. Although the cosmetics industry still supports 600 companies, eight top firms now control

hanced them cosmetically. Skin-care products became the fastest-growing segment of the cosmetics industry. Although fashion and beauty have remained the driving force behind most cosmetics sales, more consumers than ever before are willing to spend money for products that enhance their overall health.

50 percent of the business. Of those companies, most are owned by drug conglomerates.

All large, nationally advertised cosmetics firms produce hundreds of items. For sales and inventory purposes, products must thus be divided into broad categories. The typical order form of one large firm, for example, lists all the company's products, in the various sizes or colors available, under such end-use categories as skin care, facial make-up, nail care, bath preparations, hair care, fragrances, eye products, body care, and so on. If a firm produces men's as well as women's cosmetics, each of the two lines is given its own distinctive brand name, and, of course, separate sales and inventory records are kept for each brand line.

Because of fashion and product obsolescence, as well as customer boredom, manufactures are constantly updating and shipping new items to keep cosmetics customers buying new products and/or new colors. Manufacturers update formulas when they become aware of new technology and new ingredients to improve their products.

A system of product returns, unique to the cosmetics industry, aids the retailer in keeping the inventory current. The industry refers to this system as **rubber-banding,** which means that cosmetic products not sold within a specified period of time may be returned to the manufacturer to be replaced with others that will sell. This guarantees that the cosmetics retailer will never have to take a markdown on this merchandise. Only if a cosmetics company is discontinuing an item, does it permit markdowns by a store. (Other industries allow returns to vendors only for damages, overshipments, or wrong shipment.)

Briefly Speaking

Beauty 101

The day begins at 5:45 A.M. with a roll call for the first required class: exercise. Although early, there is great support and interest at this beginning of a weeklong program of mental and physical self-improvement—all at the expense of their employer, Estee Lauder.

Estee Lauder at Vassar is designed to produce corporate winners whether they are fighting for counter space, relating to a customer, or wining and dining a store president. There are obvious collegiate touches: the Vassar campus, required courses (Strategies for Winning, Power Presentation), electives (Financial Planning for the Utterly Confused), a personal essay (200 to 300 words, with suggested subjects ranging from "your special talents" to "your children"), a diploma, and graduation. The boarding school atmosphere includes the uniform (white T-shirts, shorts, pants, or skirts) and special attention to the social graces, such as ballroom dancing, the correct way to open doors, and how to entertain in restaurants.

Corporate seminars and classes are not new. But this Lauder experience emphasizes the mind, spirit, and body. After a week's session, Lauder U. expects students to realize not only their own worth but the company's as well. As Leonard Lauder says, "We want them to know they're working for the best company in the world."

This Briefly Speaking is based on information from the following source:

Pamela Street, "Beauty 101 at Lauder U.," W, July 25–August 1, 1988, p. 30.

Private-Label Manufacturers

Although dominated by giant producers of nationally advertised brand lines, the industry has many **private-label manufacturers,** producing merchandise to specification under the brand names of chain stores, mass merchants, department stores, or small independent stores and hair salons. Examples of private-label fragrance lines are "Volage" sold by Neiman-Marcus, "Bloomies," sold by Bloomingdales, and "Fireworks," sold by Bergdorf Goodman. The famous scent "Giorgio" was born in the Rodeo Drive Giorgio store. It was such a success that, although an original "private label," it is now sold in fine stores from coast-to coast.

Some of the better-known private-label manufactures are Kolmar Laboratories of Port Jervis, New York, and Private Label Cosmetics of Fair Lawn, New Jersey. Kolmar sells mass quantities to large users, but not all private-label producers are big enough to meet the large order requirements. Small private-label manufactures, such as Orlin (a division of the House of Westmore), supply smaller distributors. A beauty salon owner can walk into a private-label distributor's office, and in less than 10 days and for about $500 have a complete private-label line in his or her shop. However, this line is based on what the private-label house has already been manufacturing. Private-label manufacturers do not develop new products for individual clients.

Retailers get little help from their private-label suppliers. Private-label firms do not share advertising costs, provide gift-with-purchase offers, or accept returns.

A serious threat to the private-label industry is posed by federal ingredient-label requirements. Packing is usually kept to a minimum by private-label firms in order to keep prices low. To get the government-required ingredient label on a small lipstick, however, an additional package is required. Through its lobbying group, the Independent Cosmetic Manufacturers and Distributors Association, the private-label industry is fighting labelling requirements. At present, consumers may ask for ingredient lists at retail stores. These lists are supplied to the store by the manufacturer.

Trade Associations

The Cosmetic, Toiletry, and Fragrance Association (CTFA) is the major cosmetics trade association. Its membership markets 90 percent of all cosmetics, toiletries, and fragrances sold in the United States. The CTFA coordinates the industry commitment to scientific and quality standards. It is the industry vehicle for information exchange about scientific developments among association members, consumers, and those who regulate the industry at federal, state, and local government levels. The CTFA also keeps members informed on government regulations and offers advice on interpretation and compliance.

Federal Cosmetics Laws

Because chemicals are the basis for most cosmetic products, the Food and Drug Administration is the federal agency that polices and regulates the cosmetics industry. The Federal Trade Commission defines a **cosmetic** as any article other than soap that is intended to be "rubbed, poured, sprinkled, or sprayed on, introduced into, or otherwise applied to the human body for cleansing, beautifying, promoting attractiveness, or altering the appearance without affecting the body's structure or functions."[4]

Manufacturers are prevented by FDA regulations from using potentially harmful ingredients and from making exaggerated claims regarding the efficacy of their products.

The 1938 Federal Food, Drug, and Cosmetic Act was the first federal law controlling cosmetics. It prohibited the adulteration and misbranding of cosmetics. Amendments added to the law in 1952 made it even more stringent. Additional amendments enacted in 1960 required government review and approval of the safety of color additives used in cosmetics.

The Fair Packing and Labeling Act was passed by Congress in 1966 to prevent unfair or deceptive methods of packaging and labeling. This act covers many consumer industries beside the cosmetics industry. All cosmetics labeled since April 15, 1977, must bear a list of their ingredients in descending order of weight. To help identify potentially dangerous ingredients for manufactures, the Cosmetic Ingredient Review, an independent research group funded by the CTFA, was established in the early 1980s.

In any event, the major ingredients of most cosmetics in any price range do not vary much and mostly consist of fats, oils, waxes, talc, alcohol, glycerin, borax, coloring matter, and perfumes.

Constant surveillance by consumer and industry groups and advisory boards keeps the cosmetics industry sensitive to product liability. A formal regulatory program for cosmetics is expected to be passed and implemented soon. This legislation will require manufacturers to register their products and formulas and to establish their safety before selling them to the customer.

Market Segments

The cosmetics industry serves four major market segments in addition to the traditional women's market with its many segments. These newest market segments are the male market, the ethnic market, the international market, and the fragrance market.

The Male Cosmetics Market

The market for male cosmetics has expanded and is expected to experience

The changing male image is spurring the sale of designer-label men's cologne and after-shave lotions.

above-average growth in the future. Changing male images are opening up new and larger markets in hair care, face and body care, and fragrances. Men are buying more diversified products, such as moisturizers, cleansers, and skin toners. Men, like women, are concerned about aging.

Unlike women, they have done little about it until now. It has become socially acceptable for men to treat skin to retard the aging process.

A significant market is also being built for men's hair care products, especially treatments formulated to help prevent or reverse hair loss. Installation of complete men's cosmetic sections in department and specialty stores is a growing trend. Bloomingdale's, Macy's, and Saks, among others, have expanded their men's cosmetics areas. Menswear specialty stores have added cosmetic areas, and mail-order catalogs devote more space to men's grooming aids.

The Ethnic Market

The 1985 Census finding that 17 million Hispanics lived in the United States came as no surprise to the cosmetics industry, which had already begun wooing these active, high-spending customers, along with an even larger ethnic group made up of American blacks.[5] Blacks are estimated to spend four times more per capita than whites on health and beauty aids.[6] The two groups, collectively referred to as the "ethnic market," total 50 million persons. The ethnic market is growing at a rate of 17 percent per year, which makes retail sales to blacks and Hispanics one of the fastest-growing segments of the cosmetics industry. The cosmetics industry has begun to turn its attention to the growing Asian market.

Differences in skin shades and tones and hair texture among black women have stimulated the development of special products for this segment of the ethnic market. In the 1960s companies such as Libra and Astarte pioneered in creating mass-market lines for black women. Another early pioneer, Flori Roberts, produced the first prestige cosmetic line for blacks. Still a major force in the cosmetics industry, she also introduced the first fragrance within a black cosmetics line, initiated in-store seminars on careers for black women, and began in-store makeup demonstrations.

After Helena Rubenstein ran a makeup ad featuring black and white models in 1969, the major cosmetics companies began to pick up on the potential of the black market. Today, although specialized companies such as Flori Roberts, Fashion Fair, and Moisture Formula cater exclusively to the black market, the major cosmetics companies also produce foundation and lip products designed especially for black women.

The International Market

The foreign market for cosmetics has grown in recent years partly because the "westernization" of much of the world has made the wearing of cosmetics acceptable. Until 1980, China had a law that banned the wearing of cosmetics, and in the Soviet Union and its Eastern bloc countries, American products until recently were largely unknown. That is now beginning to change. Japan, Western Europe, South America, and the Middle East have emerged as strong markets for U.S. imports.[7]

Fortunately, cosmetics and toiletries need little or no adjustment in formulas and packaging in order to succeed in the international market, and American fragrances, body-, skin-, and hair-care products are becoming best sellers the world over.

The U.S. Commerce Department has promoted efforts by small cosmetics companies to export to the more affluent third-world countries where per capita expenditures on cosmetics products are growing rapidly. Direct distribution, private-label products produced for foreign firms, and licensing specialties for foreign production are considered the most productive prospects for this international market.

The Fragrance Market

U.S. retail fragrance sales were $4 billion in 1987.[8] Since 1960, fragrance sales have more than tripled each decade.

The term **fragrance** included cologne, toilet water, perfume, spray perfume, after-shave lotion, and environmental fragrances. Some interesting changes have occurred in this market over the past 20 years. For example, spurred by a dramatic rise in the use of colognes by men, after-shave lotions declined from 70 percent of the total men's fragrance sales to less than 30 percent. The sales of perfumes, which once amounted to 30 percent of women's fragrance sales, has declined to less than 10 percent, mostly because women are turning to colognes and toilet waters.[9] The latter are more attractive than perfumes because they cost less and are more convenient to use since the introduction of the spray bottle.

In an effort to revive perfume sales, fragrance companies have introduced eau (or esprit) de parfum, a new scent product that is intended to fit neatly (in terms of use and price) between perfume and eau de toilette, or toilet water. Many eaux des parfums are merely perfumes that have been diluted with alcohol, but they last longer than eau de toilet and cologne.

Continual innovation in fragrances is necessary to maintain growth in a fashion-conscious market. Most fragrances are available as perfume and the lower-priced, less long-lasting toilet water and/or cologne. Many also come with accessory scents such as talcum powder and hand and body lotion.

Perfumes are worn predominantly by women 25 to 44 years old—a group that

The range—from eau de cologne to eau de toilette to eau de parfum to perfume—is now available in most well-known fragrances.

is both fashion-conscious and affluent enough to buy this luxury product. Toilet waters and colognes, also worn by the aforementioned group on informal occasions, have great appeal for younger women because they are lower-priced. These lower-priced products also are used to entice the customer from any economic level to try a new product.

Target Marketing The success of a perfume or cologne depends on attractive packaging and aggressive promotion. When a perfumer creates a fragrance, he or she generally has in mind a type of person who will wear it. The ability to attract the target customer is an important factor in the success of any fragrance. To reach a target customer, fragrance advertising is designed to evoke a mood or emotion. For instance, Calvin Klein's Obsession vaulted quickly to a leadership position after its introduction in 1985, based in large part to its memorable advertising, which featured nude models and entwined bodies, and the slogan "passion without reason." The message obviously spoke to its target customer, young, modern women, since sales of the fragrance reached $30 million in the first year.[10]

Market Growth The market for fragrance will remain strong, in part because of the steadily increasing number of working women, particularly in white-collar jobs, where lighter fragrance are preferable to the heavy perfumes they may wear in the evening. The concept of a "wardrobe" of fragrances to suit the various roles a woman assumes is being promoted and has boosted demand.

Over the past 10 years, fragrances have proliferated in the marketplace. Today's consumer selects a fragrance not only for its scent, but also for its packaging, its promotion, and where it can be bought. Some stores carry a more statuslike symbol for buying and therefore many fragrances are only sold in these types of stores.

Looking ahead to the year 2000, industry forecasters speculate that fragrances will become more highly individualized, perhaps varying with specific skin biochemistry or changing with one's moods. The wearer might have more control over the formulation or the gradual release of the fragrance.

Environmental Fragrances Many industry authorities feel that home, or environmental, fragrances will be the next major breakthrough in the perfume industry. The public's growing awareness of fragrance is not restricted to personal use but includes their homes as well. Many consumers are gaining satisfaction from enhancing their environment, and are taking in-home activities, such as gourmet cooking and home entertaining, more seriously. Fashion designers were quick to pick up on the interest in environmental fragrances and many have already produced scented candles, silk flowers, paperweights, and holiday gifts.

Two of the largest prestige cosmetics and fragrance manufactures, Estee Lauder and Charles of the Ritz, led the way in producing environmental fragrances. In 1981, Estee Lauder launched a line of environmental fragrances based on its Cinnabar, White Linen, and Youth Dew scents. In 1983, Charles of the Ritz introduced a high-tech gadget that played plastic "records" injected with fragrance oil. Other companies have successfully specialized in more "low-tech" potpourris, sachets, and air fresheners. For example, Claire Burke, maker of an upscale line of home fragrances, quadrupled its volume between 1985 and 1987.[11]

Various types of potpourri and sachets are bought to make our homes and offices pleasing through fragrance.

Bloomingdale's gave its home fragrance department more prominent placement; and the Dayton-Hudson department store chain posted more than $1.5 million in sales of home fragrance products in 1986.[12] As for the total market for environmental fragrances, the New York–based Fragrance Foundation projected it would reach $600 million annually by the end of the 1980s.

Merchandising and Marketing

The cosmetics and fragrance business is a highly visible one. Its products are used nearly every day by millions of people. In the prestige cosmetics market, competition for restricted distribution to quality department and specialty stores is keen. All of the prestige brand manufacturers want to sell their lines in the most prestigious store in each town. They offer these stores exclusives, specials, and cooperative advertising to guarantee that their products will receive prime locations. Limiting the stores, or "doors," where their products are available adds to the aura of exclu-sivity and uniqueness the manufacturer of each line wishes to convey to its target customers. Such merchandising techniques are used by most prestigious cosmetics brands, including Estee Lauder, Elizabeth Arden, Clinique, Orlane, Lancome, Borghese, and Ultima II.

Distribution

The structure of distribution techniques in the cosmetics area is both distinctive and complex, involving such elements as class versus mass distribution, limited versus popular distribution, and the use of behind-the-counter brand-line representatives.

Class Versus Mass Another name for "class" is "franchise," so the proper matchup of terms is "franchise versus mass." In **franchise distribution,** the manufacturer or exclusive distributor sells directly to the ultimate retailer. No wholesalers, jobbers, diverters, rack jobbers, or intermediaries of any kind are involved. Each vending retailer is on the books of the manufacturer or distributor as a direct-receivable account. A good example of this is Estee Lauder, who sells directly to stores such as Neiman-Marcus and Saks. In contrast third-party vendors, such as wholesalers, diverters, and jobbers, play a role in mass distribution. These third parties may sell to any one of a number of retailers of any type. No control is exercised over these intermediaries. Manufacturers may not know their retailers. Furthermore, territory or other definable exclusivity does not run from manufacturer to retailer in mass distribution as it does in the franchise or class relationship. A good example of this is Revlon's Natural Wonder line, which is sold in mass merchandise outlets such as variety stores, drugstores, and chain stores.

Limited Versus Popular The franchise cosmetics business is described as being either limited or popular in its distribution pattern. In the industry, any line distributed to more than 5,000 doors is considered popular; any line distributed to fewer than 5,000 doors is limited.

Counter Brand-Line Representatives Since a need exists to inform and educate cosmetics customers about the many products that are available to them, prestige cosmetics companies place their own **brand-line representatives** behind the counter as line salespeople. These line salespeople, also called beauty counselors, are well-equipped to perform this important function. They are trained in the end-use of the hundreds of items carried in each specific line. In many instances, the salaries of these salespeople are paid by the cosmetic company directly. Sometimes the store shares in the payment of their salaries. These salespeople are also responsible for stocking inventory. They keep detailed records that show what items are and are not selling. The cosmetics companies constantly keep their brand salespeople informed about new items, new colors, and new promotions through updated training and materials. As might be expected, the limited-door stores have the best-trained salespeople.

Mass Market Distribution The **mass-distribution** cosmetics market involves drugstores, discount stores, variety stores, and large national chains such as Sears, JC Penny, and Montgomery Ward. The volume of business done in these stores is growing. As they have become increasingly interested in distribution to these types of retail outlets, large cosmetics companies have planned and implemented new merchandising activities. Until a few years ago, the mass-distribution outlets were limited to selling lines such as Cover Girl, Maybelline, or a store's own label line. Now large, nationally advertised brands such as Max Factor and Revlon have introduced their medium-priced lines into these outlets, enabling customers to select products more easily and thus increase sales. Mass-market retailers are turning to open-access display systems and mass-marketing displays. Max Factor is now selling its Pure Magic line from pegboards. Revlon's Natural Wonder line has been repackaged for distribution to the mass-market outlets, as have Coty, Aziza, and L'Erin.

Advertising and Sales Promotion

National advertising budgets of cosmetics companies are immense, especially in comparison to sales. Fierce competition for retail shelf space forces companies to spend an average of $10 million annually to support a single fragrance line, even more if it is a new product.[13] And national advertising is not the only type of sales promotion in which a company must engage.

FASHION

ESTEE LAUDER: A COMPANY MAKE-OVER BY HER SON

Shakespeare wrote that "a rose by any other name would smell as sweet." But would a cosmetics company that built its business and reputation on the name of its founder "smell as sweet" when the founder is no longer in charge? The answer is yes—if you ask Leonard Lauder.

Son of the legendary Estee Lauder, Leonard Lauder joined his mother's company in 1958 at the age of 24, became president in 1972 when Estee became chairman of the board, and was named chief executive officer in 1982. But despite the fact that Leonard has, in effect, held the reins of the cosmetics giant for about two decades, he always remained a private shadow behind his mother's public name and face.

That was the way Leonard wanted it—at least until recent years. The reason lies partly in the direction other cosmetics companies have gone when their founders were no longer there. For instance, when Helena Rubenstein passed away in 1965, her company was sold to Colgate; a year later, when Elizabeth Arden died, her company was sold as well. That left Charles Revson, founder of Revlon, whose company's sales were estimated at between $400 and $500 million when he died in 1975.[1] After his death, however, the company's course wavered and earnings slid dramatically from 1980 to 1984.[2] In 1985 Revlon was sold.

No wonder, then, that Leonard Lauder felt that it was crucial to show the public that there was an Estee Lauder behind Estee Lauder. After all, by the late 1980s, sales of the company's four cosmetics lines—Estee Lauder, Clinique, Prescriptives, and Aramis—were estimated at close to $1 billion.[3] They are also acknowledged to be the absolute leaders in the high-priced segment of cosmetics sold exclusively through department stores, accounting for 38 percent of the market.[4] The closest competitor, capturing only 14 percent of the market, is Cosmair Inc., the maker of L'Oreal and Lancome products.

And Estee herself could well be credited with much of the company's success. From the beginning, she established the firm's personal approach to marketing, training the department stores' sales staff and instructing them to "touch your customer," believing that intimacy

FOCUS

sells.[5] She also cultivated a customer base through frequent gifts of product samples, and garnered publicity through connections with rich and socially prominent women.

The Clinique line appeals primarily to women in their teens and 20s, and Prescriptives to women in their 30s and 40s, while the original Estee Lauder line appeals to those in their 50s, 60s, and 70s. Said Allan G. Mottus, a consultant to the cosmetics industry, "The trouble with the Lauder line is it's getting real old real fast."[6]

Even Leonard finally admitted that the Estee Lauder name was "turning out to be more of a liability than a help."[7] As a result, he began taking a more public role with the company, and giving a more show-business look to the company's advertising, hiring stars such as Bruce Boxleitner and Liza Minelli to tout the company's Lauder for Men line and Metropolis men's scent, respectively.[8]

Another marketing move by the company was the 1987 introduction of a new collection developed specifically for specialty stores, and called Estee Lauder Signature. Sold through such retailers as Neiman-Marcus, Bergdorf Goodman, I. Magnin, Saks Fifth Avenue, and Bonwit Teller, the line was described by a Lauder senior vice president as "the beginning of a trend back to elegance, with

new definition. We are slowly turning away from the totally utilitarian item ... not going toward the heavy or the ornate, but to a very gracefully presented product."[9]

So it would appear that Leonard Lauder is putting himself solidly in position to keep Estee Lauder strong and vital long after his mother has ceased to be the company's public persona. Already, he is grooming his elder son, William, to someday take his place. And even his wife, Evelyn, is taking on interviews that once would have been strictly Estee's domain. As Leonard summed up the direction: "No one stopped buying IBM because Tom Watson wasn't there, but they stopped buying Elizabeth Arden because she wasn't there. I don't want to be another Elizabeth Arden. I want to be another IBM."[10]

[1] Lisa Belkin, "The Make-Over at Estee Lauder," *The New York Times Magazine,* November 29, 1987, p. 66.

[2] Anthony Ramirez, "Revlons Striving Makeover Man," *Fortune,* January 5, 1987, p. 54.

[3] Belkin, p. 62.

[4] Ibid., p. 32.

[5] Ibid., p. 62.

[6] Ibid., p. 66.

[7] Ibid., p. 92.

[8] Ibid.

[9] Robin Wiest, "Lauder to Give Specialty Stores Color," *Women's Wear Daily,* March 13, 1987, p. 13.

[10] Belkin, p. 62.

This Fashion Focus is based on information from the articles cited above.

The expense of promotion and advertising is well worth the effort. A single campaign combining direct mail, television, and print exposure often results in three times the usual amount of business generated by a particular product in any given week.

Premiums An extensive publicity campaign is also mounted to introduce new products. These are often promoted by a celebrity, yet another basis for a publicity campaign. Many companies also promote their products through the use of **premiums,** a gift-with-purchase or a purchase-with-purchase offer, a concept that originated with Estee Lauder. These premiums range from the mundane—samples of products—to the elaborate—cosmetic "paint boxes," umbrellas, tote bags, scarves, even small suitcases.

Direct Mail Because of the breadth and depth of its reach, many store are finding direct mail one of the most successful forms of advertising for both promotions and regular-price cosmetics. Another advantage to the store is that direct mail campaigns are generally vendor-funded. The most common formats are order forms in four-color vendor mailers, bill insertion leaflets, and remittance envelope stubs. Estimates of sales volume from mail-order average about 2 to 3 percent of all cosmetics sales per year.

Scent and Color Strips Another promotional tool that has gained a foothold in the cosmetics industry is the use of scent and color strips, sometimes as bill insertions, but more often as part of a company's advertisement in a magazine. A new method of sampling made possible by modern technology, scent and color strips allow consumers to experiment with new eyeshadow colors or try out new fragrances in the privacy of their own homes. The success of scent and colors strips, particularly in introducing broad markets to new products, was documented by a 1986 survey conducted by *Mademoiselle* magazine. Over 90 percent of respondents reported they would buy a product as a result of a color strip, and 60 percent had already purchased a fragrance as the result of a scent-strip sampling.[14]

Industry Trends

The volume of manufacturers' shipment of cosmetics reached approximately $14.3 billion in 1987, according to the U.S. Department of Commerce, with and average 3 percent growth expected to continue annually through 1991. Sales of skin-care products are expected to grow at a faster pace than cosmetics, due to an older and more affluent population and the increasing popularity of men's products.[15] Other sectors predicted to continue solid growth include sun-care products, eye makeup, nonallergenic skin-care items, and ethnic products.

Sun Care

Sun care has become a major segment of the cosmetics industry, as consumers have become increasingly aware of the health dangers—and aging effects—of the sun's rays. As a result, even the prestige manufacturers have rushed to produced a wide range of scientifically formulated sun products. What once was a category dominated by drug stores and mass merchants has now become a major business for department stores, with some experiencing 200 percent annual sales growth on sun-care lines.[16]

TECHNOLOGY TALK

MAKEOVERS—VIA COMPUTERS

"Mirror, mirror on the wall, who is the fairest of them all?" If you are not pleased with your mirror image, computer-aided makeovers will help you become "the fairest of them all."

In 1984, both Elizabeth Arden and Shiseido began testing computer makeover simulators which let cosmetologists experiment with various shades and hues of the companies' cosmetics, using on-screen images of the customer's face. By 1988 these extraordinary machines were seen in most department store cosmetic departments across the country.

The computers simulate the actual makeup experience on a color image of the customer's face. Using that "image," the cosmetologist "paints" on various shades and hues (also by computer graphics), blending them to get the image the customer wants. The Elizabeth, with over 4,000 to 12,000 times the capacity of most home computers, remembers every color in the Elizabeth Arden line, and also has the ability to blend colors.

Both companies charge a fee for this service, applicable toward purchase of their products after the makeover. The Elizabeth allows a total of three finished makeover views on-screen so the customer can decide which "makeover" she prefers. The Shiseido machine shows two facial views on-screen. The operator can change the customer's eye color, hair style, and complete a makeover right on the screen. In both cases, the customer carries away a printout of the colors used and an exact chart of how to apply the makeup properly.

Makeup makeovers aren't the only simulators in use. Shiseido's Replica machine gives a customer a skin test in only three minutes. Then a microscopic examination allows study of the pattern of pores and lines. The cosmo-

A video, camera, monitor, and "electronic sketch pad" allow a customer to preview her appearance in different makeup.

tologist then discusses the customer's skin type and suggests cosmetic solutions to problem dry, oily, or flaky skin. Every customer is presented with a photo of the microscopic slide and is encouraged to return after 40 days of using the products to assess the results.

The technology used in these machines has added a new dimension to the importance and impact of fashion in the cosmetics industry. When new apparel and accessory fashions in new colors appear, customers can now see what new cosmetic colors best harmonize with them. Not only can they be the "fairest of them all," they can be the most fashionable of them all. A perfect pair . . . technology and fashion!

This Technology Talk is based on information from the following source:

Joyce Worley, "Makeover Simulators," *Womens Wear Daily*, Technology & Operations Section, June 1986, p. 22.

Antiaging Products

Specific-purpose cosmetic items, such as antiaging products, are also enjoying booming sales. Among the fastest-growing categories for some stores, treatment products such as Estee Launder's Eyzone Repair Gel, Lancome's Niosome Anti-Aging System, Christian Dior's Capture Complex Liposomes, and Chanel's Lift Serum Anti-Wrinkle Complex have attracted many consumers.

In-Store Salons

In-store salons that provide a full range of hair, skin, and body services are another trend. Customers can now obtain specialized advice and beauty care right on the department store floor from such lines as Lancome, Orlane, Payot, and Adrien Arpel. In-store salons have helped to introduce American women to the beauty regimens that have long been favored by European women, and in turn, the products and regimens have been simplified to fit in with Americans' fast-paced lives. In the future, regimens will become increasingly personalized as computers tailor them to individual customer's needs.

Computerized Displays

A number of cosmetics companies offer computerized assistance to help their customers chose the products that are best-suited to them. Among the most sophisticated systems are those of Shiseido and Elizabeth Arden, which have been installed in better department stores around the country.

Computers create a video image of a customer's face, on which various makeup applications—and the company's products—can be demonstrated. Borrowing on the same concept, a less complex computer system was rolled into the aisles of mass-distribution

No matter what her age, the female of the species is interested in perfume.

channels in 1987 by Noxell for its Clarion line. The Clarion computer enables customers to key in their own coloring and skin type, and the computer responds with a personalized selection of products and shades from the Clarion cosmetic line.

Scent Psychology

Very big changes are taking place in the fragrance industry. So important has the study of the physiological effects of fragrance on humans become that Annette Green, executive director of the Fragrance Foundation, coined a word, *aromachology,* to describe the phenomenon.

Studies sponsored by the Fragrance Foundation have shown how specific feelings—relaxation, exhilaration, sensuality, and happiness, to name some possibilities—can be transmitted through odor. In addition to furthering scientific research, the studies have also stimulated product development and new ideas within the fragrance industry.

In addition to its traditional emphasis on the romantic, mysterious, and intriguing qualities of perfume, experts predict that future fragrance advertising may also promote the psychological benefits of scents. And you may choose to wear a scent not so much because it is rose-based and romantic, but because it makes you feel relaxed and happy.[17]

Children's Fragrances

The children's market, around since the 1950s, is now expanding. Children's scents are catching up to their adult counterparts in sophistication and price.

Tinkerbell fragrances, long the dominant perfume product in the youth market, has recently gotten some competition in the form of designer scents. Maelle from Irene Clayeux and Ptisenbon from Parfums Givenchy are among the first to create upscale scents for babies and children. The entry into the market of Parfums Givenchy lent solid support to the baby fragrance category in department stores.

Perfume Pretty Barbie, introduced by Mattel, Inc., is packaged with Barbie dolls and also sold in a gift set that contains one fragrance for Barbie and another for Barbie's young owner.[18]

REFERENCES

[1] Lisa Belkin, "Lingerie's Great Leap Forward," *The New York Times*, August 24, 1986, p. F4.

[2] Sandra Palumbo, "Joan Collins Says Her Lingerie Is 'for the Average Woman,'" *Women's Wear Daily*, May 14, 1987, p. 11.

[3] Janet Wallach, "Innerwear/Outerwear," *Stores*, May 1987, p. 32.

[4] Definition, Federal Trade Commission.

[5] *Women's Wear Daily*, January 25, 1981, pp. 12–13.

[6] Richard Wightman, "Rising Import Flood Forecast," *Women's Wear Daily*, March 1987, p. 4.

[7] Richard Wightman, "Export Focus: Japan, Europe," *Women's Wear Daily*, March 1987, p. 6.

[8] Marguerite T. Smith, "Creating Obsession and Making It Last," *The New York Times*, November 1987, p. F12.

[9] "Consumer Expenditure Study," *Product Marketing*, August 1987, p. 7.

[10] Smith, p. F12.

[11] Colleen Troy, "Home Fragrance Success Smells Sweet," *HFD/Retailing Home Furnishings*, November 9, 1987, p. 70.

[12] Ibid.

[13] Phyllis Furman, "The Foul Scent in Fragrances," *Crain's New York Business*, December 21, 1987, p. 23.

[14] Claire Mencke, "Scent and Color Strips: Where and How Do They Fit Into In-Store Cosmetics Sales," *Stores*, September 1986, p. 64.

[15] Wrightman, p. 4.

[16] "Bare Necessities," *Women's Wear Daily*, May 8, 1987, p. 4.

[17] Kimberly Ryan, "Probing Scent Psychology," *Women's Wear Daily*, June 10, 1988, p. 66.

[18] "Kids' Scent Growing Up," *Women's Wear Daily*, June 10, 1988, p. 80.

MERCHANDISING VOCABULARY

Define or briefly explain the following terms:

At-home wear

Brand-line representatives

Cosmetics

Foundations

Fragrance

Franchise distribution

Intimate apparel

Leisurewear

Lingerie

Loungewear

Mass distribution

Premiums

Private-label manufacturers

Rubber-banding

MERCHANDISING REVIEW

1. How has the foundations industry responded to the trend toward a soft, natural look in ready-to-wear?
2. Describe the various merchandising and marketing activities currently engaged in by the intimate apparel industry.
3. How does the intimate apparel industry relate to the ready-to-wear industry?
4. Why is market segmentation by lifestyle important in the intimate apparel industry?
5. Discuss the recent trends in the intimate apparel industry.
6. How does the cosmetics industry relate to the ready-to-wear industry?
7. Summarize the Food and Drug Administration's law in regard to cosmetics.
8. Outline the major distribution methods used by the cosmetics industry.
9. Describe the various advertising and promotion activities currently engaged in by the cosmetics industry.
10. Briefly discuss the most significant trends in the cosmetics industry today.

MERCHANDISING DIGEST

1. Discuss current trends in the intimate apparel industry as they relate to (a) mergers, (b) diversification of product lines, and (c) styling.
2. Discuss the recent growth in men's cosmetics and ethnic cosmetics lines.
3. Cosmetics salespersons, or brand-line representative, exercise much more control over the products carried in their stock than do salespeople in other departments in a store. Discuss the system used, and its advantages and disadvantages.

Exploring
the Producers
of Fashion

For this project you will research and study an American apparel manufacturer who is broadly recognized under a brand name or designer label. (You may choose a women's wear, menswear, children's wear, or accessories manufacturer.) The following information must be included.

1. Name of company.
2. History of the company. Include pertinent and human-interest material about how the company got started and how it developed to its present status.
3. Where is the company located? Include headquarters, sales office, out of town locations, and factory locations.
4. Describe the company's manufacturing setup. Is the company an inside or outside shop, or both? Does it participate in dual distribution?
5. Does the company have a designer? Is the designer an owner? Is there a design staff? Is there a merchandising staff?
6. Does the company or designer have licensees who produce products other than the major items manufactured by the firm? If so, include the names of the licensees and what products they produce.
7. Who is the target audience for this manufacturer? Give a customer profile.
8. Is the line considered to be a pacesetter or advanced fashion line or mostly a mainstream fashion?
9. Does this manufacturer also own retail outlets?
10. Who are the major retail clients of this company?
11. Is the company privately or publicly held? Was it always structured the way it is now?
12. What is the company's sales volume (most currently published figures)?

UNIT THREE

the markets
for fashion

In Unit 3, you will learn how fashion reaches the retailers. When a collection has been designed, it is ready to go to market, as those who work in the business like to say. A market is a place where clothes are sold to retailers, who in turn, will sell them in their stores to the ultimate consumer.

The term "market" can actually mean a market center, a mart, or a market week. A "market center" is a city where apparel is sold at wholesale to retailers. A mart is a building or complex of buildings designed for the display and sale of apparel. A "market week" is a special time when buyers converge on a mart or a market city to see—and buy—the new collections. Market weeks are scheduled several times throughout the year.

The most important market center for fashion in the United States is New York. For many years, it was the only market center, but in the past few decades, other market centers have emerged in Los Angeles, Dallas, and Miami. In addition, various local regional markets and trade shows are sponsored throughout the year and attended by many regional buyers. New York is still the most important market, but the other market centers, each with its own unique personality, have captured large shares of the business.

The other important fashion capital is Paris, France, which is the home of high fashion and has reigned as the fashion capital of Europe and some would say, the world, for well over a century. For many years, American buyers have considered it necessary to travel to Paris as well as New York to study and buy the latest fashions.

French fashion exists on two levels: the older, established, and very expensive haute couture and the newer, more innovative, and less expensive prêt-à-porter. American buyers make arrangements with French fashion designers to buy designs, which they will then adapt to the American market.

The explosion of fashion markets across the United States also has its parallel around the world. Where American fashion buyers only traveled to Paris a few years ago, they now travel throughout the entire world. West Germany, Canada, and Latin and South America all have established themselves as important fashion centers, with their own designers, manufacturers, and fashion marts. Several Asian countries have also become extremely active competitors in the fashion business. American buyers now routinely travel to Japan, Hong Kong, the People's Republic of China, and several smaller nations in Southeast Asia.

With the emergence of so many international markets, fashion has truly become a global business. Global sourcing, the buying of foreign goods, is perhaps the most significant development in the fashion industry in recent years. American retailers now routinely do direct importing, often through store-owned foreign buying offices or commissionaires, special agents that find and buy foreign goods for resale in the United States. In addition to fairs they hold in their own countries, foreign sellers have begun to schedule fashion fairs in the United States to show off their goods. Global sourcing has led to two new kinds of buying, specification and private label, in which stores buy products made especially for their needs.

Unit 3 focuses on all the elements of fashion marketing and reveals how markets operate to help manufacturers sell their products. Chapter 13 is devoted to domestic markets, and Chapter 14, to foreign markets. The expansion into foreign markets has not been without its difficulties for the American fashion business, and Chapter 15 takes a closer look at global sourcing, including its advantages and disadvantages for the American fashion industry. It also includes discussion of the single biggest problem confronting the American fashion industry today—the need to export American fashion around the world in order to reduce the trade deficit that has arisen from so many imports.

DOMESTIC FASHION MARKETS

You cannot work in the fashion business very long without hearing people talk about "going to market." Everyone but the most jaded buyer will agree that market weeks are exciting, exhilarating, and sometimes even overwhelming. As you will learn, they also require an exhausting amount of planning, organization, and hard work.

MARKET TERMINOLOGY

Markets . . . market centers . . . marts—what are they? You will hear these terms used frequently and even interchangeably, which makes them that much harder to sort out.

Market

The word *market* has several meanings. We have already spoken of the market, or demand, for a specific product, for instance, how much people want to buy miniskirts or polo shirts. In this chapter, the word takes on yet another meaning. A **market** is the place where clothes are sold at wholesale prices to store buyers. It is an important step in the pipeline that takes clothes from manufacturer to customer. Buyers attend markets, in effect, to choose the styles we will all be wearing within a few months.

The **domestic market** refers to the place or places throughout the United States where American clothes are sold to buyers. The **foreign market** refers to places outside the United States. (These are discussed in detail in Chapter 14.)

Market Center

Actually, there is no one giant shopping mall that serves as a market for the entire American fashion industry. Instead, several **market centers,** or geographic locations, exist throughout the country. A market center is a city where fashion is produced and sold wholesale.

The first market center that comes to mind is always New York City. For many persons in and out of the fashion industry, New York City epitomizes the allure and excitement of the fashion world. Indeed, New York is the oldest market center and in many ways the most challenging to visit.

But in recent years, fashion has become regionalized, and while New York still produces much of America's fashion, it no longer produces all of it. In the past few decades, Los Angeles, Dallas, and Miami all have become flourishing market centers. Other cities that are not major apparel production centers, such as Chicago, Atlanta, and Denver, are considered markets rather than market centers, although the line between the two sometimes blurs. Chicago, for example, has always promoted itself as a market center even though it is not a major apparel production center.

Mart

A **mart** is a building or complex of buildings that houses a wholesale market, that is, an exhibition of fashions that are ready to be sold to retail stores. The grandaddy of marts was the Chicago Merchandise Mart, which opened its doors over 50 years ago. Even though Chicago is not a major producer of apparel, it was New York's only rival for years. Because it was centrally located, buyers from across the country found it convenient to meet in this huge building

The granddaddy of all the marts was the Chicago Merchandise Mart built in 1930. Look how up-to-date the offspring, called the Chicago Apparel Mart, looks.

on the Chicago River several times a year to do their wholesale buying.

In 1977, the newly constructed Chicago Apparel Mart replaced the Merchandise Mart as the fashion exhibition building. (The Mart is very much in use for other goods, such as furniture.)

Market Weeks

Buyers can and do travel to market centers at any time during the year to visit individual producers, but several times a year, they also gather for **market week.** Few buyers are willing to forego the glamour and excitement of market week. During market week, marts are filled to the rafters with producers and designers, all of whom exhibit their new lines with as much style and panache as possible. The atmosphere is electrifying, heady with new, innovative ideas and the latest trends.

As a purely physical convenience, it is immeasurably easier for buyers to take in new trends and make their buying decisions when they can see lots of clothes all at once. But beyond that, market week also gives everyone a chance to talk to each other and generally take in what's new in the industry.

Trade Shows

Finally, in this chapter, you will also learn about **trade shows:** periodic exhibits that are scheduled throughout the year in regional trading centers. Smaller than market weeks, trade shows are typically attended by buyers from one region of the country.

THE HISTORY AND DEVELOPMENT OF MARKET CENTERS

New York City was the first market center. When design and production clustered in New York, it followed that it would become a market center for buying, too. The fact that New York was the most cosmopolitan and fashion-conscious of American cities also helped it become the country's first and foremost fashion buying center. Even when travel was a strenuous undertaking, buyers at major stores tried to travel to New York twice a year. To service them, manufacturers set up showrooms near their factories in the garment district.

But for many, twice-a-year buying trips were not enough to service a store properly. And many owners and buyers for small stores across the country could not afford to travel to New York. To handle accounts between New York buying trips and to help those who did not come to New York at all, manufacturers hired **sales representatives.**

The Role of Sales Representatives

Sales representatives played an important role in making other cities into market centers. For years, they were the only link between apparel manufacturers in New York and the rest of the country. Traveling at first by train, and later by automobile, sales reps, as they were familiarly called, mailed advance notices to key customers in each city to announce the date of their arrival. In the early days of the fashion business, sales reps carried only one line. Later, as the fashion business became more sophisticated, they carried several noncompeting lines so they could offer their clients more variety. Once a rep arrived in a city, he rented one or more hotel rooms which he used to exhibit his line of apparel.

For company more than anything else (the life of a sales rep was lonely), reps began to travel in groups. Soon, groups of sales reps were jointly renting clusters of adjoining rooms, so their customers could visit not just one but several exhibits at once. When they learned that this was good for business, the next step was to rent a large hotel ballroom or exhibition hall. This gradually led to the development of regional market centers. By the 1940s, California had become a recognized center for selling sportswear, and it would soon become the second largest market center outside New York City. The Chicago Merchandise Mart, built in the early 1930s, was the first major building designed and used as a mart. It was large enough to exhibit everything from apparel and accessories to home furnishings, toys, and gifts.

The Merchandise Mart had little competition until the 1960s, when other cities began to build their own marts, and regional markets took a giant step forward in their development. In 1964, the dazzling Dallas Market Center opened and began servicing the western half of the country. That same year, the California Mart opened in Los Angeles, giving that city the capacity to sponsor a major market show rather than just sportswear shows. The successes in Dallas and Los Angeles prompted other cities to open their own marts, and throughout the 1970s, Atlanta, Seattle, Miami, Denver, Pittsburgh, Minneapolis, Charlotte, North Carolina, and Kansas City, Missouri, became important regional market centers.

The business changed, too. Sales reps still tour the country to service their customers, but the majority of their orders are now written at the marts, usually during market weeks.

The Role of Marts

Most cities' marts are a single, large central building or a complex of buildings. Most are owned and operated by independent investors. Some marts are operated by the cities themselves, and at least one, the Carolina Mart in Charlotte, is operated by a trade association. A permanent, professional staff operates the mart, although a large number of temporary employees are hired for market weeks.

Like convention centers, marts consist almost entirely of exhibition space. Some space is rented out on a full-time basis, but in many marts, the space is rented only during market weeks. These marts often balance their income by sponsoring other shows and conventions.

New York City, which, despite the rise of regional marts in many ways, still reigns as the country's premiere market center, is ironically the only market center without a mart. Part of the aura of a New York market week is the trek through the garment district from showroom to showroom.

SERVICES OF MARTS AND MARKET WEEK

Keeping buyers interested, comfortable, and happy so they will write orders is the primary goal of mart staffs and those who organize market weeks. Everything is geared to making life as comfortable as possible for the buyers who travel to market week. A market week is organized by manufacturers' associations, in cooperation with the mart staff. It is scheduled several months before the clothes will be needed in the stores.

Four or five market weeks are held each year for women's and children's wear, three to five for men's and boy's wear, and two to five for shoes. Separate market weeks are held in many marts for accessories, infants' and children's wear, lingerie, Western wear, sportswear, and bridal apparel.

The summer markets are held in January; early fall markets are held in the latter part of March or early April; late fall markets at the end of May or the first part of June; spring markets in late October or early November; and resort markets in August and early September.

Physical Facilities

Even the physical facilities of marts are designed for buyers' convenience. Exhibition space is arranged by fashion category; for example, handbags, small leather goods, and jewelry are typically located together; women's sportswear occupies another area, and lingerie still another.

WE'VE
GOT YOU
COVERED

HOLIDAY/RESORT
MARKET

August 21st through 26th.

THE DALLAS APPAREL MART
It's all here.

The Holiday/Resort Market held in August shows styles that customers will be wearing for holiday parties and for winter vacation trips in December, January, and February.

Marts include an array of meeting rooms, ranging from auditoriums and theaters for fashion shows to smaller rooms for seminars and conferences. The newer marts even have office space where buyers can take a quiet moment to relax—and add up what they have spent.

Publicity

A market week is only as successful as the exhibitors it manages to attract, so most marts mount an ongoing publicity program to draw interesting and exciting exhibitors. So the chemistry will be mutual, marts also do what they can to attract buyers. Flyers and brochures touting market weeks at various marts go out to stores and individual buyers several times a year. Buyers are also treated to buyers' breakfasts, luncheons, and cocktail parties throughout market week—all courtesy of the mart or a supporting organization.

The most popular form of publicity is the fashion shows that highlight every market week. The shows are hectic since they are so huge and so much is going on. They are also among the more extravagant and interesting fashion shows ever staged. Mostly this is because they are the work of many different designers, all of whom enter their most beautiful or interesting designs. In order to give some coherence to a market week fashion show, it is often organized around a theme, such as a particular color or, more often, an exciting new trend.

The mart's fashion director contacts exhibitors at the start of market week to confirm what they would like to contribute. Once they have decided, a flurry of activity involving fittings, programs, staging, music, and rehearsals follows. Everything is done after hours, so to speak, since exhibitors still want to display the clothes during the day. Everyone who possibly can turns out for the fashion show. It is not unusual in Dallas, one of the largest marts, for 1,200 people to cram into one auditorium for market week fashion shows.

Special Services for Market Week

The mart staffs do everything in their power to make viewing and buying of seasonal lines easy for buyers who travel to market week. The endless rounds of exhibitors are exhilarating

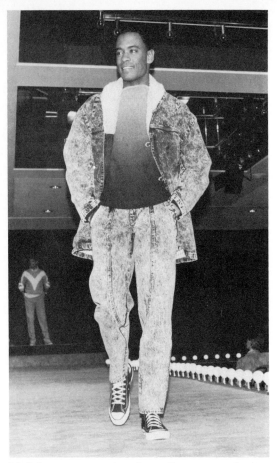

Models come prancing down the runway during a market week fashion show. This is the most popular form of publicity for market weeks at marts.

but exhausting, and no one wants to lose buyers because they were not offered enough support.

Support services begin even before the buyer leaves home. They are sent materials on hotels with special rates, shuttle service to and from the mart, and screening procedures. Only authorized manufacturers and buyers are admitted to market week, and security is high throughout the week. Travel agencies stand ready to help with travel plans or even last-minute changes in them. Ar-

rangements are even made to handle such mundane activities as check-cashing, legal, telex, secretarial, printing, and messenger services—all often within the mart.

Specialized support services are also planned. For example, models are hired to work in the showrooms in case a buyer wants to see someone wearing a particular garment. Beyond this, buyers are provided with an array of information, educational, and between-show services.

Information Services

Once the buyers arrive, they are given a **buyer's directory** and a calendar to help them find their way around and schedule events they want to see. A steady flow of daily publications—trade newspapers, flyers, brochures, and newsletters—continues throughout the week and keeps buyers abreast of breaking market week news.

Educational Services

An orientation program is typically scheduled for the first day, and consultants are on call throughout the week to discuss and deal with specific problems. Seminars and conferences are held to supply buyers with the latest information on fashion. Typical topics are what's new in fiber and fabrics, or in fashion colors, the latest merchandising techniques, advertising and promotion ideas, and sales training hints.

Between-Show Services

The level of life and services between market weeks varies from mart to mart, but the trend is for marts to stay open year-round. At the Miami International Merchandise Mart, for example, many tenants operate their showrooms year-round. The California Mart advertises that it is open 5 days a week, 52 weeks

THE DALLAS MEN'S AND BOYS' FALL MARKET

JANUARY 22 TO 24, 1989

The market opens daily at 8:30 a.m.

In Dallas, fashion makes good business not just good headlines.

THE DALLAS MENSWEAR MART
The National Gallery for Fashion Genius
© Dallas Market Center, 1988

The Dallas Men's and Boys' Market Buyer's Guide—filled with important information and a calendar of scheduled events.

a year. Some marts now have resident buying offices that were designed to serve their clients on a year-round basis. (For more on resident buying offices, see Chapter 18.)

THE NEW YORK MARKET

As a market, New York belongs in a category by itself, not only because it is the city with the most resources to offer the fashion world, but also because it has no central mart building.

Trading Area and Economic Impact

The New York market is made up of literally thousands of showrooms, which line the streets of the garment district. Generally similar-quality apparel is grouped together. In the women's whole-sale market, for example, the couture or higher-priced lines are situated primarily along Seventh Avenue in elegant showrooms. Moderate-priced lines and sportswear firms are housed around the corner on Broadway. Obviously, time and coordination are required to shop the New York market—as is a comfortable pair of shoes. Old-time buyers often joke that first-time buyers can be spotted because they are the only ones wearing high heels.

This lack of a central mart is a minor drawback compared to what many buyers consider the glory of shopping this *crème de la crème* of markets. New York, after all, is the fashion leader, the place where American fashion originates. Whatever is new will be seen here first. New York, most industry people agree, is the most dynamic and creative market center. Any buyers servicing stores of any size must come to New York to do so, regardless of the other markets they add to their schedule.

New York offers one-stop shopping. Every kind of fashion can be found here in every price range. Men's, women's, and children's wear, accessories, intimate apparel, and cosmetics are located within the garment district. Textile and fiber companies maintain showrooms in or near the garment district. Most local manufacturers feel that they must maintain a showroom here, and many regional manufacturers sponsor one as well, if only during market weeks. Many foreign manufacturers participate in the New York market.

FASHION

Shopping for customers is no easy task—when buyers plan to shop for new merchandise lines, a great deal of thought goes into not only what to buy, but where to buy it!

A typical day in the life of a buyer during market weeks often begins with a fashion show at 7 AM, and stretches through to 6:30 or 7 PM, with back-to-back showroom appointments. The new buyer can be identified by her high-heeled shoes, while the "old-timers" can be spotted by their running shoes.

Every minute counts when a buyer is shopping a market or mart, therefore premarket planning and strategy is essential. Typically, a buyer spends a great deal of time prior to market week preparing buying plans and confirming appointments with key resources. All marts send advance notices, listing schedules and special events to each buyer, so that planning can maximize the effectiveness of each market trip.

Many premarket educational seminars and workshops are planned by the regional marts, and a buyer may choose to arrive early at the mart to take part in these conferences. New-buyer orientation programs are also held before the market opens, and premarket guidance sessions are held by buying offices for the benefit of member retailers.

After registration at the mart, buyers begin a hectic back-to-back schedule, moving from one showroom to another, taking notes, making quick sketches, and checking their projected needs against market offerings. Lunchtime approaches with a rumbling of the stom-

FOCUS

ach and a quick sandwich and coffee suffice. Sometimes, there may be a fashion show combined with a luncheon, but the opportunity to relax is curtailed by the note taking which is necessary while they view the fashion show. Then it's back to the showrooms, working right through until 6:30 or 7 PM.

In the evening, a cocktail party sponsored by the mart or by a group of major manufacturers may be on the agenda. Usually, the buyer has dinner from room service, reviews the lines seen that day, watches the 11 o'clock news, and is off to dreamland.

The next morning begins again at 7:30 AM with a breakfast fashion show or seminar. Then it's on to the showrooms for more appointments, more lines to be viewed, more notes, and more sketches. Valuable contacts are made during market weeks and current information can be discussed with noncompeting buyers from other cities. Buyers and manufacturers share ideas on marketing strategies and what the trend is in fashion. Throughout the day, mini-workshops are held to show buyers how to pull together the looks of the season for display or coordinated selling, or how to coordinate the cosmetics with current colors, for example. Several marts even feature foot massages for worn-out feet!

A typical market week usually lasts 5 to 6 days, although the smaller marts often feature between-season minimarket days over a weekend and Monday. At the end of the market week, out-of-town buyers may attend postmarket analysis seminars at the mart, sponsored by resident and corporate buying offices, then devote time back home in their offices to making final decisions and writing orders.

Working the New York Market is quite different because no central mart building exists. Generally, however, similar-quality apparel and accessory items are grouped together, either within buildings or in those that are in close proximity to each other.

No matter which type of market a buyer shops, it is always exhausting, but it is also exhilarating, exciting, exasperating, expanding, and exerting! Despite the most careful planning, shopping a market can be frustrating and in many cases disappointing, if the buyer does not find the kind of merchandise to satisfy customers' needs. The mental effort coupled with the physical effort involved in viewing so many lines and new items can "do a buyer in." But when all is said and done, "to market, to market" is still the most exciting part of merchandising fashion.

This Fashion Focus is based on conversations with Gayle Smith, owner of Gayle's of Houston, Texas, and Leslie Ann Preston, owner of Preston's of Jupiter, Florida.

Other Advantages of the New York Market

Buyers who come to New York can shop not only the market but also the department stores and boutiques for which the city is known. New York is home to the flagship stores of Macy's, Bloomingdale's, Lord & Taylor, Bergdorf Goodman, Bonwit Teller, and Saks Fifth Avenue. Many smaller stores are operated by designers such as Ralph Lauren, Yves Saint Laurent, Givenchy, Sonia Rykiel, Agnes B., and Kenzo.

The city is also the hub of the fashion network. Many national organizations have headquarters here, and stand ready to provide assistance and support services to buyers. Even on a personal level, the networking possibilities are good. Local New York buyers attend market weeks as do buyers from all over the country. Buyers who can attend only a few market weeks each year generally head for New York.

Last but hardly least, part of the draw of New York is that it is the fashion capital of the United States.[1] The fashion publishing industry is located there. The Fashion Institute of Technology (FIT), founded in 1944 and located in the garment district, is still the only university in the country devoted exclusively to the fashion industry. It provides training in fashion design, production, and merchandising, and

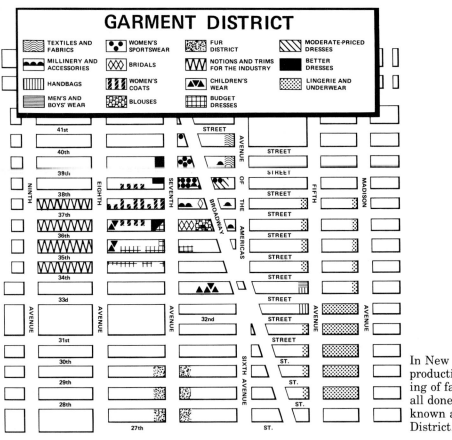

In New York, design, production, and marketing of fashion goods are all done in an area known as the "Garment District."

since the 1940s, its graduates have been making their mark on American design. The Metropolitan Museum houses one of the world's largest archives of historic fashions. New York is also home to opera, theater, and ballet—all sources of inspiration to those in the fashion world.

Disadvantages of the New York Market

The city is also not without its disadvantages, particularly with regard to its ability to maintain its preeminence as a market center in the face of competition from regional markets. To retail merchants and buyers who have shopped at the newer marts, the lack of a central mart is sometimes considered a drawback. Many manufacturers, however, oppose the idea of a central mart, arguing that the garment district itself is the mart. They question whether the huge selection of merchandise—over 5,500 women and children's lines alone—could ever fit into one building.[2]

Others—mostly those who have moved their businesses out of the city—respond that many of the buildings that house showrooms are old and deteriorating. Moving stock through New York's crowded streets and nonstop rush hour is a major undertaking. At the same time that labor costs are high, there is a shortage of adequately trained workers. The cost of doing business in New York is among the nation's highest. Rents are constantly spiraling, space shortages are a fact of life, and local taxes are high.

Many manufacturers have already moved or are moving their headquarters and production facilities out of the city, sometimes even to other regions of the country such as the Midwest, the South, and the West Coast. As they establish themselves in new regions of the coun-

try, they are more likely to support and attend regional markets. This has helped to spur the proliferation of new regional marts in the past twenty years.

Major Market Openings

The New York market is open year-round, but specific times are still set aside for market weeks. (Chapters 8–12 contain specific listings of New York market weeks by industry.)

THE REGIONAL MARKETS

Each market has its own unique flavor, as does each city, and buyers look forward to the varied experiences they will have at different markets. Many small retailers attend New York market weeks less often than they once did, relying instead on regional market weeks closer to home. Travel costs are lower, less time is spent away from the stores, and for many, the atmosphere feels more personal. As regional markets become more sophisticated, thus drawing more exhibitors, New York loses even more of its allure. If regional markets can meet their needs, buyers ask, then why struggle through what many consider to be a grueling week in New York? Some retailers have cut out New York entirely, while others have reduced the number of trips they make and fill in with trips to regional markets in Los Angeles, Dallas, or Miami.

The Los Angeles Market

Much of the look and style of California's market weeks revolves around its casual lifestyle, which it seems to sell almost as much as it sells its clothing. California leads the nation in retail apparel sales and is a leader in manufacturing, with more than 4,000 apparel-related companies in the state.[3]

Buyers shop the Los Angeles market for sportswear in pastel colors. Since the 1930s, when California introduced pants for women, the West Coast has been the source of many important trends in sportswear. Today the state is home to two of the country's largest sportswear manufacturers, Guess? and Esprit de Corp. Other recent successes are surf-fashion companies such as Ocean Pacific Sunwear Ltd., Gotcha Sportwear Inc., and David Weinstein's CP Shades.[4]

Apparel design, production, and distribution is spread out along the entire West Coast, but the heaviest concentrations are in Los Angeles and San Francisco. West Coast apparel producers have experienced phenomenal growth, in part because of the activities of the California Mart, a major regional mart located in downtown Los Angeles. The mart is open year-round and offers permanent and temporary exhibition space. A just-completed expansion of the California Mart will provide space not merely for California's lines, but for New York and Dallas lines as well, along with a growing number of foreign producers.

Not all California producers show in the mart. A number of the better women's apparel producers hold open house in their factory showrooms. Thus far, they have not found buyers reluctant to travel the extra distance to see the lines on-site.

The *California Apparel News* has established itself as an important resource covering the state's fashion news.

The Dallas Market

The mood at Dallas market weeks is strongly southwestern. Handcrafted clothes, or clothes that look handcrafted, play well, and with bright, vibrant colors are seen here. Dallas has become an important production and market center. Now the third-largest center in the country, it advertises itself as the "marketplace for the Southwest, the nation, and the world." Dallas-produced fashions are shown alongside fashions from New York, California, and around the world.

A highlight of spring market week is the presentation of the annual Dallas Fashion Awards. The much sought-after award, first offered in 1976, has been given to Oscar de la Renta, Albert Nipon, Escada, Ellen Tracy, Adrienne Vittadini, Guess ?, and Victor Costa.

The fall and spring market weeks include "Fashion/Europe/Dallas," a collection of European designers shown in sponsorship with IGEDO, Europe's largest trade fair. Buyers attend Dallas market weeks from all over the United States and 26 foreign countries.

The Dallas Apparel Mart and the separate Menswear Mart are part of a multibuilding complex that offers a million square feet of exhibition space. The Menswear Mart is the only mart in the world devoted exclusively to menswear.[5]

The Miami Market

The Miami market weeks have a highly international—mostly Hispanic and South American—flavor. Colors and styles are lively. The Miami market is also known for an outstanding selection of children's wear.

Greater Miami has become one of the most dynamic, cosmopolitan, and international fashion-producing centers in the country. Drawn by the temperate climate and quality labor force, many apparel designers and manufacturers now call South Florida home. Retailers find that Miami-produced clothing is well-made, reasonably priced, and perfect for

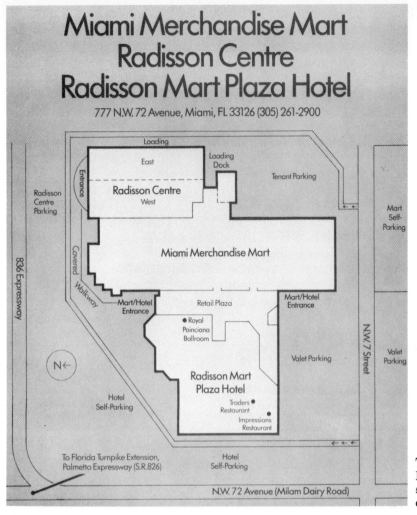

The Miami Merchandise Mart supplies a map showing where all its facilities are located.

the semitropical weather that prevails in the Sun Belt. In Miami, three strong selling seasons—cruisewear, spring, and summer—are available year-round. In addition to cruise and resort wear, Miami design and production centers around budget and moderate-priced sportswear, swimwear, and children's clothing. Miami-based designers of better-priced daytime and evening wear are becoming known for their work.

The Miami International Merchandise Mart, opened in 1968, serves this area. Some exhibitors maintain permanent showrooms, but most show only during market week. Buyers from Latin America and the Caribbean account for 13 percent of the mart's business.[6]

REGIONAL MARTS

Although they are not major centers of fashion apparel production, several cities, such as Boston, Kansas City, Minneapolis, and Denver, have proven they can hold their own against larger marts and market weeks. They do so primarily by emphasizing local design and production. Regional marts sponsor market weeks and in other ways operate much as the larger marts do. Among the regional shows that have established themselves are the Carolina-Virginia fashion exhibition, the San Francisco children's wear show, and the California handbag show.

Local marts have made inroads in servicing the stores in their trading area, and many department store buyers who regularly go to New York and Los Angeles feel they now must supplement these major buying trips with trips to their local regional market. Smaller store buyers often find the regional market is all they need to attend. (Table 13-1 lists the growing number of regional marts around the country as well as the major regional markets in Dallas, Los Angeles, and Miami.)

TABLE 13-1 • REGIONAL MARKETS AND MARTS IN THE UNITED STATES

LOCATION/ FACILITY	NUMBER OF APPAREL LINES (SHOWROOMS)	NUMBER OF MARKETS EACH YEAR	PRIMARY TRADE AREA	OTHER FACTS
Atlanta: Atlanta Apparel Mart	5,000 (1,000)	4 men's and boys' 4 women's and children's 2 activewear 1 ski 2 men's collective 2 men's, women's, and children's	11 states in Southeast U.S.	Opened 1979 Serves 90,000 buyers. 6-story atrium fashion theater seats over 1,200. Expanded in 1989.
Boston: Bayside Merchandise Mart	3,670 (200)	5 women's 3 children's 3 men's	New England states	Opened 1983. Serves 15,000 buyers. Men's shows moved from North East Trade Center.
Charlotte: Charlotte Apparel Center	3,000 (540)	5 women's and children's	N. and S. Carolina, Virginia, W. Virginia, Tennessee	Founded 1972. Owned and operated by Carolina-Virginia Fashion Exhibitors. 20,000 buyers. Moved to new facilities January 1989. Publishes *The Roadrunner*.
Charlotte: Charlotte Merchandise Mart	2,000 (400)	4 men's and boys' 5 children's 2 Western wear	N. and S. Carolina, Virginia, W. Virginia, Tennessee	Opened 1961. 36,500 buyers Expanded in 1989.

TABLE 13-1 • (Continued)

LOCATION/ FACILITY	NUMBER OF APPAREL LINES (SHOWROOMS)	NUMBER OF MARKETS EACH YEAR	PRIMARY TRADE AREA	OTHER FACTS
Chicago: Chicago Apparel Center	8,000 (850)	5 women's and children's 2 bridal 2 footwear and accessories 5 menswear	13-state Mid-western region and Canada	Opened in 1977. Located across from Chicago Merchandise Mart. Annual "Chicago is . . ." promotion features the growing number of Chicago de-signers and man-ufacturers.
Dallas: The Ap-parel Mart	14,000 (2,000)	5 women's 5 children's 2 shoes 2 bridal	All of U.S. and 26 foreign countries, especially Texas, Oklahoma, Loui-siana, N. Mexico, Arkansas, Colo-rado, Mississippi, and Kansas	Opened 1964. Over 100,000 buyers. Spring markets, held in October, declared "International Market Weeks" by U.S. Dept. of Commerce.
Dallas: The Menswear Mart	2,000 (300)	4 men's and boys' 4 Western	All of U.S. and 26 foreign countries, especially Texas, Oklahoma, Loui-siana, N. Mexico, Arkansas, Colo-rado, Mississippi, and Kansas	Opened 1983. The only whole-sale trade center in the world de-voted solely to menswear.
Denver: Denver Merchandise Mart	2,000 (400)	3 men's, wom-en's, children's, and Western 2 women's and children's 1 ski	Rocky Mountain/ Central Plains region	Opened 1965. International Western Apparel & Equipment Market draws buyers from all over the U.S. and 30 foreign coun-tries.
Kansas City: Market Center	1,000 (175)	5 women's and children's 4 men's and boys' 2 Western 1 sportswear	Missouri, Kansas, Nebraska, Iowa, Oklahoma, Ar-kansas, Illinois, Minnesota, Texas	Opened in 1979. 3,220 buyers.

TABLE 13-1 • (Continued)

LOCATION/ FACILITY	NUMBER OF APPAREL LINES (SHOWROOMS)	NUMBER OF MARKETS EACH YEAR	PRIMARY TRADE AREA	OTHER FACTS
Los Angeles: The California Mart	10,000 (2000)	5 women's 5 children's 4 men's 2 shoes 2 petite 1 large size 1 bridal 1 swim/active-wear	All of U.S., especially the South-west Opened 1964. Many guyers from the Orient	Opened 1964. Houses over 30 buying offices. Publishes *Fashion West* magazine and *Fashion West News*. Expanded in 1989.
Miami: Miami International Merchandise Mart and Radisson Centre	6,000 (525)	5 women's and children's 3 men's and boys' 7 handbags, jewelry, and accessories 1 big and tall men's 2 swimwear 1 shoes	Southern U.S., Central and South America and Caribbean.	Opened 1969. Over 125,000 buyers. Recently expanded.
Minneapolis: Hyatt Merchandise Mart	5,000 (437)	6 women's and children's 5 men's and boys'	Minnesota, N. and S. Dakota, Iowa, and Wisconsin	5,600 buyers. Adjoins Hyatt Hotel in downtown Minneapolis.
Pittsburgh: Pittsburgh Expo Mart	1,000 (51)	5 women's 4 children's 1 men's and boys' 2 shoes	Central and W. Pennsylvania, Ohio, W. Virginia, W. New York, W. Maryland	Opened 1975. 12 miles east of Pittsburgh.
Portland: Montgomery Park	475 (50)	5 women's and children's	Oregon, Washington, Idaho, N. California, Alaska	Moved 1984 to newly renovated Montgomery Park facilities: formerly at Portland Galleria.
Salt Lake City: Expo Mart	1,000 (65)	5 women's children's, and men's 2 textiles	Utah, W. Wyoming, S. Idaho, Central Nevada	Opened 1982. 1,500 buyers. Sponsored by Salt Lake City Fashion Exhibitors.

TABLE 13-1 • (Continued)

LOCATION/ FACILITY	NUMBER OF APPAREL LINES (SHOWROOMS)	NUMBER OF MARKETS EACH YEAR	PRIMARY TRADE AREA	OTHER FACTS
San Francisco: San Francisco Apparel Mart	1,400 (430)	10 women's, men's children's, and textiles	N. and S. California, Nevada, Oregon, Washington, Hawaii	Opened 1981 in restored turn-of-the-century building that is part of the Pacific center trade facility. Expansion opens 1989. Focus on better goods, new designers, and international collections. 9,000 buyers.
Seattle: Seattle Trade Center	1,500 (310)	5 women's 4 men's 2 shoes 2 winter sportswear and sports equipment	Pacific NW, Alaska, Idaho, Montana, Oregon, Washington	Opened in 1970s.

TRADE SHOWS

Trade shows, which are held in market centers throughout the year, are sponsored by **trade associations**—professional organizations of manufacturers and sales representatives. Trade shows typically last 2 to 4 days, and are much smaller than mart shows. Held in hotels and motels, civic centers, and small exhibition halls, they draw from one region only. For example, a trade show held every year in Des Moines, Iowa, attracts buyers from as far away as Chicago and Kansas City.

Often specialized, trade shows cover areas of fashion that might otherwise get lost at major market weeks. Trade shows are held for big and tall men, for example, and the Surf Expo Florida Show features surf equipment and surf-inspired sportswear.[7]

Trade shows show every sign of being able to hold their own against the proliferation of marts and market weeks. Despite Atlanta's proximity and emergence as a market center, the well-established Birmingham (Alabama) Apparel Market still sponsors four 3-day shows a year for women's and children's wear. These shows draw between 900 and 1,000 buyers to view lines by 225 sales representatives. The BAMA Men's Apparel Club of Alabama holds two shows a year, each featuring 125 sales representatives and drawing between 350 and 500 buyers. Retailers come from as far away as Tennessee, Mississippi, Georgia, and Florida.[8] A survey taken by the Bureau of Wholesale Sales Representatives, the largest organization of independent sales representatives, revealed that over 70 locations are used, each several times a year, for trade and regional shows.[9]

Trade shows are especially popular with small retailers. Their sales reps are personally familiar with their needs and can cater to them at these smaller exhibits. Buyers from boutiques find that trade shows are their best outlet for the kind of unique and unusual merchandise they seek. Trade shows are known for displaying the work of unusual or small designers who do not ordinarily exhibit at the major marts.

The disadvantage of trade shows is that the exhibitors are limited in number. Buyers have difficulty doing across-the-board buying that is easily accomplished during market weeks at major marts. Trade shows also cannot feature the ongoing service that marts do as they are increasingly open year-round.

TRENDS

The fashion industry survives through change, and the marts and markets have proven more than competent to keep up with the changes that are necessary to remain viable in a highly competitive market. Mart managements and trade associations have responded to industry growth, shifts in population, and changes in buying habits.

Expansion and Competition

Throughout the 1980s, expansion was the rule at most fashion marts. The original facilities of most existing marts expanded or moved to new locations, and many new marts were built in cities that had not previously had them. The Miami International Merchandise Mart added 60,000 square feet of exhibition space. An expansion of the California Mart in Los Angeles added a half-million square feet of new exhibition space. The Atlanta Apparel Mart expanded to more than double its original size. The Denver Mart added 65,000 square feet of exhibition space in 1986. San Francisco, with its well-established Apparel Mart at the Pacific Center, was being courted by two mart developers, each of whom wanted to sponsor its needed expansion.[10]

Even smaller local marts grew during this period. Portland, Oregon, developed a site for shows in its newly renovated Montgomery Park, once the home of a giant Montgomery Ward distribution center. In Charlotte, North Carolina, home to not one but two marts, one is expanding and another is moving into a new facility. Also under construction in Charlotte is the new Belk's Service Stores facility, created to house shows for Belk's member stores' buyers. Belk's Mart will consolidate several shows now scattered in temporary exhibit space in New York and Charlotte.[11]

Marts have also of necessity become more competitive with one another. Elaborate promotions designed to lure buyers now routinely include offers of free or reduced air fare and hotel accommodations.[12] The move toward year-round service is another response to competition. Many facilities have opened their showrooms year-round, at least on a limited basis. The Miami mart introduced Monday market days, one day a week when mart facilities are open, and other marts quickly followed suit.

The marts have joined the bandwagon in promoting the industry strategy known as **quick response,** an attempt to make the American fashion industry more competitive with foreign imports by shortening the order cycle. To re-

THE FUTURE OF MENSWEAR IS LOS ANGELES.

California Mart is bringing menswear into the 21st century by changing the L.A. skyline. Our 700,000 plus square foot Menswear Building breaks ground in '89 and is scheduled for completion in Fall '91. It will be both an architectural and industry landmark.

Seven floors of showrooms, an 800-seat fashion theater, and a 100,000 square-foot exhibition center will be dedicated 5 days a week, 52 weeks a year to the menswear industry and permanent home to CIMM, California International Menswear Market. Across the street and connected to the 3,000,000 square-foot California Mart, the new Menswear Building has access to all the Mart's resources. The future of menswear is NOW in Los Angeles...be part of it!

For leasing information call (213) 239-9260.

California Mart. 110 E. Ninth St., Suite A727
Los Angeles, CA 90079   Fax (213) 239-9325

CALIFORNIA MART
MENSWEAR
BUILDING

The trend toward expansion continues at the California Mart in Los Angeles.

spond to buyers' demands to reduce the time between buying at market and delivery to the store, many marts have also begun to sponsor more frequent market weeks so that buyers can now buy clothes closer to the time when they need them.[13] Market weeks still must be scheduled several months before the clothes can be delivered to the stores, but for domestically produced clothes, the lead time from buying at market week to delivery in the store ranges from 2 to 6 months compared to 6 to 10 months for foreign produced goods. (Men's tailored clothing still requires 6 to 10 months.)

Promoting Local Talent

The regional marts have been strong supporters of local design talent. The Chicago Apparel Center stages an ongoing promotion of local designers and manufacturers called "Chicago Is . . . ."

Chicago also recently established an Apparel and Fashion Industry Task Force, which undertook a 2-year analysis of the Chicago apparel industry involving manufacturers, labor unions, designers, and retailers. Their report, submitted in 1987, recommended the formation of a permanent apparel industry development corporation to be modeled after New York City's successful Garment Industry Development Corporation. Another task force recommendation, that an exhibit area be set aside at the Apparel Mart for local design talent, has already been initiated.[14]

San Francisco's Apparel Mart sponsors special shows designed to promote the San Francisco Design Network's talented designers and manufacturers, some of whom, like Jessica McClintock, Karen Alexander, and David Weinstein's CP Shades, have become well-established.[15] Spring market week at the California Mart now features over 130 California designers.

International Participation

Finally, a trend affecting apparel marts is the increased international participation, which has reached a level that supports specialized shows. The Italian Leathergoods Show, held in New York City, for example, is sponsored by the Italian Ministry of Foreign Trade and the Italian Leathergoods Association. At market weeks, most marts now devote special sections, and occasionally even entire floors, to just imported merchandise.

REFERENCES

[1] Bernadine Morris, "Sportswear Makes City a World Fashion Leader," *The New York Times,* April, 11, 1983, p. B3.

[2] "Marts and Markets: What's Happening Around the Country and in New York," *Stores,* April 1983, p. 47.

[3] Kathleen A. Hughes, "The Future of Fashion? California Pushes Its Way Toward the Ranks of Top Designers," *Wall Street Journal,* September 12, 1987, p. 35.

[4] Ibid.

[5] Sally Giddens, "A Buyer's Market," *Continental,* March 1987, pp. 18–22.

[6] Interview, Laura Chalberg, Public Relations Director, Miami International Merchandise Mart and a press release, Miami Merchandise Mart, September 1987.

[7] Brenda Lloyd, "AMC Purchases Surf Expo in Orlando, Florida," *Daily News Record,* January 1, 1988.

[8] Interview, Bureau of Wholesale Sales Representatives, August 20, 1987.

[9] "Show Dates and Contacts, 1987," *Bureau News,* Bureau of Wholesale Sales Representatives, April 1987, pp. 6–7.

[10] Itow, Laurie. "Showplace Square Expansion Plan," *San Francisco Examiner,* January 7, 1988.

[11] Interview, Brad Culpepper, Belk Service Stores.

[12] Diane Luber, "The Right Fit," *Greensboro News Record,* November 16, 1987.

[13] Marjorie Axelrad, "Timing Tactics," *Stores,* April 1983, pp. 44–45.

[14] "Mayor Washington Receives Apparel Report," press release, Office of the Mayor, March 26, 1987.

[15] Cecilia Hall, "S.F. Apparel Mart Kicks Off Market," *California Apparel News,* Vol. 43, No. 32, August 21–27, 1987.

MERCHANDISING VOCABULARY

Define or briefly explain the following terms:

Buyer's directory	Market center	Sales representative
Domestic market	Market week	Trade association
Foreign market	Mart	Trade show
Market	Quick response	

MERCHANDISING REVIEW

1. What criteria must be met to consider an area a market center?
2. Describe the role of the sales representative in the early days.
3. Describe the organization of the typical mart.
4. What support services for buyers are offered by the marts during market weeks?
5. What services are offered between market weeks?
6. Why is New York City considered the major fashion market center in the United States?
7. What are the disadvantages of the New York market?
8. Describe the distinctive characteristics of the three regional market centers.
9. How do regional marts that are not market centers attract business?
10. What are the advantages and disadvantages of trade shows?

MERCHANDISING DIGEST

1. If you were the women's better sportswear buyer for a major department store in the Washington, D.C., area, how would you service your department?
2. What market center and mart service the retailers in your city? If your city is not in the New York area, discuss the advantages to local retailers who use your regional mart.

FOREIGN FASHION MARKETS

Although New York City is the fashion capital of the world, fashion professionals make a twice-yearly ritual of visiting the dazzling and often frenzied foreign fashion markets. As Americans have become increasingly fashion conscious, the foreign shows have taken on greater importance.

Foreign fashion markets are designed to show off the fashion industries around the world. In the leading foreign markets, clothing is typically designed and presented on two different levels. First in prestige and cost are the **haute couture** (pronounced "oat-koo-tur") clothes. A French expression originally meaning "fine sewing," haute couture is today synonymous with high fashion. These original designs, which use luxury fabrics and are known for their exquisite detailing, are of necessity expensive and thus are made in very limited numbers. With prices that start in the thousands of dollars for a single garment, only a small, rich group of women can afford to wear haute couture design.

The next layer of fashion design is called **prêt-à-porter** (pronounced "pret-ah-por-tay"). A French term meaning "ready-to-wear," prêt-à-porter is produced in far larger numbers than haute couture. Like haute couture, it is introduced in fashion foreign markets at semiannual shows where design collections are revealed to the fashion world. Haute couture and designer prêt-à-porter provide the inspiration for the inexpensive mass market designs that dominate the fashion market.

For several centuries, the "foreign" fashion market consisted entirely of French haute couture. In the 1960s, the prêt-à-porter market emerged first in Italy and then in France. Today, cultural and economic changes and a renewed interest in nationalism and ethnicity have combined to encourage the development of fashion markets worldwide. American buyers no longer travel exclusively to France and Italy; they journey to fashion markets all over the globe.

FRANCE

France first emerged as a fashion showcase during the reign of Louis XIV (1643–1715), often called the Sun King, partly because of his lavish lifestyle. The elaborate clothing worn by his court was widely copied by royalty and the wealthy throughout Europe. The splendor of his court at Versailles created a market for beautiful fabrics, tapestries, and lace. Textile production in Lyons and lace works in Alençon were established to meet these needs. Paris, already an important city and located only a few miles from Versailles, became the fashion capital.

Paris is still considered the cradle of the fashion world. New fashion is born there. After it is seen there, it is adopted and adapted by others around the world.

Historically renowned for original, trend-setting fashion collections, more recently Paris has become an important center for ready-to-wear. In fact, Paris has played an important role in diminishing the differences between haute couture and ready-to-wear.

Paris Couture

France has been the center of haute couture since 1858, when the house of Charles Frederick Worth, generally regarded as the father of Paris couture, opened its doors. Beginning about 1907, Paul Poiret, another French couture designer, became the second great fashion legend. Poiret was the first to stage fashion shows. His oriental balls were part of the opulence that characterized Paris as the center of the fashion scene. He was also the first to branch out into the related fields of perfume, accessories, fabric design, and interior decoration.

A **couture house** is an apparel firm for which a designer creates original designs and styles. The proprietor or designer of a couture house is known as a **couturier** (pronounced "koo-tour-ee-ay") if male, or **couturière** ("koo-tour-ee-air") if female. Most Paris couture houses are known by the names of the designers who head them—Yves Saint Laurent, Givenchy, Ungaro, and Cardin, for example. Sometimes, however, a couture house may keep the name of its original designer even after the designer's death. For example, Gianfranco Ferre designs under the Dior name, and Karl Lagerfeld under the Chanel name.

Chambre Syndicale

In 1868, an elite couture trade association, called the Chambre Syndicale de la Couture Parisienne, came into being. Chambre Syndicale (which is pronounced "shahmbrah seen-dee-kahl") was by invitation only and was restricted to couture houses that agreed to abide by its strict rules. Membership in the Chambre Syndicale today requires:

- A formal written request for membership presented to and voted on by the body.
- Workrooms established in Paris. (It is preferred that the creative production also be based in Paris.)
- Collections presented twice a year on the dates in January and July established by the Chambre Syndicale.
- A collection consisting of 75 or more designs.
- Three models employed by the house throughout the year.
- A minimum of 20 workers employed in the couture operation.

The Chambre Syndicale is a strong force in the French fashion industry. From the foreign buyers' point of view, its most valuable contribution is the organization and scheduling of the twice-yearly market shows. It handles registration and issues the coveted (and limited) admission cards. It also registers

Yves Saint Laurent, a member of the *Chambre Syndicale,* receiving congratulations from his models at the finale of one of his semi-annual haute couture showings.

and copyrights new fashion designs. It is illegal in France to copy a registered fashion design without making special arrangements and paying a fee. (In the United States, there is no copyright protection for clothing designs.) From its members' point of view, the Chambre Syndicale's most valuable contribution is that it operates like an American labor union, representing its members in arbitration disputes and seeking regulation of wages and working hours.

Couture Trade Shows

The Paris couture house trade shows are held twice yearly: The spring/summer collections are shown in late January, and the fall/winter ones in late July. Four types of customers attend:

- Wealthy private customers who order the clothes for their personal wardrobes.
- Ready-to-wear apparel manufacturers who buy models (particular styles) for inspiration and adaptation or for the express purpose of having them copied.
- Retail store buyers who purchase models for direct resale to their own customers or to be copied or adapted into their exclusive ready-to-wear lines.
- Pattern manufacturers who buy models or paper patterns of models for reproduction by home sewers.

Of course, another "customer" attending the shows is the fashion press. If it is true that the couture needs the fashion press, it is even more accurate to say that the fashion press needs the couture. Couture openings have and always will be an exciting, glamourous source of news.

Private customers and the press are admitted free, although the latter must apply to the Chambre Syndicale for admission. Retailers and manufacturers, however, must pay something called a stipulated caution. This admission fee is designed to prevent attendees from stealing the designs. It may be stated as a dollar amount, but is often an agreement to purchase a specific number of models or patterns, or any combination of the above. Since they are buying copying rights, retailers and manufacturers are charged more for an individual garment than a private customer is.

Other Couture Business Activities

The sales of haute couture clothing have steadily declined in recent years as prices have risen and customers have turned to the designer ready-to-wear lines. To survive, couture houses have expanded into other, more lucrative activities, so much so that the brother and former business partner of Hubert Givenchy, Jean-Claude Givenchy, recently observed: "That we continue in couture is often a condition of the licensee contracts that we sign—and through these licenses, the couture can pay for itself."[1] Among the fashion-related business activities taken on by couture houses are the development of ready-to-wear collections, the establishment of boutiques, and the ever-present (and profitable) licensing arrangements.

Couture Ready-to-Wear

The exclusivity and cost of producing couture lines has sent many couturiers into the ready-to-wear business in recent years. In fact, the most outrageous, creative, and innovative designs are typically found in ready-to-wear lines while the more conservative, classic clothes are the realm of haute couture. Couture ready-to-wear seeks to combine the status of haute couture with the vitality of ready-to-wear.

Most couture ready-to-wear clothes are sold to department and specialty stores, which often set aside special areas or departments for display of couture-designed clothing and accessories.

Couture Boutiques

Boutique (pronounced "boo-teek") is a French word for "shop." It has come to mean, however, a shop of a certain sort, specifically one that carries exclusive merchandise. Many couturiers have installed boutiques carrying their exclusive products and ready-to-wear lines on the first floor or a lower floor of their design houses, and a few have branched out with boutiques in many different cities. Goods sold in these shops are usually designed by the couture house staff and are sometimes even made in the couture workrooms. All bear the famous label.

Yves Saint Laurent and his partner Pierre Berge launched the firm Yves Saint Laurent–Rive Gauche in 1964, and since then have expanded the operation to more than 200 boutiques worldwide. Other couture designers who followed Saint Laurent's lead include Dior, Valentino, and Givenchy.

Couture Licensing Agreements

The most lucrative business activities for couturiers are the numerous licensing arrangements they establish to sell their accessories and ready-to-wear lines and also a variety of goods produced by others on their behalf. Licensed goods range from apparel and accessories such as shoes, stockings, and perfume to home fashions such as bed, bath, and table linens—anything that will sell with a designer's name on it.

As in all licensing agreements, the designer sells the right to produce and market products bearing his or her name to various manufacturing companies. Although the licensed products are supposedly designed, or at minimum approved, by the designer, this is not always the case. Often the designer's only interest is the royalty that will be earned on wholesale sales, and little control is exercised over the design or production.

French Ready-to-Wear

The burgeoning French ready-to-wear fashion has two distinct sources: designers and mass-market producers. Young, innovative ready-to-wear designers such as Jean-Paul Gautier, Azzedine Alaia, Kenzo, and Thierry Mugler have added much-needed excitement to the French fashion industry.

To meet the needs of these ready-to-wear designers, the Chambre Syndicale expanded its membership, creating an autonomous section for the designers who work exclusively in ready-to-wear. This group, who have been designated **créateurs** (as opposed to "couturiers") now numbers 24 out of the Chambre Syndicale's total membership of 44. Their ranks are expanding rapidly. In 1985 there were only 18 créateurs. In addition to the aforementioned, the créateurs now include such important names as Karl Lagerfeld, who designs the couture collection for Chanel but creates ready-to-wear under his own name, and also Angelo Tarlazzi, Sonia Rykiel, Claude Montana, and Jean-Charles de Castelbajac. The most recent addition is Patrick Kelly, the first American and first black to be accorded this honor.

French ready-to-wear grows in importance each year, but haute couture is hardly dying out. After a downturn during the late 1960s and 1970s, it regained its prominence in the early 1980s as elegance and sophistication were once again in style. Even more recently, it received a shot in the arm by a particularly innovative designer named Christian Lacroix, hailed as the new king of the couturiers.

If anything, the push is now on to provide the créateurs with the same kind of status that has long been enjoyed by the couture houses. At present, the couture houses still dominate the high end of industry. Simon Burstein, vice president of Sonia Rykiel, noted, "The couturiers' profile has been very well maintained. The créateurs need some dynamism to make their position stronger. The intention is to improve the status of the créateurs. There's more to do in regard to [their] images."[2]

Although their influence is great, the couturiers and créateurs represent only a small part of the French fashion industry in terms of numbers and revenue. The remaining 1,200 companies are mass producers of ready-to-wear. They are represented by their own trade organization, the Fédération Française du Prêt-à-Porter Féminin. This segment of the industry reports sales of $3 billion annually.

Prêt-à-Porter Trade Shows

The French ready-to-wear producers present their collections at two market shows a year. The first, for the fall/winter collections, is held in March, and the second in October, for the spring/summer collections. Actually, two large trade shows take place simultaneously, one sponsored by the Chambre Syndicale for the prêt-à-porter designers, and a second, sponsored by the Fédération, for the mass producers of ready-to-wear.

They do not, however, take place in the same location. Couture designers' shows traditionally were held at the designer's houses, but with the onset of the créateurs, the couture and créateur shows began to be held in huge tents erected in a Paris neighborhood called Les Halles. Once the site of the Paris food market, the area has been redeveloped as a cultural and fashion center. In the Forum des Halles, a massive, multilevel building, one area has been set aside to house couture designer showrooms. Facilities for créateurs' showrooms are also nearby.

The mass market prêt-à-porter collections are exhibited at the Porte de Versailles Exhibition Center. This trade show, known as the *Salon du Prêt-à-Porter Féminin,* brings together more than 1,000 exhibitors from all over the world.

With each succeeding show, the press pays more attention and provides more coverage of this end of the French fashion business. More than 30,000 buyers attend the prêt-à-porter shows, which are rivaled only by the ready-to-wear shows in Milan and London.

A semiannual men's ready-to-wear show, *Salon de l'Habillement Masculin (SEHM),* held in February and September, is as important to the men's fashion industry as the women's ready-to-wear shows are to the women's fashion industry. It is an international show, and all of Europe's leading menswear designers exhibit there.

Export Efforts

The French fashion industry is also seeking to improve its export position. To this end, French apparel manufacturers formed a trade association, the *Fédération Française des Industries de l'Habillement,* which is roughly equivalent to the American Apparel Manufacturers Association. The *Fédération* maintains offices throughout the world, including New York. The New York office, called the French Fashion and Textile Center, plays an important role in helping member firms find U.S. agents for their products. It also assists in planning retail store promotions featuring French products and carries on a number of other, similar and related activities. Many major French designers—Yves Saint Laurent's Rive Gauche, Daniel Hechter, and Cacharel—also maintain their own offices in New York.

ITALY

Italy is France's only serious rival in the fashion industry. In certain areas, such as knitwear and accessories, Italian design is considered superior to the French. In addition to its relatively recent recognition in women's apparel, Italy has long been recognized as a leader in men's apparel, knitwear, leather accessories, and textiles.

Italian Couture

Italy has long had couture houses named for the famous designers who head them—Valentino, Tiziani, Mila Schoen, Andre Laug, Galitzine, and Fabiani. Its designers are members of Italy's couture trade group (a counterpart to the Chambre Syndicale) known as the Camera Nazionale dell'Alta Moda Italiana. Unlike French couture houses, however, Italian couture designers are not all located in a single city. They may be found in Rome, Milan, and Florence, as well as in other Italian cities.

Both Italian and French couture depend heavily on Italian fabric and yarn innovation and design. Most of the excitement today in print and woven textile design is created and produced in the fabric mills of Italy. Italian knits are also known for their avant-garde styles.

Couture Trade Shows

Italian couture collections are shown semiannually in Milan and Rome. They are scheduled one week prior to the Paris shows so that foreign buyers can cover both important fashion markets in a single trip. As in Paris, buyers and manufacturers are required to pay a caution to attend the Italian couture showings. Private customers and the fashion press are admitted free, although cards of admission are required for the latter.

Other Couture Business Activities

Like their Paris counterparts, many Italian couture houses have set up boutiques for the sale of exclusive accessories and limited lines of apparel. The designs are usually those of the couture house staff, and the apparel and accessories are sometimes made in the couture workrooms. All items offered in boutiques bear the couture house label.

In addition to their own signature lines, name designers frequently create nonname fashion collections. Giorgio Armani, for example, designs for Erreuno, Luciano Soprani for Basile, Gianni Versace for Genny, Romeo Gigli for Callaghan, and Muriel Grateau for Complice. Gianfranco Ferre consults for lines other than his, supplying ideas about color, length, and shape. Ferre believes Italian designers are motivated by "the Italian enterprise spirit."[3]

Italian couture designers also have established licensing agreements with foreign producers. Some design and produce uniforms for employees of business firms, most notably airlines and car rental agencies. Some accept commissions to create designs of fashion products ranging from menswear to home furnishings.

Italian Ready-to-Wear

Italy began to develop both its women's and men's ready-to-wear industries earlier than France did. As a result, it started exporting earlier, and today its economy relies heavily on its exporting program. Much of this exported merchandise is in the medium-high price range, especially in knitwear and accessories.

Designers

Innovative Italian ready-to-wear designers make their shows as exciting as the Paris ready-to-wear shows have become. Among the better known Italian designers who work for one or more ready-to-wear firms are Mariuccia Mandelli, Claude Montana, Luciano Soprani, Gianni Versace, and Muriel Grateau. Well-known designers who head their own firms include Giorgio Armani, Giovanna Ferragamo, and Rosita and Tai Missoni. Other well-known Italian ready-to-wear firms are Krizia, Gianfranco Ferre, Basile, Callaghan, Ken Scott, Cadette, Mirsa, Byblos, and Fendi.

Trade Shows and Market Centers

Preparing a calendar of Italian ready-to-wear events was a fairly simply matter until the late 1960s. As interest in ready-to-wear grew, and Paris began its semiannual prêt-à-porter showings, Italian ready-to-wear producers followed suit. Since many of these producers were located in Florence—a city that already had an established reputation as a fashion center—regular, semiannual showings of both ready-to-wear and accessories were initiated in the Pitti and Strossi palaces in Florence. The showings were scheduled to coincide with their French counterparts.

Along with the ready-to-wear shows, the Florence and Milan shows include some ready-to-wear shows and a knitwear show (MAIT) is held in Florence in February. This is well-attended by American buyers because of its importance in sweater design.

Men's ready-to-wear shows are held in Florence in February and September. Since 1980, Uomo Modo, the twice-a-year show of Italian menswear manufacturers in the United States, has given American and Canadian buyers a preview of manufacturers' spring designs before they are shown in Italy. These shows increase in importance as a growing number of talented designers are producing menswear apparel and furnishings.

Fiera Milano, 17-20 marzo 1989

L'UNICO MIPEL AL MONDO

COLLEZIONI AUTUNNO/INVERNO 1989/90

BORSE IN PELLE, ARTICOLI IN RETTILE,
BORSE DA SERA, IN TESSUTO, PAGLIA, BORSETTI DA UOMO - CARTELLE,
ARTICOLI DA REGALO, PICCOLA PELLETTERIA - PORTAFOGLI,
CINTURE, ARTICOLI DA VIAGGIO - VALIGIE,
OMBRELLI, BASTONI, ABBIGLIAMENTO E COORDINATI, GUANTI,
ATTREZZI PER VETRINE, PELLAMI, TESSUTI E SUCCEDANEI,
FIBBIE - CERNIERE - ACCESSORI, MACCHINARI PER PELLETTERIA.

55° MIPEL

C'È UNA NUOVA MODA.
C'È UN NUOVO MIPEL.

Mipel, the trade show for Italian-produced leather goods and accessories, is another of the important fashion trade shows held in Milan.

Accessories

Italy has always been a fashion leader in the design and manufacture of leather accessories. Shoes, handbags, gloves, and small leather goods are a major part of Italy's fashion industry. Other accessories that are world-famous are silk scarves and knitted hats, scarves, and gloves. Because of the Italian finesse in designing these accessories, they have become major exports to the rest of the world.

The importance of accessories to the well-dressed European public is well known, and this message has been carried to the United States by buyers who have attended the Italian fashion markets. Today, well-designed accessories have become a fashion must for the well-dressed, fashion-conscious American public. Accessories fairs are held all over Italy. The most famous are those held in Lake Como, Florence, Milan, Bologna, and Rome.

Mipel is the name of the trade show for Italian-produced handbags and other accessories such as luggage, belts, umbrellas, hats, and scarves. This important show is held in Milan in January and June (see page 321). Because the Mipel show is sometimes too late to allow American buyers to place orders and receive delivery by the start of the coming season, an earlier show, called Europel, was instituted in 1974. This show concentrates on handbags and small leather goods and features exhibitors from all over Europe, as well as Italian producers. Although originally sponsored by Italian handbag manufacturers, Europel has held shows in Paris, Düsseldorf, and Berlin, as well as in Rome and Florence.

The famous shoe show held in Bologna in March is well-attended by foreign buyers because of the importance of Italy's shoe industry and the large quantity of shoe exports. Among famous Italian shoe manufacturers are Ferragamo and Gucci.

The glove industry, centered around Naples, is represented in many fashion fairs, as is women's neckwear, produced mainly in the Lake Como and Milan areas.

Another interesting fashion fair is the famous Ideacomo, held at Lake Como in early May. It is here that the Italian fashion fabric producers show new designs and fabric textures for use in the following year's fashion apparel and accessories.

GREAT BRITAIN

For many years, London was for menswear what Paris has been for women's apparel—the fountainhead of fashion inspiration. In recent years its dominance has diminished, and Italy has become the main source of European-styled menswear. But London still remains the major fashion center for impeccably tailored men's custom apparel.

Britain's most important fashion strength, however, lies in tweeds, woolens, and knitwear for both men and women. The materials for these garments come from the mills of the Midlands of England and also from Scotland and Northern Ireland. Britain is also a growing market center for leather apparel for both women and men.

London Couture

The British Fashion Council, which was formed in 1982 by Britain's fashion industry, is supported by the Clothing Export Council, the British Clothing Industry Association, and the Fashion in Action group. It is working to boost London's reputation as an international fashion center. The BFC, as it is known, has given top priority to making London the fashion mecca it was for a brief period in the sixties. It was during these years that London's mods and rockers, with their wide ties and miniskirts, set the fashion tone for the youth revolution. In conjunction with the London

Fashion Fair, which it sponsors, the BFC produces a diary of all events that take place during London fashion week, including designer shows. The London Fashion Fair is held at the Olympia Exhibition Center.

British Ready-to-Wear

Although England has never supported a couture industry in the way that France has, the British have nonetheless tended to rely on made-to-measure apparel. Its ready-to-wear industry was a minor industry until after World War II. The fact that it entered a period of expansion after the war is largely due to the efforts of the government. According to one English fashion authority, the government became "the fairy godmother" responsible for "the survival of [British] couture and the rapid development of [Britain's] large and excellent ready-to-wear trade."[4]

Women's Apparel

Like its American and continental counterparts, British ready-to-wear for women is divided into three categories: high-fashion (usually high-priced), moderate-priced, and mass-produced (popular-priced). High-fashion ready-to-wear. is usually the product of couture houses in Britain, but has rarely been considered trend-setting. British moderate- and popular-priced ready-to-wear was considered of little fashion importance until the 1960s.

Early in the 1960s, however, a London designer named Mary Quant recognized an emerging youth trend and began designing clothes for the young. Other London designers quickly followed her lead, and almost overnight London became the world's fashion market center for junior apparel.

In 1968—from Little Rock, Arkansas—Mary Quant (at right) waves hello as she brings her "mod" styles from Britain to the U.S.A.

The fashion trend in the early 1970s, however, moved toward longer, softer, more romantic styles. When the British ready-to-wear industry failed to follow, London lost fashion importance again. But backed by the British government and led by three London designers— Jean Muir, Zandra Rhodes, and Ossie Clark—who had sprung to prominence in the 1960s, a new group of young designers began to exert impact on the London fashion scene. By the late 1980s, London became hot fashion news again.

New, young, innovative designers, products of England's famous design schools, such as the Royal College of Art, the London College of Fashion, and St. Martin, were once again shocking, teasing, and tempting the fashion world with their outrageous designs. Vivienne Westwood, Stephan Linard, Janice Wainwright, Bruce Oldfield, Belleville Sassoon, and Jasper Conrans are all talents sparking the fashion scene in Great Britain.

London is the center of Britain's women's ready-to-wear industry, and the major manufacturers' trade associations have headquarters there. Most permanent showrooms of ready-to-wear producers are located there, although there also are showrooms in the Midlands and in Scotland. The major ready-to-wear shows take place in London. The International Fashion Fair, sponsored by the Clothing Export Council in Great Britain, is held each April and October.

Despite their best promotional efforts, the British fashion industry has been unable to capitalize on its design talents enough to move it into the first ranks of fashion producers. Designers attribute their failure to achieve the prominence they would like to production problems. British manufacturers still tend to view themselves as a cottage industry.[5] Britain's designers say that the industry overall has begun to see itself in a more businesslike light. This, they hope, will enable them to compete more successfully than they have done in the past with Paris and Milan.

Menswear

London and Harrogate are important market centers for menswear. The major trade associations are located in London. So are many of the permanent showrooms of menswear producers, although others are located elsewhere in England and Scotland. One important trade show, the International Men's and Boy's Wear Exhibition, has some 200 British and continental firms exhibiting and is held in London in February. However, a bigger menswear show, the Menswear Association Convention and Exhibition, is held in Harrogate in September. At this show, about 300 exhibitors (90 percent British and 10 percent from the Continent, Australia, Japan, and Yugoslavia) show their lines. For the American customer, the major British menswear designers and manufacturers can be seen at the previously noted SEHM show in Paris. The best-known companies also have showrooms or representatives in the United States.

Savile Row is the name of a historic London street and also an adjective that, when used to modify the word "suit," conjures up visions of impeccably tailored men's suits. Savile Row is a wonderful place where each suit is hand-crafted for its new owner, a process known as "bespoke tailoring." (Bespoke, an archaic word meaning to have reserved in advance, is applied in England to men's clothing that is made to measure, a process that takes 6 to 10 weeks.)[6] Many shops require three individual fittings. All this effort adds up to high prices—as much as $1,500 and up for a suit. However, a Savile Row suit can be expected to last 20 to 50 years. For years, experts have predicted that because of its high prices and time-consuming tailoring, and the more frequent changes in male fashions and tastes, Savile Row is doomed. But somehow it hasn't disappeared.

WEST GERMANY

Until the mid-1980s, most American fashion buyers skipped West Germany, and few West German designers were well-known outside Europe. But a new wave of high-fashion women's designers is changing this. And although West Germany's fashion industry is relatively small, its international trade fairs have become a major source of fashion inspiration for new fabric and designs.

Changing Fashion Image

For years, German fashion was considered somewhat stodgy. Their major fashion export seemed to be the unisex green Loden coat, a fashion classic that was hardly high fashion. Recently, though, two apparel firms, Escada and Mondi, have had success with their high-fashion lines, and other firms have wasted no time in following their lead. The Loden coat seems to have taken a back seat to newer, brighter high fashion, and the rest of the world is taking another look at West German fashion. Ellin Saltzman, senior vice president and corporate fashion director of Saks Fifth Avenue, reported: "More and more people are discovering the German manufacturers. Their quality and detailing are simply excellent. They have done their research and are filling a void here. It seems the German fashion industry has come into its own."[7]

Igedo is the largest European fashion fair for women's ready-to-wear.

FASHION

Every year, groups of Americans pack their bags, get on planes, and head for some of the most exciting cities in Europe. But we're not talking about tourists off on a vacation—we're referring to fashion merchandising and executives from leading retail companies in search of new design collections for their customers.

Because virtually all department and specialty stores try to stay at the "cutting edge" of fashion, buying trips to the European fashion shows are considered *de rigueur*—even in years when the value of the U.S. dollar may be weak against foreign currencies. In the fall of 1987, for instance, when exchange rates were particularly unfavorable, major fashion retailers Neiman-Marcus, Saks Fifth Avenue, and Bloomingdale's still sent 17, 20, and 37 executives, respectively, to cover the markets in Paris, London, and Milan.[1]

What's more, although a weakened dollar makes the cost of merchandise higher as well, many department stores have actually been increasing their attention to and emphasis on European designers in recent years—recognizing that those designers hold a special cachet for fashion-forward customers on this side of the Atlantic. Many, in fact, have enjoyed increases in recent seasons of 10 percent to more than 15 percent in sales of their foreign designers, includ-

ing Giorgio Armani, Emanuel Ungaro, and Valentino.[2] And because of the success of certain European designer collections, Bloomingdale's increased its buying budget for one recent trip by 10 percent.[3]

"We definitely have customers for these designers, customers who follow their moves and wait for their new collections," stated the fashion merchandising director at Rich's, Atlanta. And, echoed the vice president of fashion marketing at Burdine's, Miami: "Every season we look to buy new and exciting fashions for our customers—and some of the most exciting come out of Europe."[4]

Of course, not all U.S. retailers approach the European designer in the same way. Some focus on the designer collections of one particular country;

FOCUS

others feature a broad international scope. And some highlight individual European designer names on their sales floor, while others make their visual statement based on a look more than a name. Whatever the approach, it is based on a knowledge of what their own customers want in the way of fashion-forward merchandise—coupled with a good sense of economics as prices shift with a higher or lower dollar value.

As the fashion director for Marshall Field, Chicago, noted, when pricing gets high, it "makes you more selective. You can't simply use the broad brush approach, but rather you have to view every collection individually regarding its fashionability for your customer. Then you choose what's best from the collections, asking yourself whether it is intrinsically worth the price, in all aspects."[5]

Certainly the runways and showrooms of Paris, London, and Milan have traditionally been the key markets shopped by U.S. fashion merchandising executives. But during the late 1980s, there was also interest blossoming in new design collections from West Germany; and a number of U.S. retailers either traveled to or talked of exploring the fashion scene at major shows in Düsseldorf and Munich. One German designer name, Escada, for instance, was first test-marketed in the U.S. in 1981,

and by 1987, annual sales had grown to $30 million.[6]

Whatever foreign markets they shop, however, savvy U.S. fashion retailers not only look for new collections from established European designers, but also seek out fresh new talent, in order to offer their customers the latest fashion looks. Today there is little copying of the Paris couture collections. World attention is focused on the young vibrant talents of the ready-to-wear.[7] As the vice president of fashion merchandising for Woodward & Lothrop, Washington, D.C., stated: "It's important for us to be on top of the fashion directions coming out of Europe, which is why we'll continue to pursue that avenue of the designer business. It definitely creates a strong fashion image for us."[8]

[1] "A Listing of Executives Making the Trip," Women's Wear Daily, October 7, 1987, p. 14.

[2] "European Designs Strong at Stores," Women's Wear Daily, October 6, 1987, p. 1.

[3] "Stores Braced for Europe's Prices," Women's Wear Daily, October 7, 1987, p. 14.

[4] Penny Gill, "European Designers: Middle Market Stores and the Big Names," Stones, December 1987, p. 18.

[5] Ibid., p. 16.

[6] Irene Daria, "Escada: Expanding Retail Network," Women's Wear Daily, Sportswear Report, October 7, 1987, p. 20.

[7] Bill Cunningham, "Couturist Class," Details, November 1988, pp. 119–138.

[8] Daria, p. 18.

This Fashion Focus is based on information from the articles cited above.

International Trade Fairs

The women's ready-to-wear industry is centered in Düsseldorf, but West Germany promotes its fashion industry through a series of large fairs held around the country. A major show is the international textile trade show, Interstoff, held in Frankfurt in May and November. It is an important place to do research on new fabrics and fashion ideas. Another important trade show is the gigantic Igedo, held in Düsseldorf in April and October, and supplemented with smaller fairs scheduled throughout the year. Igedo is Europe's largest fashion fair for women's ready-to-wear, accessories, and intimate apparel. More than 2,500 exhibitors come from 27 countries to fill the 1.25 million-square-foot exhibition space.

Fashion fairs are also held in Munich each March. The Overseas Export Fashion Fair takes place in Berlin every September. Cologne, the center of the menswear industry, is host to the week-long International Men's Fashion Week every February and August. Other shows include a footwear fair in Düsseldorf, a semiannual international children's fair in Cologne, a semiannual swimwear and underwear show in Düsseldorf, and numerous accessory fairs, the most notable of which is the leather goods fair in Offenbach in February and August.

SCANDINAVIA

While each of the four Scandinavian countries—Norway, Sweden, Denmark, and Finland—has its own fashion industries and specialities, these countries also form a single identifiable market center. This is partly because they tend to work with the same basic materials: leather, fur, some wool, an increasing amount of textiles made of artificial fibers, some gold, and silver. However, the main reason is that the four countries, while they do make individual marketing efforts, hold major trade fairs and maintain permanent showrooms in one location: Copenhagen. This is the center of the Scandinavian fashion world.

Conservative, high-style wool apparel, including coats, dresses, and suits, has long been the specialty of the Danish apparel industry. Prices are generally high.

Moderate-priced apparel is particularly strong among the Swedish, Finnish, and Norwegian offerings. Some are made from cotton knit, but manmade fibers and cotton blends are more common. Styling is often youthful; a Swedish sportswear producer claims to have introduced the string bikini to the United States in the fall of 1973.

Leather apparel, primarily in menswear, is a popular Swedish product. Both Sweden and Norway are among the important suppliers of mink and other furs to countries around the world. Birgir Christiansen is a leading furrier.

Scandinavia offers some interesting textile designs. Both American producers and retail buyers, who are interested in unusual fabrics, watch the Scandinavian textile offerings closely, especially the work of Finland's Marimekko.

Excellent jewelry in all price ranges is available in Scandinavia. The area has long been known for its clean-cut designs in gold and silver. Today, an increasing amount of costume jewelry is being produced there, particularly in Sweden.

CANADA

For many years, Canadian designers lived in the shadow of their American and European counterparts. Recently,

Joining the ranks of the fashion leaders, Canada, through its Festival of Canadian Fashion, is showing the world that Canada has fashion flair.

though, Canada has stepped out of the shadow and taken on a personality of its own. The development of a group of new and innovative designers has given the Canadian fashion industry a growing sense of confidence that has paid off in real growth. The fashion industry is the fifth largest employer in Canada and gets bigger every year.

Canadian Designers

Well-known Canadian designers include such names as Wayne Clark, Mariola Mayer, Debbie Shuchat, Donna Stephens, Edie Johne, Pat McDonagh, Romona Keneza, and Alfred Sung. Pat McDonagh got her start designing clothes for Diana Rigg in the television series *The Avengers,* and Alfred Sung, who made history as the first Canadian designer to become a publicly held company, recently expanded his product line to include bed and bath linens.

Much of the current recognition of Canadian fashion designers has been the inspiration of a trade group called Fashion Canada/Mode du Canada. Chartered by the Canadian government in 1973–1974, it has instituted a fashion scholarship program and fosters an international marketing program to promote Canadian fashion designers.

Trade Shows

The Festival of Canadian Fashion, held annually at the Metro Toronto Convention Center, aims to prove that Canada does indeed have an exciting fashion industry. As the ad on page 329 shows, fashion industry leaders as well as major buyers find the Festival a valuable experience. Total attendance for the five-day festival grows every year as does the attention paid to this fair by foreign buyers. Bob Emmet, vice president of Jacobson's, a Michigan specialty chain, reflected the new attitude toward Canadian fashion when he commented: "If we're willing to go to Europe for those incredible prices, if we're willing to go to the Far East twice a year, why not go to Canada for the weekend?"[8] The festival does its part, too, and in 1988, for the first time, accessories were featured, and the show was open to the public on evenings and weekends.

Not surprisingly, since Canada's history is intertwined with that of fur and skin trading, outerwear and furs are Canada's fashion specialty. The Canadian Outerwear Fashion Fair (COFF), an annual show held in Winnipeg, is the largest such show in North America.

CENTRAL AND SOUTH AMERICA

By the mid-1970s, the Central and South American market could be added to the growing list of international fashion markets. The fashion world began visiting market centers in Rio de Janeiro, Buenos Aires, São Paulo, and Bogotá, which represented the emerging fashion industries in Central and South America and the Caribbean.

Two factors contributed to this new presence in the fashion world. The first was inflation, which drove American buyers to seek cheaper sources and suppliers. The second was the conveniently corresponding development of a fashion industry in Central and South America.

Actually the region was a natural area for the development of a fashion industry, since it is a source of both cheap materials such as cotton, wool, and leather and cheap labor. But it was not until various governments began to encourage the expansion of the fashion industry that the fashion world began to travel to this new market. Central and South American governments saw the fashion industry as a means of increasing their gross national product and their status in the world marketplace.

Fashion Products

The Central and South American fashion industry offers fashion on three levels. First, several countries have developed their own high-fashion, or couture, industries, many of which are ripe for import to the United States and Europe. The second level revolves around the development of fashion products that reflect each country's national heritage of crafts. With a renewed interest in ethnicity throughout the world, such products are welcome. Third and finally, Central and South America, with its cheap production facilities and labor, has the ability to be an "off-shore" source of products made to North American manufacturers' specifications.

The Central and South American fashion business also tends to be specialized. Argentina, Brazil, and Uruguay are important centers of women's and men's apparel. Argentina and Uruguay produce clothing in the moderate-to upper-price ranges and specialize in clothing made from wool, while Brazil is known for its sportswear.

Handbag buyers seek out the better-quality goods of Argentina and go to Brazil for moderate-quality goods. Uruguay is another important source of moderate- to high-quality handbags.

The most important shoe center is Brazil, where manufacturers concentrate on creating a stylish product made from lasts that fit North American feet. Belts and small leather goods are the specialty of Brazil, Argentina, and the Dominican Republic.

Costume jewelry is another important product from this region. A number of Central and South American countries have begun to export silver and gold jewelry of native design. Thus far, Ecuador and Peru have provided some of the most interesting offerings.

Trade Shows

The single most important market center in South America is São Paulo, Brazil. An international textile and textile products fair is held there every January and June, with exhibitors not only from Latin America but from other areas of the world as well. This trade show draws over 60,000 buyers.

Other important international fairs featuring textiles and textile products as well as fashion accessories are held in Bogotá, Colombia; Lima, Peru; and San Salvador, El Salvador. All three are annual fairs.

THE FAR EAST

The United States imports more apparel from the Far East than from any other area in the world. However, the major portion of these imports has been low-priced, high-volume merchandise, and hardly any of the apparel has qualified as "designer merchandise." There are definite signs that this situation is beginning to change, and now fashion buyers can find exciting, innovative styles offered by new design-oriented Asian stylists.

Buyers have used certain countries in the Far East as a market in which to have fashions they saw in the European fashion centers copied and adapted. A fashion buyer needs to know which areas in the Far East are best equipped to handle specific types of manufacturing. Japan and Hong Kong were once the two major contract or copyist countries. But these countries have upgraded their fashion images, so that today they are producers of outstanding high-styled, high-priced fashion apparel.

Japan

The success of the Japanese in marketing cars and consumer electronics is legendary, and they have begun to apply the same effort and skill to the apparel and textile business with high hopes for similar success. Apparel accounts for more than half of the finished goods that Japan exports to the United States, and in medium- to high-priced clothing, the

Japanese have made a significant impact on the U.S. fashion industry.

Many Japanese boutiques in Tokyo, Japan's fashion center, have their own design staffs who create exciting new looks. Because of their ability to produce fashion goods quickly, the Tokyo fashion scene is often 6 months to 1 year ahead of other fashion centers.

Japanese Ready-to-Wear

In the 1950s and 1960s the Japanese faithfully copied Western trends. Ironically, in the 1970s as Western dress had finally won acceptance in Japan, a group of highly original Japanese designers—Hanae Mori, Kenzo Takada, Issey Miyake, and Kansai Yamamoto—emerged. They first worked in Paris, where their lines were design sensations that rivaled the French prêt-à-porter designers. For over a decade, in fact, these daring, designers were thought of as French rather than Japanese.

Today, Japan's designers, who have become even more innovative and ex-

Japanese designers, even the most avant-garde, stress mobility and comfort.

perimental in a clearly Japanese sense, work out of and are clearly identified with Japan. While popular in the West, Japanese style has remained individualistic and often has few reference points to Western design. Japanese designers, for example, pay little attention to waistlines and rarely go out of their way to emphasize any particular body part. They consider hem lengths irrelevant. The emphasis is on mobility and comfort.

Japanese Designers

In the early 1980s a mostly new wave of avant-garde designers—Issey Miyake, Kansai Yamamoto, Rei Kawakubo of Comme des Garçons, Yohji Yamamoto, and Matsuhiro Matsuda—stormed the American fashion scene. Even their business operations were considered innovative. In an arrangement that is not unusual in Japan, Kansai Yamamoto, for example, designs, manufactures, wholesales, and retails his clothing all over the world. In Japan, he operates over 200 retail outlets and free-standing stores, and leases space in over 40 department stores. He employs and trains people to work in his leased departments much as American cosmetics companies train their own department store staffs.

Although the new wave of Japanese designers continues to be a force in the domestic fashion world, the initial excitement over their work has subsided. United States retailers had trouble mass merchandising the designs, which appeal mostly to customers who are looking for strikingly unusual shapes and fabrics. The American dollar, which sank to unprecedented lows compared to the Japanese yen, also took its toll on the Japanese fashion wave. Japanese fashions became so expensive that few American stores and customers could afford them.

Fashion Trade Shows

The most prominent Far Eastern trade event is the Tokyo Fashion Week. Held in January and July, this semiannual trade fair is the combined effort of over 150 Tokyo apparel producers. In the 1980s the show assumed new importance. As the Japanese high-fashion industry wanes abroad, however, it remains to be seen whether the Western buyers will continue to travel to Tokyo.

Hong Kong

Hong Kong also upgraded its fashion image in the 1980s, primarily by shifting from the execution of contract work to the production of its own designs. To help foster its attempt to become a fashion leader as well as a production center, Hong Kong sponsors a fashion week each year, inviting buyers from all over the world to view its exquisite and exotic fabrics and fashions and to meet its designers.

Despite its shift in emphasis, Hong Kong production facilities have always been and continue to be an important resource for Western manufacturers. Designers such as Yves Saint Laurent, Calvin Klein, Pierre Cardin, Hubert Givenchy, Oscar de la Renta, Giorgio Armani, and Dior have used Hong Kong manufacturing facilities for years. Even though it is the world's largest exporter of fashion apparel, Hong Kong's strength continues to be in production more than in the introduction of new designs. It is the hope of the Hong Kong fashion industry, however, that its future will include a reputation for innovative design as well as production.

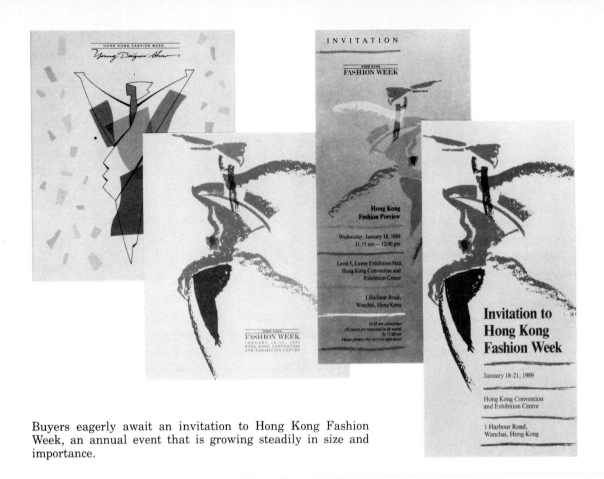

Buyers eagerly await an invitation to Hong Kong Fashion Week, an annual event that is growing steadily in size and importance.

Trade Shows

In 1988, over 8,000 buyers traveled to Hong Kong for its fashion week. In a territory where apparel is the primary money spinner, accounting for 34 percent of its total exports, the government is still working hard to make this event one of international prominence.[9]

The first Hong Kong Fashion Week was held in 1967, but it was not until the late 1970s that it attracted much attention. Because of its steady growth in size and importance, the 1990 fair will be held in the new 4.3 million-square-foot Convention Center, Asia's largest exhibition space.[10]

Hong Kong Fashion Week differs from its Western counterparts in two main respects. First, it is held only once a year rather than twice. Second, it is more of a collective effort than one witnesses at the Western fairs. Emphasis is on promoting Hong Kong's overall image rather than on promoting individual designers.

Hong Kong Fashion Week is organized by the Hong Kong Trade Development Council, which also promotes the colony's designers in American and European trade shows. The council arranges for Hong Kong designers to make personal appearances in stores throughout Europe and North America.

Designers

Although successful locally, Hong Kong designers have yet to make an impact on the international fashion scene. Some names—Ragance Lam, Walter Ma, Ophelia Leung, Rene Ozorio, Lim Ying Ying, Eddie Lau, Hannah Pang, and Diane Freis—have gained recognition among fashion professionals, but are not yet known to consumers. To help remedy this, Hong Kong designers have formed their own group, the Hong Kong Fashion Designers Association, which sponsors shows of its members' designs.

The Hong Kong fashion industry has shown itself to be interested in fostering new talent. As part of fashion week, young hopefuls present their designs and compete for a $1,200 prize and a 2-week trip to the Paris collections.

People's Republic of China

The People's Republic of China is considered a sleeping giant with the potential to become a major force in the fashion world. At present, Americans are buying only a small amount of fashion apparel from China, although fabrics from China, particularly silk and cotton, are important export items. Many retailers expect Chinese–U.S. trade to increase. Over the past few years, many American department and specialty stores have staged elaborate promotions of Chinese imports.

The People's Republic of China holds an important semiannual trade fair in Guangzhou (formerly Canton), but admission is by invitation only, and only a few hundred foreign firms are invited. Recently, more American apparel buyers and producers have been invited to visit China, and hopes are high that long-range plans can be made to establish a flourishing trade.

China is Hong Kong's largest supplier of low- to medium-priced piece goods, which account for 42 percent of Hong Kong's imports. There is no reason to think they could not sell these goods to the rest of the world, too.[11]

China's real forte, however, is silk fabrics. It is the world's largest silk producer, although a lack of modern technology has prevented China from becoming a major exporter of silk. Steps have been taken to remedy this problem, and China is working to improve its weaving, printing, and dyeing technology. It is also training its own fashion designers.

Chinese officials project that production and sales will reach 11 billion yuan (about $2.7 billion) by 1990.[12]

South Korea

With much the same design history as the Japanese, Korea has some exciting young designers creating for the Korean fashion-conscious market. One of them, Maria Kim, has also established a successful volume-priced knitwear business in the United States.

Much of the production of ready-to-wear in Korea is still contract work. But because of the fashion design movement among young Koreans, this is slowly beginning to change.

Taiwan

In Taiwan there is a definite upgrading in the quality of work being produced. Taiwan closely follows Hong Kong in the variety and innovation of knitwear technology. To stimulate and build a more fashion-oriented and higher-priced market, the Taiwan Textile Federation was established. Under its aegis, young Taiwanese designers and technicians are being trained in fashion design and execution. In addition, Garmen Taipei, an interesting showcase of Taiwanese products, is held in Taipei each October.

Southeast Asia

Singapore, Indonesia, Thailand, Malaysia, and the Philippines took to the fashion runway at the 1987 Singapore Apparel and Fashion Week. This special show, called the "Best of the Asian Designers," was a highlight of the week, which has been held annually since 1983.

The Singapore Apparel and Fashion Week is a joint effort of the Singapore Trade Development Board, Tourist Promotion Board, and Textile and Garment Manufacturers Association.

Singapore itself, with 524 apparel companies employing over 30,000 people and turning out over $510 million in goods annually, is the leading fashion producer in this part of the world.[13] Many American designers and manufacturers cite Singapore's shipping facilities, technology, work ethic, and political stability as reasons for its popularity. Thus far, however, despite its excellent reputation and success in turning out casual sporty clothes, Singapore has failed to find its fashion personality. Several industry experts believe that Singapore could become a fashion capital once it finds its particular niche.[14]

India

India's centuries-old textile industry continues to make it a major force in the Asian textile market. It is the home of the largest handloom industry in the world. Over 13.5 million handlooms are in operation in India. Cotton and silk are the strongest growth areas of the Indian textile industry. India is the only country in the world that produces all

Exquisite Indian silks and embroidered cottons make fashions from India unique and full of fashion excitement.

four silk varieties: mulberry, tussah, eriand, and muga. Its textile industry employs 10 million people, second only to the number who work in agriculture.

The Trade Development Council of India conducts promotions and fashion events with major retailers and assists American and European designers in developing sourcing contacts in India.[15]

Recognizing the need for professionally trained personnel, the Indian government, in collaboration with the Fashion Institute of Technology in New York City, has sponsored the National Institute of Fashion Technology (NIFT), a specialized college of design and technology.

REFERENCES

[1] Susan Heller Anderson, "The Sun Never Sets on His Empires," *The New York Times,* September 6, 1981, p. F5.

[2] Dennis Thim, "Chambre Goal: Raise RTW Image," *Women's Wear Daily,* December 18, 1987, p. 11.

[3] Michael Gross, "Moonlighting's in Fashion for Italy's Top Designer," *New York Times,* March 16, 1987, p. C12.

[4] Madge Garland, *The Changing Form of Fashion.* Praeger Publishers, New York, 1971, p. 73.

[5] James Fallon, "London Building a Fashion Empire," *Women's Wear Daily,* February 17, 1987, p. 30.

[6] Terry Trucco, "Beyond Savile Row," The Business World, *The New York Times Magazine,* Part 2, April 2, 1989, p. 58.

[7] Wendy Green, "German Fashion: Making It a Business," *Women's Wear Daily,* December 30, 1985, pp. 30, 31.

[8] Pat Kivestu and Angela Kryhul, "Toronto Fair Makes a Fashion Impact," *Women's Wear Daily,* April 24, 1987, p. 12.

[9] Cathy Netherwood, "Hong Kong Fair Gets a Hot Start," *Women's Wear Daily,* January 13, 1988, p. 14.

[10] Ibid., p. 14.

[11] Paul Charles Ehrlich, "The China Connection," *Women's Wear Daily,* September 28, 1987, p. 19.

[12] Ibid., p. 19.

[13] Christine Bookalill, "Singapore Show Gets $14.5M in Orders," *Women's Wear Daily,* April 15, 1987, p. 25.

[14] Christine Bookalill, "Singapore Fashion Week," *Women's Wear Daily,* April 22, 1987, p. 16.

[15] Dianne M. Pagoda, "India: Balancing Old and New," *Women's Wear Daily,* September 28, 1987, p. 12.

MERCHANDISING VOCABULARY

Define or briefly explain the following terms:

Boutique	Couturier	Haute couture
Caution	Couturière	Prêt-à-porter
Couture house	Créateur	

MERCHANDISING REVIEW

1. Name and describe the two levels of fashion design in France.
2. What are the most important functions of the Chambre Syndicale?
3. What four types of customers attend the couture trade shows?
4. What business activities have the Paris couture houses undertaken to offset the decline in sales of haute couture clothing?
5. Name the fashion products for which Italy is considered a leader.

6. Describe the development of the British women's ready-to-wear industry since the 1960s.
7. What is West Germany's current fashion image?
8. Name the fashion products for which Scandinavia and Canada are known.
9. Why have Central and South America recently become international fashion markets?
10. What are the distinctive characteristics of Japanese fashion design?

MERCHANDISING DIGEST

1. The reputation of Paris as a prime source of fashion inspiration began to develop several centuries ago as the result of many interrelating factors. Identify those factors and discuss their importance in the development of any major fashion design center.
2. What major countries make up the Far East? Discuss the importance of that geographic area to producers and retailers to fashion goods.

GLOBAL SOURCING

A major development of the 1980s was that the fashion industry became truly global, so much so that those who work in the business invented a term to describe the process of shopping for and purchasing imported goods: **global sourcing.** When a country, such as the United States, buys foreign goods, it **imports** them. The country that furnishes the goods **exports** them. Most countries are both importers and exporters, although, as we shall see, they do not necessarily do each activity in equal amounts.

Both retailers and customers have learned to expect the variety and sophistication that imports provide. The world of international trading is undeniably a fascinating one; this is its great appeal. For many years, though, in the fashion industry, the extent of foreign buying had consisted of buyers traveling to France a few times a year for the haute couture shows. Even then, very few Americans actually bought haute couture for their personal use. Buyers bought ideas and patterns—and then came home to have them produced by American manufacturers. Eventually, as the world experienced a strong and growing post-World War II economy, other European countries, Italy at first, and then other Western European nations, developed their own fashion industries and began luring foreign—that is, American—buyers.

The rest of the world soon followed. The Orient, long a source of import goods in home furnishings and a few other specialized areas, went after the U.S. fashion market. The Central and South American countries have been the most recent to tap into the mother lode that many consider the American fashion consumer market to be.

Today, American buyers have expanded their sources to cover, quite literally, the globe. There is no place in the world that American apparel buyers do not travel to in order to obtain goods. Where the Far Eastern circuit once meant shopping the markets in Hong Kong and

Taiwan for raw materials, it now also means traveling to Japan for high fashion and places such as Sri Lanka, Indonesia, Malaysia, and the Philippines for their growing number of fashion specialties. American buyers have learned to use a global market to their advantage, molding it to current trends such as private-label manufacturing and specification ordering. They have learned to work their way through the labyrinth of federal and international restrictions that regulate international trade.

IMPORTING BY RETAILERS

Retailers are the primary importers of foreign goods in the fashion industry, although manufacturers have also begun to seek global sourcing. Retailers like imports for several reasons: their uniqueness, quality, cost, and the variety they add to their stock. In a time when department stores such as Bloomingdale's and Neiman-Marcus can turn a lackluster year into a blockbuster year by sponsoring a storewide, foreign-theme promotion such as Bloomingdale's 1988 Chinese "Year of the Dragon" campaign, retailers are well aware of the advantageous uses of imports. They constantly seek merchandise that will make their stores stand out in special and unique ways that will set them apart from the competition. Foreign merchandise often fills that bill.

Global sourcing is a complex and often complicated business. What makes a foreign source attractive—its low cost and promise of higher profits—can be lost or diminished in a matter of minutes if something goes wrong. A shipment of dresses can languish in a warehouse in Sri Lanka, for example, if the importer has not paid attention to quotas. In the Caribbean, a man's pants with a flap but no pocket can suddenly be reclassified at a higher duty rate because of the nonfunctional flap.[1]

Anyone who intends to buy goods from a foreign country needs to have a thorough knowledge of its local laws and regulations, particularly the laws that regulate exporting and importing, the efficiency of the transportation system, and the availability and skill of the labor force. The buyer must be well-versed on the tax system and exchange rates. He or she must understand local and national customs and must be well-informed about the current political and economic climate. Finally, he or she must be up-to-date on U.S. import-export regulations, including any pending legislation,[2] and must know all this for any country in which he or she intends to do business. This is why importing is best done by someone with entree to good suppliers and extensive experience in dealing with foreign manufacturers and import regulations.

To gain entree to foreign fashion markets, as well as to cover them extensively, U.S. buyers rely on the help and experience of intermediaries. These specialists help U.S. buyers shop in the international markets successfully. Foreign-made goods can be purchased:

- In foreign fashion markets.
- By store-owned foreign buying offices.
- By commissionaires or independent agents.
- At import fairs held in the United States.
- By importers.

Buyers' Visits to Foreign Fashion Markets

Buyers like and need to travel to foreign fashion markets so they can observe new trends first-hand and buy goods suited to their customers. The interna-

There are 5 million people and 60 thousand factories in Hong Kong.

But we were there to meet only one man, who still made jewelry that was simply one-of-a-kind.

To reach him we would have to go to the much less populous New Territories.

Where, thanks to a typhoon in the South China Sea, roads were rivers.

Fortunately, at Bloomingdale's, to find truly unique merchandise we're not only prepared to travel halfway around the world.

We're quite willing to get our feet wet.

"*Where is the man who makes this jewelry?*" *I said.*

"*Not far,*" *answered my guide,* "*but the roads are a bit wet this time of year.*"

bloomingdale's

No one goes as far as we do.

© 1988 Bloomingdale's, Inc.

Traveling the globe in both good and bad situations is an everyday experience for today's buyers.

tional markets offer a variety of goods, but not all of them are suited to the American marketplace. By personally shopping in international markets, often during fashion weeks, American buyers can be sure that they are obtaining goods that will sell at home. They are also able to soak up the cultural and social climates of the countries to which they travel, which, in turn, helps them translate what is new and exciting to their customers.

Store-Owned Foreign Buying Offices

Some stores—those that are large enough to do so or whose image is very special—own and maintain their own foreign buying offices. Buyers who work in these offices support the work of domestic buyers by surveying the market for new trends, advising store buyers, supervising purchases, and following up on delivery. Because they are an extension of the store, buyers in foreign buying offices are often authorized to make purchases just as domestic buyers are when they shop in foreign and domestic markets. Stores generally locate their buying offices in major fashion capitals such as Paris, Rome, London, Hong Kong, and Tokyo, from which their buyers can travel to smaller markets around the world.

Macy's, BAT, and the May Company all maintain store-owned buying offices, as do the big general-merchandise chains such as Sears and JC Penney. Some stores subscribe to the services of independently owned buying offices with foreign facilities such as Frederick Atkins and the Associated Merchandising Corporation, which shop exclusively for their member stores.

Foreign Commissionaires or Agents

In contrast to store-owned foreign buying offices are **commissionaires,** or foreign-owned independent agents. Commissionaires, whose offices are also located in key buying cities, tend to be smaller than store-owned offices. Commissionaires also represent both retailers and manufacturers.

Apart from these differences, though, they provide many of the same services as store-owned foreign buying offices.

They often have specialized buyers, or market representatives, who work closely with clients, keeping them abreast of what is generally available and helping them locate specific goods. As is the case with store-owned buying offices, a substantial part of the staff's time is spent following up on purchases to make sure they are delivered when they are needed. If the purchase is part of a new trend, stores need the goods when they are still new and customers are still eager to buy them. If it is part of a foreign theme promotion, goods must be delivered while the promotion is in progress. Delivery—especially timely delivery—has been a major problem with imported goods.

Unlike store buyers, who are authorized to purchase on the store's behalf, commissionaires do not purchase unless they have been authorized to do so.

Commissionaires are paid on a fee basis. Usually, they take a percentage of the **first cost,** or wholesale price, in the country of origin.

Foreign Import Fairs in the United States

A newer way to buy foreign goods is to attend one or more of the foreign import fairs that are now regularly held in the United States. Many foreign countries now participate in such shows or stage their own fashion fairs in the United States. The New York Pret—a semiannual event in New York City—is one of the largest and most prestigious of these United States–based shows.

These shows perform two important functions. First, they give foreign manufacturers and designers the same chance to observe American culture that Americans get when they buy in foreign fashion markets. The result is usually closer collaboration between buyers and manufacturers to adapt styles and quality to American tastes. Second, they increase the size and depth of the import market by giving buyers of small and intermediate-sized stores who would not ordinarily tap into the foreign market a chance to do so. To provide their customers with imported merchandise, these buyers need not maintain foreign representatives or shop in the foreign markets, neither of which would be cost-effective for their operations.

American Importers

Last but hardly least in a market that relies increasingly on foreign goods, American buyers purchase from American-owned importing firms. Import firms shop in the international markets to purchase their own "lines," which they put together and display to retailers. Shopping these lines gives small retailers an opportunity to purchase foreign fashion merchandise that would not otherwise be available to them. The only drawback to this method is that it does not allow for the customized ordering that buyers from big stores and chains have come to expect.

SPECIFICATION AND PRIVATE-LABEL BUYING

Many retail operations have learned that they can, with careful planning and supervision, also do specification and private-label buying from foreign sources.

Specification buying is a type of purchasing that is done to the store's rather than the manufacturer's standards. Retailers provide the standards and guidelines for the manufacture of clothes they order. Standards cover everything from the quality of materials and workmanship to styling and cost.

Today, computer-aided designs are a critical component of the global specification buying scene.

Clothes made to specification by foreign producers must also conform to an array of industry and government standards. In fact, specification buying has become so specialized that many stores now employ a **specification manager** or **product manager** who is trained in specification buying. While keeping an eye on industry and government standards, specification managers work closely with manufacturers to ensure that their ventures will be economically successful for both the retailer and the manufacturer.

As they grow more successful with specification buying, stores have begun to use it for their private-label lines. Initially intended as a way to keep production at home, a growing amount of private-label stock is now purchased offshore. When stores began to pit their private-label merchandise against national brands, they often found that foreign manufacture was one way to control the cost.

Whether it is done at home or abroad, though, private-label manufacturing must be done right. Not only does private-label merchandise compete with national brands, but these days, when a customer buys a store's label, he or she is buying the store's image.

Among the special concerns that arise when private-label goods are manufactured offshore are the quality of the merchandise and the need to meet delivery schedules. Foreign producers are learning to meet American quality standards, but they are still likely to lose out to American manufacturers over delivery time.

IMPORTING BY MANUFACTURERS

Even though American manufacturers continue to be upset about the growth of direct importing done by retailers, they have increasingly turned to offshore sources. They maintain they are forced into global sourcing by high domestic labor costs and competition from other importers, such as retailers who do specification and private-label buying in large quantities. Manufacturer importing has become so pervasive that in 1984, after years of opposing imports, the American Apparel Manufacturers Association announced that its members should consider offshore sources as legitimate suppliers.

Manufacturers import for the same reasons that retailers do: price advantage, exclusivity, workmanship. Many manufacturers say the most important factor in the decision to import is the need to get the product made in the best possible way for the least amount of money, something that has not always been possible with domestic manufacture in recent years. Alfred Fusco, chairman of the Palm Beach Company, described what many see as an industrywide problem with U.S. apparel manufacturers over the past few years: "In the United States manufacturers want to mass-produce one style of blouse, and they tell us what their needs are, and

what we should be doing, instead of letting us design . . . what we want."[3]

INTERNATIONAL BALANCE OF TRADE

Just as there are two sides to every coin, there are also two sides to the global market. Throughout the early 1980s, the expanding international market seemed to work to everyone's advantage. The global market came about largely because the early 1980s were a period of prosperity at home and abroad. There was nothing wrong with a fashion market that was truly international so long as a balance was maintained between exports—what Americans sold abroad—and imports—what they bought abroad. For several decades, foreign countries were eager to import American-made goods, which were much sought-after for their high quality.

Unfortunately, by the mid-1980s, the down side of a global market—what happened when the trade balance shifted—revealed itself. The American dollar grew weak, which meant that American goods became expensive, often too expensive to be of interest for export. The American reputation for producing quality goods suffered by comparison as other nations learned how to turn out quality products. The Japanese were soon beating Americans at their own game—cars and electronics. And the clothing industry proved itself woefully inept at competing at all. At first, Americans bought foreign clothes because they were so much cheaper than domestically produced goods. Eventually, though, they began to buy them because of their excellent quality. In fact, for certain kinds of sophisticated workmanship, industry experts agree, domestic manufacturers have not proven themselves equal to the task.[4]

When the dollar weakened, foreign countries only increased their exports to the United States. The resulting tidal wave of imports caused severe trauma to American industry generally and to the U.S. apparel manufacturing industry specifically. As foreign producers gained ground, domestic producers lost out. Imports, which accounted for a then shocking one-fourth of all consumption in 1982, are expected to grow to an even more incredible two-thirds of all consumption by 1995.[5]

The story of the global market, however, encompasses much more than a few cold statistics, however telling they may be. It is also the story of how the fashion business lost its competitive edge and then began, as it is now doing, to rebound.

In order to understand what can go wrong in the import-export market, it is important to know something about the **balance of trade.** This is the difference between the value of exports and the value of imports. When the value of goods that a country imports exceeds the value of its exports, it experiences a **trade deficit.** When a country's exports exceed its imports, it has a **trade surplus.** Since the mid-1980s, the United States has imported more from the Japanese than it has sold to them. Thus, the United States has suffered from a trade deficit with Japan, while Japan has experienced a trade surplus with the United States. A trade surplus is advantageous; a trade deficit hurts a country's economy. See the chart below.

The United States' deficit problems are not limited to Japan. In recent years, the United States has become the world's largest clothing importer, buying nearly one-third of all the imported clothing in the world. Hong Kong, in contrast, a British colony that operates as a free port, is the world's largest exporter in dollar volume. Nearly one-seventh of the world's clothing exports come from this 400-square-mile area.[6]

The United States is not the only country with deficit problems. Around the world, trade statistics show that the industrial countries are relying more and more on imports while the developing countries are becoming the ex-

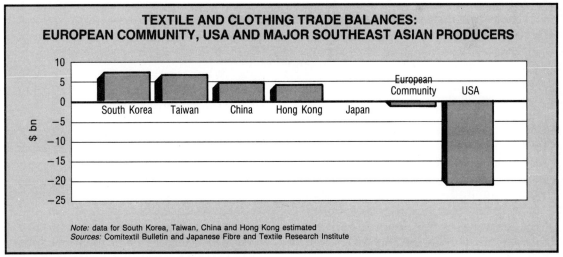

TEXTILE AND CLOTHING TRADE BALANCES: EUROPEAN COMMUNITY, USA AND MAJOR SOUTHEAST ASIAN PRODUCERS

Note: data for South Korea, Taiwan, China and Hong Kong estimated
Sources: Comitextil Bulletin and Japanese Fibre and Textile Research Institute

Textile Outlook International, July 1987. The Economist Publications Limited

porters. Although indications are that the growth in the U.S. trade deficit has slowed, the United States remains the single largest contributor to the world trade imbalance.

The traditional restraints on consumers to purchase domestic goods—a devalued dollar and heightened tariffs—seem to have done little to slow the American public's craving for foreign goods. While the promotion "Crafted with Pride in the U.S.A.," which urges Americans to buy American, has created a sentimental support for buying domestic goods, consumers seen unable to resist foreign goods at the point of purchase. And why should they? They are part of a 25-year-old trend in which foreign goods have been viewed with special glamour and status regardless of what they cost.

As a result, some people believe that sterner measures—higher tariffs and stricter import quotas among them—are necessary to protect American industry from imports. Others oppose such measures. They argue that the real problem is the inefficiency of American industry, which will not be made stronger by import restrictions. These two groups belong to two opposing schools of ideological thought regarding the conduct of American business.

Protectionism is the name given to an economic and political doctrine that seeks to exclude or limit foreign goods. The opposing doctrine, **free trade,** supports the free exchange of goods among nations. Since the balance of trade affects the nation's economic health, and the federal government is constantly passing and revising legislation about importing and exporting, advocates of both doctrines are well represented in Washington, D.C., by lobbyists who seek to promote legislation supporting their views.

Protectionism

The first import restrictions on goods brought into the country date back to 1789, when the United States, a newly founded republic which was still mostly rural, feared that it would not be able to compete with the world's industrial powers. To reduce its considerable reliance on imported goods, it slapped a 50 percent tariff, or import tax, on seventy different articles imported from France and England. Tariffs have come and gone, but the debate over whether protectionism is good—or necessary—has persisted for the 200 intervening years.

In the fashion industry, the leading supporters of protectionist legislation are manufacturers, who are most hurt when Americans buy imported rather than domestic goods. Industry trade associations and unions offer the most organized support for protectionism. Most consumers recognize their work through their consumer campaigns, "Crafted with Pride" and "Made in the U.S.A." which encourage people to buy American. But the manufacturers have also mounted a behind-the-scenes campaign designed to inform retailers about the advantages of buying domestically produced goods.

The industry has also changed its attitude in recent years, moving from a "Here's what we can do for you" stance to a "What can we do for you?" posture. Among industry strategies for promoting domestic buying are a renewed emphasis on quality and a new emphasis on flexibility.

Free Trade

Free traders believe that restrictions on trade will threaten the nation's ability to grow and compete in the global marketplace. Retailers and most consumers are among those who support free trade.

The Trouble With Imports Is That It Takes Months To Move The Junk.

Our fabrics are on hand, not on water. So we can send 500 yards or more of your favorite fabrics in Kodel® polyester and cotton blends immediately. Even our exclusive prints have shorter lead times than imports. So don't wait. Call Hank Grossman at 212-556-6191. *From the company you thought you knew so well.*

Springs

KODEL is an Eastman Kodak Company reg. TM.   Apparel Fabrics Division, 104 West 40th Street, New York 10018   © 1986 Springs Industries, Inc.

Quick Response is based on having the merchandise quickly—when the customer wants it! In this trade ad a USA textile firm informs manufacturers that wanted fabrics are on hand—not on the water.

They believe the buying public should be free to buy imported as well as domestic goods.

Except for those times when protectionists are active, free traders do not do much to promote their cause. When the domestic apparel industry began to demand trade restrictions in the mid-1980s, free trade advocates organized in response. Retail associations in all 50 states, along with hundreds of corporate members, organized the Retail Industry Trade Action Coalition in 1985. It serves as the retail industry's lobbying arm in Washington, D.C. A counterbalance to the textile and apparel manufacturers, they promote their basic tenet that unfettered economic expansion means greater economic growth, which, in turn, translates into prosperity for the consumer and retailer.[7]

The struggle over free trade versus protectionism is played out in several arenas, such as international trading laws, U.S. regulations, and preferential programs sponsored by various trading nations.

INTERNATIONAL TRADING LAWS

In 1947, the United States and 23 other nations met in Geneva, Switzerland, to write an agreement known as the General Agreement on Tariffs and Trade, or GATT. Since then, the world's nations have practiced far more free trade than protectionism. Under the liberal trading terms of GATT, many countries have enjoyed unprecedented prosperity. In the past decade, however, faced with growing trade deficits worldwide and wildly fluctuating currencies in such previously stable economies as the United States, nations have once again begun to erect trade barriers. And as trade barriers have gone up, nations have begun to supplement trade agreements like GATT with individual trade treaties with one another.

A **bilateral agreement** is one in which two countries reach a separate agreement regarding their trade arrangements. The United States has negotiated one-on-one trade treaties over the past few years with its five major Asian suppliers—Hong Kong, Taiwan, China, Japan, and South Korea. These treaties have been successful in reducing the general level of imports to the United States from these countries, but at the same time, other countries such as Indonesia, Malaysia, Singapore, and the Philippines have taken up the slack, so there have been no overall reductions in imports from these areas.[8]

General Agreement on Tariffs and Trade (GATT)

Since its initiation in 1947, the number of GATT countries has grown from 23 to 92. GATT has played a major role in reducing trade barriers and unifying trading practices among member nations.

GATT representatives meet every few years to negotiate new trade arrangements among member nations. At most meetings, the main order of business has been to interpret GATT regulations, but the GATT session in 1986 was an ambitious departure from past negotiating sessions. GATT representatives set about overhauling the present trading rules, an action they thought was necessary to forestall the growing demand for protectionism and to cope with the problems that have resulted from the emergence of a truly global economy. The new rules, impressive on paper, will matter little, however, if governments go their individual ways and seek out bilateral trade agreements.

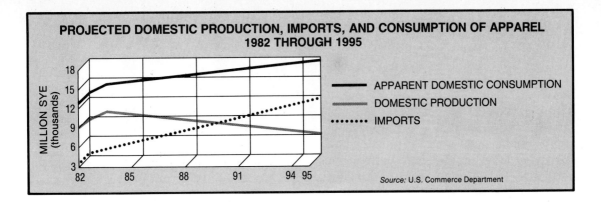

PROJECTED DOMESTIC PRODUCTION, IMPORTS, AND CONSUMPTION OF APPAREL
1982 THROUGH 1995

MILLION SYE (thousands)

APPARENT DOMESTIC CONSUMPTION
DOMESTIC PRODUCTION
IMPORTS

Source: U.S. Commerce Department

Multi-Fiber and Textile Arrangement (MFA)

In 1973, the United States and 53 other nations signed the first multinational agreement specifically regulating the flow of textile products. A primary purpose of the agreement was to establish ground rules for bilateral agreements and unilateral actions designed to restrict the free flow of these products.

The MFA was renewed twice without any essential changes in its stated purpose or goals. It was also renewed in 1986, but this time not without controversy. The 1986 renewal attempted to deal with two changes in the status of textile trade: (1) growing pressure in the United States to enact tighter quotas on textile imports and (2) United States' insistence that the Big Three textile-importing nations—Hong Kong, Korea, and Taiwan—revise their bilateral agreements with the United States.

Despite the substantial revision, many American producers feel it does not give them the measure of relief they sought. They point out, for example, that the MFA limits the number of units that can be brought into the country rather than the cost value of merchandise. Faced with quantity limits, many foreign producers have merely shifted to higher-priced merchandise, a move that hurts the domestic market even more than limiting cheap imports does.

Future Trends in Regulation

On the one hand, the growing concern among U.S. producers over competition from both inexpensive and high-priced apparel and textile imports is not likely to abate, at least not until the domestic industry gets back on its feet through its own initiative or gets some relief in the form of protectionist regulation. If imports continue to grow at their present rate, they will soon account for over 65 percent of men's, women's, and children's wear.[9]

On the other hand, those who support free trade worry about the effects of restrictive legislation, some of which is likely to be passed. They argue that it will not work. Americans, for example, have proven unwilling to stop buying foreign goods, even when the price goes up. If they did stop buying, this might trigger a recession. And free trade supporters fear that any recession will be worldwide since the nations' economies are so interlocked after over 40 years of relatively unrestricted trade. Free trade supporters also worry that other nations may retaliate if the United States enacts overly restrictive trade barriers.

FASHION

When we think of exciting, glamorous, captivating, pulsating fashion capitals of the world . . . Prague, Czechoslovakia is not the first one that comes to mind. But, in September 1985, one of fashion's most exciting, glamorous, pulsating names was opening a shop there, the first for a Western manufacturer since the start of the Communist regime in 1948. The name was Benetton—an outstanding example of global sourcing and marketing.

The store in Prague was one of the most exotic offspring of the Benetton Group, the Italian corporation whose sudden appearance and resounding success has caused a sensation in the international fashion industry and has made Benetton the subject of Harvard Business School case studies.

There are Benetton stores in over 79 countries, and over 700 stores in the United States alone. Pretty terrific for a small Italian family enterprise, consisting of Luciano Benetton the oldest brother, and the sparkplug of ideas and concepts, his sister Giuliana, and their younger brother, Gilberto and Carlo. Ben-

FOCUS

etton had its start in 1965 and is today one of the largest knitwear manufacturers and marketers in the world.

To do this, Luciano Benetton travels the world, and when he travels he spends a lot of time walking the sidewalks of the cities of the world, studying the ins and outs of street fashion and trying to hear that "special buzz" that shows the direction of fashion trends.

Benetton delegates a large percentage of work to a network of contractors and subcontractors located mostly in small towns in northern Italy. However, recently, Benetton has found its way into other parts of the world and has established contractors in Hong Kong, Taiwan, and Korea.

Benetton has always held the concept of a global customer, believing that what is attractive to their target customer in Asia will be just as attractive to their customers in Europe, South America, and North America. What Benetton is offering clearly appeals to people all over the world.

Two terrific advertising campaigns fixed the image of Benetton in the eyes of the world. One showed crowds of children of all races and nationalities wearing Benetton clothes—with the slogan—"Benetton, All the Colors in the World." The second one showed the same inter-racial crowds of children wearing Benetton clothes, and the flags of the various countries, with the slogan "United Colors of Benetton." With this type of advertising, it is no wonder that Benetton truly represents a global image.

In 1988, the Benetton management decided to try a new marketing approach, and decided to have less growth in the number of stores . . . moving from more stores to better stores. They opened superstores that were four and five times larger than the usual Benetton store and called them "United Colors." However, large or small, the global image of the Benetton label and the international spirit of the company will lead the way for other innovative, risk-takers to look at fashion merchandising from a global perspective.

This fashion focus is based upon the following articles:

"Benetton Targets a New Customer—Wall Street," *Business Week,* May 29, 1989, p. 32.

Peter Fuhrman, "Benetton Learns to Darn," *Forbes,* October 3, 1988, pp. 122–123.

Phyllis Furman, "The New Colors for Benetton," *Crain's New York Business,* September 19, 1988, p. 1 and p. 32.

Andrea Lee, "Profiles: Being Everywhere," *The New Yorker,* November 10, 1986, pp. 53–74.

David Orgel, "Benetton Plans Expansion of 'Superstores'," *Daily News Record (DNR),* September 15, 1988, p. 14.

Dara Schechter, "Margins Are Thinning at Benneton's" *Women's Wear Daily,* April 27, 1989, p. 18.

U.S. REGULATION OF TEXTILE AND APPAREL IMPORTS

Some of the specific measures the United States—or any other country—is liable to undertake or has undertaken to promote its own trade interests are tariffs and duties, quotas, and preferential programs.

Taxes: Tariffs and Duties

Most fashion merchandise is subject to an import tax, called a **duty** or **tariff.** This is a fee assessed by the government on certain goods that it wishes to restrict or limit. Tariffs and duties are imposed on imported goods that the government wishes to make more competitive in price with domestically produced goods. The tax varies depending upon the category of merchandise, but it is usually a percentage of the first cost.

Import Quotas

Import quotas are limits set to restrict the number of specific goods that may be brought into the country for a specific period of time. Quotas, which are established either by presidential proclamation or legislation, are either absolute or tariff-rate.

Absolute Quotas

Absolute quotas limit the quantity of goods that may enter the United States. When the limit is reached, no more goods of that kind may be imported until the quota period ends. Absolute quotas may be global or directed to specific countries. Imports in excess of a quota may be exported or detained for entry during the next quota period.

Tariff-Rate Quotas

Tariff-rate quotas set a limit after which a higher duty is charged on goods entering the country. When a certain number of goods have entered at the lower rate, customs raises the duty on any additional goods, which, in effect, also raises their price in the market.

PREFERENTIAL PROGRAMS

Over the years, the United States has been a proponent of aid to developing countries. Among the incentives offered in its many preferential programs is one that permits the imports from certain favored nations to enter the country quota- and duty-free.

Tariff Schedules 807 and 807A

These two tariff schedules provide for preferential access of goods that originate or are partly manufactured in the United States and are also partially made abroad. These schedules favor American manufacturers. Item 807 of the United States tariff schedule allows cut piece goods and trim items to be exported from the United States, assembled or sewn abroad, and then returned to United States with duties owed only on the value that was added abroad. In other words, duty is paid only on the labor that was done abroad.[10]

A revision, 807A, requires that the piece goods taken out of the country be of U.S. origin. Approximately 80 percent of the value of 807A exports comes from the United States. 807A is also referred to as Super 807, because it provides special access for goods that are domestically cut and made of U.S. fabrics.

These two provisions have proven helpful to domestic manufacturers. In many instances, items produced under 807 and 807A cost less than items produced entirely in the Far East.[11] Items produced under 807 and 807A must bear a special label. "Assembled in——of U.S. components" is the most common form of the label.

Caribbean Basin Initiative

Latin American imports have been an area of growing concern to Americans. The import of textiles, apparel, and footwear has increased a phenomenal 80 percent in less than a decade.[12] While U.S. manufacturers worry that a flood of imports from Latin America will hurt domestic industry, Americans also have a special interest in promoting their neighbors' economic development. The Caribbean Basin Initiative (CBI) was designed to do two things: offer trade protection to U. S. manufacturers at the same time it encourages the growth of an import industry in Latin America.

Passed in 1983 with an expiration date of 1995, the CBI is designed to permit the one-way, duty-free entry of goods from 21 beneficiary countries to the United States once certain conditions are met. These are:

1. The product must be imported directly into the United States.

2. The appraised value of the product must have been raised by at least 35 percent in one or more CBI countries.

3. Any product that includes foreign components from countries other than CBI members must have been substantially transformed into a "new and different article of commerce" by a CBI country before entry into the United States.

PENETRATION OF THE UNITED STATES ECONOMY BY FOREIGN INVESTORS

The dramatic drop in the dollar since the mid-1980s together with the stock market crash in 1987 have made direct investment in U.S. properties and businesses extremely attractive to foreigners. The imposition of quotas in the textile and apparel industries has been a further incentive for foreign buyers to use their surplus dollars to buy American companies.

To date, most of the investment has been by West Germany and Japan. Japan's investment in the United States grew by more than $23 billion, or 21.3 percent in 1986 alone. West Germany invested $17 billion for a growth rate of more than 17 percent.[13]

Foreign Manufacturers

Since so many textiles and apparel items are imported in the United States, foreign investors have long been interested in buying into American textile and apparel manufacturing companies. Only recently have they succeeded in doing so. Foreign investors, mostly from Europe and the Far East, have taken two routes to ownership: joint ventures and total ownership.

In 1981, Sanyo Shokai, Ltd., became the first totally Japanese-owned apparel manufacturing company in the United States when it opened a $4.2 million, state-of-the-art sewing facility in Oneonta, New York. The factory, which employs 110 workers, sells rainwear under the Sanyo label through the company's U.S. subsidiary, Sanyo Fashion House.[14]

In 1988, Tal Apparel Ltd., a Hong Kong manufacturer with an estimated annual sales of $169 million, bought a 900-employee plant from Burlington Industry. South Korean interests own the Kunja Industrial Company, a sweater factory, and Jonesville Fancy Yarns Mills, an upholstery fabric company, in South Carolina.[15]

Licensing

Actually, investment by foreign manufacturers in the fashion industry is not entirely new. Licensing arrangements, which often involve ownership of American companies, were initiated over 25 years ago by companies such as Christian Dior, Pierre Cardin, and Hubert Givenchy.

Foreign Retailers

While the purchasing of manufacturers is a relatively new form of foreign investment, many retail operations have been foreign-owned for some time, and there is even more activity in this sector than in manufacturing. Saks Fifth Avenue has been owned by the British-based BAT Industries for years, and they recently bought Marshall Field. Other foreign firms active in retailing in the United States are Australia's Hooker Corporation, which owns Bonwit Teller and B. Altman in New York, Sakowitz in Texas, and The Parisian in Birmingham, Alabama, and the Netherlands company, Vendex, which has minority ownership shares in Dillard Department Stores. Two other relatively recent foreign retailing successes are Laura Ashley, which is British-owned and Benetton, which is Italian-owned. Even newer to the retail scene is Britain's famous retail chain Marks and Spencer, which through its Canadian subsidiary owns and operates several stores in upstate New York called D'Allairds.[16]

The largest and most impressive foreign penetration, however, has been that of the Campeau Corporation of Canada. In 1986, they bought Allied Stores, and in 1988, they outbid Macy's Corporation in a bitter takeover battle to buy Federated Department Stores. After the purchase, they sold Brooks Brothers, the prestigious menswear retailer, to England's Marks and Spencer.

PENETRATION OF FOREIGN MARKETS BY U.S. COMPANIES

In order to counterbalance foreign investment, American business has been interested in investing in foreign countries, where their management is often welcomed because American know-how and standards for high quality are much-respected commodities. U.S. investment in foreign countries also helps the balance of trade.

Licensing

Just as foreign manufacturers first penetrated the U.S. retail market with licensed products, so too, have American companies been able to license products abroad. American products such as Mickey Mouse, Kermit the Frog, Superman, and Miss Piggy have been great successes as licensing ventures.

Joint Ownership

While the United States permits total ownership by foreign investors, most other countries only allow foreign investors to be partners or joint owners. Among the American companies that are joint owners in foreign manufacturing firms is Blue Bell, producer of Wrangler jeans in Asia, Italy, and Spain.

U.S. EXPORTING

Because the "Made in the U.S.A." label is desirable all over the world, the United States can export its fashion products around the globe. Increased U.S. exports, in fact, are seen by many industry experts as the solution to the U.S. trade deficit. The United States does not need to keep out foreign competitors as much as it needs to sell and promote its products abroad.

Naturally, when the United States exports its goods, it is often subjected to the same kinds of trade restrictions that it imposes on other countries. U.S. manufacturers seeking to export their products must work their way through a maze of foreign country quota, duty, and tariff regulations.

Because the United States is a major industrial giant, it is not the beneficiary of foreign-sponsored preferential programs such as it frequently sponsors for other nations. But recently, many domestic programs have been developed to help U.S. manufacturers become more successful exporters. The new programs are usually sponsored by the federal and state departments of commerce.

One active program is the Textile and Apparel Export Expansion Program, sponsored by the U.S. Department of Commerce. At the Fashion Institute of Technology, the Export Advisory Service Extension (EASE) maintains an active program for fashion industry exporters. EASE counsels individual manufacturers on the advisability of exporting their products and through conferences, workshops, and seminars, works closely with members of the fashion industry to encourage exporting.

With programs like EASE, there is every reason to believe that the American textile and apparel industry will soon be a major player in the global economy. The industry, caught unawares by the tidal wave of imports, is only now beginning to realize that it has something to give back. What it has to give the world is its expertise and know-how in manufacturing that most American of products—fashion.

REFERENCES

[1] Manuel Gaetan, "Going for the Gold in 807/CBI," *Bobbin,* June, 1988, p. 88.

[2] Ibid, p. 92.

[3] Interview with Alfred Fusco, chairman of the Palm Beach Company.

[4] Allan Klinger, "The 807 and 807A Production Alternatives," *Body Fashions, Intimate Apparel,* February 1987, p. 19.

[5] U.S. Department of Commerce, Washington, D.C.

[6] Robert Hartlein, "Allure of Asia Continues High for U.S. Firms," *Women's Wear Daily,* February 24, 1988, p. 11.

[7] Hank Gilman, "More Apparel Makers Turn Abroad," *The Wall Street Journal,* May 9, 1985, p. 6.

[8] Manuel Gaetan, "The Source Be With You," *Bobbin,* May 1987, p. 132.

[9] Hartlein, p. 11.

[10] Textile Outlook International, *The Economist Publications Limited,* July 1987, p. 18.

[11] Anne Imperato Colgate, "The Other Side of the Story," *Bobbin,* October 1987.

[12] Industry statistic supplied by Office of Textiles and Apparel (OTEXA), United States Department of Commerce, Washington, D.C.

[13] Robert A. Armstrong, "Sale-Priced U.S. Assets Pulling Foreign Cash," *Women's Wear Daily*, February 11, 1988, p. 13.

[14] "Sanyo Shokai Ready to Open Upstate New York Facility," *Women's Wear Daily*, June 4, 1987, p. 15.

[15] Robert A. Armstrong, "Direct Investment from Overseas on Rise," *Women's Wear Daily*, February 11, 1988, p. 14.

[16] Ellen Forman, "Foreign Interest Grows in U.S. Retail," *Women's Wear Daily*, February 11, 1988, p. 16.

MERCHANDISE VOCABULARY

Define or brief explain the following terms:

Absolute quota	Free trade	Specification manager/
Balance of trade	Global sourcing	product manager
Bilateral agreement	Import	Tariff
Commissionaire	Import quota	Tariff-rate quota
Duty	Protectionism	Trade deficit
Export	Specification buying	Trade surplus
First cost		

MERCHANDISING REVIEW

1. What advantages do imports give retailers?
2. Name the five ways foreign-made fashion merchandise can be purchased.
3. What are the two important functions of foreign import shows in the United States?
4. What are the concerns that arise when retailers do specification buying of private-label merchandise?
5. Describe the "down side" developments that have taken place in the global market since the mid-1980s.
6. Who are the advocates of protectionism in the fashion industry? Why?
7. Who are the advocates of free trade in the fashion industry? Why?
8. What is the purpose of the General Agreement on Tariffs and Trade? The Multi-fiber and Textile Arrangement?
9. What are the provisions of Tariff Schedules 807 and 807A?
10. What forms do American investing in foreign countries fashion industries take?

MERCHANDISING DIGEST

1. As a fashion consumer, do you advocate protectionism or free trade? What major items of your current wardrobe would you have been unable to purchase if broad protective legislation prohibiting imports had been in place?
2. What are the advantages of using a store-owned foreign buying office? A commissionaire?

Exploring
Import Buying

A development of major importance to the U.S. fashion industry is the intensive penetration of imports into our domestic markets. Producers of apparel and textile have proliferated in almost every country in the world and are competing for a larger share of the U.S. consumer dollar.

There have been many efforts to stem this tide of imports as well as many counter efforts to allow it to continue and take the course of allowing free trade. These contradictory efforts depend on who the people are and the types of businesses they represent.

In Part A of this project, you will research the import situation in the U.S. fashion industry and be prepared to discuss the pros and cons of imports from the point of view of the following people:

1. A representative from a consumer's group.

2. A major American sportswear producer (choose a specific one).

3. A CEO of a large retail organization.

4. A representative of a fashion industry union (e.g., ILGWU).

Be prepared to explain and defend your "stand" on imports from the perspective of each of these different people.

In Part B of this project, you will assemble a list of garments and accessories that you yourself have recently bought, and the various countries in which they were produced. Give your reasons for purchasing any of these goods that were made in foreign countries. Do you think that you represent a typical consumer? Why or why not?

UNIT FOUR

the merchandising of fashion

The business of merchandising clothing to the user, or ultimate consumer, is the subject of Unit 4. Like the creation of fashion, the merchandising of fashion is also something of an art. It is the retailer's job to interpret, translate, and display apparel attractively enough to make people want to buy it. Merchandisers must also constantly update and refine their ideas in order to keep the customer interested. The merchandising of apparel is the final step in the process of creating fashion.

Because there are so many types of consumers of fashion, there are also, not surprisingly, many different kinds of retailers. Apparel is sold to consumers by general merchandisers, who market other goods in addition to apparel, and specialty merchandisers, who market only apparel and accessories.

Many thousands of stores sell clothing. Retail apparel stores range from the relatively modest mom-and-pop operation to the sophisticated, full-service department stores such as Macy's and Marshall Field's. Fashion has traditionally been sold in department stores, specialty stores, leased departments, and since the 1960s, in boutiques and franchises.

In Chapter 16, you will study each of the various kinds of retail operations to learn how they function to attract customers. Not all stores can—or want to—attract the same kinds of customers. Stores use their merchandising and operating policies to attract different kinds of customers. An upscale specialty store, for example, will pay attention to its decor, providing its elite customers with a luxurious ambiance in order to support its high prices, whereas a chain operation will emphasize its self-service, bare bones atmosphere as a means of promoting its lower prices.

The new kinds of retailers have helped to revolutionize the merchandising of fashion. In Chapter 17, you will explore the newest trends in retailing and learn how the established, traditional retailers have responded to this competition. Following the lead of chain and discount organizations, most department stores have adapted some form of centralized buying.

Chapter 17 also focuses on the broader changes that have occurred in fashion retailing. Retailers experienced a particularly tumultuous decade in the 1980s, as many department stores changed hands, either merging with other stores or becoming part of department store conglomerates. Other stores were reorganized for greater efficiency or expanded in order to compete on a more equal footing with the conglomerates.

The future of fashion retailing is also examined. Two new kinds of retailers—hypermarkets and electronic shopping—loom on the horizon and are expected to make a major impact on the retailing business in the coming decade.

Chapter 18 focuses on the auxiliary services available to the fashion merchandiser. Retailers have an intense need for information. They must, for example, be constantly engaged in identifying, digesting, and reacting to new trends and ideas. Information is so important to fashion merchandising, in fact, that an array of support services dedicated exclusively to promulgating fashion information has developed over the years.

FASHION RETAILING

Retailing is the business of buying and selling goods to those who will use them, the ultimate consumers. **Fashion retailing** involves the business of buying and selling—or merchandising—apparel and accessories. It is the way clothes are moved from the designer or manufacturer to the customer.

Retailing is in many ways the heart of the fashion industry. It is the most challenging end of the fashion business, existing as it does in a constant state of change. Retailers must, for example, be among the first to spot and act on new trends. They must be attuned to their customers' needs and desires to a degree that is required in few other businesses. Retailers must react to a constantly changing and often unsettled economic climate.

An extraordinary amount of planning and effort goes into the merchandising of fashion products. To take just one example, let's say that paisley scarves have become the hot fall accessory—the one article of clothing that women want most to buy. It is the retailer's responsibility first to estimate demand and then to make sure that enough paisley scarves have been ordered to meet it. Since manufacturers will be making many different kinds of scarves, the retailer must select scarves that will appeal to the customer in terms of style, quality, and price. If the customer is high-end, expensive wool challis or even cashmere paisley scarves can be stocked. If the customer is budget-minded, less expensive polyester paisley scarves will do.

Perhaps most important, the retailer must make sure that the scarves arrive in the stores at the right time—when women are eager to buy them. Women typically shop for fall clothes in late summer and early autumn. Customers will not be eager to buy in December when the fad has begun to wear itself out and paisley scarves no longer look new.

Finally, the retailer needs to let the customers know that the scarves are available and will probably promote them by running newspaper advertisements. All of this effort goes into merchandising a single product—and fashion retailers merchandise not one but thousands of products.

HISTORY AND DEVELOPMENT OF FASHION RETAILING

People have been swapping, trading, or selling each other various goods for thousands of years. In the Orient and eastern Mediterranean lands, bazaars and marketplaces still operate on the sites they have occupied for centuries. Not until the mid-1800s and the opening of the first department store—the Bon Marché in Paris—did modern merchandising as we know it begin to develop. Even then, it developed differently in the United States than in Europe. In this chapter, we shall explore the development of retailing in the United States.

Retailing in the United States grew directly out of the frontier. It was an attempt to meet the needs of countless numbers of settlers who were moving west to populate a huge country. The first settlements in the United States were situated along its eastern coast. There, settlers built cities and towns that resembled what they had left behind in Europe. Philadelphia, New York, and Boston were soon populous centers of commerce and culture. Their shops were patterned after those in London and Paris. On the frontier, however, such sophistication was not possible, nor would it have served the needs of western buyers. Instead, three elements— general stores, peddlers, and mail-order sellers—each uniquely geared to life on the frontier, combined to give birth to modern retailing in the United States.

General Stores

When the West was in the very early stages of settlement, there were no stores—and very few women to buy anything in them anyway. Apart from the settled areas along the East Coast, most of North America was populated by Indians, fur traders, and explorers. Groups of Indians had long traded goods among themselves, and the Europeans who traveled west soon learned to follow suit. They began by trading with Indians, but soon European traders opened trading posts. There, fur traders swapped furs for basic supplies.

Gradually, as the West became more settled, and pioneer men and women moved across the country, trading posts evolved into **general stores.** Where trading posts had carried only such basics as guns, gun parts, and food supplies, general stores sought to expand their stock by adding such goods as saddles, salt pork, lamp oil, and even ladies' bonnets. Money was a scarce commodity on the frontier, so general stores were still willing to take goods as well as cash for payment. A farmer's wife might make bonnets or lace collars to exchange for the few supplies she needed from the general store. As people became more settled, they became interested in buying more than basic supplies, and general stores were soon stocking a greater variety of items such as dress fabric, sewing notions, and fancier bonnets.

Not surprisingly, in a place where life was spartan and store-bought goods were one of life's few pleasures, people liked to linger over their purchases. As a result, general stores also functioned as community social centers as well as gathering places for political debate. To this day, general stores still serve many small communities in rural areas of the United States.

Gradually, as settlers became more prosperous, the general stores stopped bartering and began to operate on a cash-only basis. The new influx of capital could be used for expansion. Over time, some general stores—such as Meier & Frank in Portland, Oregon, and Filene's in Boston—grew into full-fledged department stores.

Peddlers

Even with general stores located in communities and trading posts scattered along well-traveled trails, many homesteads were too isolated to make regular use of them. Itinerant peddlers began to service these remote customers. A peddler visited some areas only once a year, so he was accorded a warm welcome.

In many ways, peddlers were the first marketing experts. In addition to their wares, which typically consisted of pots and pans, shoes and boots, sewing notions, and a few luxury items such as lace, combs, and ribbons, they carried news of the latest fashions being worn in the cities back east. The reverse was also true, and they carried word back east about specific items that pleased or displeased customers in the Midwest or West.

Mail-Order Sellers

The final element in the development of modern retailing was the mail-order seller. Mail-order companies, which began in the late 1800s, serviced the rural areas of the United States. At that time, the United States was largely rural, so

In the latter part of the 19th century, the Montgomery Ward catalogs opened a whole new world of fashion to rural Americans who lived far away from shops.

this meant almost everyone was a mail-order customer. Montgomery Ward, which mailed its first catalog in 1872, was the first company to do the bulk of its business by mail. By 1886, it had a competitor, Sears Roebuck, and the mail-order business was in full swing. Such companies were only able to operate after the establishment of rural free delivery (RFD), a system of free mail delivery to rural areas, and later, parcel post, a system of low-cost mail delivery that replaced RFD.

The mail-order catalog brought a new and expansive world to the lives of rural Americans. Hundreds of fashion items, furnishings for the home, and tools for the farm were offered in the catalogs. The illustrations were clear, goods were described in detail, and best of all, from a farm woman's point of view, prices were reasonable. The catalogs did not offer high fashion, but to rural women their variety and prices were still enough to delight. Women who had been limited to the scant provisions that a peddler was able to carry on his wagon or the barely filled shelves of general stores now felt as if the world was at their fingertips.

By 1895, a mere 9 years after its first issue was mailed, the Sears catalog had expanded to fill 507 pages. The fledgling company posted astonishing sales of $750,000 that year.

Despite the growth of towns and cities, which brought far more cosmopolitan shops to the entire country, the appeal of mail-order shopping never completely lost its luster, and today, mail-order remains a major segment of retail business.

Retailing Today

As the frontier turned into towns and cities, peddlers became sales representatives and general stores and mail-order businesses evolved into something entirely different from their ancestors. Today, hundreds of thousands of retail stores exist to serve the over 248 million consumers in the United States.

TYPES OF FASHION MERCHANDISE RETAILERS

Retailers usually can be classified into one of two broad categories—general and specialized—depending upon the kinds of merchandise they carry. In each of these categories are many different kinds of retail operations: department stores, specialty stores, chain operations, discount stores, and leased departments. Almost all retail stores offer some form of mail-order buying service, and there are also retailers that deal exclusively in mail order. Some stores have grown into giant operations, but many others are still small independently owned and operated business.

The retail scene is dominated by **general merchandise retailers.** These retailers typically sell many kinds of merchandise in addition to clothing. They try to appeal to a broad range of customers. Most general merchandisers very broadly target their merchandise to several price ranges, and only a few limit themselves to narrow price ranges.

Specialty retailers, in contrast, offer limited lines of related merchandise targeted to a more specific customer. They define their customers by age, size, or shared tastes. Their customers are more homogeneous than those of general merchandisers.

Department Stores

The **department store** is the type of general retailer most familiar to the buying public. Many are even tourist landmarks. Few persons, for example, visit New York without seeing Macy's or Bloomingdale's. People also make special trips to see Marshall Field's in Chicago, John Wanamaker in Philadelphia, and Rich's in Atlanta.

Department stores are in a state of flux that makes them difficult to define. The Census Bureau defines a department store as any establishment that is engaged in the selling of hard goods (furniture, home furnishing, electronics, and appliances) and household linens and dry goods in addition to clothing and accessories. Despite this official definition, however, many department stores have eliminated their hard goods departments. And at least one major trade magazine, *Stores,* includes "multidepartment soft goods stores (or specialized department stores) with a fashion orientation [and] full markup policy" on its list of traditional department stores.[1] Both the government's lapse and the magazine's eagerness to revamp the definition of a department store are indicative of the changing image of department stores, and for that matter, other stores today. But before getting into the ways in which stores are changing, let's take a look at how various kinds of retailers operate and merchandise themselves.

As general merchandisers, department stores typically serve a larger portion of the community than other stores

TABLE 16-1 • THE TOP 25 DEPARTMENT STORES IN THE UNITED STATES

Rank	Company/Division	Affiliation	Number of Stores	Volume* (millions)
1.	Dillard's (Little Rock)	(Ind)	135	$2,206.3
2.	Nordstrom (Seattle)	(Ind)	56	1,920.2
3.	Macy's, New York	(RHM)	23	1,780
4.	Macy's (New Jersey)	(RHM)	26	1,635
5.	Dayton Hudson (Minneapolis)	(DH)	37	1,552.3
6.	Macy's (California)	(RHM)	25	1,450
7.	Foley's (Houston)	(Fed)	38	1,170
8.	Bloomingdale's (New York)	(Fed)	16	1,120
9.	Saks Fifth Avenue (New York)	(Bat)	44	1,110
10.	The Broadway (Southern California)	(CHH)	43	1,090
11.	Marshall Field (Chicago)	(Bat)	25	988
12.	Lazarus (Cincinnati)	(Fed)	44	945
13.	Lord & Taylor (New York)	(May)	46	938
14.	Neiman-Marcus (Dallas)	(NMG)	22	890
15.	May Co. (California)	(May)	34	853
16.	Burdine's (Miami)	(Fed)	29	850
17.	Abraham & Straus (Brooklyn)	(Fed)	14	805
18.	Bullock's (California)	(Fed)	29	775
19.	Emporium-Capwell (San Francisco)	(CHH)	22	710
20.	Rich's (Atlanta)	(Fed)	20	710
21.	Hecht's (Washington)	(May)	23	700
22.	Jordan Marsh (New England)	(All)	25	690
23.	Maas Brothers/Jordan Marsh (Florida)	(All)	38	615
24.	Robinson's (Los Angeles)	(May)	24	576
25.	Macy's, Atlanta	(RHM)	16	575

†Four quarters ended Jan. 30, 1988
*All figures without a decimal are estimates; others are sales reported in company financial reports or other public statements.
Affiliation code: All, Allied Stores; Bat, Batus Retail Group of Batus Inc.; CHH, Carter Hawley Hale; DH, Dayton-Hudson; Fed, Federated Department Stores; Ind, Independent; May, May Department Stores; NMG, Neiman-Marcus Group; RHM, R. H. Macy & Co., Inc.
Source: Reprinted from *Stores* magazine, National Retail Merchants Association, 1988.

The traditional department store "look" features separate, departmentalized classifications, as in Rich's menswear department in their Atlanta store.

and often offer a variety of quality and price ranges. Department stores have also traditionally enjoyed a certain prestige that often extends even beyond the communities they serve. They are usually actively involved in their communities. A department store, for example, will eagerly stage a fashion show for a local charity or lend space for an art show or club meeting, knowing that such activities create goodwill and enhance the store's overall reputation.

Organization for Buying and Merchandising

Department stores are organized into special areas, or departments, such as sportswear, dresses, men's clothing, and furniture. Generally, buyers purchase for their departments, although in very large department stores, even the departments may be departmentalized, with individual buyers purchasing only part of the stock for a department. In some sportswear departments, for example, one buyer may purchase shirts, while another buys pants, and still another skirts, and so on.

Most department stores have a flagship, or parent, store, and many also operate branch stores. Buyers may buy for the branches as well as for the main store, or if the branches are located in another town or very far from the parent stores, they may have their own buyers.

Specialty Stores

A **specialty store** carries a limited line of merchandise, whether it is clothing, accessories, or furniture. Examples of specialty stores include shoe stores, jewelry stores, and boutiques. As noted, specialty merchandisers tend to target a more specific customer than do general merchandisers.

Most of us are familiar with specialty stores but do not realize how varied they are. A specialty store can be a tiny **mom-and-pop store,** run by the proprietor with few or no hired assistants, or it can be a large, multidepartment store such as I. Magnin or Saks Fifth Avenue, both of which specialize in apparel. The latter are the type that *Stores* recently reclassified as full-fledged department stores.[2]

The majority of specialty stores in the United States are individually owned and have no branches. The composite sales of these single-unit specialty stores, however, represent only somewhat less than half of the total sales volume of all specialty stores.

Organization for Buying and Merchandising

In small specialty stores, the buying and merchandising are done by their owner or a store manager, sometimes with the assistance of a small staff. Large multidepartment stores are organized along the lines of department stores, with buyers purchasing merchandise for their own departments. Multiunit specialty stores belonging to chain organizations are set up in a unique way that is described in the next section.

Chain Organizations

A **chain organization** is a group of centrally owned stores, four or more according to the Census definition, each of which handles similar goods and merchandise. A chain organization may be local, regional, or national, although it is the national chains that have had the largest impact on retailing. They also may be general or specialty merchandisers, and depending upon the kind of stores they are, they will target their customer broadly or narrowly. A chain organization can be a mass merchandiser known for its low prices, or a specialty merchandiser selling exclusive designs at high prices. Apparel chains may focus on a special size, age, or income group.

The oldest and best-known chain organizations are JC Penney, Sears, Roebuck, and Montgomery Ward. New ones include K mart and Zayre. Prestigious special chains are Bonwit Teller and Brooks Brothers. Loehmann's is an example of a discount specialty chain, and The Limited, The Gap, and Lerner Stores are examples of women's apparel specialty chains. Lane Bryant is a chain organization that caters to large-sized women, while Kids R Us targets the children's market.

Organization for Buying and Merchandising

Most chain stores are departmentalized, but not in the same way as department stores. Chain-store buyers are typically assigned to buy a specific category or classification of apparel within a department instead of buying all categories for a department the way a department store buyer does. This practice is referred to as **category buying** or **classification buying.** Buyers in department stores, in contrast, are said to be responsible for **departmental buying.**

A departmental buyer in a sportswear department, for example, would buy swimwear, tops, jeans, sweaters, and slacks. A chain-store buyer who bought in the sportswear department might buy only swimsuits or only swimwear accessories. Category buying is necessary because huge quantities of goods are needed to stock the individual stores of a chain operation. Some chain operations have merchandise units numbering in the hundreds of thousands.

In addition to centralized buying and merchandising, most chains also have a system of central distribution. Merchandise is distributed to the units from a central warehouse or from regional distribution centers. Computer systems keep track of stock so that it can be

Lane Bryant is a chain organization that caters to the fashion needs of the large-size woman.

what makes chain operations different from these stores. The simple answer is that merchandise for a chain operation is bought and controlled from a central office, which is not attached to a store, whereas department stores and non-chain specialty stores are merchandised and controlled from a parent store.

A more complicated answer is that, more and more often these days, the differences are not so clearly defined. It has become increasingly difficult to distinguish a department store from a chain operation. To understand what is happening, one must understand how buying operations have changed in all stores in recent years.

Not too long ago, department and specialty store buyers not only purchased merchandise, but they were also responsible for selling the merchandise on the floor of the stores. As stores opened more branches, at first in local shopping centers and then in cities some distance from the parent store, buyers of necessity relinquished some of their dual responsibilities. They still traveled to the stores, but they no longer had the hands-on, day-to-day responsibility for what happened on the selling floor that they had once had. The day-to-day operation of departments became the responsibility of a department (or sales) manager.

At about the same time that this change was occurring in department and specialty stores, chain organizations emerged to complete the separation of buying and selling functions. In fact, chains had always separated the buying and selling function—and this provided further impetus to department stores to do so even more.

Today, most of the buying for Bloomingdale's stores is done from a central office and it can be considered a chain store. Macy's has stores in many states,

reordered as needed and also keep buyers informed of what is selling.

Although central buyers are not responsible for sales in their departments, they have adopted some of the functions of traditional department store buyers. They do not assist in the training of sales personnel, but they distribute trend and other information to individual stores.

Chains Versus Department Stores

Chain organizations have had an enormous impact on retailing. Since department and specialty stores can and do have branches, an obvious question is

and an argument might be made that it, too, functions as a chain. The retailing mergers that occurred throughout the late 1980s were an attempt by department stores and the department store conglomerates that bought them to consolidate the buying functions of many stores under one huge staff. Many of the department and specialty stores—Gimbel's in New York City, to name but one—that did not change their buying and merchandising operations to keep up with the times were forced to close their doors, while stores that revamped are surviving the competition from chain organizations.

Discount Stores

The discount business got its start after World War II, when servicemen and servicewomen came home with a well-thought-out agenda for their lives: get married, establish a home, and start a family. Within a few years, with the help of the G.I. bill, which funded both education and mortgages, they had managed to achieve at least one of their wishes. Millions of new houses had been built in "new" suburban towns. The next step was to furnish them.

Discounters saw a need and began to fill it. The first discounters sold household goods. They ran weekend operations, usually setting up shop in an empty warehouse, barn, or lot just outside the city limits. Their stock varied from week to week, but they managed to have what people needed. One weekend toasters were featured; on another bath and bed linens were on sale. The selection was not particularly good, but the prices were right, so people came to buy. Through word-of-mouth, discount businesses began to grow. Some even expanded into permanent stores.

Briefly Speaking

Who Killed Roger Retail?

Can a retailer studying the failure of others recognize the path to disaster? The problem is that most retailers learn their mistakes by hindsight . . . and by then it is too late. Here is a list of ten "retail killer" mistakes made not only by those who fail but also by those who hang on wondering why they don't do better.

1. Staying too long with an unsuccessful concept.
2. Insufficient commitment to a fashion concept.
3. Staying with bad real estate. What's bad? Poor location, narrow, complex buildings, high rentals, and bad access.
4. Not really knowing the customer.
5. Inadequate customer service.
6. Taking unrealistic markup.
7. Poor training and stability of buyers.
8. Taking someone else's success strategy and copying it.
9. No clear, definable focus. Customer must know what you stand for.
10. Poor communication both inside and outside the store.

The best way to avoid mistakes is . . . not to make them! But good retailers will make mistakes if they're worth their salt, in a risk-taking business like retailing. The real way to learn and profit is from mistakes.

This briefly speaking is based on information from the following source:

Isadore Barmash, "Retailer Killers: The 10 Most Common Reasons Retailers Fail." *Sportswear International,* October 1987, pp. 20, 22.

The discounters sold name-brand merchandise at less than retail prices. They did it by keeping their overhead low and offering minimal services—two facets of discount selling that prevail to this day. Cash-and-carry was the rule.

Fair trade laws made the sale of goods at more than retail or "list" price illegal. Discounters discovered, however, that the fair trade laws did not apply to selling lower than list price. Soon they were doing exactly that. In a sense, the fair trade laws, designed to prevent gouging by retailers, made the discounter's low price more recognizable and reputable.

Today a **discount store** is any retail operation that sell goods at less than full retail prices. Discounters are called "discount stores," "mass merchandisers," "promotional department stores," and "off-pricers," a term used exclusively by the fashion industry. Discounters, who may be either general or specialty merchandisers, sell everything from cosmetics, accessories, and apparel, to health and beauty aids, to major appliances.

As noted, discounters make a profit by keeping their overhead low and service minimal. Most discount stores have centralized checkout counters and rely on self-service. Volume and size are used to compensate for low markups. Discount stores typically aim to do a minimum annual sales volume of $500,000 and maintain stores with at least 10,000 square feet.

Discount stores may be independently owned or part of a chain operation such as K mart or Zayre. Even department stores have gotten into the act, opening wholly owned divisions of the parent firm. Target Stores, for example, is a discount operation of the Dayton-Hudson department store group, and Volume Shoes is the successful discount footwear chain in May Department Stores.

The first fashion discounters established themselves in New England. They rented warehouses and factories that had once been textile mills. Today, fashion discount operations have begun to resemble other retailers. Credit cards are often accepted. Self-service and centralized checkouts are still the rule, but there is a trend toward more personalized service on the floor.

Discounters make a profit by keeping their overhead low; most rely on self service, so aisles must be clearly marked.

Organization for Buying and Merchandising

Early discounters searched the marketplace for closeout and special-price promotions. Their inventories consisted almost entirely of this type of goods. Today, discounters specialize in low-end open-market goods or special lines made exclusively for them. Most conventional retail operations do not want their buyers to purchase goods that will be sold to discounters, but this has not stopped manufacturers from making special lines for discounters. Some designers and manufacturers use discount outlets to sell their overstocks or slow-moving items.

Independently owned and nonchain discounters follow the same buying and merchandising practices as other retailers of similar volume and size. Chain discounters follow the usual practices of their business, with one exception. In chain discount buying, buyers are usually responsible for several departments rather than a single category of merchandise.

Experts estimate that over 50 percent of all fashion goods are now sold at discount. Discounters have a tremendous stake in the future of fashion retailing.

Leased Departments

Leased departments, which were first discussed in Chapter 7, are sections of a retail store that are owned and operated by outside organizations. The outside organization usually owns the department's stock, merchandises and staffs the department, and pays for its own advertising. It is, in turn, required to abide by the host store's policies and regulations. In return for the leasing arrangement, the outside organization pays the store a percentage of its sales as rent.

Leased departments work best where some specialized knowledge is required. Jewelry, fur, and shoe departments are often leased, as are beauty salons. Glemby Company and Seligman and Latz, for example, lease many of the beauty salons in stores. Marcus and Co. leases the fine jewelry department of B. Altman. The Fur Vault maintains leased fur operations in Bloomingdale's and Rich's. U.S. Athletics leases athletic shoe departments in Foley's and Bloomingdale's.

Department stores, chains, and discount organizations will lease both service and merchandise departments, while specialty stores usually restrict leased operations to services, such as jewelry or shoe repair or leather and suede cleaning.

Organization for Buying and Merchandising

Leased operations vary from the independent who operates in only one store to major chain organizations that operate in many stores. In chain organizations, centralized buying and merchandising prevail. Supervisors regularly visit each location to consult with local sales staff and department store managers. At such meetings, they assess current sales, deal with any problems, and plan for the future.

As the buying and selling functions have become increasingly separate from one another, operators of leased departments enjoy a unique and at this point rather old-fashioned position within the fashion industry. Most operate in a variety of stores. They are furthermore buyers who maintain daily contact with their markets and their suppliers, which allows them to make excellent projections about future trends as well as giving outstanding fashion guidance to their customers.

FASHION

In the 1960s, everyone seemed to be discussing the "generation gap"; so in 1969, when Donald and Doris Fisher opened a youth-oriented basement store selling nothing but Levi's jeans and records, they called it The Gap.

During the 1970s, The Gap stores grew in number, adding sweats and faddish tops to their assortment, while dropping the records. But by the early 1980s, Donald Fisher, now chief executive officer, realized that the children of the 1960s and 1970s had grown up, that his customer base was stagnant, and that "The Gap needed a new and effective merchandising thrust to grow successfully over the long term."[1]

So Fisher acted fast—and in 1983, hired Millard (Mickey) S. Drexler as president to revitalize and revamp the chain. The result? One apparel management consultant called it "one of the fastest turnarounds ever."[2]

Drexler, a former merchandiser for Bloomingdale's, Macy's, and Abraham & Straus, was perhaps best known for his outstanding repositioning of the Ann Taylor specialty chain in the early 1980s. Like a whirlwind, Drexler went to work on The Gap, sweeping out the old and changing both the face and structure of the retail operation.

With the new president at the helm, out went the vast expanses of nothing but blue denim, and in came such fash-

Millard S. Drexler.

ion-focused items as periwinkle sweats, oversize fuschia sweaters, candy-striped rugby shirts, and Technicolor socks. Also out were drab metal display fixtures and T-racks, while in their place came clean-looking tiered tables to hold piles of neatly folded sweaters and sweat suits in every hue. Almost a dozen different private labels were reduced to one: The Gap Clothing Company. The stale "fall into The Gap" jingle was retired in

FOCUS

favor of classier print ads in fashion magazines like *Glamour* and *GQ*.

The "new" Gap decidedly struck a chord with its new target customer audience of more affluent 20- to 45-year olds. By 1987, Gap sales had almost doubled from their 1983 level; and profits that year were expected to be more than four times the 1983 results.[3] Suddenly, The Gap was going head-to-head—and successfully so—with such heavyweight specialty apparel chains as Benetton and The Limited.

A main ingredient in The Gap's recipe is its simplicity: all its merchandise works together. It is a sure bet that the yellow socks picked out by a customer will perfectly match that yellow sweater nearby, as well as that yellow baseball cap and yellow canvas belt elsewhere on the sales floor. And once a sweater, for example, is selected, a shirt that coordinates with it is just a step or two away, with lots of compatible pants close by.

Of course, The Gap has not forgone completely its traditional base of blue jeans and sweat suits. It has simply given front-and-center focus to more fashion-forward looks, which are updated frequently. Drexler himself visits his stores every week, always checking to see whether the "merchandise has a familiar look to it. If I feel that way, so does the customer. Staying fresh is the challenge in this business. You have to make the shopper eager to come in."[4]

Eager those shoppers do appear to be—so much so that in 1987, The Gap (which also owns Banana Republic) announced it was launching another chain called Hemisphere, which would be even more upscale than The Gap stores themselves.[5] And the odds are good that the new venture will fly, based on the company's shrewd reading of the market in revitalizing its original chain. As the apparel management consultant put it: "The Gap is exemplar of the retailer of the future in its classification. It has taken the pulse of who it services and understands what turns them on."[6] And that is what fashion retailing is all about.

[1] Jean Sherman, "Bridging the Gap," *Working Woman,* June 1987, p. 58.
[2] Pamela Ellis-Simons, "A Cinderella Story," *Marketing & Media Decisions,* Winter 1986, p. 47.
[3] Howard Rudnitsky, "Put the Zipper on the Back," *Forbes,* June 29, 1987, p. 89.
[4] Ibid., p. 90.
[5] Howard G. Ruben, "The Gap to Test Upscale Market with New Stores," *DNR,* May 1987, p. 2.
[6] Ellis-Simons, p. 47.

This Fashion Focus is based on information from the articles cited above and from these sources:

Marcia Biedman, "Chain of Too Many Gaps?" *Crain's New York Business,* February 13, 1989, p. 1.
Jeff B. Copeland with Dody Tsiantar, "Exploring a New Hemisphere," *Newsweek,* September 14, 1987, p. 57.
Ellen Forman, "Widening the Gap," *DNR The Magazine,* May 26, 1987, pp. 35–39.

MERCHANDISING POLICIES

Regardless of whether a retailer is a chain or mom-and-pop operation, a general or specialty merchandiser, it seeks to maximize its profits by going after a target group of customers. In order to better target their customers, retailers establish **merchandising policies.** These are general and specific guidelines and goals established by store management and adjusted according to current trends and marketplace needs to keep the store on target.

Of the many elements that go into a store's merchandising policies, the most important are the store's overall general goals regarding (1) the stage of the fashion cycle that will be emphasized, (2) the level of quality that will be maintained, (3) the price range or ranges that will be offered, and (4) the depth and breadth of merchandise assortments. Store management also must set policies regarding brands, exclusivity, customer service, selling services, promotional activities, and fashion coordination. All these policies must be maintained and monitored with a careful eye on what are always rapidly changing retail patterns, as well as external economic conditions. Merchandising policies are outlined in Table 16-2.

TABLE 16-2 • MERCHANDISING POLICIES OF VARIOUS TYPES OF FIRMS THAT SELL FASHION MERCHANDISE

Merchandising Policies	Nonchain Department Store	Nonchain Specialty Store	Chain Organization	Discount Organization	Off-Price Retailer	Firm Using Direct Mail
Fashion cycle emphasis	Mainly late rise and early culmination; early rise in prestige departments; full to late culmination in budget departments	Particular stage of cycle favored by majority of its customers	Mainly culmination stage; some specialty chains feature styles in earlier stages of cycle	Styles well into the culmination of their fashion cycles	Same as department and specialty chains	Particular stage of cycle favored by majority of its customers
Quality	High quality in prestige departments; quality at a price in moderate or budget departments	Highest quality as to materials and workmanship	Serviceable quality consistent with price	Quality may vary; "irregulars" and "seconds" may be carried	Varies from highest quality to serviceable depending on price	Quality consistent with targeted group of customers

TABLE 16-2 • (continued)

Merchan-dising Policies	Nonchain Depart-ment Store	Nonchain Specialty Store	Chain Or-ganization	Discount Organi-zation	Off-Price Retailer	Firm Using Direct Mail
Price ranges	Mainly moderate; high in prestige de-partments; low in budget de-partments	Mainly moderate but de-pends on stage of fashion cycle its customers prefer	Department store chains: lower and promotional pricing; some spe-cialty chains: moderate to high price ranges	Lower than convention-al retailers	Moderate-to-high-priced	Mainly moderate but de-pends on stage of fashion cycle its customers prefer
Depth and breadth of assort-ments	Broad and shallow at start of new selling sea-sons; nar-rower and deeper as customer preferences become known	Typically broad and shallow	Department store chains: nar-row range of proven styles in considera-ble depth; moderate-to high-priced spe-cialty chains: broader and shallower	Mainly broad and shallow	Broad and shallow	Narrow range of proven styles in considera-ble depth
Brand poli-cies	National brands em-phasized	Major em-phasis on own store labels or designer la-bels	Own pri-vate labels emphasized	Unbranded; own brand or with brand label removed	Designer labels em-phasized, with many national brands also	Major em-phasis on own brand or national brands
Exclusivity	Use of store brand or la-bel ensures some exclu-sivity	Uses con-fined goods—es-pecially de-signer or home la-bels—to gain exclu-sivity	Mainly specifica-tion buying and "store own" mer-chandise	No exclu-sivity un-less bought by specifi-cation	No exclu-sivity	Much ex-clusivity because goods are produced for them alone

Source: Reprinted from *Stores* magazine, July 1984, p. 29, National Retail Merchants Association, 1984.

Fashion Cycle Emphasis

As a means of establishing its image, every retailer decides to emphasize one phase of the fashion cycle over others. It then chooses its merchandise to fit that phase. Most stores want to ride the tide of new fashion. Few knowingly highlight styles once they have reached the decline stage, but stores still must choose whether to emphasize styles in their introductory, rise, culmination, or peak stages.

A retailer who chooses to buy styles in the introductory phase is opting to be a fashion leader, while a store that waits for the styles to become slightly established, that is, to enter at the rise stage, has decided to aim for being a close second to the fashion leader. Finally, a retailer may buy clothes in the culmination or peak stages, thus making itself a follower of fashion trends—as indeed most women are. The majority of stores across the country probably fall into this category.

Naturally, a store's choice about fashion emphasis must accord with its targeted customers' needs and wants. Henri Bendel's in New York, which for many years had a reputation for extreme trendiness, knew that its target customers were a small, elite group of young and very stylish women who wanted to be the first to wear whatever was new. When The Limited bought it, they changed its target customer and shifted the store's emphasis, moving from a position of fashion leadership to one of being a close second.

Quality

Retailers can choose from three general levels of quality:

- The top level, which involves the finest materials and workmanship.
- The intermediate level, which exhibits concern for quality and workmanship but always with an eye to maintaining certain price levels.
- The serviceable level, which involves materials and workmanship of a fairly low level, consistent with equally low prices.

Just as retailers are known for their chosen emphasis within the fashion cycle, they are also known for their decisions regarding quality. Quality and high fashion, however, do not always go hand in hand. Although most introductory styles are high-priced, this is not always the case. Some stores that assert themselves as fashion leaders do not bother with high quality, preferring merely to push what is new and exciting. In contrast, retailers that emphasize the rise or culmination stage also often stake their reputations on the high quality of their merchandise. They are thus able to emphasize their apparel's lasting qualities in ways that fashion leaders often cannot and do not want to.

Once a store has set its quality policies, it must make more specific decisions, such as whether it will accept nothing less than perfect goods or whether it will permit irregulars and second-quality goods to be offered.

Price Ranges

What people earn affects what they can spend, especially for clothing, where a variety of choices regarding quality and price are available. As a result, pricing policies are an important merchandising decision. A store's pricing policies play a major role in determining the kinds of customers it will attract.

There is actually no direct correlation between price and quality. Items of relatively low quality may carry a high price tag if there is a reason for them to do so, such as the presence of a designer's name or the fact that they are in the introductory phase of the fashion cycle. Despite the lack of a correlation, however, most retailers do attempt to tie their price ranges to quality standards. A store policy of buying only top quality also permits high price ranges, whereas a store that features intermediate quality usually sets some bottom limits that it will not go below. Stores that emphasize serviceable quality usually tend to also emphasize their low prices.

Depth and Breadth of Assortments

An **assortment** refers to the range of stock a retailer features. A store can feature a **narrow and deep assortment,** in which it stocks relatively few styles but has them in many sizes and colors. Or it can stock a **broad and shallow assortment** in which it offers many different styles in limited sizes and colors.

The two are mutually exclusive since space and cost are limiting factors in retail operations. A policy of stocking a broad assortment usually limits the depth to which those items can be stocked, and conversely, if depth is desired, variety must usually be limited.

Prestige stores and departments tend to stock broad and shallow assortments, offering small stocks of many styles in limited sizes and colors. In stores that cater to mid-range fashion and quality, assortments are broad and shallow early in a season when new styles are being tested. Once the demand for a style has become clear, the store begins concentrating on narrow and deep assortments of proven styles. Mass merchandisers focus on narrow and deep assortments of styles in the culmination stage.

Brand Policies

Stores also must establish policies regarding the brands they will carry. A **brand** is a name, trademark, or logo that is used to identify the products of a specific manufacturer or seller. Brands help to differentiate products from their competition. Some brands, those associated with exclusive designers, for example, acquire a special status that permits them to be sold at higher prices. Status and price, however, are not the only things that help a brand sell well. National brands and private labels have also become important.

A **national brand,** which identifies the manufacturer of a product, is widely distributed in many stores across the country. National brands, which hold out the promise of consistent quality, have become the backbone of many retailers' stocks. Today the names of some designers, such as Pierre Cardin and Sassoon, to name but two, have become so well-known to consumers that their labels are considered national brands. These name brands have acquired a value in the consumers' mind that is distinct from any intrinsic value in the products themselves. In order to minimize competition over national brands, some major retailers insist on buying exclusive, or **confined, styles** from national brand manufacturers.

Retailers are also riding the wave of popularity of brand names by promoting their own **private labels** or **store brands.** Store brands have proven to be an excellent way to meet price competition and achieve exclusivity.

Prestige specialty stores tend to feature their own store labels and designer names, a strategy that department stores have begun to adopt with great success. Mass merchandisers have always offered their own private labels, typically sold alongside unbranded merchandise, as a means of keeping prices low. Even mass merchandisers, however, have been swept into the tidal wave of brand names and now carry them.

Exclusivity

Exclusivity is something many stores strive for but few are able to achieve. Several store policies can help retailers establish a reputation for exclusivity.

1. Retailers may prevail upon vendors to confine one or more styles to their store for a period of time and/or within their trading area.
2. They can buy from producers who will manufacture goods to their special designs and other specifications.
3. They can become the sole agent within their trading area for new, young designers.
4. They can seek out and buy from domestic or foreign sources of supply that no one else has discovered.

However, the first two policies (confined lines and specification buying) are options only when a store can place a large enough initial order to make production profitable for the manufacturer.

The last two policies do not necessarily demand high volume. They are thus invaluable to prestige stores who need exclusivity as part of their images but cannot hope to compete in volume with mass merchandisers or even big department stores.

OPERATIONAL STORE POLICIES

After a retailer has defined its target customers and set its merchandise policies in a manner designed to attract them, it must next establish **operational policies.** Often more specific in nature than merchandising policies, these are primarily designed to keep the customers once they are attracted enough to come into the store. What merchandising policies do to establish a retailer's image, operational policies do to build a store's reputation. Operational policies also serve to enhance merchandising policies. They establish such things as the store's ambiance, its customer services, its selling services, its promotional activities, and last but hardly least, its fashion services.

Ambiance

Ambiance, the atmosphere you encounter when you enter a store, does much to create the image of a store. Prestige department and specialty stores work hard to provide pleasant and even luxurious surroundings. The store is pleasing to the eye and even to the other senses. (Some stores emanate a store-wide scent). Decor matters, and usually consists of carpeted or wood floors, wood counters and display cases, chandeliers and other expensive lighting. Dressing rooms are numerous, large, and private.

In contrast, at low-range and discount stores, ambiance may count for little. The intention is to send the customer a clear message: Shop here in less-than-luxurious surroundings and we will give you the lowest possible price. Fitting room space may be limited or may consist only of a large, shared dressing room, commonly referred to as a "snake pit" by customers.

Customer Service

Department stores pioneered in offering customer service. They were the first retailers to offer their customers store charge privileges and generous return

The "ambiance" of the accessories section of a Neiman-Marcus store is luxurious!

policies. Their willingness to accept merchandise returns, in fact, originated with John Wanamaker and his Philadelphia store of the same name. His first store, opened in 1876 in an old railroad freight station, was a men's clothing store. A year later, he added departments for ladies' goods, household linens, upholstery, and shoes, for a then unheard of total of 16 departments. Wanamaker further shocked the retail world by advertising that if anything did not please "the folks at home" or was unsatisfactory for any other reason, it could be returned for a cash refund within 10 days.

Today, it is commonplace for department and specialty stores to offer their customers an array of services designed to increase their edge over the competition. The more familiar customer services include a variety of credit plans, liberal merchandise return policies, telephone ordering, free or inexpensive delivery, in-store restaurants, free parking, and a variety of services such as alterations and jewelry repair. As competition, particularly from chains and discounters, has increased, general merchandisers have met it by offering still more services. Newer customer services include travel bureaus, ticket agencies, mailing facilities, expanded telephone-order facilities, and extended shopping hours.

Chain stores offer a more limited range of services than do department and specialty stores. The usual credit plans prevail, with greater emphasis on installment plans. Chain stores took a lead in establishing extended hours.

At discount stores, transactions are usually on a cash-and-carry basis, although many have started to accept major credit cards. A few offer their own credit plans. Refund policies are less liberal than those of department stores; however, most discounters will accept unused goods (often for credit rather than cash) if they are returned in a specified period of time, usually 7 to 10 days. Delivery service, if available, is restricted to bulky items and may cost extra. Phone orders are almost never taken.

Selling Services

In all but the higher-priced specialty stores these days, self-service is the rule. In discount stores and low- to moderate-priced chain stores, clerks are present on the selling floor to direct customers to merchandise and ring up sales. In most department and specialty stores, salespersons are available on the sales floor to answer some questions and complete sales transactions. The old service of catering exclusively to one client at a time, bringing clothes into the dressing room, and offering fit and style advice is gone, probably forever. An exception to this rule is Nordstrom's department stores, which has maintained a high degree of selling services. In fact, it is the success of its sales help that has made Nordstrom's one of the most successful department stores in America.

High-level service is usually available only in high-end department and specialty stores where salon selling prevails. In **salon selling,** merchandise other than that used for display purposes is kept out of sight, and a salesperson chooses apparel items from the stockroom to bring out for the individual customer's inspection. The sales staff in such an organization is often instructed in highly personalized selling techniques, which include remembering what individual customers have purchased in the past and alerting them by phone or mail to new merchandise that may interest them.

Promotional Activities

All retailers engage in some promotional activities, whether it is advertising or publicity. Advertising and publicity are a store's two chief means of communicating with its customers. How much a retail organization promotes itself, however, varies depending upon the type of retail operation.

Discount stores are the heaviest promoters and they rely almost entirely on advertising as opposed to publicity or public relations. All kinds of advertising—newspaper, television, radio, and direct mail—are employed to get their message across. Their advertising emphasizes low prices and in many instances invites customers to comparison shop. Discount operations tend to run frequent sales or special promotions.

Compared to the discounters, general merchandisers like department and chain stores and specialty stores engage in only a moderate amount of promotional activity, although, of course, large budgets are allotted for this purpose. Department stores rely most heavily on newspaper advertising, although some prestigious department and specialty stores also advertise in the major fashion magazines. Specialty chains like The Gap and Esprit have begun to use general magazines as much as fashion magazines to reach their target customers. The more prestigious stores use direct mail. Monthly bills, stuffed with advertising and special catalogs, are mailed regularly to charge customers.

These retailers also do a moderate number of "special sale" and "special purchase" advertising campaigns. Sales are usually tied to special events, such as a holiday (the Columbus Day coat sales are one example), an anniversary, or an end-of-the-month clearance. Department stores were the leaders in pioneering traditional seasonal sales: white sales in January and August, back-to-school promotions in late summer and early fall.

The content of advertising varies with the type of retailer. Discount and mass merchandisers' ads are heavily product-oriented, displaying the product and its price in a direct manner. The prestige stores run some advertisements for individual items, but their advertisements are more likely to feature a designer or a new design collection. Advertisements may emphasize a new fashion look or trend at the expense of promoting the apparel in the ad.

TECHNOLOGY TALK

RETAILING IS ON A NEW WAVELENGTH

As new technology charges in to reshape the fashion industry, retailers, manufacturers, and others in the fashion pipeline are racing to keep pace with a changing and challenging world.

For retailers, who stand at the end of the fashion pipeline, the ability to communicate is the vital link to survival in today's high-tech world.

As a new way to cut across and sharpen their competitive edge, major retailers are taking to the airwaves, turning to video broadcasting as a means to get their messages across. While it usually takes millions of dollars to get this technology up and running, industry giants see it as an investment that gives them broad flexibility with a relatively quick payoff.

Sears, Roebuck is only one of the major retailers to invest in video conferencing via satellite as a means of improving communications and expediting decision making. Sears, Roebuck expects video conferencing to whittle down travel costs and make internal communications more timely and efficient. Programming on the video network will be varied, including training programs, executive messages, and product presentations.

Wal-Mart and K mart are two other retail giants that have successfully implemented video conferencing. Wal-Mart inaugurated live programming with an address to over 1,200 stores. But executive messages are only part of Wal-Mart's use of video broadcasting. Like other chains, Wal-Mart presents new merchandise or corporate strategies over the network from its Bentonville, Arkansas, headquarters.

JC Penney, a leader in the use of satellite television, reports that it is saving about 80 percent of the costs of bringing in sample lines of merchandise by broadcasting them on their own TV. Conferencing via personal computer lets buyers discuss what changes they would like to see in sample lines and have the changes electronically transmitted back in very short time frames.

Chain stores have led the pack in installing new, comprehensive communications systems. However, the whole of the retailing industry is paying more attention to this aspect of operations. Communications networks are going to be used more heavily in the future because they bring everybody closer together—providing greater ability to manage better.

This Technology Talk is based on information from the following source:

Holly Haber, "Retailing '88—On a New Wavelength," *WWD/DNR Retailing Technology & Operations,* April 1988, pp. 26–27.

Merchandise from many departments is brought together to complete the "coordinated look" of sportswear.

Fashion Services

Prestigious chain organizations and department stores and large specialty stores often employ a fashion coordinator or director whose job is to make sure that the apparel displays throughout the store, as well as the assortments on the racks, reflect current fashion trends as well as the store's image. These days, an important part of the fashion coordinator's job is to coordinate departments storewide. For example, the coat department displays and mannequins may play up scarves, even though they are sold in another department, if they are the hot accessory of the moment. Departmental displays and mannequins tend to be more fully outfitted than in the past, when only the apparel items actually sold in a department were displayed or promoted within it.

Specialty stores have always tried to offer fashion coordination services, although few small stores have a fashion coordinator on staff. Instead they train their sales staff to handle this task. Since small specialty retailers do less volume business than a department store or chain, one way they can increase their profits is to sell a fully accessorized outfit. Since most specialty stores occupy smaller physical surroundings than department stores, their salespeople are in a better position than department store staff to accessorize an outfit for a customer. In a department store, the scarf a salesperson wants to recommend to go with an outfit may be five floors away; in a specialty store, it is only a few steps away.

Discounters and low-priced mass merchandisers do little fashion coordination. Goods are often displayed only on sales racks, and the mannequin or other displays that exist are more utilitarian. While there has been some upgrading of merchandising methods in these stores, it has not yet reached the level of full-blown fashion coordination and may never do so.

CHANGING RETAIL PATTERNS

Retail operations not only must constantly respond to change in their environments, but they themselves must change if they are to survive. One theory, suggested by Malcolm P. McNair, retailing authority and professor emeritus at the Harvard Business School, describes the way in which retail organizations naturally change or evolve. According to McNair, most retail organizations begin life as lower-priced distributors. They offer strictly functional facilities, limited assortments, and minimal customer services.

As time elapses, the successful businesses need to grow in order to survive, so they begin to trade up in an effort to broaden their customer profile. Facilities are modernized. Store decor becomes more attractive. Assortments become more varied and of higher quality. Promotional efforts are initiated or increased, and some customer services are introduced.

The process of trading up, however, involves considerable capital investment in the physical plant, equipment, and stock. Operating expenses spiral. As a result, retailers are forced to charge higher prices to cover the increased cost of doing business. To justify the higher prices, they also begin to stock more expensive merchandise.

Barney's in New York City is an example of a retail organization that underwent this dramatic change over a period of about a decade. Initially a discount men's clothier, Barney's became so successful that it had no choice but to upgrade its facilities. In the process it began to carry more expensive merchandise. Soon it was carrying top-quality merchandise, and the discount prices were gone. Its men's facility, services, and promotional activities were upgraded accordingly with each change. Finally, Barney's expanded into a nearby brownstone, where it created a luxurious and very expensive store for women's wear. To promote its new image, it began advertising in fashion magazines and was one of the first department stores to experiment—successfully—with television advertising.

According to McNair's theory, as Barney's and other retailers move out of the low-priced end of the market into the moderate-to-high-priced field, they create a vacuum at the bottom of the retailing structure. The vacuum does not exist for long, though. Enterprising new retailers move quickly to fill the vacated and temporarily uncompetitive low-priced area to meet the demands of customers who either need or prefer to patronize low-priced retailers. This pattern keeps repeating itself as successful retailers trade up and new ones move into the vacuum.

Even those who move up must still constantly cope with the ever-changing nature of the fashion business. In the next chapter, the most important challenges and trends confronting today's retailers will be discussed.

REFERENCES

[1] Joan Bergmann, "What Is a Department Store? Why Does It Matter?," *Stores,* July 1987, p. 81.
[2] Ibid.

MERCHANDISING VOCABULARY

Define or briefly explain the following terms:

Ambiance
Assortment
Brand
Broad and shallow assortment
Category buying or classification buying
Chain organization
Confined style
Department store
Departmental buying

Discount store
Fashion retailing
General merchandise retailers
General store
Leased department
Merchandising policies
Mom-and-pop store
Narrow and deep assortment

National brand
Operational policies
Private or store brand or private label
Retailing
Salon selling
Specialty retailers
Specialty store

MERCHANDISING REVIEW

1. Name and briefly explain the characteristics and importance of three early forms of rural distribution in the United States.
2. How is the buying function handled by a department store?
3. What is a specialty store? How are buying and merchandising handled in a specialty store?
4. What is a chain organization? How are buying and merchandising handled in chain operations?
5. How do successful discounters make a profit?
6. What is a leased department and how does it operate? Name the departments in a retail store that are frequently leased.
7. What are the four major merchandising policies that must be set by each store?
8. What stage or stages of the fashion cycle would most likely be emphasized by (a) a high-end specialty store, (b) a department store, and (c) a discount operation?
9. What operational policies must each store set in order to keep its customers and build its reputation?
10. According to Malcolm P. McNair, how do retail organizations typically evolve?

MERCHANDISING DIGEST

1. Compare and contrast the fashion coordination efforts of (a) prestigious chain organizations, department stores, and large specialty stores and (b) discounters and low-priced mass merchandisers. Give examples of fashion coordination efforts of different types of retailers in your community.
2. What examples in your community can you cite which support Dr. McNair's theory of trading up by retailers?

TRENDS IN FASHION RETAILING

As the end of the twentieth century draws near, industry insiders and experts are asking themselves what retailing will be like in the twenty-first century. Retailing overall underwent profound and often tumultuous changes during the 1980s. The department stores were beset by merger mania. The 1980s also saw the rise of several new kinds of retailers—discounters, chain organizations, and hypermarkets. New, unanticipated trends—the growth of private labels—also changed the face of retailing. While the upheavals of the 1980s can be expected to slow in the 1990s, the era of important change has not ended, nor will it anytime soon. Retailing, after all, is a business built on change.

For the most part, the changes have been good. In many ways they have left the industry stronger and more competitive. American fashion is creative, forceful, and respected worldwide for its innovative and classic designs. But it is also faced with many challenges. It is in the midst of learning to cope with the flood of imported fashion goods. At the same time, the American fashion industry must learn how to take its merchandise abroad more successfully. New merchandising strategies have been devised for coping with the increased competition at home. The department stores that survived the 1980s did so because they were able to adapt some of the merchandising techniques developed by the chains and discounters. One important trend, in fact, has been the blurring of distinctions between the various kinds of retailers as merchandising techniques have become more universal.

In the first half of this chapter, we shall examine three of the general trends that are affecting all retailers. These are merger mania, the decline of customer loyalty, and the rise of private labels. In the second half of the chapter, discussion will focus on the changes that are occurring in individual segments of the retailing industry.

MERGERS AND ACQUISITIONS

Until the 1930s, most department stores in the United States were independently owned. Most, in fact, were owned by the families whose names they bore, names such as Marshall Field, John Wanamaker, Gimbel Bros. and J. L. Hudson. By the 1980s, most of these long-established stores had changed hands, and with these changes in ownership came new images and sometimes even new names.

So much change has occurred in the retail business recently that you need a scorecard to track the remaining players. Consolidations, changes in distribution channels, altered buying organizations, and foreign investments have all caused the retail scene as we knew it to change.

Just when you thought that big retailers were really big enough, they got bigger! Five companies—Allied/Federated, Macy's, Dillards, the May Company, and Carter Hawley Hale—now own most of the big city department stores, and account for over $40 billion in sales. Former leading retail names like Gimbels no longer exist.

Although mergers have taken their toll on the department stores, causing some old, established stores to close their doors, some good has been served. Without mergers, many of the established department stores would not have survived the onslaught of competition from chains and discounters. In fact, mergers generally occur for one of two reasons: a need to reorganize for greater efficiency and a need to expand.

Merging for Efficiency

In the early 1980s, chain organizations, with their centralized buying, had developed a competitive edge over department stores even though department stores had tried to keep up by expanding the number of branch stores. The department stores soon realized that the real way to meet the competition was to develop more streamlined, efficient internal organizations. This was often achieved by merging one or more internal divisions in order to create a parent organization large enough to sponsor centralized buying, shipping, and merchandising.

Macy's, after years of operating the New Jersey department store, Bamberger's, streamlined both organizations by merging the merchandising and operational functions; Bamberger's lost its name in the process.

Merging for Expansion

Faced with the rapid expansion throughout the 1980s of huge national chains, retail department stores began to merge with one another and with parent organizations so they, too, could join the expansion boom. It is obviously easier and less expensive to expand by acquiring an established retail outlet than it is to build an entire new store from scratch.

In cities where a store is a recognized leader, the parent company may find it advantageous to keep the store's name and image intact. This was the case in 1986 when Washington-based Woodward & Lothrop purchased Wanamaker's, Philadelphia's most prestigious department store. Both stores kept their own names. In contrast, the Arkansas-based Dillard's vaulted itself into the position of the country's number-one ranked department store through a series of acquisitions of other department stores—all of which were immediately converted to Dillard's stores.

Inevitably, even the parent companies ended up merging. In fact, one of the mergers that had a major impact on the industry was not between two or more divisions of a parent company but was instead between two of the largest department store companies in the country: Associated Dry Goods and the May Department Store Company. Operating under the May name, the merged organization accounted for over $10 billion in sales in 1986 alone. Among its lucrative divisions are Lord & Taylor of New York, Hecht's of Washington, D.C., Robinson's of Los Angeles, Famous-Barr of St. Louis, Kaufmann's of Pittsburgh, and L. S. Ayres of Indianapolis.[1]

Hostile Takeovers

Not all mergers are by invitation. Some are hostile and therefore unwanted and opposed by the company that is taken over. Retailing has seen more than its share of hostile takeovers. David Dworkin, president of Neiman-Marcus, was referring to the cutthroat competition among retailers when he described the business as one of "trench warfare."[2] But he might just as easily have been describing the series of hostile takeovers and takeover bids that rocked the retail industry throughout the last half of the 1980s.

The tone was set by the aggressive Campeau Corporation, a Canadian-based real estate company, which sought to take over the Allied Stores, then the parent organization of such stores as Block's, The Bon, Jordan Marsh, Garfinkel's, Joske's, Miller & Rhoad's, Pomeroy's, Stern's, and Dey Brothers. After months of discussion, court challenges, and competitive bids from other companies (known as white knights because Allied asked them to bid in order to save them from being bought by Campeau),

Campeau succeeded in buying Allied. Almost immediately it set about selling off more than half of the organization's retail divisions. Other organizations were quick to pick up Campeau's discards: Dillard's snatched up Joske's; Federated grabbed Block's; Hess's bought Miller & Rhoad's, and May Department Stores acquired Dey Brothers.

DECLINE OF CUSTOMER LOYALTY

The increased competition among retailers has not been without its price. Retailers soon discovered that the rise of discounters was directly tied to a decline in customer loyalty, something department and specialty stores had been able to count on for over a century. Presented with more variety—in styles, quality, and price—than they had ever before encountered, customers began to shop wherever they got the best buy, even if that included the previously unprestigious discounters. While the status of individual designers and labels grew, the prestige of shopping in a particular store decreased.

The age of consumerism also created very sophisticated shoppers. Today's customers are alert observers of what is offered in the marketplace, and they shop where they believe they will get the most—and the best quality—for their money.

GROWTH OF PRIVATE LABELS

In order to compete with chain organizations such as The Gap and The Limited, which have had great success with their private labels, department and large specialty stores began promoting

A growing trend in fashion merchandising is for stores to feature their own labels as opposed to only store labels.

their own private-label merchandise. Private labels became more attractive when national brands and designer merchandise began showing up in discount stores, making them, in the eyes of department store management, less desirable. Department stores thought they could fill an empty niche—the market for status clothes—by developing their own exclusive labels.[3] Once a decidedly unglamourous aspect of retailing, private labels were now seen as a means of adding prestige to a store's image—and boosting profits.

Most department stores had always carried some private-label merchandise; the difference is the aggressiveness with which private labels are being merchandised and the upgrading of the labels themselves. Where private labels previously consisted of a store's own lines of socks, underwear, and other such basics, they are now seen on everything from high-end women's career apparel to sheets to Christmas decorations.

Bloomingdale's pioneered in the realm of the private label, capitalizing on the status of its name by putting it on everything from candy to leather goods to toilet paper. By the late 1980s, it had even opened "Bloomie's Express" gift shops in airports—stores that sold nothing but Bloomingdale's signature merchandise.

Today, the private label has moved from its earlier use of presenting basic house lines to one of promoting entire lifestyle concepts. Dayton-Hudson's Boundary Waters label appears, for example, on housewares as well as apparel. Stores have taken private labels one step further, as they move from sponsoring their own names on private labels to developing private labels that will stand on their own. Carson, Pirie, Scott in Chicago discontinued using its own name in favor of private brand names it developed for different departments. It uses "Impulse" for junior wear, "Corporate Level" for upscale working women, and "Year One" for baby clothes.[4]

Private labels offer several advantages to retailers. They enable them to control the design, production, and merchandising of goods. Mostly, though, private-label goods hold out the promise of greater profits because stores can generate a quality product in their own fashion colors, at a competitive price that can generate extra profit. Or the savings may be passed on to consumers.

Industry experts predict that retailers will continue their love affair with private labels in the future. Estimates are that major department stores such as Macy's, which has developed what may be the strongest private-label program of any department store, will do as much as 30 percent of its business in private-label merchandise.[5] In departments such as menswear, where private labels have been especially well-received, the figure may go even higher. Stores will probably offer fewer rather than more labels, however, as they devote more attention and effort to merchandising the strongest labels.

Macy's has done so well with its Aerospace private label that it has even opened what may be the first in-store boutique devoted entirely to a private label. Unfortunately, when something grows in a store, something else must be abandoned, and Macy's created a stir in the business when it dropped the well-known sportswear label Chaus in order to offer more support to Aerospace. Some industry experts feel that retailers' headlong rush into private labels may be a mistake, particularly when a successful line like Chaus is dropped to make way for a private label. Bernard Olsoff, executive vice president of Frederick Atkins, a buying and research office, commented that his organization did not recommend building up a private label at the expense of brand identification. Private label, in his eyes, is meant to support, not replace, brands.[6] For the moment, however, most retailers look to private labels to provide greater profits and more status, and they are not likely to turn away from this trend any time soon.

TRENDS IN INDIVIDUAL RETAILING OPERATIONS

While most of the excitement over the past decade has been in department stores, they are not the only retailers who have had to adapt to internal and external forces. Among the retailers who have seen specific kinds of growth are discounters, who have experienced growth in off-price retailing and factory outlets, and mail-order sellers, who are now opening catalog showrooms and offering electronic shopping.

Discounters

Industry experts predicted that 25 to 30 percent of all name-brand goods would be sold at discount in the United States by the end of the 1980s. Sales figures have fallen slightly short of that mark,

To retain its customers' loyalty, Sears has returned to the policy of "everyday low prices."

but there is no question that discounters are having a tremendous impact on the merchandising of fashion goods. Unlike regular-priced retailing, which has suffered from overexpansion (and endured the takeovers that often result), discount retailing has room to grow.[7]

Off-Price Retailing

One area that is experiencing strong growth is **off-price retailing,** the selling of brand-name and designer merchandise at lower-than-normal retail prices when they are at the late rise or early peak in the fashion cycle. In contrast, regular discounters sell merchandise in the late peak and decline stages of the fashion cycle.

Off-price retailers attribute part of their success to the fact that they pro-vide an invaluable service to manufacturers and price-conscious customers. Because manufacturers must commit to fabric houses so far in advance (up to 18 months before garments will be in the stores), they risk not having enough orders to use the fabric they have ordered. For many years, manufacturers took a loss when this happened. Today, however, when they have fewer orders than anticipated, they turn to off-pricers who will often pay full price for the fabric if the manufacturers will make it into garments at a lower cost. The manufacturers can more easily afford to cut their production costs than the cost of material they have already paid for. Off-pricers have in effect helped to smooth out the cyclical and often financially disastrous course of apparel manufacturing. Customers, in turn, benefit from being able to buy the same garments that are being sold in exclusive stores for less than they would pay in those stores.

The first major off-price retailer in the United States was Loehmann's, which set up shop in Brooklyn in 1920 to sell "better" women's wear. Until then, high-quality women's garments had been available only through exclusive department stores.

The regular-priced stores, for their part, did not fail to notice the arrival of Loehmann's on the retail scene. Department stores demanded that the discounter remove the labels so customers would not know what they were buying. To this day, Loehmann's and other reputable off-pricers scissor out name brands before putting garments on the racks. Savvy shoppers, of course, have long since learned to identify their favorite brands without labels.

The growth of off-price retailing in the 1980s drew other retailers into the market. Melville Corporation began off-price retailing of men's, women's, and children's fashions through its Marshall's Stores, which was the fifth largest specialty retailer in the country in 1986.[8] The Zayre Corporation started two off-price chains, T. J. Maxx and Hit or Miss. Even small off-pricers, such as Syms and Suzanne S., experienced phenomenal growth in the 1980s.

Off-pricers managed to capture an important share of the brand-name market. The success of brand names such as Pierre Cardin, Bill Blass, and Calvin Klein meant that designers no longer had to give department stores exclusives, and they were soon selling their products to off-pricers.

Only one disadvantage seems to be built into off-price retailing: Off-price retailers get the goods later than regular-priced retailers. While a department store puts designer spring and summer clothing on the selling floor during the winter, the off-pricer does not get the same merchandise until several months later. As a result, the off-pricer has a shorter selling season than the regular-priced retailer.

Industry experts worry that off-pricers will overextend themselves, as retailers did during the mid- to late 1980s, in the rush to cash in on a strong market. Woolworth's, for example, started and quickly closed its off-price chain, J. Brannam, after losing $9 million on the stores in 1984.[9]

Other signs indicate that off-price retailing has still more muscle to flex. Zayre's T. J. Maxx division turned in $1 billion in sales in 1986, a remarkable demonstration of the consumer's appetite for brand-name and designer garments at reduced prices.

Zayre's T. J. Maxx stores successfully fill the consumer's appetite for brand-name and designer clothes at discounted prices.

Factory Outlet Stores

Factory outlet stores, a discount operation run by a manufacturer, or increasingly these days, by a designer, are the other booming area of discount retailing. Industry figures indicate that factory outlets are growing at a faster rate than department stores, specialty stores, and off-price stores.[10]

Factory outlet stores began decades ago, and for many years, experienced little or no growth. A manufacturer would open a little store in one corner of a plant to sell company products—slightly defective goods and overstocks—at reduced rates to company employees. Kayser-Roth and William Carter Co. were among the first to sponsor factory outlet stores. Other manufacturers followed suit, usually opening their outlets on the premises, which also always meant in the Northeast where

the apparel factories were located. Over time, manufacturers opened their stores to the buying public—that is, those who drove by their often obscure locations.

The proliferation of factory outlet stores can be traced to a recession in the early 1980s, which created a market for stores that could meet the demand for bargain-hungry shoppers. Not only did the already-established factory outlets, such as Warnaco, Inc., Manhattan Industries and Blue Bell continue to operate, but big-name designers such as Calvin Klein, Anne Klein, and Harve Bernard and brand-name organizations like Addidas, Bass Shoes, Jack Winter Sportswear, and Van Heusen menswear opened factory outlet stores.

Factory stores also left the factory, often to band together with one another in malls. The latest development is the emergence of entire communities, such

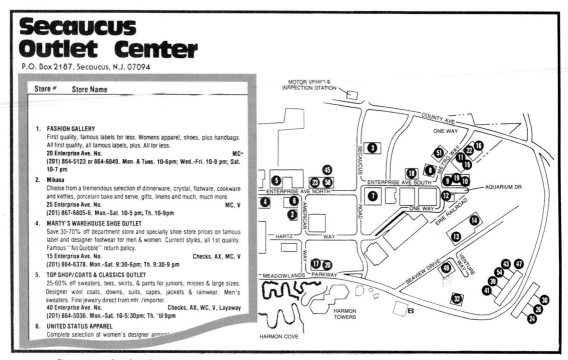

Secaucus Outlet Center is an example of the huge factory outlet mall, where designer and brand-name merchandise is offered at bargain prices.

as Freeport, Maine, Manchester, Vermont, and Secaucus, New Jersey, devoted almost exclusively to the selling of factory outlet goods. (The draw in Freeport was the presence of L. L. Bean, an established force in mail catalog retailing that expanded its factory store outlet throughout the 1980s from a small outpost to a huge multibuilding operation.)

Like off-price discounters, factory outlets offer certain advantages to manufacturers and customers. Most important is the fact that they provide manufacturers and designers with a backup channel of distribution, which improves inventory control. Canceled orders and overstocks can be funneled into discount stores, which, if run correctly, also can be enormous image enhancers. Not to be underestimated is the possibility of strong profits. An outlet buys merchandise from the parent company for 30 percent off the regular wholesale prices and sells it for the same markup percentage as regular-priced retailers.[11]

Designers and brand-name manufacturers use their outlets for overstocks and canceled orders while large manufacturers, such as Kayser-Roth and Carter, are careful to use their outlets only for closeouts and seconds. The latter are unwilling to risk offending department stores and other major customers with more direct competition.

The recession was followed by a boom in the mid- and late 1980s that helped all retailers, including the factory store outlets. The strong market also encouraged factory outlets to upgrade. Before the boom, most outlet stores were pipe-rack operations in dingy surroundings. Many looked like the factories out of which they had originally operated. Now factory outlets have begun to resemble regular-priced retailers more and more, offering attractive merchandise displays and customer service that compares to that offered by full-priced retailers.

There seems to be room for further expansion of factory outlet stores, as well as further upgrading of facilities and service. Most factory outlets, for example, are still located east of the Mississippi, leaving a huge huge untapped market along the Pacific Coast.

Many designers are expanding by opening showcase stores. A **showcase store** is a factory outlet that sells merchandise at the introductory and early rise stages of the fashion cycles. In addition to generating income, showcase stores are testing grounds for new products. Calvin Klein, Ralph Lauren, Esprit, and CP Shades operate showcase stores in addition to factory outlets.

Experts speculate on how well factory outlets will do when the hot market cools off, as it inevitably will, and as already appears to be happening. Customers' expectations regarding factory outlets have been raised by the proliferation of attractive, full-service, professionally run designer shops. Yet, ironically, factory outlet customers are not people who must look for bargains. Instead, they are people with incomes far above average; nearly 50 percent have incomes in excess of $35,000.[12] For these customers, bargain hunting is a leisure pastime, one that could easily be given up if factory outlet stores had to raise prices or cut services.

Another potential trouble area for factory outlet stores is the same kind of overexpansion that derailed regular-priced retailers in the mid-1980s. These fears are minimal, however, and most industry experts expect continued growth for factory outlet stores. They believe this new store has carved out a permanent niche in the retail world. [13]

FASHION

Ralph Lauren began his career in the fashion business as a salesperson for a necktie manufacturer. He found himself pondering fashion trends as he made his sales rounds. Fashionably put together himself (in high school he had worked part time to earn money to buy classically cut clothes at Brooks Brothers), he says, "I would walk [into a room] and my clients would say 'I want what you are wearing.' My instincts were there. I didn't think I was a designer, but I had ideas."[1]

It did not take long for those ideas to blossom. In 1967, he designed for another men's furnishings company a very successful line of neckties, to which he gave the name "Polo." The next year, he struck out on his own, and began producing an entire menswear line that was more flamboyant than the contemporary Ivy League look, yet not as brash as the era's psychedelic style.[2] The clothing caught on quickly at such chic department stores as Bloomingdale's and within four years, Lauren expanded his talents to women's wear. Cologne and boy's wear were added in 1978, girls' wear in 1981, luggage and eyeglasses in 1982, home furnishings in 1983, and women's handbags in 1985.

While Ralph Lauren's creations had a definite impact on the fashion scene, his merchandising strategies have had an even stronger impact on the fashion re-

tailing scene. Almost from the beginning, the designer has insisted that department stores carrying his collections display them the way *he* wants them to be displayed. When he launched his splashy Western Wear collection in 1978, for example, he demanded that retailers surround the apparel with props including cacti, split-rail fences, and wagon wheels. He was also the first designer to require department stores to devote space to give his clothing boutiques of their own.[3]

Because of Lauren's definite ideas about how his products should be merchandised, it is perhaps not surprising that the designer decided to open stores of his own. In addition to the almost 150 Polo/Ralph Lauren boutiques in department stores, he now maintains over 60 freestanding stores worldwide.[4] Among them is the lavish, 20,000 square-foot store opened in 1986 on New York's fashionable Madison Avenue.[5] It is Lau-

FOCUS

ren's ultimate showcase, as well as a testing ground for new merchandise and display ideas.

Said Lauren of his store's setup and what it offers other retailers: "This way they can see the whole vision I have of the clothes. I could explain it all day long, but until I had the store they couldn't see it."[6] And, noted the fashion editor of the *Washington Post:* "Lauren is the only designer with the product range to have such a store."[7]

Indeed, the success of Ralph Lauren's retailing venture may inspire other designers to try their own. Some already have opened their stores, but not all have enjoyed the same success as Lauren, particularly in Europe. Calvin Klein, for instance, opened a retail outlet in Milan in 1982, but closed it soon after because of slow sales. Lauren, on the other hand, has highly successful shops in Paris and London, among other cities. In fact, the London shop—whose patrons include the Prince and Princess of Wales—had to triple its space 5 years after opening in 1981![8]

With sales and consumer traffic growing steadily at the freestanding Polo/Ralph Lauren stores, has Lauren been losing customers for his department store boutiques? A minor drop-off may have occurred when the Madison Avenue store first opened, but not for long.[9] Rather, department stores took their cue and developed their own strategies to beef up the business. Saks Fifth Avenue, for one, completely renovated its own Lauren department to coincide with the opening of the Polo flagship. And as for Bloomingdale's? It also remodeled its Ralph Lauren women's shop in the style of the Lauren flagship—tripling the floor space and subsequently running a 90 percent sales increase in the first four days the renovated shop was open![10]

Lauren is not one to rest on his laurels. "There will always be a new challenge ahead, something to learn about, I love discovering new worlds. I want to perfect my craft. You can never sit back and think you've done it. There will always be room for improvement."[11]

[1] Stephen Koepp, "Selling a Dream of Elegance and the Good Life," *Time,* Sept. 1, 1986, p. 57.

[2] Ibid., p. 58.

[3] "Ralph Lauren: The Dream Maker," *U.S. News & World Report,* February 8, 1988, p. 78.

[4] Samuel Feinberg, "Lauren Saga: Lots of Sizzle Made Him Rich," *Women's Wear Daily,* January 4, 1989, p. 12.

[5] Koepp, p. 61.

[6] Lisa Belkin, "Lauren Look Permeating City," *The New York Times.*

[7] Koepp, p. 61.

[8] Ibid.

[9] Pete Born, "Lauren Store Tops $30 Million in First Year," *Women's Wear Daily,* July 14, 1987, p. 1.

[10] Pete Born, "Bloomingdale's Remodeled Lauren Shop Is a Big Hit," *Women's Wear Daily,* August 28, 1987, p. 2.

[11] Kathleen Boyes, "Ralph Lauren Telling Stories," *Women's Wear Daily,* October 24, 1988, p. 31.

This Fashion Focus is based on information from the articles cited above.

Mail-Order Retailers

By 1982, the explosive growth of mail-order retailers had reached such proportions that *Time* magazine ran a cover story on it. Mail-order retailing has expanded every year since then; in 1988, it chalked up sales totalling $64 billion. The yearly rate of growth for direct-mail and catalog sales has been averaging 10 percent compared to 6 percent for store retailers.

The computer has been an important tool in increasing direct-mail and catalog sales. With computers, companies were able to target their customers in very specific ways, by age, income, geographic region, lifestyle, and interests. As a result, almost 90 percent of all catalog sales are now from specialized catalogs. Other boosts to mail-order selling are the toll-free 800 telephone number and the ability to use bank credit cards to pay for merchandise.[14]

Mail-order houses have benefited from the growing numbers of women who now work and no longer have much leisure time to shop. Working women are the primary users of direct-mail sales, and not surprisingly, they are followed by single men. The group that relied least on direct mail are the wives of professional men.

Not willing to rest on its laurels, mail-order sales companies have also sought new ways to develop their business. Some of the new methods that are expected to remain strong throughout the 1990s are "magalogs," which are catalogs with magazine articles.[15]

Direct-mail selling has become so lucrative that other retailers have established their own programs, and department store bills now arrive stuffed with offers to purchase through direct mail. Bloomingdale's, to cite one typical example, achieved $60 million in direct-mail sales out of a total store volume of $800 million just 3 years after they launched their catalog sales program.[16]

Catalog Showrooms

A **catalog showroom** gives customers a chance to study samples of merchandise, which they can then order on the spot or through catalogs. The showrooms are a way of speeding up the delivery of products. Orders are filled from a stockroom so customers may take their purchases with them when they leave.

Two of the largest catalog showroom chains are Service Merchandise and Best Products. These distributors have not yet begun to sell much fashion merchandise except for watches and other kinds of jewelry, but apparel and accessories would be a natural area for expansion in the 1990s. One Ohio outfit, Investment Clothiers, has opened a fashion-oriented catalog showroom. It has been so successful that plans are underway to franchise the operation.

Electronic Shopping

One of the most talked about developments in retailing has been the growth of electronic or "home" shopping, a form of retailing that takes the catalog sales techniques one step further. By the year 2000, one of every three or four consumer dollars will be spent on televideo shopping.[17]

The potential of television as a direct-mail sales tool has long been recognized; witness the late-night gadget demonstrations and the ubiquitous storm window and "golden oldies" record advertisements. Not until the advent of cable television, however, with its lower production standards and lower costs, was it feasible to set up home shopping services that sold an array of goods.

The glamour of television production adds to the excitement of home-shopping.

The pioneer in the business was Home Shopping Network. On the air 24 hours a day, 7 days a week, with over 400 operators standing by to take telephone orders, Home Shopping Service did nearly $1 billion in sales in 1987.[18] Orders are entered directly into a computer, which keeps track of inventory, and if all goes well, are sent out within a week. Other television shopping services include Cable Value Network, ValueTelevision, and Quality Value Network, all of which offer on-screen demonstrations of merchandise that ranges from simple cookware to sophisticated electronics and includes apparel and accessories.

In 1988, Sears, Roebuck joined with IBM to launch Trintex, an interactive home shopping service using videotext. Viewers can turn to a channel showing videotaped (videotext) presentations of merchandise, which can then be ordered either by push-button telephone or computer. Such prominent retailing names as Neiman-Marcus, Chanel, and Levi Strauss & Co. signed on.

The future of electronic marketing is unclear, mostly because the technology has not yet become widespread enough to demonstrate its strength. Electronic shopping works best when customers have the equipment to shop this way. While virtually every American has a television, fewer are equipped with push-button telephones, computers, and telephone modems.

New Retailers

With discounters and mail-order houses bursting at the seams with business, where will the growth be in the next decade? If the economy remains strong, there will be room for still more expansion. Industry experts predict that hypermarkets, strong in Europe, are the wave of the future. Other relatively new forms of retailers that have shown gains are franchises and boutiques.

Hypermarkets

In the late 1980s, the very newest retailing concept made its way across the Atlantic from Europe, where it has been popular for decades. **Hypermarkets,** huge combined supermarket-discount stores that are sometimes described as "malls without walls," sell an array of goods that typically include food, furniture, housewares, hardware, electronics, and apparel.

The first domestic hypermarket was opened in Cincinnati, Ohio, in the mid-1980s by Euromarche, a French company. In 1988, a Philadelphia hypermarket was opened by Carrefour, the largest hypermarketer in Europe and Wal-Mart opened the first American-owned hypermarket in Garland, Texas. In 1989, K mart opened a hypermarket in Atlanta, called American Fare.[19]

No one knows whether the concept will catch on in the United States to the

Don't know what to do today? Spend the day at a hypermarket—where it takes all day just to browse through its thousands of products from food to fashion.

extent that it already has in Europe. Europe lacks the array of discounters that the United States has, and these firmly entrenched firms will offer tough competition to hypermarketers. As the first totally new retailing concept to come along in a few years, however, hypermarkets will attract a great deal of consumer attention—and sales may well follow. Retailing analyst Walter F. Loeb says of these new stores: "The blend of food and general merchandise will be extremely important to the future growth of retailing. These bigger stores probably will cannibalize the business of other food and general merchandise stores."[20]

Franchises

Franchises established themselves as a viable form of retailing in the 1970s when shops featuring bath linens, cookware, fabrics, unfinished furniture, electronics, and computers were successfully franchised. With the exception of one or two bridal wear franchises and the maternity shop Lady Madonna, the fashion industry was not part of the initial franchise boom.

It seems to have made up lost time, however, in the second wave of franchising that proliferated during the 1980s. Athletic footwear, tennis apparel, and men's sportswear have all produced lucrative and popular franchises. The latest trend is for designers to get in the act. Examples of successful franchises by designers are Ralph Lauren's Polo Shops, Calvin Klein shops, and Yves Saint Laurent's Rive Gauche shops.

Industry experts see no signs that franchising will slow its pace and many feel that this form of retailing will continue to grow.

Boutiques

Although boutiques originated as small shops with French couture houses, they really came to life as small, individually owned shops in the antiestablishment 1960s. The first boutiques opened in London and quickly spread to the

TECHNOLOGY TALK

UPC: WHAT IT IS, HOW IT WORKS, ITS BENEFITS

The Universal Product Code (UPC) is one of a variety of bar codes used today for automatic identification of items scanned at a retail point-of-sale. UPC is the symbol that has been most widely accepted by retailers and manufacturers.

Bar codes are made up of a pattern of dark bars and white spaces of varying widths. A group of bars and spaces represents one character. Scanning equipment performs three functions to read the bar code:

- The scanner provides a source of intense light that illuminates the symbol. The dark bars tend to absorb the light, and the lighter spaces reflect the light back to the scanner.
- The scanner collects the reflected patterns and converts them into an electrical signal that is sent to a decoder.
- The decoder translates the electrical signal to binary digits for use by the point-of-sale terminal or computer.

The changeover to bar-code identification and data capture is a complex task for retailers, but UPC marking represents a major opportunity for retailers to improve the efficiency of their business in three basic areas: more accurate sales and inventory data; faster point-of-sale transactions; the ability to use vendor marking that identifies merchandise at the size/color level.

The benefits of more reliable data to a retailer's business is of ultimate importance. Buyers have data they can trust and can use with confidence to make merchandising decisions. Fast-moving items are accurately reported and out-of-stock situations reduced. Inventory is accurately reflected, and this reduces the need for manual stock counts at the stores. Also, better data results in better planning for next season's inventory assortment.

Customer service, too, is greatly enhanced because buyers now know what particular sizes and colors are selling in each individual store.

The UPC symbol does not contain the price of the merchandise, however, and many retailers are experimenting with ways to determine the best method to indicate price to the customer. Some retailers are applying their own tickets to indicate the price while tracking the style at the size/color level via UPC.

Retailers are also evaluating the potential benefits of UPC marking in these areas:

- *Training:* faster and easier register training for sales associates.
- *Inventory:* ability to take an accurate physical inventory, at the item level, using portable scanners.
- *Receiving:* ability to track receipts as they travel through the distribution center.

In this age of technology, there are many new programs available to the retailer, and it will be the early innovators, the ones who are willing to try the new technologies, who will become the victors.

This Technology Talk is based on information from the following source:

"UPDATE: UPC & EDI—For General Merchandise Retailing," STORES, Section 2, an AIM Advertising Supplement, December 1988, pp. 1–16.

United States. Their appeal lies in their potential for quirky individuality. These stores are often owned and operated by highly creative persons who are eager to promote their own fashion enthusiasms. Their target customers are like-minded souls who share their unique attitudes about dressing.

Some boutique owners design their own merchandise; others buy and sell other people's designs. Boutiques are one of the few outlets for avant-garde merchandise that is too risky for department and specialty stores to carry.

Department stores have not, however, been above capitalizing on the success of boutiques. Bloomingdale's and Bendel's in New York City revolutionized merchandising display in the 1960s when they created special shops-within-shops on their selling floors. Frequently organized around the collections of a single designer, in-store boutiques offered customers a more complete fashion look. They were a fad that did not pass, and many department stores are now organized along boutique lines.

The newest trend in boutiques has been for designers to open their own small shops. The French designers were the first to experiment with free-standing boutiques in the United States, but American designers soon followed suit. Among the French who have opened successful U.S. boutiques are Cardin, Valentino, Yves Saint Laurent, and Givenchy; Americans include Calvin Klein, Ralph Lauren, Liz Claiborne, Adrienne Vittadini, and Tommy Hilfinger. Successful British firms that pioneered in boutique selling on both sides of the Atlantic were Laura Ashley and Liberty of London. As such prominent names join the ranks of boutique selling, there is little doubt that this form of retailing will continue to prosper in the coming decade.

REFERENCES

[1] "Retail Corporate Results for Fiscal 1986," *Stores,* July 1987, p. 18.

[2] Sam Feinberg, "American Retailing: A Century of Transition," *WWD/75 Years in Fashion, 1910–1985,* p. 68.

[3] Muriel J. Adams, "Private Label: Now Trump," *Stores,* June 1988, p. 12.

[4] Isadore Barmash, "Private Label: Flux," *Stores,* June 1988, p. 18.

[5] Adams, p. 12.

[6] Ibid., pp. 12–13.

[7] Harry Bernard, Colton Bernard Inc., "The Outlet Metamorphosis," *A Special Report from the Factory Outlet Stores Committee,* September 1988, unpaged.

[8] Ranking of Top 100 Speciality Chains, *Stores,* August 1987, p. 26.

[9] Isadore Barmash, "Piece by Piece, the Big Stores Rebuild," *The New York Times,* February 4, 1988, p. D2.

[10] AAMA Report, unpaged.

[11] Ibid.

[12] Ibid.

[13] Isadore Barmash, "At Factory Outlets, a Bright Outlook," *The New York Times,* April, 1989, p. 31.

[14] Samuel Feinberg, "Nonstop Growth for Non-Store Sales Channels," *Women's Wear Daily,* October 25, 1988, p. 14.

[15] Wayne Curtis, "What's New In Mail Order," *The New York Times,* May 14, 1989, p. F15.

16 Feinberg, "American Retailing," p. 72.

17 Feinberg, "Nonstop Growth," p. 14.

18 Paul D. Colford, "Shopping at Home with TV as Your Guide," *Newsday,* May 22, 1987, p. 3.

19 Georgia Lee, "K mart Expecting Big Hypermarket Draw," *Women's Wear Daily,* January 31, 1989, p. 19.

20 Thomas C. Hayes, "The Hypermarket: 5 Acres of Store," *The New York Times,* February 4, 1988, p. D2.

MERCHANDISE VOCABULARY

Define or briefly explain the following terms:

Catalog showroom	Hypermarket	Showcase store
Factory outlet store	Off-price retailing	

MERCHANDISE REVIEW

1. Describe how the merger of department stores increases efficiency.
2. What is a hostile takeover? Describe Campeau's hostile takeover of Allied Stores.
3. What are the major advantages of private labels for retailers?
4. What is the difference between an off-price retailer and a regular discounter?
5. What are the advantages of a factory outlet store for manufacturers and designers?
6. Name and briefly describe four factors that have benefited mail-order retailing.
7. What two new methods are mail-order retailers using to develop their business?
8. Why do some industry experts predict success for hypermarkets in the United States?
9. Describe the development of franchising in fashion retailing.
10. How are department stores and designers using boutique selling to merchandise their products?

MERCHANDISE DIGEST

1. Explain and discuss the following statement, citing current examples to illustrate how its applies to fashion retailing: "Today, the contents of major mail-order catalogs bear little resemblance to those early offerings to rural America."
2. Discuss how the major trends in fashion retailing have affected retailers in your own community. Have there been mergers? Which types of retailers have grown?

FASHION AUXILIARY SERVICES

The fashion industry is so huge and all-encompassing that it requires many support, or auxiliary, services. Some services—computer, bookkeeping, legal—are typical of those needed by any business, and may not be particularly tailored to the fashion business. Others, though, are specific to the fashion industry. They have either been created specifically to serve it, as in the case of buying offices, or their function has been tailored to the fashion industry's specific needs, as in the case of advertising and public relations agencies, fashion magazines, and the variety of consultants and marketing groups that exist to serve the fashion industry. In this chapter you will learn about the most important auxiliary services such as fashion magazines, trade publications, the broadcast media, advertising and public relations agencies, resident buying offices, and consulting and market research groups.

CATEGORIES OF FASHION AUXILIARY SERVICES

Fashion auxiliary services fall into three broad categories: advertising, publicity, and public relations. **Advertising,** which appears in everything from magazines and newspapers to radio and television, is space and time that is paid for. **Publicity** is the free and voluntary mention of a firm, product, or person in the media. Its purpose is to inform or enhance public interest about something specific. **Public relations,** a broader term than publicity, is also free and voluntary mention, but it is designed to enhance a long-term goal, such as the shaping of a company's public image. All three efforts are important elements of the remaining auxiliary services.

One difference between advertising and publicity/public relations is the amount of control a manufacturer or retailer can exercise over each. Since advertising is purchased, a great deal of control can be exercised over its execution. Public relations and publicity can be carefully developed and well-presented to the media, but there is no guarantee that the material and information supplied will be used well—or used at all.

Fashion Magazines

Fashion magazines, which combine advertising, publicity and public relations, came into existence about 150 years ago in the form of a single publication called *Godey's Lady's Book*. Prior to that, women discussed the newest fashions with one another but had no authoritative source from which they could learn what was new and exciting. The magazine's first editor, Sara Joseph Hale, is now best remembered for her early feminism, especially her struggle to help women win acceptance in professions, but her influence on fashion was equally important. *Godey's Lady's Book* reported on the latest styles and was the forerunner of such fashion magazines as *Vogue, Harper's Bazaar, Mademoiselle, Glamour,* and *Seventeen* for young women. For years, these magazines held sway and while they competed with one another, they were not subject to new competition. In recent years, though, several new magazines have established themselves as fashion arbiters, most notably, *Elle,* which competes with *Glamour* and *Mademoiselle,* and *Details,* which specializes in avant garde fashion. Some magazines have even become specialized: *Savvy, Ms., and Working Woman* cover career fashions; *Lear's* and *Mirabella,* geared to women over 40; and *Modern Bride* and *Bride's* report on wedding fashions. *Esquire, M,* and *Playboy* cover men's fashions.

Fashion magazines' pages are filled with advertisements for apparel. The business of reporting and interpreting the fashion news, however, is their primary function. They also provide a unique kind of publicity called an **editorial credit.** In order to feature clothes on their editorial pages, fashion editors visit manufacturers' showrooms, where they choose the latest fashions to photograph for the editorial pages of their magazines. When these clothes appear, they are accompanied by an editorial credit that names the manufacturer. Retail stores where the clothes may be purchased are also listed. This invaluable form of publicity benefits even stores that are not listed in the credits, for if they have seen a magazine in advance, they can often stock the fashions.

Trade Publications

One of the most important aids to the merchandising of fashion is the **trade publication.** Unlike the fashion magazines, trade newspapers and magazines are published just for the industry.

Just as general publications like city newspapers and national news magazines keep the public informed about what is going on in the world, trade publications keep their special readers informed about what is going on in the fashion world—from the acquisition of raw materials to reports on retail sales. These publications announce new technical developments, analyze fashion trends, report on current business conditions, and generally help all who work in the fashion industry keep up-to-date on a staggering number of new products, techniques, and markets. Even government regulations are covered.

Mix manic stripes
with fistfuls of
beads and
bracelets, or spark
sultry solids with
an Indian-inspired
leather belt.
Near right:
Cardigans, T-shirt,
leggings, stretch
belts, bracelets,
earrings; Missoni.
Watch, Watchout,
$45. Bead
necklaces, Jay
Feinberg. Hat,
Patricia Underwood,
$200. At Ultimo,
Chicago.
Far right: Pants,
$320, suede shirt,
$351; Mario
Valentino. Belt,
Omega, $49. For
details, see Retail
Guide. Hair, Valentin
for Jean Louis David;
makeup, Craig
Gadson for Yellen,
Inc., NYC.

SUN-DRENCHED SAFFRON

Editorial credits, such as these in *Elle,* provide valuable information to consumers and priceless promotion for manufacturers.

Women's Wear Daily

The best-known fashion trade publication is *Women's Wear Daily,* often referred to as the bible of the industry. It is one of the oldest publications of its kind, having first been published in 1890. Since its inception, it has played a prominent role in the fashion business. *Women's Wear Daily,* called *WWD* by those who read it, is published daily five times a week. It covers every aspect of the fashion industry from fiber and fabric to apparel, from day-to-day developments to new directions and trends. In the last 20 years, *WWD* has even covered the social scene, reporting on fashions worn by trendsetters at social events and parties. In addition, it is an advertising vehicle, and business notices, employment opportunities, and arrivals of buyers in the New York market are also reported. The Monday, Thursday, and Friday issues highlight children's wear, lingerie and loungewear, and fashion accessories, respectively.

Other Trade Publications

Numerous trade publications serve the needs of specialized segments of the fashion industry. *Accessories* and *Footwear News* cover their specialties as intensely as *WWD* covers the overall industry. The youth market is covered in *Children's Business.* Department store and specialty store management and merchandising executives read *Stores* and *Chain Store Age.* The fiber and fabric professionals read *Bobbin Magazine* and *Textile World.* The *Daily News Record*, published daily five times a week, specializes in textiles and menswear.

General Consumer Publications

General interest consumer publications also play a role in disseminating fashion news. Practically every newspaper reports on fashion, and some, such as *The New York Times, The Los Angeles Times, Chicago Tribune, and Washington Post,* devote regular weekly sections to apparel and home fashion design. Their fashion editors cover fashion openings, press weeks, and trade shows around the world. *Time, Newsweek, People,* and *Us* provide irregular but important fashion coverage, as do the traditional women's magazines such as *Good Housekeeping* and *Ladies' Home Journal.* So important, in fact, has fashion become that *Women's Wear Daily* has spun off a successful weekly publication called *W* geared to general consumers.

The publicity departments of most stores across America usually have no difficulty getting their messages across in local newspapers since apparel stores are a major source of advertising revenue for newspapers.

The Broadcast Media

Fashion merchandisers have a choice of standard broadcast mediums: television, cable television, and radio. Unlike the print medium, the broadcast media are time- rather than space-oriented. Radio and television stations sell three levels of commercials, in descending order of cost: network, spot, and local.

Television

One cannot turn on television today without learning something about current apparel fashions. The fashion industry obtains invaluable publicity from the simple fact that everyone who acts in a show or hosts or appears on a newscast or talk show wants to—and usually does—wear the latest fashions.

In addition to this general across-the-board exposure, short segments on fashion are generally presented in many news and talk shows. News of the fashion world is reported, as are the latest

Tall & Big Men

Choose from a greater selection of styles, in your size than you'll find anywhere else in the big (or tall) apple.

HE MAN Shops

61 West 48th Street • NYC • (212) 581-5020

*Forest Hills • Valley Stream • Huntington Station • Yonkers • Short Hills
Paramus • East Brunswick • Willow Grove • Stamford • Hartford*

Ads in general consumer publications like newspapers and magazines are a "must" for many retailers.

styles. Occasionally manufacturers and designers get a chance to exhibit their work.

Network television advertising is expensive enough to be prohibitive to all but a few fashion giants. Until the early 1980s, only huge companies such as Sears Roebuck and JC Penney or fiber firms like DuPont and Monsanto could afford to advertise on television. Increasingly, though, retailers and manufacturers have built television advertising into their budgets because they have seen that this is the best way to reach a generation reared on television. Manufacturers of sportswear—specifically, makers of jeans—were among the first to use television, but now designers such as Anne Klein II and Calvin Klein have learned to use television to transmit their fashion message.

Because of the technical expertise and high level of quality required for network television, outside advertising agencies are usually hired to produce television advertising. Agencies develop an idea, present it in storyboard form to their client, photograph the advertisement, obtain or create the music, and provide tapes to individual stations for on-air viewing.

Cable Television

Cable television has become an increasingly attractive option for fashion advertisers, largely because it costs so much less than network television. Many more outlets also exist for cable

All is not glamour in fashion advertising photography. Much time is spent on tiresome details such as checking the lighting.

television, which reduces the competition to buy space. The market for cable television is just taking off, but it is a large one that is far from saturated.

Radio

While television is unsurpassed as a fashion advertising medium because of its visual qualities, radio is popular because it is inexpensive and can reach large but target audiences. Stations exist that serve only the youth market; others, such as classical radio stations, are geared to an older market. Others broadcast news and can deliver a virtual captive audience during the morning and evening commutes.

The use of radio to sell fashion was tied to the rise of rock music in the 1950s and the youth-oriented market it created. The youth market has remained strong, but radio advertising, if chosen carefully, also reaches adults and families.

Radio is also a source of publicity as products and fashion news are discussed on regular shows.

As with television, most retailers and manufacturers rely on outside agencies to write and produce radio commercials, although some use their in-house talent to prepare commercials and then hire time-buying groups to place them.

Advertising, Publicity, and Public Relations Agencies

Advertising, publicity, and public relations agencies do far more for the fashion industry than prepare and sell advertising. An agency in any of these three areas may be deeply involved in creating a multimedia campaign designed to shape the public's image of a client company. They are used for ongoing maintenance of a company's image as well as for an image change.

Briefly Speaking

Lights, Camera, Action!

Videos *not* starring legendary song and dance teams, beautiful models, or handsome leading men have become the "hot sellers" of a new licensed department in stores. It is called *On Location* and can be found on the children's floor in Macy's New York where it draws a variety of customers who ham it up in a small video studio to the music and moving backdrop of their choice. About 10 minutes and $18.95 later, they emerge with a videotape featuring them as a pop star, Superman, or Superwoman. The clientele is split 50–50 between kids and adults. Parents often bring their children in for "video portraits."

The studio is operated by Center Stage of Houston, Texas, which started with a recording studio in Macy's where customers make cassette tapes of themselves singing to recorded music. Macy executives have stated that having these studios has helped to bring people into the store, which, after all is what sales promotion is all about!

Center Stage officials expect to construct many more video studios in stores in major metropolitan areas. The Center Stage audio recording studio is set up as a freestanding store in 15 regional shopping malls in addition to the department in Macy's New York. The company expects to license the video studios to upscale department stores across the country.

This Briefly Speaking is based on information from the following source:

Holly Haber, "On Location With Macy's," *Retailing Technology and Operations WWD/DNR*, September 1988, p. 52.

Advertising Agencies

Advertising agencies provide many services, all of which are tied to the selling of commercial advertising space and/or time. Some agencies are specialized and deal only with one medium or one type of client, while others are general, offering a full range of services for many different types of clients. Agencies vary from a one-person shop to a giant agency that employs hundreds of persons. Small agencies claim to offer personal attention, but even large agencies divide their staff into creative teams so they, too, promise and often deliver a specialized service.

Only the very large fiber and apparel companies regularly use advertising agencies. Smaller manufacturers and retailers and even fairly large department stores tend to rely on in-house advertising departments for all advertising except television and radio.

Public Relations Agencies

Public relations firms are involved in the creation of publicity as well as in public relations. Publicity and public relations require that the agency work closely with its client, keeping abreast of what is new and newsworthy and announcing it to the world, either through press releases, often accompanied by photographs, or with story ideas presented to trade and consumer magazines and newspapers. As noted, public relations also involves, on a much deeper level, the shaping of a company's image. To this end, a public relations agency may suggest or help to plan and coordinate an event or activity, such as the rendering of a public service or gift to a charity or community or the presentation of a scholarship or endowment to an institution or foundation. For example, the presentation of the Cutty Sark Fashion Award, given annually to a designer, is an industry-wide public relations activity.

The larger the company, the more likely it is to depend on an outside public relations firm. Retailers, however, largely tend to have their own in-house publicity departments that work closely

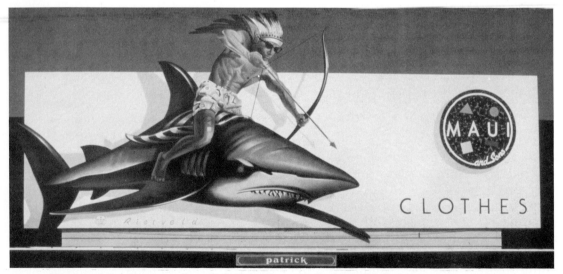

Print and broadcast media aren't the only game in town for fashion goods . . . check out this dramatic billboard.

with top management to present the company's best face to the public. Among the respected public relations agencies that specialize in the fashion industry are Eleanor Lambert, Inc., Ruth Hammer, Jody Donahue, Madeline De Vries, Christina Gottfried, and Mildred Collins.

TECHNOLOGY TALK

VIDEO CATALOGS EXPAND . . . BUT DON'T ALWAYS SUCCEED

When JC Penney Co. flipped the "on" switch to its Telaction network in 1987, after testing it in 39 Chicago suburbs, it heralded the service as a quick and easy way to shop at home using a TV and a pushbutton phone.

Unlike other TV shopping services that have announcers demonstrating sales items, Telaction resembled a video catalog offering viewers merchandise ranging from groceries to sweaters to pants to vacations.

Viewers used push-button phones to enter an electronic "mall" of more than 30 stores, then paged through items of a certain category or from a specific store. Consumers could shop or order 20 hours a day.

Besides Penney's, other stores featured in the electronic mall included Sears Roebuck, Spiegel, Marshal Field's, and Neiman-Marcus, as well as a jewelry store, a bank, a fabric store, and some traditional catalog houses.

For direct marketing, services like Telaction held the promise of a vast flow of additional information to direct marketers in the years ahead. For example, the system's tracking capability let marketers know how many people look at a video catalog and what interests individual viewers. Telaction's research indicated that electronic marketers had to be sensitive to what consumers want and expect. Also, consumers who know that a company has hundreds of items in its mailed catalog would be disappointed if only 30 items were in the electronic version.

Penney officials saw such interactive home shopping as the wave of the future. But the wave never crested. On March 30, 1989, after spending $106 million on Telaction, Penney scrapped the entire venture.

With Penney's retreat from interactive home shopping and other companies' failure in high-tech retailing, it suggests that retailers might be trying an idea whose time has not yet come. These failures raised doubts about how many consumers prefer to shop electronically rather than at stores. Yet some retailers still foresee a bright future for low-tech varieties of home shopping; because new technology greatly increases the number of callers who can respond to TV advertising. Currently, consumers are spending over $1 billion through TV programs that allow them to order by telephone, and industry experts suggest that it will continue to grow. At present, the business is dominated by the Home Shopping, Cable Value, and QVC networks.

However, the glory days of interactive retailing networks will only come when the home computer becomes a staple in homes—a staple like a TV and phone. Even if some of these high-tech concepts don't always work, moving two steps forward and one step back is better than standing still.

This Technology Talk is based on information from the following sources:

Judith Graham, "Computers Are Standing By," *Advertising Age,* February 6, 1989, p. 41.

Ira Teinowitz, "Penney's Video Catalog Text Expands," *Advertising Age,* February 6, 1989, p. 30.

"Penney's Drops Home Shopping," *Women's Wear Daily,* March 31, 1989, p. 11.

Brian Bremmer, "Penney's Isn't the Only Casualty in High-Tech Home Shopping," *Business Week,* April 17, 1989, p. 90.

Other Information Resources

The fashion business is so huge and complex that no one individual or company can keep abreast of everything that is happening in it. It is a business made up in large part of trends and news in addition to its products. As a result, an auxiliary service is provided by fashion consultants and research agencies whose job it is to supply information to the industry.

Fashion Consultants

Fashion consultants are individuals and groups who provide information and services to producers and retailers.

Tobé The most famous consultant, a pioneer in fashion consulting, was Tobé Coller Davis, who founded her agency Tobé Associates in 1927. Now owned and operated by Marjorie S. Deane, it remains an important source of information for the industry.

Tobé Associates produces "The Tobé Report," a weekly update on fashion news and trends, as well as its videotape counterpart, "Tobé on Tape."

The Fashion Group, Inc. Another vital source of industry information is The Fashion Group, Inc. An association of thousands of professional women who work in the industry, its original purpose was to create executive jobs for women, but it has become an important consulting and research agency. Its services are offered to members and, in some instances, nonmembers.

The Fashion Group is known for its exciting and prophetic fashion presentations. Through lavish fashion shows and fiber displays, it offers the fashion industry its expert and insightful analysis of upcoming trends. It covers the American, European, and Far Eastern fashion scene. It also publishes monthly news bulletins.

Market Research Agencies

Market research agencies have emerged to provide the fashion industry with the raw data it needs to spot and analyze trends. Among the better-known agencies is Yankelovich, Skelly, and White, respected for its extensive work in demographics and psychographics.

Trade Associations and Trade Shows

Associations of manufacturers and retailers assist fashion buyers in many ways. The nature and frequency of assistance available, though, are not uniform throughout the industry, and buyers soon learn how much assistance will be forthcoming from their particular trade association.

Buyers Groups Specialized associations or buying clubs provide an opportunity for an exchange of opinions and ideas among members. Retail buyers' groups also transmit the preferences of their members on matters as varied as the dates when lines should be opened to the sizes of stock boxes that are needed for specific products. Trade associations are often subsidized by outside sources, either the industry itself or a trade publication.

One of the newest associations is a group called Value Retailing, which is devoted to helping discounters. It was begun in 1980 with only 60 discount stores; by 1990 its membership had soared to 340, with chapters springing up all over the country. Value Retailing publishes a trade newspaper called *Value News.*

Trade Shows Retail and manufacturing groups, as well as independent organizations, sometimes sponsor trade shows, at which many exhibitors gather to show their products and lines in one place, usually a hotel or convention center. Trade shows save time that would otherwise be spent trudging from showroom to showroom and also provide buyers with a chance to meet and exchange ideas with one another. They are especially helpful in fashion areas made up of many small firms.

The shoe, notions, piece goods, and men's sportswear industries regularly sponsor trade shows. Other well-known shows are the Prêt-à-Porter show, the

FRENCH ACCENT
at New York Pret™

— March 5-7, 1989 —

The best of Paris at New York Prêt Fall-Winter 89

FEDERATION FRANÇAISE DU PRET A PORTER FEMININ

JACOB K. JAVITS CONVENTION CENTER
NEW YORK, N.Y.

FRENCH FASHION AND TEXTILE CENTER
CONTACT : BARBARA ENDE · TEL. (212) 213-0170

Trade shows, like the famous "NY Pret," save buyers time and money, and allow them to view lines that they would not normally be allowed to see.

New York Boutique Show, the International Fur Fair, the National Variety Show, and the Premium Show.

Fashion Bulletins Trade associations also regularly publish bulletins designed to report on news and trends in the industry and how they can be applied to special groups of buyers.

Specialized Consultants Some trade associations have staff experts whose job is to consult with group members and to make suggestions about the advertising, display, promotion, and selling of current fashions.

Retail Conventions Retail trade groups regularly sponsor conventions or meetings geared to their members' interests. Workshops provide a forum for discussing trends, news, opportunities, and problem areas. Members, of course, meet informally to exchange ideas at conventions.

One general convention is sponsored by the National Retail Merchants Association in New York City. A special feature at this convention is a session devoted to outstanding fashion promotions during the previous year. A new convention caters exclusively to discounters and is sponsored by the Value Retailing Association.

RESIDENT BUYING OFFICE

Another type of auxiliary service is the resident buying office, which is an organization that exists to serve the ongoing needs of a store or group of stores for a steady supply of new merchandise. Buying offices support the store's own buyers; they do not replace them. But a store's buyers work out of the store and only travel several times a year to fashion centers around the world, whereas a resident buying office is located at the market center and can provide ongoing, daily attention to the client stores' needs.

Although their main job is to buy and coordinate orders, buying offices provide many support services. They watch and report on fashion trends, provide information on product development, help with strategic planning, make vendor recommendations, and coordinate imports. They help to organize fashion weeks and ensure that they go smoothly for their client stores' buyers. A good buying office continually adds to its list of services, and many have even expanded into areas such as sales promotion and advertising, personnel operations, and computer processing.

Originally, resident buying offices existed only to place orders for out-of-town retailers. Today, their functions have become so diverse that the terms "resident office" or "buying office," which are used interchangeably, no longer seem adequate to explain the array of services these organizations provide for their client stores.

Types of Resident Buying Offices

Resident buying offices are either independent or store-owned. An independent office works for noncompeting stores that it seeks out as clients, while a store-owned office is owned by a group of stores, or less often one store, for whom it works exclusively.

Independent Offices

Independent offices are more numerous than store-owned offices. These can be further divided into those that are fee, or salaried, and those that are nonfee offices.

N E W Y O R K C O L L E C T I O N S

SEVENTH AVENUE TURNS ITS BACK ON FALL

Bill Blass did it, so did Carolyne Roehm and Geoffrey Beene—Blass even did it in broad daylight. They scooped the backs out of otherwise severe dresses, often anchoring racing-back straps with gold or diamante buttons. At Blass, daytime suit and coat outfits offer the surprise of a sweater with a cutout back.

One of GEOFFREY BEENE's "Metamorphosis" dresses—monastically severe in front with a cut-out back.

BILL BLASS' bare backs: by day, a double face wool Balmacaan and matching skirt in brown and red window pane check worn with a red cashmere turtle neck backless sweater; by night a red wool jersey backless gown is teamed with a red brocade jacket.

This is an example of an information resource provided by a fashion research agency.

FASHION

If you have ever doubted the power of the press, look at John Fairchild, the publisher of the fashion industry's "bibles"—*Women's Wear Daily* and *W.*

Fairchild Publications, a leading publisher of trade journals, was founded by John Fairchild's family and sold in 1968 to Capital Cities Communications. John Fairchild himself joined *Women's Wear Daily (WWD)* in the 1950s, became its publisher in 1960, and enhanced its prestige in 1972 by creating *W,* a color tabloid aimed at socialites.

Fairchild spent his summers working as a copyboy in Fairchild Publications' Paris offices. After college and a 2-year stint in the Army, he joined the family company full-time, before returning to Paris to become the company's European director in 1955.[1]

Having learned the ropes of fashion reporting from the bottom up—and obviously helped by the fact that his family owned the company—John Fairchild quickly found himself in a position to influence the way the press reported on fashion. Instead of publishing just pedestrian photos of runway fashion shows, *WWD* under his leadership began filling its page with photos from the street and from society parties to record the fashion worn by trend-setters.[2] And virtually singlehandedly, he changed fashion journalism from "elegant puffery" to hard-nosed reporting.[3]

For instance, early in his *WWD* career, two French couturiers barred press coverage of their collections until a month after the collections were shown to buyers. Feeling that it was unfair to his readers to hold back newsworthy information, Fairchild went ahead and published the fashion photos and sketches before their release dates. Banished from the couturiers' showrooms, he sometimes disguised his reporters as messengers to gain entry—or even had them stand in windows of buildings opposite fashion houses, in order to see and sketch the new styles![4]

Because of his "no holds barred" methods of reporting on fashion, it is perhaps not surprising that certain "feuds" have taken place between Fairchild and various designers. After all, he wields enormous power over who is "in" and who is "out." And while those

FOCUS

decisions may sometimes appear arbitrary—"He has a fickle star system that changes with the wind," says a former *WWD* writer[5]—they are also based on a tremendously sound knowledge and feel for fashion: "For years, he has sensed what's good, better, and faster than anyone else in the fashion industry."[6]

Agrees James Brady, a syndicated columnist and former *WWD* staffer: "It takes a rare critical quality to be able to sit through a collection of some 300 dresses, coats, and suits . . . and still be able to emerge declaring with absolute confidence that No. 276, the red wool scalloped suit with the soft waist, is the one 'Ford' that millions of women will be wearing next year . . . John Fairchild has that knack."[7]

Playing favorites appears to be highly fashionable in fashion writing. Friends of Fairchild, including Bill Blass and Oscar de la Renta, have been lavishly covered in his pages over the years; while Givenchy, Balenciaga, and Beene, to name a few, are among the respected designers who have been periodically banned from *WWD*'s pages.[8] The reasons? In Beene's case, the designer himself cites several *"faux pas,"* including refusing to reveal to Fairchild an advance sketch of Lynda Bird Johnson's wedding dress and purchasing only a small ad in *W* for a new fragrance he was launching.[9]

On the other hand, while established designers the likes of Yves Saint Laurent and Geoffrey Beene were being exiled from the pages of *WWD* and *W,* a relative newcomer was enjoying the *WWD* fashion spotlight. Christian Lacroix, within months after opening his own Paris salon, found himself and his creations splashed on the covers of Fairchild's publications. And inside, the society pages were filled with women in Lacroix designs. Of course, a "wrong move" and all that could change instantly—as Lacroix' business director, Jean-Jacques Picart, noted, saying "All we've won today, we can lose in two seasons."[10] It can work both ways. But that's the power of the press . . . and the power and talent of John Fairchild to tell the fashion world what's *haute* and what's out.

[1] James Brady, "Clothes Encounters with John Fairchild," *New York,* August 4, 1980, p. 29.

[2] Patrick Reilly, "At 75, Threadbare Spots Mar *WWD*'s Hold on Fashion World," *Crain's New York Business,* December 9, 1985, p. 1.

[3] Ibid., p. 30.

[4] Michael Gross, "Women's Wear Daily and Feuds in Fashion," *The New York Times,* May 8, 1987, p. J.

[5] Andrea Gabor with Richard Z. Chesnoff and Maia Wechsler, "Of Power, Glory and the Rich and Famous," *U.S. News & World Report,* August 24, 1987, p. 55.

[6] Ibid.

[7] Brady, p. 29.

[8] Ibid.

[9] Gross, p. J.

[10] Ibid.

This Fashion Focus is based on information from the articles cited above.

Fee Offices A **fee, salaried,** or **paid office** charges the stores for whom it works an annual, stipulated fee, which is based on the store's sales volume.

Fee offices typically represent noncompeting moderate-priced department and specialty stores in mid-sized and secondary markets. To avoid conflicts, most buying offices restrict themselves to one client in each trading area, although they do specialize in one type of store or retail operation. A buying office familiarizes itself with each client's needs, however, and then attempts to meet those needs with as wide a range of services as possible.

Nonfee Offices A **nonfee office,** in contrast to a fee office, does not charge its clients for its services. Instead it takes a fee from manufacturers. The fee is based on a dollar percentage of the orders placed for clients. While it might appear that a buying office would be more involved with the manufacturers' interests than those of the client stores, well-run nonfee offices have been able to overcome this handicap and serve their clients as well as fee offices. Nonfee offices are a good solution for small fashion stores whose sales volume is not large enough to permit them to hire the services of a fee buying office. One of the largest nonfee offices is Apparel Alliance.

Store-Owned Offices

Store-owned offices are either associated or corporate-owned.

Associated Offices An **associated** or **cooperative office** is cooperatively owned and operated by a group of privately owned stores for their mutual use. It never takes outside private clients. Membership is by invitation only. It is considerably more expensive than if the store were a client of an in-

dependent office since members buy shares in the cooperative when they join. The amount of shares that must be purchased is keyed to member stores' sales volume.

One advantage of belonging to an associated office is that it provides member stores with an important exchange of information. Since the stores that belong to an associated office are homogeneous, their relationship to one another is an intimate one that often includes an exchange of financial information as well as merchandising experience.

Two of the best-known and largest associated buying offices are Frederick Atkins, and Associated Merchandising Corporation (AMC).

Corporate-Owned Offices The **corporate-owned,** or **syndicated office** as it is sometimes called, is maintained by a parent organization exclusively for the stores it owns. One advantage of this type of organization is that it can be given more authority than an independent office, although some corporate-owned offices still require authorization from store buyers for major purchases. The Macy corporate office is an example of this type of office.

Organization of Resident Buying Offices

All buying offices are organized with one goal in mind: to provide member stores with products and information they need to maintain a cutting edge in the fashion business. To this end, buying offices offer a broad—and generally expanding—variety of services to their client stores. Not surprising, when one considers their function, most buying offices are organized along the lines of a department store. Their four main divisions are merchandising, sales promotion, operation and research, and personnel.

Merchandising Division

The merchandising division's primary responsibility is to buy merchandise for client stores. Merchandise managers supervise groups of **market representatives,** who are the equivalent of store buyers. As is the case with store buyers, each market representative specializes and buys only within a specialty.

A fashion director is responsible for promoting and coordinating overall fashion trends for client stores. The fashion director's staff watches and interprets fashion trends and supplies information on them to the merchandising managers and client stores.

Sales Promotion Division

The sales promotion division, typically bolstered by an in-house staff of artists, provides sales assistance to member stores. All buying offices provide special materials for their clients. These consist of regular bulletins and more elaborate brochures for seasonal or special events such as Christmas, or back-to-school.

Operations and Research Division

The operations and research division studies and reports to client stores on their business operations. Sales, merchandising, and financial data is regularly supplied to client stores.

Personnel Division

The personnel division is dedicated to keeping client stores up-to-date on the numerous government regulations regarding personnel. Many small stores do not have their own personnel departments, so this service is especially important to them. The personnel division also provides placement assistance to client stores. It may do so formally by conducting a search, or informally by passing the word throughout the marketplace on behalf of a client.

Foreign Buying Division

In response to the increasingly global nature of the fashion business, many resident buying offices have begun maintaining overseas, or commissionaire, divisions in key foreign cities. (A commissionaire is an agent that represents stores in foreign markets.) Overseas divisions work closely with the merchandising division and with client stores.

Trends in Resident Buying Offices

Because of the mergers and acquisitions occurring among retailers, buying offices have declined in number. This is because buying offices lose clients when these mergers occur.

Buying offices have also been subject to some mergers and acquisitions of their own. Size appears to be an important trend in buying offices' reorganizations. Abbey Doneger, president of Henry Doneger Associates, recently said: "To succeed, buying offices have to be very big or very small."[1] Henry Doneger Associates has emerged as one of the larger offices. In the 1980s, it merged with Steinberg-Kass, Jerry Bernstein, and the Independent Retailers Syndicate.

Small operations, which offer exclusivity to their customers, sometimes even exaggerate their smallness by downplaying the number of stores they handle. They note that in a business consumed by "mergermania," they are better able to service their clients, who may themselves be expanding, by continuing to provide personalized and individual service.

Specialization

Some buying offices have responded to the decline in business by becoming even more specialized. While buying offices have always specialized to some degree in order to better serve their clients, the specialization today has gone to even greater depths. Atlas Buying Corporation, for example, has carved out its own niche by specializing in discount stores owned by department store chains. Other offices, work only with stores selling off-price merchandise. A number of firms have followed the broader industry trend toward niche selling and specialize in large-, half-, and petite-sized fashions.

Private-Label Programs

Corporate buying offices have played an important role in the development of private labels. Most corporate-owned buying offices have a private-label program for their member stores.

Associated Merchandising Corporation and Frederick Atkins have established a particularly strong retail presence with the private labels among its member stores. AMC is known for its Preswick & Moore label, aimed at the high-end, traditional customer, and Architect, geared toward the young, career-oriented customer. AMC has devoted considerable time and attention to developing its private label program, researching everything from names to package design and point-of-sale display. It has even begun national advertising in major fashion magazines.[2]

Corporate offices have also aggressively pursued private-label business. Among their names are Macy's Loft & Brownstone, Dayton Hudson's Boundary Waters, and The Limited's Forenza. Some offices have also contracted with designers to create merchandise exclusive lines.[3]

REFERENCES

[1] Samuel Feinberg, "Buying Offices: Thinking Small," *Women's Wear Daily,* September 7, 1988, p. 24.
[2] Isadore Barmash, "Private Label: Flux," *Stores,* April 1987, p. 19.
[3] Jacqueline Bivens, "Buying Office Status Report," *Stores,* May, 1989, pp. 54–61.

MERCHANDISING VOCABULARY

Define or briefly explain the following terms:

Advertising
Associated or cooperative office
Corporate-owned or syndicated office

Editorial credit
Fee, salaried, or paid office
Market representative
Nonfee office

Public relations
Publicity
Resident buying office
Trade publication

MERCHANDISING REVIEW

1. What is the major function of the resident buying office? What additional services do they perform? Why are resident buying offices particularly advantageous to the small store?
2. List and briefly describe the differences between the four major types of resident buying offices.
3. Describe the organization of a typical resident buying office today.
4. Describe the sales promotion services of a resident buying office.
5. What are the current trends in the development of resident buying offices?
6. What is the difference between advertising and publicity/public relations?
7. Describe the contents of *Women's Wear Daily*.
8. What are the advantages of television and radio for fashion exposure?
9. What tasks do public relations firms undertake for their clients?
10. What is the role of a fashion consultant? Name two major fashion consultants in the industry today.

MERCHANDISING DIGEST

1. You own a small boutique that caters to upscale young women. What type of resident buying office would be most advantageous for you? Why?
2. As a consumer, where do you get your information about fashion? What media influences your buying decisions the most?

Exploring Fashion Retailing Policies

T he objective of this project is to allow the student to synthesize the information learned in this unit and to assess its impact on different types of retailers and how they function.

A. Choose three different types of fashion:
- One should be the local department store in town
- One should be a specialty store in town
- One should be a choice of your own from any of the following types of retail distributors—discount store, off-price store, mass merchandiser, mail order catalog firm

Compare and contrast each of the three different types of retail distributors on the following points:
- Target customer
- Type of merchandise assortment
- Place on the fashion cycle
- Quality standards
- Foreign vs. domestic merchandise
- Selling and other customer services

B. Choose one major department or classification of goods (i.e., sportswear, dresses, shoes, etc.) in each store that you used in question A above. (It should be the same for all stores!) Compare these departments on the following points:
- Manufacturers carried (brand names, designer names, store name labels, etc.)
- Type of advertising used (clip ads over a three-week period, comparing and contrasting the ads on your chosen classification.)
- Publicity or promotional events used by each retailer

C. Set up a chart (model it after Table 16-2 in Chapter 16) that shows information for each of the retail distributors you chose.

D. Cut and mount one ad from each retailer showing the retailer's merchandising and advertising policies. Explain the differences between them.

Appendix 1
Choosing a Career in Fashion

The person who embarks on a fashion career today enters a field that is far-flung and many-faceted. In this field there is freedom to grow, freedom to change jobs or direction, and freedom to move to different cities or even to different countries without having to begin in an unrelated type of work.

PERSONAL QUALITIES AND SKILLS REQUIRED IN FASHION FIELDS

The fashion field is many-faceted, and the positions open to people starting a career are numerous and diverse. Some fields, such as designing, advertising, and display, usually demand a high degree of creativity and originality. Others, such as fiber and fabric research and development, require an interest and education in scientific subjects. Still others, such as plant management and retailing management, call for in-depth business know-how and administrative skills.

A pleasing personality, a genuine interest in people, and a willingness to work and learn are indispensable in the fashion field. A strong constitution and healthy feet are also helpful in the market work of retail buyers, buying office representatives, magazine editors, fashion coordinators, and their assistants. Skills in writing, sketching, typing, and photography are much in demand in the fashion field. Sewing and draping skills, even without a designer's creativity, can lead to such interesting work as sample making. In personnel, supervisory, and training work, an ability to teach is very helpful. This ability can also lead to a position as a teacher in one of the many schools devoted to fashion training.

Education and experience requirements vary even between one business and another within the same industry. Many large retail organizations, for example, will not even interview a person for a position in the store's executive training program unless he or she has a baccalaureate degree. Others will accept associate degrees and certificates from specialized fashion schools. Still others hire for management training primarily those individuals on their sales staff who show the most promise. The wide variation in requirements, therefore, makes advance planning and research doubly important to the individual planning a fashion career.

EVALUATING CAREER GOALS

An individual's career is usually the single most important factor in determining his or her lifestyle. Consideration should therefore be given to the effect career choice will have on such things as geographic location, family life, monetary compensation, degree of pressure and responsibility the job requires, and number of hours devoted to the job.

Too often dissatisfaction with a job is not the fault of either the job or the worker, but rather the result of a mismatch between the two. The scope and variety of job opportunities within the fashion field means that there is a fashion-related position for almost anyone who is interested, and a realistic evaluation of career goals will help eliminate many future disappointments.

IN-DEPTH JOB STUDY

Obviously, a wise decision cannot be made until the options are known. The importance of making an in-depth study of the career being considered cannot be overemphasized. As is true with many glamour jobs, there are a great many unrealistic perceptions of what a fashion career is really like. College graduates often expect to become buyers within a year, and are very surprised when they are asked to sell and do stock work, literally starting from the bottom in what might seem to be painfully slow progress toward their ultimate goal.

IMPORTANCE OF FIRST JOBS

First jobs in any industry can be critical, and the fashion business is no exception. Obviously, experience and training can be gained in any job, but will the job be a real plus on a résumé? What is the reputation of the firm or individual? What type of training program or apprenticeship is offered? The value of a good reference from an individual who is well respected in the industry cannot be overemphasized! And, it is often better to accept a lower-paying job that offers outstanding training, rather than a higher-paying position with narrower opportunity in the long run.

CAREER PATHS

A **career** is a lifelong activity, involving all of the jobs an individual may have, both paid and unpaid. An aspiring designer may, for example, begin his or her career designing clothes for family and friends. As opportunities for education and experience occur, choices are made, and so an occupational **career path** or **career ladder** is formed: the order of occupations or periods of work in a person's life.

A **job** is a specific position within an industry. In fashion retailing, typical **entry-level jobs,** requiring little or no specific training and experience, include salesperson, cashier, and stock person. **Mid-management positions,** requiring some experience and training and involving a higher degree of responsibility, include department manager or manager of a small store. **Management positions** include buyer, merchandise manager, and manager for a large store.

Those individuals who do some advance planning, who determine the goals they wish to pursue in the fashion industry, and what education, training, and experience are necessary to achieve those goals, are more likely to recognize a good opportunity when they see it. They make things happen!

FINDING A JOB IN FASHION

One of the first steps in career selection should be a self-evaluation to determine what the individual truly wants from a career. Listed below are some of the questions that should be answered to narrow down some of the many choices available to the fashion graduate:

- Do you want a career that will let you live in the same area that you live in now?
- Would you be willing to move to another area in the future if it meant a better job?
- Would you like to travel for your job?
- Would you be willing to work on the weekends and have your days off during the middle of the week?

- Which of the following things do you want from your career? Which is most important? Which is least important?

Money	Self-satisfaction
Prestige	Challenges
Independence	Chance to be
Security	creative
Interesting	Other things
experiences	(list)

Each response should be considered in light of various careers considered by the student. When career choices have been narrowed, a thorough investigation of each should be made to determine how well a career area meets the needs of the individual.

As mentioned previously, part-time experience is an excellent way to explore job possibilities. Field experience and internship programs in colleges provide such opportunities, and students have the advantage of being able to share experiences with other students.

LOOKING FOR OPPORTUNITIES

Where can the student look for full-time jobs in fashion? One possible source—and often the best—is the campus interview. Each spring, retailers from all over the United States send recruiters to various campuses in an effort to select personnel for executive training programs in their stores. Former part-time employers can also be an excellent source of information for employment; often if they have no position available, they can give leads to other sources.

Many personnel agencies specialize in specific types of job placement. A telephone survey of possible agencies can save time and make job hunting much more effective.

Finally, networking among friends in the fashion field can be one of the best ways to pick up leads. The job seeker should let everyone know that he or she is actively looking for employment. This multiplies the effort and can therefore often shorten the search.

AFTER YOU ARE HIRED

The true professional never stops growing, whether through participation in professional organizations, taking advanced courses and seminars, or reading journals and other publications. It is also important to stay aware of opportunities for growth through promotion or moves to other firms. Such information is often acquired through a network of professional friends—valuable assets to any career. Such a network must be cultivated, however, which means at least in part that the policy to follow when moving from one organization to another is "Don't burn your bridges behind you!"

Appendix 2
Careers in Manufacturing

The principal manufacturing industries in the fashion field require fashion-oriented and fashion-trained people to guide their production, market their products to the industries they serve, and keep both their customers and fashion consumers informed about their products.

RAW MATERIALS INDUSTRIES

The greatest number and variety of fashion careers in the raw materials field are found among the producers of fiber and fabrics. Similar positions, but in smaller numbers, are also to be found with other raw materials producers, such as leather and furs, and their respective industry associations.

Fashion Expert

Fiber producers and fabric firms have fashion departments headed by individuals with a variety of titles who attend worldwide fashion openings, keep in close touch with all sources of fashion information, and disseminate the fashion story throughout their respective organizations. Candidates for such positions either may have already acquired fashion expertise in other areas of the fashion business or are employees of the firm who have demonstrated an ability to handle such responsibilities.

The fashion department's activities usually require personnel with the ability to coordinate apparel and accessories, to stage fashion shows, to work with the press, to assist individual producers and retailers with fashion-related problems, and to set up fashion exhibits for the trade or for the public.

Fabric Designer

It takes both technical and artistic skills to produce a fabric. Fabric companies employ designers who have not only technical knowledge of the processes involved in producing a fabric but also artistic ability and the ability to successfully anticipate fashion trends. The fabric designer, who works months ahead of the apparel trades, needs fashion radar of superlative quality. The chief designer for a fabric mill makes fashion decisions that can involve vast capital investments every time a new season's line is prepared.

Fabric Stylist and Colorist

Many fabric companies employ a fabric stylist and/or colorist to revise existing fabric designs for a new seasonal line, try out various color combinations for an existing design, or adapt designs for specific markets.

Fabric Librarian

Most major synthetic fiber sources maintain libraries of fabrics that are made from their fibers. These libraries consist of fabric swatches clipped to cards on which detailed descriptions and sources of supply are recorded. The librarian in charge is expected to be thoroughly capable of discussing fashion trends and fabric matters with interested designers and manufacturers.

Publicity Executive

In both fiber and fabric companies, the publicity staff keeps in close touch with technical as well as fashion matters and makes information about company products readily available to the trade and consumer press. Usually product stories can be tied to fashion information, enhancing their appeal to editors and readers alike.

In the major fiber-producing companies, there may be a corps of publicity executives, each specializing in one or two closely related industries. One may concentrate on the use of specific fibers in apparel fabrics, for instance, while another may specialize in the use of the company's fibers in rugs and carpeting. In smaller organizations, there may be only one such executive.

Jobs in Textile Technology

Positions within the industry are also available for individuals with technical training in the production of textile products. Converters oversee the various processes in the transition of greige goods to finished fabric. Lab technicians perform tests on fabrics, yarns, fibers, and garments to determine durability, colorfastness, and shrinkage. Other positions involve responsibility for quality control, design of graphs for knits, fabric analysis, and color research.

Marketing Fibers and Fabrics

Both fiber and fabric industries offer career opportunities in sales, market research, and promotion. These are not always fashion jobs, however, and they are rarely open to beginners. Some experience within the company and some specialized skill in the field are likely to be more important in getting such jobs than a knowledge of fashion alone.

APPAREL TRADES

For creative people, the plum of the fashion apparel trades is the designer's job. But the climb to this top job is often laborious and uncertain, and the footing at the top may be slippery. New talent is always elbowing its way in, and even the most successful couture designers are haunted by the prospect of a season when their ideas do not have customer appeal.

Designing

Because so much of an apparel firm's success depends upon the styling of its line, the designing responsibility is rarely entrusted to a beginner, even a highly talented one. There are matters of cost and mass-production techniques involved, for example, and there is also the business of judging accurately the point in the fashion cycle at which the firm's customers will buy.

For moderate-priced and mass-market producers, the designer's job may be one of adapting rather than creating. Immense skill may be required, nevertheless, to take a daringly original couture idea and modify it so that it appears bright and new but not terrifyingly unfamiliar to a mass-market or middle-income customer.

The beginner, aside from offering designs on a freelance basis, can seek a number of jobs below the designer level in hopes of working up to that top level. Entry-level design jobs include assistant designer, sketcher-stylist, junior designer, pattern maker, sketcher, and sample maker.

Apparel Production

Positions in this field are with apparel manufacturing plants or offices. Skilled jobs for fashion graduates are available in both apparel production management and in pattern making.

Apparel Production Management

Entry-level positions in this field include junior engineers, costing engineers, assistant plant managers, production assistants, and quality control engineers.

Pattern Making

Entry-level positions in this field include assistant pattern maker, cutting assistant, grader trainee, and marker trainee.

Advertising and Publicity

An advertising manager, with possibly an assistant or two, may handle the advertising and publicity for an apparel manufacturer. Publicity, usually a part of the advertising job, involves sending out press releases to interest consumer publications in some of the firm's new styles. Promotion kits for retailers are prepared under the direction of the advertising manager, as are statement enclosures and other direct-mail pieces offered for retail use.

Sales Opportunities

Sales representatives who call upon retail stores should know the fashion points as well as the value points of their merchandise. Today, sales representatives are expected to be able to address retail salespeople, if invited to do so, or even to take part in consumer forums and clinics.

An understanding of retail merchandising, promotion, and fashion coordination is extremely helpful in all sales jobs in the apparel field. When selling to retailers, it is important to understand their needs, problems, and methods of operation, as well as what stage of the fashion cycle is of major interest to their customers. With such a background, sales representatives can present a line more effectively and can also gather and develop sound retail merchandising and promotion ideas for their accounts.

One of the best ways to begin a career in fashion is as a salesperson in a retail organization. Experience in selling to customers is a must for all people interested in any career in the fashion field. For it is the salesperson who has direct contact with the customer, and in the fashion field it is the customer who is always right.

MERCHANDISING CAREERS

The starting place for most merchandising careers is in selling. Here one experiences face-to-face encounters with customers and the problem of anticipating what they will want.

Traditionally, the merchandising career ladder has moved from a sales position up through the ranks to the buyer's position. However, in recent years many large firms with many branches have provided a choice: an aspiring fashion merchant may choose either the traditional sales-to-buyer route or a strictly management route.

The Buying Route

A person who chooses the buying route can go from head of stock to assistant buyer to buyer to divisional merchandise manager and finally to general merchandise manager. The responsibilities of each position are given below.

Head of Stock

This is a position in which one may do some selling, but it mainly involves replenishing stock in the selling area from the stockroom, reporting "outs," noticing and reporting slow sellers, and advising the buyer on unfilled customer wants.

Assistant Buyer

The assistant buyer's job is the next step upward. As an understudy to the buyer, the assistant buyer may be called in to view the line of a visiting sales representative and may be taken occasionally to the market on a buying trip. Usually, however, the assistant buyer relieves the buyer of floor supervision, helps to train and supervise salespeople, processes branch questions and requests, and writes up reorders for basic stocks subject to the buyer's approval.

Buyer

Buyers are virtually in business for themselves, in the sense that they have to budget and plan their expenditures, select the actual merchandise for resale, and decide what is to be advertised or displayed and why. The job usually involves from two to a dozen or more market trips a year.

Divisional Merchandise Manager

In large stores, buyers of departments handling related merchandise are supervised by a divisional merchandise manager. Examples of related departments are infants' and children's wear, women's ready-to-wear, menswear, boys' wear, and home furnishings.

The merchandise manager coordinates the efforts of a group of departments, with or without the aid of a fashion director, so that the fashion picture each department presents to the public is related in theme, timing, and emphasis to those presented by the others.

General Mechandise Manager

The final rung on the merchandising career ladder is general merchandise manager, a top management position that demands, in addition to fashion and merchandising know-how, an understanding of every phase of store operation, from housekeeping to finances.

The Management Route

A person who chooses the management route can go from assistant group sales manager to group sales manager to divisional sales manager and finally to store manager. The responsibilities of each position are given below.

Assistant Group Sales Manager

The assistant group sales manager works closely with the group sales manager in directing the activities of several related departments in a branch store.

Group Sales Manager

The group sales manager (GSM) coordinates the personnel, merchandising, and operations aspects of several departments in a branch store. The person employed in this position must be both a merchant and a manager of people, learning to delegate responsibility in increasingly larger areas with a growing staff. A very large chain of stores might have several levels of group sales manager positions, with top-level GSMs managing the activities of two or three other executives.

Divisional Sales Manager

The divisional sales manager is responsible for a large segment of a store. It is the responsibility of the divisional sales manager to develop the skills of the group sales managers so that they can better manage, control, and direct the efforts of their areas to maximize profitable retail sales volume.

Store Manager

Store manager positions are near the top of the career ladder in management, second only to the chief executive officer and board of directors of the organization. The store manager is responsible for the total store operation in a single location.

SALES PROMOTION CAREERS

Career opportunities in sales promotion include jobs on the advertising staff, the publicity and public relations staff, and the display staff.

Copywriters and Artists

Copywriters and artists who begin in retailing usually enjoy a tremendous advantage ever afterward. If they leave the field and go into advertising agencies or go to work for producers, they carry with them an understanding of consumer reaction that can be learned in no better school than the retail store.

Public Relations

Publicity assignments usually grow out of copywriting jobs, although outsiders are sometimes hired for this work. Involved are such diverse activities as alerting the local press to newsworthy happenings, arranging for television interviews of visiting celebrities, and working up elaborate events—whether in the name of fashion, community, or charity—that will brighten the store image.

Visual Merchandising and Display

Visual merchandising and display executives usually start as assistants with a willingness to work hard. They advance in position if they demonstrate artistic sense, a knowledge of fashion, the ability to speak in visual terms to the store's customers, and the ability to pick up important selling points about merchandise.

FASHION COORDINATION AND FASHION DIRECTION

Partly merchandising and partly promotion, the jobs of fashion coordinator and fashion director are ideal for people who are extremely interested in fashion, know how to work with others, and have an unlimited supply of energy! These jobs involve working with a great many people, from merchandise or fashion information resources to store staff to customers, and their goals are accomplished largely through recommendations and advice rather than direct orders.

The fashion director is often one of the key store executives in a large chain who travel with buyers and merchandise managers to overseas markets as well as domestic markets. He or she may also be a member of a buying committee that travels to the Orient to contract for large orders to be produced exclusively for the chain according to store specifications.

As exciting as these jobs are, there are actually very few full-time fashion directors or coordinators employed, even in large cities.

SALES-SUPPORTING CAREERS

Retail stores have openings in fields not directly related to the buying, selling, and promoting of merchandise. These activities, which may involve more than half the employees of a store, include personnel employment and training, accounting, customer services, and adjustments, among many others. Even in the rapidly growing area of data processing jobs, fashion knowledge can be a valuable asset. For instance, add a knowledge of fashion merchandising to an understanding of computer programming, and the result is the kind of background that can lead to a career in computer program design for fashion-oriented companies.

PROFESSIONAL FASHION SALES CAREERS

Surprisingly enough, many commissioned salespersons in top fashion stores earn more than the buyers or store managers! Individuals who truly enjoy working one-on-one with a customer, who take a personal interest in the customer's lifestyle and clothing needs, and who derive a great deal of pleasure from completing a sale and seeing a satisfied customer walk out of the store should consider professional sales as a career.

CHAIN AND MAIL-ORDER CAREERS

Chain and catalog firms offer careers that are similar to those offered by independent stores, with this important exception: Buying, merchandising, publicity, and fashion coordination are handled by the headquarters staff rather than by the individual stores.

Career advancement up the retail management ladder, if one starts in a unit of a chain or in a catalog organization, begins with selling and moves to department manager, merchandise manager, store manager, and finally to district, regional, or central management. Those interested in such fields as buying, fashion coordination, promotion, catalog preparation, merchandising, and quality control start as assistants in regional or central headquarters, where central buyers and merchandise managers are located.

Many highly specialized jobs in the chain and catalog companies call for intimate knowledge of the fashion business. For instance, the quality control department of one chain was called upon by the merchandising division to devise a size range for girls who fell between two size ranges currently offered by the children's market. The chain then made its new size range measurements available to any producers who wished to adopt them, whether or not they were resources of that chain.

Whatever special assets the beginner presents—apparel production techniques, laboratory know-how, or experience in copywriting, art, selling, buying, or coordination—the chain and the catalog companies can use them, but not always in the city or region where the applicant lives.

Appendix 4
Careers in Fashion Auxiliary Services

A wide variety of job opportunities is available in the service organizations that aid and assist the wholesale and retail fashion industries. These service organizations, such as advertising and publicity agencies, consumer and trade publications, trade associations, and consulting firms, perform functions that have a show-business quality about them. Work in these fields is hectic and, for those suited to it, fun. Each area has its own requirements, but in all of them there are important jobs in which an understanding of fashion is vital.

ADVERTISING AGENCIES

Beginners, even those with special skills, often have a hard time entering the agency field. College graduates complain that they go to dozens of agencies and are offered nothing more exciting than a mail room or receptionist job. A solution to the beginner's problem may be to avoid the biggest and best-known agencies and seek a starting job in an agency of modest or small size. There the pay is likely to be small, the office tiny, and the future problematic, but the opportunities to work and learn are good and provide the experience necessary to qualify later for a good job in a major agency.

The careers in advertising agencies in which a fashion background can be useful include account executive, copywriter, illustrator, layout artist, and fashion consultant.

CONSUMER PUBLICATIONS

Nearly all consumer publications carry some sort of fashion material, and some are devoted exclusively to fashion. Career opportunities with such publications are immensely varied, ranging from editorial work to those numerous, behind-the-scenes activities that go into the publishing of a magazine or newspaper.

Fashion Editor

When fashion is presented in a publication, that publication's fashion judgment must be authoritative. Whether the publication is devoted entirely to fashion or simply runs a fashion section, the editor's job is to discover what the reader responds to, locate those fashions in the market, and illustrate examples of them at the right time. The editorial job can be all the more complicated because of pressures from publicity-hungry producers. An editor may cover the entire fashion market or just one segment of it, depending on the type of publication and the size of the publication's staff.

Merchandising Editor

Behind the scenes, the merchandising editors of national publications and their staffs work to make sure that readers anywhere in the country can buy the merchandise that is featured editorially. They do this by reporting to retailers in advance of publication the details of what is to run, why it is important, and from what resources it is available. With their formidable knowledge of markets, merchandise, and retailing, these editors are also well equipped to offer retailers practical suggestions about how to successfully merchandise, promote, and display the items featured in their publications.

Advertising Sales Rep

Selling advertising space is the major source of revenue for a publication. The many aspects of selling accommodate various talents. Those who like selling deal with producers and their advertising agencies. People with a flair for research help the sales representatives to sell advertising space in the publication by supplying facts that indicate the publication's ability to enlist retail cooperation or that measure the buying power of the publication's readers. Those with a flair for persuasive writing may find a place on the advertising promotion staff, where presentations are developed to help the sales reresentatives conduct meetings with prospective advertisers.

TRADE PUBLICATIONS

Some trade publications are very narrowly specialized, such as *Accessories* and *Body Fashions and Intimate Apparel,* and are likely to be published monthly. Some are less specialized, such as *Retail Week,* and tend to be published weekly or semimonthly. A few, such as *Women's Wear Daily* (covering the women's apparel field) and *Daily News Record* (covering the menswear and textile fields), provide in-depth coverage of a specific field and are published 5 days a week, Monday through Friday, except holidays. All may offer opportunities for beginners with an interest in fashion.

CONSULTING SERVICES TO THE FASHION INDUSTRY

The most glamorous of the consulting services involved in the fashion field is, of course, the fashion consultant. Of these, the oldest and best-known is the Tobé service, founded in 1927 by the late Tobé Coller Davis. As a young woman, she was hired to advise a retail store on its fashion merchandise by bringing the customers' point of view to bear on merchandise selections and promotions. From this start, she developed a syndicated service to which stores all over the country subscribed. With what is now a large staff, the firm continues to cover and interpret fashion news in such a way that buying, merchandising, and coordination executives can be guided by the views of skilled observers in every important fashion center. Reports, bulletins, clinics, videotapes, and individual advice are the subscribers' diet.

Resident Buying Office Careers

Fashion careers in resident buying offices center around market work. Market representatives "live" in their markets, see every line that is important (and many that are not), and know supply and delivery conditions in those markets as well as they know the fashion aspects of the merchandise. Market representatives also learn to work with any number of bosses: their own supervisors, the heads of the client stores, and the buyers in the stores they serve.

Entry into the market representative's job is through the position of apprentice. Beginners work as assistants, literally running errands in the market all day. The major job of an assistant is to follow up on details, to check with resources on deliveries and other questions that may arise, and to save the time of the market representative. In the process, the beginner gets to know the markets, the buying office routines, and the needs of the client stores. If the work is done against a background of fashion training, it is more easily mastered and promotion is apt to be more rapid.

CONSULTING SERVICES TO THE CONSUMER

In recent years, fashion consumer consulting services have grown in popularity. Consulting services may be offered by fashion-trained individuals who wish to begin their own business on a part-time basis, and can often grow to a full-time, profitable business. Such businesses can be started with relatively little capital, but need a considerable amount of promotion from self-starting individuals with previous experience in the field of fashion to succeed.

Image and Wardrobe Consultant

Wardrobe, or image, consultants act as wardrobe counselors to individuals who wish to look fashionable and project an individual image. Such consumers may lack confidence in their own ability to plan a wardrobe, or may simply lack the time and knowledge necessary to choose the fashions that are most flattering and suitable for their lifestyle.

Color Consultant

Another type of consumer consultant that has become popular is the color consultant or specialist. The extent of services offered varies widely, as do the background and training of these individuals. Many color specialists offer only one service, that of developing a color chart for the individual client illustrating the client's best colors. This color chart is then used for all clothing purchases so that the individual can closely coordinate his or her wardrobe, thus avoiding costly mistakes in purchasing items that do not match other garments in the wardrobe. Other color specialists also offer services such as recommending the client's best fashion "type" or look, whether it be sophisticated, ingenue, or country.

Many color specialists develop workshops each season to present fashion looks to their clients, drawing from the selections offered in many stores in their shopping area. Workshops are also presented to corporate groups who want to improve the personal image of their employees.

In recent years, the Association of Image Consultants has been organized, seeking to professionalize both the Wardrobe/Image Consultant's job and the Color Consultant's job. Certification courses are available in schools throughout the country, as well as through workshops offered by the organization.

TELEVISION AND AUDIOVISUAL PRODUCTIONS

Fashion-oriented specialists are beginning to find exciting careers in television. Many advertising agencies today engage outside companies to create fashion commercials for client producers or retailers. The high cost of television time and production limits its appeal to retailers, but some make good use of television to present fashion. National advertising by major manufacturers and retailers—for example, Calvin Klein and Sears, Roebuck—is most common.

TRADE ASSOCIATIONS

One of the more interesting areas of employment in the fashion field is trade association work. Industries, retailers, and professionals of all types form associations and hire executive staffs to do research, publicity, and public relations work. These associations also handle legislative contacts, run conventions, publish periodicals, and run trade shows. The associations often perform any other services members may require.

Small or large, a trade association provides a great variety of work to its staff. Versatility is thus a paramount requirement. An assistant entering trade association work will find a background in the specific field served helpful, but the ability to communicate well is just as important.

TEACHING

Opportunities to teach fashion-related courses are varied. Individuals with extensive experience in the industry can often teach in private schools offering 1- or 2-year training programs, without the necessity of a college degree. Teachers in secondary schools with specialized fashion merchandising and design programs generally are required to have a 4-year degree, often with additional college hours in teaching methods. To teach on the junior college or baccalaureate level, a master's degree is usually required. In any case, credibility is greatly enhanced by a solid background of direct experience in the fashion business. Other opportunities for teaching include working in the training department of a large store or chain, and providing freelance seminars on fashion-related topics.

Glossary

Absolute quota A limit to the quantity of goods entering the United States.

Active sportswear The sector of sportswear that includes casual attire worn for sports such as running, jogging, tennis, and racketball.

Adaptations Designs that have all the dominant features of the style that inspired them, but do not claim to be exact copies.

Advertising The paid use of space or time in any medium. This includes newspapers, magazines, direct-mail pieces, shopping news bulletins, theater programs, catalogs, bus cards, billboards, radio, and television.

Ambiance The atmosphere encountered when entering a store.

Apparel contractor A firm whose sole function is to supply sewing services to the apparel industry.

Apparel jobber (manufacturing) A firm that handles the designing, planning and purchasing of materials, and usually the cutting, selling, and shipping of apparel, but does not handle the actual garment sewing.

Apparel manufacturer A firm that performs all the operations required to produce a garment.

Assortment The range of stock a retailer features.

At-home-wear Trade term for robes, pajamas, and hostess gowns.

Auxiliary level Composed of all the support services that are working with primary producers, secondary manufacturers, and retailers to keep consumers aware of the fashion merchandise produced for ultimate consumption.

Balance of trade The difference between the value of exports and the value of imports.

Bankruptcy A legal procedure by which a person or business unable to pay debts is relieved of debt by having a court divide their assets among the creditors.

Bilateral agreement Two countries reaching a separate agreement regarding their trade arrangements.

Board of directors Chief governing body of a corporation.

Boarding (hosiery) A heat-setting process through which hosiery acquires permanent shape.

Bodywear Coordinated leotards, tights, and wrap skirts.

Boutique A shop associated with few-of-a-kind merchandise, generally of very new or extreme styling, with an imaginative presentation of goods. French word for "shop."

Branch store division A separate function or division within a large retail firm's organizational structure that is responsible for seeing that the firm's policies are carried out in the branches.

Brand A name, trademark, or logo that is used to identify the products of a specific maker or seller and to differentiate the products from those of the competition.

Brand-line representative (cosmetics) A trained cosmetician who advises customers in the selection and use of a specific brand of cosmetics, and handles the sales of that brand in a retail store.

Bridge jewelry Merchandise ranging from costume to fine jewelry in price, materials, and newness of styling.

Bridge (menswear) The area that spans young men's and men's collections; serves customers between ages 25 and 40.

Broad and shallow assortment An assortment of goods with many styles but only limited sizes and colors carried in each style.

Business The act of creating, producing, and marketing products or services for a profit.

Career A lifelong activity, involving all of the jobs an individual may have, both paid and unpaid.

Career path or ladder The order of occupations in a person's life.

Catalog showroom A place where customers study merchandise catalogs and sample merchandise on display. Orders are filled from a stockroom on the premises and customers take their purchases with them.

Category or classification buying A practice whereby a chain store buyer located in a central buying office is usually assigned to purchase only a specific category or classification of merchandise instead of buying all categories carried in a single department. See *Departmental buying.*

Caution A fee charged for viewing a couture collection.

Chain organization A group of 12 or more centrally owned stores, each handling somewhat similar goods, which are merchandised and controlled from a central headquarters office (as defined by the Bureau of the Census.)

Chambre syndicale (pronounced "shahmbrah seen-dee-kahl") A French elite couture trade association providing many services for the entire French fashion industry.

Classic A style or design that satisfies a basic need and remains in general fashion acceptance for an extended period of time.

Classification An assortment of units or items of merchandise which can be reasonably substituted for each other, regardless of who made the item, the material of which it is made, or the part of the store in which it is offered for sale.

Commissionaire (pronounced "ko-me-see-ohn-air") An independent retailers' service organization usually located in the major city of a foreign market area. It is roughly the foreign equivalent of an American resident buying office.

Confined style(s) Styles that a vendor agrees to sell to only one store in a given trading area. See *Exclusivity.*

Conglomerate A group of companies that may or may not be related in terms of product or marketing level but which are owned by a single parent organization.

Conglomerate merger A merger between two companies with unrelated product lines.

Consignment selling A manufacturer places merchandise in a retail store for resale but permits any unsold portion to be returned to the wholesale source by a specific date.

Consumer The ultimate user of goods or services.

Consumerism The efforts of consumers to protect their own interests.

Contemporary menswear A type of styling that is often also referred to as "updated," "better," or "young men's." Applies to all categories of male apparel and furnishings.

Contract or specification buying A "development sample" of an item is made up so that it can be copied or adapted for sale at a price more advantageous to producers or customers. This type of buying is commonly used by chain organizations and mail order firms and often in foreign buying, as well.

Contract tanneries Business firms that process hides and skins to the specifications of converters but are not involved in the sale of the finished product.

Contractors See *Apparel contractor.*

Converter, leather Firms that buy hides and skins, farm out their processing to contract tanneries, and sell the finished product.

Converter, textiles A producer who buys fabrics in the greige, contracts to have them finished (dyed, bleached, printed, or subjected to other treatments) in plants specializing in each operation, and sells the finished goods.

Cooperative advertising Retail advertising, the costs of which are shared by a store and one or more producers on terms mutually agreed to.

Corporation An artificial being, invisible, intangible, and existing only in contemplation of law.

Cosmetics Articles other than soap that are intended to be rubbed, poured, sprinkled, or sprayed on the person for purposes of cleansing, beautifying, promoting attractiveness, or altering the appearance (as defined by the Federal Trade Commission).

Costume jewelry Mass-produced jewelry made of plastic, wood, glass, brass, or other base metals, and set with simulated or nonprecious stones. Also called fashion jewelry.

Couture house (pronounced "ko-tour") An apparel firm for which the designer creates original styles.

Couturier (male) or **couturiere** (female) (pronounced "ko-tour-ee-ay" and "ko-tour-ee-air") The proprietor or designer of a French couture house.

Créateurs French ready-to-wear designers.

Culmination (stage) See *Fashion cycle*.

Custom-made Clothing fitted specifically to the wearer.

Customer A patron or potential purchaser of goods or services.

Customer demand Customer needs and wants for consumer goods.

Decline (stage) See *Fashion cycle*.

Demographics Studies that divide broad groups of consumers into smaller, more homogeneous target segments; the variables include population distribution, age, sex, family life cycle, race, religion, nationality, education, occupation, and income.

Departmental buying A practice whereby a department buyer is responsible for buying all the various categories of merchandise carried in that department. See also *category buying*.

Department store A store, as defined by the Bureau of the Census, that employs 25 or more people and sells general lines of merchandise in each of three categories: (1) home furnishings, (2) household linens and dry goods (an old trade term meaning piece goods and sewing notions), and (3) apparel and accessories for the entire family.

Design A specific version or variation of a style. In everyday usage, however, fashion producers and retailers refer to a design as a "style," a "style number," or simply a "number."

Details The individual elements that give a silhouette its form or shape. These include trimmings, skirt and pant length and width, and shoulder, waist, and sleeve treatment.

Direct mail A form of sales promotion aimed at an individual customer and sent through the mail. Includes letters, catalogs, statement inserts.

Discount store A departmentalized retail store using many self-service techniques to sell its goods. It operates usually at low profit margins, has a minimum annual volume of $500,000 and is at least 10,000 sq. ft. in size.

Discretionary income The money that an individual or family has to spend or save after buying such necessities as food, clothing, shelter, and basic transportation.

Disposable personal income The amount of money a person has left to spend or save after paying taxes. It is roughly equivalent to what an employee calls "take-home pay" and provides an approximation of the purchasing power of each consumer during any given year.

Diversification The addition of various lines, products, or services to serve different markets.

Divestiture Sale of part of a company for economic gain or debt management.

Domestic market A fashion market center located in the United States.

Downward-flow theory The theory of fashion adoption which maintains that to be identified as a true fashion, a style must first be adopted by people at the top of the social pyramid. The style then gradually wins acceptance at progressively lower social levels. Also called the "trickle-down" theory.

Drop (menswear) Refers to the difference between the waist and chest measurements of a man's jacket. Designer suits are sized on a 7-inch drop; traditional suits are styled with a 6-inch drop.

Dual distribution A manufacturer's policy of selling goods at both wholesale and retail.

Duty See *tariff*.

Editorial credit The mention, in a magazine or newspaper, of a store name as a retail source for merchandise that is being editorially featured by the publication.

Entrepreneurs People who start new business ventures.

Entry-level job One requiring little or no specific training and experience.

Environment The conditions under which we live that affect our lives and influence our actions.

Erogenous Sexually stimulating or newly exposed.

European styling (menswear) Features more fitted jackets that hug the body and have extremely square shoulders.

Exclusivity Allowing sole use within a given trading area of a style or styles. An important competitive retail weapon.

Export When a country provides goods to another country.

Factor Financial institution that specializes in buying account receivable at a discount.

Factory outlet store Manufacturer-owned store that sells company products at reduced prices in austere surroundings with minimum services.

Fad A short-lived fashion.

Fashion A style that is accepted and used by the majority of group at any one time.

Fashion business Includes all industries and services connected with fashion: manufacturing, distribution, advertising, publishing, and consulting—any business concerned with goods or services in which fashion is a factor.

Fashion coordination The function of analyzing fashion trends in order to insure that the fashion merchandise offered is appropriate in terms of style, quality, and appeal to the target customer.

Fashion director A store's ranking fashion authority. Sometimes referred to as a fashion coordinator.

Fashion cycle The rise, widespread popularity, and then decline in acceptance of a style. *Rise:* The acceptance of either a newly introduced design or its adaptations by an increasing number of consumers. *Culmination:* That period when a fashion is at the height of its popularity and use. The fashion then is in such demand that it can be mass-produced, mass-distributed, and sold at prices within the reach of most consumers. *Decline:* The decrease in consumer demand because of boredom resulting from widespread use of a fashion. *Obsolescence:* When disinterest occurs and a style can no longer be sold at any price.

Fashion forecasting A prediction of the trend of fashion as determined by the prevailing elements in all the fashion industries.

Fashion image That aspect of a store's image that reflects the degree of fashion leadership the store strives to exercise and the stage of the fashion cycle that its assortments represent.

Fashion industries Those engaged in producing the materials used in the production of apparel and accessories for men, women, and children.

Fashion influential A person whose advice is sought by associates. An influential's adoption of a new style gives it prestige among a group.

Fashion innovator A person first to try out a new style.

Fashion jewelry See *Costume jewelry*.

Fashion marketing The marketing of fashion related apparel and accessories to the ultimate consumer.

Fashion merchandising Refers to the planning required to have the right fashion-oriented merchandise at the right time, in the right quantities, in the right place, with the right promotion, and at the right prices for the target group(s) of customers.

Fashion retailing The business of buying fashion-oriented merchandise from a variety of resources and assembling it in convenient locations for resale to ultimate consumers.

Fashion trend The direction in which fashion is moving.

Fiber A hairlike unit of raw material from which yarn and, eventually, textile fabric is made.

Fine jewelry Jewelry made of such precious metals as gold and all members of the platinum family (palladium, rhodium, and iridium), which may be set with precious or semiprecious stones.

First cost The wholesale price of merchandise in the country of origin.

Filaments Fibers of continuous, indefinite lengths produced by forcing liquid through a spinnerette.

Fords Styles that are widely copied at a variety of price lines.

Foreign market Markets outside the United States. See also *Markets*.

Foundations The trade term for such women's undergarments as brassieres, girdles, panty-girdles, garter belts, and corselettes.

Fragrance Includes cologne, toilet water, perfume, spray perfume, aftershave lotion, and environmental fragrances.

Franchise A contractual agreement in which a firm or individual buys the exclusive right to conduct a retail business within a specified trading area under a franchisor's registered or trademarked name.

Franchise distribution (cosmetics) The manufacturer or exclusive distributor sells directly to the ultimate retailer.

Free trade The free exchange of goods between nations.

Free trade zone Secure areas, usually located in or near customs ports of entry, that are regarded as legally outside a nation's customs territory.

Freelancing Working independently on an individual job or on a contractual basis for a variety of clients.

Fur farming The breeding and raising of fur-bearing animals under controlled conditions.

Fusing A process in which various parts of a garment can be melded together under heat and pressure rather than stitched.

Garment District The center of the women's apparel market in New York City.

Gemstones Natural stones used in making jewelry. Precious stones include the diamond, ruby, and real pearl. Semiprecious stones include garnet, jade, cultured pearl.

General merchandise stores Retail stores which sell a number of lines of merchandise—apparel and accessories, furniture and home furnishings, household lines and dry-goods, hardware, appliances, and small-wares, for example—under one roof. Stores included in this group are commonly known as mass-merchandisers, department stores, variety stores, general merchandise stores, or general stores.

General store An early form of retail store which carried a wide variety of mainly utilitarian consumer goods.

Global sourcing Term used to describe the process of shopping for and purchasing imported goods.

Going public Turning a privately-owned company into a public corporation and issuing stock for sale.

Graded Developed from a style's sample pattern; adjusted to meet the dimensional requirements of each size in which the style is to be made. Also referred to as "sloped."

Grade 6 + suit Man's suit that requires between 120 and 150 separate hand-tailoring operations and up to 15 hours of an experienced tailor's time for its production. Considered the finest quality available.

Grade X suit Man's suit that can be produced in 90 minutes with only 90 stitching and pressing operations. An acceptable but lower-quality, high-volume suit made possible by recent technological advances.

Greige goods (pronounced "gray goods") Unfinished fabrics.

Group purchase The purchasing from a given resource of identical merchandise by several stores at one time so that all participants may share in the advantages of a large-volume purchase.

Haute couture (pronounced "oat-koo-tour") The French term literally meaning "fine sewing" but actually having much the same sense as our own term "high fashion."

Hides Animals skins that weigh over 25 pounds when shipped to a tannery.

High fashion Those styles or designs accepted by a limited group of fashion leaders—the elite among consumers—who are first to accept fashion change.

Holding company A type of parent corporation that exercises little control over its subsidiary corporation, just "holding" its stock as investment.

Horizontal-flow theory The theory of fashion adoption that holds that fashions move horizontally between groups on similar social levels rather than vertically from one level to another. Also called the "mass-market theory."

Horizontal integration Merging with or acquiring other firms that function at the same marketing level, such as the merger of two fabric producers or one retail store with another store or store group.

Hostile takeover Situation in which an outside party buys enough voting stock in a corporation to gain control of it against the wishes of the Board of Directors and the corporate officers.

Hot items Items, new or otherwise, that have demonstrated greater customer acceptance than was anticipated.

Hypermarket A combined supermarket-discount store which sells food, furniture, housewares, hardware, electronics, and apparel.

Import When a country buys goods from a foreign country.

Import quota Limits set to restrict the number of specific goods entering the country.

Impulse items Items a customer buys on an impulse rather than as a result of planning.

Inflation A substantial and continuing rise in the general price level.

Inside shops Garment factories owned and operated by menswear manufacturers who perform all the operations required to produce finished garments.

Intimate apparel The trade term for women's foundations, lingerie, and loungewear. Also called inner fashions, body fashions, and innerwear.

Job A specific position within an industry.

Jobber A middleman who buys from manufacturers and sells to retailers. See also *Apparel jobber*.

Kips Animal skins weighing from 15 to 25 pounds when shipped to a tannery.

Knocked-off A trade term referring to the copying, at a lower price, of an item that has had good acceptance at higher prices.

Laissez-faire economy A government policy of noninterference with business.

Last (shoe) A form in the shape of a foot over which shoes are built.

Leased department A department ostensibly operated by the store in which it is found but actually run by an outsider who pays a percentage of sales to the store as rent.

Leisure-wear Trade term for robes, pajamas, and hostess gowns.

Let-out (furs) A cutting and re-sewing operation to make short skins into longer-length skins adequate for garment purposes.

Leverage Use of borrowed funds to finance a portion of an investment.

Leveraged buyout Situation (financial arrangement) in which an individual or group of investors purchases a company with debt secured by the purchased company's assets.

Licensed trademark (fibers) A fiber's registered trademark used under a licensing agreement whereby use of the trademark is permitted only to those manufacturers whose end products pass established tests for their specific end use or application.

Licensing An arrangement whereby firms are given permission to produce and market merchandise in the name of the licensor, who is paid a percentage of sales for permitting his or her name to be used.

Licensing agreement A contract whereby the licensor usually agrees to pay the licensee a royalty for use of the licensee's name.

Line An assortment of new designs offered by manufacturers to their customers, usually on a seasonal basis.

Line-for-line copies These are exactly like the original designs except that they have been mass-produced in less expensive fabrics to standard size measurements.

Lingerie A general undergarment category that includes slips, petticoats, camisoles, panties of all types, nightgowns, and pajamas. Slips, petticoats, and panties are considered "daywear," while nightgowns and pajamas are classified as "sleepwear."

Long-run fashion A fashion that takes more seasons to complete its cycle than what might be considered its average life expectancy.

Loungewear The trade term for the intimate apparel category that includes robes, bed jackets, and housecoats.

Mail-order company A firm that does the bulk of its sales and delivery by mail.

Manufacturer See *Apparel manufacturer.*

Marker (apparel manufacturing) A long piece of paper upon which the pieces of the pattern of a garment in all its sizes are outlined and which is placed on top of many layers of material for cutting purposes.

Market (1) A group of potential customers. (2) The place or area in which buyers and sellers meet for the purpose of trading ownership of goods at wholesale prices.

Market center A geographic center for the creation and production of fashion merchandise, as well as for exchanging ownership.

Market representative A specialist who covers a narrow segment of the total market and makes information about it available to client stores.

Market segmentation The separating of the total consumer market into smaller groups known as "market segments."

Market weeks Scheduled periods throughout the year during which producers and their sales representatives introduce new lines for the upcoming season to retail buyers.

Marketing A total system of business activities designed to plan, price, promote, and place (distribute) products and services to present and potential customers.

Marketing concept A company's attempt to identify the consumer's needs and wants, in order to create goods and services to satisfy them.

Marketing mix A combination of product, pricing, promotion and place that respond to the needs of the intended consumer.

Marketing strategy An overall marketing plan for a product.

Markup The difference between the wholesale cost and the retail price of merchandise (sometimes called "mark-on" by large retail stores).

Mart A building or building complex housing both permanent and transient showrooms of producers and their sales representatives.

Mass distribution (cosmetics) Third-party vendors, such as wholesalers, divertors, and jobbers, often interposed between the manufacturer and the retailer.

Mass or volume fashion Refers to those styles or designs that are widely accepted.

Merchandise assortment A collection of varied types of related merchandise, essentially intended for the same general end-use and usually grouped together in one selling area of a retail store. *Broad:* A merchandise assortment that includes many styles. *Deep:* A merchandise assortment that includes a comprehensive range of colors and sizes in each style. *Narrow:* A merchandise assortment that includes relatively few styles. *Shallow:* A merchandise assortment that contains only a few sizes and colors in each style.

Merchandising The planning required on the part of retailers to have the right merchandise at the right time, in the right place, in the right quantities, at the right price (for the specific target group(s) of consumers), and with the right promotion.

Merchandising policies Guidelines established by store management for merchandising executives to follow in order that the store organization may win the patronage of the specific target group(s) of customers it has chosen to serve.

Merger A sale of one company to another with the result that only one company exists.

Mid-management position One requiring some experience and training and involving a higher degree of responsibility.

Mom-and-Pop store A small store run by the proprietor with few or no hired assistants.

Monopoly When a single company has total control over products and prices and has no competition.

Narrow and deep assortment One in which there are relatively few styles, but these styles are stocked in all available sizes and colors.

National brand A nationally advertised and distributed brand owned by a manufacturer or processor. Offers consistent guarantee of quality and fashion correctness.

Obsolescence (stage) See *Fashion cycle.*

Officers (corporation) Those responsible for carrying out the business objectives of the firm.

Off-price apparel stores Sell home-brands and

designer merchandise at prices well below traditional department store levels.

Off-price retailing The selling of brand name and designer label merchandise at lower-than-normal retail prices, but still at the late rise or early peak of the fashion cycle.

Off-shore production Domestic apparel producers who import goods either from their own plants operating in cheap, labor-rich foreign areas or through their long-term supply arrangements with foreign producers.

Oligopoly An industry where there are few competitors. Example: Auto industry.

Organization chart A visual presentation of the manner in which a firm delegates responsibility and authority within its organization.

Outside shops See *Apparel contractor*.

Parent company A company that owns or partially owns other companies which it supervises. See also *Subsidiary corporation*.

Partnership An association of two or more persons to carry on as co-owners of a business for a profit.

Patronage motives (consumer) The reasons that induce consumers to patronize one store rather than another; why people buy where they do.

Pelt The skin of a fur-bearing animal.

Personal income The total or gross amount of income received from all sources by the population as a whole. It consists of wages, salaries, interest, dividends, and all other income for everyone in the country. See also *Disposable personal income* and *Discretionary income*.

Personnel division A separate function or division within a retail firm's organizational structure that is responsible for employment, training, employee records, executive recruitment and development, and related activities.

Piece-work A production method in which an operator sews only a section of the garment to speed the production process. See *Section work*.

Plateau See *Fashion cycle*.

Policy A settled, clearly defined course of action or methods of doing business deemed necessary, expedient, or advantageous.

Precious stones Include the diamond, emerald, ruby, sapphire, and real, or oriental, pearl.

Premiums A gift with purchase offered by a manufacturer to promote a product.

Press release A written statement of news that has occurred or is about to occur, specifying the source of the information and the date after which its use is permissible.

Prêt-à-porter (pronounced "pret-ah-por-tay") French term meaning ready-to-wear.

Price line A specific price point at which an assortment of merchandise is regularly offered for sale.

Price lining The practice of determing the various but limited number of retail prices at which a department's or store's assortments will be offered.

Price range The spread between the lowest and the highest price line at which merchandise is offered for sale.

Price zone A series of somewhat continuous price lines that are likely to have major appeal to one particular segment of a store's or department's customers.

Primary level Composed of the growers and producers of the raw materials of fashion—the fiber, fabric, leather, and fur producers who function in the raw materials market.

Primary supliers Producers of fibers, textile fabrics, finished leathers, and furs.

Prime resources Those producers from whom a department has consistently bought a substantial portion of its merchandise in past seasons.

Private corporation Ownership is usually held by a few owners and no shares of stock are sold on the open market.

Private label or store brand Merchandise that meets standards specified by a retail organization and which belongs exclusively to it. Primarily used to insure consistent quality of product as well as to meet price competition.

Private label manufacturers Produce merchandise to specification under the brand name of stores.

Product managers See *Specification manager*.

Profit The amount of money a business earns in excess of its income. See also *Net income*.

Prophetic styles Particularly interesting new

styles that are still in the introductory phase of their fashion cycles.

Protectionism An economic and political doctrine that seeks to exclude or limit foreign goods.

Psychographics Studies that develop fuller, more personal portraits of potential customers, including personality, attitude, interest, personal opinions, and actual product benefits desired.

Public corporation Sells shares of its stock on the open market to the public.

Public relations Works to improve a client's public image and may develop long-range plans and directions for this purpose.

Publicity The free and voluntary mention of a firm, brand, product, or person in some form of media.

Purchasing power The value of the dollar as it relates to the amount of goods or services it will buy. A decline in purchasing power is caused by inflation.

Quick response A strategy used by manufacturers to shorten the ordering cycle to compete with foreign imports.

Ready-to-wear (RTW) Apparel made in factories to standard size measurements.

Recession A low point in a business cycle, when money and credit become scarce and unemployment is high.

Regular tanneries Those companies that purchase and process hides and skins to the specifications of converters but are not involved in the sales of the finished products.

Resident buying office A service organization located in a major market area that provides market information and representation to its noncompeting client stores. *Associated/Cooperative:* One that is jointly owned and operated by a group of independently-owned stores. *Private:* One that is owned and operated by a single, out-of-town store organization and which performs market work exclusively for that store organization. *Salaried, Fee or Paid:* One that is independently owned and operated and charges the stores it represents for the work it does. *Syndicate/*

Corporate: One that is maintained by a parent organization which owns a group of stores and performs market work exclusively for those stores. *Commission/Merchandise Broker:* One that is independent, whose fees are paid not by the store but by manufacturers.

Resource Vendor, source of supply.

Retail level The ultimate distribution level—outlets for fashion goods directly to the consumer.

Retailing The business of buying goods from a variety of resources and assembling these goods in convenient locations for resale to ultimate consumers.

Rise (stage) See *Fashion cycle.*

Royalty fee Percentage of licensee sales paid to the licensor. See also *Licensing* and *Licensing* agreement.

Rubber-banding Cosmetic products that can be returned to the manufacturer and replaced with other products, if not sold within a specified period of time.

Sales promotion The coordination of advertising, display, publicity, and personal salesmanship in order to promote profitable sales.

Sales representatives Company representatives who exhibit merchandise to potential costumers.

Salon selling The most exacting type of personal selling: Little or no stock is exposed to the customer's view except that which is brought out for the customer's inspection by the salesperson.

Secondary level Composed of industries—manufacturers and contractors—that produce the semifinished or finished fashion goods from the materials produced on the primary level.

Section work The division of labor in apparel manufacturing whereby each sewing-machine operator sews only a certain section of the garment, such as a sleeve or hem.

Self-selection selling The method of selling in which merchandise is displayed and arranged so that customers can make at least a preliminary selection without the aid of a salesperson.

Self-service The method of selling in which customers make their selections from the goods on display and bring their purchases to a check-out counter where they make payment and their purchases are prepared for take-out.

Semi-precious stones Include the amethyst, garnet, opal, jade and other natural stones that are less rare and costly than precious stones.

Shop A small store or area within a large store that is stocked with merchandise for special end-use purposes; intended for customers with specialized interests.

Short run (apparel production) The production of a limited number of units of a particular item, fewer than would normally be considered an average number to produce.

Short-run fashion A fashion that takes fewer seasons to complete its cycle than what might be considered its average life expectancy.

Showcase store A factory-outlet store that sells merchandise at the early stages of the fashion cycle. They also serve as testing grounds for new products.

Silhouette The overall outline or contour of a costume. Also frequently referred to as "shape" or "form."

Skins Animals skins that weigh 15 pounds or less when shipped to a tannery.

Sloped See *Graded*.

Slop shops A name associated with the first shops offering men's ready-to-wear in this country. Garments lacked careful fit and detail work found in custom-tailored clothing of the period.

Sole proprietorship An individual owns the business, assumes all risks, and operates the business for his or her own personal interest.

Specialty store A store that carries limited lines of apparel, accessories, or home furnishings (as defined by the Bureau of the Census). In the trade, retailers use the term to describe any apparel and/or accessories store that exhibits a degree of fashion awareness and carries goods for men, women, and/or children.

Specification buying See *Contract buying*.

Specification manager Manager who oversees the purchasing and manufacturing process for a private label.

Spinnerette A mechanical device through which a thick liquid base is forced to produce fibers of varying lengths.

Stockholders Owners of the corporation.

Stockkeeping unit (SKU) A single or group of items of merchandise within a classification to which an identifying number is assigned and for which separate sales and stock records are kept.

Store image The character or personality that a store presents to the public.

Store policies Guidelines that affect areas other than merchandising, such as customer services, selling services, promotional activities, and fashion coordination.

Structured apparel Menswear garments whose construction involves many different hand-tailoring operations that give them a shape of their own when not being worn.

Style A characteristic or distinctive mode of presentation or conceptualization in a particular field. In apparel, style is the characteristic or distinctive appearance of a garment, the combination of features that makes it different from other garments.

Style number The number manufacturers and retailers assigned to a design. The number identifies the product for manufacturing, ordering, and selling.

Subsidiary corporation A corporation owned or partially owned by another corporation which supervises it. See also *Parent company*.

Sumptuary laws Laws regulating consumer purchases, for example, dress, on religious or moral grounds.

Sweatshop A garment manufacturing plant employing workers under unfair, unsanitary, and sometimes dangerous conditions.

Tailored clothing firms Those menswear firms that produce structured or semistructured suits, overcoats, topcoats, sportcoats, and/or separate trousers in which a specific number of hand-tailoring operations are required.

Tanning The process of transforming animal skins into leather.

Target market A specific group of potential customers that manufacturers and retailers are attempting to turn into regular customers.

Tariff A fee assessed by government on certain goods that it wishes to restrict or limit.

Tariff-rate quota A set limit after which a higher duty is charged on goods entering the country.

Taste The recognition of what is and is not attractive and appropriate. Good taste in fashion means sensitivity not only to what is artistic but to these considerations as well.

Textile fabric Cloth or material made from fibers by weaving, knitting, braiding, felting, crocheting, knotting, laminating, or bonding.

Textile converter See *Converter.*

Texture The look and feel of material, woven or unwoven.

Trade association Professional organizations for manufacturers or sales representatives.

Trade deficit When the value of goods that a country imports exceeds the value of its exports.

Trade publications Newspapers or magazines published specifically for professionals in a special field, such as fashion.

Trade shows Periodic merchandise exhibits stages in various regional trading areas around the country by groups of producers and their sales representatives for the specific purpose of making sales of their products to retailers in that area.

Trade surplus When a country's exports exceed its imports.

Trunk show A form of pre-testing that involves a producer's sending a representative to a store with samples of the current line, and exhibiting those samples to customers at scheduled, announced showings.

Unstructured apparel Menswear garments whose construction involves few if any hand-tailoring operations. A sports jacket, for example, often lacks padding, binding, and lin-ing; it takes its shape in part from the person who wears it.

Upward-flow theory The theory of fashion adoption that holds that the young—particularly those of low-income families as well as those of higher income who adopt low-income lifestyles—are quicker than any other social group to create or adopt new and different fashions.

Variety store A store carrying a wide range of merchandise in a limited number of low or relatively low price lines.

Vendor One who sells goods to others; source of supply, resource.

Venture or start-up capital Funds available for investment in the ownership element of a new enterprise; comes from a variety of sources.

Venture capitalist Investment specialist who provides money to finance new businesses in exchange for a position of the ownership with the intent of making a profit on the investment.

Vertical integration The acquisition or merger of firms at different marketing levels, for example, a fiber mill with a fabric mill or a garment producer with a fabric producer.

Video shopping In-home shopping using cable television and/or home computers.

Visual merchandising Everything visual that is done to, with, or for a product and its surroundings to encourage its sale. This includes display; print, broadcast, or film advertising; publicity; store layout; and store decor.

Voluntary associations (retailers) Stores affiliated loosely with one another on a voluntary basis. Each store retains its own identity.

Yarn A continuous thread formed by spinning or twisting fibers together.

Index

Large sizes in women's apparel, 182, 367
Last, 237
Latin American fashion market, 330–331, 353
Lauren, Ralph, 394–395
Layout artist, 431
Leased departments, 160, 238, 254, 371
Leather industry, 94, 144–151, 312
  gloves, 147, 255–257, 321–322
  handbags, 248–250, 321–322
  Italian, 312, 321–322
  (*See also* Fur industry; Shoe-making industry)
Legislation, federal, 17, 57–58, 96–98, 104, 124, 138–139, 163, 164, 275–276, 348–352
Leisure time and fashion, 33–34, 54
Leisurewear, 264–266, 268
Lerner Stores, 367
Let out, 160
Leverage, 105
Leveraged buy-outs, 105, 176
Levi Strauss & Co., 210, 211, 228
Licensed trademarks, 124
Licensing, 106–110, 220–221
  in children's wear, 202–203
  definition of, 106
  foreign investment in U.S., 354
  French couture, 317
  hosiery, 246
  international programs, 110
  Italian couture, 320
  retail programs, 106–109, 178–179, 190–191
  in textile fiber industry, 124
  by U.S. companies overseas, 354
  women's apparel, 178–179, 190–191
Lifestyle, 19
Limited, The, 104, 270–271, 367, 376, 387, 418
Line:
  definition of, 75
  designing, in menswear, 217–223, 230
  development of, 171–174
  production of, 174–175, 222–224, 230–232
Line-for-line copies, 48
Linen, 120, 121
Lingerie, 264
Lingerie industry, 264–268
Loehmann's, 367, 391
London couture, 322–323
London Fashion Fair, 322–323
Long-run fashions, 50–52
Loom, evolution of, 129–130
Lord & Taylor, 99, 182, 212, 302, 365, 387
Loungewear, 264
Loungewear industry, 264–266, 268
Lycra spandex, 247, 262

Macy's, 105, 182, 212, 264, 268, 277, 302, 342, 354, 364, 365, 368–369, 386, 389, 407, 418
Magazines, fashion, 403–405
  (*See also* Publications)
Mail-order companies (*see* Cata-log sales, mail-order)
Male cosmetics market, 276–278
Man-made fibers, 31, 50, 122–124
  and change in fashion, 16
  classification of, 120–121
  definition of, 119
  versus leather, 151
  major trade names in, 123
  marketing of, 124–129
  (*See also* Textile fiber industry)
Management positions, 422
Manufacturers, 94
  and creation of fashion, 75
  definition of, 177
  factory outlet stores, 392–393
  foreign, investment in U.S. by, 353–354
  fur industry, 158–160
  and growth of garment district, 169
  importing by, 344
  licensing programs, 107
  of menswear, 213–216
  as retailers, 189–190, 392–393
  textile fabric, 135–136
  types of, 75
  and unionization, 170–171
  women's apparel, 174–175
Manufacturing:
  careers in, 424–426
  technological advances in, 30–31
Marcus and Co., 371
Marker, 174
Marker trainee, 426
Market:
  definitions of, 111, 291, 293
  organization of, 295–296
  regional (*see* Regional mar-kets)
  trends in, 310–312
  working the, 300–301
Market calendar for the year, 298–299
Market centers:
  for children's wear industry, 197
  definition of, 291, 294
  foreign (*see* Foreign fashion market centers)
  for fur industry, 162, 164, 166
  for handbag industry, 248
  history and development of, 295–296
  for hosiery industry, 245
  for intimate apparel industry, 266
  for jewelry industry, 254
  for leather industry, 146
  marts, 294–299, 303–309

Market centers (*continued*
  for menswear industry, 225–226
  in New York, 291, 299–303
  regional, 303–305
  for shoemaking industry, 237
  for textile fabric industry, 133
  trade shows in, 309–310
  for women's apparel, 168–170, 342–343
Market representative, 417
Market research agencies, 410
Market segments:
  cosmetics industry, 276–280
  definition of, 28, 111
  intimate apparel, 268
  in menswear, 221–225
Market terminology, 293–294
Market weeks, 340–341
  definition of, 291, 294–295
  services rendered during, 296–299
Marketing, 110–111
  concept, 111
  definition of, 4, 110
  fashion, 1, 4–5, 28
    careers in, 425
    by children's wear industry, 200–203
    by cosmetics and fragrance industries, 280–284
    definition of, 4
    by intimate apparel industry, 263–264
    by menswear industry, 226–227
    by textile fabric industry, 134–136, 140–141, 425
    by textile fiber industry, 124–129, 425
    (*See also* Merchandising)
  production-driven, 110
  sales-driven, 110
  strategy, 111
  study of customer in, 65
Marketing mix, 111
Marks and Spencer, 354
Marshall Field's, 182, 212, 254, 354, 364, 365, 386
Marshall's Stores, 391
Marts:
  definition of, 291, 294
  organization of, 295–296
  regional, 294–299, 303–312
  trends in, 310–312
Mass distribution, 281
Mass fashion, 7
Mass-market theory of fashion adoption, 78–80
Mass-merchandise brand, 246
Mass merchants, 76
Maternity clothing, 182–184
May Company, 254, 342, 365, 370, 386, 387
Mechanization in textile indus-try, 142
  (*See also* Automation)